D0152496

WORLD FASCISM

WORLD FASCISM

A HISTORICAL ENCYCLOPEDIA

VOLUME 1: A–K

Cyprian P. Blamires, Editor
with Paul Jackson

A B C 🌊 C L I O

Santa Barbara, California • Denver, Colorado • Oxford, United Kingdom

Library of Congress Cataloging-in-Publication Data

World fascism : a historical encyclopedia / Cyprian P. Blamires, editor ; with Paul Jackson.
p.   cm
Includes bibliographical references and index.
ISBN 1-57607-940-6 (hard cover : alk. paper)—ISBN 1-57607-941-4 (ebook)
1. Fascism—History—Encyclopedias.   I. Blamires, Cyprian.   II. Jackson, Paul.
JC481.W67 2006
335.603—dc22
20006021588

10   09   08   07   06   05 / 10   9   8   7   6   5   4   3   2   1

This book is also available on the World Wide Web as an ebook.
Visit abc-clio.com for details.

ABC-CLIO, Inc.
130 Cremona Drive, P.O. Box 1911
Santa Barbara, California 93116–1911

Production Editor: Vicki Moran
Editorial Assistant: Alisha Martinez
Production Manager: Don Schmidt
Media Editor: Sharon Daughtery
Image Coordinator: Ellen Dougherty
Media Resources Manager: Caroline Price
File Manager: Paula Gerard

This book is printed on acid-free paper ∞ .
Manufactured in the United States of America

Contents

Advisory Board

Contributors

ADAMSON, Göran
London School of Economics
    and Political Science, UK

ANTLIFF, Mark
Duke University, USA

BAILER GAILANDA, Brigitte
Documentation Center of
    Austrian Resistance, Vienna,
    Austria

BALE, Jeffrey M.
Monterey Institute of
    International Studies, USA

BALLING, Pamela
Bowdoin College, USA

BARNETT, Victoria
US Holocaust Memorial Museum,
    Washington DC, USA

BAR-ON, Tamir
George Brown College, Toronto,
    Canada

BASTOW, Steve
Kingston University, UK

BEIT-HALLAHMI, Benjamin
University of Haifa, Israel

BEN-GHIAT, Ruth
New York University, USA

BERGGREN, Lena
Umea University, Sweden

BERLET, Chip
Political Research Associates, USA

BETZ, Hans-Georg
York University, Toronto,
    Canada

BEYLER, Richard H
Portland State University,
    Oregon, USA

BILLIG, Michael
Loughborough University, UK

BLAMIRES, Cyprian
UK

BROWDER, George
State University of New York
    College at Fredonia, USA

BRUSTEIN, William I
University of Pittsburgh, USA

BURSTOW, Bonnie
University of Toronto, Canada

BYFORD, Jovan
Open University, UK

CAMPI, Alessandro
University of Perugia, Italy

CAREW, Meredith
St Antony's College, University
    of Oxford, UK

CHANG, Maria
University of Nevada, Reno, USA

COOGAN, Kevin
New York, USA

COUPLAND, Philip
University of Glasgow, UK

CRONIN, Michael
Boston College, Dublin, Ireland

CROWE, David
Elon College, NC, USA

DAHL, Göran
Lund University, Sweden

DAHL, Hans Fredrik
University of Oslo, Norway

DAVIES, Peter J
University of Huddersfield, UK

DE GRAND, Alex
North Carolina State University,
    USA

DEZE, Alexandre
Institut d'Etudes Politiques de
    Paris, France

DOENECKE, Justus
New College of Florida, Sarasota,
    USA

DÜMLING, Albrecht
Musica Reanimata, Berlin,
    Germany

DURHAM, Martin
University of Wolverhampton,
    UK

EAR, Sophal
Center for Khmer Studies and
    UC Berkeley, USA

EAR, Susan
University of California,
    Berkeley, USA

EARLE, Ben
Birmingham University, UK

ERB, Peter
Wilfrid Laurier University,
    Waterloo, Ontario, Canada

FALASCA-ZAMPONI, Simonetta
University of California, Santa
    Barbara, USA

FELDMAN, Matt
University of Northampton, UK

FINZI, Roberto
University of Trieste, Italy

FLOOD, Christopher
University of Surrey, UK

GASMAN, Daniel
John Jay College and the
    Graduate Center, City
    University of New York, USA

GELLOTT, Laura
University of Wisconsin-
    Parkside, USA

GENTILE, Emilio
University of Rome, Italy

GISPEN, Kees
University of Mississippi, USA

GIVENS, Terri
University of Texas,
    Austin, USA

GÖTZ, Norbert
University of Greifswald,
    Germany

GÖKMEN, Özgür
University of Leiden, the
    Netherlands

GOLOMB, Jacob
Hebrew University of Jerusalem,
    Israel

GOODRICK-CLARKE, Nicholas
University of Exeter, UK

GOWARD, Stephen
Oxford Brookes University,
    UK

GRIFFIN, Roger
Oxford Brookes University, UK

GRIFFITHS, Richard
King's College, London, UK

GRUMKE, Thomas
Ministry of the Interior,
    Northrhine-Westphalia,
    Germany

HAGTVET, Bernt
University of Oslo,
    Norway

HAMMERSTEIN, Notker
Johann Wolfgang Goethe
    University, Frankfurt am
    Main, Germany

HATTSTEIN, Markus
Germany

HEER, Hannes
Germany

HEXHAM, Irving
University of Calgary, Canada

HOLM, Adam
Denmark

HUYSSEUNE, Michel
Vrije Universiteit Brussel and
    Vesalius College, Brussels,
    Belgium

INGIMUNDARSON, Valur
University of Iceland

JACKSON, Paul
Oxford Brookes University, UK

JAMSHEER, Hassan
University of Lodz, Poland

JASKOT, Paul
DePaul University, Chicago, USA

KALDIS, Byron
Hellenic Open University,
    Greece

KALLIS, Aristotle
Lancaster University, UK

KASEKAMP, Andres
University of Tartu, Estonia

KASZA, Gregory
Indiana University, USA

KING, Christine E.
Staffordshire University, UK

KOLLER, Christian
University of Zurich, Switzerland

KÜRTI, László
University of Miskolc, Hungary

LAUDERBAUGH, George
Jacksonville State University, USA

LLOYD-JONES, Stewart
Contemporary Portuguese
    Political History Research
    Centre, UK

LONDON, John
London University, UK

LOWE, Sid
Sheffield University, UK

LYNCH, Derek
University of Huddersfield,
    UK

MACKLIN, Graham
National Archives, Kew,
    UK

MARES, Miroslav
Masaryk University, Brno,
    Czech Republic

MARTIN, James
Goldsmith's College,
    London, UK

MCHENRY Jr, Dean
Claremont Graduate University,
    USA

MENÉNDEZ, Agustín José
University of León, Spain

MEURS, VAN, Philip
Belgium

MINICHIELLO, Mario
Loughborough University,
    UK

MOOS, Carlo
University of Zurich,
    Switzerland

MORGAN, Philip
Hull University, UK

MÜLLER, Christoph Hendrik
University College Dublin,
    Ireland

MULLOY, Darren
Wilfrid Laurier University,
    Waterloo, Ontario,
    Canada

OLSEN, Jonathan
University of Wisconsin-
    Parkside, USA

PANKOWSKI, Rafal
Poland
PAPPAS, Takis
University of Macedonia, Greece

PATEL, Kiran
Humboldt University, Berlin,
    Germany

PAXTON, Robert O.
Columbia University, USA

POCAI, Susanne
Germany

POEWE, Karla
University of Calgary,
    Canada

POLLARD, John
Trinity Hall, Cambridge, UK

POWER, Margaret
Illinois Institute of Technology,
    Chicago, USA

QUINN, Malcolm
Wimbledon School of Art, UK

REICHARDT, Sven
University of Constance,
    Germany

RENTON, David
UK

RUIZ JIMENÉZ, Marta
Spain

RYCHLAK, Ronald
University of Mississippi,
    USA

SAVARINO, Franco
Escuela Nacional de
    Antropologia e Historia,
    Mexico City

SAX, Boria
Mercy College, Dobbs Ferry, NY,
    USA

SCHÄBITZ, Michael
Germany

SEIDEL, Hans-Christoph
Ruhr University, Bochum,
    Germany

SPEKTOROWSKI, Alberto
Tel Aviv University, Israel

SREBRNIK, Henry
University of Prince Edward
    Island, Canada

TURNER, Steve
University of South Florida,
    USA

UMLAND, Andreas
National Taras Shevchenko
    University of Kiev, Ukraine

VANHAELEMEERSCH, Philip
Belgium

VIRCHOW, Fabian
University of Marburg,
    Germany

VOGT, Stefan
University of Amsterdam, the
    Netherlands

WANROOIJ, Bruno
Georgetown University
    Fiesole, Italy

WEAR, Rae
University of Queensland,
    Australia

WEINBERG, Leonard
University of Nevada, USA

WEINDLING, Paul
Oxford Brookes University,
    UK

WELCH, David A.
University of Kent, UK

WEVER, DE, Bruno
Ghent University, Belgium

YEOMANS, Rory
UK Criminal Justice Performance
    Directorate

YOUNG, Ron
Georgia Southern University,
    USA

ZIEMANN, Benjamin
University of Sheffield,
    UK

ZIMMERMANN, Ekkart
Technische Universität, Dresden,
    Germany

List of Entries

Editor's Foreword

This work of reference fills a significant void in the field of modern historical/political studies. There are existing individual encyclopaedic dictionaries dedicated respectively to the Third Reich and to interwar Italian Fascism as well as smaller reference works taking a global approach to far-right movements (and I have found all of these most useful as a reference resource for the editorial work); but there is to date no substantial English-language encyclopedia giving in-depth global coverage on this scale to the modern phenomenon of fascism from its first stirrings in the nineteenth century up to the beginning of the new millennium. The present work gives comprehensive coverage to movements, ideologies, ideologues, and events generally associated with fascism across the globe. Our aim is to give coverage firstly to those openly identifying themselves as 'fascists' (e.g., Mussolini, Mosley), secondly to some at least of those who have been associated—often wrongly in our view—with the idea of fascism in the public mind (e.g., General Pinochet of Chile), and thirdly, to some whose ideologies seem to have certain affinities to fascism (e.g., General Qadhafi of Libya).

The person who spotted this gap in our resources and decided to do something about it was Robert Neville, a former ABC-CLIO editor based in the Oxford office in the UK, so many thanks are due to him. Without the interest and the enthusiastic backing of Professor Roger Griffin of Oxford Brookes University in the UK our project would not have got off the ground, and he can certainly be regarded as the midwife of this particular baby. As the project developed he proved to be an unfailing source of information, contacts, advice, and general wisdom as well as being a major contributor to the content, and in my capacity as editor I owe him an inestimable debt. Alongside him the Advisory Board has also provided invaluable support and encouragement. I would in addition like to express my thanks to all the one hundred and twenty-plus contributors from all over the globe who have worked unsparingly to make the *Encyclopedia* a success. They are based at universities in twenty-four different countries, and the range of nationalities they represent is even wider. One of the greatest pleasures for me in the preparation of this *Encyclopedia* has been the emailing relationships the work has led me to establish with so many scholars all over the world. In addition I should say a word of thanks to my son Robert who was kind enough to devote some time to studying the text and commenting on it at a formative moment in its development and to David O'Donoghue, who inspired the addition of an important entry to our original list. I must thank my wife Trudi too for her stoic endurance of the the intrusions of this project into our family life. Finally, a particular accolade to Paul Jackson, not simply for his various weighty articles, but also for having read the whole text through at a crucial stage and offered his wisdom about it; in addition, I am grateful to him for undertaking to compose the chronology and general bibliography and to add many bibliographical items to a number of entries.

DISCLAIMER

The term 'fascist' as used in the present work is not being used for purposes of abuse of individuals but is a taxonomic category of political analysis. The selection of a particular passage from an author's writings does not imply his or her guilt by association for the sufferings inflicted on millions of persons as a result of the policies pursued by the two fascist regimes half a century ago, nor for the acts of criminality and violence carried out by contemporary fascist movements committed to racist or terrorist violence. 'Fascism' in the present work designates a political myth or ideology. There are numerous cases of modern ideologues who produce texts that could be identified as 'fascist', but who stay aloof from paramilitary or mass movements and repudiate violence, seeing culture, not the streets or parliament, as the prime arena in which the battle for national, European, or Aryan regeneration is to be fought. They would be likely to resent their ideas being categorized as 'fascist' whatever structural links there might be between those ideas and the core ideas of fascism as understood by the contributors to the present work. Moreover, it is quite possible to contribute to some of the newer discourses of fascism, such as revisionism or the New Right, without harboring any sympathy with organized fascism at all, but simply by having written works that can be cited as mitigating circumstances for the atrocities committed by Nazism, or as theoretical justification for the rejection of egalitarian ideals. For further clarification of these issues, see the Introduction by Professor Roger Griffin.

Cyprian P. Blamires

Introduction

Part I: Defining Fascism

Unlike most reference books, *World Fascism: A Historical Encyclopedia* cannot, in the very nature of things, avoid being controversial. There are two reasons for this. One is that not all scholars are prepared to accept the idea that the original Italian Fascism and other political systems share some kind of common mentality or ideology; to them, German Nazism, for example, was so different from Italian Fascism that it is completely erroneous and false to historical fact to call them both *fascist*. Nazism was specifically and uniquely Germanic in its thinking and its mentality, whereas Italian Fascism was specifically and uniquely Italian. The wartime alliance between Mussolini and Hitler was an accident of history, and it provides no indication whatsoever of a common mind between them. They were both totalitarian dictatorships, but history is littered with such dictatorships, the vast majority of which could not by any stretch of the imagination be labeled "fascist." Historians of such "nominalist" persuasion are unlikely to be convinced to join the fold of comparative fascist studies by the entries in this volume, whatever their empirical content.

The second reason why this encyclopedia is controversial is that even those scholars (the majority) who do accept that a phenomenon called *fascism* (spelled with a lowercase *f*, to distinguish it from specifically Italian Fascism—that is, the creed, practices, and policies of the Italian Fascist Party—spelled with the uppercase *F*)

can be identified as a common feature in many political systems, differ as to the common elements that compose it. For example, some have focused on the shared technique of the mass rally and the promotion of politics as spectacle, as a theatrical display of military and state power; some have focused on the leader cult, some on the doctrine of corporatism, and some on the resort to the tactics of terror. Several major scholars have defined it in such a way that it excludes Nazism as one of its manifestations. Indeed, until quite recently scholarly disagreement about what is to be understood by the generic term *fascism* would have made it almost unthinkable even to contemplate an encyclopedia of fascism whose entries broadly share a common perspective on the central topic.

However, the last few years have seen the growth—at least within the non-Marxist and Anglophone human sciences—of a convergence of scholarly opinion about the main features of fascism that I have referred to as the "new consensus" in fascist studies, though it is a consensus that is inevitably partial and contested.[1] As a result, it has become possible to contemplate a global treatment of fascism as a worldwide phenomenon originating in nineteenth-century Europe and that continues to be advocated and propagated in the third millennium, a treatment that will be broadly acceptable to the majority of experts working in fields relating to fascism, nationalism, and racism. The following is a working definition of how this emergent consensus views the phenomenon of global fascism:

A revolutionary form of ultra-nationalism bent on mobilizing all "healthy" social and political energies to resist the perceived threat of decadence and on achieving the goal of a reborn national or ethnic community. This project involves the regeneration both of the political culture and of the social and ethical culture that underpins it, and in some cases involves the eugenic concept of rebirth based on racial doctrine.

This definition contains three core elements that are fundamental to the definition of generic fascism adopted in this encyclopedia.

THREE CORE ELEMENTS

Ultra-nationalism

The term *ultra-nationalism* is absolutely fundamental, and it must be understood as something totally different from traditional nationalism. Modern nationalism in the West is widely understood as based on "civic" concepts of nationality arising from legal processes that grant permanent rights of citizenship and residence even to culturally unassimilated ethnic or religious groups. But *ultra-nationalism* regards as "mechanistic" (*see* MECHANISTIC THINKING) and meaningless the notion that the mere granting of a passport or even the acquisition of a language is a sufficient prerequisite for an immigrant's acquiring a nationality. Instead, it promotes an "ethnic," "organic," or "integral" concept of nationality that stresses the primacy of identity, of belonging to a supposedly homogeneous culture, shared history, or race that it sees as undermined by such forces as individualism, consumerism, mass immigration, cosmopolitanism, globalization, and multiculturalism. Fascist ideology builds on a concept of the nation as a living organism that can thrive, die, or regenerate, a suprapersonal community with a life history and destiny of its own that predates and survives "mere" individuals and imparts a higher purpose to their lives. (At the same time, it must of course be borne in mind that fascists may well choose to adopt the outward guise of a democratic political party or invoke apparently liberal principles such as freedom of speech as part of their tactics to increase popular support and gain power.)

The ultra-nationalist component of fascism means that it has assumed a wide variety of ideological permutations simply because of the extraordinary diversity of unique historical, religious, linguistic, political, military, or colonial factors involved in the emergence of modern nation-states and national communities. It has also embraced strikingly different notions of national belonging, ranging from purely cultural and historical attachments to the incorporation of scientistic notions of genetics, eugenics, and racial hygiene; in the case of the Third Reich, the nation itself was defined in terms of both cultural and biological racial purity, so that nationalism and racial pride became virtually identical. In Nazi parlance, to be German thus meant belonging both to a nation-state, a national culture, and to a discrete racial entity, even though the historical, geopolitical nation of Germany was far from coterminous with the imagined entity called the "German race." So it is no more than a paradox when some fascists celebrate both their own (mythicized) nation and belonging to a supranational "home," such as the White Race or Europe. It is on the grounds of this plural sense of belonging that a British Nazi can feel a much deeper sense of kinship with nationalistic "Aryans" in other countries, especially German Nazis, than with those of his own liberal fellow-citizens who lack a real sense of "roots," let alone with (nonwhite/non-Europeanized) "immigrants."

It is true that extreme forms of nationalism together with the aspiration to revolutionize society have been evident in certain regimes dedicated to "really existing socialism" in the twentieth century—not only in Russia and China but also in smaller nations such as Romania and North Korea. However, although as regimes they share some features with fascist totalitarianism, they cannot be regarded as coming under the definition of fascism offered here. In contrast to fascism, their core ideology centered not on reversing the nation's decline, so as to bring about its rebirth, but on overthrowing a superseded social and economic system, whether feudal or bourgeois, in the name of a new phase of human history that would eventually emancipate all workers or all nations everywhere from the shackles of capitalism and the scourge of alienation. That kind of utopia is anathema to fascists, for it ultimately destroys both the nation and any sense of national belonging. (However, there have been attempted hybrids of fascism and communism; *see,* for example, NATIONAL BOLSHEVISM.)

Revolution

Our definition takes fascists at their word and accepts their claim that they are engaged in a revolutionary struggle to reverse decadence and inaugurate a national rebirth. It excludes from the category of fascism organized forms of chauvinism and racism such as the Austrian Freedom Party (*see* HAIDER, JÖRG) or France's

National Front; for, although these may exhibit many features of interwar fascism, have roots in historical fascism, and even attract the vote of "genuine" fascists, they lack the revolutionary agenda of creating a new postfeudal, postliberal, or post-Soviet order.

No single template can be identified for the type of national community that would result from a successful fascist revolution, since in each case a unique constellation of historical factors conditions the policies on such issues as territorial expansion, technology, the participation of the working class and the peasantry, religion, art, demographic policy, women, or race. According to our definition, there have historically been only two actual government regimes that can properly be defined as fascist, Fascist Italy and the Third Reich, and they differed strikingly in such areas as the ambition of their colonial policies, the deployment of state terror, the implementation of policies of racial purification and ethnic cleansing, and the control of "cultural production" (painting, literature, architecture, and the like). These regimes also illustrate the fact that fascist movements can host deeply contrasting attitudes toward artistic modernism, the retention of private industry and finance capitalism, the role of the countryside as the source of racial regeneration, and the need to create a fascist International to induce the rebirth not just of individual nations but also of Europe itself.

Rebirth

Perhaps the most distinctive feature of the definition we have offered, and certainly its hallmark as representative of the emerging new consensus in fascist studies, is the centrality it accords to the vision of regeneration, rebirth, or "palingenesis" (from the Greek *palin,* "again," and *genesis,* "birth"), all three terms with organic connotations of reversing decay and of revitalization rather than of merely overthrowing one system to replace it by another. It is a myth closely connected to the idea of "cleansing," "purifying," or "redeeming" the nation as stressed in other definitions of fascism convergent with the one explored here. The destruction of the existing liberal or conservative system, the extensive deployment of highly invasive forms of social engineering, the elaborate displays of ritual politics, even the leader cult itself, all prominent features shared by Italian Fascism and Nazism once in power, were in fact not ends in themselves but means to an end: the transformation of society into the basis of a regenerated national community. The erection of a new political system and the militarization of society were not the principal loci of the fascistization of the nation but rather the preconditions or concomitants of a deeper metamorphosis that fascists wanted to bring about in the nature of society: their final goal—like that of the communists—was to create a new national character, a new man.

Far from being a modern notion, rebirth is one of the fundamental archetypes in the history of human myth-making, playing a crucial role in the cosmology and ritual, whether metaphysical or secular, of virtually every human society that has existed since Neanderthal times. One has only to think of the power that continues to emanate for devout Christians from the image of Christ's resurrection, or of how much the notion of renewal permeates all forms of New Age therapy, practice, and "alternative" belief, to realize the persistence of its mythic resonance. When combined with the modern ideology of ultra-nationalism, itself capable of generating enormous affective energy in times of collective danger or of outstanding achievement by a military, cultural, or sporting elite, it forms a mythic compound ("palingenetic ultra-nationalism") that in the crisis conditions endemic to interwar Europe proved able to unleash a huge mobilizing power both as an elitist movement and as a populist force.

The importance that the promise of comprehensive social renewal acquires within the dynamics of fascism is not confined to the emotional affect it can produce on an elite of dedicated fanatics. The very nebulousness of the myth of rebirth is vital in enabling a fascist movement to recruit support from people with widely differing social backgrounds, heterogeneous values, and conflicting theories of how particular failings of society or symptoms of decadence may be remedied. Fascism's ability under the "right" historical conditions to weld into a unified movement diffused and fragmented constituencies of disaffection and utopianism is due in no small measure to the power of the notion of an ill-defined renewal or palingenesis to override the conflicts between rival visions of the new order, which, without this all-purpose mythopoeic "glue," would lead to irreversible fractionalization. This "override" effect resembles the way in which the experience of being in love can be so overwhelming to a couple as to make a host of practical objections or problems seem trivial. Because "rebirth" is ultimately a metapolitical phenomenon, a spiritual or psychological metaphor of radical change rooted in archaic notions of accessing a "sacred" higher dimension of time itself, its pervasive role in fascist ideology means that the same movement can host a wide range of projects for renewal in such different spheres as the military, foreign policy, imperialism, the role of women, demographic policy, art, economics, technology, and sport, while accommodating contrasting elements of elitism and populism, together with deep divisions over the role that the past should play in inspiring the present renewal of society.

Perhaps the most significant aspect of fascism's palingenetic component, however, is the alchemical property that it displays in the most intimate symbolical sphere of the human imagination: its capacity to transmute despair into hope, absurd death into sacrifice, end into beginning, twilight into dawn, ruthless destruction into ritual cleansing, symptoms of decline into harbingers of a new era, the bleakest winter into a new spring. To inhabit a palingenetic mind-set is to experience all issues and events as if they partook of a magical dimension invisible to the uninitiated, turning what to outsiders might seem like chaos and darkness into a dramatic narrative of decay's mysterious metamorphosis into renewal shot through with shafts of light. Palingenetic mythopoeia lies at the very heart of the human capacity to sanctify the profane, sacralize the secular, and create a web of religious sentiments and presentiments that bind the seeming confusions of reality into a world infused with transcendent meaning. When, as in fascism, the object of this faculty is the national community, then its very history is endowed with spiritual, transcendental, sacral meaning; if a fascist movement actually succeeds in conquering power, it will tend naturally to institute a "political religion" that sacralizes both the nation and the state, which is now charged with instituting the new order. Even before that, it will tend as a movement to espouse overtly charismatic, spectacular, ritual forms of politics that make the liturgical aspect of the "civic religion" fostered by liberal democracy (for example, the state opening of Parliament in Britain or the State of the Union Address in the United States) pale into insignificance.

The definition of generic fascism given above may be illustrated by two samples of the fascist style of ideological discourse taken from speeches made by fascist leaders. The first comes from a speech by Mussolini on the eve of the March on Rome in October 1922, a major step in Italian Fascism's "conquest of the state." The second comes from an address by Hitler at the Nuremberg Rally of September 1935, two years after the Nazi "seizure of power."

Mussolini

We have created our myth. The myth is a faith, a passion. It is not necessary for it to be a reality. It is a reality in the sense that it is a stimulus, is hope, is faith, is courage. Our myth is the nation; our myth is the greatness of the nation! And it is to this myth, this greatness, which we want to translate into a total reality, that we subordinate everything else.

For us the nation is not just territory, but something spiritual. There are States which have had immense territories and which have left no trace in human history. It is not just a question of size, because there have been minute, microscopic States in history which have bequeathed memorable, immortal specimens of art and philosophy.

The greatness of the nation is the totality of all these qualities, of all these conditions. A nation is great when it translates into reality the force of its spirit. Rome becomes great when, starting out as a small rural democracy, it gradually spreads out across the whole of Italy in accordance with its spirit, till it encounters the warriors of Carthage and must fight them. It is the first war in history, one of the first. Then, gradually, it bears its standards to the ends of the earth, but at every turn the Roman Empire is the creation of the spirit, since the weapons were aimed, not just by the arms of the Roman legionaries, but by their spirit. Now, therefore, we desire the greatness of the nation, both material and spiritual.[2]

Hitler

At some future date, when it will be possible to view these events in clear perspective, people will be astonished to find that just at the time the National Socialists and their leaders were fighting a life-or-death battle for the preservation of the nation the first impulse was given for the re-awakening and restoration of artistic vitality in Germany. It was at this same juncture that the congeries of political parties were wiped out, the opposition of the federal states overcome, and the sovereignty of the Reich established as sole and exclusive. While the defeated Center Party and the Marxists were being driven from their final entrenchments, the trade unions abolished, and while National Socialist thought and ideas were being brought from the world of dream and vision into the world of fact, and our plans were being put into effect one after the other—in the midst of all this we found time to lay the foundations of a new Temple of Art. And so it was that the same revolution that had swept over the State prepared the soil for the growth of a new culture.

Art is not one of those human activities that may be laid aside to order and resumed to order. Nor can it be retired on pension, as it were. For either a people is endowed with cultural gifts that are inherent in its very nature or it is not so endowed at all. Therefore such gifts are part of the general racial qualities of a people. But the creative function through which these spiritual gifts or faculties are expressed follows the same law of development and decay that governs all human activity.[3]

Clearly, there are important differences between these passages. While both are resoundingly nationalistic, the references to culture as the expression of racial qualities distinguishes the German speech from the purely cultural nationalism alluded to in the Italian. Mussolini's invocation of the Romans as the role model for the greatness of a nation would make no sense in Hitler's speech (unless it were part of a general eulogy of the past cultural glories of Aryan peoples). There is furthermore an element of biological determinism in the second passage foreign to the first (although, as a matter of historical fact, Fascist Italy did eventually attempt to "Aryanize" and biologize its conception of the Italian race). Nor should it be inferred from these two passages that the two fascist leaders had the same view of art. In practice, Mussolini displayed an almost total indifference to aesthetic issues and presided benevolently over a plethora of contrasting artistic styles and creeds following a principle that has been called "hegemonic pluralism." Hitler's speech, on the other hand, is one of many that he made as the ultimate arbiter of cultural issues, in which capacity he was about to launch a ferocious campaign against artistic modernism as an expression of decadence (involving the selling off or destruction of thousands of works of art, not to mention the persecution of their creators). This drive to purge Germany of aesthetic decadence ("cultural Bolshevism") was a direct corollary of the mission to destroy all the ideological and racial enemies of the New Germany that became the thrust of World War II.

Despite all these points of contrast, the parallels between the two passages remain striking. At the heart of both lies the vision of national greatness to be realized in order to replace a decadent liberal system. In both, the key to the revolution is the will or spirit needed to translate dream or myth into practice, thereby transforming the course of history itself. Moreover, the speeches from which these extracts were taken are in fact to be seen as *performative* acts—that is, they are not intended simply to reflect on the times but actually to shape them through the power of ideas to inform actions directly—and thus, to use a phrase from another speech by Mussolini, to "make history." Despite the vast differences in their personalities, both men came to embody the idea of providential and redemptive forces of rebirth spontaneously generated from the depth of the national soul, to save the nation in its hour of need. Once the collective hopes for renewal were projected onto them, they were transfigured among their supporters into "charismatic" leaders, a blend of head of state, war-lord, legendary hero, savior, and seer. They

thus came to incarnate the spirit of the new order and of the "new man" necessary for history to enter a new era and for time to begin again.

We have to remember that whereas for us today the words they uttered are now frozen impotently on the page, the fanatical devotees among their first hearers responded to them in the context of what to them was no ordinary event, but one that took place in a higher, ritual time in which an invisible bond was renewed between them and their leader. For them, what they were listening to was no mere "propaganda" but liturgical confirmation of the fundamental axioms of the fascist worldview. Even these brief passages convey some of its key elements: the violence of military intervention and the dismantling of democracy is, in the mind of the fascist, not destructive or barbaric but regenerative and cathartic, forming the precondition to national renewal; the nation is first and foremost a spiritual entity, a sum far greater than its visible parts, so that the sphere of politics is organically linked to the sphere of art and culture, which is no longer conceived as an independent realm of innovation and self-expression but rather as the externalization of the genius of a whole people; the imminent flourishing of art is to be seen in terms of renaissance, as a revival of an earlier high tide of creativity, whether that of the Romans or the heyday of premodernist German art.

Both speeches imply that the spirit of the revival is not that of backward-looking reaction born of nostalgia for premodern idylls (even if the German text refers to "restoration") but of rebirth. In other words, political renewal is intimately bound up with cultural renewal, pointing to the "total" conception of the nation and the interconnectedness of all its component spheres that underlies fascist totalitarianism. Approached in this way, the nation itself, with its institutional, political, economic, military, social, and human resources, comes to be seen by the fascist elite as the raw material to be molded and sculpted into a living community, retaining from the decadent old order everything capable of transformation, and discarding the remainder as waste. If the spirit of the nation can be reawakened and purged of the forces of decadence, then the revolution will take place in every sphere of society, great achievements will follow in politics and art, and the new man, *Homo fascistus,* will be born. In the words of a Nazi ideologue: "The new human being lives in conscious service of the community, but with a deeply personal sense of responsibility. He is not a person 'in his own right,' and not the embodiment of a class, but of his people. He does not live for himself, but as an integral part of a living whole."

Hence for Mussolini, Fascism does not strive to conquer external territory for its own sake, and certainly not primarily for economic ends, but as a symbolic gesture, part of the project of colonizing the inner space of Italy so as to turn its inhabitants into modern Romans capable of achieving greatness once more. Similarly for Hitler, the reversal of the terms of the humiliating Versailles Treaty and the acquisition of an empire is not just a question of military might and political will. Its premise is the rebirth of Germany, the "growth of a new culture" whose hegemony on the world stage will save the West from terminal decline.

SOURCES OF CONFUSION

Taking fascist ideology at face value

The approach being taken here to the phenomenon of "fascism" is suspect to some commentators, simply because it takes seriously the claims of fascists about their creed. Curiously, it has long been legitimate in some academic circles to apply one standard to the apostles of communism, whose belief-systems have been generally reckoned sincere in intent even if misguided and horrendously destructive in implementation, while applying another standard to the propagandists for fascism. These have been widely assumed to be using their ideology merely as a cloak to cover a naked desire for dictatorial tyranny or destruction for its own sake—without actually believing in it themselves. In particular, simply to take at face value fascists' claims about the revolutionary nature of their cause was for a long time unthinkable for many experts within fascist studies, and it is still anathema to most convinced Marxists. For the latter, the driving force behind fascism is precisely the desire to crush the only true revolutionary process of the modern age—namely, the bid by socialists to overthrow capitalism and usher in the next stage in the evolution of humanity toward a communist society. Fascism is thus, for them, inherently reactionary, no matter how much it adopts the rhetoric and outward trappings of popular revolution in order to deceive the masses about its true purpose. As a result, some Marxist intellectuals have even read apologetic intentions into the new consensus, as if the attempt to understand Nazism's worldview somehow meant justifying it (which is no more logical than suggesting that a cancer specialist approves of cancer).

A key premise behind the definition applied in this introduction therefore needs to be spelled out—namely, that it is perfectly legitimate to apply to fascism the same principle used by academics when defining any ideological phenomenon, whether a premodern cultural system or a modern political movement—that is, "methodological empathy." This is the deliberate attempt to understand policies and events not from "outside" but from "within," in the way that those responsible conceived them, and hence to achieve a deeper grasp of their inner rationale and logic.

This principle is part of the stock-in-trade of cultural anthropology. Thus, however much aspects of ancient Egyptian or Aztec societies, for example, can be explained in generic categories such as "superstition," "feudal oppression," or "patriarchy," the starting point for understanding them is their cosmology, accepted in its own terms as a way of interpreting the world. Reconstituting the belief-system that led to the building of pyramids as the vehicle for the pharaoh's passage to immortal life, or as the sacred site for the constant flow of human blood required for the Fifth Sun to continue its orbit, is not a matter of justifying irrational notions about the cosmos or rationalizing suffering. It serves rather as a technique for learning more about the societies that held those beliefs. It is not apologetic, but heuristic.

The same is true of historians engaged in the study of particular episodes in the evolution of Western society. No matter how much inhumanity or corruption has been presided over by political systems associated with Christianity, absolute monarchy, conservatism, or liberalism, it is normal historiographical procedure to characterize their underlying ideologies in terms of the values, aspirations, and worldview of their major protagonists and thinkers—rather than on the basis of how they were experienced and perceived by their victims. To approach the Thirty Years' War solely as the clash of rival territorial ambitions, or the colonization of Latin America solely from the perspective of the inhabitants of an Incan city that had just been looted by conquistadors, would be considered poor, even perverse, historiography, no matter how much light those events might throw on the exploitation of Christianity by secular interests as the rationale for wealth and power, or on the "phenomenological" realities of conquest for its victims.

Inevitably, the unprecedented scale on which crimes against humanity were mass-produced by the policies of the Third Reich, and the inconceivable number of lives lost as a result of the war to defeat it, between 1939 and 1945, made it virtually impossible for the generation of academics who lived through those events to apply methodological empathy to understanding what had just happened. Fascism was naturally interpreted as the breakdown of civilization, as an orgy of nihilism and barbarism, or as a display of capitalism's most terroristic and destructive "imperialist" impulses. Children of their age, most academics instinctively characterized it in terms of what it was against, rather than what it was for, portraying it as the ruthless enemy of whatever they upheld as valuable—whether freedom, socialism, liberalism, humanism, Christianity, culture, progress, or reason. Fascism, now equated in the public mind with Nazism, was the product of a pathological national culture, an aberrant path to modernity, the last-ditch stand of a doomed imperialist system, or the megalomania of evil genius.

Some scholars, even those of the stature of Hugh Trevor-Roper and Denis Mack Smith, were so bemused by the seeming contradictions between the proclaimed beliefs of fascist leaders and their actual practice that they simply conjured away the importance of the vision of national redemption in interpreting their actions, dismissing fascist ideology as little more than euphemistic claptrap cloaking a traditional Machiavellian pragmatism. But between 1960 and 1980 a small number of scholars began pioneering a more sophisticated way of approaching fascism, explaining it as the product of a profound structural crisis in liberal society and, in its own terms, as a revolutionary bid to resolve that crisis and create a new type of national culture. Although their theories inevitably had idiosyncratic elements and might conflict on key issues, Ernst Nolte, Eugen Weber, Juan Linz, Stanley Payne, Zeev Sternhell, and George Mosse together established comparative fascist studies as a legitimate field of academic enquiry. In doing so they made it possible to treat the external features of fascism in interwar Europe (with which it had become identified)—uniforms, leader cult, militarism, spectacular or religious politics, social engineering of conformism and collective enthusiasm, elimination of individual freedoms and of the rights of workers—not as definitional traits but as the outer trappings of a movement that was working to achieve a "higher" purpose, one that it treated with deadly earnest. In different ways they all accepted that the propaganda machines of fascist parties and regimes were attempting not to brainwash the masses in order to enslave them but to induce them to share genuinely held beliefs and aspirations.

In that respect George Orwell's *1984,* though undoubtedly a brilliant evocation of the terrifying experience of living under a modern totalitarian state for someone with deep-seated humanistic instincts and convictions, is also quite misleading, since it implies that at the very heart of the regime lay an ideological vacuum, the absence of any genuine ideals other than those of a pathological sadist. What pioneers of fascist studies had in common was the belief that it was a perfectly legitimate scholarly enterprise to describe fascism in the terms that its ideologues themselves employed, as a movement of extreme nationalism bent on creating a new type of sociopolitical order, whose generic contents and "style" were dictated (in interwar Europe, at least) by the peculiar sociopolitical climate of crisis and disorientation that emerged in the aftermath of World War I. Equipped with this definition it was possible to identify the common ground shared by movements that called themselves fascist (for example, Italian Fascism, the British Union of Fascist, *Le Faisceau* in France), but, more important, to classify as fascist for the purposes of comparative study a large number of ultra-nationalist movements whose ideologues did not necessarily have recourse to the term themselves (as in the case of Nazism and the Romanian Iron Guard).

The relationship between fascism and conservatism

In its own terms then, fascism was not simply another reactionary or conservative force, for it had genuinely revolutionary aspirations. Just as many international socialists interpreted World War I as the externalization of a structural crisis of liberal democracy that heralded the age of socialism, so ultra-nationalists were predisposed to see in the chaotic events that burst upon Europe after 1914 the signs that a process of decay, affecting not just their nation but the whole of the West, was about to give way to a new age. It also follows from this methodological premise that, in marked contrast to the earlier generation of historians, scholars working in harmony with the "new consensus" take seriously the claim of many fascist ideologues to want to bring about a new type of culture. Fascism's stress on the primacy of values, ideals, and the will, its tendency to "aestheticize" politics through elaborate liturgical displays of mass energy, and the importance that it attaches to artistic, intellectual, and cultural activity are not therefore to be dismissed as the cynical propaganda of a fundamentally barbarian, nihilistic ideology. Rather, they are to be viewed as part of a drive by a modern regime to bring about a total change in values and ethos, an anthropological revolution. It is this drive that in turn explains their improvisation of an elaborate "political religion" that sets out to sacralize the state and induce the collective experience of living through the inauguration of a new historical era in the life of the nation.

Undeniably, the regimes of Hitler and Mussolini both devoted vast resources to propaganda and social engineering, but that was not in order to manipulate or "brainwash" people for the sake of it, nor to conceal a vacuum of cynicism, perversion, and nihilism; at least some of their adherents were undoubtedly true believers in a new faith who took themselves to be collaborating to achieve its rebirth. The ultimate goal of fascists was not territorial expansion or total control, but a regenerated culture in the "total" sense familiar from anthropology when it talks of Hindu or Mayan culture.

Many nationalist parties or movements have wanted the benefits of civil society to be enjoyed only by an indigenous population that culturally or ethnically fully "belongs" to the nation (the product of deeply utopian and ahistorical imaginings). They are not "fascist," however, according to our definition, unless they pursue an agenda (whether overt or covert) not only of "regime change" but also of "system change"—the wholesale replacement of liberal democracy by a new order. There have been episodes even in the history of liberalism that have an affinity with fascism, as when Robespierre attempted to purge France of the enemies of the revolution through the Terror, or when World War I temporarily but effectively turned liberal nations into authoritarian states, condemning millions of their citizens to the horrors of trench warfare. But lacking a vision of a postliberal new order, revolutionary France and World War I Britain did not come close to developing anything that could justly be called fascism.

A far more serious source of confusion for the novice to the comparative study of fascism is its complex relationship with conservatism. Interwar Europe retained a considerable political and social legacy from the age of absolutism, and in a number of countries right-wing nationalist regimes were in place based upon authoritarian forms of monarchical or military power. In Latin America too, several military or personal dictatorships were established, while Imperial Japan became ever more aggressively expansionist abroad and totalitarian at home. It has become part of the "common-sense" view of the history of the period for all of these to be seen as symptoms of the so-called era of fascism—a perception apparently corroborated by the way in which so many of these regimes deliberately adopted elements of the fascist style of rule, such as vast displays of spectacular politics, a youth movement, the cult of the nation, the portrayal of the head of state as a charismatic leader, and the militarization of society. The equation of authoritarian conservatism with fascism was seemingly corroborated by the help offered to Franco's war against the Spanish Republic by Hitler and Mussolini: the net impact of this on global opinion was for the cause of Franco to be equated with the cause of fascism. Later on, Japan's alliance with Germany and Italy in the Axis encouraged the belief that Japan too was fascist. The anticommunist and anti-Soviet stance adopted by all authoritarian right-wing regimes after 1917 also seemed to bear out the Marxist classification of them as "fascist."

However, from the perspective of the definition adopted in the present work, fascism is in principle as hostile to conservative forces as it is to liberal ones. But in the interwar period, fascism was forced into collusion with conservative forces for tactical reasons whenever the prospect of gaining power opened up, for it lacked the mass support to carry out the national revolution on its own. Mussolini's Fascism is exemplary in that respect. Mussolini's movement started out in 1919 with a radical program of anticlericalism and republicanism partly conceived in the Futurist spirit of making a radical break with the past. But within a decade the "anti-party" had become the basis of a deeply hierarchical single-party state that upheld the monarchy, had signed a pact with the Vatican, was instituting a cult both of "Romanness" and the state, and had become heavily dependent on Italy's existing military establishment, business and industrial sector, and civil service for its survival. Its leadership, youthful enough at the time of the March on Rome in 1922, was by the early 1930s well on the way to becoming a gerontocracy, a reactionary old guard hated by a new generation of fascists as obstructing the second wave of revolutionary energy that many youthful idealists wanted to see spread not just through Italy but also the whole of Europe.

Franco's Spain demonstrates another permutation of the tangled nexus between fascism and conservatism. Although aided by the fascist dictators, General Franco was by instinct true to his profession as an army commander, and deeply aware of the threat to the traditional ruling elites posed by national revolutionaries fighting for a "New Spain." As a result he kept his options open with Mussolini and Hitler, cultivating enough of the image of a fascist dictator to make them believe that he might become a full partner in the New European Order and incorporating the fascist Falange into his regime rather than eliminating it. That was a shrewd move, since its paramilitary squads had fought alongside Franco's regular troops in the Civil War; by institutionalizing the Falangists he was able to maintain a facade of revolutionary dynamism and youthful activism while essentially perpetuating the institutional structures of preliberal Spain—notably the aristocracy and the Catholic Church.

In fact then, conservative forces classically take every opportunity to eliminate, marginalize, or neutralize fascism, and only when they require the populist appeal supplied by fascism to reinforce their own political legitimacy are they prepared to deal with fascism, on a temporary basis. The notable exceptions to this rule are Fascist Italy and Nazi Germany, where conservatism supplied the tail to the fascist dog; only in the Third Reich, however, was revolutionary nationalism able to achieve a high measure of ascendancy over the civil service, industry, the military, and the church (the monarchy had been abolished in 1918). Yet here too conservatives played a crucial role in enabling fascism to seize power in both cases, having persuaded themselves that it would help destroy the threat from the Left and restore law and order.

As for Imperial Japan, there is no doubt that in the course of the 1930s its ruling elites were increasingly impressed by the territorial expansion of Italian Fascism and Nazism, as well as their open contempt for the League of Nations. The Third Reich became a role model for the country's bid to create a vast Asian colonial empire based on the alleged cultural and racial superiority of the Japanese and their right to achieve geopolitical hegemony in the Far East. However, the fact that it attempted to realize this utopia with its feudal social and political system intact—and hence not under a charismatic leader but a divine emperor—makes parallels with European fascism specious. The invasion of Manchuria in 1931 was not the expression of a revolutionary bid to bring about the rebirth of Japan out of its decline, but of the attempt by hawkish elements within the dominant military faction to maneuver the political caste into pursuing policies that would enable Japan to fulfill its considerable potential as a colonial power in the East, now that the age of European imperialism was drawing to an end. It had been placed in that position thanks to an extraordinarily rapid program of modernization, industrialization, and militarization carried out by an arch-conservative "ancien regime" with the minimum of democratization, secularization, or need to mobilize mass populist energies. The Japan that formed the Anti-Comintern Pact with Fascist Italy and Nazi Germany in 1937 certainly displayed features that can be illuminated by some generic terms deployed by Western specialists in the human sciences and historians, such as "conservatism," "militarism," "feudalism," "nationalism," and "totalitarianism." However, the peculiarities of its modernization and rise to nationhood mean that approaching its behavior as a twentieth-century military and colonial power Eurocentrically in terms of its relationship to fascism is likely to lead to more misunderstanding than insight, distracting attention from features of its imperialism for which there is no Western counterpart and that must be explored from within Japan's own history and culture. It is a history that demonstrates the power of conservatism to operate as a modern form of imperialism in a way foreign to the Western experience.

The relationship between fascism and modernity

A further confusing area is that of the relationship between fascism and modernity. The sharp contrast between the level of economic development in Italy and Germany on the eve of their respective fascist takeovers, and the vast gap separating (for instance) the Britain of the British Union of Fascists from the Romania of the Iron Guard, make it clear how fallacious it would be to locate the genesis of fascism within a particular stage of modernization. A corollary of fascism's antagonism to traditional conservatism is that it would be equally erroneous to assume that it is intrinsically hostile to modernity. Rather, its aspiration to inaugurate a new age has made many fascists believe themselves to be hypermodern, with the qualification that they have seen their task as restoring to modern life those roots and communal ethical boundaries without which it seems to them to become essentially vacuous and nihilistic. What fascism does viscerally oppose is not modernity, as such, but those elements within modernity that it considers to be fueling national decay and the erosion of that sense of a higher purpose to existence that fascism associates with membership in an organic community. While opposing cosmopolitanism and the spread of materialism, fascism can at the same time celebrate modern technology and the triumphs of the corporate economy; while envying the dynamism of the capitalism and technology of the United States, it can reject America's exaggerated individualism and moral decadence.

Similarly, there was no contradiction if Nazism celebrated Aryan values and the glories of the Germanic knights while also taking pride in its newly created motorway system; the autobahn was precisely the demonstration of the eternal Aryan genius for technology and culture, and a symbol both of the synthesis of ancestral land and forests with modernity and of the opening up of the nation to the whole people made possible for the first time through the "People's Car," the Volkswagen.

Nor was it inconsistent with the myth of a Thousand-Year Reich if the Nazis used the latest IBM technology to keep tabs on some of the millions consigned to rot or die in the concentration camps as victims of what, seen by those not under the thrall of Nazism, are clearly ancient reflexes of hatred and prejudice rationalized by pseudo-scientific theories of racial purity and decadence. The Nazis saw themselves as pioneering a new age, fusing the healthiest parts of the earlier ages with the best of modernity. It was the spirit of the past that fascists looked to in order to inspire the new era of greatness. They had no intention of restoring the various ways this spirit had externalized itself in more glorious days by abandoning the fruits of the industrial and technological revolutions.

This paradoxical relationship with the past gave fascism a complex relationship with aesthetic modernism in the interwar period. There was no inconsistency if some fascists celebrated the thrust to transcend decadence and inaugurate a new era at the heart of much modernist art, while others saw in it a symptom of rootless cosmopolitanism, the privatization of the artists' vision, the boundless commercialization of art, or the symptom of a loss of racial instinct. At this point it became a symbol of decadence rather than its transcendence. Underlying both responses was the same longing for art to reflect the health and dynamism of the national community, rather than the originality or genius of the artist. As such, fascism itself can be seen as one manifestation of modernism, understood not in the narrow artistic sense, but as a drive to counteract the disembedding, disenchanting, decentering impact of modernity that could manifest itself not only in movements of social revitalization, such as eugenics, utopian town planning, or youth movements, but also in revolutionary forms of politics with ambitious social programs to put an end to modern degeneracy.

Fascism's relationship to religion

Many fascists under Mussolini and Hitler experienced no fundamental contradiction between their religious faith and commitment even to the most extreme policies of the regime, and some clergy were enthusiastic party members and contributors to the leader cult. In Italy, where Catholicism permeated social and political life, this gave rise to the phenomenon called clerico-Fascism, which, in terms of our working definition, is a hybrid of fascism with Christianity rather than a variant of fascism itself, symptomatic of the highly developed human capacity to live out value systems containing components that are theoretically contradictory and incompatible. In Romania, the Iron Guard incorporated elements of the imagery and rhetoric of the Orthodox Church into its ideology, but that is to be attributed to the fact that in multiethnic, multicultural Romania, Orthodoxy was an indicator of "Romanianness." To make it an integral part of the consciousness of *omul nou* (the New Man), the Orthodox metaphysical element of religion was subtly replaced by the component of secular nationalism: Christ was stripped of genuine otherworldly mystery and was reduced to a metaphor for national redemption and the ultimate sacrifice demanded of "true" Romanians. A similar process of the perversion of religion into an ingredient of ultra-nationalism is exhibited in the relationship to Catholicism of the Falange in Franco's Spain, the Hungarian Arrow Cross, the Croatian Ustasha, and the Belgian Rex, in the use of Dutch Reformed Christianity by the prewar South African *Ossawabrandweg* and the postwar *Afrikaner-Werstandsbeweging,* and the invocation of Lutheranism in the Finnish People's Patriotic Movement.

A close study of such examples will confirm the fact that fascism promotes a fundamentally secular worldview. It postulates a supra-individual realm, but one that does not extend beyond the strictly this-worldly transcendence afforded by the epic history of the "organic" nation, rather than a metaphysical eternity made possible in a supraterrestrial spiritual, divine dimension. As Hitler declared in a moment of lucidity, "To the Christian doctrine of the infinite significance of the individual human soul . . . I oppose with icy clarity the saving doctrine of the nothingness and insignificance of the individual human being, and of his continued existence in the visible immortality of the nation." From this perspective Nazism's "Positive Christianity" was as much a euphemism as the "resettlement" of Jews or the "selection" of concentration camp inmates. It is consistent with this that Italian Fascism and Nazism developed elaborate forms of "political religion" that aped Christianity, and that their more radical and coherent ideologues wanted to impose as an ersatz faith and liturgy, substituting for belief in Christ a pagan cosmology and secular values centered on the nation and race. There is no doubt that in the long run Nazi leaders such as Hitler and Himmler intended to eradicate Christianity just as ruthlessly as any other rival ideology, even if in the short term they had to be content to make compromises with it.

Despite the clarity of such examples, fascism's relationship with religion is made problematic by the difficulty of drawing a neat demarcation line between the secular and the religious. In the United States, radical-right forms of Christianity, such as Christian Identity, and pagan variants of white supremacism, such as Aryan Nations, pose thorny taxonomic issues; some experts (notably Walter Laqueur) argue that radical religion itself—such as radical Islam and radical Hinduism—constitutes a form of "clerical fascism" that shows every sign of growing in importance in the new millennium. However, the policy of the present work is to regard such phenomena as more appropriately treated in an encyclopedia of religious politics or fundamentalism, no matter how many surface affinities there are between right-wing fanaticisms of any denomination.

These are just some of the issues that continue to generate controversy in comparative fascist studies, and we have not even attempted to discuss perhaps the most crucial one of all for historians—namely, how the ideology and values of fascism relate to its praxis, and to the concrete events in which individual variants of it have been involved as a sociopolitical force in modern history. In considering such questions it is worth bearing in mind that ultimately, like all taxonomic and generic concepts, the label *fascism* is a "cognitive construct," or what Max Weber called an "ideal type." It has been abstracted from the data relating to a cluster of singular phenomena between which a certain kinship is sensed, such as different variants of "feudal system," "revolution," "bourgeoisie," "modernity," or "totalitarian state." Ideal types cannot be "true" in the absolute sense, but they can have differing degrees of usefulness to the academic researching a particular area. The definitional essence of fascism is not some priceless treasure to be found only through a daring leap of the romantic or historical imagination, or what one historian sarcastically likened to the Holy Grail. It resembles rather an industrial diamond in being an entirely "man-made" product, a conceptual entity constructed through an act of idealizing abstraction in which flights of speculation are strictly controlled by down-to-earth data. It is thus a deliberate cognitive act that takes place at the beginning of an empirical investigation in the human sciences for mundane, strictly heuristic purposes. Defining fascism is not an idealistic quest but a functional starting-point for writing aspects of its history.

Roger Griffin

Notes

1. For more on the "new consensus" and the evolution of fascist studies hitherto, see Roger Griffin. "The Primacy of Culture: The Current Growth (or Manufacture) of Consensus within Fascist Studies." *Journal of Contemporary History* 37, no. 1 (2002): 21–43; Aristotle Kallis, ed. 2002. *The Fascist Reader.* London: Routledge; Roger Griffin, ed., with Matthew Feldman. 2003. *Critical Concepts: Fascism.* Vol. 1. London: Routledge.

2. Benito Mussolini, Il discorso di Napoli, [The Naples speech], October 24, 1922, text in *Il Popolo d'Italia*, No. 255, October 25, 1922; and in E. and D. Susmel, eds. 1951–1981. *Omnia Opera di Benito Mussolini.* Florence: La Fenice, Vol. 18, pp. 453–458, cited in Roger Griffin, ed. 1995. *Fascism.* Oxford: Oxford University Press, pp. 43–44.

3. Adolf Hitler, "Art and Politics," in M. Muller and Son. 1935. *Liberty. Art. Nationhood,* pp. 33–42, cited in Roger Griffin, ed. 1995. *Fascism.* Oxford: Oxford University Press, pp. 139–140.

Part II: A Short History of Fascism

THE ORIGINS OF FASCISM

It is consistent with these reflections on the nature of fascism that it has assumed radically contrasting expressions according to the specific national culture and political situation in which it has attempted to transform the status quo. It has also undergone profound changes in external expression and specific ideological content, according to whether it was born out of the structural crisis of liberal civilization and capitalism in the decade following World War I, or whether it has had to adapt to the very different threats to the (supposedly) "organic nation," "national community," or the mythic European motherland of individual ethnicities posed by the general return to stability and prosperity in the liberal capitalist world after 1945 and the emergence of the Soviet Empire.

As a fusion of the rebirth myth with ultra-nationalism, fascism has naturally emerged in societies in which two conditions have prevailed: (a) an established tradition of ultra-nationalism that rejects not just feudal or absolutist notions of dynastic power, and conservative ideas of restoring a preliberal social system (the "ancien regime"), but also liberalism itself; and (b) a prevailing sense of national decadence, weakness, and decline. In late-nineteenth-century Europe that conjuncture came about when the explosive forces of "modernity" precipitated the subjective crisis in the myth of rationality and progress associated with the "revolt against positivism" and the closely connected modernist revolt against "decadence." This expressed itself in the widespread preoccupation within artistic and intellectual circles with moral and cultural decline and renewal (for example, Dostoevsky, Nietzsche, Wagner), which in turn formed the backcloth to intense speculation about how to stop the rot and recenter a world sliding into spiritual anarchy through a revolution that would have to be as much ethical and metapolitical as political. At the end of the nineteenth century, "palingenetic" forms of ultra-nationalism remained utopian, with no real sense of the need to mobilize the masses, but by 1900 several countries were producing varieties of such forms that warrant the label "proto-fascism": notably Germany, Italy, and France, all of which went on to produce vigorous fascist subcultures after 1918.

Where and when a fully fledged form of fascism first manifested itself is a more tricky issue to resolve. By the turn of the twentieth century there was abundant writing both fictional and nonfictional available to Germans expressing the *völkisch* longing for the nation to throw off the decadent forces that were threatening its cultural and racial essence and bring about a total rebirth. Italy too hosted rich seams of cultural nationalism calling for the newly formed nation to complete its Risorgimento by discovering a unifying vision that would finally allow it to become a great nation and put an end to Giolitti's liberal regime, which was allegedly condemning it to mediocrity, disunity, and impotence. On the other hand, some scholars have argued that, ideologically, fascism already existed fully formed in France by the outbreak of World War I, born out of the fusion of antimaterialist Marxism with "tribal" nationalism. This resulted from the collaboration of syndicalists searching for a myth that would unleash the forces of popular revolution, with ultra-nationalists influenced by Maurras's attempt to find a way of mobilizing the populist energies necessary to regenerate France. It has even been suggested that the key ideas of French fascism were subsequently imported by Italian syndicalists to become the germ of Mussolini's movement. Yet that remains a minority view.

Scholars associated, wittingly or not, with the "new consensus" alluded to above broadly agree that the period from 1880 to 1914 was crucial for incubating fascism and producing all of its key ideological ingredients: for example, the organic conception of nationalism, the rejection of Enlightenment reason, the obsession with decay and renewal, the call for new elites, the cult of the body as the vehicle of health and beauty, eugenic notions of degeneration and the improvement of the race, and the conception of the modern state as charged with the task of realizing the ideal society (the

so-called "gardening state"). However, a majority opinion is that World War I was indispensable to the actual birth of fascism, supplying the vital factor that turned utopian fantasies about palingenesis into a practical form of politics bent on bringing about a national revolution. It was the war that mobilized millions in the name of a "sacred duty" to save the nation, that placed the masses at the center of politics, that gave the modern state license to make unprecedented incursions into the lives of its citizens, that displayed the awesome destructive power both of technology and of mobilizing myths, that pulverized the myth of progress, that provided a glimpse of the awesome transformations that the symbiosis of state power, technology, and mass man could achieve through the process of "total mobilization," and that created the conditions for the collapse of the ancien regime in Europe and for the Bolshevik revolution to take place in Russia. It was the war that made it "common sense" for millions, and not just for the intelligentsia, that the world was either experiencing the death throes of the liberal era—and even the death of Western civilization itself—or the birth pangs of a new order whose final contours and nature were beyond the scope of the imagination. Seen from that point of view, fascism first appeared as a fully fledged political force in Italy and Germany in the immediate aftermath of the armistice of 1918.

It was World War I that first gave Mussolini the visionary certainty that the demobilized soldiers returning from the trenches could form a new elite destined to regenerate Italy. In 1919, Mussolini formed the Fasci di combattimento in Milan, and Gabriele D'Annunzio, former decadent artist and self-styled Nietzschean but now Italy's foremost nationalist poet, became the self-consciously charismatic leader of the occupation of the city of Fiume on the Dalmatian coast by disaffected troops and their officers who believed that the Italian victory had been betrayed in the peace treaties. Even as Mussolini and D'Annunzio proclaimed the birth of a "new Italy," the far more severe conditions of national humiliation and social breakdown in Germany had given rise to several intensely racist and anticommunist parties attacking the fledgling Weimar Republic and campaigning for the establishment of a new Germany based on a reborn national community. One was the Deutschvölkischer Schutz- und Trutzbund. Another was the Deutsche Arbeiterpartei (DAP), an obscure *völkisch* nationalist party with links to the arcane Thule Society, disseminating an occultist form of anti-Semitic racism called Ariosophy, an offshoot of the wave of occultism that in the 1890s and 1900s had been one of the West's major revitalization movements at a populist level. The DAP found its fortunes transformed when a few months later it recruited a certain Adolf Hitler as one of its key speakers and added "National Socialist" to its name to form the NSDAP. If a symbolic date has to be chosen for the birth of fascism, it thus seems appropriate for it to be 1919, though it is unwise to identify it with any one person, group, or event.

THE STRUCTURAL DIVERSITY OF FASCISM

This approach to the origins of fascism rejects the "diffusionist" view that fascism spread outward from one place or movement as factions in different countries succumbed to its influence. Instead it stresses a "structuralist" interpretation that sees similar phenomena being produced by similar historical conditions in different countries. It also interprets attempts to emulate a particular manifestation of revolutionary nationalism (Italian Fascism, Nazism) as the sign that ultra-nationalists in different countries needed successful role models if they were to translate their vision of national regeneration into reality, but not that they were simply copying for its own sake. Fascism was not "imported" from Italy, Germany, or France but appeared wherever indigenous factors and conditions created the need and the "political space" for revolutionary nationalist politics, each variant generating its own unique ideological contents and policies. As a result it is extremely hazardous to generalize about the origins or contents of fascism at the level of specific ideological contents or policies. For example, all fascisms are concerned with reviving the "greatness of the nation," and hence have a built-in tendency to develop overtly racist policies. Yet it is the specific history of the nation in which a particular variant of fascism arises that determines the content of the racial policies (which particular core historical or ethnic groups are to be regenerated, and which if any are regarded as racial enemies), the type of racism (how far it draws on anthropological, cultural, historical, linguistic, religious, genetic, or eugenic components), and whether it argues for racial superiority in a way that leads to persecution or "merely" to segregation on the basis of the need to preserve difference. The example of Nazi Germany underlines the dangers of generalization about this aspect of fascism: not only was its anti-Semitism far from being homogeneous—its importance as an issue, the rationales offered for it, and the solutions envisaged for the "Jewish problem" varied considerably among committed Nazis—but the official

policies Nazism adopted as a movement and regime to purge the national community of decadence underwent extensive transformation as time went on.

Similarly, it was the pre-fascist condition of a nation and its specific situation in the aftermath of World War I that dictated whether fascism adopted an expansionist foreign policy and what its contents would be. To take an extreme example, it was only natural that interwar Hungarian fascism was intensely irredentist, since so many millions of Hungarians found themselves living within Romania's expanded borders as a result of the peace settlement of World War I—in particular, the Treaty of Trianon of June 1920—which used territorial penalties and rewards to punish the losers and reward the victors. Yet at the same time this settlement ensured that Romanian fascism did not nurture expansionist plans, since as part of the victorious coalition it had been richly rewarded with new territory at Hungary's expense; thus it was in this respect at least a "sated" nationalism (like British nationalism, for the British Empire was still the most powerful on earth).

If it is futile trying to identify core fascist policies, it is no less counterproductive to attempt to trace the origins of fascism back to particular currents of thought, such as social Darwinism, elite theory, vitalism, or millennialism, let alone individual thinkers, such as Barrès, Sorel, Pareto, Nietzsche, Haeckel, or even Mussolini himself. Not only does the ultra-nationalism of fascism mean that the origins and development of each of its variants has to be seen in its unique national context, but also that each variant proves on closer inspection to be a highly eclectic blend of ideas and influences that defy tidy theoretical analysis, with individual ideologues drawing on different sources for their ideas even within the same movement, and several different currents of rebirth myth jockeying for position.

Thus fascism's resistance to conventional political or intellectual analysis is partly due to the fact that many of its most important activists in the interwar period, true to the late-nineteenth-century spirit of vitalism (the "revolt against positivism") celebrated the primacy of action over theory and showed contempt for party political programs, coherent doctrines, and theoretical rationales. But it is also because, despite its desire to appear homogeneous, each movement of appreciable size and momentum is liable to contain rival variants of the vision of the reborn nation, each one representing a different synthesis of ideas, even at the highest level. Leading Nazis such as Adolf Hitler, Gregor Strasser, Walther Darré, Joseph Goebbels, Heinrich Himmler, Alfred Rosenberg, and Fritz Todt, for example, held a wide range of opinions on the need to overhaul capitalism and create a corporate economy, workers and peasantry in the national revolution, the appropriate aesthetic expression of Nazi technological and technocratic modernity, the centrality of "racial hygiene," and the role to be played by pagan and occultist theories of the Aryan race. There were even significant differences in the intensity and "biologism" of their anti-Semitism and the radicalness of the solutions they envisaged to the "Jewish problem." What enabled them to make common cause was their shared passion for the cause of national rebirth, combined with their belief in Hitler and the NSDAP as the embodiment of and vehicle for that rebirth.

Fascism's eclecticism and heterogeneity means that it defies straightforward analysis in terms of specific ideological axioms or the Left/Right political spectrum. In different ways, Italian Fascism and Nazism combined a conservative view that human potential is constrained by natural forces, the belief in private property, and the need for hierarchy with "left-wing" ideas of the possibility of creating a "new man," direct state involvement in welfare and in the regulation of the economy, and the formation of a classless (though still hierarchical and unequal) society through the agency of the so-called national community. Both also advocated the need for a new elite of political soldiers, while stressing the need to mobilize popular energies, and both synthesized a belief in the value of the past as a repository of eternal values with the commitment to an intense program of technological modernization carried out in a radical spirit that gave them few qualms about breaking with any traditional institutions and values that did not serve the higher interests of the nation. Other forms of fascism manifest similar paradoxes. Movements in Romania and South Africa, for example, combined elements of conventional Christianity with pagan ideas of race and destiny.

Such syncretism not only operated in different fascisms to produce contrasting policies on art, demographic growth, the role of women, the economy, and technology, but also could produce a proliferation of different theories on the same issue within the same movement. Thus Italian Fascism attempted to institute a "corporatist" economy, but the state made little effort to resolve the glaring differences between left-wing currents of corporatist theory, which retained remnants of a socialist commitment to class equality, and right-wing currents, which saw the experiment as a way of neutralizing class conflict in the interests of the state and capital. There was also a rival Christian variant of corporatism promoted by the Vatican with its own spokesmen under the Italian Fascist regime. This prolif-

eration of corporatisms partly explains why the so-called corporatist state never became a reality. By contrast, in the sphere of artistic production, Italian Fascism deliberately adopted a hands-off policy while encouraging the public to identify Italian Fascism with all outstanding cultural achievements in the spirit of "hegemonic pluralism," referred to earlier, resulting in a large number of conflicting aesthetic codes whose protagonists invariably claimed theirs to be the most expressive of the spirit of the New Italy. Nazism, on the other hand, though it launched a four-year economic plan and set up enormous state enterprises, such as Hermann-Goering Works and the Todt Organization, never embraced an economic theory of corporatism. Yet in practice it comprehensively corporatized all aspects of cultural life and production within the Reichskulturkammer (the "Reich Chamber of Culture").

Meanwhile the British Union of Fascists (BUF) adopted an Italian-style corporatist theory enriched with elements of home-grown Keynesian economics, while its stand on artistic decadence came to be increasingly modeled on the antimodernist and anti-Semitic policies of Nazi Germany, even if its own racism was never overtly biological or eugenic. Predictably, the party press claimed that a BUF victory would usher in a new golden age, not just of British military strength and colonialism but also of art, emulating the glories of the Elizabethan or Shakespearean Age, the last time Britain had experienced the longed-for conjuncture of political and cultural greatness. The theory of history espoused by BUF leader Sir Oswald Mosley, however, drew not just on a highly selective version of Christian ethics but on the Nietzschean superman theory as well (partly mediated by George Bernard Shaw) and on Spengler's theory of the decline of the West, to which he believed international fascism provided the answer. His own vision of the Greater Britain was highly technocratic (though it retained the monarchy), even if one of his better-known followers, Henry Williamson, developed a deeply anti-urban and proto-Green variant conceived to save Britain's countryside from the ravages of cosmopolitanism along the lines of Darré's Blood and Soil in Germany. The BUF had other idiosyncrasies, not just in its choice of national heroes (Robin Hood and King Arthur were treated as forerunners of national socialism), but also in celebrating pacifism and appeasement rather than war—but on condition that Britain retain her vast colonial empire and thus uphold, not liberal humanist ideas of peace, but the Pax Britannica. No matter how derivative in its genesis, the BUF was thus very English in ethos and iconography. It is clear from these examples that any attempt to look for a core set of fascist ideological components or policies beyond one as nebulous as national rebirth is misguided. Instead it is more fruitful for attempts to understand the nature of fascism as a revolutionary political project to start by concentrating on the historical conditions in which it arose.

ITALIAN FASCISM AND GERMAN NAZISM

Fascism took concrete form as a movement at a time when Europe had just emerged from a war that had mobilized and demobilized millions of uniformed men, raised national consciousnesses to fever pitch, and militarized the ethos even in states that had not participated in the war. The aftermath of the war saw the collapse of the ancien regime in Europe, the removal of the German monarchy, the redrawing of the maps of Germany and central Europe, the Russian Revolution, and attempts by Bolsheviks to internationalize it throughout the capitalist world. It was an age of upheaval, crisis, and revolution, shattering the illusion of indefinite stability, progress, and peace that had characterized the Belle Epoque and creating a mood of the times in which Spengler's *Decline of the West* became a best-seller on the strength of the title alone. The war produced a Europe of crowds, rallies, and thronged squares, where media technology had developed enough to produce a powerful propaganda machine capable of reaching millions of ordinary lives yet to be privatized by consumerism, the car, multichannel television, video games, and cellular phones. In these extraordinary conditions any political movement that wanted to revolutionize the status quo naturally expressed itself as a mass uniformed movement run on military lines by a leader whose image was that of a soldier rather than a statesman, and poured energy into staging spectacular forms of charismatic politics once the necessary critical mass had been achieved in terms of public support. That is why outwardly Fascism, Nazism, and Soviet Communism under Stalin look so similar on the newsreels to the untrained eye: an orgy of brainwashing propaganda, megalomania, and state terror.

The background to the emergence of Italian Fascism was the incomplete nature of the Risorgimento, as summed up in d'Azeglio's famous remark that unification had succeeded in making Italy but not in making Italians. Vast areas of the peninsula were in social and economical terms chronically underdeveloped, compared with Germany, Britain, or even France, and the

nation lacked the industrial, military, and colonial might to be a Great Power. The traditional corruption and weakness of the political system made it unable to deal with the pressing problems posed by the primitiveness and ungovernability of "the South," the persistent refusal of the Church to recognize the Italian state, or the militancy of revolutionary socialists. It also proved unresponsive to the longing for an improvement in living conditions that was rife among the millions of ordinary people from all over Italy whose lives had been affected, and in many cases devastated, by the sacrifices necessitated by participation in the war. The treatment of Italy by its allies in the peace settlement of 1919, which was shabby, even if it was not the "mutilated victory" D'Annunzio claimed it to be, only reinforced the widespread sense (which had for decades been common among the intelligentsia and ruling elites) that Italy was in the vicelike grip of decadence.

It was against this background that Italian Fascism achieved power. It did not "conquer the state" through a surge of mass electoral and social support, or a tide of mass charismatic energy, but it exploited the ineffectiveness of Giolitti's government in tackling the threat from the revolutionary Left. However, when Mussolini set about replacing the parliamentary system with a totalitarian state in 1925, no mass protest movement arose to voice its opposition. Indeed, the majority of Italians actively or passively welcomed the Fascist experiment, not just as the basis for the imposition of law and order after years of instability and social unrest but also as the only way in which their nation would reverse the decline and become great again. From then on Fascism's popularity grew, arguably reaching its highest point when, in May 1935, Mussolini was able to announce from his balcony to an ecstatic crowd in the square below and to millions more Italians listening to his speech at home that "Ethiopia is Italian."

By contrast, the Germany that emerged from the war in 1918 had already "nationalized" its citizens to a high degree. This was an undertaking considerably aided by the fact that, at the turn of the twentieth century, even if Britain remained the greatest colonial power on earth, Germans knew that their country had become the most productive military, industrial, and cultural power in Europe. Their formerly secure sense of national identity was now to suffer a series of blows that followed on from a surrender that took many Germans by surprise and bequeathed the myth of the nation's having been "stabbed in the back" by (Jewish) Social Democrats: the abdication of the emperor and the end of the Second Reich; the brief seizure of power by communists in Berlin and Munich; the imposition of a deeply humiliating and economically punitive peace settlement at Versailles, including the loss of Alsace and Lorraine; the occupation of the Ruhr by foreign troops; an acute monetary crisis that culminated in the hyperinflation of 1923; not to mention the wave of horrendous social distress that swept across the nation as hundreds of thousands of demobilized soldiers, many mutilated by injuries sustained in battle or psychologically damaged, tried in vain to reintegrate themselves into a society in which millions mourned loved ones who now seemed to have died for nothing. This collective misery was lived out within a nation already saturated with the hypercharged chauvinist sentiments that affected all combatant nations in the cauldron of World War I but that had been given a particularly aggressive dynamic by a powerful tradition of belief in the cultural superiority and unique destiny to greatness of Germany. The latter had been first articulated in response to the occupation of German provinces by Napoleonic troops a century earlier. By the last decade of the nineteenth century the belief was finding expression in a proliferation of *völkisch* literature that evoked the myth of a "true Germany" which had been travestied by the modern nation-state, as well as in forms of pangermanism and anti-Semitism that were emerging in German and Austrian political subcultures with increasing virulence.

What imparted a particular coloring and intensity to German ultra-nationalism was the fact that the rapid urbanization and secularization of society, accompanied by the growth of science and technology in an area of Europe that not long before had been predominantly rural, had, by the late nineteenth century, given rise both to powerful "antimodern" (but modernist) currents of nostalgia for connectedness with virgin nature, and to pseudo-scientific, biological and eugenic forms of a highly modernized racism. To make matters worse, there was also a long and complex history of anti-Semitism in the German-speaking world that created a backlash against the growing emancipation and integration of Jews under the Second Reich. Apart from influential nationalistic associations such as the Pan-German League, Wilhelmine Germany also hosted numerous societies devoted to paganism and esotericism, some of which in the early 1900s were refining occultist varieties of racism and anti-Semitism almost unknown elsewhere in Europe. The result was that when the collective national identity underwent the trauma of 1918, a wave of brooding anomie (a sense of social and moral vacuum) gripped many Germans who lacked deep spiritual anchors in a personal or metaphysical sphere immune from the vicissitudes of history, thus swelling currents of hyper-nationalism that had started flowing well before the outbreak of war. A powerful ultra-Right subculture came into existence almost immediately, articulated by authors who in different ways argued that Weimar was not a true state: what was needed was a German revolution that would allow the nation to arise from the ashes of defeat and humiliation and become once more the great cultural and political nation it essentially remained, despite defeat, betrayal, and humiliation.

It was against this backcloth of a highly diffused, multifaceted, and racist ultra-nationalism (one that had no real equivalent in Italy) that the spark of national revolution represented by the minute Deutsche Arbeiterpartei could be fanned by Hitler into the flames of the NSDAP. Upon its reformation in 1925 the party became a populist movement and parliamentary party—albeit one with a very small electoral base till 1930; within three years Hitler had managed to use it as the vehicle for bringing together into a single ecumenical force all the major currents of German ultra-nationalism that existed at the end of the war. These ranged from extreme anti-urbanization and "blood and soil" ruralism to an intense commitment to modernization and technology, from pagan and occultist blood mysticism to eugenics, from overtly religious to extremely secularized varieties of thought that could appeal to representatives of all academic disciplines and artistic milieux as long as they were committed to the vision of German rebirth. Nazism could also build on the existence of a highly developed civic society and on the widespread Prussian cult of obedience, efficiency, and duty that had no counterpart in Italy.

For all their array of distinctive features, Italian Fascism and German Nazism actually had a striking amount in common. Both of them cultivated an organic view of the nation and a cyclical vision of the fundamental processes of history, according to which it could be periodically "renewed"; both rejected materialism, conservatism, communism, socialism, and liberalism in principle in the name of a new order. Both tended to promote a vitalistic and idealist concept of reality that celebrated action, the will, and the power of myth. The structural parallels go even deeper. From a sociological or anthropological perspective, both regimes offered a solution to the ailments of modernity, analyzing those ailments in terms of anomie, alienation, and decadence. At an experiential level these translate as an acute sensation, not necessarily expressible in words, of the breakdown of genuine community and a shared cosmology, and the loss of a center and a collective identity; of the atomization of society; of the erosion of the spiritual and metaphysical dimension to life resulting from the spread of materialism and individualism; of the reduction of culture to self-expression, sensuality, or sensationalism to the point where artists and intellectuals had ceased to be the interpreters and articulators of the healthy values of the "people"; of the decay of tradition, traditional values, and hierarchies through the impact of egalitarianism, democracy, and secularization.

To reverse this decay, neither regime attempted to return to an idealized past of the nation (as conservatives would have it). Instead, both set out to forge a mythic link between the present generation and a glorious stage in the past (the Roman Empire, the pristine age of the Aryans) that would enable the "eternal values" that it embodied to live once more in the new order. Both regimes thus upheld a cyclical vision of historical time and intended their revolution to inaugurate a renewed era of national greatness. Their politics were informed by a totalizing view that naturally expressed itself in a "totalitarian" style of politics, not in the sense of oppression but in the attempt to make each Italian and German belong mind, body, and soul to the regime. They were meant to internalize the cosmology and values of Fascism and Nazism as fully as medieval Christians were meant to live out the values of Christianity in every aspect of their lives. The natural expression of this concept of politics was in both cases a highly developed theatrical and liturgical style, creating a "political religion" that implicitly sacralized the regime and its leaders as objects of veneration. Certainly Hitler and probably Mussolini (whose private thoughts on such issues are more difficult to glean) intended belief in the new order they had created eventually to replace conventional religious faith, no matter how many concessions to Christianity were necessary in the short term.

Even in areas where major differences between the regimes become apparent—such as the relative absence of anti-Semitism in Fascist Italy before 1938 compared with the Third Reich, or the Italian Fascist enthusiasm for artistic modernism (notably Futurism) compared with Nazism's rejection of it—closer consideration reveals that here too the regimes are more kindred spirits than has often been assumed, especially by historians who insist that Nazism was a product of Germany's "special path" to modern nationhood, so that attempts to apply comparative perspectives are fruitless. For example, some Italian Fascist artists cultivated an anti-urban, "back to nature" form of art known as *strapaese,* which had parallels with the Nazi art associated with the cult of "blood and soil," and while Nazism is reputedly antimodernist, a genre of art existed that celebrated the construction of motorways and factories in a triumphalist technophile spirit related to Futurism, even if stylistically remote from it. A small but vociferous faction of Nazi art theorists argued that expressionism (a German form of modernism) was pervaded with a deeply antidecadent Aryan dynamism, and they lost out to the vehemently antimodernist Rosenberg lobby only in 1935.

As for the question of race, from early on Italian Fascism energetically pursued a policy of demographic growth through a whole raft of state measures to encourage births. It also instituted a cult of athleticism and sport that was linked to the celebration of the Romans as a physically and spiritually gifted world-historical race with a special historical destiny now being renewed under Fascism. In the aftermath of the colonization of Ethiopia, antimiscegenation laws were introduced to preserve the purity of Italian blood from contamination by contact with "natives." There were also currents of anti-Semitism within Italian Fascism from early on that, in the 1930s, grew in outspokenness not only under the impact of Nazi Germany but also as a response to the increasing radicalness of Zionism in its call for Jews to be given their own homeland in Palestine. It is thus simplistic to regard the Fascist race laws promulgated in 1938 that declared the Italians an Aryan race into which Jews could never be assimilated as a simple import from Nazi Germany, especially since there is no evidence that Hitler applied direct pressure on Mussolini to address the "Jewish problem" in Italy.

Stereotypes about Italian Fascism and Nazism reinforced in the popular cinema (which paradoxically reflect widespread racist stereotypes about Italians and Germans in general) make it tempting to assume that everything about Mussolini's regime was messy, chaotic, improvised, and relatively benign, in stark contrast to a Third Reich that was monolithic, well coordinated, punctiliously planned, and irremediably evil. Film versions of World War II have created stock images of German soldiers as humorless fanatics readily obeying orders, while their Italian opposite numbers could not wait to fling off their uniforms and revert to their good-natured humanity and love of life, women, and music. In fact, however, despite the rhetoric of total unity, collective will, and the leaders' seer-like long-term vision of the future, both regimes contained conflicting currents of ideology, many centers of power (they were "polycentric" and "polycratic"), and a great deal of improvisation (they were, in a manner of speaking, palingenetic ad-hocracies). There were fanatical Fascists in Italy prepared to commit atrocities, and there were Nazis who disobeyed orders and risked their lives to help victims of the Third Reich. But the most fundamental kinship between the two regimes, the one that underlies the surface similarities of institutions, political style, and policies, lies in a shared vision of national rebirth that enabled their most fervent activists and ideologues to feel that they were part of the same revolution, which was inaugurating a new era in history.

Specimens of the same political genus they may have been, but a vast gulf separates the impact of the respective policies of Italian Fascism and German Nazism on their own populations and on the history of the twentieth century. Both regimes were expansionist, as befitted a fascist state in an age in which national greatness was equated with colonial possessions. For its part, Fascist Italy set out primarily to complete some unfinished business of liberal Italy by conquering Ethiopia, thereby avenging the famous defeat of Italian troops at the hands of the Abyssinians at Adowa in 1896, and enabling the regime to claim that it had fulfilled yet another part of its mission by giving Italy an African Empire to emulate the Romans and join the league of Great Powers. It was drawn into supporting Franco in the Spanish Civil War largely so as not be eclipsed by Nazi Germany and to be seen to play a leading role in the war against Bolshevism and the defense of "Christian" civilization. It became embroiled in World War II against the instincts of Mussolini, who was aware that he was the junior partner in the Rome-Berlin Axis and that his military resources were deficient. At the same time, however, he was reluctant to surrender the initiative entirely to Hitler and so lose the spoils of what seemed at the time like Nazism's inevitable victory in Europe. Left to its own devices, Italian Fascism is unlikely to have aspired to much more than turning Italy into a modest colonial power with a high profile on the international stage, widely respected abroad for its modern armed forces and its resolute stand against Bolshevism and social chaos, even if that meant defying challenges to its sovereignty by the League of Nations.

By contrast, Nazi expansionist policy evolved considerably over time and was driven not by one but by a cluster of goals. Hitler's *Mein Kampf* had already committed the NSDAP to reversing the terms of the Versailles Treaty and redeeming the "blood sacrifice" of the millions of war dead by ending foreign occupation of the Ruhr and incorporating all ethnic Germans in the new Reich, which in practice involved annexing the Czech area of Czechoslovakia (home of the Sudeten Germans) and Austria, and taking back Alsace and Lor-

raine from the French (the Alto Adige could not be "redeemed" immediately because of the alliance with Mussolini). It also revived old dreams of an empire in the East, which under Hitler meant the colonization of Poland, the Baltic States, and Russia, so as to provide a vast supply of food, raw materials, oil, industrial capacity, and labor, as well as the elimination of Bolshevism from Europe. Once the war had started, plans emerged for Germany to rule a geopolitical area of privileged status formed by the Germanic peoples (which might also have been extended to include the British Isles) and to create a New European Order dominated by Germany. The prerequisite for a vast program of conquest and colonization, elements of which were deeply rooted in German history (such as the enmity with France and Poland) while others evolved or were improvised in the light of unfolding events and the opportunities they brought, was the creation of a war machine of an unprecedented level of material and human strength.

By 1937 the speed and level of Nazi rearmament had created a domestic situation in which only the acquisition of colonies and vassal states could avert a deep economic crisis, which in practice meant a new European war, something that Nazi military forward planning took for granted. What enabled such a policy to be envisaged in the first place was that, unlike Italy, Germany on the eve of World War II was one of the most technologically advanced and productive industrial nations in the world, dominating nearly every sector of manufacture and technical innovation, not least military technology. Moreover, Germany had displayed the ability to mount a military campaign of awesome power in World War I, and had been defeated economically and diplomatically rather than by force of arms. It thus had the military, industrial, and technological means, as well as the human resources and public consensus, necessary to undertake a program of military conquest that was quite inconceivable in Italy.

Another factor that contributed to the distinctiveness of the Nazis' scheme of territorial expansion was their racial concept of nationhood and history. In contrast to the founders of Italian Fascism, the Nazi elite embraced from the outset a belief in the nation not just as a cultural but also as an ethnic entity, a conviction rationalized both through the deeply "Romantic" currents of nineteenth-century nationalism and through genetics, physical anthropology, social Darwinism, and eugenics. This scientist vision of the nation not only led to the rationalization of anti-Semitism in biological as well as cultural terms but also had an impact on every aspect of Nazi ideology. The belief in the Aryan stock of modern Germans as an anthropological and genetic reality, and the resulting idea of national greatness and decay as a function of racial health and purity, informed the Nuremberg race laws, the genocide of the gypsies, the sterilization and euthanasia programs, the campaigns to eradicate homosexuality and "social parasitism," the war on decadent art and attempts to engineer a healthy German substitute, the new pseudoscience of "racial hygiene," the demographic policy to breed more Germans, the Nazification of school curricula, the cult of sport, and the vision of the "new man." Biological racism also underlay the Third Reich's claim on ethnic German populations outside Germany's state borders, as well as conditioning the spirit in which territorial expansion was carried out. Collaborating French, for example, were treated relatively benignly, because they were considered citizens of a civilized country heavily influenced in its history by Aryans and Germans, whereas Poles and Russians were assumed to be intrinsically subhuman; the utter brutality of their occupation and colonization reflected that premise. In the Russian campaign both the military and civilian populations of the enemy territories were generally treated by convinced Nazis with the same contempt that in the main the Spanish and Portuguese armies had shown the indigenous populations of Latin America in the sixteenth century, or that was expressed by many European colonialists in their attitude to native Africans when slavery was at its height By contrast, Italian Fascism only belatedly adopted a "scientifically" racist and anti-Semitic concept of the nation, and then half-heartedly, though it should be remembered that "normal" European assumptions of the primitiveness of non-European peoples were demonstrated in abundance in the brutal Italian colonization of Ethiopia.

It is the program to commit the systematic genocide of the Jews that has understandably become the most notorious manifestation of Nazi racism, though it is important not to forget the many more millions of Russian and Polish civilians and soldiers murdered by the Nazis, the genocide of the Roma and Sinti peoples, the mass murder of the "hereditary ill," the ruthless persecution of communists, homosexuals, and Jehovah's Witnesses, "decadent" artists, defiant Protestants and Catholics, and many other categories of racial and ideological "enemies," as well as the use of forced labor on a gigantic scale, involving the exploitation of "human resources" from many creeds and nations to keep the Third Reich's arms industry in full production to the bitter end. The Holocaust remains in the collective historical imagination of postwar generations one of the defining events of the twentieth century, on a par

as a calculated act of mass destruction of human life with the purges carried out by Stalinist communism and the dropping of the two atom bombs on Japan in the summer of 1945 (though the rationale for each is, of course, entirely different). Its enormity as an episode of painstakingly planned and executed mass murder carried out by a highly advanced and nominally Christian European state with an extraordinarily rich cultural heritage and highly educated and "civilized" population is one of the most important reasons why historians, especially in Germany, are still reluctant to apply the generic perspective offered by fascist studies to the Third Reich: the Holocaust seems to set the German case definitively apart, as something entirely sui generis—unique and disconnected from the world outside.

Fascist studies must not, of course, be used to detract from or "relativize" the uniqueness of a human catastrophe that historical analysis can never adequately capture, nor to mitigate the element of personal responsibility, moral failure, and guilt involved in every single act of persecution, torture, and murder. However, even here, where explanatory powers, understanding, and the language of humanism are stretched to the limit, the theory of fascism as advocated by the "new consensus" has something important to offer. Once Nazism is located within generic fascism, three important aspects of the Holocaust are thrown into relief. First, the ultra-nationalism of the Third Reich, of which it was one of the ultimate expressions, was far from being a product of something peculiarly German, since it is common to all fascisms, which in turn were incubated by the ultra-nationalist cultural climate of Europe as a whole. Even its virulent anti-Semitism was far from unique. Not only was it found in less intense forms in Italian Fascism and in the British Union of Fascists but it also existed in intense, eliminatory forms in the Croatian Ustasha, the Hungarian Arrow Cross, the Romanian Iron Guard, and in Nazi-dominated regimes such as Vichy France and the Salò Republic, as well as among those elements of the populations that collaborated in the genocide in Poland, the Baltic States, Ukraine, and Russia. What makes Nazism unique is that it was the only fascist movement that actually acquired power in an advanced industrialized nation-state, which placed it in a position to apply huge resources to the ruthless implementation of its eugenic vision of the new order.

Second, seeing Nazism as a form of fascism highlights the role played by modernity in making the "final solution" possible. Fascism draws on the past for mythic inspiration but is forward-looking, pursuing the realization of an alternative, rigorously "futural" temporalization. It does not reject modernity, only its "decadent," nation-destroying elements. It enthusiastically embraces whatever elements of modernity can help bring about the national revolution. In many respects the Holocaust is a product of the hyper-modernity and hyper-rationality of the modern state in the permutation of it created by the Third Reich, rather than of "antimodernity" or of regressive, reactionary barbarity. Once the modern state takes upon itself the task of deploying its enormous material and human resources to pursuing what it has designated a higher cause, or creating the ideal society at whatever cost in terms of the suffering inflicted on its own citizens and those of other states, then atrocities can occur with a minimum of individual responsibility and personal will being involved.

Finally, the "new consensus" highlights the ritual and cathartic dimension of the Holocaust. Far from being conceived in a purely destructive, nihilistic spirit, or being the emanation of Hitler's own pathological anti-Semitism, let alone the product of the personal sadism and hatred of his many thousands of "willing executioners," the destruction of European Jewry was conceived by many of those who participated in it, and by all the Nazi leaders, as just one major episode in the necessary process of purging Europe of decadence. It was informed by the same logic as the eradication of the hereditarily ill in the so-called euthanasia program, or the burning of decadent books and paintings: the unhealthy must be purged to make way for the healthy, death is the necessary prelude to rebirth (a principle known as "creative destruction" or "German nihilism"). A deep ritualistic impulse informs such a logic, fusing the instrumental rationality of modernity with man's most archaic psychological mechanisms for imbuing time with meaning, and endowing all those whose sense of purpose and morality is locked into this logic with the conviction that they are carrying out a higher and sacred mission, beyond the comprehension and judgment of profane minds. A member of the Red Cross who made an unofficial inspection of Nazi death camps in 1944 was asked by a BBC journalist why he did not attempt to confront the commanders of Auschwitz with the moral enormity of what was happening in their camp. He answered that the very idea was preposterous: "These people were proud of their work. They were convinced of being engaged in an act of purification. They called Auschwitz the anus of Europe. Europe had to be cleansed. They were responsible for the purification of Europe. If you cannot get your head round that you will understand nothing at all." A

chilling palingenetic logic of "creative destruction" runs through all the cultural, racial, and foreign policies enacted so meticulously and ruthlessly by Nazism and the events they unleashed: Nazism was at once irreducibly unique and yet simultaneously a manifestation of generic fascism.

THE FASCIST ERA?

To devote so much time to the Third Reich's relationship to Italian Fascism and generic fascism runs the risk of endorsing the "Nazi-centric" view of fascism that it is one of the purposes of the present publication to challenge. There has been a regrettable tendency in reference works and in survey histories for Nazism to become the subliminal template for the essential "nature of fascism," the manifestation of its deepest impulses and essence. This false premise creates two significant distortions in the understanding of fascism as a generic ideological and historical force. First, it detracts attention away from the sheer diversity of interwar fascisms and from a recognition of their almost universal failure to achieve power. Second, it makes the evolution of fascism after 1945 almost incomprehensible.

One of fascism's outstanding general traits when compared with conservatism, liberalism, or socialism is the vast gap between the ambitious rhetoric of total renewal and its actual achievements. Italian Fascism's dream of a Third Rome proved to be wildly unrealistic, and the mass Fascistization of the Italians, which might have seemed partly realized when a wave of excited patriotism swept Italy on the conquest of Ethiopia in May 1935, turned out to have been a clamorous failure once World War II was under way. Although Nazification initially made great inroads into German society, when the war turned against the Third Reich the genuine enthusiasm of millions for the regime decayed into mass conformism maintained through the increasingly intensive use of propaganda, social engineering, and state terror, even if the Hitler myth itself proved stubbornly resistant.

The most obvious pattern to emerge from a comparative survey of fascisms outside of Italy and Germany in the interwar period is that of their chronic political weakness and widespread marginalization. A unique configuration of factors accounts for each failure in detail, but one common denominator stands out: the "political space" available for a revolutionary nationalist project to establish a new order was simply too small because of the structural stability of the conservative, liberal, or (in the case of Russia) communist system that they were attempting to overthrow—in some cases reinforced by displays of popular opposition to the threat that fascism posed. Fascists made few inroads into the power of the state outside Italy and Germany. In England, BUF membership peaked at 50,000, at most, in 1934, and Mosley's "Greater Britain" remained a chimera; in Ireland, the most radical component of the Blue Shirts that followed their openly fascist leader, Eoin O'Duffy, to form the National Corporate Party (the Greenshirts) in 1935 had a minimal impact on events, beyond intensifying the general climate of political crisis and uncertainty in the newly liberated nation-state. Minute, easily marginalized movements, whether parties or pressure groups, emerged on Italian Fascist lines (in the 1920s) or increasingly Nazi lines (in the 1930s) in Czechoslovakia, Poland, and every Scandinavian and Benelux country, but the only ones to achieve any importance historically were those that formed the basis of collaborationist parties under Nazi occupation—namely, Quisling's Nasjonal Samling in Norway, Mussert's Nationaal-Socialistische Beweging in Holland, and Degrelle's Rex in Belgium, which became overtly fascist only after war broke out.

In Finland the virulence of anticommunism caused by the proximity of Soviet Russia, and the legacy of the civil war between nationalists and communists, provided the habitat for a more substantial ultra-Right movement, leading eventually to the emergence of the IKL (People's Patriotic Movement). The IKL was both a party and an extraparliamentary movement, with a typically fascist vision of the Finns' special historical and cultural mission as a race and the imminence of its rebirth as a Greater Finland. As it happened, though, it too was kept safely at bay by the liberal system. Only one other European democracy hosted a more significant ultra-Right subculture after 1933—namely, France. There a cluster of minute formations and much larger paramilitary movements espoused anticommunist and ultra-nationalist ideas, some of which were influenced by Nazism; most, however, drew on the country's long tradition of ultra-conservative opposition to Republican liberalism and socialism. Their total membership probably represented a constituency of hundreds of thousands at the peak of nationalist agitation against the Blum government in 1934, and there are grounds for seeing the veterans' league of the Croix de Feu as one of the largest fascist movements of the interwar years—that is, before its ban and subsequent domestication within the Parti Social Français. However, the extreme fragmentation of the French ultra-Right deprived its supporters of the cohesion, prag-

matism, and leadership of a movement like the NS-DAP, factors that were necessary to challenge the stability of the Second Republic, however much of a threat they seemed to pose at the time. Outside Europe, movements inspired by Nazism in the United States and Australia remained minute, while the home-grown movements of Afrikaner ultra-nationalism in South Africa, the Ossawabrandweg and the Greyshirts, never threatened British dominance of interwar South Africa (although the Greyshirts misjudged their strength sufficiently to make an abortive attempt to launch a pro-Nazi civil war). Overall, then, with the outstanding exceptions of Italy and Germany, liberalism effectively withstood the attempts by domestic fascist movements to overthrow it.

It might be assumed that conservative authoritarian regimes could afford to be more hospitable to fascism, especially since in theory they both shared some important core values (such as nationalism and "family values") and had common enemies (for example, communism, individualism, and materialism). Yet, though fascism may subsume many traditional conservative elements, its revolutionary, palingenetic, populist thrust makes it the archenemy of authoritarian conservatism and the social elites whose interests it serves. Therefore it should not be surprising that fascism was also neutralized whenever it showed signs of undermining the hegemony of traditional preliberal ruling elites. Thus in Portugal, Salazar had no scruples in suppressing Rolão Preto's National Syndicalists (Blue Shirts) when they threatened to mount a coup. In Vichy France, genuine fascists such as Déat and Doriot were given no chance under Marshal Pétain to become part of the ruling cadres and generally preferred to remain in the Nazi-occupied zone, where they enjoyed more freedom to nourish their utopian fantasies of playing a proactive role in the European New Order in the company of numerous artistic and intellectual fellow-travellers of Nazism. In Latvia the leader of the Peasant's League, Ulmanis, suppressed the Perkonkrust, or Thunder Cross, after he set up an authoritarian regime to solve the state crisis. In Hungary, Horthy's right-wing authoritarian government imprisoned Szálasi when his Arrow Cross–Hungarist movement experienced a sudden surge in popularity in 1938. It was only when the Third Reich forced Hungary into becoming a puppet state that he was made its nominal head, a compliant tool in the imposition of the "final solution" on the substantial Jewish population. In Austria, the threat posed to the authoritarian state by the fascist element in the paramilitary Heimwehren was neutralized until the country's annexation by the Third Reich (the

Anschluss), despite the assassination of Dollfuss by Austrian Nazis in 1934 (a vivid demonstration of the underlying hostility between fascism and conservatism).

The two movements that break with this pattern are the Falange in Spain and the Legion of the Archangel Michael (Iron Guard) in Romania, both of which can be argued to have shared government power. However, Franco's incorporation of the Falange into his regime was a calculated move to enable him to exploit its image of dynamism, radicalism, and youth while effectively neutralizing it as a revolutionary force. In Romania, both King Carol and General Antonescu cynically attempted to use the legion to the same ends. King Carol did so only once he realized that his attempts to crush it were undermining his popularity, though his abdication soon put an end to the experiment. Antonescu tried to channel the significant popular enthusiasm for the legion into support for his National Legionary State. However, he could not control its most radical elements, and with the approval of Hitler he finally deployed the army to wipe it out root and branch in an extreme display of state terror.

The same basic pattern was exhibited elsewhere. In 1937, General Vargas crushed Brazilian Integralist Action (AIB), the largest fascist movement outside Europe. Led by Plínio Salgado, who had given his movement a sophisticated ideology and historical vision of renewal, the AIB's elaborate organizational structure and "political religion" had developed a significant presence in Brazilian society, its membership by 1934 numbering more than 200,000; but it was still no match for state troops. In Chile the National Socialist Movement's attempted coup of 1938 was easily put down by the military regime, whereupon it mutated into a democratic party. Elsewhere in Latin America various blends of military dictatorship with democratic institutions maintained power in the interwar period, largely untroubled by the numerous populist nationalist movements that arose without the mass support or clear-cut revolutionary agenda to pose a real threat or to be classified as unambiguously fascist. Japan in the 1930s hosted a cluster of right-wing projects and groupings, but one of the few attempts to create a movement of populist ultra-nationalism on European lines was the minute "Eastern Way," modeled on Nazism. This made a significant ideological break with the fundamental principle of Japanese conservatism by turning the emperor into a purely symbolic national figurehead. Immediately it showed signs of raising its public profile through mass meetings it was banned and its leader, Nakano Seigo, placed under house arrest, whereupon he committed the ritual suicide of the samurai warrior.

There are, however, two at least partial exceptions to this pattern of fascism's abject failure. There are convincing arguments for seeing Argentina's postwar Peronist government as an attempt to steer the country into social and economic stability by fusing the familiar elements of Latin American rule—namely, military junta and personal dictatorship—with features drawn from Italian Fascism, especially the combination of nationalism, militarism, trade unionism, and genuine populism, and the palingenetic rhetoric of a new order, a reborn national community, and a "new man" modified to adapt to the conditions of postwar history. Peronism thus emerges as a rare example of a hybrid of fascism and conservatism in power. The other major exception is China, where Chiang Kai-shek, deeply impressed by the continuous displays of youthful enthusiasm and disciplined nationalism being staged at the time in both the Italian Fascist and Nazi regimes, gave official backing to two movements, the Blue Shirts and New Life, in an attempt to infuse his Nationalist Party regime with genuine populist and revolutionary fervor. Although both movements were eclipsed by the United Front, formed to fight the Japanese in 1937, they seem to represent a unique case of fascism's being promoted by a nationalist regime from above to revolutionize the masses, and not simply used for its propaganda value.

In every other instance, conservative reaction prevailed over revolutionary fascism whenever the latter posed a serious threat to its interests. Nor should it be forgotten how far Italian Fascism's revolutionary zeal was dampened in practice by the extensive compromises it had to accept with a multitude of conservative forces in Italy, and that it was the monarchy that sealed Mussolini's fate in July 1943, when Victor Emmanuel III placed him under arrest. It was also conservative elements within the military that came within a table leg of killing Hitler in the Stauffenberg Plot of 1944.

Given the almost universal impotence of fascism to break through in the period from 1918 to 1945, and the compromise and failure that characterized it when it did, it is legitimate to ask if the phrase "fascist era" is justified at all. Certainly it should not be inferred from it that fascism was the dominant form of government of the day—far from it. Yet a cluster of factors makes the phrase telling. First, the Spanish Civil War was widely seen at the time as a trial of strength between communism and fascism. Given the material and military support that Italian Fascism and Nazism gave Franco, and that Stalin gave the Republican government, those who fought against the Nationalists can be forgiven for interpreting the war as a stand against the rise of international fascism, no matter how unconvincing Franco's own fascist credentials. Had support for the Republicans by democratic nations led to the defeat of Franco along with his allies, there is every likelihood that it would have had a considerable impact on restraining Hitler's foreign policy—at least in the short term. Second, Nazism's policies of territorial expansion and racial purification had such terrible consequences for the world that they have left a profound mark in the way the whole era has entered the collective memory, and at a popular level of the historical imagination Nazism is widely equated with fascism. Third, fascism was strongly identified by the Right as the rising force of the age at a time when liberalism was seemingly in terminal decline. Consequently, there was hardly a single authoritarian right-wing regime in the world by 1940 that had not partially fascistized itself outwardly, whether in Portugal or Spain, in Austria or Yugoslavia, in Latvia or Estonia, in Vichy France, Poland, or Greece, in Brazil, Argentina, or Japan. Fascism was a product of the peculiar historical conditions of post–World War I Europe, but it came to dominate the minds of all Europeanized nation-states to a point where the future of human civilization itself could be seen as a Manichean struggle between communism and fascism, with liberals mostly condemned to look on impotently from the wings.

POSTWAR FASCISM

Even after the Allied victory in 1945 some fascists continued to dedicate their life's energy to the cause of national revolution as an immediate possibility. However, once liberalism had recovered its stability and capitalist economics and technology had delivered greater prosperity to ever more citizens of the "One-Third World," the preconditions for fascism to become a mass revolutionary movement disappeared; many came to believe that, despite the growing signs of decadence, national rebirth had to be indefinitely postponed until the present "interregnum" was over. Their function as activists and ideologues has thus changed from directly bringing about the new order to preparing the ground for it, and adapting the core values of national revolution to the development of modern history away from the initial conditions that had engendered it after World War I.

One of the more conspicuous results of this process of adaptation to new realities is that, although some forms of revolutionary nationalism (that is, fascism) still promote a narrowly chauvinistic form of ultra-nationalism, its dominant forms now see the struggle for national or ethnic rebirth in an international and supranational context, an aspect of fascism that in the interwar period was comparatively underdeveloped. Thus Nazism has been adopted throughout the Westernized world as the role model for the fight for Aryan or white supremacy, producing what can be called "universal Nazism." Within Europe most national fascisms see their local struggle as part of a campaign for a new Europe, one far removed from the vision of Brussels or Eurolandia. Third Positionism, meanwhile, especially in its more outspokenly anticapitalist, National Bolshevik forms, campaigns for a radical new world order in which the dominance of the economic, cultural, and military imperialism of the United States has been ended. It looks forward to an entirely new economic system and international community, and its struggle against the present system fosters a sense of solidarity with nonaligned countries such as Libya, the Palestinians, and even Iraq and Yugoslavia when they are "victims of U.S. imperialist aggression," thus blurring traditional divisions between extreme Left and Right.

The second change is a pervasive "metapoliticization" of fascism. Many formations have vacated party-political space altogether, and important areas of it have even abandoned the arena of activist struggle, choosing to focus on the battle for minds. The most clear expression of this development can be seen in the New Right, which grew out of the recognition that dawned in French neofascist circles in the 1960s of the need for a radical change of "discourse" with which to regain the credibility for revolutionary forms of antiliberal nationalism that had been destroyed by World War II and its aftermath. Taking the concept of "cultural hegemony" to heart resulted in a "right-wing Gramscism" that aimed to undermine the intellectual legitimacy of liberalism by attacking such core features of liberal democracy as individualism, the universality of human rights, egalitarianism, and multiculturalism. They did so not on the basis of an aggressive ultra-nationalism and axiomatic racial superiority, but in the name of a Europe restored to the (essentially mythic) homogeneity of its component primordial cultures by the application of a "differentialist" concept of culture. This seeks to put an end to the rampant vulgarization and ethnic miscegenation that they see as endemic to modern, globalized multicultural societies. At the heart of such an ideal lurks the belief in the decadence of the present system and the possibility that a new historical era may yet arise.

Later versions of the extraordinarily prolific, but still hopelessly marginalized, New Right (the Russian offshoot of which is called Eurasianism) have placed increasing stress on the need to transcend the division between Left and Right in a broad antiglobal front. Fascism's metapoliticization is also a central feature of the other main "supranational" forms of rebirth ideology already referred to—namely, Third Positionism, and its close cousin National Bolshevism (though some forms of Third Positionism are violently anticommunist). All these advocate in different ways the inauguration of a new global order that would preserve or restore (through policies and measures never specified) the unique ethnic and cultural identities (first and foremost European/"Indo-European" ones) allegedly threatened by globalization.

The battle "to take over the laboratories of thinking," as one German New Right ideologue put it, takes place on other fronts as well. Historical Revisionism and Holocaust denial are widely dispersed and highly deliberate assaults on the collective memories of the postwar generations. These are calculated to exploit the power of the academic register of historical and scientific enquiry, to rewrite history in such a way as to minimize, relativize, or cancel out altogether the crimes against humanity committed by fascist regimes. The 1960s counterculture also bred New Age, neopagan, and occultist variants of the Hitler myth and forms of nationalism that embrace various visions of the threat to humanity posed by materialism and globalization, one strand of which led to Tolkien's *Lord of the Rings* becoming a prescribed text for the intellectuals of the Italian New Right. Other currents of fascism have taken on board ecological concerns, often as an integral part of the New Right critique of the Western concept of progress.

Contemporary fascism's absence of ties with mass party-movements or regimes with centralized hierarchies of command or directorates of propaganda allows it to retain considerable ideological flexibility. In the United States, that has enabled it to enter into a sufficiently close relationship with certain forms of fundamentalist Christianity to produce new forms of collaboration and hybrid between religious and secular racism (in particular, white supremacism and anti-Semitism, the Christian Identity network being the outstanding example). Other revolutionary nationalists have used the popularity among proletarian racists of (appropriated and suitably adapted/perverted) punk rock and heavy metal to create a highly productive "white noise" music scene geared to the legitimization of racial hatred and violent xenophobia. At least the lyrics of fascist punk music make no attempt to disguise its racism under layers of New Right "metapolitical" or "differentialist" discourse. Nor do they euphemize the palingenetic dream of "purging"

the nation from decadence though an apocalyptic racial war, a vision that is the main artery of continuity between this culture and interwar Italian Fascism and Nazism. Thus one of the songs of the seminal white noise band, Ian Stuart Donaldson's Skrewdriver, roared out to its audience:

> *Hail and thunder, the lightning fills the sky*
> *Not too far it comes before the storm*
> *Hail and thunder, we're not afraid to die*
> *Our mighty fearless warriors marching on.*
> *With high ideals we make our stand*
> *To cleanse the poison from our land.[. . .]*
> *They spread a flame, a wicked spell*
> *To keep our people locked in Hell.[. . .]*
> *But now the devil's cover's blown*
> *The strength of light is going to break the evil seal.*

The fact that White Noise CDs and concerts set out to whip up racial hatred and inspire racially motivated crimes underlines how misleading it would be to imply that fascism's metapoliticization and ideological diversification have led to its abandoning the sphere of activism and violence altogether. The difference is that, instead of being absorbed into paramilitary formations of the mass party, such as the Nazi SA, activism is now often concentrated within minute, specially formed cadre units such as the Combat 18 group in the United Kingdom or the numerous "black terrorist" cells that carried out bomb attacks in Italy during the 1970s. Even more significantly, racist violence is increasingly carried out not by members of fascist parties but by groups of racists acting on their own initiative. Similarly, a number of terrorist outrages have been committed by "lone wolves" who were not under any centralized command at all, but who had formed a deep sense of personal mission to further the cause as communicated to them by a variety of sources. The outstanding examples from the 1990s are the "Oklahoma bomber," Timothy McVeigh, and the London nail-bomber, David Copeland. The way in which McVeigh and Copeland internalized an extreme right-wing worldview and carried out their self-appointed mission in a spirit of "leaderless resistance" is symptomatic of the biggest change of all to affect fascism in the "post-fascist age": groupuscularization. In the context of extreme right-wing politics in the contemporary age, "groupuscules" can be defined as numerically negligible political (frequently metapolitical but never party-political) entities formed to pursue palingenetic ideological, organizational, or activist ends with an ultimate goal of overcoming the decadence of the existing liberal-democratic system. Although they are fully formed and autonomous, they have small active memberships and minimal if any public visibility or support. Yet they acquire enhanced influence and significance as a result of the ease with which they can be associated—even if only in the minds of political extremists—with other ideologically and tactically similar grouplets whose activities complement their own efforts to institute a new type of society.

The groupuscule thus has a Janus-headed characteristic of combining organizational autonomy with the ability to create informal linkages with, or reinforce the influence of, other such formations. This enables groupuscules, when considered in terms of their aggregate impact on politics and society, to be seen as forming a nonhierarchical, leaderless, and centerless (or rather polycentric) movement with fluid boundaries and constantly changing components. This "groupuscular Right" has the characteristics of a political and ideological subculture rather than a conventional political party movement, and it is perfectly adapted to the task of perpetuating revolutionary extremism in an age of relative political stability.

Far from dying out since 1945 then, fascism has in reality displayed a vigorous Darwinian capacity for creative adaptation and mutation. It has diversified, specialized, and groupuscularized in order to fill as many civic (and uncivic!) spaces as possible, now that mainstream political spaces are denied it. It may have withered on the vine as a would-be party-political mass movement, but it has assumed a new capillary form and operates like some small organism resistant to hostile environments. Collectively these keep an extremist agenda of revolutionary nationalism alive in forms that are practically uncensurable, since the groupuscular Right shares with the Internet it uses so readily the property that the information and organizational intelligence it contains is not lost through the suppression of any one of its nodes.

In its New Right adaptation, which in some countries (notably France, Germany, Italy, and Russia) has achieved a degree of respectability within orthodox culture, fascism can help rationalize and legitimate neopopulist attacks on multiculturalism and feed fears about the erosion of national or ethnic identity (albeit in a "differentialist" and pseudo-xenophile rather than an openly xenophobic spirit). This in turn can reinforce a climate that breeds traditional xenophobic racism and help to ensure that the default position of liberal democracy in particular countries shifts to the right rather than the left on such issues as international trade, citizenship, immigration, and economic asylum seekers.

To that extent New Rightists would be justified in claiming at least some measure of success for their attempts to undermine the hegemony of actually existing liberal democratic values, though these are under threat even where it is not a perceptible presence in political culture. As a movement capable of transforming society, whether through military coup, electoral victory, political trade-off with the ruling elite, or the extensive ideological subversion of pluralistic democracy, fascism may be a spent political force able to mobilize only a minute percentage of the population into active support, however large the tacit support for its racism, chauvinism, and xenophobia in milieux with exacerbated social and racial tensions. Nevertheless, those who consult this historical encyclopedia with the notion that fascism is purely a phenomenon of the past should be mindful of the words of Pierre-André Taguieff, one of the most astute observers of contemporary French extremism:

Neither "fascism" nor "racism" will do us the favour of returning in such a way that we can recognize them easily. If vigilance was only a game of recognizing something already well known, then it would only be a question of remembering. Vigilance would be reduced to a social game using reminiscence and identification by recognition, a consoling illusion of an immobile history peopled with events which accord with our expectations or our fears.

Roger Griffin

SUGGESTED READING

Gregor, A. James. 1999. *Phoenix*. New Brunswick, NJ: Transaction. *A text that provides insight into the continuity between interwar and postwar fascism, while both offering a vigorous critique of Griffin's "new consensus" and corroborating some of its fundamental tenets about the ideological dynamics of fascism.*

Griffin, Roger, ed. 1995. *Fascism*. Oxford: Oxford University Press. *An influential primary-source documentary reader that covers the interwar and postwar eras and the history of fascist studies, while presenting an early formulation of the "new consensus" on the fascist minimum (the smallest number of traits that a movement or regime must have before it becomes classifiable as 'fascist').*

Griffin, Roger, ed., with Matthew Feldman. 2003. *Critical Concepts: Fascism*. London: Routledge. *A five-volume "library" collection of secondary sources on fascism that demonstrates the extreme diversity both of the phenomenon and of the critical perspectives it has generated.*

Kallis, Aristotle, ed. 2002. *The Fascist Reader*. London: Routledge. *An excellent secondary source reader on interwar fascism that also takes stock of the current state of the debate within fascist studies.*

Laqueur, Walter. 1996. *Fascism: Past, Present, and Future*. New York: Oxford University Press. *Another example of an interpretation of generic fascism and assessment of its current prospects as a political force by a specialist who operates on the basis of an ideal type of fascism that conflicts with the "new consensus."*

Larsen, Stein, ed. 2001. *Fascism outside Europe.* New York: Columbia University Press (Boulder Social Science Monographs). *A seminal collection of essays on non-European fascisms edited by a major expert on comparative fascism who offers an interpretation of its global diffusion radically divergent from that offered in this introduction.*

Mann, Michael. 2004. *Fascists.* New York: Cambridge University Press. *An impressive attempt to write a panoramic, empirically detailed history of interwar fascism and explain its nature as a political and historical phenomenon from a sociological perspective, thereby complementing and challenging the one-sidedly "ideological" approach consciously adopted in Griffin's work, including the entries to this encyclopedia.*

Morgan, Philip. 2002. *Fascism in Europe, 1918–1945.* London: Routledge. *An excellent textbook on interwar European fascism by someone who consciously applies the approach to fascism proposed by the "new consensus," though with the typical misgivings that many so-called empirical historians have when using social science concepts.*

Mosse, G. L. 1998. *The Fascist Revolution.* New York: Howard Fertig. *A collection of seminal essays on different aspects of fascism's attempted "cultural revolution" by the pioneer of comparative fascist studies and the "new consensus."*

Paxton, Robert O. 2005. *The Anatomy of Fascism.* London: Penguin. *A controversial attempt to get away from abstract theorizing about the nature of fascism and to focus instead on different stages in the realization of fascist visions of a reborn nation exhibited in the twentieth century. It provides much useful empirical and bibliographical material about the history of fascism and the extreme variety of its manifestations.*

Payne, Stanley. 1995. *A History of Fascism.* London: UCL. *The most authoritative, comprehensive, and scholarly overview of the history of fascism and the way in which the academic debate surrounding it had evolved by the mid-1990s.*

ABSTRACTION

Term of abuse current in interwar fascist vocabulary to denigrate the principles of the upholders of such values as human rights, the brotherhood of man, egalitarianism, and internationalism, which fascists dismissed as "unreal" abstractions. To generalized "human" rights, fascists preferred the rights of the Italian or the German or the Aryan; to the hoped-for brotherhood of man they preferred the bonds of the national community; to aspiration to an ideal of egalitarianism they preferred acceptance of the "natural" hierarchies and elite structures endemic to human societies and seemingly required by Social Darwinism; to the "pipe dream" of internationalism (*see* LEAGUE OF NATIONS, THE) they preferred the existent reality of the nation; to Rousseau's claim that "all men are born free" they preferred a focus on each individual's dependency from birth on family and wider community. In all this they saw themselves as having a preference for concrete and realistic styles of thought over idealistic and unrealistic theorizing, and hence as preferring "science" to "fantasy." They believed that they stood for a realistic, scientific, rooted modernity in preference to the liberal modernity of abstract individualism.

Much of this is at least as old as Aristotle, who held, for example, that men are by nature divided into "sheep" and "shepherds," and Machiavelli. But it also tapped into the nineteenth-century reaction to the French Revolution, beginning with Edmund Burke (1729–1797), whose *Reflections on the Revolution in France* first appeared in 1790. Burke believed that society requires its members to observe the laws and customs in which they have been brought up, rather than to agitate for some vague "rights of man," which in his view could lead only to division and anarchy. This argument was taken up by the Traditionalists in France, who followed Burke in focusing on the dependence of each child born into the world on the nourishment, nurture, and support of family and the wider society; thus the individual's obligations to the community must trump all other considerations. The Traditionalist critique of revolutionary abstraction found its way into the integral nationalism of Maurras and the Action Française. However, it is often overlooked that there were parallel critiques of revolutionary abstraction on the Left, where the argument was made that liberals offered their abstract slogans like "liberty, equality, fraternity" simply as sops to the poor, who felt better for them but still had no bread. (There was also, of course, a critique of revolutionary "abstractions" from the Anglo-Saxon utilitarian school, which denied that concepts like "the rights of man" have any meaning at all: the English legal reformer Jeremy Bentham dismissed them contemptuously as "nonsense on stilts.")

The preference for the defense of existing customs over revolutionary "abstractions" became a hallmark of nineteenth-century conservatism, but in the hands of Romantic nationalism it transmuted into a harsh advocacy of the superiority of the ethos and principles of whatever nation it was to whom the ideologue in question belonged. Nazi ideologues in particular—and they represented the culmination and extreme exaggeration of nineteenth-century Romantic nationalism—promoted the idea of "Germany" (not just the nation with her existing borders but an idealized nation of all ethnic Germans) as bearer of a uniquely powerful understanding of nature and the world arising out of her special history and her "soul." Pro-Nazi philosophers like Hermann Glockner and Ferdinand Weinhandl claimed that Germans had a special ability to "look at" (*anschauen*) the world through a direct manner of perception; they contrasted this with the abstract "rationalist" way of thinking *about* the world practiced in the Franco-British tradition of philosophizing that derived from Descartes. Some Nazi hard-liners in the scientific world criticized the physics of Einstein as too "abstract" and "Jewish" and not sufficiently "intuitive." Ironically, this alleged earthiness and concreteness of the German way of seeing had itself now become detached from the defense of traditional national institutions, for the Nazi creed was itself ruthlessly revolutionary.

Mussolini too condemned his "internationalist" enemies for their "abstraction." But appropriately, perhaps, it was the far-right French Vichy regime that embodied this aspect of fascist ideology most succinctly when it boldly replaced the hallowed (abstract) slogan of the French Revolution *Liberté, Egalité, Fraternité* with the new trio of *Patrie, Famille, Travail* ("Fatherland, Family, Work"). These are names for concrete and familiar entities that the individual can easily visualize. Moreover, during the Vichy regime, busts of *Marianne* (not a real person, but a symbolic idealization of the supposed beauty of the French Revolutionary ideal) in public places were replaced by busts of the regime's leader, the very real person Marshal Philippe Pétain.

Cyprian Blamires

See Also: ACTION FRANÇAISE; ARYANISM; BLOOD AND SOIL; COSMOPOLITANISM; EGALITARIANISM; ENLIGHTENMENT, THE; EXPANSIONISM; FRENCH REVOLUTION, THE; GERMANNESS (*DEUTSCHHEIT*); GERMANY; INDIVIDUALISM; LEAGUE OF NATIONS, THE; LIBERALISM; MAURRAS, CHARLES; MICHELS, ROBERTO; NATIONALISM; NATURE; NAZISM; NORDIC SOUL, THE; ORGANICISM; PANGERMANISM; PETAIN, MARSHAL HENRI PHILIPPE; ROOTLESSNESS; SCIENCE; TRADITIONALISM; VICHY; *WELTANSCHAUUNG*

References
Gentile, G. 2002. *Origins and Doctrine of Fascism.* New Brunswick, NJ: Transaction.
Gregor, A. James. 2001. *Giovanni Gentile: Philosopher of Fascism.* New Brunswick, NJ: Transaction.
Hughes, S. H. 1961. *Consciousness and Society.* New York: Vintage.
Mosse, G. L. 1966. *The Crisis of German Ideology.* London: Weidenfeld and Nicolson.
Redner, H. 1997. *Malign Masters: Gentile, Heidegger, Lukacs, Wittgenstein.* London: Macmillan.
Stromberg, R. N. 1981. *European Intellectual History since 1789.* Englewood Cliffs, NJ: Prentice-Hall.

ABYSSINIA: *See* ETHIOPIA
ACCADEMIA D'ITALIA: *See* ART; SCIENCE

ACERBO LAW, THE

Law passed by the Italian Chamber of Deputies on 15 July 1923 that opened the door for the Fascists to gain control of the Parliament. It was drafted by Undersecretary of State Giacomo Acerbo (1888–1969), and it provided that the electoral list that received the greatest number of votes—provided it amounted to more than 25 percent of the total—would be entitled to two-thirds of the total number of seats (535). The rest of the seats were to be shared out proportionally among the parties. Many liberals supported the bill, which they hoped would introduce more stability into the political order. In the next elections, in April 1924, Mussolini was able to secure the election of 374 of his supporters (including 275 fascists), and that prepared the way for his subsequent destruction of the parliamentary governmental system.

Cyprian Blamires

See Also: FASCIST PARTY, THE; ITALY; MOSCA, GAETANO; MUSSOLINI, BENITO ANDREA; PARLIAMENTARISM

References
Gallo, M. 1974. *Mussolini's Italy: Twenty Years of the Fascist Era.* London: Abelard-Schuman.
Lyttelton, A. 2004. *The Seizure of Power: Fascism in Italy 1919–1929.* London: Routledge.

ACTION FRANÇAISE (FRENCH ACTION)

French royalist league founded before World War I, often regarded as a forerunner of fascism. It was set up on 8 August 1898 by various opponents of Dreyfus: Jacques Bainville, Henri Vaugeois, Maurice Pujo, and Charles Maurras. The following July a bimonthly paper, also named *Action Française,* was brought out. It became a daily paper on 21 March 1908, run by Maurras and Léon Daudet. The Action Française (AF) advocated monarchism, saw the nation as the foundation of society, showed respect for Catholicism and established traditions, and claimed to be in a struggle against international plutocracy and the influence of Jews and freemasons. The AF was notable for the originality of its fusion of political intellectualism—both through the publications of the various intellectuals attached to the movement and through the courses provided by the Institut d'Action Français—with a muscular form of political activism, particularly through the formation in 1908 of the Camelots du roi ("king's street peddlers") action groups.

An extremely potent political force in the years before World War I, the AF went into a relative decline after the mid-1920s. One reason was that many of the people who had joined the AF because they saw it as a potentially revolutionary force, capable of producing a synthesis between nationalism and syndicalism, became disillusioned with its failure to do so. One of the key figures in that disillusionment, Georges Valois, left the movement in 1925 to form the first French fascist party, Le Faisceau ("The Bundle"). A further factor in the movement's decline was the decision by the Vatican on 29 December 1926 to place it out of bounds for Catholics, forcing thousands of them to withdraw. New members did join, but many recruits got caught up in mobilization for what they saw as more radical movements. That would be the case for many of the young activists who joined the movement at the beginning of the 1930s. Such activists as Robert Brasillach, Pierre Gaxotte, Lucien Rebatet, Dominique Sordet, Claude and Gabriel Jeantet, and Eugène Deloncle passed through the AF before moving in the direction of fascism as the 1930s progressed. Despite their traditional hostility to Germany, Maurras and the AF supported the national revolution under Pétain after the

Charles Maurras was the leading figure in the French nationalist movement Action Française, often considered to be a precursor of interwar fascism. (Hulton Archive/Getty Images)

collapse of France in 1940. The last edition of *Action Française* came out on 24 August 1944, and the movement was dissolved after the war.

Steve Bastow

See Also: ANTICLERICALISM; ANTI-SEMITISM; BLANCHOT, MAURICE; BRASILLACH, ROBERT; DREYFUS CASE, THE; FRANCE; FREEMASONRY/FREEMASONS, THE; INTEGRAL NATIONALISM; MAURRAS, CHARLES; MONARCHISM; NATIONALISM; PERONISM; PLUTOCRACY; PROTOFASCISM; REBATET, LUCIEN; SYNDICALISM; TRADITIONALISM; VICHY

References

Davies, P., 2001. *France and the Second World War: Occupation, Collaboration and Resistance.* London: Routledge.

Mazgaj, P. 1979. *The Action Française and Revolutionary Syndicalism.* Chapel Hill, NC: University of North Carolina Press.

Nolte, E. 1965. *Three Faces of Fascism.* London: Weidenfeld and Nicholson.

Weber, Eugen. 1962. *Action Française.* Stanford: Stanford University Press.

ACTUALISM

The name of the philosophy espoused by Giovanni Gentile, generally recognized to have been the philosophical mentor to Mussolini's regime and the only truly fascist philosopher to be accorded a respected place in the history of philosophy. Actualism was rooted in the tradition of idealism, and it sprang from the difficulty experienced by eighteenth-century philosophers in finding a philosophical proof of the reality of the external world. Idealists concluded that in the absence of such a proof we have only the content of our thinking that we can be sure of. There were various versions of idealism, but Gentile's actualism held that the only defensible idealism was an absolute kind. He denied that our convictions about the world are the result of passive observation, alleging that all knowledge arises out of a conscious choice made by our minds; we choose from the waves of impressions that we receive those that seem to work, or those that we can fit into the achievement of some goal or aim. This applies not simply to individuals but also to communities and their collective goals.

Thus it is our minds that construct reality, not the reality we experience that molds our minds. Actualism in fact holds that it is our purpose and our role as humans to construct or fashion ourselves through thinking, a process that it denominates "self-actualization." With regard to other persons, we experience them as having something called "spirituality," and with them we find that we share something different and more profound than we can share with mere things. Other persons call up in us a longing for mutual affection and sympathy, and philosophy becomes ethical. Indeed Gentile defined his system of pure idealism as in essence a system of ethics. Moreover, since each individual has within his mind the concept of "the other," we can say that the concept of society is immanent in every person. This implies a rejection of the classic liberal opinion as incarnated in the French Revolution, that society is composed of isolated individuals having inalienable rights who choose of their own volition to come together to create a society. Gentile conceived of individuals in society as belonging together in a single transcendent self that gives them a common consciousness. What is real is the collectivity, not the individual. Only communities are transcendent; individuals are transient, and the transcendent reality is embodied in the state. So the state is very far from being an arbitrary construction put together at the behest of a number of individuals. Since it represents an organic continuity that actually transcends the existence of any individual within it, the state has priority over the individual, not just philosophically but also in terms of ethics.

What bonded Gentile's thought particularly strongly to fascism was his argument that whereas in a previous era it was the church that represented the foundation of each individual's social consciousness, in modern times it is the nation that unites individuals in the state. But twentieth-century men are heirs to a long tradition of individualism that has distorted their perceptions; what they most need is to be reminded that they cannot find the self-fulfillment that they crave except by consciously identifying themselves with the transcendent historic community to which they belong. That can be achieved only through a sacrificial commitment by which the individual, exercising or undergoing an iron discipline, buries his own individuality in that of the state. If the individuals within a state are to make such a commitment, they must be educated to do so, and the state itself must take responsibility for that education: the state must become the educator of its citizens. Both in his writings and in his professional career, Gentile strove to promote the importance of education.

Actualism gave to the Italian Fascist regime a philosophical rationale, at a time when many intellectuals were turning away from the positivism and scientism that had been predominant in pre–World War I Europe. Although Gentile drank deep at the sources of German Neo-Hegelianism and was generally indebted to German thought, actualism did not play any part in German Nazism, which sought its intellectual justification precisely in the scientism that Gentile rejected. Although it proclaimed that "Germanness" implied a unique way of looking at the world that was entirely different from the Enlightenment rationalism that prevailed in France and the Anglo-Saxon world, Nazism based itself on a conviction that the "scientific" deliverances of a certain kind of anthropology and biology and "racial science" could be relied upon. However, although the Nazis regarded themselves as perfectly at home with science, they had a particular conception of what that meant, in the sense that they believed not simply in the empirical study of the deliverances of the senses but also in a certain uniquely "Nordic" way of perception that was some kind of intuitionism or "seeing" (*schauen*) that gave them a uniquely superior Weltanschauung.

Cyprian Blamires

See Also: ABSTRACTION; ANTHROPOLOGY; *ENCICLOPEDIA ITALIANA,* THE; ENLIGHTENMENT, THE; FRENCH REVOLUTION, THE; GENTILE, GIOVANNI; GERMANNESS; INDIVIDUALISM; LIBERALISM; MUSSOLINI, BENITO ANDREA; NAZISM; NORDIC SOUL, THE; ORGANICISM; RACIAL DOCTRINE; *WELTANSCHAUUNG*

References
Gentile, Giovanni. 2002. *Origins and Doctrine of Fascism.* New Brunswick, NJ: Transaction.
Gregor, A. James. 2001. *Giovanni Gentile: Philosopher of Fascism.* New Brunswick, NJ: Transaction.
———. 2005. *Mussolini's Intellectuals: Fascist Social and Political Thought.* Princeton: Princeton University Press.

ADORNO, THEODOR W.: *See* PSYCHOLOGY
AESTHETICS: *See* ARCHITECTURE; ART; MODERNISM; STYLE
AGRICULTURE: *See* FARMERS

AHNENERBE (FORSCHUNGS- UND LEHRGEMEINSCHAFT) (GERMAN ANCESTRAL HERITAGE SOCIETY)

A German society established in 1935 to look for support for the racial theories of some National Socialists in the study of prehistory. In 1937 it was integrated into the SS. It attracted academics in good standing and carried out some useful research—for example, the excavation of a Viking fortress, and expeditions to Tibet and the Near East. During World War II anthropological research was conducted on the skulls of Auschwitz victims, which were measured to compare with those of Aryans. The organization was also involved in the medical experiments carried out by Rascher in Dachau and by Mengele in Auschwitz.

Cyprian Blamires

See Also: ANTHROPOLOGY; ARYANISM; AUSCHWITZ; HIMMLER, HEINRICH; MENGELE, JOSEF; MEDICINE; RACIAL DOCTRINE; SS, THE; TIBET

References
Hale, Christopher. 2003. *Himmler's Crusade: The Nazi Expedition to Find the Origins of the Aryan Race.* Hoboken, NJ: Wiley.
Kater, Michael. 1979. *Das 'Ahnenerbe' der SS 1935–1945: Ein Beitrag zur Kulturpolitik des Dritten Reiches.* Stuttgart: Deutsche Verlags-Anstalt.
Lumsden, Robin. 1999. *Himmler's Black Order: A History of the SS, 1923–1945.* Surrey: Bramley.

ALBANIA

In 1939, Italy invaded Albania. A satellite government led by Shefquet Vërlaci was established. However, real power lay with Mussolini's son-in-law, Galeazzo Ciano. Albanian society was subjected to fascist influences, and the new government promoted the Albanian state as the core of a future Greater Albania to which Kosovo would be annexed. For years, Albanians in Kosovo (Kosovars) had complained about being oppressed by Slavs. With the German invasion of Yugoslavia, Kosovo was annexed to Albania, and its new leaders—Rexhep Mitrovica, Iliaz Agushi, and Bedri Pejani—exacted a terrible revenge on non-Albanians: 100,000 Serbs were expelled, and many thousands were massacred. Paramilitary organizations such as the Vulnari and the Balli Kombëtar, inspired by myths of Albanian masculinity, were responsible for these atrocities. The shock troops ignored the protests of the Italians, whom they considered unmanly. The Mrdita paramilitaries and Xhafer Deva's police also wreaked havoc. The most violent Kosovar force was the SS Skanderbeg, created in 1944 as an elite death squad. In addition to massacring Serb civilians, it also hunted down Jews.

After Italy's capitulation in September 1943, German forces invaded Albania and placed in power a regime led by the Kosovars Vehbi Frashëri and Deva. In gratitude to the Nazis for "liberation" from Slav rule, the Kosovars proposed that Albanians were "Aryans of Illyrian heritage." However, by September 1944 the Albanian state was close to collapse, and the capital, Tirana, had fallen by November. Nationalist resistance in Kosovo lasted longer. Led by Deva, nationalists endeavored to purchase weapons from retreating Germans with the aim of carrying out a "final solution" of Slavs in Kosovo. The overwhelming force of the Yugoslav partisans prevented this, but although the insurrection was crushed, it was not until 1947 that Kosovo was fully reintegrated into Yugoslavia.

Rory Yeomans

See Also: ARYANISM; CIANO, COUNT GALEAZZO; CORFU; EXPANSIONISM; HONOR; IMPERIALISM; ITALY; PARAMILI-TARISM; SERBS, THE; SLAVS, THE (AND GERMANY); SLAVS, THE (AND ITALY); WARRIOR ETHOS, THE; YUGOSLAVIA

References

Fischer, Berndt J. 1999. *Albania at War, 1941–1945.* London: Hurst.

Malcolm, Noel. 1995. *Kosovo: A Short History.* London: Macmillan.

Vickers, Miranda. 1998. *Between Serb and Albanian: A History of Kosovo.* London: Hurst.

ALMIRANTE, GIORGIO (1914–1988)

Originally a schoolteacher from Parma, Almirante became the editor of two racist Fascist journals during the Mussolini dictatorship in Italy. After the latter's collapse in 1943, Almirante served as chief of staff in the Ministry of Popular Culture for the Salò Republic. In 1946, Almirante helped to found and became the first leader of the MSI, a party that quickly became the principal neofascist force in Italian politics over the succeeding decades. He was removed from his leadership post in 1950 by conservative figures who wanted to make the MSI a respectable participant in parliamentary life. When that attempt eventually failed, Almirante resumed the MSI's leadership in 1969. Under his direction, the MSI welcomed back into its ranks Giuseppe "Pino" Rauti and a number of individuals linked to Italy's violent neofascist underground. During the turbulent late 1960s and early 1970s, Almirante was accused of promoting a "strategy of tension," of simultaneously appealing to a "silent majority" of Italians who wanted a restoration of law and order while covertly promoting right-wing violence. The aim of this strategy, many journalists argued, was to create a sense of sufficient disorder in Italy that the public would tolerate a coup d'etat and the advent of a military neofascist dictatorship. The accusations, probably exaggerated, led to demands that the MSI be placed outside the law and that Almirante be prosecuted for antidemocratic scheming. These efforts did not succeed, but neither did the "strategy of tension." In the 1980s, Almirante was replaced as MSI secretary and spent the remainder of his life as the party's ceremonial president.

Leonard Weinberg

See Also: ITALY; MOVIMENTO SOCIALE ITALIANO, THE; MUS-SOLINI, BENITO ANDREA; POSTWAR FASCISM; RAUTI, GIUSEPPE "PINO"; SALÒ REPUBLIC, THE; TENSION, THE STRATEGY OF

Reference

Weinberg, Leonard. 1979. *After Mussolini: Italian Neo-Fascism and the Nature of Fascism.* Washington, DC: University Press of America.

AMERICA: *See* AMERICANIZATION; U.S.A.

AMERICANIZATION

Term of abuse in the vocabulary of fascists in the interwar era, when such new cultural imports as jazz music and Hollywood movies were felt by some in Europe to embody the penetration of "alien" values into their world. The rise of the modern cinema and popular music industries were tied in by the celebrated car maker and anti-Semitic propagandist Henry Ford to "Jewish" influence, on account of the strong representation of Jews in the production of Hollywood films and in the promotion of modern music; Ford and others denounced "showbiz" as a source of "Jewish" corruption in U.S. society. Such arguments were picked up enthusiastically by the Nazis, for whom "Americanizing" influences might often be a code for "Jewish" influences.

In postwar fascism, the term *Americanization* has a different, though not totally unrelated, set of connotations. Some fascists have taken on board the agenda of antiglobalization, anticapitalist, and ecological movements, and they turn the fire on the United States as the archetypal capitalist nation, which is home to many of the world's great multinationals. They also attack the United States as the world's major polluter. There are elements too for whom fascism has become a defense of "European" values against not only the influence of nonwhite immigrants but also the homogenized culture of "McDonaldization."

Cyprian Blamires

See Also: ANTI-SEMITISM; CAPITALISM; COSMOPOLITANISM; DECADENCE; ECOLOGY; EUROPEAN NEW RIGHT, THE; FILM; FORD, HENRY; GLOBALIZATION; GREECE; IMMIGRATION; NAZISM; NIHILISM; PERONISM; POSTWAR FASCISM; RADIO; SEXUALITY

References

Campbell, N., J. Davies, and G. Mckay, eds. 1996. *Americanisation and the Transformation of World Cultures: Melting Pot or Cultural Chernobyl?* New York: Edwin Mellen.

Payne, S. G. 1995. *A History of Fascism, 1914–1945.* London: UCL.

Ramet, S., ed. 2003. *Kazaaam! Splat! Ploof!: The American Impact on European Popular Culture since 1945.* Oxford: Rowman and Littlefield.

AMIN AL-HUSSEINI: *See* PALESTINE

ANIMALS

The eclectic nature of fascism, so often obscured by militant rhetoric, is very evident in policies regarding animals. The early Italian Fascists glorified technology, romanticized war, and dismissed humane issues as effete sentimentality. Mussolini, for example, said that Italian Fascism denied the equation which said that well-being = happiness, an equation that regards men as mere animals content to eat and drink and get fat as though they had only a vegetative existence. Nevertheless, the Fascist government in Italy did pass an animal protection law in 1931 that contained the strongest restrictions on animal experimentation in Europe to that date. It was to serve as a partial model for similar legislation in Nazi Germany and elsewhere. The law allowed experiments on warm-blooded vertebrates to be performed only by authorized scientific institutions and under the supervision of the director. It also regulated the care and handling of laboratory animals, and demanded that they be anesthetized during experiments, provided that was not incompatible with the purpose of the research.

Internal contradictions within fascism are even more apparent in Nazi attitudes toward animals. While deliberately cultivating brutality toward human (and often animal) life, the Nazis introduced the most comprehensive humane legislation in the world and laid the foundations for the study of animals throughout much of the twentieth century. The composer Richard Wagner, who was an important influence on Hitler and other Nazis,

had become a crusader for animal protection toward the end of his life. He popularized the idea that animal experimentation, or "vivisection," exemplified the "sterile rationalism" of Jewish thought, while kosher slaughter was ritualized cruelty. These notions enabled the Nazis to rationalize anti-Semitic measures with appeals to animal welfare. Shortly after they came to power in 1933, the Nazis enacted a comprehensive law on the slaughter of animals that effectively banned kosher practices.

In turn the law on slaughter inaugurated a comprehensive series of laws regulating the treatment of animals in meticulous detail, including a comprehensive animal protection law of 1934 that was revised and expanded in 1938. Practices such as cock-fighting and the use of hunting dogs were forbidden. A law on transportation of animals, passed in 1938, carefully regulated how much space, food, and water various animals were to receive during transport, while Jews and others were being indiscriminately crammed into cattle cars destined for concentration camps. The enforcement of animal protection laws was, however, erratic. Members of organizations such as the Hitler Youth and the SS were sometimes forced to practice cruelty toward animals—for example, by strangling pigeons or dogs—in order to teach unquestioned obedience.

Animals were important in the symbolism and the applied science of the Nazi regime. Predators such as the eagle and wolf were invoked to inspire fierceness in battle. Dogs, especially, were used to model the ideal of pure blood, which was central to the Nazi eugenics programs. Konrad Lorenz, a prominent member of the Nazi regime's Office of Race Policy, articulated a theory of genetic degeneration based on an analogy between careless breeding of animals in the barnyard and racial miscegenation of human beings in cities.

Groups that draw on fascist traditions, especially in Europe, have continued to emphasize animals, for example by protesting ritual slaughter performed by Muslims and Jews. Today it is common for opposing parties to invoke fascism as a negative paradigm in debates on issues involving animal protection. The organization PETA, for example, launched an advertising campaign in 2003 entitled "The Holocaust on Your Plate," comparing the meat industry to Nazi death camps. On the other hand, critics of animal rights often point out that severe restrictions on animal experimentation under Nazism accompanied grisly experiments on unwilling human subjects.

Boria Sax

See Also: ANTI-SEMITISM; BLOOD; CONCENTRATION CAMPS; ECOLOGY; EUGENICS; FASCIST PARTY, THE; HITLER, ADOLF; HOLOCAUST, THE; LORENZ, KONRAD;

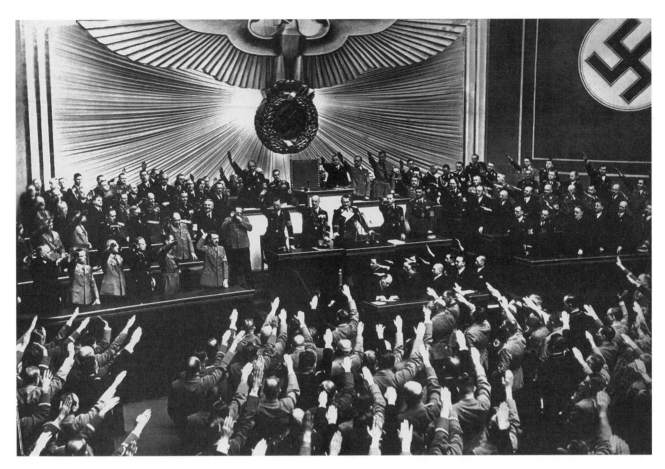

The Berlin Reichstag (parliament) greets Hitler's announcement in March 1938 of the annexation of Austria to Germany with rapturous applause. This was the first step toward the fulfillment of the Nazi dream of a greater German Reich uniting all the Germans of Europe. (National Archives)

MUSSOLINI, BENITO ANDREA; NATURE; RATIONALISM; SS, THE; TECHNOLOGY; WAGNER, (WILHELM) RICHARD; WAR; YOUTH

References

Deichmann, U. 1996. *Biologists under Hitler.* Trans. T. Dunlap. Cambridge: Harvard University Press.

Mussolini, B. 1968 [1935]. *Fascism: Doctrine and Institutions.* New York: Howard Fertig.

Rupke, N., ed. 1987. *Vivisection in Historical Perspective.* New York: Croom Helm.

Sax, B. 2000. *Animals in the Third Reich: Pets, Scapegoats and the Holocaust.* New York: Continuum.

ANSCHLUSS, THE

Roughly translates from German as "union"; effectively referring to the annexation of Austria—thereafter la-

beled the *Ostmark* in the terminology of the Nazis—by the Third Reich in March 1938. Such an annexation was specifically prohibited by the terms of the various peace settlements following World War I, and again in 1931 in relation to a proposed "customs union" between Austria and Germany under the Weimar Republic. The *Anschluss* may be understood as Hitler's final repudiation of the provisions of the Versailles Treaty.

By 1920 the Austro-Hungarian Empire had been dissolved into various smaller states, with Austria comprising 7 million German-speaking inhabitants and occupying a pivotal strategic area in Central Europe. In the same year, the first point of Nazism's Twenty-Five Point Program demanded unification of all Germans into a Greater Germany (*Grossdeutschland*). Austria was to become a major aim of Nazi revanchism during the Weimar Republic, and in 1934 a failed coup d'etat by Austrian Nazis—in Vienna, yet coordinated from Berlin—resulted in the death of the chancellor, Engelbert Dollfuss, the formation of the so-called Stresa

Front to contain German expansionism, and heightened political tension in Austria.

However, by 1938 the international state of affairs was much more conducive to the aggressive foreign policy increasingly pursued by the Nazi regime, especially given German domestic strength, international relations with Fascist Italy, and the evident appeasement pursued (particularly) by Britain and France. Conflict with Austria loomed after a meeting between Hitler and Austria's conservative chancellor, Kurt von Schuschnigg, at Berchtesgaden on 12 February 1938, at which Hitler issued political ultimatums with strong martial overtones. Demanded were an amnesty and a free rein for all Austrian Nazis, the appointment of two Nazis to the Austrian cabinet, as well as the development of economic ties between the two countries. Schuschnigg accepted before the three-day deadline, but he retaliated with a surprising decision on 9 March 1938 to hold a referendum (constructed in a manner unfavorable to the Nazis) on Austrian independence four days thereafter.

A range of options in response were hastily discussed by Nazi functionaries—particularly Hitler, Goering, and Goebbels—including invasion, propaganda leaflets to be distributed by airplane, and renewed threats. Bolstered by Mussolini's diplomatic support, Hitler made military preparations while simultaneously insisting upon Schuschnigg's resignation as well as a restructuring and postponement of the plebiscite. Despite much negotiation between Vienna and Berlin, by midnight on 11 March 1938, Schuschnigg had resigned; the Nazis' puppet in Austria, Arthur Seyss-Inquart, had been made chancellor; and Austrian armed forces had been ordered not to resist the invading German forces. On 12 March, German troops marched into Austria, and the next day the Law for the Reunion of Austria with the German Reich was drafted; on 15 March 1938, Hitler spoke to a crowd of hundreds of thousands of jubilant Viennese as their new head of state.

Matt Feldman

See Also: AUSTRIA; AUSTRO-HUNGARIAN EMPIRE/HABSBURG EMPIRE, THE; CLERICO-FASCISM; DOLLFUSS, ENGELBERT; GOEBBELS, (PAUL) JOSEPH; GOERING, HERMANN; HITLER, ADOLF; ITALY; NAZISM; PANGERMANISM; SCHUSCHNIGG, KURT VON; SEYSS-INQUART, ARTHUR; THIRD REICH, THE; VERSAILLES, THE TREATY OF; WEIMAR REPUBLIC, THE

References
Kershaw, Ian. 2000. *Hitler: Nemesis 1936–1945*. London: Penguin.
Noakes, Jeremy, and Geoffrey Pridham. 1997. *Nazism 1919–1945*. Vol. 3: *Foreign Policy, War and Racial Extermination*. Exeter: University of Exeter Press.

ANTHROPOLOGY

The subfields of physical, social, and colonial anthropology—as well as a racially adapted theory of diffusion and the idea of an Indo-Germanic culture circle—contributed substantially to the Nazi version of the fascist conception of a nation in crisis and in a state of decadence, from which only an ultranationalist worldview that envisioned national regeneration could save it. While the relationship of academic anthropologists in universities and university research institutes to National Socialism was complex, that of popular anthropologists or of anthropologists working for Ahnenerbe, the research institute of the SS, was formative.

Academic anthropologists like Eugen Fischer and Diedrich Westermann, for example, were close to the regime. In the Prussian Academy of Science, following a lecture by the physical anthropologist Eugen Fischer on the 8 May 1941 about "White Africa," Fischer and Westermann formed a commission to organize interdisciplinary research on Northern Africa. The topic "White Africa" was chosen not only for its German colonial interests but also for its affirmation of the diffusion theory of Himmler and the SS—namely, that the *Herrenschicht*, here applied to Africa, were "white Africans" who came from the north, established larger statelike organizations, but eventually disappeared among the black masses, thereby losing their hegemony.

Already in 1910, Eugen Fischer had published his book *Social Anthropology and Its Meaning for the State*. Here he warned that the same fate of cultural decline awaited Germany that had befallen Portugal, Spain, and Italy, and that was even then afflicting France. The idea of decadence, turning *Völker* into masses owing to Westernization and international wars, found its greatest expression in the writings of the popular anthropologist of race studies Hans F. K. Günther. His writing became popular after the defeat in World War I and the Treaty of Versailles. Basing his thought on the race theories of Gobineau, Chamberlain, and Galton, Günther saw the root cause of decadence in three processes: (1) rapid urbanization (*Verstädterung*); (2) the degeneration of *Volk* into mass (*Masse*); and (3) the counterselection (*Gegenauslese*) that occurs following major wars. Major wars destroy exemplary officers, soldiers, and hereditarily qualified families (*erbtüchtige Familien*), while urbanization and massification produce moral decline and reproductive irresponsibility. Since all Occidental peoples are racially mixed already, the three processes lead to biocultural catastrophe. Salvation lies in a "racial renewal" movement.

Schemann's translation of Gobineau's work, *The Inequality of Human Races*, had a major impact on the "racial renewal movement" in Germany. It was claimed that racial inequality justified favoring Nordic elements in Occidental peoples. Likewise, Houston Stewart Chamberlain's work, *Foundations of the Nineteenth Century*, helped to give credence to the idea that race plays a vital role in the life and history of peoples. The works of Vacher de Lapouge, *Les Selections sociales*, (1896) and *L'Aryen, son rôle social* (1899), further raised the importance of the role of the Nordic race in the history of Indo-Germanic language speakers. German anthropologists Otto Ammon (1842–1915) and Ludwig Woltmann (1871–1907), who was a student of Haeckel and popularizer of Gobineau, reinforced the special meaning of the Nordic race by highlighting its political and religious dimensions.

Günther and Ludwig Ferdinand Clauß (1892–1974), an anthropologist who taught race psychology in the philosophical faculty of the University of Berlin, soon linked racial with religious renewal within Hauer's German Faith Movement. A former missionary to India who exchanged a hatred of Jewish-Christianity for a love of Hinduism and Buddhism, Hauer developed a race-based religion that he considered to be the essence of National Socialism. To him, a specific type of pre-Christian primordial godliness permeates a people and culture (that is, a race), and it is the task of an elite minority and persuasive personality to re-establish this collective representation as the ruling idea of a regenerative movement that answers the specific political yearnings of a specific people. To Hauer, Hinduism and Buddhism were vital parts of Indo-Germanic culture, which was determined by the Nordic race. Inevitably it clashed with Near-Asian-Semitic culture. Unlike the disintegrative thrust of Near-Asian-Semitic cultures, Indo-Germanicism acts as a reintegrative force of all forms of life under the formidable power of faith, with National Socialism as its guarantor. Hauer and company concocted an ideological mix that not only dazzled the anthropologists and indologists of Ahnenerbe but also pervaded the SS generally, from Himmler on down.

Karla Poewe

See Also: AHNENERBE; ARYANISM; *BHAGAVADGITA*, THE; BLOOD; BUDDHISM; CHAMBERLAIN, HOUSTON STEWART; EUGENICS; GERMAN FAITH MOVEMENT, THE; GOBINEAU, JOSEPH ARTHUR COMTE DE; GÜNTHER, HANS F. K.; HAUER, JAKOB WILHELM; HIMMLER, HEINRICH; NATION-ALISM; NAZISM; NORDIC SOUL, THE; PALINGENETIC MYTH; RACIAL DOCTRINE; SS, THE; TIBET; UNIVERSITIES; VACHER DE LAPOUGE, GEORGES; *VOLK, VÖLKISCH*

References

Günther, Hans F. K. 1929. *Kleine Rassenkunde des deutschen Volkes*. München: J. F. Lehmanns.

Hauer, W. J. 1938. *Glaube und Blut*. Karlsruhe/Leipzig: Boltze.

Kater, M. H. 2001. *Das "Ahnenerbe" der SS 1935–1945*. München: Oldenbourg.

Poewe, Karla. 2005. *New Religions and the Nazis*. London: Routledge.

Stocking, George W. 1989. *Bones, Bodies, Behaviour: Essays in Biological Anthropology*. Madison: University of Wisconsin Press.

"ANTI-" DIMENSION OF FASCISM, THE

Fascism has frequently been identified more with what it is against than with what it is for, but the "positive" goals generating its negations, violence, and destructiveness are now being increasingly recognized by scholars. All ideologies have a built-in "anti-dimension," because a corollary of asserting any set of core ideals is the rejection of values that conflict with them. Liberalism, for example, is by definition opposed to absolutism, communism, religious fanaticism, anarchy, and all forms of tyranny. One of the features that used to mark fascism out from other political ideologies, however, is that it was routinely described by political scientists, not from the point of view of its own protagonists but from the perspective of its enemies and victims. That is in marked contrast with the conventional academic treatment of ideologies such as liberalism and anarchism, whose attempted implementation has in the past led to violence against the established order, or of Marxism-Leninism, which, once adopted as the state ideology of the Soviet Union, was partly responsible for atrocities and abuses of human rights on an enormous scale.

The first analyses of fascism as an international (generic) species of politics—that is, as a phenomenon not confined to Italy—were carried out by Marxists. In the 1920s they established a tradition that persists to this day of interpreting fascism as the product of a crisis of capitalism. They argued that behind its dynamic, populist facade, fascism was driven by the drive to crush the revolutionary movement for proletariat emancipation by resorting to a pseudo-revolution that exalted the supraclass interests of the nation while actually defending the vested interests of the ruling elites. By the 1930s the term *fascism* was being employed ever more frequently in liberal circles as well to describe both ultranationalist movements and extreme right-wing authoritarian regimes that seemed to be modeled on Mussolini's Fascism. However, the prevailing uncertainty about what it stood for as a positive ideology meant that it was widely characterized in terms of its rejection of democracy, humanism, culture, civilization, and progress—or, even more loosely, in terms of its cult of violence and its theatrical, charismatic, or megalomaniac style of political display.

The unprecedented scale of destruction of civilian life and of mass-produced human atrocities caused by the Third Reich and its allies during World War II were naturally identified in the public mind with barbarism, madness, and evil. It is thus understandable if academics from both antifascist camps perpetuated the characterization of fascism after 1945 purely in terms of what it was against. Marxists, including those working under communist regimes, produced theories of varying degrees of sophistication, all of which axiomatically denied it an autonomous revolutionary dynamic. Meanwhile, Western liberal academics tended to treat it either as a subcategory of totalitarianism—an overwhelmingly negative concept in the context of the Cold War—or as generated by dysfunction, whether in the development of nationhood or the process of modernization, or by the personal pathology of its leaders. It is thus hardly surprising that the first major academic attempt to explore the ideological dynamics of fascism in their full complexity, Ernst Nolte's *Three Faces of Fascism* (1965; German ed., 1963) still presented the "fascist minimum" as both a reaction against and emulation of Marxism on one level, and on another as "resistance to transcendence," a concerted effort to reverse the human drive toward self-emancipation expressed in liberalism and socialism.

It was in the same decade that comparative fascist studies finally began to be enriched by the publication of theories which, in contrasting ways, recognized that the driving force of fascism lay in its bid to overcome decadence and achieve a "new order," and that this project involved not just an economic and political revolution but also a cultural and anthropological revolution conceived in a totalitarian spirit—that is, one that aspires to produce a new type of human being through the vehicle of a secular political religion. Foremost among the pioneers of this approach in Anglophone scholarship, which is used increasingly now by historians studying aspects of fascism, were Eugen Weber, Juan Linz, George Mosse, Zeev Sternhell, and A. J. Gregor. For example, Juan Linz's 1976 definition spoke of fascism as a hypernationalist/pan-nationalist movement which, in addition to having on its agenda the planned destruction of a whole list of political opponents, had the positive aim of "national social integration through a single party and corporative representation. . . . [W]ith a distinctive style and rhetoric, it relied on activist cadres ready for violent action combined with electoral participation to gain power with totalitarian goals by a combination of legal and violent tactics." Linz argued that fascist ideology and rhetoric appealed "for the incorporation of a national cultural tradition selectively in the new synthesis in response to new social classes, new social and economic problems, and with new organizational conceptions of mobilization and participation, which differentiate them from conservative parties."

Building on Linz's work, Stanley Payne evolved his highly influential "typological description" of fascism in 1980. This groundbreaking approach to the problem of defining fascism outlined its "ideology and goals" in terms of wanting to create a "new nationalist authoritarian state" and to "realize a new form of modern, self-determined, secular culture." However, even this theory still opened with "the fascist negations"—namely, antiliberalism, anticommunism, and anticonservatism.

A feature of the "new consensus" in fascist studies (*see* INTRODUCTION) is that the "inhuman," negative effects of fascism are now interpreted as the direct product of its bid to achieve what, in its own perception, are positive goals, rather than of its inherently destructive or nihilistic nature. In other words, what to an outsider appears wanton destruction is considered by the fascist activist to be the precondition of and prelude to nothing less than the rebirth of the entirety of society (*see* INTRODUCTION, PALINGENETIC MYTH). In the case of the most extreme form of fascism that actually seized state power, Nazism, this principle expressed itself in the chilling "palingenetic logic" that was to run through all the major policies and actions of the Third Reich. The ruthless destruction of the Weimar parliamentary system, of the working-class movement, of decadent culture, of racial and ideological enemies, and all those considered morally or racially unfit to become full members of the regenerated national-racial community, the *Volksgemeinschaft*—all these are to be seen as the concomitants of, and ritual preparations for, the rebirth of Germany.

Roger Griffin

See Also: INTRODUCTION; ENLIGHTENMENT, THE; COLD WAR, THE; CONSPIRACY THEORIES; CULTURE; DECADENCE; DEMOCRACY; FREEMASONRY/FREEMASONS, THE; FRENCH REVOLUTION, THE; LIBERALISM; MARXIST THEORIES OF FASCISM; MUSSOLINI, BENITO ANDREA; NEW MAN, THE; NIHILISM; PALINGENETIC MYTH; RELIGION; REVOLUTION; SOCIALISM; TOTALITARIANISM; WEIMAR REPUBLIC, THE; *VOLKSGEMEINSCHAFT*, THE

References

Griffin, Roger. 1993. *The Nature of Fascism.* London: Routledge.

Linz, J. J. 1979. "Some Notes toward a Comparative Study of Fascism in Sociological Historical Perspective." In *Fascism: A Reader's Guide,* edited by W. Laqueur. Harmondsworth: Penguin.

Mosse, George. 1999. "Towards a General Theory of Fascism." In *The Fascist Revolution.* New York: Howard Fertig (reprinted in Griffin, Roger, with Matt Feldman, eds. 2003. *Fascism.* Critical Concepts in Politics Series, vol. 1. London: Routledge).

Payne, Stanley. 1995. "Interpretations of Fascism." Pp. 441–461 in id., *A History of Fascism 1914–1945.* London: UCL.

Stern, Fritz. 1961. *The Politics of Cultural Despair.* Berkeley: University of California Press.

Sternhell, Zeev. 1991. "Fascist Ideology." In *Fascism: A Reader's Guide: Analyses, Interpretations, Bibliography,* edited by Walter Laqueur. Aldershot: Scholar Press (reprinted in Griffin, Roger, with Matt Feldman, eds. 2003. *Fascism.* Critical Concepts in Politics Series, vol. 1., 325–406. London: Routledge).

ANTICLERICALISM

A number of European interwar fascist movements were heirs to a tradition of anticlericalism going back to the French Revolution, and to the Enlightenment before that. Mussolini's early propaganda called for the "de-Vaticanization" of Italy, though he subsequently realized that this would alienate many potential sympathizers and became much more supportive of the Church in his public utterances. Hitler and the Nazi leadership were contemptuous both of the Catholic Church and of the Lutheran Church. Hitler despised Franco for his Catholicism. In France, matters were more complicated. There were those on the Right who retained the visceral anticlericalism of the republican heirs to the French Revolution, for whom the Church represented the forces opposed to the Revolution and its philosophy, but the predominant mood was probably one of sympathy for the Catholic

Church. Charles Maurras, for example, whose nationalism was of a Mediterranean type that exalted Latin culture and France's role as a bearer of it, saw the logic of accepting the importance of the Catholic Church's role in preserving Latinity and keeping that culture alive. At the same time, however, he himself did not practice the Catholic faith, and he saw his Action Française movement placed beyond the pale for Catholics by the Church, with a consequent dwindling of support. Although he was far from being anticlerical, his slogan *la politique d'abord* ("politics first") was bound to set him on a collision course with a body that stood for the primacy of the spiritual. The Action Française could draw on a strong reservoir of Catholic monarchism in early-twentieth-century France, but the papal interdict on the movement merely made official the obvious contradiction between extreme nationalism and membership in a global church. In Croatia and in Austria there arose for a time a type of authoritarian right-wing government known as clerico-fascism that involved an alliance between state and Church. In pre-Soviet and post-Soviet Russia there was a strong tradition of pro-Orthodox anti-Semitic nationalism that was and remains susceptible to the message of fascist and fascistic political movements. Postwar fascism has proved mainly heterodox in religion, the most outstanding example being that of the European New Right, with its open advocacy of paganism.

Cyprian Blamires

See Also: ACTION FRANÇAISE; ANTIFASCISM; ANTI-SEMITISM; AUSTRIA; CATHOLIC CHURCH, THE; CLERICO-FASCISM; CROATIA; DEGRELLE, LEON; EUROPEAN NEW RIGHT, THE; FRANCE; FRANCO Y BAHMONDE, GENERAL FRANCISCO; FRANCOISM; FRENCH REVOLUTION, THE; HITLER, ADOLF; LUTHERAN CHURCHES, THE; MAURRAS, CHARLES; MUSSOLINI, BENITO ANDREA; NATIONALISM; NAZISM; ORTHODOX CHURCHES, THE; PIUS XI, POPE; PIUS XII, POPE; POSTWAR FASCISM; RUSSIA; SALAZAR, ANTÓNIO DE OLIVEIRA

References

Koon, Tracy. 1985. *Believe, Obey, Fight: Political Socialization of Youth in Fascist Italy, 1922–1943.* Chapel Hill: University of North Carolina Press.

Lewy, Guenter. 1965. *The Catholic Church and Nazi Germany.* New York: McGraw-Hill.

Mack Smith, Denis. 1981. *Mussolini.* London: George Weidenfeld and Nicholson.

Rychlak, Ronald J. 2000. *Hitler, the War, and the Pope.* Huntington, IN: Our Sunday Visitor.

Sánchez, José M. 1987. *The Spanish Civil War as a Religious Tragedy.* Notre Dame, IN: University of Notre Dame Press.

Weber, Eugen. 1962. *Action Française.* Stanford: Stanford University Press.

ANTI-COMINTERN PACT, THE

On 25 November 1936, Germany and Japan signed a treaty designed to create a common front against international communism, designated under the word *Comintern*. Although it did not specify any particular country in this connection, there was a secret protocol that was directed against the Soviet Union. Italy joined the pact formally on 6 November 1937.

Cyprian Blamires

See Also: AXIS, THE; COMINTERN, THE; ITALY; JAPAN AND WORLD WAR II

ANTIFASCISM

I. POLITICAL

The antifascist response on the political level to the rise to power of Hitler and Mussolini in the 1930s was not homogeneous. Liberals, socialists, communists, and others could draw on different traditions in opposing fascism. Yet there were some lessons that tended to be accepted by antifascists across party divisions. A common argument on the Left was that the whole Left was threatened by the rise of the Right. Antifascists should put aside all temporary divisions and work together to prevent the rise of this great enemy. Yet diverse traditions advocated different forms of unity. The main form of antifascist unity in 1920s Italy was the Arditi del popolo, an alliance of former soldiers with radical unionists. However, the movement was isolated and defeated. The socialists and communists had no time to grasp the threat ahead of them before Mussolini took power. Between 1930 and 1932, German communists again argued for antifascist unity, and the result was the Iron Front, an alliance of communists with some members of the SPD's paramilitary Reichsbanner. The Communist Party was able to run what should have been a united project. Many interwar Marxists, including Antonio Gramsci, Ignazio Silone, Victor Serge, and Leon Trotsky, defended a different strategy, the "united front." In criticism of the German communists, they insisted that genuine unity required more than just one

Oskar Schindler—known to posterity through the Hollywood movie Schindler's List—*was one of many who strove to save Jews from the fate the Nazis planned for them. (Keystone/Getty Images)*

party repackaging itself under another name. They argued instead for a combination of all socialists. The best strategy for confronting fascism, they argued, would be one of working-class alliance. If a confident and cohesive working class confronted fascism, then the leaders of the Fascist Party would prove unable to hold their supporters together in opposition to it.

These and similar arguments did not go unnoticed. In Germany, copies of pamphlets calling for unity sold in the tens and hundreds of thousands. Breakaway parties were formed to the left of the socialists or to the right of the communists, calling for both to adopt united front politics. Independent journalists and artists took up the call. Yet the leaders of the socialists and communists alike failed to grasp their chance. On 30 January 1933, Adolf Hitler's Nazis took power. Within four months the left-wing parties and the trade unions were banned. After Italy and Germany, the third place where antifascist tactics were tried was in

Spain. Tens of thousands of Spaniards died in the battle against Franco. They were joined by large numbers of international volunteers. The best activists of the European and American Left served in the International Brigades. They fought and died for an internationalist cause. Some of the most famous conflicts between fascists and antifascists (such as the "Battle of Cable Street" in London) took place outside Spain, while the Civil War continued and in the very shadow of that cause. Yet the politics of the Civil War were complicated by changes in communist tactics. After 1935 the spokesmen of the Communist International argued for a new form of antifascist alliance, the Popular Front. Unity was now to be sought with any force, right up to the edges of the fascist party itself. Internal disputes undermined the opposition to Franco. Anarchists and others called for a revolutionary war against Franco. They suggested vital, creative tactics, such as the arming of popular volunteers (which was accepted) and the acceptance of the national right to independence as a means to undermine Franco's hold over his Moroccan troops (which was not tried). Meanwhile, communists, liberals, and some right-wing socialists devoted themselves to the opposite task of downplaying the Spanish revolution for the sake of a potential alliance with the moderate socialists of Britain and France.

In addition to historical experiences, certain books, songs, plays, paintings, and other cultural forms have been shared by antifascists across Europe in the postwar era. Many were first produced for audiences of workers or intellectuals in the interwar years. One such has been Ignazio Silone's novel *Fontamara*, a plausible account of an antifascist uprising in an isolated village in southern Italy. Silone's own reputation has since come under fire from within his native Italy. His book has continued to be popular, however, as have the plays derived from it. Other forms of antifascist culture from the 1920s and 1930s include the pacifist essays of Albert Einstein; the antiwar paintings of Pablo Picasso, including his classic work *Guernica*, painted in response to Franco's bombing raids; the poems and montage art of the Volksbühne circle, including John Heartfield; the radical sexology of Wilhelm Reich; the pessimistic cultural essays of Walter Benjamin; and the books written by such Holocaust survivors as Primo Levi. The British novelist Virginia Woolf fired her own broadside against fascism. Her book *Three Guineas* argued that fascist violence depends on certain images of male virtue that can be found even in liberal or mainstream texts.

The Nazis dubbed Weimar art and music "degenerate." Not surprisingly, antifascists have used it as a common resource to draw upon since. The outstanding examples of such culture were the plays produced by Bertolt Brecht, Max Reinhardt, Erwin Piscator, and Kurt Weill. The antifascist theater of the 1920s and 1930s did not see its task as being to provide high-brow thrills to the middle classes, but rather to create a new art, owned by plebeian audiences. The playwrights introduced bawdy songs and situations modeled on boxing fights or union meetings. In the proletarian citadel of Wedding, they drew on a network of workers' choirs and acting groups. They forced their audience to think, to test their own ideas, and to challenge all authority. In a number of poems, Bertolt Brecht also attempted to put a demotic, even humorous case against fascism. His "Song of the SA Man" asked why individual workers had signed up for Hitler's party; couldn't they see that they and their brothers would lose out too? Another poem, "But for the Jews Advising against It," made the ironic point that if the Jews were so extraordinary and so powerful, then why had Hitler not used them (rather than the Germans) to take on the world? Long before Hitler threatened to take power, Brecht railed against the society in which fascism could flourish. Certain other cultural forms, evolved in one country to meet a specific need, have tended to become general and now form part of the common iconography of antifascist campaigns across Europe and North America. They include the three antifascist arrows of interwar German antifascism; the yellow "lollipop" symbol, employed by the Anti-Nazi League in 1970s Britain; punk dress and music, derived from the same campaign; and the outstretched yellow hand of the French movement SOS-Racisme, often with the slogan "Don't touch my friend" attached to it.

The greatest problem faced by postwar antifascists is that interwar fascism and postwar fascism have not been entirely alike. We can list just a few differences here. First of all, postwar fascism has frequently attempted to conceal its own past. Neofascists in France deny that they have a link to the interwar years. Their Italian equivalents describe themselves as "postfascists." Second, the far Right has been less obsessed with the task of building a mass activist party, in competition with the far Left. One reason for that has been the relative decline of the old communist parties, and their replacement by a more diffuse series of anticapitalist "lefts." Another has been the relative success that the far Right has achieved through electoral rather than street politics. Third, the main popular slogans of postwar fascism have been immediately racial rather than economic in character. Fourth, the far Right has grown in areas in which it was previously much weaker, including Third World countries. Fifth, the postwar years have seen fascistic parties sharing in government power, but without the economic crisis of the interwar years, or (as of yet) the same calamitous results.

The conversion of neofascist parties to an electoralist strategy has raised tactical problems. In contrast to the 1920s and 1930s, the immediate postwar years were ones of rapid economic growth and relative prosperity. Meanwhile, the fascist parties were hampered by their association with Nazi genocide and an unpopular war. Such organizations as the Italian MSI have argued that only the adoption of more moderate-seeming tactics could increase their support. Antifascists have found that certain prewar tactics, such as the mass march designed to prevent a fascist mobilization, have had less success than previously, largely because the fascists themselves have not been marching. While the tactics of mass mobilization have remained important to antifascists, many have also had to develop new forms of electoral work.

The slogans of postwar fascists have been shaped by anti-immigrant racism. Race is perhaps even more ubiquitous in their propaganda than it was for the equivalent parties before 1933. Yet the process has been contradictory, for Europe has witnessed growing racial integration even as the popular press has expressed its hatred of successive waves of labor migrants and refugees. Whatever the complexities, the task facing electoral antifascists has been to win an argument in defense of peaceful racial cohabitation. In comparison to interwar antifascism, its postwar forms have been much more "cultural" and less "economic." Antifascists have had to respond to the participation of postwar fascist parties in local and national government. Each far-right advance has been met by waves of popular protest. The greater the initial success, the greater has been the public resistance. Yet the experience of fascist advance has also created an expectation of further success. Widespread protests met the election of Berlusconi's first Italian government, which included two far-right parties, the National Alliance and the Northern Leagues. The early response to the election of Berlusconi's second government was far more muted. Antifascists have also been charged with explaining the difference between the experience of interwar and postwar fascism in government. Both Mussolini and Hitler entered government as leaders of minority parties in cabinet. Yet buoyed up by the support of extraparliamentary armies, they were able to achieve a reordering of the state. Postwar fascist parties governing as minority members of coalitions inside Europe (Italy, Austria) or outside Europe (India) have not attempted any similar "fascization" of the nation. Some antifascists have con-

cluded that postwar fascism has indeed been more moderate than its predecessors. Another response has been to point out that the particular radicalism of the 1920s and 1930s depended not just on the ideology of the new fascist parties but also on the total economic and social context in which they took power. Were Europe or the world to enter such a period of catastrophic economic decline as was witnessed after 1929, then the contemporary far Right would be far better placed than it was, even in the interwar years, to turn its dystopia into reality.

David Renton

See Also: ANTI-NAZI LEAGUE, THE; ART; AUSTRIA; AVENTINE SECESSION, THE; BOLSHEVISM; CABLE STREET, THE BATTLE OF; COMINTERN, THE; CROCE, BENEDETTO; DEGENERACY; EDELWEISS PIRATES, THE; FASCIST PARTY, THE; FRANCO Y BAHAMONDE, GENERAL FRANCISCO; GRAMSCI, ANTONIO; GUERNICA; HITLER, ADOLF; HOLOCAUST, THE; IMMIGRATION; INDIA; INTERNATIONAL BRIGADES, THE; ITALY; JULY PLOT, THE; KREISAU CIRCLE, THE; MARXIST THEORIES OF FASCISM; MOVIMENTO SOCIALE ITALIANO; MUSIC (GERMANY); MUSSOLINI, BENITO ANDREA; NAZISM; ORWELL, GEORGE; POSTWAR FASCISM; REICH, WILHELM; *SEARCHLIGHT;* SOCIALISM; SOVIET UNION, THE; SPANISH CIVIL WAR, THE; STALIN, IOSIF VISSARIONOVICH; STAUFFENBERG, CLAUS SCHENK GRAF VON; TRADES UNIONS; TROTSKY, LEON; TROTT ZU SOLZ, ADAM VON; WARRIOR ETHOS, THE; WHITE ROSE; WIESENTHAL, SIMON

References
Behan, T. 2002. *The Resistible Rise of Benito Mussolini.* London: Bookmarks.
Copsey, N. 2000. *Anti-Fascism in Britain.* Basingstoke: Macmillan.
Gluckstein, D. 1999. *The Nazis, Capitalism and the Working Class.* London: Bookmarks.
Mason, T. 1993. *Social Policy in the Third Reich: The Working Class and the National Community.* Oxford: Berg.
Merson, A. 1985. *Communist Resistance in Nazi Germany.* London: Lawrence and Wishart.
Renton, D. 1999. *Fascism, Theory and Practice.* London: Pluto.
Renton, D. 2000. *Fascism, Anti-Fascism, and the 1940s.* London: Macmillan.
Thompson, E. P. 1997. *Beyond the Frontier: The Politics of a Failed Mission, Bulgaria 1944.* London: Merlin.

II. RELIGIOUS

All over Europe, there were courageous Christian leaders and individuals who took a stand against interwar and wartime fascism in the name of their faith. Alongside the multitudes of Jews in the concentration camps, there were also Catholic and Lutheran clerics and laypeople incarcerated because of their opposition to

Nazism. In Dachau three barracks were reserved for some 1,600 clergymen. On the German Lutheran side, the names of Bonhoeffer and Niemoeller are legendary. On the Catholic side, Cardinal Faulhaber was a thorn in the flesh for the Nazi regime, and some of those who spoke out vigorously have since been recognized by the Catholic Church as saints and martyrs: the names of the Polish Franciscan St. Maximilian Kolbe, who died in Auschwitz, and the Dutch Carmelite Fr. Titus Brandsma, who died in Dachau, are among the most eminent. Perhaps we may legitimately include the White Rose resistance movement in Germany under the Catholic umbrella, insofar as the Kolls who founded it were advised by a Catholic professor. There were also more subtle ways in which hostility to fascism could be expressed. The psychiatrist Karl Stern, a Jew by birth who was born in Austria but escaped the Holocaust, recorded that on the day when news came through to their community of Nazi anti-Jewish legislation, he was out in the street with his father. The Catholic priest, who had up to that point been unknown to them, came up to his father and made a special point of greeting him and shaking him by the hand.

III. HUMANITARIAN

The success of the Hollywood movie *Schindler's List* is a reminder that some individuals fought against fascism from within the system, not out of political or religious conviction but seemingly on general ethical or humanitarian grounds. Oskar Schindler was an example of a minor industrialist who not only saved as many Jews as he could but also went out of his way to produce substandard armaments in his factory, to speed the defeat of fascism. Others sought to protest by directly addressing fascist leaders, as was the case with industrialist Fritz Thyssen. Having initially been a supporter of Hitler, he became disenchanted with the Nazi regime and on 28 December 1939 left Germany for Switzerland. From there he sent a long letter to Hitler complaining of the persecution against Christianity and the Jews. He told the Fuehrer that the alliance with Stalin was the last straw. He made it clear that he wanted to avoid undermining the German war effort, but he appealed to the conscience of the German people against Hitler. "Listen to me and you will hear the voice of the tormented German nation that is crying out to you: 'Turn back, let freedom, right, and humaneness rise again in the German Reich.'" This is a reminder that, along with the many Jews who fled Germany and the Occupied Territories, there were also many principled non-Jews whose

costly decision to emigrate and to abandon their homes and possessions was made on grounds of hostility to fascist regimes. Among the most celebrated cases is that of the Austrian Von Trapp family, whose rejection of Nazism motivated their abandonment of the family estates and their emigration, which eventually took them to the United States. Their story was immortalized in the 1960s musical *The Sound of Music*.

IV. MILITARY

The brunt of the military fight against fascism was borne by the citizens of the Allied powers in World War II, but it should be remembered that many emigrants or escapees from fascist regimes joined the Allied forces in this war. Poles, Czechs, Frenchmen, and others played an important part in the military defeat of fascism. Equally, there were those who refused military service on conscientious grounds in what they considered an unjust war, suffering the ultimate penalty for it. The case of the Austrian Franz Jägerstaetter, who was executed after refusing to take the oath of loyalty to Hitler when he was called up, along with that of Carl von Ossietzky (*see* PACIFISM), is emblematic in this respect. Finally, many nationals in territories occupied by the Germans engaged in guerrilla resistance activities at great personal risk, often paying with their lives.

Cyprian Blamires

See Also: ANTI-SEMITISM; BARBIE, KLAUS; BONHOEFFER, DIETRICH; CATHOLIC CHURCH, THE; CHRISTIANITY; CHURCHILL, SIR WINSTON LEONARD SPENCER; CONFESSING CHURCH, THE; EDELWEISS PIRATES, THE; FAULHABER, CARDINAL MICHAEL VON; GALEN, CARDINAL CLEMENS AUGUST VON; JULY PLOT, THE; KREISAU CIRCLE, THE; LUTHERAN CHURCHES, THE; NIEMOELLER, MARTIN; ORTHODOX CHURCHES, THE; PACIFISM; PIUS XI, POPE; PIUS XII, POPE; POLITICAL CATHOLICISM; PROTESTANTISM; RELIGION; ROOSEVELT, FRANKLIN DELANO; *SEARCHLIGHT*; SKINHEAD FASCISM; WHITE ROSE; WIESENTHAL, SIMON

References
Anon. 1940. *The Persecution of the Catholic Church in the Third Reich.* London: Burns and Oates.
Barnett, Victoria. 1992. *For the Soul of the People: Protestant Protest against Hitler.* Oxford: Oxford University Press.
Bergmann, Georg. 1988. *Franz Jägerstätter: Ein Leben vom Gewissen entschieden von Chrisus gestaltet: mit dem gesamten schriftlichen Nachlass von Franz Jägerstätter.* Stein am Rhein, Switzerland: Christiana.
Crowe, David. 2004. *Oskar Schindler: The Untold Account of His Life, Wartime Activities, and the True Story of His List.* New York: Basic Books.

Duncan-Jones, A. S. 1938. *The Struggle for Religious Freedom in Germany*. London: Gollancz.

Ericksen, Robert P., and Susannah Heschel. 1999. *Betrayal: German Churches and the Holocaust*. Minneapolis: Fortress.

Feige, Franz G. M. 1990. *The Varieties of Protestantism in Nazi Germany*. Lewiston, NY: Edwin Mellen.

Hanley, Boniface. 1983. *No Strangers to Violence, No Strangers to Love*. Notre Dame, IN: Ave Maria.

Kenneally, Thomas. 1994. *Schindler's List*. London: Hodder & Stoughton.

Mommsen, Hans. 2003. *Alternatives to Hitler: German Resistance under the Third Reich*. Trans. Angus McGeoch. London: I. B. Tauris.

Montclos, Xavier de. 1983. *Les Chrétiens face au Nazisme et au Stalinisme. L'épreueve totalitaire*. Paris: Plon.

Stern, Karl. 1951. *The Pillar of Fire*. New York: Harcourt Brace

Trapp, Maria Augusta. 2002. *The Story of the Trapp Family Singers*. London: HarperCollins.

ANTI-NAZI LEAGUE, THE

Launched in 1977, following clashes between the police and antifascists at Lewisham in South London, the Anti-Nazi League (ANL) was a mass movement in opposition to the UK National Front. Its main innovation was the use of music in the Rock against Racism carnivals. By 1979 the league could boast of having distributed some 9 million leaflets and 750,000 badges. Approximately 250 ANL branches mobilized some 50,000 supporters. The league claimed to have played a large part in the decline of the National Front vote, and to have contributed to the pushing back of fascism in Britain. It was dissolved in 1982 and relaunched in 1992.

David Renton

See Also: ANTIFASCISM; GREAT BRITAIN; NATIONAL FRONT (UK), THE; POSTWAR FASCISM; *SEARCHLIGHT*

Reference
Renton, David. 2005. *When We Touched the Sky: The Anti-Nazi League 1979–1981*. Cheltenham: New Clarion.

ANTI-SEMITISM

As a consequence of the Holocaust, it is often assumed that anti-Semitism and (generic) fascism are synony-

mous, but in fact the situation is a great deal more complex. Although it was a major plank in the ideology of Nazism, "biological" anti-Semitism was not a major element in the worldview of Italian Fascism until the late 1930s, by which time Mussolini had already been in power for fifteen years. In other words, Mussolini and his Fascist Party did not gain such support as they enjoyed in the general public on the basis of an overtly anti-Semitic platform, as the Nazis did, nor did their program once in office involve a campaign against Jews. Indeed, there were even Zionists attracted to Italian Fascism (*see* ZIONISM). There was certainly a level of classic "anti-Judaism" among Fascist Party supporters and their leaders, but that was a common feature in all sectors of European society at the time. Mussolini himself had a Jewish mistress, Margherita Sarfatti, for more than fifteen years, and he was quite happy for her to publish a (very adulatory) biography of him in 1925; it is impossible to imagine Hitler encouraging or permitting someone Jewish to write his biography. Indeed, Sarfatti prospered so much under Mussolini's regime that she became one of the most powerful women in Italy in the late 1920s. Mussolini was certainly a racist with regard to black people in Ethiopia, but the list of his chosen enemies comprised mainly liberals, democrats, socialists, and freemasons rather than Jews, and a significant proportion of Italian Jews actually supported the Fascist Party until Mussolini's introduction of anti-Jewish legislation in 1938. Mussolini's list of "enemies" was much the same as Hitler's, but he did not (as Hitler did) perpetually see lurking behind these enemies the figure of the Jew pulling the strings. Anti-Semitism cannot therefore be regarded as an essential part of the core of generic fascism—that is, of the shared nucleus of doctrines that were common to Italian Fascism and German Nazism.

Anti-Semitism had been around for a long time when the Nazis appeared on the scene, but not as long as is generally thought. Strictly speaking, modern anti-Semitism has its roots in the Enlightenment, and Voltaire was the classic anti-Semite. Modern anti-Semitism, in fact, is a phenomenon of a very different kind from the traditional anti-Judaism with which it is frequently conflated, a phenomenon that can be traced back to pre-Christian antiquity. Many of those who write about this topic gloss over or ignore the crucial difference between anti-Judaism, which is hostility to Jews on account of their religion (predating the appearance of Christianity), and anti-Semitism, which is hostility to Jews (purportedly at least) on grounds of race—that is, that Jews are believed to be a corrupt and corrupting race whose blood contaminates that of "pure" races where there is intermarriage. The difference is crucial. From the anti-Judaist standpoint there is at least a way for Jews to redeem themselves: by conversion to Christianity. That route was taken by countless Jews down the centuries in Christian countries. Indeed, Margherita Sarfatti herself was baptized and received into the Catholic Church in the late 1920s. From the standpoint of biological anti-Semitism, however, there is simply nothing a Jew can do to integrate into society, because he is by virtue of his blood and race a harmful bacillus; the Holocaust was merely the chilling conclusion to an argument that the Nazis believed to be scientific, for they appealed both to currents within anthropology and to social Darwinistic ideas. Although baptized Jews initially escaped incarceration and deportation to the death camps, eventually they too were targeted for extinction. One of the most celebrated victims was the philosopher Edith Stein, a Jewish convert to Catholicism who had become a Carmelite nun.

Anti-Judaism as hostility to Jews on account of their religion can be traced back to antiquity. Originally it was provoked by the resolute monotheism that led the Jews to refuse to respect other gods than their own—and this kind of anti-Judaism can of course be found in the First/Old Testament. Christian anti-Judaism was hostility to Jews specifically on another religious ground: their rejection of the claim that Christ was the Messiah. This new variant of anti-Judaism became embedded in the Catholic world, subsequently being absorbed at the Reformation into Protestantism. Generally speaking, conversion of Jews to Christianity was regarded as perfectly acceptable, and biology was not an issue.

Paradoxically, the roots of the anti-Semitism embraced by Nazism are not to be found in this traditional Christian anti-Judaism at all, but in the opposite camp, in the campaign against the Christian faith waged by certain Enlightenment thinkers. These thinkers sought to undermine traditional Christianity and in particular the Catholic Church by destroying its foundation in the idea that the Israel of the First/Old Testament was a people to whom a special divine revelation had been given. In other words, although there appears on the surface to be a continuous tradition of hostility to the Jews in Europe, the anti-Semitism propagated by the Nazis actually arose out of a new movement of ideas that took its rise only with the Enlightenment and that had a new agenda: to pour scorn on the idea that the Jews were God's chosen people and so to destroy Christianity and the churches. This movement saw that the New/Second testament made no sense without the Old/First Testament. Christians saw themselves as "the new Israel," and they buttressed their claims about Christ by pointing to the way that his coming was a fulfillment of the words of the Hebrew prophets. Following the English deists, Voltaire ridiculed the idea that a tiny desert tribe in the Middle East could have been the bearers of divine revelation, mocking Israel's political and cultural insignificance as contrasted with great and powerful civilizations like those of Ancient Greece, Rome, and China. This was part of his program to rewrite the history of Europe: in place of the history in which the Bible and the rise and spread of Christianity played a central place, Voltaire put forward an account based on a humanistic appreciation of the literary, philosophical, and cultural glories of the historical empires. This was picked up by the celebrated British historian Gibbon, whose classic *The Decline and Fall of the Roman Empire* largely blamed the rise of Christianity for the fall of Rome. For such thinkers, Christianity was penetrated with the "fanatical" and "barbaric" spirit of the ignorant desert people of Israel, and as such was the enemy of all true culture and civilization. Their association of Christianity and Judaism as common enemies of civilization was later to be picked up by the Nazis.

French Revolutionary leaders largely turned away from Voltairian anti-Judaism, however, and espoused the tolerantism inherent in the notion of the Rights of Man, which led them to introduce measures to grant citizenship rights to Jews. (This was one of the reasons for Nazi hostility to what the French Revolution represented.) The spread of the ideals of the French Revolution in Europe led to a gradual Europewide repeal of anti-Jewish legislation, and that enabled Jews openly to take up positions of leadership and influence in European societies for the first time in the course of the nineteenth century. That in itself began to provoke fresh resentment against them in some quarters. The international nature of Judaism made it into an object of suspicion to nationalism, which was in the ascendancy over much of Europe during the nineteenth century; at the same time, the pluralistic cultures that began to develop in the aftermath of the collapse of the old-regime idea of the "Christian state" proved unsettling for many Catholics and Protestants. A tendency developed among them to find comfort in conspiracy theories that blamed the new state of affairs since the French Revolution on targets with global networks, such as the Freemasons or the Jews or, later, the Bolsheviks—or all of them at once.

At the same time, the development of the "scientific" study of races in the nineteenth century (often itself motivated by a desire to "prove" crude racial theories) led some ideologues to a belief in a superior Aryan Nordic race whose healthy blood was threatened with corruption by intermingling with the inferior Semitic breed. (Of course, strictly speaking, the Jews are only one among many "Semitic" races, but the term *anti-Semitic* came to be used only in relation to the Jewish people.) Darwinistic ideas about the survival of the fittest sharpened and intensified the racial panics whipped up by anti-Semitic propagandists. It is no accident that it was a biologist (and, curiously, an Englishman, though one completely unknown in England) named Houston Stewart Chamberlain who wrote the bible of Nazi anti-Semites, *The Foundations of the Nineteenth Century,* a best-seller so successful in Germany that it even led the author into a prolonged correspondence with Kaiser Wilhelm II. Chamberlain and others like him tried to rebuild an acceptably "Aryan" or "Nordic" version of Christianity by severing Jesus entirely from Judaism. They built on the work of German Protestant critics of the Bible to preach that Jesus himself had not in fact been a Jew; to do this they exploited the idea of his Galilean origins: Galilee (in northern Palestine), it was claimed, having been inhabited by heathen, non-Jewish tribes, as opposed to Judah (in southern Palestine, around Jerusalem). There was said to be a pure, original version of the non-Jewish teachings of Christ, which had been traduced after his death by the Jew St. Paul.

The critique of the Old Testament and St. Paul by propagandists like Chamberlain and his acolytes actually followed the lines of a classic Protestant polemic against the Catholic Church. This polemic had assumed that the supreme difference between the Old Testament religion and the New (the authentic one as preached by Christ) resided in a polarity between a "materialistic" Old Testament religion based on "externalism" (rituals of purification, outward obedience to the law, a system of ritual sacrifices) and a New Testament religion based on inward spiritual values (inward purity of heart rather than outward purification rituals, obedience of the heart to God rather than outward conformity with the requirements of the law, etc). It had long been a classic argument of Protestants that Catholicism had in fact lost sight of this inward religion of the heart and lapsed into a materialistic practice of rites and ceremonies (the sacramental system, and the like), which was nothing more than a replay of the old Judaism. Both these themes—the "materialism" of the Old Testament and the "Jewish distortion" of the authentic "spiritual" message of Jesus into the "materialistic" religion preached by the Catholic Church—were picked up by Nazi ideologues.

Nazi propagandists like Rosenberg followed in the footsteps of Chamberlain in arguing that it was the great hero Luther who had first led the Germans out of their Babylonish captivity to Catholic/Jewish materialism, preaching an inward spiritual religion against the materialistic focus on externals practiced by Catholicism and inspired by Judaism. In this view Luther was, however, only the pioneer; he was still himself not fully freed from the materialistic version of Christ's teaching because he still continued to preach the reality of a divinely ordained positive religion based on a core of credal orthodoxy, and it was not until the nineteenth century that the significance of his emancipation from Rome was properly understood. Then it was finally grasped that Luther represented the resurgence of a peculiarly "Germanic" religious outlook definable simply as a magnificently unique inwardness and spiritual depth. This was claimed to be the true lost message of the real Jesus, who had in fact called for the complete obliteration of Old Testament "materialism" rather than for its incorporation into new rites and rituals as in the Christian churches.

This kind of traditional hostility to Jewish/Catholic "materialism" merged with the new "scientific" anti-Semitism in the approach of Nazi propagandists. Confusion has arisen because of the historical prominence of a parallel but rather different species of anti-Judaism in France in the late nineteenth century taken up by right-wing Catholics as part of their hostility against the secular governments of France. This was essentially a rerun of the old Catholic anti-Judaism, now dressed up in a different garb. Its foremost prophets were Alfonse Toussenel and Edouard Drumont. These writers and their imitators spread the fashion in French (Catholic) conservative circles of blaming the Jews for the French Revolution and for the "ills" of the republican secularist tradition that had emerged from it. Like Balzac and Carlyle and other satirists, they claimed that the nineteenth century was an era dominated by materialism and greed and financial speculation, a way of life that they contrasted starkly with the "noble" and "heroic" culture of an earlier pre-Revolutionary age. (This was the kind of tune played by the Irish politician Edmund Burke in his celebrated attack on the Revolution in 1790, *Reflections on the Revolution in France,* which inspired generations of conservative hostility to the Revolution.) They regarded the Jews as the very incarnation of this decadent spirit. Having emerged to prominence in the last quarter of the nineteenth century (when there was a Europewide upsurge in anti-

Semitic propaganda following large-scale immigration of Jews into Western Europe after pogroms in the East), this brand of hostility to the Jews in France reached a paroxysm in the notorious Dreyfus case, which resulted in a defeat for the anti-Jewish lobby. That episode made a massive impact at the time and went down in history, partly owing to the onslaught against the anti-Semites by the novelist Emile Zola in his celebrated pamphlet *J'Accuse*. But the philosophy of those hostile to Jews in France at this point was poles apart from that of their epigones in Germany. The anti-Dreyfusards attacked the Jews as enemies of what they saw as the great traditions of French Catholic civilization; the anti-Dreyfusards were continuing the French Catholic Church's long war against the French Revolution, its Enlightenment anticipators, and the secular republic that it had spawned. (The Church did not finally begin to come to terms with the republican status quo in France until the very end of the nineteenth century, when Pope Leo XIII called for an end to hostilities.)

The anti-Dreyfusards were in fact viscerally hostile to the Enlightenment. They were at the opposite pole from the specifically anti-Catholic anti-Semitism that inspired the Nazis, based on the "scientific" rationalist and secularizing movement of hostility to Christian teaching that had developed out of the Enlightenment. A German photograph from the 1930s shows a charabanc draped with a banner expressing hatred for "Jews and Jesuits," and Rosenberg's classic textbook of Nazism repeatedly brackets together these great enemies of Nazi values. The Jesuits were singled out as representative of the spirit of Catholicism because they were not subject to the episcopal hierarchies of the national churches but were directly answerable to the pope, so that they represented the very acme of that internationalism that the Nazis so detested.

The "scientific" argument for anti-Semitism prevalent in Germany and favored by the Nazis built on the work of a Frenchman, Arthur de Gobineau, who claimed that race alone is the decisive factor in the rise and fall of civilizations, rather than such things as governments, ideas, or the influence of religion. In Gobineau's view, history shows that races rise to power in their pure state and fall when they have suffered contamination. He claimed that the purest contemporary race was the Aryans, believed to be the ancient forebears of the Anglo-Saxons. He argued that force and conquest were essential to the nature of the Aryans, aristocrats among their contemporaries. However, their racial purity was subject to contamination by interbreeding with lesser races, and that would spell their inevitable decay. Gobineau's ideas were popularized in

Germany by Ludwig Schemann, who evolved a classically antimodernist worldview that identified the horrors of modernity with values derived from technology and science. In 1925 he claimed that the prime need for the Germans was to rid themselves of the delusion that big cities, machines, and the emancipation of the Jews were signs of progress. The Nazis appointed Schemann to the Reichsinstitut for modern history, and he was awarded the Goethe medal for his services to the nation and the race—though his hostility to technology and science was far from being embodied in Nazi practice.

In Houston Stewart Chamberlain's *Foundations of the Nineteenth Century*, the hypotheses of a "German" science and a "German" religion were used as weapons of anti-Semitic propaganda. Religiously speaking, the history of mankind was held to center on a bitter struggle between God as embodied in the Germanic race and the devil as embodied in the Jewish race. The Teutonic peoples had been bearers of all the best spiritual and cultural values in Greek and Roman civilization, but they were remorselessly opposed by the Jews with their materialism, shallowness, and culturelessness. The "scientific" backing for this thesis was to be found in the work of anthropologists going back to Franz Josef Gall, who conducted research that purported to indicate a relationship between external physical characteristics such as skull shapes and internal qualities of character. This built on a long anthropological tradition that had sought a racial classification of tribes and nations with attributions of superiority and inferiority.

The kind of anti-Semitism that the Nazis tapped into may be seen as a manifestation of the sort of social panic instigated a century earlier in Europe by the theories of the English demographer Thomas Malthus. In proposing his thesis that population was increasing much faster than the food supply, Malthus created a panic about overpopulation that has persisted to the present day. Those who subscribed to "scientific" racial theories that identified the Jews as the ongoing threat to the purity of a superior Aryan race naturally promoted a panic about a Jewish threat to civilization. Unfortunately that panic met up with the anti-Judaism traditionally current in Christian societies, so that anti-Semitism actually increased the attractiveness of the Nazi movement to many active churchgoers, and even to church leaders. This was especially so when anti-Semitic propagandists claimed that Bolshevism too was a Jewish movement, since Christians were all too aware of the visceral hatred of Bolshevism for Christianity and the murderous and destructive measures being implemented by the Soviets to destroy the Christian faith in their country. The idea that Bolshevism was a "Jewish plot" could seem all too plausible to Christian believers at that time. In propagating anti-Semitism, Nazis could even seem then to be advancing the cause of the Christian faith. All too few Christian leaders in the German-speaking world resisted such conclusions, which proved equally attractive to many Christians in other parts of the world. The long-standing tradition of anti-Judaism as a response to the Jewish rejection of Christ (though it was an attitude not supported by the Bible, and especially not by St. Paul) was so widespread in Christian countries that the open advocacy of anti-Semitism did little to damage the image of Nazism worldwide and indeed to many was a positive commendation.

Some observers saw the Nazi exploitation of anti-Semitic feeling as a tactic intended to woo working-class support away from the socialists. On this argument, the Nazis had no intention of eliminating capitalism or marginalizing the big industrialists, so they needed to provide the workers with another scapegoat—hence the convenience of the Jews in that role. However, that in itself does not seem to explain the extreme lengths to which the Nazis went, diverting vital resources at the height of the war—when it would have made sense to throw every resource into the military struggle—to the business of exterminating Jews. It must be assumed that some among them at least believed fanatically in their own anti-Semitic ideology, which, allegedly based on scientific premises, they considered unanswerable. The fanatical extremes to which the Nazis went in their devotion of energies, manpower, transport, and other facilities to the business of the Holocaust has proved a very thorny issue for Marxist commentators on fascism, who prefer to locate the reasons for human actions in immediate or long-term material gain to the actors. In fact, the Holocaust does have its logic, however, if the Nazis did actually believe what they claimed to believe—that the Jews were the prime cause of the decay of European civilization, that they were a parasite in an otherwise healthy body, and that they must be exterminated with the same ruthlessness that a surgeon would apply to the excision of a cancer.

The main thrust of Nazi anti-Semitic policy was embodied in the Nuremberg Laws of 1935, which created two categories of German citizenship, relegating Jews to an inferior civic status. The Law for the Protection of Blood and Honor forbade intermarriage between the two categories. A further 250 decrees followed in the years up to 1943, excluding Jews from an increasing range of professions and posts, obliging them to wear the yellow Star of David, and confining them to ghettos. The final decree made them outlaws in Germany. In the meantime, the gas ovens had been busily implementing the decision of the Nazi leadership at the Wannsee Conference to embark on a systematic elimination of Jews from Europe by mass murder. Governments in all the invaded or occupied territories were pressured into taking part in the war of extermination against Jews, and in some cases the collaboration was enthusiastic. The Nazis were able to tap into a widespread suspicion of the Jews in Europe, but some countries were much less cooperative than others—a higher percentage of Jews was protected in France, The Netherlands, and Italy, for example.

Among Mussolini's associates in the Fascist leadership, Roberto Farinacci was one of the most violently hostile to the Jews: he was also known for being particularly pro-Nazi. The only major Italian ideologue sympathetic to Fascism who espoused Nazi anti-Semitism was Julius Evola. Some among the tiny Italian Jewish population (47,000 in 1938) actually helped fund Fascism in the early days, while by the mid-1930s about one in three Jewish adults was a member of the Fascist Party—a higher proportion than among the Gentile population. Ettore Ovazza, one of 230 Jews who took part in the March on Rome, later founded a stridently pro-Fascist journal. In 1933, Mussolini informed Emil Ludwig that anti-Semitism could not be found in Italy. He went on to observe that Italian Jews were good citizens, courageous soldiers, and prestigious academics, officers, and bankers. Biological racism had never been part of his program. Mussolini was at that time in fact somewhat contemptuous of Nazi racial theories. But in the late 1930s (when he had already been in power for fifteen years) he became increasingly convinced of the need to ally with Nazi Germany, and (in part at least) for that reason he pronounced the "Manifesto of Fascist Racism" to win over Nazi sympathies. This manifesto spoke of the Jews as "unassimilable" and proscribed intermarriage between Jews and "Aryans." A series of anti-Semitic decrees based on the Nazi model were then promulgated, introducing a variety of restrictions on Jews. In general these decrees were not enforced with anything like Teutonic thoroughness, however, and 80 percent of Italian Jews eventually survived the war, though most had had to go into hiding. Up to the collapse of his regime in 1943, Mussolini told his diplomatic representatives in areas controlled by Italy not to hand over Jews to National Socialist forces. Under the Salò Republic the atmosphere changed dramatically, and members of the regime turned to active collaboration with the Nazis in rounding up Jews and surrendering them to the German forces in Italy.

Hitler's two pet hates were the Slavs and the Jews. The Slavs Hitler believed he could enslave—he admired the British Indian Empire and planned to imitate it in Russia, controlling a huge colonial territory with a small number of men, as the British had done in India. He did not want the Slavs eliminated; on the contrary, the idea was that they should be kept ignorant and unschooled, with just enough about them to enable them to act as lackeys and servants of the Master Race. And he knew that there would be nobody outside Russia who would care if that happened. But the Jews he could not control, because they were by definition and in very essence international. Nazism was hypernationalism; it exalted the German soul, but the Jews would forever be alien to that soul and could never be absorbed into it. In that light we can see that Hitler must have considered that exterminating the Jews was contributing to the war effort, because the Jews would always potentially be stabbing Germany in the back, as he accused them of having done in 1918. In eliminating the Jews he was eliminating a fifth column and thereby, in his eyes, making a crucial contribution to an eventual German victory. This is yet another reminder of the way that bitterness among the generation that fought in World War I sought an outlet in scapegoating, the favorite scapegoat for the Nazis being the Jews.

But eliminating the Jews would still not eliminate the "Jewish" spirit, as represented by materialism, egalitarianism, and internationalism; Hitler's *Table Talk*—transcripts taken down by official stenographers of his remarks made at dinner parties—makes it clear that the elimination of the Jews was but the prelude to an attack on the churches as propagators of the "Jewish" spirit, a campaign that Hitler planned to undertake once the war was over. In his mind the two campaigns were two stages in the same battle for the establishment of a properly Germanic empire purged of all taint of alien elements.

After the war anti-Semitism remained endemic in many places. For example, U.S. Hitler sympathizer and celebrated aviator Charles Lindbergh was living in a suburban enclave in Darien, Connecticut, that legally excluded Jews as well as blacks from owning property. The town was so notorious for its hostility to Jews that the makers of a film about anti-Semitism in the United States entitled *Gentleman's Agreement* actually used it as the setting for the film. The horrors of the Holocaust only gradually began to emerge into the consciousness of the world after the war's end. So appalling and indescribable did this genocidal project seem to most people, once knowledge of the facts was widely disseminated in the 1950s and 1960s, that anti-

Semitism seemed unthinkable. During the 1960s, when the minority rights issue first became fashionable, stories of guest houses in the United States with signs saying "No Jews" became an occasion of shock-horror reactions among listeners. Legislative measures in various countries often made such public discrimination an offense. (Unofficially, however, it could be practiced; the author recalls a search for lodgings in a French town in the early 1990s when a potential landlord was concerned to know if he was Jewish.) The mainline Christian denominations in Germany underwent a period of soul-searching about their past attitudes and attempted to make amends. However, anti-Semitism never went away; it has remained a particularly pronounced feature of neo-Nazism in the United States. In modern far-right Christian Identity circles some even hold to the theory that the Jewish race sprang originally from the sexual union of Eve with Satan.

In Europe, however, postwar fascism has generally focused on the issue of immigration in preference to that of anti-Semitism; indeed, it could be argued that the immigrant plays the same role for postwar fascism that the Jew played in prewar Nazism. Why should the modern fascist scapegoat the Jew when he knows that he can count on much more public sympathy by scapegoating the immigrant? However, desecration or vandalism of Jewish cemeteries is a not uncommon experience.

The issue of the past treatment of Jews in Europe is definitely a factor in the Middle East question. For many, support for Israel is a way of atoning for a sense of guilt about the Holocaust, but naturally Palestinians find that abhorrent; they argue that they are being made to pay the price for European guilt about something in which they had no involvement. Many Jews consider it important to distinguish between anti-Zionism (as rejection of the policies or goals of the state of Israel) and anti-Semitism. Equally, the existence of the state of Israel and of the Palestinian refugee campsite is made a reason for hatred of all Jews everywhere among many Muslim propagandists and their supporters; historical anti-Semitic libels, such as the "Protocols of the Elders of Zion," continue to circulate freely in the Arab world.

Cyprian Blamires

See Also: INTRODUCTION; AMERICANIZATION; ANTHROPOLOGY; "ANTI-" DIMENSION OF FASCISM, THE; ARENDT, HANNAH; ARYANISM; AUSCHWITZ (-BIRKENAU); BLOOD; BLOOD AND SOIL; BOLSHEVISM; BUDDHISM; BUTLER, RICHARD GIRNT; CAPITALISM; CARTO, WILLIS; CATHOLIC CHURCH, THE; CHAMBERLAIN, HOUSTON STEWART; CHRISTIAN

IDENTITY; CHRISTIANITY; COLLINS, SEWARD; CONCENTRATION CAMPS; CONSPIRACY THEORIES; COUGHLIN, FR. CHARLES EDWARD; DEGENERACY; DEMOCRACY; DREYFUS CASE, THE; DRUMONT, EDOUARD ADOLPHE; DÜHRING, (KARL) EUGEN; ECKART, JOHANN DIETRICH; EICHMANN, OTTO ADOLF; EVOLA, JULIUS; FORD, HENRY; FREEMASONRY/FREEMASONS, THE; GERMANIC RELIGION, THE; GERMANY; GOBINEAU, JOSEPH ARTHUR COMTE DE; GÜNTHER, HANS FRIEDRICH KARL; HITLER, ADOLF; HOLOCAUST, THE; ITALY; JESUITS, THE; *KRISTALLNACHT;* LAGARDE, PAUL DE; LANGBEHN, JULIUS; LEESE, ARNOLD SPENCER; LIBERALISM; LINDBERGH, CHARLES AUGUSTUS; LUEGER, KARL; LUTHER, MARTIN; MATERIALISM; MEDICINE; *MEIN KAMPF;* MUSIC (GERMANY); MUSSOLINI, BENITO ANDREA; NAZISM; NOVEMBER CRIMINALS, THE; NUEVA GERMANIA; NUREMBERG LAWS, THE; ORTHODOX CHURCHES, THE; PALESTINE; PAPACY, THE; PELLEY, WILLIAM DUDLEY; PIUS XI, POPE; PIUS XII, POPE; POUND, EZRA; *PROTOCOLS OF THE ELDERS OF ZION, THE*; RACIAL DOCTRINE; RACISM; ROOTLESSNESS; ROSENBERG, ALFRED; SARFATTI-GRASSINI, MARGHERITA; SCHÖNERER, GEORG RITTER VON; SCIENCE; SLAVS, THE (AND GERMANY); SOCIAL DARWINISM; SOCIALISM; STOECKER, ADOLF; *STÜRMER, DER;* TECHNOLOGY; THEOLOGY; UNIVERSITIES; VIERECK, GEORGE SYLVESTER; WAGNER, (WILHELM) RICHARD; WANNSEE CONFERENCE, THE; WEBSTER, NESTA; WINROD, GERALD BURTON; ZIONISM; ZIONIST OCCUPATION GOVERNMENT, THE

References

Cannistraro, Philip V., and Brian R Sullivan. 1993. *Il Duce's Other Woman: The Untold Story of Margherita Sarfatti, Benito Mussolini's Jewish Mistress, and How She Helped Him Come to Power.* New York: William Morrow.

Chamberlain, Houston Stewart. 1911. *The Foundations of the Nineteenth Century.* London: J. Lane.

Ericksen, Robert P., and Susannah Heschel, eds. 1999. *Betrayal: German Churches and the Holocaust.* Minneapolis: Fortress.

Fischer, K. P. 1998. *History of an Obsession: German Judeophobia and the Holocaust.* London: Constable.

Ford, Henry. 1964. *The International Jew: The World's Foremost Problem.* Los Angeles: Christian Nationalist Crusade.

Hay, M. V. 1960. *Europe and the Jews: The Pressure of Christendom on the People of Israel for 1900 Years.* Boston: Beacon.

Hertzberg, A. 1990. *The French Enlightenment and the Jews: The Origins of Modern Anti-Semitism.* New York: Columbia University Press.

Hitler, A. 1973. *Hitler's Table Talk, 1941–1944: His Private Conversations.* London: Weidenfeld and Nicolson.

Keith, Graham A. 1997. *Hated without a Cause? A Survey of Anti-Semitism.* Carlisle, UK: Paternoster.

Klemperer, Victor. 2000. *Language of the Third Reich.* Trans. Martin Brady. London: Athlone.

Leo Baeck Institute Year Book. 1987. *Nineteenth-century Anti-Semitism and Nazi Rule.* Vol. 32. London: Secker and Warburg.

Masden, V. E., trans. 1931. *Protocols of the Meetings of the Learned Elders of Zion.* London: Britons Publishing Society.

Mussolini, B. 1936. *My Autobiography.* London: Hurst and Blackett.

Ozment, Steven. 2004. *A Mighty Fortress: A New History of the German People.* London: Granta.

Poliakov, L. 1974. *The History of Anti-Semitism.* 5 vols. London: Routledge and Kegan Paul.

Pulzer, P. G. 1988 [1964]. *The Rise of Political Anti-Semitism in Germany and Austria.* London: Peter Halban.

Sarfatti, M. 1925. *The Life of Benito Mussolini: From the Italian of Margherita G. Sarfatti.* London: T. Butterworth.

Stein, André. 1989. *Quiet Heroes: True Stories of the Rescue of the Jews by Christians in Nazi-occupied Holland.* New York: New York University Press.

Steinweis, Alan E. 2006. *Studying and the Law: Scholarly Anti-Semitism in Nazi Germany.* Cambridge: Harvard University Press.

Taguieff, Pierre-André, and Patrick Camiller. 2004. *Rising from the Muck: The New Anti-Semitism in Europe.* Chicago: Ivan R. Dee.

Zimmerman, Joshua D., ed. 2005. *The Jews of Italy under Fascist and Nazi Rule: 1922–1945.* Cambridge: Cambridge University Press.

ANTONESCU, GENERAL ION (1882–1946)

Far-right Romanian interwar politician. Appointed prime minister of Romania by King Charles II on 5 September 1940, after which he forced the king to abdicate in favor of his son Michael. Antonescu proclaimed the "National-Legionary State" in Romania on 14 September, with key positions for the Legion of the Archangel Michael, often known as the "Iron Guard." He suppressed a rebellion by the legion four months later and eliminated the movement. Under Antonescu, Romania fought with Germany against Russia, hoping to regain the territories she had lost to the Russians. He was arrested by King Michael on 23 August 1944, detained in Russia from 1944 to 1946, and brought to trial and executed in Romania on 1 June 1946.

Philip Vanhaelemeersch

See Also: CODREANU, CORNELIU ZELEA; LEGION OF THE ARCHANGEL MICHAEL, THE; ROMANIA; WORLD WAR II

References

Ioanid, R. 1990. *The Sword of the Archangel Michael: Fascist Ideology in Romania.* Boulder: Eastern European Monographs.

Nagy-Talavera, N. 1970. *The Green Shirts and Others.* Stanford: Stanford University Press.

APARTHEID: *See* SOUTH AFRICA

APPEASEMENT

A term applied to the policy adopted by British prime minister Neville Chamberlain and French leaders (especially Edouard Daladier) in the face of the aggressive policies of Hitler and Mussolini in the late 1930s. The policy was in part motivated by a widespread sense at the period that Germany had been much too harshly treated in the Versailles settlement. Its most notorious features were the toleration of Mussolini's conquest of Ethiopia, Hitler's entry into the demilitarized Rhineland and annexation of Austria, German and Italian intervention in the Spanish Civil War, and finally Hitler's annexation of the Sudetenland, which Chamberlain naively imagined would be the German dictator's final demand. Even Hitler's invasion of Poland in September 1939 was met with a tame response from the British and French governments, despite their declarations of war, but the German march to the west in 1940 confirmed the short-sightedness of the appeasement policy. Hitler himself was surprised by the lack of sustained opposition to his belligerent policies.

Cyprian Blamires

See Also: *ANSCHLUSS, THE*; CZECHOSOLOVAKIA; ETHIOPIA; GERMANY; HITLER, ADOLF; ITALY; MUNICH AGREEMENT/PACT, THE; MUSSOLINI, BENITO ANDREA; POLAND AND NAZI GERMANY; SPANISH CIVIL WAR, THE; SPORT; SUDETENLAND, THE; VERSAILLES, THE TREATY OF; WORLD WAR II

References

Haraszti, Eva H. 1983. *The Invaders: Hitler Occupies the Rhineland.* Trans. Z. Laszlo. Budapest: Akademiai Kiado.

Kershaw, Ian. 2004. *Making Friends with Hitler: Lord Londonderry and the Roots of Appeasement.* London: Allen Lane.

McDonough, Frank. 2002. *Hitler, Chamberlain and Appeasement.* Cambridge: Cambridge University Press.

Sbacchi, Alberto. 1997. *Legacy of Bitterness: Ethiopia and Fascist Italy 1935–1941.* Trenton, NJ: Red Sea.

ARAB WORLD, THE: *See* BA'THISM; MIDDLE EAST, THE; PALESTINE

ARCHITECTURE

No art form has been more consistently associated with fascism than architecture. Yet architecture under fascism was more diverse than is popularly thought and cannot be reduced to a specific "fascist style." Fascist architecture is more correctly defined by how it was used to support or carry out specific ideological aims or political goals, rather than as a coherent set of symbolic forms. As evidenced in particular by the sponsorship of large-scale public works in Italy as well as the personal involvement of Hitler in architectural projects in Germany and Austria, monumental building became a key element upon which a political ideology could be projected and, in some cases, through which specific policy goals could be enacted. While most interwar states favored some variation of classicism for their major public buildings, for several fascistic regimes, architectural production was more central to their cultural and social concerns. This was particularly true in Germany and Italy. By the end of World War II, a series of high-profile architects and major public commissions had become firmly associated with their respective governments and leaders. Because of the massive scale of the projects, the involvement of political leaders, including the dictators themselves in specific instances, and the use of building and construction for the enactment of political and ideological goals, architecture continues to be crucial for our understanding of the relationship of art and politics under fascism.

Italy was not only the first state in which a fascist party came to power but also the first to use public commissions to establish an ideological connection between architecture and fascist politics. In the capital, many of these projects related to Mussolini's interest in connecting his regime to the political symbols of Augustan Rome, a period of consolidation of political authority that was also well represented in such famous works as the *Ara Pacis* in the forum. Not only were Augustan sites like this forum excavated and studied but, in addition, imperial building types like the triumphal arch and the classical temple front were reintroduced in commissions for memorials and party buildings in Bolzano, Genoa, and Florence, among other cities. In addition, the interest in the urban form of the ancient forum, marked by an open space at the intersection of a major east/west and north/south axis, was also revived, particularly in plans for new cities such as the provin-

Paul Troost was commissioned by Hitler to build this Temple of Honor ("Ehrentempel") to commemorate those who died in the abortive Munich putsch of 1923. The annual reenactment of this event became part of the Nazi calendar. (Library of Congress)

cial city of Littoria (1932; now named Latina) and the famous Rome Universal Exposition (EUR) grounds begun in 1937. The latter was to be the site of a proposed 1942 World's Fair, but the buildings were subsequently turned over to government administrative work. The prominent architect Marcello Piacentini led the team that developed EUR's marble-clad buildings with stripped-down neoclassical details. Piacentini had already shown early on in the regime his ability to adapt classical prototypes to contemporary state and party ideological needs. Such ideological claims became active policy in 1935, with the very real expansion of imperial interests through the invasion of Ethiopia, after which Addis Ababa was remodeled and some sections of the city based on classical Roman urban prototypes.

Yet while a modified neoclassicism was used in particular projects, it is important to emphasize that no single official style can be claimed for Fascist Italy. The streamlined and modernist-inspired work of the group of architects known as the Italian Rationalists, as well as regional variations by lesser-known designers that invoked vernacular medievalist traditions, could also be adapted to an often contradictory Fascist ideology. The range of building styles and types reflected the interest of particular patrons, regional administrations, and immediate propagandistic needs that could encompass claims of Italy's modernity and technological sophistication alongside arguments for a premodern return to the land. For example, the abstract forms and structural emphasis of the Rationalists were not rejected as too removed from the classicism favored in other commissions but rather celebrated in cases such as the famous *Casa del Fascio* in Como (1932–1936) by Giuseppe Terragni. Still, Terragni's modern structural expression nevertheless was complemented by the use of traditional materials like marble that could be interpreted with a specifically nationalist rhetoric, as well as interior decorations that included not only abstract sculpture but also images of Mussolini.

The range of stylistic options that allowed for a variety of patrons and propagandistic interpretations of architecture existed as well in National Socialist Germany. However, given the key role of Hitler and his greater influence on major commissions, the plurality of formal variations was more limited for major commissions and the political instrumentality of the building process more intense than in other authoritarian regimes. Architecture in Germany was not only a matter of promoting the physical presence of the Nazi Party—for example, through such commissions as Paul Ludwig Troost's party buildings for the Königsplatz in Munich (1933–1937). It was also a matter of enabling and promoting the governing principles of the regime in terms of a polycratic system of patronage for which Hitler was the final arbiter. Reflecting his interest as a young adult in becoming an artist and his experience in trying to live off of his sketches of buildings and tourist locations prior to World War I, Hitler had strong opinions about what he considered suitable state and party architecture. He was more decisive in his intervention in architectural production than were other fascist and authoritarian leaders.

Architecture had been crucial to National Socialist politicians and propagandists even in the struggle for power at the end of the Weimar Republic. Hitler signaled the importance of architecture to the Nazi Party by proclaiming in his autobiography, *Mein Kampf,* that powerful architecture was an expression of a strong *Volk,* praising dynastic cultures like ancient Egypt and Rome while decrying Berlin and its Jewish department stores. But further, Nazi denunciations concerning the supposedly internationalist and Bolshevik tendencies of the flat-roofed architecture of the Bauhaus and other modernist architects became one part of the antidemocratic propaganda.

Yet once in power after 1933, neither party leaders nor Hitler came out with an officially decreed style. Rather, different kinds of architecture tended to be favored by specific patrons, while politically or ideologically suspect architects were purged from public commissions. In this sense, architecture followed the general *Gleichschaltung,* or coordination, of other cultural administrations. So, for example, the SS often favored medievalist architecture for its buildings, and certain industrial and military complexes like those of the Luftwaffe might use the steel and glass of modernism. Still, for large-scale public and party commissions involving Hitler, architects tended to stick to a stripped down neoclassicism massive in scale and solid in its masonry. Such buildings could be variably interpreted as either examples of an ideology of racial purity, in which contemporary Germany was linked to the supposedly Aryan peoples of classical Greece, or as manifestations of a new and powerful imperial state rivaling that of ancient Rome. Different patrons in the Nazi Party proposed these varying meanings for the built environment. Beginning in 1937 and the architect Albert Speer's announcement of plans to rebuild Berlin as the first of five "Hitler Cities" (including Munich, Nuremberg, Hamburg, and Linz), it had become clear to all who wanted to gain Hitler's attention that architecture and urban planning would be key to his peacetime initiatives.

But architecture served not only practical and ideological goals within the Nazi state. Architectural production was also integrated into specific policy initiatives and hence functionally related to the radicalization of racism and militarism. Speer's architectural office in Berlin, for instance, began to promote as early as 1938 a new policy for the concentration of the Berlin Jewish community and the deprivation of its property rights. For the architects, this was a way of gaining control over the property of displaced German Jews that could then in turn be used for non-Jewish citizens who needed to be compensated should the government appropriate their property for the massive site clearing necessary for the rebuilding plans. Furthermore, architects and urban planners also took part in streamlining specific aspects of the most extreme anti-Semitic policies. For example, the ghettoization of Jews in Eastern Europe depended on the manipulation of space and structures by professionals; most grotesquely, the SS architectural staff at Auschwitz helped make it possible through efficient planning of space to kill even more of European Jewry. In these instances, as in others, the Nazi state was the extreme example of how far architecture could be instrumentalized to promote a fascist project.

While fascist patrons made use of architecture in Italy and Germany to the greatest extent, architecture could also play a significant role at particular moments for other fascistic or right-wing authoritarian states. Most famously, at the 1937 Paris World's Fair, not only was the face-off of the Soviet and Nazi pavilions much discussed, but, in addition, the steel and glass structure for the Spanish Pavilion by Josep Lluis Sert and Luis Lacasa was seen with its art (including Picasso's *Guernica*) as a modernist rejection of the massive masonry structures of both the fascist and Soviet states. As a Republican building, it signaled the Popular Front policy of the government, which extended from the liberal to the left in their struggles against Franco. Yet while the pavilion might appear ideologically neutral because of its simple materials, the context of the other monuments of the fair, the content of the Spanish exhibition, and the use of the facade as a support for statements promoting the Republican government meant that the architecture naturally paralleled the antifascist message. After defeating the Republicans, Franco did not devote his regime to architecture anywhere as much as Hitler did, but he did patronize several large-scale ideological projects, such as the massive complex in the Valley of the Fallen (1959) to memorialize supposedly both the fascist and antifascist soldiers who had died in the Civil War, although the antifascist message remains unclear at best.

With the defeat of the Axis powers at the end of World War II, the scale of the interwar projects and, particularly, those that focused on neoclassical masonry construction became associated not only with the extreme fascist Right but also the bombast of the Stalinist Eastern Block. Such associations further played a postwar role as polarized definitions of fascist or communist architecture were juxtaposed to the apparently democratic architecture of modernism, even though such easy transparencies between architecture and ideology would not have been recognized before the Cold War. Civic and corporate patrons in democratic capitalist cities increasingly favored modernist architects and steel and glass structures as a way of distinguishing themselves from the interwar politicization of masonry construction. Public interest continued to be drawn most intensely to Hitler's biography (including his early years as a failed artist) and the revelations brought forward by Speer, who completed several autobiographical accounts after his release in 1966 from Spandau Prison. In the postwar period, while modernists like Terragni had been relatively easily accepted as a focus of aesthetic study, Speer and other more traditional architects were not systematically treated in relation to their contribution to cultural policy. That situation began to change, particularly with the publication of several foundational texts from the late 1960s and early 1970s that confronted the role of architecture in fascist states.

Paul Jaskot

See Also: ANTI-SEMITISM; ART; AXIS, THE; BOLSHEVISM; COLD WAR, THE; DECADENCE; FASCIST PARTY, THE; FUTURISM; GERMANY; GHETTOS, THE; *GLEICHSCHALTUNG;* GUERNICA; HITLER, ADOLF; HOLOCAUST, THE; ITALY; LUFTWAFFE, THE; MARINETTI, FILIPPO TOMMASO; *MEIN KAMPF;* MODERNISM; MUSSOLINI, BENITO ANDREA; NAZISM; NUREMBERG; NUREMBERG RALLIES, THE; PROPAGANDA; RACIAL DOCTRINE; ROME; SARFATTI-GRASSINI,

MARGHERITA; SPAIN; SPANDAU PRISON; SPEER, ALBERT; SS, THE; STYLE; WEIMAR REPUBLIC, THE

References

Ades, Dawn, et al., eds. 1996. *Art and Power: Europe under the Dictators, 1930–45.* London: Hayward Gallery.

Etlin, Richard. 1991. *Modernism in Italian Architecture.* Cambridge: MIT Press.

Ghirardo, Diane. 1989. *Building New Communities: New Deal America and Fascist Italy.* Princeton: Princeton University Press.

Jaskot, Paul B. 2000. *The Architecture of Oppression: The SS, Forced Labor, and the Nazi Monumental Building Economy.* New York: Routledge.

Miller Lane, Barbara. 1968. *Architecture and Politics in Germany, 1918–1945.* Cambridge: Harvard University Press.

Scobie, Alex. 1990. *Hitler's State Architecture: The Impact of Classical Antiquity.* University Park: Penn State University Press.

ARDITI, THE: *See* ANTIFASCISM

ARENDT, HANNAH (1906–1975)

German-American philosopher and political theorist, famous for her theory of totalitarian dictatorship. Born into a Jewish family in Hanover, she studied philosophy, theology, and Greek at Heidelberg, completing a doctoral dissertation at the age of twenty-two. She studied under Jaspers and Heidegger. In 1933, Arendt fled first to Paris, where she worked for Zionist bodies sending Jewish orphans to Palestine, and then seven years later to New York. Her three-volume work *The Origins of Totalitarianism* (1951) inaugurated a new understanding of modern tyranny of Right and Left as essentially of a piece, exemplified by Hitler's Nazi Germany from 1933 to 1945 and Stalin's regime in the Soviet Union from around 1930 to 1953. She saw these dictatorships (much less, if at all, Mussolini's Italy) as a specifically modern and novel form of rule. Its prime feature is the combination of unprecedented state violence and control over all spheres of life with an all-embracing, historicist secular ideology. The social underpinning of this ideology is provided by a mass mobilizing movement geared toward total elimination of whole categories of people, not for what they may or may not have done, but because of their mere existence.

Arendt sees the essence of totalitarianism in "total terror" as practiced in Nazi concentration camps. In

American political philosopher Hannah Arendt is famous for her reflections on the nature of totalitarianism and for her commentary on the trial of Nazi war criminal Adolf Eichmann. (Library of Congress)

are characterized by the insistence on logical consistency ("logiciality"): the leader's relentless and automatic process of deduction from race- and class-premises to the total elimination of the movement's putative "objective adversaries" (in the case of Nazism, European Jewry; for Stalin, kulaks and other "class enemies"). This element of total destruction of entire categories of people is deduced from a notion of "historical necessity," whether in the form of inexorable "laws" of history or biological "laws" of race. The goal of ideologies of this kind is to create "fictitious" worlds: modern utopias devoid of any contradictions and therefore inaccessible to any sort of empirical verification or refutation. That proved to be an idea with enormous appeal for masses uprooted from their social and mental moorings in times of upheaval and social fragmentation—for instance, in the wake of wars like World War I.

Strictly speaking, Arendt did not offer a coherent theory of the causes of totalitarianism but rather an historical account of the elements, as she put it, that "crystallized" into it—that is, made it possible or comprehensible. Two important conditioning elements of this kind were European imperialism and anti-Semitism. She uses these historical phenomena to trace the background of the totalitarian regimes to different experiences of the "superfluousness" of people, chief among which is the phenomenon of statelessness following the breakdown of the European system of nation-states after World War I, which in turn caused the demise of the rights of man. The Achilles heel of the European concept of individual rights was its attachment to citizenship. Groups lacking the rights bestowed by citizenship simply became a nuisance and were deprived of protection, even in liberal states. People who are "superfluous" in this sense are ideal victims of scapegoating and eliminationist terror in totalitarian regimes (for example, Jewish, Sinti and Roma, and homosexual "class enemies").

One of Arendt's basic themes is the fragility of civilization once the protective walls of the nation-state and its class system have broken down and are replaced by the barbarism of dynamic and ideology-driven mass movements principally recruited from among helpless people ("the mob"). This criminal underworld is generated by the unsettling dynamism of inflation, war, and unemployment. Imperialism in the nineteenth century had exported unscrupulous criminal elements like these across the globe and imparted in them a total loss of proportion, a sense that "everything is possible." The nihilism and lawlessness of this mentality was reimported to Europe and brought to bear on the diverse

these camps the eradication of all individuality and a completely arbitrary control over human life was achieved. Unlike the coercion used by traditional tyrants, oppression in these total institutions seemed not to have a utilitarian purpose, such as repressing opposition or spurring economic growth. (On that score Arendt may have underestimated Stalin's use of the Gulag system as an integral part of the Soviet economy, and Albert Speer's coalition with German corporations and their massive exploitation of prisoners of war and work camps to bolster the German war effort.)

In Arendt's view, the distinguishing characteristic of totalitarian ideologies is their metahistorical character. They are thought systems purporting to explain the origins and inner workings of history and provide a reliable guide to the future. By virtue of their power to simplify empirical reality, these ideologies facilitate mass action through ideological fervor. Above all, they pan-movements (that is, Panslavism and Pangermanism). These boundary-transcending movements sought to unify peoples across existing state borders by appealing to their putative collective ethnic, religious, or racial identities. In this imperialist heritage of limitless expansion and loss of moderation (that is, a sense of proportion), Arendt sees one of the most important sources of relentless totalitarian violence.

Arendt's theory must be seen in contrast to another strand of theorizing about totalitarian regimes, the tradition exemplified, for example, by Z. Brzezinski and C. Friedrich. That tradition underscores the rigidity, uniformity, and immobility of totalitarian regimes. Arendt's view is rather to interpret totalitarian political structures as excessive, dynamic, limitless, chaotic, nonutilitarian, and manically destructive. The experience of Mao's Cultural Revolution, North Korea under Kim, Cambodia under Pol Pot, the ethno-nationalism of the former Yugoslavia, and the sweeping genocide in Rwanda lends support, however, to Arendt's principal purpose: to warn against the alluring and immense power of totalitarian thought-systems to turn humans into beasts by encouraging them to suspend normal moral sentiment in order to facilitate the pursuit of highly simplistic utopian goals.

In her controversial book on the Eichmann case (1963), Hannah Arendt coined the phrase the "banality of evil." The most striking quality of Eichmann was not sadism, wickedness, or depravity, she wrote, but equally pernicious: "thoughtlessness," the inability to empathize with the victims or to grasp what he was doing in all its moral, psychological, and cognitive ramifications. She asks: "Do the inability to think and a disastrous failure of what we commonly call conscience coincide?" The exact meaning of these assertions has spawned a huge literature. In the context of her theory of totalitarianism, it seems fair to say that Eichmann forced Arendt to modify her position on the pervasiveness and terrifying motivational force of ideology. Eichmann seems to have shared most of the Third Reich's prejudices toward Jews, but Eichmann himself claimed that he was not a Jew-hater. Rather, he claimed, he would have preferred to "solve" the Jewish question through deportation to Africa or the creation of a Jewish state in Palestine. In Jerusalem, Arendt was struck by the lack of Nazi sloganeering or thought-forms in his defense—in fact, his seeming lack of fanaticism, his "ordinariness." This perverse "normality," or in Arendt's word "banality," of the man's character—not especially evil, rather mundanely bureaucratic—led her to characterize Eichmann as someone who "never realized what he was doing." Eichmann exhibited "a remoteness from reality" and an inability to see or feel his victims' sufferings, as well as a cognitive incapacity to view an argument from an opposite angle. Instead, he loyally performed his duties as he would in any other job (though he also served in an overzealous manner, as in Hungary in 1944). That this mental and moral detachment, this "thoughtlessness," "can wreak more havoc than all the evil instincts taken together which, perhaps, are inherent in man—that was, in fact, the lesson one could learn in Jerusalem," Arendt wrote.

Bernt Hagtvet

See Also: INTRODUCTION; ANTI-SEMITISM; CONCENTRATION CAMPS; EICHMANN, OTTO ADOLF; GERMANY; HEIDEGGER, MARTIN; HITLER, ADOLF; HOLOCAUST, THE; HOMOSEXUALITY; ITALY; MASSES, THE ROLE OF THE; MUSSOLINI, BENITO ANDREA; NAZISM; PALESTINE; PANGERMANISM; RELIGION; ROMA AND SINTI, THE; SOVIET UNION, THE; SPEER, ALBERT; THIRD REICH, THE; TOTALITARIANISM; UTOPIA, UTOPIANISM; ZIONISM

References

Arendt, H. 1963. *Eichmann in Jerusalem.* New York: Viking.
———. 1966. *The Origins of Totalitarianism.* New York: Harcourt.
Baehr, Peter, and Melvin Richter, eds. 2004. *Dictatorship in History and Theory: Bonapartism, Caesarism, and Totalitarianism.* Washington, DC: German Historical Institute.
Brzezinski, Z., and C. Friedrich. 1956. *Totalitarian Dictatorship and Autocracy.* Cambridge: Harvard University Press.
Burrowes, R. 1969. "Totalitarianism: The Standard Revised Edition." *World Politics* 21: 272–294.
Canovan, M. 1992. *Hannah Arendt: A Reinterpretation of Her Political Thought.* Cambridge: Cambridge University Press.
Hagtvet, B. 1981. "The Theory of Mass Society and the Collapse of the Weimar Republic: A Re-Examination." Pp. 66–118 in *Who Were the Fascists: Social Roots of European Fascism,* edited by Stein Ugelvik Larsen, Bernt Hagtvet, and Jan P. Myklebust. Bergen: Universitetsforlaget.
Linz, J. 2000. *Totalitarian and Authoritarian Regimes.* Boulder: Lynne Rienner.
Villa, D., ed. 2000. *The Cambridge Companion to Hannah Arendt.* Cambridge: Cambridge University Press.

ARGENTINA

At first sight it is surprising that in spite of Latin America's long history of dictatorships and authoritarianism, fascist movements did not take root there. Probably the one country that might challenge that view is Argentina, not only because of the rise of

Peronism, which could be considered a local brand of fascist populism, but especially because of the development of an intellectual fascist public sphere in the 1920s and 1930s that contributed to delegitimize any prospect for democratic development in Argentina for years to come.

Perón's period was preceded by a decade or more of ideological turbulence that served as the intellectual background for the two attempts to establish a corporatist regime in Argentina. The first attempt was led by general Felix de Uriburu, who overthrew the democratic populist regime of Hipolito Yrigoyen. Influenced by the ideas of the nationalist poet Leopoldo Lugones and the ideological laboratory initiated at the journal *La Nueva Republica,* which brought together a new brand of antidemocratic integral nationalist intellectuals, Uriburu strove to replace popular democracy with a national corporatist regime. His attempt did not prosper, because of the strength of the conservative elites, who shifted the "corporatist revolution" into a type of corrupted limited democracy in which political parties were legitimated—except for the populist wing of the Radical Party, which was banned from politics. The period, known as the "infamous decade" because of the political corruption and economic dependency on Great Britain, was shaped by an intellectual flourishing of right and left nationalist ideas that prepared the ideological arena for a new political and economic development. This intellectual upheaval, which preceded the military fascist revolution of 1943, was marked by the synthesis of right and left nationalism into a single critique of the Argentinian liberal establishment. Despite differences in their intellectual sources, both right-wing and left-wing intellectuals shared a common critique of the liberal interpretation of Argentina's history and of British economic imperialism. They shared a common repugnance for liberal democracy and a common support for Argentina's "pro-Axis" neutrality in World War II. They both promoted a new type of nonliberal nationalist state above political parties.

The right-wing intellectuals who promoted this model were the brothers Julio and Rodolfo Irazusta, Juan Carulla Ernesto Palacio, Bruno Jacovella, and others. They were all influenced by Italian and French fascism, and especially the writings of Charles Maurras. Most of them rejected Yrigoyen's populist democracy from 1916 to 1930 and contributed to setting the ideological context for overthrowing the regime; however, during the 1930s they shifted to national populism, because they became convinced that fascism, unlike au-

thoritarianism, should be populist. During the 1930s they promoted the organization of a fascist public sphere marked by the flourishing of nationalist leagues like the Legion Civica, the Liga Republicana, the Alianza Nacionalista, and others. They stormed Buenos Aires streets and portended the commencement of a new fascist era for Argentina.

The nationalist Left was composed of a young group of intransigent radicals who rejected the conservative tendencies in the Radical Party. Known as FORJA, they focused on re-establishing "popular sovereignty" through popular mobilization and economic and cultural anti-imperialism. The most prominent figures within FORJA—Arturo Jauretche, Dario Alessandro, Manuel Ortiz Pereyra, Luis Dellepiane, and even Raul Scalabrini Ortiz (who was never a direct member of the group)—were far from being fascist counter-revolutionaries, despite being antiliberal nationalists. They supported a new type of "antipolitical party" populist democracy, and conceived of the nation as an organic unit mobilized by authentic leaders. Therefore, although their critique was focused on Argentina's liberalism and the sources of economic imperialism, they developed a concept of republican populism and a direct approach to democratic justice that largely delegitimated formal democratic procedures. Both trends set the ideological basis for the military revolution of 1943 that preceded Peronism, and should be considered the harbingers of a local brand of Argentinian fascism. Indeed, the impact that this intellectual tradition had on Argentina's political development, and especially on the military revolution of 1943 and the Peronism that followed it, is undeniable.

Argentina in the 1940s was a rich country with great potential to become an industrial democracy. Yet the military revolution of 1943 adopted the nationalist discourse of peripheral modernity and shifted Argentina's path of political and economic development from liberalism to autarkic development (*see* AUTARKY). This was not merely an authoritarian upheaval; it was a nationalist uprising that operated on a different vision of political modernization. More than once in Argentina, liberals have called for military intervention to "save" the constitutional order from populist, left-wing, and, nowadays, fundamentalist pressures. As some scholars have already noted, the propensity toward authoritarian politics has also been a part of the liberal political tradition. However, the category of integral nationalism goes beyond the idea of an authoritarian "solution" to conjectural crises of liberalism. The new nationalism did not want to save liberalism but to go beyond it. Argentina's liberal-conservatives had been authoritarian, even while paying tribute to a liberal constitution, whereas the integral nationalists of the 1930s strove to redefine the idea of democracy from liberal to populist, and they replaced the liberal and socialist path to modernity with a new rhetoric of cultural and political anti-imperialism that was to become an integral part of Argentina's political culture.

Although several analysts are inclined to define as fascist the 1976 military regime in Argentina, that is not plausible. The 1976–1982 military junta led by General Videla was a criminal military regime, but it can hardly be defined as fascist. More akin to fascism are the examples of Aldo Rico and Muhamed Sinheldin, military men of lower rank who attempted a military uprising during Alfonsin's democratic rule. They were certainly ideological heirs of the nationalists of the 1930s and 1940s, and promoted a synthesis between right-wing national authoritarianism and left-wing anti-imperialism.

Alberto Spektorowski

See Also: AUTARKY; AUTHORITARIANISM; AXIS, THE; CORPORATISM; DICTATORSHIP; INTEGRAL NATIONALISM; MAURRAS, CHARLES; MILITARY DICTATORSHIP; ORGANICISM; PERÓN, JUAN DOMINGO; PERONISM; WORLD WAR II

References
Johnson, J. 1958. *Political Change in Latin America: The Emergence of the Middle Sectors.* Stanford: Stanford University Press.
McGee Deutsch, S., and R. H. Dolkart, eds. 1993. *The Argentine Right: Its History and Intellectual Origins.* Wilmington, DE: SR.
Rock, D. 1992. *Authoritarian Argentina: The Nationalist Movement, Its History and Impact.* Berkeley: University of California Press.
Silvert, K. 1961. *The Conflict Society: Reaction and Revolution in Latin America.* New Orleans: Hauser.
Spektorowski, A. S. 2003. *The Origins of Argentina's Revolution of the Right.* Paris: University of Notre Dame Press.
Whitaker, A. 1996. "Argentina, Nostalgic and Dynamic Nationalism." In *Nationalism in Contemporary Latin America,* edited by D. Jordan. New York: New Press.

ARISTOCRACY

Fascists have a long tradition of regarding themselves as flatly opposed to the egalitarianism that they associate both with traditional socialisms and with liberalism. Where they have propagated their own version of socialism, as in National Socialism, the term *national* has carried connotations of elitism. The "nation" in question is not conceived as an association of those holding documents attesting their citizenship but as a mythical society of those holding to the true values of the nation, which, in the case of German Nazism, entailed purity of blood resulting from untainted Germanic descent without "alien" admixtures. Both Mussolini and Hitler regarded themselves as founders of a new aristocracy, a warrior race or nation that would embody true "Italian" or "German" values. Undoubtedly they both absorbed some of the thinking of Friedrich Nietzsche, who promoted a "heroic" morality of virility as an antidote to Christian ideas of meekness and the penitential spirit. A similar mind-set can be found in the Victorian Scottish writer Thomas Carlyle, who was also an influence on them, and it has definite echoes of Machiavelli as well.

A current of thought within National Socialism tried to float the idea of a new rural peasant aristocracy, but it never had any great influence in practice and was marginalized when the Nazis came to power. Hitler and Mussolini were both resolutely proindustry and protechnology.

Neither Hitler nor Mussolini had any time for the aristocratic classes of their day; Hitler in fact criticized Mussolini in his *Table Talk* for not having gotten rid of the monarchy in Italy and therefore for being in thrall to a court. Ironically, however, the policy pursued under his regime of "racial purity" and the requirement to show evidence of untainted "Aryan" ancestry, particularly for membership in the elite SS, is reminiscent of the practice prevailing in ancien regime France of requiring genealogical proofs of aristocratic ancestry as a qualification for certain positions—for example, officerships in the army.

Cyprian Blamires

See Also: AHNENERBE; ARYANISM; BLOOD AND SOIL; CARLYLE, THOMAS; DARRE, RICHARD WALTHER; EGALITARIANISM; ELITE THEORY; FASCIST PARTY, THE; HITLER, ADOLF; LIBERALISM; MASSES, THE ROLE OF THE; MONARCHY; MUSSOLINI, BENITO ANDREA; NAZISM; NIETZSCHE, FRIEDRICH; RURALISM; SOCIALISM; SS, THE; WARRIOR ETHOS, THE

References
Blinkhorn, M., ed. 1990. *Fascists and Conservatives.* London: Unwin Hyman.
Nye, R. A. 1977. *The Anti-democratic Sources of Elite Theory: Pareto, Mosca, Michels.* London: Sage.
Sontheimer, Kurt. 1978. *Anti-demokratisches Denken in der Weimarer Republik.* München: Deutscher Taschenbuch.

ARROW CROSS, THE (NYILASKERESZTES PÁRT)

A Hungarian pro-German, racist, and extremely nationalistic party, the Arrow Cross was created by Ferenc Szálasi on 23 October 1937. As a symbol, the arrow cross (the German swastika) predates the foundation of the Hungarian National Socialist Party (Magyar Nemzeti Szocalista Párt). The party had nearly 500,000 members by 1939, when it won thirty-one parliamentary seats. It espoused the ideal of a "greater Hungary," and that brought it into conflict with Hitler and his ambitions for Central Europe. After having been banned at the outset of World War II, the party was legalized again in March 1944 under German pressure and was installed in power by the Germans some months after the German occupation of Hungary on 19 March 1944.

Arrow Cross leaders did not fully embrace German Aryanism and objected to the German occupation of Hungary, arguing that the Hungarist Movement alone could solve the country's problems. At that time, the party counted about 150,000 paying members. It rose to power on 15 October 1944, when Regent Horthy offered the prime ministerial position to the leader of the party, Ferenc Szálasi himself. The Arrow Cross terrorized Hungary, rampaging through cities and creating fear in Budapest. Looting, killing, and causing havoc, the Arrow Cross gangs were led by its feared leader, Pater Andás Kun (1911–1945), a Catholic monk who ordered several mass murders in Budapest alone. For this crime he was hanged as a war criminal in 1945. The party's brief tenure of government ended in January 1945, after the fall of Budapest to the Soviets the previous month. After the war, Szálasi and other Arrow Cross leaders were put on trial as war criminals by the Hungarian courts. Arrow Cross ideology has not completely vanished from Hungary; "Hungarism" is still propagated in the journal of the neofascist Hungarian Welfare Association, Magyartudat (Hungarian Awareness).

László Kürti

See Also: INTRODUCTION; ARYANISM; CATHOLIC CHURCH, THE; HORTHY DE NAGYBÁNYA, MIKLÓS; HUNGARY; NATIONALISM; POSTWAR FASCISM; RACISM; SZÁLASI, FERENC

References
Lackó, M. 1969. *Arrow-Cross Men, National Socialists, 1935–1944.* Budapest: Akadémiai Kiadó.
Macartney, C. A. 1957. *October Fifteenth: A History of Modern Hungary, 1929–1945.* Edinburgh: Edinburgh University Press.
Nagy-Talavera, N. 1970. *The Green Shirts and Others.* Stanford: Stanford University Press.

ART

Mussolini and Hitler (a painter himself) both understood the power of art and sought to make it serve their political visions. In Italy, Fascist artists and architects did not have to follow anything as dogmatic as an officially defined policy, but Mussolini's theme of "modernization" informed his totalitarian state. That meant developing a new way of thinking about every aspect of life. This was the catalyst to make art that would change the values, ideals, and aspirations of all Italians; "art was to reflect modern life," and there were three principal movements: Futurism, Novecento, and the Rationalists.

Futurism was initially a literary movement created by Filippo Tommaso Marinetti, who produced violent polemics against all traditional art and aesthetics. Marinetti's 1909 "Manifesto of Futurism" states: "It was time to create a new art, forged out of the beauty of speed and a glorification of war: art, in fact, can be nothing but violence, cruelty, and injustice." He wanted art to be made that would speed the movement from rural to urban life, from peasant to industrial, and from democratic to fascist. The movement was so concerned with speed that poems such as *mots in libertà* contained no adjectives, adverbs, finite verbs, punctuation—nothing to slow it down. Futurists believed that they had invented a new language: onomatopoeia. This they defined in their technical manifestos as consisting of four basic types: realistic, analogical, abstract (the "sound of a state of mind"), and psychic harmony (the fusion of two or three of the abstract representations). This was the art of action, movement, and dynamism, often depicting idealized figures engaged in heroic action. It was vital that the work related to the space round it and had a direct relationship to it. This reflected the idea that there is an unbreakable connection between a political movement and the environment or culture it inhabits. This so-called art of everyday life would manifest itself through all art and design, and especially through architecture, or "environmental sculpture" as the Futurists termed it.

The Novecento, which simply means the "new century," was a movement that sought to build modern thinking with respect for, and continuity with, the past. The Novecento understood the potential benefits of reflecting the achievements of the past, particularly connecting through art elements of the Roman Empire to the "modernization" of Italy. The work of architect Piero Portaluppi exemplifies how Novecento combined the traditional with the modern. His *Corso Venezia* building in Milan retains the large central arch favored by traditional design, but the height of each floor is different, the finishes on the facades range from smooth to rough stone, and the windows are irregularly framed. The movement began in the gallery of Lino Pesaro in Via Manzoni in Milan, now the Museum Poldi Pezzoli. This was the first exhibition of the seven founding group members. The most famous painters were Emilio Malerba, Funi, Dudreville, Oppi, Bucci, Marussig, and Sironi. Mussolini and his influential mistress, the critic and Italian intellectual Margherita Sarfatti, supported the first exhibition. The work combined modern ideas of stillness, shallow perspective, and a cool, calm air that displayed a control over the self and the world around, reflecting at least in some degree the aim of Fascist aspirations.

The Rationalists were primarily an architectural movement founded by a group of seven idealistic students in Milan around 1927. Their best known members were Guiseppe Pagano, Piero Bottoni, Dullio Torres, and Gino Levi-Montalcini. They were focused on functionalism, removing anything that could be seen as decoration. The apartments they designed survive to this day—for example, the Palazzo Gualino complex. These brutal buildings have a rigid uniformity of structure, color, and surface texture, like boxes stacked upon each other. One unusual feature that seemed to ape the physique of Mussolini was that the windows are wider than they are tall. Torres redesigned the facade of the Italia Pavilion at the Venice Biennale in 1932 when Mussolini was at the height of his powers. This is a linear building whose lines are interrupted only by a simple winged lion, to represent St. Mark, the symbol of Venice, next to an imperial eagle, the Fascist symbol.

Italian art and culture under Mussolini were allowed to flourish without too many dogmatic rules (unlike in Russia and Germany). Mussolini used art to give his party credibility and status; to help to define their place

in history, he even developed "the Academy" (Accademia italiana) as the intellectual authority of the country, emphasizing Italy's international cultural importance. However, members of the Academy did have to be loyal and active Fascist Party members. Mussolini's support for the great Fascist exhibitions ensured that these were well attended by the public. The Venice Biennales, the Milan Triennales, and the Mostra della rivoluzione fascista ("Exhibition of the Fascist Revolution") were propaganda exhibitions that encouraged Fascist art, where Fascist thinking could be portrayed as normal and modern.

When Hitler, an unsuccessful artist, became Fuehrer, he took revenge on the art world, personally supervising the Exhibition of Degenerate Art, held in 1937, which declared war on modern art. This was part of the so-called cleansing of German culture. Hitler defined true art as linked with the country life, with good health, and with the Aryan race. This was "national realism": "We shall discover and encourage the artists who are able to impress upon the State of the German people the cultural stamp of the Germanic race" (Hitler, Party Day speech, 1935). Joseph Goebbels, the Nazi propaganda minister, and cultural theorist Alfred Rosenberg developed Nazi cultural policy—an absolutist policy, dogmatically and violently applied. Like Mussolini, Hitler used the power of architecture to further the Third Reich, building the Olympic stadium in Berlin. This powerful venue designed by Albert Speer would hold the Olympic Games and was intended to show the world the supremacy of the master race. Many of the forced laborers died during its construction. It was the essence of totalitarian design in the service of power, fitted to stage many Nazi rituals and rallies, something Hitler loved.

The Nazis were the great destroyers of art and intellectual thought. They disposed of the Bauhaus, describing it as a haven for socialists, Bolsheviks, liars, and Jews. Hitler wanted art that idealized the Aryan race and brought their stories to life, thus strengthening the Nazi myth-making and propaganda machine. Technique was prized over expression. Personal ideas and experimentation were seen as the work of Bolshevik thinking, which would be replaced with unambiguous story-telling that gave a clear model of life as it should be lived. To achieve this the Nazis exploited technology, producing works on a scale never seen before. These included *Der Giftpilz,* a range of anti-Semitic children's books with titles such as *The Poisonous Mushroom* and *How to Tell a Jew;* newspapers including Julius Streicher's anti-Semitic *Der Stürmer,* with many cartoons to help the illiterate; and *Brennessel,* a Nazi humor magazine that was also highly illustrated throughout. They used photography, too, and made propaganda films such as *Der ewige Jude (The Eternal Jew).* They used filmmakers, sculptors, graphic designers, architects, and artists. Ernst Vollbehr (1876–1960) painted in gouache the party convention in Nuremberg. Other artists included T. Rieger, Herbert Schimkowitz, Maximilian Spilhaczek, and Arno Breker ("The Guard," "The Warrior Departs," "The Party and the Army," "Preparedness"), Adolph Wissel ("Farm Family from Kahlenberg"), Hubert Lanzinger ("The Flag Bearer"), Albert Janesh ("Water Sports"), and Ernst Liebermann ("By the Water"). Where Mussolini used modernist art selectively to promote Italian Fascism, the Nazis were brutal in its suppression, even down to the smallest detail. Goebbels replaced sans-serif type (seen as a Jewish invention) with what he regarded as the more German-looking *Fraktur;* sans-serif, however, was more legible and could be set with narrow leading, thus packing more text onto a page, and so it did eventually replace the ornate *Fraktur* as the German typeface.

The Nazis admired Greek art, but their cultural policy created bland, arrogant, bombastic work that now looks like the stuff of kitsch cartoon fantasy comics. At the same time the great art of Germany was obsessively listed, rounded up, and sent to its own concentration camp, including paintings by Otto Dix, Braque, Derain, Chagall, Kirschner, Nolde, Heckel, van Doesburg, Ensor, and Beckmann. Hitler planned to sell off much of the more famous work but had many paintings destroyed, replacing them with works of which he approved. After the war this Nazi art was taken to the United States, perhaps to help pay for the huge cost of the war. While much of the graphics was kept as historical documentation and the posters formed a collection in the Library of Congress, the paintings and sculptures, housed in an airplane hangar in Virginia, were eventually offered back to Germany, which politely declined to receive them. It is widely believed that in the end this unwanted work was also destroyed.

Mario Minichiello

See Also: INTRODUCTION; ANTI-SEMITISM; ARCHITECTURE; ARYANISM; BERLIN OLYMPICS, THE; BOOKS, THE BURNING OF THE; CULTURE; DECADENCE; DEGENERACY; FILM; FORCED LABOR; FUTURISM; GOEBBELS, PAUL JOSEPH; GUERNICA; HERO, THE CULT OF THE; HITLER, ADOLF; MARINETTI, FILIPPO TOMMASO; MODERNISM; MUSIC; MUSSOLINI, BENITO ANDREA; NORDIC SOUL, THE; NUREMBERG RALLIES, THE; PROPAGANDA; RIEFENSTAHL, LENI; ROME; SARFATTI-GRASSINI, MARGHERITA; SPORT; STREICHER, JULIUS; TOTALITARIANISM; WAGNER, (WILHELM) RICHARD; WAR

References
Arnheim, Rudolf. 1992. *The Genesis of a Painting: Picasso's "Guernica."* Berkeley: University of California Press.
Braun, Emily, ed. *Italian Art in the 20th Century.* London: Royal Academy of Arts.
Brenner, H. 1972. "Art in the Political Struggle of 1933–1934." In *From Republic to Reich: The Making of the Nazi Revolution,* edited by H. Holborn, New York: Pantheon.
De Grazia, V. 1981. *The Culture of Consent: Mass Organizations of Leisure in Fascist Italy.* Cambridge: Cambridge University Press.
Dorrdan, D. P. 1988. *Building Modern Italy: Italian Architecture 1914–1936.* New York: Princeton Architectural Press.
Hensbergen, Gijs van. 2004. *Guernica: The Biography of a Painting.* London: Bloomsbury.
Hinz, B. 1979. *Art in the Third Reich.* Oxford: Basil Blackwell.
Joll, J. 1961. *Three Intellectuals in Politics.* New York: Pantheon.
Lyttelton, A. 1987. *The Seizure of Power: Fascism in Italy 1919–1929.* 2d ed. Princeton: Princeton University Press.
Miller-Lane, B. 1988. "Architects in the Service of Power." In *Art and History: Images and Their Meaning,* edited by R. Rothberg and T. Rabb. Cambridge: Cambridge University Press.
Morgan, P. 1995. *Italian Fascism, 1919–1945.* New York: St. Martin's.
Mosse, G. L. 1966. *The Crisis of German Ideology: Intellectual Origins of the Third Reich.* London: Weidenfeld and Nicolson.
Tannenbaum, E. 1972. *The Fascist Experience: Italian Society and Culture 1922–1945.* London: Basic.
Traldi, A. 1987. "The Myths of Fascist Propaganda" and "The Peculiar Relationship between Fascism and Fiction." In *Fascism and Fiction: A Survey of Italian Fiction on Fascism,* edited by Traldi. London: Scarecrow.

ARTAMAN LEAGUE, THE

A 1920s nationalist anti-Slav youth organization in Germany, imbued with ruralist thinking and calling for a return to the soil. Heinrich Himmler was a member for a time.

Cyprian Blamires

See Also: BLOOD AND SOIL; DARRE, RICHARD WALTHER; HIMMLER, HEINRICH; RURALISM (GERMANY); SLAVS, THE (AND GERMANY)

ARYAN MYTH THE: *See* ARYANISM

ARYAN NATIONS, THE

Formed in Idaho in the early 1970s, the Church of Jesus Christ Christian and its political arm, Aryan Nations, is a leading exponent of Christian Identity, a doctrine which claims that whites are the real descendants of the biblical Israelites. Led for many years by Richard Butler, it preaches that Jews are the product of Satan's sexual congress with Eve in the Garden of Eden. Following an incident in 1998 in which a woman and her son were assaulted by Aryan Nations security guards, a court case led to the organization's losing its land; bitter disputes as to its future followed.

Martin Durham

See Also: ARYANISM; BUTLER, RICHARD GIRNT; CHRISTIAN IDENTITY; RACIAL DOCTRINE; UNITED STATES, THE (POSTWAR); WHITE SUPREMACISM

Reference
Ridgeway, James. 1995. *Blood in the Face: Ku Klux Klan, Aryan Nations, Nazi Skinheads and the Rise of a New White Culture.* New York: Thunder's Mouth.

ARYANISM

Aryanism was one of the most important ideological elements in German National Socialism, and it remains important for many modern neo-Nazi movements in various countries today. Adolf Hitler and the early Nazi ideologues believed in an Aryan Master Race that had a mission to dominate all other peoples and races. The term *Aryan* was popularized in the late nineteenth century by the Anglo-German scholar Max Müller (1823–1900) as an alternative to *Indo-European.* "Indo-European languages" were treated as a particular category of languages that included Sanskrit, Persian, Greek, Latin, Celtic, Teutonic, and Slavonic. Müller used the term *Aryan* only of language speakers, but others began to apply it to racial groupings, a practice that he himself never considered acceptable.

The story of how so-called Aryanism came to play such an important role in Nazi thinking is complex and goes back to the Early Modern era. In the sixteenth century there developed in German-speaking Europe an aspiration to find ways of expressing the cultural unity of German-speakers, or "Germanness," which some felt transcended actual territorial political divisions. That gave rise to attempts to "unmix" Germany as a melting-pot of different peoples in favor of a "pure Germanness." The specifically "German" peoples were pictured as set apart from their neighboring peoples; the Germans were depicted as men who were original, rooted in the soil, free-spirited, and with a developed sense of honor, distinguished from other peoples by their positive qualities. Ulrich von Hutten (1488–1523) contrasted the "manliness" of the Germans as a "world-dominating" people with the "womanliness" of the Romans. The development of the notion of a "German special way" in spirit, culture, and race was encouraged by the German Reformation, especially in its sectarian form. That movement soon acquired (as did later the whole Aryan myth) a decidedly anti-Church and anti-Roman tendency, on the basis of theories which claimed that the originally free Germans adhering to a "natural religion" had been weakened in spirit and enslaved by the yoke of the Roman Church and had become "mixed in" with other culturally inferior peoples. Some humanists saw German as "the language of heroes" and aspired to "purify" it from supposedly later admixtures. Even Leibniz believed that German was closer to the lost "Adamitic primitive language" than Hebrew or Arabic. When Aryan studies began in the eighteenth century, the Germans were portrayed as the leaders of the noble Aryan Master race, set apart from other peoples by their "purity."

Inspired by the discovery of new peoples and continents, and following older medieval theories according to which there were "pre-Adamitic peoples" who did not go back to the forefather Adam, some Enlightenment thinkers developed a theory of the distinct origins of the human races. This was intended as a rival to the Christian teaching that saw Adam and Eve as the original couple of all of humanity. These Enlightenment figures assigned to the blacks, whom they regarded as standing on a low spiritual level, all the lowly and primitive qualities, and to the creative white master races (Aryan and European) all the noble and higher qualities. Carl von Linnaeus (1707–1778), the great classifier of nature, called the European "inventive . . . white, full-blooded. He is governed by laws." At the other end of his scale (below the intermediate stages of Americans and Asiatics) stood the African: "foolish, lazy, apathetic . . . black, phlegmatic . . . ruled by the arbitrary power of his master" (*Systema naturae,* 1793). Pupils of Linnaeus developed dualistic theories according to which the whites were the original race while the blacks had emerged through a "mixture" of the whites with apes. David Hume (1711–1776) called "Negroes and generally all other species of men . . . inferior to whites by nature. . . . There has never been a civilized nation of other than white skin, not even a single one, which distinguished itself in trade and thought."

Again as part of an anti-Christian propaganda war, Voltaire attributed to the spiritual culture of India temporal precedence over biblical Hebrew culture, tracing "Abraham" back to the Indian "Brahma." Along with other rather bizarre theoreticians, he inspired the German Romantics in their love affair with India.

In Germany both Enlightenment and Romantic thinkers aspired to look beyond the Jewish-Christian horizon of the West. They were fascinated by the early Indian thinkers, now seen as the earliest representatives of a spiritual culture of humanity. India was regarded as the source of "the ways of humanity" and the "lawgiver to all peoples" in the words of travel writer Pierre Sonnerat (1748–1814). Johann Gottfried Herder (1744–1803) inspired a Romantic cult of "Mother India"; India was for him both the source and place of origin of mankind itself and the source of the "religion of natural revelation," of which the Hebrew Bible was only a "faithful copy." For Herder, the Indians were perfect representatives of wisdom, science, nobility, and restraint; he celebrated the common origins of the "IndoAryans" and the racial and cultural-linguistic relationship between Indians, Persians, and Germans as representatives of the "high and noble." Herder's contemporaries at the German universities now sought to draw the outlines of an Aryan high culture that had developed separately from "Semitic" cultures and languages. In his work *Über die Sprache und Weisheit der Indier* (*On the Language and Wisdom of the Indians,* 1808), Friedrich Schlegel (1772–1829) claimed that a people of Aryan culture came from north India to the West, which meant that many ideas from ancient India were to be found among the old Germans.

His brother August Wilhelm Schlegel (1767–1845) was the first to give the Aryan idea a nationalistic turn, making an association between the root "Ari" and the German word *Ehre* ("honor"). Through E. M. Arndt and F. L. Jahn, "Aryan" or "Indo-German" studies in Germany took on a decidedly anti-Semitic coloring by the mid-nineteenth century, initially on the basis of the idea that the old Indian wisdom books represented the original revelation of God more perfectly than the Hebraic-biblical texts. This idea was formulated in increasingly dualistic terms: the original pure texts of the IndoAryans, a world-dominating master people, were watered down and falsified by the uncreative and ultimately culturally "parasitic" Semites.

The French historian Jules Michelet (1798–1874) spoke in his *Histoire romaine* (1831) of the "long struggle between the Semitic world and the Indogermanic world"; for him, too, India was the "Mother of the Nations." Other propagandists of Aryan studies, mostly theologians and Sanskrit scholars, constructed an "Aryan Christ" who had taught a master religion of the noble and the subjection of non-Aryan peoples—for example, the French Orientalist Ernest Renan (1823–1892), in his extremely successful work *The Life of Jesus* (7 vols., 1863–1883). Others accepted that the roots of Christendom were Semitic but argued that it had experienced its high point in the Middle Ages, when it was marked by the culture of the German Reich.

In the course of the nineteenth century, Aryan theories got mixed with a series of ideas prevalent at the time into an inextricable tangle; thus with race theory, which propagated the "racial pride" of the white races as the "motor of history"; with a crude form of social Darwinism that started from the struggle of the races with each other; also with "physiological" anthropology, which argued from physical racial characteristics, especially through skull measurements, to the spiritual and ethical superiority of the whites or the inferiority of the blacks. In Germany, Great Britain, and France, anti-Semitic cultural theories constructed the "cultural genius" of the Aryans over against the "cultural sterility" of the Semites. The Genevan linguistics scholar Adolphe Pictet called the Aryans the "civilizers of the world": "[T]he race of the Aryans, chosen before all others, is the most important tool of the plans of God for the destiny of humanity" (*Les origines indo-européennes ou les Aryas primitifs,* 1859). For Gobineau, who brought together almost all of these theories and had his greatest influence in Germany, the white Aryan races had arisen in north India and were from the beginning led by "Providence" (later a favorite term of Hitler's). In his four-volume work *Essai sur l'inégalité des races humaines* (*Essay on the Inequality of the Human Races,* 1853–1855), which made him the most influential prophet of Aryan superiority, Gobineau categorized nearly all known races according to the degree of their "mixture" with others, especially with Aryans or Semites. He saw in the "bastardizing of the Aryans" the main reason for the collapse of civilizations and cultures, which were condemned to general "mediocrity" by it. It was Gobineau who gave a history-of-philosophy orientation to the Aryan/Jewish polarity.

The theory of the different origins of the Aryan and Semitic peoples became virtually a religious dogma for all anti-Semitic currents in Germany. Prescription of the separation of races and depiction of the dangers of a "mixing of races" became a fixed idea, with prophets of doom forever repeating the claim that the "inferior races" damaged the "higher" ones ("bad blood corrupts the good!"). In the nineteenth century, race researchers had speculated that an Aryan woman who had been "tainted" even just the once by a Jewish man could thenceforth bring into the world only "Jewish bastards."

In parallel with the cult of the Germans in the second half of the nineteenth century there developed a no less exaggerated cult of the Aryans with religious-type features, and that also drew many representatives of early National Socialism under its banner. One of the main prophets was the German Orientalist Lagarde, who wanted to set the figure of Jesus Christ free from a Jewish context and outlined a Germanic or Aryan "religion of the future." His example inspired a whole flood of writings that aimed at "Aryanizing" Jesus. Most of them were rather comical, such as the theory of Ernst von Bunsen (1817–1893), according to which the Bible had originated in an Aryan religion of the sun, and the first man, Adam, was an Aryan; the serpent in Paradise, by contrast, had been "Semitic" (*Die Uberlieferung,* 1889). The young Richard Wagner had in 1850 compared Christ to the highest German god, Wotan, while the expatriate Englishman Houston Stewart Chamberlain was a tireless "prophet of Aryanism" who claimed that he had "demonstrated" the "non-Jewish descent" of Jesus Christ. His anti-Semitic *Foundations of the 19th Century* (1899) had a direct influence (down to the choice of title) on Rosenberg's "Myth of the Twentieth Century" and on his Aryan mysticism.

Clearly then, in many respects the Nazi ideologues with their Aryan mystifications needed only to harvest where others—including some of the leading minds of the nineteenth and twentieth centuries—had already sown. But in *Mein Kampf,* Hitler gave to the idea of the Aryan as "founder of culture" a peculiarly violent turn, claiming that the Aryan alone was worthy to bear the name "human," so that all other peoples and races were no more than "subhumans." This strict dualism between the "racially pure" Aryans and all others—especially Jews and Slavs—led in

Nazism to the radical outlawing of all "non-Aryans" and to their enslavement and attempted annihilation. The "Aryan Paragraph" formulated for the first time in the *Gesetz zur Wiederherstellung des Berufsbeamtentums* (Law for the Restoration of the Civil Service) of 7 April 1933 (which went back to a demand of Georg von Schönerer in the nineteenth century) decreed that all civil servants of "nonAryan descent" be retired. After this the Aryan Paragraph served for the systematic outlawing of Jews from all areas of public life. The identification of Aryanism and Germanness was recognized by the National Socialist state in a memo from the Reich Ministry of the Interior of 26 November 1935, in which the concept "Aryan" was replaced by "of German blood," and later by the formula "those belonging to German or related blood." The accompanying "Aryan proof" obliged Germans, especially applicants for official posts, to show an unbroken "testimony of descent" of "Aryan purity of blood" of their ancestors back to the year 1800. Official Nazi linguistic usage designated the taking of Jewish property into Aryan hands as laid down in the Aryanizing Decrees of 26 April and 12 November 1938 as "Aryanization": the alienation of Jewish property without compensation in favor of "Aryan members of the nation," who could acquire alienated Jewish goods. This is a typical example of the way that the "Aryan" idea served the Nazis both as a propaganda tool in their war against the Jews and as a cover for robbery and exploitation.

Significantly, the term *Aryanism* does not even figure in the index to Cannistraro's *Historical Dictionary of Fascist Italy,* let alone as an individual entry. That is a powerful indicator of the lack of interest in Italy for the whole Aryan myth, which in fact is one of the key indicators of the profound differences between Italian Fascism and Nazism—alongside of their similarities. As with "Nordic thinking," it seems to have been designed to make Protestant Germans and their secularized compatriots feel that they had a past to be proud of—both vis-à-vis the pride of the Latins in their Greco-Roman forebears and vis-à-vis the Catholic sense that the whole of Church history belonged to them. It is true that French scholars played an important role in developing the Aryan myth, but perhaps their agenda was different. As secularist heirs to the Enlightenment, writers like Gobineau and Renan were continuing the tradition of promoting a story of the past rival to the biblical account.

Markus Hattstein
(translated and enlarged by Cyprian Blamires)

See Also: AHNENERBE; ANTHROPOLOGY; ANTI-SEMITISM; ARYAN NATIONS, THE; BLOOD; BLOOD AND SOIL; CHAMBERLAIN, HOUSTON STEWART; ENLIGHTENMENT, THE; EUGENICS; GERMANNESS; GOBINEAU, JOSEPH ARTHUR COMTE DE; HERO, THE CULT OF THE; HITLER, ADOLF; HOLOCAUST, THE; LAGARDE, PAUL DE; NATIONALISM; *MEIN KAMPF;* MYSTICISM; NAZISM; NEO-NAZISM; NORDIC SOUL, THE; *NUEVA GERMANIA;* NUREMBERG LAWS, THE; RACIAL DOCTRINE; RACISM; ROSENBERG, ALFRED; SCHÖNERER, GEORG RITTER VON; SCIENCE; SLAVS, THE (AND GERMANY); SOCIAL DARWINISM; SS, THE; THEOLOGY; TIBET; TRADITION; *UNTERMENSCHEN* ("SUBHUMANS"); VACHER DE LAPOUGE, GEORGES; WAGNER, (WILHELM) RICHARD; WARRIOR ETHOS, THE

References

Burleigh, M., and W. Wippermann. 1991. *The Racial State: Germany 1933–45.* Cambridge: Cambridge University Press.

Goodrick-Clarke, N. 2003a. *Black Sun: Aryan Cults, Esoteric Nazism, and the Politics of Identity.* New York: New York University Press.

———. 2003b. *The Occult Roots of Nazism: Secret Aryan Cults and Their Influence on Nazi Ideology.* London: Tauris Parke.

Mosse, G. L. 1966. *The Crisis of German Ideology: Intellectual Origins of the Third Reich.* London: Weidenfeld and Nicholson.

Noll, Richard. 1997. *The Aryan Christ: The Secret Life of Carl Gustav Jung.* London: Macmillan.

ARYANS: *See* ARYANISM

ASOCIALS

Label given by the Nazis to persons whose way of life or weaknesses or deviant behavior they regarded as making them incapable and unworthy of being a part of society. They included beggars, prostitutes and the sexually nonconformist, alcoholics, destitute families, the work-shy, and travelers (*see* ROMA AND SINTI, THE). Persecution of "asocials" was instituted from the start of the Nazi regime in 1933, and many were imprisoned or sent to concentration camps. Some were forcibly sterilized.

Cyprian Blamires

See Also: AUSCHWITZ; BLOOD AND SOIL; CONCENTRATION CAMPS; EUGENICS; EUTHANASIA; HOLOCAUST, THE; MEDICINE (GERMANY); NAZISM; ROMA AND SINTI, THE; SEXUALITY.

AUSCHWITZ (-BIRKENAU)

Although there were a large number of Nazi concentration camps, the one that since World War II has come to represent them all and act as a symbol of the atrocity of the Holocaust is Auschwitz-Birkenau, whose remains continue to be visited by many thousands of tourists every year. Situated just outside the Polish town of Oswiecim, near Krakow, Auschwitz-Birkenau is also the largest mass murder site documented anywhere in history. Established first in May 1940 on territory occupied by Germany at the onset of World War II, Auschwitz soon emerged as the central killing center for Jews murdered by National Socialism and its allies. In less than five years some 1.1 million victims perished, overwhelmingly Jews, but also 75,000 Poles, 25,000 Roma and Sinti travelers, 15,000 Soviet POWs, and thousands of others—including many clergy and other persons opposed to Nazism on conscientious grounds. Its sheer size, slave labor facilities, and its bureaucratic management of genocide have made Auschwitz a central—often exemplary—part of the Holocaust story.

The development of Auschwitz-Birkenau was initially an exercise of trial and error under Rudolf Höss, camp commandant until his transfer in November 1943. On 14 June 1940, 728 Polish prisoners arrived to commence enlarging the camp in the first deployment of slave labor at Auschwitz. As the numbers of incarcerated Polish intellectuals and political dissidents increased, conditions further deteriorated—to the point that most prisoners died, through work, malnutrition, or, more and more commonly, execution. Even in its transformation from a disused Polish army base to concentration camp, and even before the large extermination facilities were operational, Auschwitz already meant death for the vast majority of those guarded by 300 members of the SS. The creation of Auschwitz-Birkenau as an industrial killing center owes to various factors: the increase of prisoners within expanding SS camps; investment of private capital; the onset of a "war of annihilation" against the Soviet Union; and especially, the Nazis' radicalizing plans for a "solution to the Jewish question."

In March 1941, Heinrich Himmler ordered Höss to enlarge the camp massively beyond the initially envisaged 10,000 prisoners, thus turning Auschwitz into the largest concentration camp and source of enforced labor within the Third Reich. In turn, that decision was largely motivated by the willingness of the private German firm IG Farben to establish operations near Auschwitz, subsidizing prisoners' expenses so as to harvest some of the valuable raw materials nearby (such as coal and lime) for the German war effort; in addition, facilities were constructed for the production of synthetic rubber and fuel at a satellite labor camp called Monowitz, and later Auschwitz III (opened October 1942). Other companies benefiting from enforced labor included Krupp, Wichsel Metall-Union, Allgemein Elektrizitätsgesellschaft (AEG), and Oberschlesiche Hydrierwerk; they were soon operating in some three dozen satellite camps, ultimately surrounding the original site of Auschwitz. Finally, Nazi population policy—especially following the invasion of the USSR in June 1941—grew more intense and ambitious toward "undesirable elements." By the summer of 1941, Russian prisoners quickly outnumbered surviving Polish workers at Auschwitz, receiving even worse treatment and being worked to death at even greater rates: of nearly 12,000 laborers, only 150 Russian POWs survived their first year building Auschwitz. In a related development for "solving" Nazism's "demographic problems," Russian POWs were also the first group gassed by the pesticide Zyklon-B, in September 1941, at the initiative of Höss's deputy, Karl Fritsch, in the infamous punishment cells of Block 11. Previous attempts at mass murder by the Third Reich through shooting, explosives, injections, and carbon monoxide tanks and engine fumes were all superseded by the efficiency and availability of Fritsch's successful experiment with Zyklon-B.

By the time of the 20 January 1942 Wannsee Conference, organized by Reinhard Heydrich and Adolf Eichmann, most of the enormous facilities were in meticulous preparation to transform Auschwitz into the scythe of Nazism's attempted elimination of European Jewry. Over the course of 1942, some 200,000 Jews from across Europe, from Slovakia to France, were transported on sealed trains to Auschwitz I; 70 percent died upon arrival, through "selection" by SS doctors like Josef Mengele, following gassing and mass burial. Further challenges to the enlargement of the killing facilities and the disposal of bodies were overcome in the spring of 1943 with the completion of nearby Birkenau (renamed Auschwitz II by the new commandant, Arthur Liebehenschel, in November 1943), containing eight gas chambers, four crematoria, and forty-six ovens, in all capable of "processing" 4,416 human beings every day. From the moment of design until the end of the gassings in November 1944, the facilities at Birkenau were intended to annihilate "enemies of the state" of all types: those wearing insignias of pink (homosexuals), brown (travelers), green (criminals), black ("asocials"), red (dissidents), violet (Jehovah's Witnesses), and especially yellow stars (Jews). Supplementing this genocidal machinery were about 3,000 SS staff, specialists, and military personnel; a railway terminus with elaborate techniques of deception and arrangements for the seamless disposal of thousands of victims simultaneously; as well as a constellation of laboring slaves and mechanisms of internal control—from electrified fences to inmate guards (*Kapos*).

The apex of extermination was reached over 1944, when some 400,000 Hungarian Jews were deported and gassed at Auschwitz in just over three months. Primary documents, recovered architectural studies, and painstaking historical research nevertheless confirm what wartime political leaders could not or would not accept, and which Holocaust deniers, anti-Semites, and neo-Nazis continue to question or trivialize: by the cessation of production-line genocide in November 1944, 1 million Jews had died at Auschwitz-Birkenau. The barking dogs, punishing roll calls, severe malnutrition and disease, tattooed prisoners and savage guards, storehouses of pillaged clothes or gold teeth, and smell of burning human remains—all ceased only because of the imminent defeat of the Third Reich. With the advancing armies closing on Germany, SS guards took about 60,000 prisoners on a "death march" toward central Germany; when liberating Soviet troops entered Auschwitz-Birkenau in late January 1945, only about 8,000 diseased and malnourished inmates remained behind. Such is the symbolic and representative nature of Auschwitz-Birkenau to the Holocaust as a whole that Holocaust Memorial Day falls annually on the day the camp was liberated, 27 January.

Matt Feldman

See Also: ANTI-SEMITISM; BLOOD; BLOOD AND SOIL; CONCENTRATION CAMPS; DEMOGRAPHIC POLICY; EICHMANN, ADOLF OTTO; GERMANY; HEYDRICH, REINHARD; HIMMLER, HEINRICH; HITLER, ADOLF; HOLOCAUST, THE; HOLOCAUST DENIAL; HOMOSEXUALITY; I G FARBEN; JEHOVAH'S WITNESSES, THE; KRUPP VON BOHLEN UND HALBACH, ALFRIED; MENGELE, JOSEF; NAZISM; NEO-NAZISM; SOVIET UNION, THE; SS, THE; THIRD REICH, THE; WANNSEE CONFERENCE, THE; ZYKLON-B

References

Dwork, Deborah, and Robert van Pelt. 1996. *Auschwitz: 1270 to the Present*. Newhaven, CT: Yale University Press.

Friedrich, Otto. 1996. *The Kingdom of Auschwitz*. London: Penguin.

Gutman, Yisrael, and Michael Berenbaum. 1994. *Anatomy of the Auschwitz Death Camp.* Bloomington, IN: Holocaust Memorial Museum.

Hilberg, Raul. 1985. *The Destruction of the European Jews.* London: Holmes and Meier.

Höss, Rudolf. 1992. *Death Dealer: The Memoirs of the SS Kommandant at Auschwitz.* Buffalo, NY: Prometheus.

Levi, Primo. 1987. *If This Is a Man* and *the Truce.* London: Abacus.

AUSTRALIA

It is difficult to determine which groups in Australia qualify as "fascist." Although numerous extreme right-wing groups have existed in Australia since the country's federation in 1901, there has been little agreement among experts about how to classify them. Some of the most significant groups were formed in the 1920s and 1930s, the high-water mark for fascism in Australia. The aftermath of World War I, economic depression, fear of communism, and the election of a radical labor government in the state of New South Wales produced a number of quasi-fascist and fascist paramilitary movements. In addition, local fascist branches were formed by Italian and German consular authorities and by Australians liaising with the British Union of Fascists.

The best known of the native organizations were the Old Guard, formed in 1930, and the New Guard, which split off a year later. There were, however, antecedents to these groups. One of them, probably the Australian Protective League, is thought to have formed the basis of the secret organization described by D. H. Lawrence in *Kangaroo,* which he wrote in Australia in 1922. At its height, the Old Guard had an estimated secret membership of 30,000, which included members of Australia's business elite with connections to conservative politicians.

The New Guard was created by Lieutenant Colonel Eric Campbell and was a more public, working-class, and extreme organization than the Old Guard. It is remembered mainly for the intervention of one of its members at the opening of the Sydney Harbour Bridge in 1932: Francis De Groot slashed the ceremonial ribbon in order to prevent that honor's falling to the state premier. After a visit to Europe, Campbell introduced uniforms and the fascist salute to the New Guard, innovations that caused some members to leave. With the declaration of war in 1939, members of fascist organizations and fellow travelers such as P. R. Stephenson, from the anti-Semitic Australia First Movement, were interned.

In the postwar period the most influential extremist group was the League of Rights, established in 1946 by Eric Butler. Although the league's origins lie in the Social Credit ideas of Major C. H. Douglas, it disseminates fascist propaganda and has links with neofascist groups in Britain. Support for the league has been strongest in rural areas, but its membership is aging; it has faced competition from the LaRouchite Citizens Electoral Councils. All were overtaken in popularity by Pauline Hanson's One Nation Party, which emerged in 1997 and in 1998 secured one in four votes for the Queensland state legislature. That was the high point for the party, which has since all but disappeared. Although a few commentators described Hanson as fascist because of her racism and ultranationalism, and because some people attracted to her party had been members of neofascist organizations, most analysts placed her in the Australian populist tradition. Groups such as National Action, formed in 1982, and the breakaway Australian National Movement, provide less contested examples of fascist organizations. Members of both groups have been convicted of racist violence. Other groups, such as the racist Adelaide Institute, use the Internet to spread their views. The institute's director, Dr. Frederick Töben, was arrested in Germany in 1999 and convicted of denial of genocide and incitement to racial hatred. Such extremist groups attract little public support.

Rae Wear

See Also: ANTI-SEMITISM; CYBERFASCISM; GREAT BRITAIN; HOLOCAUST DENIAL; LAROUCHE, LYNDON HERMYLE; NATIONALISM; PARAMILITARISM; POSTWAR FASCISM; RACISM; WALL STREET CRASH, THE; WORLD WAR I

References

Greason, David. 1994. *I Was a Teenage Fascist.* Ringwood, Victoria: McPhee Gribble.

Leach, Michael, Geoffrey Stokes, and Ian Ward, eds. 2000. *The Rise and Fall of One Nation.* St Lucia, Queensland: University of Queensland Press.

Moore, Andrew. 1989. *The Secret Army and the Premier: Conservative Paramilitary Organisations in New South Wales 1930–32.* Kensington, New South Wales: New South Wales University Press.

———. 1995. *The Right Road: A History of Right-Wing Politics in Australia.* Oxford: Oxford University Press.

AUSTRIA

The period known variously as Austria's authoritarian, clerico-fascist, or Austro-fascist era encompassed the years 1933 to 1938. It grew out of Austria's troubled post–World War I experience and serves as a prelude to the *Anschluss* and Austria's absorption into the Third Reich. The story is a complex one, incorporating the chancellorships of former Christian Social politicians Engelbert Dollfuss and Kurt von Schuschnigg; the establishment of a one-party state under the Fatherland Front; the adoption of a corporatist, authoritarian constitution; a native fascist movement in the form of the Heimwehr; an Austrian Nazi party enjoying varying degrees of support from Germany; and the role of the Catholic Church, an issue in the frequent labeling of the Dollfuss and Schuschnigg regimes as "clerico-fascist." A further source of conflict was the widespread lack of confidence in the viability of Austria as a second German state in an era influenced at the outset by the Wilsonian doctrine of national self-determination and increasingly by the might of Hitlerian Germany.

As a homogenous state (94 percent German), Austria was spared the ethnic strife that bedeviled the other successor states to the Austro-Hungarian Empire. But the breakup of what had been a unified economic entity of 54 million left Austria deprived of resources and markets and plagued by high unemployment. Out of a population of just over 7 million, nearly 2.5 million lived in Vienna alone. Robbed of its imperial status, the city could no longer employ the university-educated middle class or many of the bureaucratic and military elements that had formerly found a comfortable niche in the imperial apparatus.

Moreover, the country was polarized between two political camps, Social Democrats and Christian Socials, each representing vastly different social, economic, and cultural worldviews. The Christian Social Party was strong in the rural Catholic heartland, while the Social Democrats found their supporters in urban industrial areas, notably Vienna and Linz. In Vienna the Christian Socials too had a strong following among middle- and lower-middle-class elements, small business and property owners, and loyal adherents of the Catholic Church. Present also was a German nationalist movement, heir of the nineteenth-century Panger-

mans who had scorned the multinational "mongrel" Habsburg Empire, desiring instead unity within a *Grossdeutschland.* This movement, defeated and embittered after 1866 and Austria's exclusion from the Bismarckian Reich, had gained strength as the Habsburg Empire faltered. Pangermanism would be one of the spiritual progenitors of the Austrian Nazi Party as well as elements of Heimwehr fascism, a movement that enjoyed its greatest popularity in regions bordering the new Czechoslovak, Yugoslav, and Hungarian states.

In the immediate aftermath of World War I and the collapse of the Habsburg Empire, Austria's provisional government adopted the name "German-Austrian Republic," declaring its intentions to merge into a greater Germany inspired by the idea of national self-determination that was shaping the formation of the other successor states to that empire. But the treaties of Versailles and St. Germain forbade this early and peaceful *Anschluss.* Austria's postwar political history, then, properly began with the adoption of the Constitution of 1920. Austria was to be a federal state, with Vienna granted the status of a province. In the first regular elections held since the war, the Christian Social Party attained a slim majority of seats in the parliament, or Nationalrat. The Christian Socials would retain a small majority in nearly every subsequent election, and would likewise retain their hold on the chancellorship. But the party did so only in coalition with nationalist groups—notably, by 1930, the fascist Heimwehr. In May 1932, when Engelbert Dollfuss became chancellor, the Christian Social majority had been reduced to a single vote.

The rise to power of Adolf Hitler in January 1933 began the threat to Austrian independence that would culminate in March 1938 with the *Anschluss.* Hitler appointed Theo Habicht as his inspector general for Austria. From Munich, Habicht directed the Austrian Nazi Party in a campaign of propaganda and terror against the Dollfuss government and the Austrian people. Swastikas defaced public buildings, and bombs killed and wounded civilians. Dollfuss was portrayed in radio broadcasts as a lackey of Jewish, clerical, and foreign interests. In June 1933, Dollfuss banned the Nazi Party in Austria, a move that drove the organization underground, where it infiltrated the bureaucracy and police departments. Hitler retaliated by levying a 1,000 Reichsmark tax on any German citizen traveling to Austria, an astronomical sum aimed at crippling the tourist industry in Austria. Dollfuss believed that the way to preserve Austria's independence was to steer a middle course between the Nazis and his Socialist rivals, and to do so under the auspices of an authoritarian government with trappings borrowed from populist fascist regimes abroad. In this he was encouraged by Mussolini—with whom he enjoyed both a personal friendship and a political alliance—and by his Heimwehr allies, upon whose eight votes in the Nationalrat he depended to bolster his one-vote Christian Social majority.

The pretext for the end of parliamentary government occurred on 4 March 1933, during a procedural vote in the Nationalrat. Karl Renner, speaker of the assembly, Social Democratic Party leader, and a former Austrian chancellor, resigned the speakership in order to be able to cast a vote. The next two men in line of succession for the speaker's chair resigned as well, plunging parliament into chaos. The next day Dollfuss, invoking the obscure 1917 War Economy Emergency Powers Act, declared the Nationalrat indefinitely suspended. For the next fifteen months he ruled by emergency decree, abolishing the Communist Party in May 1933 and, as noted, the Nazi Party in June. In May he unveiled his Fatherland Front, a state party given the appearance of mass support by a network of auxiliary organizations: a labor front, professional organizations, women's and youth groups. He moved forward with plans to implement a corporatist constitution modeled on those of Mussolini's Italy and Antonio Salazar's Portugal, as well as on the 1931 papal encyclical *Quadragesimo Anno.*

The new constitution would not be implemented until 1 May 1934, following a series of dramatic events. At Mussolini's urgings, and in an attempt to neutralize opposition on the left, on 12 February 1934 government and Heimwehr forces launched a number of raids in search of weapons held by the Socialist Party's paramilitary organization, the Schutzbund. Socialists in Linz fought back, and in Vienna the Social Democrats called for a general strike. Fighting in the capital concentrated around the working-class housing complexes ringing the city. Constructed in the 1920s and early 1930s, these dwellings were the proud achievement of the Socialist-dominated municipal government in Vienna, which had benefited from the taxation powers granted by its provincial status. These massive projects (the most famous of which, the Karl Marx Hof, boasted more than 1,300 apartments) had attracted international attention among urban planners. Critics and pundits alike often noted the fortresslike character of these housing blocks; they now in fact became defensive

fortresses. The Schutzbund, however, armed with rifles, was no match for the heavy artillery employed by government forces. (Dollfuss reportedly wanted to use tear gas; the lack of stockpiles led to the decision to employ artillery.) During the ensuing five days of fighting, heavy damage was inflicted on the structures. Casualty statistics vary; the most reliable cite around 300 dead and 800 wounded, with losses fairly evenly divided. Schutzbund resistance collapsed. The brief civil war provided justification, if further were sought, for the suppression of the Socialist Party. Dollfuss then abolished all remaining political parties, including his own Christian Social Party, in June of 1934.

On May 1 the corporate constitution was promulgated. That same day the new concordat with the Catholic Church took effect. Modeled on the 1929 Lateran Treaty between the Vatican and the Italian government and on the *Reichskonkordat* between the Vatican and Germany in May 1933, the concordat assigned the Catholic Church a leading role in education and guaranteed the autonomy of the Church's youth and other social and corporate organizations, provided these confined themselves to religious activities. In fact, as would be the case in Italy and Germany, tensions and rivalries would occur between church and state in Austria as the government sought to expand the role of its Fatherland Front auxiliary organizations into precisely those areas jealously guarded by the Church: youth, education, women, and family. Such tensions undercut, at critical junctures, Church support for the regime and they serve as a caveat against any too-facile use of the "clerico-fascist" label in describing the Austrian regime between 1934 and 1938.

Dollfuss's triumph was short-lived. On 25 July 1934 a band of 150 Austrian Nazi sympathizers, dressed in improvised uniforms, entered the Ballhausplatz chancellery, seized hostages, and assassinated Dollfuss. The failure of the putsch can be credited to Dollfuss's actions: with less than an hour's advance notice from a participant-turned-informer, Dollfuss had suspended the cabinet meeting then in session and directed ministers to scatter to their respective offices across Vienna. A communications failure separated leaders of the putsch from its participants. The small force dispatched to kidnap Austrian president Wilhelm Miklas, vacationing in Carinthia, was foiled by a suspicious local police. Instead Miklas swore in Kurt von Schuschnigg, formerly the justice and education minister, as the new chancellor over the telephone. From the Defense Ministry, where the cabinet reassembled, Schuschnigg directed a collaborative police, army, and Heimwehr effort. The putschists were arrested, its leaders tried and executed. Mussolini strengthened the existing deployment of 50,000 Italian troops at the Brenner Pass with an additional four divisions, warning Germany to make no further advances on Austria. Hitler disavowed the putsch, fired Habicht, and appointed the former Catholic Center Party leader Franz von Papen as his envoy to Vienna.

Dollfuss, who had risen to prominence on the basis of his work with farmers' organizations and local chambers of agriculture, had never lost a certain populist appeal. Schuschnigg, however, was reserved, even aloof. A lawyer, an intellectual, and a Habsburg legitimist by sentiment, Schuschnigg was an individual upon whom the mantle of fascist leader proved a poor fit. Moreover, his frequent use of the word *German* in describing the independent Austria to which he was strongly committed served to complicate the very question of national identity that he sought to solidify. Schuschnigg continued Dollfuss's policies at home and abroad. He strengthened ties with Italy and Hungary. He consolidated his position as chancellor in a series of measures against the Heimwehr. In April 1936, Schuschnigg reintroduced military conscription (in violation of the Treaty of St. Germain) in order to lessen the government's reliance on Heimwehr paramilitary forces. In May 1936 he forced Heimwehr leader Ruediger von Starhemberg out of his dual role as vice chancellor and head of the Fatherland Front. In October, Schuschnigg abolished the Heimwehr itself, absorbing its members into the Fatherland Front militia and expelling Heimwehr members from all remaining cabinet posts, while proclaiming himself *Front Fuehrer.*

Schuschnigg continued to walk a tightrope between an increasingly expansionist Nazi Germany and the growing stridency and violent actions of the underground Nazi Party. Moreover, as Germany and Italy drew together, culminating in the Axis alliance of October 1936, Schuschnigg lost a key ally. Attempting to clarify Austria's position vis-à-vis Germany, Schuschnigg entered into an agreement with Hitler on 11 July 1936. Each nation promised to respect the sovereignty of the other, but the wording in the agreement by which Austria acknowledged that it was a "German state" was one more example of Schuschnigg's near-mystical conviction that Austria represented the Christian *Deutschtum,* an authentic Germany that was heir to the Holy Roman Empire and the Habsburgs, a Germany that had been betrayed first by Bismarck's Reich and then by Nazism.

Such idealistic formulations, however, were of decreasing value in the face of forces bent ultimately on another variant of the *Grossdeutsch* solution.

Austria's authoritarian era moved hastily toward its conclusion. Hitler's march of aggression, begun with the repudiation of the disarmament clauses of the Versailles Treaty and his occupation of the Rhineland, now focused upon Austria. Hitler summoned Schuschnigg to Berchtesgaden on 12 February 1938, where, under duress, Schuschnigg agreed to an amnesty for Austrian Nazis, including participants in the July 1934 putsch, relented to Hitler's demand for the inclusion of Nazis in the cabinet, and agreed to admission of Nazis into the Fatherland Front. Hitler then upped the ante in a speech on 20 February, promising "protection" for the 10 million Germans residing outside the Reich, a statement seen as a provocation by the Schuschnigg government. On 1 March, Nazi-led street violence broke out in Graz and spread to other areas of the country. In desperation Schuschnigg turned to the remnants of the Socialist Party, offering them a role in government. On 9 March he announced a plebiscite, scheduled for 13 March, asking Austrians to vote "for a free and German, independent Christian and social Austria." In a final indication of the authoritarian character of the regime, only "yes" ballots were to be provided. It was, however, a moot point. On 11 March, Hitler issued an ultimatum demanding postponement of the plebiscite, Schuschnigg's resignation, and the appointment of the Nazi Arthur Seyss-Inquart—since February 1938, minister of the interior—to the office of chancellor. Desiring to spare Austrians any bloodshed in what he deemed would be futile resistance, Schuschnigg capitulated and broadcast news of these developments, along with a farewell to the Austrian people. On 13 March, the day originally planned for the plebiscite, Seyss-Inquart instead proclaimed the *Anschluss* of Austria with Germany. Schuschnigg was arrested and would be held prisoner, for the most part at the Sachsenhausen concentration camp, until his liberation by the Allies in May 1945. Other political opponents of the Nazi "New Order," representing the full array of interwar Austrian political life and strife—Socialists, Christian Socials, Catholic lay activists, Fatherland Front and Heimwehr followers—were arrested. Jews were subject to particularly vicious acts of humiliation and suffering, a prelude to horrors yet to come.

The Nazi plebiscite of 10 April 1938 yielded a 99.75 percent "yes" vote for the *Anschluss.* Judging public sentiment, however, is difficult, given the arrests and intimidation of opponents that preceded the vote and the likelihood of fraudulent reporting of results. Studies of public opinion between 1938 and 1945 reveal a complex picture of shifting and evolving attitudes toward the Hitler regime. Nazi attempts to win working-class support by portraying the party as anticlerical (and thus the heir to the Social Democrats), to woo large and small business, and to draw sharp contrasts between themselves and the "philo-Semitism" of the Schuschnigg regime highlight both the impossibility of viewing the pre-1938 era as indistinct from what came after, and the divisions of opinion in Austria that the Nazis hoped to exploit. At the same time, Austria did not forge a resistance movement on a par with those in other occupied countries. One of the more infamous concentration camps, Mauthausen, was located in Austria. A significant number of Austrians (many with Heimwehr connections) occupied high places in the party hierarchy: Ernst Kaltenbrunner was Himmler's deputy in the SS; several SS chiefs in occupied Eastern European countries were Austrians; and Arthur Seyss-Inquart was one of only ten Nuremberg Trials defendants to be executed.

Austria's postwar existence and its delayed confrontation with its interwar and wartime experience can be traced to the Moscow Declaration of 1 November 1943, wherein the Allies proclaimed Austria "the first free country to fall a victim to Hitlerite aggression." At the same time, the declaration noted that Austria bore "a responsibility which she cannot evade, for participation in the war on the side of Hitlerite Germany." The latter caution was subordinated to the Cold War aim of securing a neutral, albeit Western-friendly, Austria. The former identification provided the Second Austrian Republic with a foundational myth, and delayed what the German language calls *Vergangenheitsbewaeltigung*—coming to terms with the past. That confrontation with the past—inconclusive as it proved to be—occurred during the presidential campaign of Kurt Waldheim in 1986. Waldheim, secretary-general of the United Nations from 1971 to 1981, had returned to Austria to seek the largely ceremonial office of president as a capstone to a long diplomatic career. Instead, the Austrian weekly *Profil,* The *New York Times,* and the World Jewish Congress published information that disproved Waldheim's account of those years—that his military service spanned the years 1941–1942, ending when he was wounded on the Eastern front, at which time he returned to the University of Vienna as a law student. In fact, Waldheim had returned to military service in 1942 and was a member of Army Group E, charged with carrying out the de-

portation of Jews from Greece and operations against Yugoslav partisans.

Legal judgments of a Nuremberg tribunal stating that officers of Waldheim's rank were not criminally liable for activities carried out by Group E, and the judgment of commentators that his affiliation with Nazi student groups owed more to opportunism than to conviction, proved insignificant in the face of the resulting international furor. Waldheim's own defense, that he had merely "done his duty," echoed earlier discussions in Germany about collective guilt, and followed directly upon the 1985 "Bitburg Affair"—President Ronald Reagan's and Chancellor Helmut Kohl's visit to a military cemetery where SS officers were interred. Waldheim's supporters complained of an international [Jewish] "campaign." In the United States many saw Waldheim's election as evidence of an unrepentant fascist nation. In 1987 the U.S. Justice Department placed the president on a "watch list" and barred him from entering the country. If anything, international opinion against the president only strengthened Waldheim's standing in Austria, but the episode did occasion public discussion of what had long been taboo or ignored. Waldheim served only one term, leaving office in 1992. By then Austria was occupied with a dramatically changed situation in Central and Eastern Europe: the fall of communism in Eastern Europe, the Balkan Wars of the 1990s, and its own pending admission to the European Union in 1995. These new circumstances would bring to the fore another politician, Jörg Haider, since 1986 leader of the Freedom Party (FPOe).

The FPOe's origins can be traced to the 1949 League of Independents, or VdU. This "third camp" provided a political home to everyone not a member of the two dominant parties: the Social Democrats (SPOe) and the Peoples Party (OeVP). It thus embraced a wide range of views, from free-market liberals to populists to former Nazis, and enjoyed the tacit support (before 1955) of the U.S. occupation administration as well as leaders of the Volkspartei, who saw it as a coalition partner. By 1955/1956 the VdU had evolved into the Freedom Party. Its importance was relatively short-lived, however. FPOe disillusionment with the OeVP, a vacuum in its leadership, and the long SPOe domination under the chancellorship of Bruno Kreisky (1970–1983) all served to diminish its role until the late 1980s. While news media attention abroad would focus on Haider's praise of the full employment policies of the Nazis, or his remarks praising Wehrmacht veterans as men of character, within Austria Haider's popularity resulted from growing discontent with the long dominance of the two major parties. The SPOe and OeVP had presided over a consensus in Austria supportive of a generous welfare state, EU membership, an "Austrian Mission" that embraced the nation's neutral status in a continent divided by the Cold War (a position rendered irrelevant by the early 1990s), and a commitment to providing a "first haven" for refugees (a role that became increasingly burdensome with the dismantling of fortified borders in the East and the outbreak of the Balkan wars). The postwar era, moreover, had witnessed the transforming social forces of secularism, feminism, and urbanization, reminiscent of changes that had swept European society in the 1930s.

Haider's calls for strict limits on immigration, his anti-EU stance, and his opposition to generous social welfare benefits led many, at home and abroad, to see in the FPOe the ghosts of the 1930s and of fascism. Countering this is the argument that Haider and those of his ilk represent not a return to the past but a threat to a future Europe marked by a strong European Union as an ever more important player in a globalized world.

Laura Gellott

See Also: *ANSCHLUSS,* THE; ANTI-SEMITISM; AUSTRO-HUNGARIAN EMPIRE, THE; AUSTROFASCISM; CATHOLIC CHURCH, THE; CENTER PARTY, THE; CLERICO-FASCISM; COLD WAR, THE; CONCENTRATION CAMPS; CORPORATISM; DOLLFUSS, ENGELBERT; EDUCATION; EUROPE; EXPANSIONISM; FAMILY, THE; FEMINISM; GERMANNESS (*DEUTSCHHEIT*); GERMANY; GLOBALIZATION; HAIDER, JÖRG; HEIMWEHR, THE; HIMMLER, HEINRICH; HITLER, ADOLF; HOLY ROMAN EMPIRE, THE; ITALY; KALTENBRUNNER, ERNST; KORNEUBURG OATH, THE; LUEGER, KARL; MUSSOLINI, BENITO ANDREA; NAZISM; NUREMBERG TRIALS, THE; PANGERMANISM; PAPACY, THE; PAPEN, FRANZ VON; POLITICAL CATHOLICISM; PORTUGAL; POSTWAR FASCISM; SALAZAR, ANTÓNIO DE OLIVEIRA; SCHUSCHNIGG, KURT VON; SEYSS-INQUART, ARTHUR; SOCIALISM; SS, THE; SWASTIKA, THE; VERSAILLES, THE TREATY OF; WEHRMACHT, THE; WOMEN; WORLD WAR II; YOUTH

References

Bischof, Gunter, Anton Pelinka, and Alexander Lassner. 2003. *The Dollfuss/Schuschnigg Era in Austria: A Reassessment.* Contemporary Austrian Studies. Somerset, NJ: Transaction.
Botz, G. 1980. "The Changing Patterns of Social Support for Austrian National Socialism (1918–1945)." In *Who Were the Fascists?: Social Roots of European Fascism,* edited by J. Larsen, B. Haftvet, and J. Myklebust. Bergen: Universitetsforlaget.
Bukey, Evan Burr. 1986. *Hitler's Home Town: Linz, Austria, 1908–1945.* Bloomington: Indiana University Press.
Hoebelt, Lothar. 2003. *Defiant Populist: Joerg Haider and the Politics of Austria.* West Lafayette, IN: Purdue University Press.
Kitchen, Martin. 1980. *The Coming of Austrian Fascism.* Montreal: McGill Queens University Press.
Maas, Walter B. 1972. *Assassination in Vienna.* New York: Charles Scribner's Sons.
Mann, Michael. 2004. *Fascists.* Cambridge: Cambridge University Press.
Parkinson, F., ed. 1989. *Conquering the Past: Austrian Nazism Yesterday and Today.* Detroit: Wayne State University Press.
Pauley, Bruce. 1981. *Hitler and the Forgotten Nazis: A History of Austrian National Socialism.* Chapel Hill: University of North Carolina Press.

AUSTRO-HUNGARIAN EMPIRE/ HABSBURG EMPIRE, THE

Major political power in Central and Eastern Europe prior to the end of World War I, ruled by the Habsburg dynasty and regarded by Hitler, who lived within its borders in his youth, as embodying the decadence of his day: not only was it a multiracial polyglot empire but, in addition, it allowed far too much of a say to its Slav inhabitants and wielded too much power over its German minority. After 1918 the territories of the empire were partitioned among Italy, Czechoslovakia, Poland, Hungary, Romania, and Yugoslavia, with the Germanic rump remaining as the Republic of Austria. One of the dominant themes in Hitler's *Mein Kampf* is the unsatisfactory racial mixing and cohabitation of this "mongrel" empire, for which he had nothing but contempt. To him it represented the antithesis of the ideal of the greater Germany that he wished to create, freed of Jews—whose presence and wealth in Vienna he had bitterly resented—firmly and decisively ruled by Germans, and with Slavs reduced to the status of a source of slave labor.

Cyprian Blamires

See Also: AUSTRIA; CZECHOSLOVAKIA; GERMANNESS; HITLER, ADOLF; HUNGARY; ITALY; *MEIN KAMPF;* POLAND; ROMANIA; SLAVS, THE (AND GERMANY); SLAVS, THE (AND ITALY); VERSAILLES, THE TREATY OF; WORLD WAR I

References

Cornwall, Mark, ed. 2002. *The Last Years of Austria-Hungary: A Multi-national Experiment in Early Twentieth-century Europe.* Exeter: University of Exeter Press.
Jones, J. Sydney. 2002. *Hitler in Vienna, 1907–1913: Clues to the Future.* New York: Cooper Square.
Kershaw, I. 1998. *Hitler, 1889–1936: Hubris.* London: Allen Lane.
Watt, D. C. 1974. *Hitler's "Mein Kampf."* Trans. Ralph Mannheim. London: Hutchinson.

AUSTROFASCISM

A label frequently applied to the authoritarian system of government prevailing in Austria between 1934 and 1938; it is also sometimes referred to as "semi-fascism" or "imitation fascism," and some have seen it as a variety of "clerico-fascism" (qv). The term was actually used by defenders of the regime, but its appropriateness remains a subject of dispute among historians. Although they were certainly a dictatorship and incarcerated their opponents in special camps called *Anhaltelager,* and although they actually employed fascist symbols, the Dollfuss and Schuschnigg regimes lacked the typical mass basis of fascist parties. Dollfuss wanted to adopt only the outward trappings of fascism at a time when they were fashionable (and partly as a sop to a belligerent Nazi Germany) to cloak what was in reality an attempt to revive an authoritarian Catholic-conservative form of government.

Cyprian Blamires

See Also: AUSTRIA; CLERICO-FASCISM; DOLLFUSS, ENGELBERT; KORNEUBURG OATH, THE; SCHUSCHNIGG, KURT VON

References

Kitchen, Martin. 1983. *The Coming of Austrian Fascism.* Montreal: McGill-Queens University Press.
Linz, J. 2000. *Totalitarian and Authoritarian Regimes.* London: Lynne Rienner.

AUTARKY

The policy of economic self-sufficiency pursued by both Fascist Italy and Nazi Germany. While the ideological origins of the policy lay in both regimes' commitment to expansion and war, the circumstances of the Great Depression in Europe, which persuaded a number of powers, both dictatorial and democratic, to pursue protectionist trade policies, played an important role in encouraging autarky.

Arguably, the Italian Fascist regime first moved in the direction of autarky when Mussolini, in his "Pesaro Speech" of 1926, vowed to defend the value of the lira to the last drop of his blood. The "Battle for the Lira," the first of Mussolini's "economic battles," was as much a political as an economic policy. What was at stake in defending the lira at the parity of ninety to the pound sterling (its value when Fascism came to power) was the prestige of Mussolini and the regime, a positively Nietzschean battle for "the triumph of the will." But economically speaking it was expensive, and insofar as it overpriced Italian exports, it thus ensured that when the Great Depression hit Italy, its effects would be seriously felt. The "Battle for Grain," as a means of rectifying Italy's dependence upon expensive imports of wheat and other cereals, was another result of the Pesaro Speech. Like the "Demographic Battle," it was not a success.

The adoption of a more explicit policy of economic autarky was prompted by the Italo-Ethiopian War and the economic sanctions that the League of Nations imposed upon Italy as a result. In 1935 attempts were made to conserve currency holdings in preparation for war, and to purchase and stockpile necessary raw materials and machine tools. After the end of that war, more systematic attempts were made at import substitution by alternative domestic supplies or by artificial products, which resulted in the discovery of natural gas in the Po Valley region and in the development of textile and petrochemical industries. But such a policy inevitably had its limits in a country that had never been well endowed with natural resources. As Italy once more faced balance of payments problems in the late 1930s, the regime resorted to manufacturing cartels, tariff barriers, currency restrictions, and massive regulation of economic activity to plug the gap. Mussolini effectively admitted the failure of *autarkia* in 1939, when he cited Italy's massive shortfalls in crucial raw materials, energy resources, and military goods as his reason for not joining Nazi Germany in its war against Britain and France. Italy's subsequent disastrous experience of combat, following his declaration of war upon Britain and France in June 1940, confirmed the inefficacy of autarky as far as Fascist Italy was concerned.

The need to bring about recovery from the effects of the Great Depression clearly played a very important role in the development of economic policy after National Socialism came to power in Germany in 1933, including the withdrawal of Germany from various sectors of the world economy to avoid reparations payments. An early form of autarky was the establishment of the *Reichsnahrstand,* an institution bringing about the vertical organization of the agriculture and food industries under the *Blut und Boden* enthusiast Darré.

His explicit aim was to make Germany as far as possible self-sufficient in foodstuffs in order to avoid the consequences of the Allied blockade during World War I, which had caused huge food shortages and undermined the war effort.

Another major element in the Nazi policy of autarky was the creation in 1937 of the Reichswerke AG Herman Goering, a new, state-owned and -managed firm whose purpose was to exploit to the full all ores on German (and later Austrian) territory, even if not as high grade as imported ones, in order to make Germany self-sufficient in iron and steel. In the Goering-directed Four Year Plan, the development of ersatz products—synthetic rubber, oil, and so forth—played a key part. As well as domestic production targets, part and parcel of the plan was a system of controls on tariffs, exports, currency holdings, and cartelization in key industries very similar to the Italian regulations, but which provided a more effective instrument of state management of the economy for the purposes of rearmament and war.

In fact, when Germany eventually did go to war, measures of autarky played a less important role than the exploitation of the economic resources of the countries that German armies invaded and occupied between 1939 and 1942—resources including foodstuffs, ores, other metals, energy sources, manufactured goods, and forced labor, as well as the resources of neutrals like Switzerland and Spain. The overall shape of the German war economy, while not seriously diminishing the weight of private capitalism, certainly tended more and more toward a National Socialist form of the "war socialism" practiced by other belligerents, most notably Britain and the Soviet Union.

John Pollard

See Also: BANKS, THE; BLOOD AND SOIL; DARRE, RICHARD WALTHER; DEMOGRAPHIC POLICY; ECONOMICS; ETHIOPIA; FASCIST PARTY, THE; FORCED LABOR; GERMANY; INDUSTRY; INFLATION; ITALY; LEAGUE OF NATIONS, THE; MUSSOLINI, BENITO ANDREA; NATIONALISM; NIETZSCHE, FRIEDRICH; PERONISM; SOCIALISM; TRADE; WALL STREET CRASH, THE; WORLD WAR II

References
Cannistraro, P. V. 1982. *Historical Dictionary of Fascist Italy.* Westport, CT: Greenwood
Noakes, J., and G. Pridham, eds. 1984. *Nazism, 1919–1945.* Vol. 2: *State, Economy and Society, 1933–1939.* Exeter: Exeter University Press.
Overy, R. 1994. *War and Economy in the Third Reich.* Oxford: Oxford University Press.
Pollard, J. F. 1999. *The Fascist Experience in Italy.* London: Routledge.

AUTHORITARIAN PERSONALITY, THE: See FROMM, ERICH; PSYCHOANALYSIS; PSYCHOLOGY; SOCIOLOGY; REICH, WILHELM

AUTHORITARIANISM

Fascism and *authoritarianism* are often treated as virtually interchangeable terms in common parlance, and early students of fascism like Arendt and Wilhelm Reich often focused their attention on the flagrant abuse of power in fascist regimes. This approach was particularly influenced by research in the field of psychology. However, as Arendt herself saw, authoritarianism was not a trait peculiar to fascism, for the same phenomenon was observable in the Soviet Union. Hence the coining of the term *totalitarian* to apply to the dictatorial regimes of the interwar era. It might perhaps be argued that whereas communist ideologues at least *claimed* to be promoting egalitarianism and the liberation of the world's poor from tyrannical oppression by a minority, and that they were therefore authoritarian "by accident" rather than by design, their fascist counterparts had no qualms about advocating a hierarchical authoritarian society as a permanent feature of their utopia. But although that could be taken to distinguish fascism from communism, it does not distinguish it from traditional conservatism, which also takes a hierarchical authoritarian social order as a given for all time, eschewing egalitarianism as a damaging pipedream. An excessive focus on the authoritarian nature of fascist thought and action in fact made it more difficult in the decades after World War II to understand the novelty and uniqueness of the phenomenon of fascism, which certainly does not reside in some uniquely "authoritarian" feature of its worldview.

Cyprian Blamires

See Also: INTRODUCTION; ARENDT, HANNAH; CONSERVATISM; DICTATORSHIP; EGALITARIANISM; MILITARY DICTATORSHIP; PSYCHOANALYSIS; PSYCHOLOGY; REICH, WILHELM; TOTALITARIANISM; UTOPIA

References
Blinkhorn, M. 2001. *Fascism and the Right in Europe, 1919–1945.* Harlow: Longman.

———, ed. 1990. *Fascists and Conservatives.* London: Unwin Hyman.

Germani, Gino. 1978. *Authoritarianism, National Populism, and Fascism.* Piscataway, NJ: Transaction.

Linz, J. 2000. *Totalitarian and Authoritarian Regimes.* London: Lynne Rienner.

AUTOBAHNS, THE

System of German motor roads, often considered to be one of the Nazis' greatest achievements. In fact, however, several associations in Germany had already developed plans for motor roads in the 1920s, but those projects did not materialize, mainly for economic reasons. Before its rise to power, the NSDAP had actually been quite ambivalent about the issue: as mass motorization was still in its beginnings, sections of the party saw *Autobahnen* as a superfluous luxury for the privileged. Only weeks after his rise to power, Hitler nevertheless announced a large *Autobahnen* program. On 27 June 1933, a law was passed to build up a special agency for this purpose. Head of the organization was the *Generalinspekteur für das deutsche Straßenwesen,* Fritz Todt (1891–1942). On 19 May 1935 the first stretch—from Frankfurt to Darmstadt—was opened. By mid-1936 some 125,000 workers were employed on the *Reichsautobahnen,* the highest number ever during the Third Reich. By the end of 1938, 3,000 kilometers had been completed. During World War II, POWs and forced laborers, Jewish and otherwise, were put to work on the *Autobahnen,* but the whole project lost priority because of the war effort. By the end of 1941 all the construction sites had been closed. By then, 3,870 kilometers had been completed, and another 3,000 kilometers were under construction.

The *Autobahnen* did not have a primarily military motivation, as is sometimes suggested: before 1939, those considerations did not play a large role. Also, the contribution of the *Autobahnen* in the fight against the Great Depression should not be overestimated. Their relevance for German traffic was not very significant either: in 1935, for example, only 16 out of 1,000 Germans owned a car (in the United States, it was 204 out of every 1,000). All in all, the "the Fuehrer's roads" (an expression popularized by Todt) primarily played a cultural and symbolic role as expressions of the regime's self-stylization. This is clearly reflected in Hitler's *Table Talk,* in which he speaks frequently about his love for fast cars on the open road (Mussolini's equivalent passion being for flying). Despite their economic, military, and ecological shortcomings, as well as their low significance for German traffic at the time, they became the most successful propaganda product of the Reich and a reminder that Hitler, like Mussolini, was unabashedly at home with modern technology and had no time for those fascist propagandists who wanted to promote rural values. Mythologized while still under construction, the autobahns are praised by neo-Nazis and other apologists of the regime even today.

Kiran Patel

See Also: ECONOMICS; EMPLOYMENT; FORCED LABOR; GERMANY; HITLER, ADOLF; INDUSTRY; LEADER CULT, THE; MODERNITY; NAZISM; PROPAGANDA; RURALISM; STYLE; TECHNOLOGY

References
Overy, Richard. 1995. "Cars, Roads, and Economic Recovery in Germany, 1932–1938." Pp. 68–89 in *War and Economy in the Third Reich,* edited by Overy. Oxford: Clarendon.

Schütz, Erhard, and Eckhard Gruber. 1996. *Mythos Reichsautobahn: Bau und Inszenierung der "Straßen des Führers" 1933–1941.* Berlin: Ch. Links.

Shand, J. D. 1984. "The *Reichsautobahn:* Symbol of the New Reich." *Journal of Contemporary History* 19, no. 2, pp. 189–200.

Zeller, Thomas. 2002. *Straße, Bahn, Panorama: Verkehrswege und Landschaftsveränderung in Deutschland von 1930 bis 1990.* Frankfurt: Campus.

AVENTINE SECESSION, THE

Expression of protest against Mussolini's regime on the part of members of the Chamber of Deputies from various parties. In June 1924, soon after the kidnapping of Matteotti by Fascists, 150 or so deputies withdrew together from the chamber and declared themselves to be the only true representatives of the Italian people, calling for the overthrow of the regime. Most of them were committed to constitutional means and hoped for support from King Victor Emmanuel III, but it was not forthcoming. Participants in the protest drifted away from the movement for various reasons, but after Mussolini assumed dictatorial powers in January 1925, they were left powerless; in 1926, Mussolini declared all the Aventine deputies stripped of their seats. The name

"Aventine"—after one of the hills of Rome—echoed the protest of Gaius Gracchus under the ancient Republic of Rome.

Cyprian Blamires

See Also: ANTIFASCISM; FASCIST PARTY, THE; ITALY; LIBER-ALISM; MATTEOTTI, GIACOMO; MUSSOLINI, BENITO AN-DREA; PARLIAMENTARISM; VICTOR EMMANUEL/VITTORIO EMANUELE III, KING

Reference
De Grand, A. 2000. *Italian Fascism: Its Origins and Development.* London: University of Nebraska Press.

AXIS, THE

Name for the German-Italian alliance sealed in May 1939, later expanded with the entry of Japan. Japan signed on to a tripartite axis in September 1940 when the German occupation of France and The Netherlands made French Indochina and the Dutch East Indies obvious targets for a Japanese takeover. Japan needed the backing of Germany in particular because of the danger of U.S. intervention in the event of Japan's pursing an expansionist policy in the areas. In March 1941, Hitler promised German support in any war with the United States and honored his pledge after Pearl Harbor.

The relationship between Hitler and Mussolini effectively began in the autumn of 1936, but it became a full offensive military alliance only in May 1939. (It was widened by the Anti-Comintern Pact, formally including Japan in 1937). Until the spring of 1936, relations between the two fascist dictators had been cool. Mussolini had been concerned about the potential threat to the independence of Austria posed by a resurgent Germany committed to *Anschluss;* he saw Austria as an indispensable buffer on Italy's northern frontier. In July 1934, when Austrian Nazis murdered the Austrian chancellor Dollfuss, Mussolini sent troops to the Brenner frontier with Austria to warn off Hitler. In May 1935, he even signed the Stresa agreement with Britain and France against Germany.

The situation changed dramatically after the Italian invasion of Ethiopia in October 1935, when the League of Nations imposed economic sanctions on Italy. This threw Mussolini into Hitler's arms. The outbreak of the Spanish Civil war in July 1936, in which both fascist states intervened on the side of Franco, strengthened the new relationship. Mussolini talked of a "Rome-Berlin Axis" around which, he declared, politics in Europe would henceforth gravitate. The Axis was strengthened by Mussolini's visit to Berlin in 1937, when he renounced his "protectorate" over Austria. Thus, in March 1938 he did not protest when Hitler annexed Austria.

In May 1939, Mussolini's foreign minister, Ciano, signed the "Pact of Steel" with his German counterpart, committing Italy to an offensive alliance with its Axis partner. Although Mussolini and Ciano did not yet abandon negotiations with Britain and France, the pact demonstrates that Mussolini believed that only through an alliance with Nazi Germany would he be able to defeat Britain and France and wrest from them the territories that would constitute his much-vaunted "second Roman Empire." For his part, Hitler envisaged the pact as a diplomatic move, a way of keeping the Italians out of the clutches of the democratic powers, rather than one of military significance. Despite the pact, Mussolini did not join Hitler when Britain and France declared war upon Germany in September 1939. Offended by the Soviet-German Non-Aggression Pact, fearing that Hitler had bitten off more than he could chew, and conscious that Italian public opinion was against war, he declared that Italy would remain "non-belligerent," as he described it. But after Hitler's victories against Scandinavia, the Low Countries, and France in the Blitzkrieg, Mussolini became impatient to get in at the kill and declared war on Britain and France on 10 June, 1940. He pursued a "parallel war" to that of the Germans as a means of keeping them out of Italian spheres of influence. But the overstretching of already inadequate Italian economic and military resources and abysmal strategic decisions on Mussolini's part led to defeats in Egypt and Greece that brought the Germans into the Mediterranean. Mussolini worsened Italy's strategic situation in the summer of 1941 by insisting on sending an Italian division to support the Germans on the Eastern Front. In December 1941, following the Japanese attack on Pearl Harbor, Mussolini joined Hitler in gratuitously declaring war on the United States. Following Mussolini's overthrow in July 1943 and the Allied invasion of Italy, Hitler was forced to divert resources from the campaign against Russia inaugurated in June 1943. It is therefore arguable that Hitler's alliance with Mussolini ultimately contributed to his defeat in 1945.

The Axis was briefly revived following Mussolini's rescue by Skorzeny and the restoration of his regime in the form of the Salò Republic in September 1943. But in the words of Deakin, it was by now a "brutal friendship." Mussolini's restored Fascist state was essentially a puppet of Nazi Germany; Italy was under SS-Gestapo control, and a substantial part of northeastern Italy, Kustenland, was directly ruled by the German occupying authorities. The final humiliation was that in April 1945 the German authorities in Italy negotiated surrender to the advancing Allies behind Mussolini's back.

John Pollard

See Also: *ANSCHLUSS,* THE; ANTI-COMINTERN PACT, THE; AUSTRIA; BLITZKRIEG; CIANO, COUNT GALEAZZO; DOLLFUSS, ENGELBERT; ETHIOPIA; FRANCE; FRANCO Y BAHA MONDE, GENERAL FRANCISCO; GERMANY; GESTAPO, THE; HITLER, ADOLF; HITLER-STALIN PACT, THE; ITALY; JAPAN AND WORLD WAR II; LEAGUE OF NATIONS, THE; MUSSOLINI, BENITO ANDREA; NETHERLANDS, THE; PEARL HARBOR; ROME; SALÒ REPUBLIC, THE; SKORZENY, OTTO; SPANISH CIVIL WAR, THE; SS, THE; WORLD WAR II

References

Deakin, W. 1962. *The Brutal Friendship: Mussolini, Hitler and the Fall of Italian Fascism.* Harmondsworth: Penguin.

Pollard, J. F. 1998. *The Fascist Experience in Italy.* London: Routledge.

Wiskemann, Elizabeth. 1966. *The Rome-Berlin Axis: A Study of the Relations between Mussolini and Hitler.* London: Collins.

BA'ATHISM: *See* BA'THISM

BADOGLIO, PIETRO
(1871–1956)

Chief of staff of the Italian army, governor of Libya, and then Emilio de Bono's replacement to spearhead the invasion of Ethiopia in 1936. Born in the province of Asti, Badoglio pursued a military career and rose to the rank of general during World War I. His war record was not untarnished, as he carried some responsibility for the catastrophic defeat at Caporetto in 1917. Initially he opposed Mussolini, and the latter marginalized him by appointing him ambassador to Brazil. By 1924, however, he had reconciled himself to the regime and was appointed army chief of staff. After his success in capturing the Ethiopian capital, he was given the title of Duke of Addis Ababa. He resigned his army position in December 1940.

On 25 July 1943, King Victor Emmanuel III appointed Badoglio to replace Mussolini as head of government. Badoglio declared a state of martial law, had his former chief arrested, and opened peace negotiations with the Allies. The aggressive response to this by the German army obliged the new government to take refuge first in Pescara and then in Brindisi and to avail itself of the protection of the Allies. Badoglio signed Italy's surrender papers on 23 September 1943, and his government declared war on Germany on 13 October. In June 1944 he was dismissed and replaced as head of government by Ivanoe Bonomi.

Cyprian Blamires

See Also: CAPORETTO; ETHIOPIA; ITALY; LIBYA; MUSSOLINI, BENITO ANDREA; SALÒ REPUBLIC, THE; VICTOR EMMANUEL/VITTORIO EMANUELE III; WORLD WAR II

References
Badoglio, P. 1976. *Italy in the Second World War: Memories and Documents.* Westport, CT: Greenwood.
Cannistraro, Philip V. 1982. *Historical Dictionary of Fascist Italy.* Westport, CT: Greenwood.

BAEUMLER, ALFRED
(1887–1968)

German philosopher and art historian, one of the leading academic advocates of National Socialism, to which he remained loyal until its collapse in 1945. Baeumler studied languages and art history in Munich from 1908, later applying himself with increasing enthusiasm to the study of Kant, upon whom he wrote his doctoral thesis in 1914. At the end of World War I, Baeumler gradually fell under the spell of the so-called conservative revolution; he read Thomas Mann and Oswald Spengler. He put his ideas into writing in *Metaphysik und Geschichte (Metaphysics and History)* in 1920. Baeumler was promoted to professor at the Technical University of Dresden in 1924. Around 1930 he drew nearer to National Socialism, confirming his commitment by joining the NSDAP following the elections in March 1933. Baeumler's lifelong veneration for Nietzsche was echoed in his National Socialist writings. He politicized and nationalized Nietzsche's "Will to Power," by reinterpreting it to apply to the political science of a Germanic hegemonic Reich. He was the most influential commentator on Nietzsche as a "proto-Nazi," presenting him as a prophet of National Socialism in spite of Nietzsche's open rejection of anti-Semitism and avowed distaste for nationalism.

In 1933, Baeumler was appointed to the newly created chair of political pedagogy at the University of Berlin. In his inaugural address he called for the burning of books considered antithetical to the Nazi philosophy, and that actually took place on the same day all over Germany. Baeumler's Germanism was constitutive for his thinking: its features were "honor" as the highest value, the heroic affirmation of "life" as a struggle, the Fuehrer principle, and the "instinct" of the "Nordic" man in opposition to rationalism. Baeumler's anti-Semitism was closely connected with his anticommunism. In his essay "The Jew in German Intellectual History: Karl Marx" (1944), Baeumler arrived at the conclusion that "the Jew" is merely parasitic and not capable of real intellectual productivity. Baeumler's concept of race was based upon his assumption that the "Germanic race" in its efforts toward superiority was subject only to a general "rule of life." At the same time it must be kept "pure" of foreign elements. After the war Baeumler was interned in camps for three years. In his hearing in front of the Denazification Committee, Baeumler was initially classified as "tainted," but after an appeal he was later reclassified as "untainted" and thereby acquitted.

Susanne Pocai

See Also: ANTI-SEMITISM; BOOKS, THE BURNING OF THE; CIVILIZATION; DENAZIFICATION; GERMANIC RELIGION, THE; GERMANNESS; *GLEICHSCHALTUNG;* HEIDEGGER, MARTIN; LEADER PRINCIPLE, THE; NAZISM; NIETZSCHE, FRIEDRICH; NORDIC SOUL, THE; RACIAL DOCTRINE; ROSENBERG, ALFRED; SOCIAL DARWINISM; SPENGLER, OSWALD; UNIVERSITIES; VITALISM; *VOLK, VÖLKISCH*

References
Brinton, Crane. "The National Socialists' Use of Nietzsche." *Journal of the History of Ideas,* vol. 1 (1940): 131–150.
Giesecke, Hermann. 1993. *Hitlers Pädagogen. Theorie und Praxis nationalsozialistischer Erziehung.* München: Juventa.
Kuenzli, Rudolf E. "The Nazi Appropriation of Nietzsche." *Nietzsche Studien* 12 (1983): 428–435.
Mosse, George L. 1981. *Nazi Culture: Intellectual, Cultural and Social Life in the Third Reich.* New York: Schocken.
Strong, Tracy B. "Nietzsche's Political Misappropriations." In *The Cambridge Companion to Nietzsche,* edited by Bernd Magnus and Kathleen M. Higgins. Cambridge: Cambridge University Press.
Woods, Roger. 1996. *The Conservative Revolution in the Weimar Republic.* London: Macmillan.

BALBO, ITALO (1896–1940)

One of the founders of *squadrismo*. After taking part in World War I as an officer, Balbo helped to lead the March on Rome as a "quadrumvir." In 1929 he became minister of aviation. A passionate flyer, in 1931 and 1933 he organized two transatlantic flights from Europe to Brazil and the United States. Thanks to these adventures he became the most popular Fascist leader in Italy and the world after Mussolini. In 1934 he went to Libya as governor general, demonstrating great organizational capacities in that office. He unsuccessfully opposed the anti-Semitic legislation of 1938 and the military alliance with Germany. He died on 28 June 1940, a few days after Italy's entry into the war: in the course of a reconnaissance flight his plane was shot down by Italian antiaircraft forces by mistake.

Alessandro Campi (translated by Cyprian Blamires)

See Also: FASCIST PARTY, THE; ITALY; LIBYA; MUSSOLINI, BENITO ANDREA; QUADRUMVIRS, THE; *SQUADRISMO;* WORLD WAR I

References
Cannistraro, Philip, ed. 1982. *Historical Dictionary of Fascist Italy.* Westport, CT: Greenwood.
Segré, C. 1987. *Italo Balbo: A Fascist Life.* London: University of California Press.

BALILLA: See YOUTH MOVEMENTS (ITALY)

BANKS, THE

It is clear that the collapse of the banking system in Central Europe in 1931 had a catalytic effect on the growth of fascism. Within two years Hitler was in power in Germany, and in Austria, with the demise of Credit Anstalt, foreign investment ceased; Dollfuss became chancellor in 1932, and the drift toward "Austro-fascism" had begun. We can see the same pattern in Italy. Banks such as Credito Italiano, Banca Commerciale, and the Bank of Italy suffered as part of the post-1918 economic malaise; they carried the can as firms went bust and repayment schedules went out of the window. When Mussolini arrived in power he was quick to throw a lifeline to key organizations, most famously Banca Italiana di Sconto and the (Catholic) Banco di Roma. That became the fascists' policy across the board—propping up down-on-their-luck financial institutions.

In the same period, it is apparent that Hitler in particular saw bankers, banks, and banking as part of a multilayered "antinational conspiracy." As early as April 1921, he attributed the desperate state of Germany's economy to those who had profited by her collapse, noting that "Banks and Stock Exchanges are more flourishing than ever before."

When we assess the reality of fascism in power, we must conclude that the banking sector was subject to enormous control. This was not socialist "nationalization" or "collectivization" but simply control. Hitler was keen to emphasize the distinction here. In a letter to Herman Rauschning, he declared: "Let them [those on the left] own land or factories as much as they please. The decisive factor is that the State, through the Party, is supreme over them regardless of whether they are owners or workers. All that is unessential; our [national] socialism goes far deeper. It establishes a relationship of the individual to the State, the national community. Why need we trouble to socialize banks and factories? We socialize human beings." In Italy private banks were taken over and heavily regulated. In 1931 the Italian Fascist regime established the Istituto Mobiliare to control and manage credit; later on, the Institute for Industrial Reconstruction (IRI) acquired all shares previously held by banks in industrial, agricultural, and real estate enterprises. And it was the IRI's task to take on the work of the formerly private banks in fostering industrial development. In

this way the banking system evolved and survived, and by 1939 the IRI controlled the key companies in the key sectors: steel, shipping, construction, and communications. It could be argued plausibly that Mussolini's dealings with the banking sector were quite successful.

There is also a sense in which the banks and key individuals within the banking sector in certain countries became involved in the fascist "project"—perhaps even as "silent partners." Mussolini surrounded himself with financiers and bankers, including Count Giuseppe Volpi, a man who emerged as one of the most prominent finance ministers of the Fascist era. We also know that Deutsche Bank benefited considerably, in a financial sense, from Nazi patronage. That said, we must also note that in countries like Norway, which was invaded by the Germans and then became subject to Nazi diktats, the national bank was shorn of all its assets by Hitler's agents.

The relationship between fascism and the banking sector did not end with the end of the fascist era. The postwar years have been littered with unsavory scandals in which specific financial institutions have been accused of inappropriate links with fascist governments. In 1999, for example, a French government commission, investigating the seizure of Jewish bank accounts during World War II, stated that five U.S. banks—Chase Manhattan, J.P. Morgan, Guaranty Trust Co. of New York, Bank of the City of New York, and American Express—had taken part. It stated that their Paris branches had handed over to the Nazi occupiers about one hundred such accounts. At the time this occurred, the United States was not at war with Germany, and the U.S. banks could have behaved differently. Moreover, the Nazis stashed millions of U.S. dollars' worth of assets, gold, and bonds belonging to Europe's Jews in Swiss bank accounts during the war. Reportedly, 76 percent of Nazi gold transactions went through Switzerland and the volume of trade between Swiss private banks and wartime Germany was very substantial. Swiss commercial banks bought $61.2 million worth of gold during the Nazi era, the value of which (at rates applying in the late 1990s) would be more than $700 million. The Swiss National Bank, SNB, acquired $389.2 million, worth more than $4 billion at today's prices. The SNB had previously admitted to buying 1.2 billion Swiss francs' worth of gold. The Bergier commission accused the Nazis of stealing $146 million in gold from Holocaust victims, including at least $2.5 million seized by the SS from inmates of Auschwitz and other death camps in Eastern Europe.

And as a postscript, we should note the fact that in July 2004, Barclays Bank shut down various accounts held by the British National Party. Reuters stated: "Barclays is closing accounts held by the far-right BNP after the BBC filmed party members saying they had assaulted Muslims."

P J Davies

See Also: AUSCHWITZ; AUSTRIA; AUSTROFASCISM; AUTARKY; BRITISH NATIONAL PARTY, THE; CONSPIRACY THEORIES; DOLLFUSS, ENGELBERT; ECONOMICS; FARMERS; FASCIST PARTY, THE; FINANCE; HITLER, ADOLF; HOLOCAUST, THE; INDUSTRY; MUSSOLINI, BENITO ANDREA; NAZISM; RAUSCHNING, HERMANN; SS, THE; STATE, THE; SWITZERLAND; WALL STREET CRASH, THE

References

James, H. 2004. *The Nazi Dictatorship and the Deutsche Bank.* Cambridge: Cambridge University Press.

James, H., H. Lindgren, and A. Teichova eds. 2002. *The Role of Banks in the Interwar Economy.* Cambridge: Cambridge University Press.

LeBor, Adam. 1997. *Hitler's Secret Bankers: The Myth of Swiss Neutrality during the Holocaust.* Secaucus, NJ: Birch Lane.

Milward, Alan S. 1972. *The Fascist Economy in Norway.* London: OUP.

Vincent, I. 1997. *Hitler's Silent Partners: Swiss Banks, Nazi Gold, and the Pursuit of Justice.* New York: William Morrow.

Whittam, J. 1995. *Fascist Italy.* Manchester: Manchester University Press.

BARBAROSSA, FREDERICK, HOLY ROMAN EMPEROR (ca. 1123–1190)

One of the historical models whose example was prized by Hitler, who used his name as a codeword for the launch of his Russian campaign in 1941—Operation Barbarossa. Considered one of the greatest German monarchs, Frederick engaged in an ongoing struggle with the papacy to assert his rights as emperor on the throne of Charlemagne. He died while on Crusade in Cilicia, but legend had it that he had actually gone to the east in search of the roots of his tribe and of the wonder-working relic known as the grail, a theme taken up by Richard Wagner in his writings. It was said that one day he would return to revive Germany's greatness.

Cyprian Blamires

See Also: BARBAROSSA, OPERATION; HITLER, ADOLF; HOLY ROMAN EMPIRE, THE; *MEIN KAMPF;* WAGNER, (WILHELM) RICHARD; WEHRMACHT, THE; WORLD WAR II

BARBAROSSA, OPERATION

Hitler's code name for his invasion of the Soviet Union, launched on 22 June 1941. It was the greatest military conflict of the modern era and the greatest land invasion in the history of modern warfare. It was also one of the greatest betrayals of history, since Stalin had obviously believed that Hitler's commitment to the Hitler-Stalin Pact was genuine. Placed under the aegis of the great German medieval emperor Frederick Barbarossa, it was intended to signal Hitler's determination to assert German imperium over Slavdom. It was also meant to demonstrate the superiority of the Germans, members of the master race, over the Slavs, considered in Nazi racial theory to be *Untermenschen*—"subhumans." Special orders were given as to the treatment of captured Russians and Russian civilians, for whom the normal rules of war were not to apply.

Cyprian Blamires

See Also: BARBAROSSA, FREDERICK, HOLY ROMAN EMPEROR; HITLER, ADOLF; HITLER-STALIN PACT, THE; *MEIN KAMPF;* RACIAL DOCTRINE; SLAVS, THE (AND GERMANY); SOVIET UNION, THE; STALIN, IOSIF VISSARIONOVICH; *UNTERMENSCHEN;* WEHRMACHT, THE; WORLD WAR II

References

Glantz, David. 2003. *Before Stalingrad: Hitler's Invasion of Russia, 1941.* Stroud: Tempus.

Overy, Richard. 1999. *Russia's War.* London: Penguin.

BARBIE, KLAUS (1913–1991)

Notorious as the "Butcher of Lyons" for his brutal "cleansing" of Lyons during the German occupation and for his belated trial in Lyons in the late 1980s (which made him the focus of intense news media interest), Barbie was born in Bad Godesberg on the Rhine, the son of two Catholic schoolteachers. In 1925 the family moved to Trier. He developed a particular hatred for the French because he believed that his father's death (in 1933) had resulted from a war wound received at the Battle of Verdun. In 1935 he joined the SD, and in 1937 he was assigned, along with his unit, the task of "cleansing" Berlin of its population of Jews, homosexuals, and "undesirables." In April 1940 he became a second lieutenant in the SS. He subsequently earned a reputation for extreme brutality, even by SS standards, in the "purging" of Amsterdam's Jewish population. Transferred to Lyons to carry out a similar task in 1943, Barbie deported huge numbers of Jews to the death camps and had many French civilians thought to be complicit with the Resistance put to death. Among those he executed was the French Resistance hero Jean Moulin, and his achievement in dealing with Moulin resulted in an award from Hitler himself. After the war, Barbie was taken under the wing of the U.S. Counterintelligence Corps and enabled to escape to Latin America. He was sentenced to death in absentia by a French court but, although identified under his alias in Bolivia in 1971, he was not extradited to France until 1983. In 1987 he was given a life sentence, and he died in prison in 1991.

Cyprian Blamires

See Also: ANTI-SEMITISM; ASOCIALS; BOLIVIA; CONCENTRATION CAMPS; FRANCE; HOLOCAUST, THE; HOMOSEXUALITY; ODESSA; SD, THE; SS, THE

Reference
Bower, T. 1984. *Klaus Barbie: The Butcher of Lyons.* London: Michael Joseph.

BARDECHE, MAURICE (1909–1998)

Although only a minor figure as a French prewar fascist, contributing from 1938 to the fascist newspaper *Je Suis Partout,* Bardèche (brother-in-law of Robert Brasillach) was prominent as a postwar French neofascist. He wrote a series of key texts aimed at legitimating prewar fascism (notably *Lettre à François Mauriac,* 1947) and Holocaust denial (*Nuremberg ou la Terre promise,* 1948), and promoting neofascism (*Qu'est-ce que le fascisme?,* 1961)—the first time that a member of the French far Right had dared proclaim himself explicitly fascist. He also promoted the work of other neofascists through management of the publishing house Les Sept Couleurs and his direction of the journal *Défense de*

l'Occident from its foundation in 1952 until December 1982. He co-founded the Mouvement Social Européen (European Social Movement) in 1951 with Mosley, Priester, and Engdahl, serving as its vice president; and he was involved in the Comité national français (French National Committee) with René Binet.

Steve Bastow

See Also: BRASILLACH, ROBERT; FRANCE; HOLOCAUST DENIAL; MOSLEY, SIR OSWALD; POSTWAR FASCISM; SWEDEN

References
Barnes, I. 2000. "Antisemitic Europe and the 'Third Way': The Ideas of Maurice Bardèche." Pp. 57–73 in *Patterns of Prejudice,* vol. 34, no. 2, April 2000.
Barnes, I. 2002. "I Am a Fascist Writer: Maurice Bardèche—Ideologist and Defender of French Fascism." Pp. 195–209 in *the European Legacy,* vol. 7, no 2, April 2002.

BARMEN DECLARATION, THE: *See* CONFESSING CHURCH, THE; LUTHERAN CHURCHES, THE

BARRES, AUGUSTE MAURICE (1862–1923)

French writer, journalist, and politician whose work is seen by some commentators as producing an ideological fusion of nationalism and socialism that fed into the development of fascist ideology. Barrès's family had to flee from Prussian troops during the Franco-Prussian War of 1870–1871, and this inspired in him a desire for revenge over Germany and a love for his native Lorraine. Educated in the law faculty at Nancy from 1880, he moved to Paris in 1882, where he became known as a symbolist and a decadent. In 1888 he published the first volume of his trilogy *Le culte du moi,* articulating an extreme individualism in which the self is the only reality. Boulangism, however, made him aware of the realities of the wider national community. Barrès successfully stood for parliament on 22 September 1889 in Nancy on a left boulangist platform in which anti-Semitism was used as the ideological nodal point unifying elements of socialism and nationalism (though he failed to get reelected in 1893). Over the next few years he developed his doctrine of *la terre et les morts,* in which he argued that the individual "I" is supported and fed by society: "I have been an individualist. . . . I have preached the development of the personality by a certain discipline of internal meditation and analysis. Having for a long time looked deeply into the idea of the 'Me' with the sole method of poets and novelists, by internal observation, I descended . . . to find at the bottom, and for support, the collectivity" (cited in Girardet 1983, 185–186). This identification of the "me" with the nation leads to an emphasis on rootedness, as revealed in his novel *Les déracinés,* published in 1897 as the first novel in a new trilogy, the *Roman de l'Energie nationale.*

In 1889, Barrès was a founding member of the Ligue de la Patrie Française (League for the French Fatherland), serving on its executive committee from 1899 to 1901. In May 1898 he failed to be elected in Nancy, this time on the list of a National Socialist Republican Committee. He was finally re-elected MP in 1906, in Paris, but only as a consequence of having abandoned the anti-Dreyfusards. He remained in parliament until 1923, growing progressively more conservative and abandoning his antiparliamentarism.

The importance of Barrès's thought lies in the claim that it was an intellectual precursor of fascism. Sternhell, for example, argues that in Barrès's thought could be seen a break with traditional conservatism, announcing a new discourse of the Right that prefigured the rise of fascism. Barrès, he claims, "waged a Nietzschean struggle against the French Enlightenment, Cartesian rationalism, the Kantian categorical imperative, the rights of man, liberal democracy, the idea of progress, and democratic education," fusing this with a historical, cultural, and racial determinism completely foreign to Nietzsche.

Steve Bastow

See Also: ACTION FRANÇAISE; ANTI-SEMITISM; BOULANGISM; CONSERVATISM; DEMOCRACY; DREYFUS CASE, THE; ENLIGHTENMENT, THE; FRANCE; INDIVIDUALISM; INTEGRAL NATIONALISM; MAURRAS, CHARLES; NATIONALISM; NIETZSCHE, FRIEDRICH; PARLIAMENTARISM; PROGRESS; PROTOFASCISM; RATIONALISM; ROOTLESSNESS; SOCIALISM; TRADITION

References
Carroll, D. 1995. *French Literary Fascism.* Princeton: Princeton University Press.
Girardet, R. 1983. *Le nationalisme français. Anthologie 1871–1914.* Paris: Seuil.
Soucy, R. 1972. *Fascism in France: The Case of Maurice Barrès.* Berkeley: University of California Press.
Sternhell, Ze'ev. 1972. *Maurice Barrès et le nationalisme français.* Paris: Armand Colin.
———. 1978. *La droite révolutionnaire: Les origines françaises du fascisme.* Paris: Seuil.

Weber, E. 1962. *Action Française: Royalism and Reaction in Twentieth Century France.* Palo Alto, CA: Stanford University Press.

BARTH, KARL: See THEOLOGY

BATAILLE, GEORGES (1897–1962)

Author of *The Psychological Structure of Fascism,* French avant-garde intellectual of the interwar and postwar periods whose work on transgression in a number of domains (economics, philosophy, eroticism) has been very influential on French theory. Bataille was the co-founder in 1935, with André Breton, of the antifascist group Contre-Attaque (Counter-attack). His attempt to use this group to counter fascism with equal force, organizing a "parallel mobilization" that would liberate rather than subjugate the masses and highlight "the anachronistic character of classical proletarian movements" (Richman 1982, 65), led to accusations that Bataille himself had fascistic tendencies. Bataille also co-founded a secret society, the Acéphale Group, whose journal of the same name published a special edition in January 1937 on "Nietzsche and the Fascists," including an article by Bataille of the same title.

Steve Bastow

See Also: ANTIFASCISM; FRANCE; NIETZSCHE, FRIEDRICH

References
Richman, M. 1982. *Reading Georges Bataille: Beyond the Gift.* Baltimore: Johns Hopkins University Press.
Surya, M. 2002. *Georges Bataille: An Intellectual Biography.* London: Verso.
Wolin, Richard. 2004. *The Seduction of Unreason: The Intellectual Romance with Fascism from Nietzsche to Postmodernism.* Princeton: Princeton University Press.

BA'THISM

Secular radical nationalist ideology developed in the 1940s by Western-educated Syrian educators who sought, like earlier European fascists and various other types of revolutionary nationalists, to conjoin diverse currents of nationalism and socialism and thereby forge a new type of revolutionary movement. Elements of Ba'thist doctrine, which was inspired in certain respects by both fascist and traditional socialist conceptions, subsequently undergirded the "official" ideologies of dictatorial regimes established by reformist military officers in both Syria and Iraq.

The principal creator of Ba'thist ideology was the Syrian Michel 'Aflaq (1910–1989), who was born into a Greek Orthodox family in Damascus. After studying history at the Sorbonne between 1928 and 1932, he returned home and became a teacher. In the spring of 1934, a group of Arab nationalist and Marxist-oriented writers, journalists, and teachers from Syria and Lebanon—including 'Aflaq, future Ba'th Party cofounder Salah al-Din al-Bitar (1912–1980), and several disillusioned former Lebanese communists—held a meeting in the Lebanese town of Zahla to discuss common concerns. The result was the issuance of a statement entitled "In the Path of Arab Unity," which promoted the unification of the "Arab Fatherland"—that is, "the entire area between the Taurus and the Sahara and the Atlantic and the Arab [Persian] Gulf"—under a single party on the basis of language, culture, history, customs, and common interests, a scheme that was later adopted by the Ba'th. In 1935 these same activists created a short-lived journal called *al-Tali'a (The Vanguard)*, which indicated that they saw themselves as the vanguard of this greater Arab nation and the spokesmen for a new generation that had emerged to educate and defend "the popular masses." It was from this milieu, where "rightist" and "leftist" activists interacted (in a manner reminiscent of the proto-fascist *Cercle Proudhon* in pre–World War I France), that vaguely socialist ideas were grafted onto pan-Arab nationalism.

In 1943, having already inspired and gathered together a group of pupils and European-educated nationalists, 'Aflaq and Bitar established a small vanguard organization known as al-Ba'th al-'Arabi (Arab Rebirth). This group later merged with two other organizations, former Parisian philosophy student Zaki al-Arsuzi's *al-Ihya' al-'Arabi* (Arab Revival) group in 1947, and Akram al-Hawrani's pro-peasant *Hizb al-Ishtiraki al-'Arabi* (Arab Socialist Party) in 1953, after which the combined group was known as the *Hizb al-Ba'th al-'Arabi al-Ishtiraki* (Socialist Arab Rebirth Party). Organizationally, the new formation fell into the category of what French sociologist Maurice Duverger has referred to as a "cell party." This type of party, which is also characteristic of communism and fascism, is particu-

larly well suited to clandestine and covert activities, and is essentially a pyramidal, centralized structure in which orders are transmitted from above down to the smallest organizational components. At the top of the Ba'th Party pyramid was a secretary general ('Aflaq himself between 1943 and 1965) and an executive body known as the National Command, whose members were elected by regional leaders during a biannual national convention. Below that were regional commands that represented individual countries in which the party had established its main branches (Syria, Iraq, Lebanon, Jordan, and "Palestine") and then, in descending order, branches, divisions, companies, and three- to seven-person geographical, sectoral, and recruiting cells. Perhaps not surprisingly, the party operated on the Leninist principle of "democratic centralism," whereby internal debate and criticism were permitted only until a decision was reached, after which disagreement was no longer tolerated. 'Aflaq functioned both as a movement theorist who operated above the mundane political fray and as a mediator between the party's right- and left-wing factions, whereas Bitar was a key movement organizer and tactician who later held several government posts in Syria.

It is difficult to provide a concise summary of Ba'thist ideology, since 'Aflaq was an exhortatory, passionate, optimistic, and quasi-mystical writer who emphasized youthful energy and self-sacrifice, as opposed to a dry, systematic thinker. The official slogan of the Ba'th Party was "Unity, Freedom, and Socialism," which referred, respectively, to pan-Arab nationalism, independence from foreign political and psychological control, and vague notions of social justice. 'Aflaq's conceptions of nationalism were essentially derived from those of Sati' al-Husri (1882–1968), who had adapted and applied nineteenth-century German romantic, antirationalist, and illiberal nationalist ideas, with their focus on the unique characteristics of particular historically formed ethnocultural groups, to the Arabs. In a context marked by the imposition of British and French colonial control over Arab territories, it is not surprising that 'Aflaq carried these Germanophile sentiments even further. For him, it was above all necessary to revive the underlying soul of the great "Arab nation," whose essence was to be tapped by the party and personally embodied in all of its members, and in the process to supplant the corrupt, backward-looking elites in the Arab world. He also promoted the "structural transformation" (*inqilab*) of Arab society. However, his concept of "Arab socialism," like "German" socialism or the variants of socialism promoted by fascist theorists, was not only subordinated to nationalism in practice but also antithetical to Marxism. Far from being an advocate of class struggle, 'Aflaq insisted that all members of the Arab nation needed to work together harmoniously. As he put it, Arabs should never "lose" their nationalism or "confuse it with the felonious notion of class interests." Thus, although the Ba'th Party criticized the exploitation of the masses by "colonialists" and traditional elites, it saw itself as a corporatist-style arbitrator between social classes rather than as the champion of only one class. Likewise, although he viewed Islam as an expression of Arab genius, his overriding concern for national unity also turned 'Aflaq, who was himself a member of a religious minority in Muslim Syria, into a bitter critic of religious sectarianism.

'Aflaq and his civilian colleagues later lost effective political control of the movement they had created. During the 1960s, Ba'th-supported coups in Syria and Iraq temporarily brought more left-leaning elements of the party to the fore, whether rural officers from its Syrian Military Committee or quasi-Marxist "neo-Ba'thist" Iraqi civilians. After a long process of factional infighting, Hafiz al-Asad and Saddam Husayn established reform-minded, anti-Western militarized dictatorships that, in part because of their establishment of close Cold War–era relations with the Soviet Union, adopted certain Soviet organizational features. Yet both regimes brutally suppressed domestic communists along with proto-democrats, Islamists, and other opposition groups; their leaders—who developed considerable hostility toward one another—created personality cults and portrayed themselves as nationalist champions of the entire Arab world.

The above summary suggests that Ba'thism may have been a Middle Eastern variant of fascism, even though 'Aflaq and other Ba'th leaders criticized particular fascist ideas and practices. The Ba'th movement undoubtedly shared certain characteristic features of European fascism—the attempt to synthesize radical, illiberal nationalism and non-Marxist socialism, a romantic, mythopoetic, and elitist "revolutionary" vision, the desire both to create a "new man" and to restore past greatness, a centralized authoritarian party divided into "right-wing" and "left-wing" factions, and so forth; several close associates later admitted that 'Aflaq had been directly inspired by certain fascist and Nazi theorists.

Still another Middle Eastern movement with an apparent fascist character was the Ba'th Party's Syrian rival, the *Hizb al-Qawmi al-Ijtima'i al-Suri* (SSNP: Syrian Social Nationalist Party) of Antun Sa'ada (1904–1949), which openly praised European fascism, established an armed party militia, adopted a racialized conception of the nation, and promoted the forcible creation of "Greater Syria," a more limited and parochial nationalist notion. In that sense the SSNP seems to have been more typical of interwar fascist movements, whereas Ba'thism (like Jamal 'Abd al-Nasir's *Harakat al-Dubbat al-Ahrar* [Free Officers' Movement] in Egypt), with its less sectarian pan-Arab agenda, is arguably more akin to the pan-European ("Nation Europa") notions promoted by many postwar neofascist movements. (Indeed, neofascist activists in Europe have periodically offered support, and not only rhetorically, to their "comrades" in the Ba'th movement.)

Jeffrey M. Bale

See Also: *CERCLE PROUDHON,* THE; COLD WAR, THE; CORPORATISM; ELITE THEORY; HUSSEIN, SADDAM; IRAQ; LEADER CULT, THE; MARXISM; MIDDLE EAST, THE; NATIONALISM; NAZISM; NEW MAN, THE; PALESTINE; PALINGENETIC MYTH; PARAMILITARISM; PHALANGE; POSTWAR FASCISM; PROTOFASCISM; QADHAFI, MU'AMMAR; RACIAL DOCTRINE; SOCIALISM

References

Abu Jaber, Kamel. 1966. *The Arab Ba'th Socialist Party: History, Ideology, and Organization.* Syracuse, NY: Syracuse University Press.
'Aflaq, Mishil. 1986. *Fi sabil al-Ba'th.* 5 vols. Baghdad: Hurriyya lil-Tiba'a.
Aflak [sic], Michel. 1977. *Choice of Texts from the Ba'th Party Founder's Thought.* Florence: n.p.
Choueiri, Youssef M. 2000. *Arab Nationalism: A History.* Oxford: Blackwell.
Farah, Elyas. 1978. *Arab Revolutionary Thought in the Face of Current Challenges.* Madrid: Alberreja.
Kienle, Eberhard. 1990. *Ba'th v Ba'th: The Conflict between Syria and Iraq, 1968–1989.* London: I. B. Tauris.
Olson, Robert. 1982. *The Ba'th and Syria, 1947–1982: The Evolution of Ideology, Party and State.* Princeton, NJ: Kingston.
Seale, Patrick. 1986. *The Struggle for Syria.* New Haven: Yale University Press.
Tibi, Bassam. 1990. *Arab Nationalism: A Critical Inquiry.* New York: St. Martin's.

BATTLE OF BRITAIN, THE

Legendary air combat over southern England that marked Hitler's first major setback in the military campaign he had opened on 1 September 1939 with his assault on Poland. Hitler had been convinced by Goering, chief of the Luftwaffe, that it would be able to crush the RAF as an essential preliminary to a planned invasion of Britain (Operation Sealion). The Battle of Britain, opened on 13 August 1940, was essentially over by 15 September, in that the Luftwaffe had suffered heavy losses, and from that point the attacks on British targets began to decrease. Their tireless and sleepless devotion to duty, their courage, and their supposed insouciance—together with the fighting qualities of the *Spitfire* planes they flew—have made the fighter pilots who fought this campaign into semimythical embodiments of heroic British resistance to the all-conquering Goliath of the Nazi war machine. That war machine had successfully crushed the resistance of countries from Poland to France over the prior twelve months.

Cyprian Blamires

See Also: CHURCHILL, SIR WINSTON LEONARD SPENCER; GOERING, HERMANN; LUFTWAFFE, THE; WORLD WAR II

References
Bungay, Stephen. 2001. *The Most Dangerous Enemy: A History of the Battle of Britain.* London: Aurum.
Weinberg, G. L. 1994. *A World at Arms: A Global History of World War II.* Cambridge: Cambridge University Press.

BAYREUTH

A place of pilgrimage for many Nazis—not least Hitler himself—as the home of Richard Wagner and location of the Bayreuth Festivals. After Wagner's death the Bayreuth Festivals were carried on by his widow, Cosima Wagner (1837–1930), until 1906, and they continued to be associated with a clear German National tendency that excluded Jewry. As Wagner's son-in-law and one of his most fervent admirers, Houston Stewart Chamberlain became another point of ideological attractiveness for the Nazi movement with his theory that history is a struggle between races. Hitler's visit to Chamberlain in 1923 marked the beginning of a very close relationship between Hitler and the House of Wagner, especially with Winifred Wagner. In 1930, Winifred Wagner, a convinced Nazi who had joined the NSDAP in 1926, took over the management of the festivals, and Hitler frequently visited the Wagner family, the children calling him "uncle Wolf." Not surprisingly, then, the Bayreuth Festival got financial support from the NS regime after 1933 and changed its fre-

quency from biennial to annual performances. Each year Hitler and other prominent Nazi leaders went to the festival and let themselves be seen with the Wagner family. During the war the festivals gained further importance as soldiers and workers from armament factories were brought along by the thousands in order to boost their morale.

Fabian Virchow

See Also: ANTI-SEMITISM; CHAMBERLAIN, HOUSTON STEWART; GERMANNESS *(DEUTSCHHETT)*; HITLER, ADOLF; MUSIC (GERMANY); NAZISM; RACIAL DOCTRINE; WAGNER, (WILHELM) RICHARD; WAGNER, WINIFRED

References
Katz, Jacob. 1986. *Richard Wagner: The Darker Side of Genius: Richard Wagner's Anti-Semitism.* Hanover: University Press of New England.
Spotts, Frederic. 1994. *Bayreuth: A History of the Wagner Festival.* New Haven: Yale University Press.
Weiner, Marc. 1995. *Richard Wagner and the Anti-Semitic Imagination.* Lincoln: University of Nebraska Press.

BELGIUM

Fascism in Belgium had some specific characteristics, because it developed along the lines of the cleavage between the (Dutch-speaking) Flemings and the (French-speaking) Walloons. As with several other countries, the roots of the diverse fascist movements in Belgium are situated in World War I. As a consequence of that war, certain social groups became frustrated. The earliest fascist organizations were mainly shaped by French-speaking, conservative and Catholic former soldiers who turned against a broadening Belgian democracy after the introduction of universal suffrage (1919) and the subsequent electoral success of the socialists and the Christian Democrats. They recruited in the right wing of the Catholic Party. The most important organization was the Légion Nationale (National Legion) under the direction of Paul Hoornaert, with some 7,000 followers in the 1930s.

Another frustrated social group was the radical Flemish movement that stood for the recognition of Dutch as the official language of the Flemings. During the war this radical wing became a Flemish Nationalist movement that demanded Flemish independence. Some radicals collaborated with the German occupation and were punished after World War I for high treason. After the war, Flemish nationalism depended on democracy to enlarge its following. In 1931, Joris Van Severen founded the Verbond van Dietse Nationaal Solidaristen (Verdinaso; League of Pan-Netherlandic Solidarists). Verdinaso was primarily a militia ideologically trained as a crack regiment and with the purpose of organizing a coup. Verdinaso did not take part in the elections. At first the group aimed at the destruction of the Belgian state and wanted to link up Flanders with The Netherlands to form a unified territory they proposed to call Dietsland. When the Belgian government issued a prohibition on militias, Verdinaso became a Belgian New Order movement that worked for the fusion of Belgium, The Netherlands, and parts of northern France. Verdinaso had some 5,000 members, living mainly in Flanders, but also a few hundred inhabitants of the Walloon provinces and The Netherlands. In 1933 the Vlaams Nationaal Verbond (Flemish National League; VNV), under the direction of Staf De Clercq, was founded. The VNV had the same objects in view as Verdinaso in its early anti-Belgian phase, but in a more moderate way. The party took part in the elections and had a moderate wing that agitated for an independent form of authoritarian government in Flanders. In 1936 this party got 13.6 percent of the Flemish votes (= 7.1 percent in Belgium).

The revelation of the 1936 elections was Léon Degrelle and his Rex Party, which managed to get 11.5 percent of the Belgian votes (three-quarters from French-speaking Belgium). Degrelle was a young Catholic politician who left the Catholic Party out of disagreement with its moderate attitude. In 1935 he founded Rex, which tried to attract discontented groups like Catholic conservatives, former soldiers, shopkeepers, and the unemployed. Degrelle had a flamboyant personality with a talent for public appearances, but he overestimated his political power. In an attempt to destabilize the Belgian regime, he made a compromise with the far-right winner in Flanders, the VNV. As a consequence of that agreement, he lost a part of his rank and file who considered the VNV to be a party of traitors to the state. Moreover, the head of the Catholic Church rebuffed Degrelle at the insistence of the Catholic Party leadership, and Rex began to disintegrate. In 1939, it gained only 4.4 percent of the votes. The remaining membership radicalized under the impulse of Degrelle to become a more fascist party. Degrelle tried to contact foreign fascist organizations, including in Germany. That was one of the reasons why cooperation with the extremely patriotic Légion Nationale proved impossible.

On the eve of World War II the fascist movements in French-speaking Belgium were divided and alienated. They were also weak, because they had chosen the Belgian king as a symbolic leader above the party system. King Leopold III had some authoritarian sympathies, but he could not be tempted to an unconstitutional adventure and did not respond to agitation by Rex. The anti-Belgian Flemish Nationalist VNV was less hindered by patriotic ambiguities and divisions and managed to maintain its strength. In 1939, the party got 15 percent of the votes in Flanders. During the election contest the traditional parties treated the VNV as a fascist fifth column of Nazi Germany. That did not stop the Flemish wing of the Catholic Party from making policy contracts with the VNV on a local level, so that the VNV did not become isolated from the broad Flemish-minded Catholic movement of the Right. Nevertheless VNV leader De Clercq was aware of the fact that he could not realize his totalitarian and anti-Belgian ambitions in a democratic way. He counted on a new European war and made contacts with Nazi Germany with the intention of making political capital out of the coming conflict. He declared to the German military security agents (*Abwehr*) that he had a VNV-section in the Belgian army at his disposal that would follow his orders, even at the risk of the accusation of high treason. Belgian state security was aware of these contacts and arrested some VNV members and some politicians who were considered dangerous to the state, such as Van Severen and Degrelle. De Clercq remained a free man, but he was not able to carry out his strategy because of the actions of Belgian state security and the sudden surrender of Belgium—the Belgian army capitulated after eighteen days on 28 May 1940. Nevertheless, De Clercq had a meeting with the German military governor on 3 June and promised the collaboration of his party and its 30,000 active members.

De Clercq stole a march upon his more moderate supporters, who saw that the party-militants were ready and able to collaborate. The VNV cherished many ambitions. Although the military administration was not allowed to make decisions concerning the future of Belgium, Hitler gave orders that the "Germanic" Flemings should be favored over the "Latin" Walloons. Probably the memory of Flemish Nationalist collaboration during World War I influenced the decision. Some Flemish collaborators who had immigrated to Germany after World War I had close ties with Nazi organizations. That was why the VNV became the privileged partner of the new rulers. The conditional character of this collaboration became clear when the VNV was no longer permitted to propagate its pan-Netherlandic goal. An "independent"

Flanders in a German empire was the most they could aspire to. That did not hinder De Clercq from entrusting Hitler with his own destiny, with the future of his party, and with the future of Flanders. German National Socialist ideology (including anti-Semitism) became official VNV party ideology. The German military authority did not want the VNV to change its name into the Flemish National Socialist Party because it wanted to act carefully regarding the Belgian establishment—King Leopold III (who remained in the occupied country), the Church, the magistrates, the industrial groups, and of course the French-speaking Belgians. The idea of the VNV leader that the Walloon provinces stood for *Lebensraum* for Flanders, and that the ethnic Walloons could be deported to France, was rejected.

Léon Degrelle returned to Belgium after his imprisonment in France with the ambition of regaining his former status. His position was not very favorable, though, both because of Hitler's instruction concerning the Walloons and because he had acquired the reputation of being a political charlatan. In May 1941 the military authority forced Degrelle to fuse the Rex divisions in Flanders with the VNV. Verdinaso (which became leaderless after the death of its leader in French imprisonment) was compelled to do the same. That was why De Clercq could take the leadership of the unified VNV and cherish the hope that this would be the immediate precedent for a Flemish one-party state. He immediately discovered that the rulers in Berlin had other intentions. The VNV was opposed by a Pangerman movement that agitated for the unification of Flanders and Germany (with the support of the SS). At first this movement was called the Flemish SS; from 1941 on it became the Duits-Vlaamse Arbeidsgemeenschap (DeVlag) (German-Flemish Labor Community) under the direction of Gottlob Berger, right-hand man of SS leader Heinrich Himmler. The intense struggle between the VNV and the DeVlag/SS became obvious in things like the "contest" to recruit as many volunteers as possible on the German side in the war. Except on the nationalist level, there were no fundamental ideological differences between the two groups, though DeVlag took greater interest in typical National Socialist themes like anti-Semitism.

Soon Léon Degrelle realized that participation in the war effort was a way to get political attention. After the beginning of the German-Soviet war, he volunteered for the German army and formed a Walloon anti-Bolshevist division on the Eastern Front with a few hundred supporters. Degrelle distinguished himself as a soldier but remained a politician first and foremost. His experiences in Flanders had taught him that the SS was his most powerful ally. He succeeded in getting recognition for the Walloons as French-speaking "Germanics," which gave him the opportunity to integrate the Walloon Eastern Front soldiers into the Waffen-SS. Degrelle himself was decorated with the highest SS order and met Hitler in person, something that no other Belgian collaboration leaders managed to do. In fact, Degrelle became the leader of the Walloon annexationist Pangerman party, and Rex became a mere reservoir for Waffen-SS recruitment. In June 1944, Berlin acknowledged Degrelle as "Leader of the Walloon part of the nation," by the side of the leader of DeVlag, who became "Leader of the Flemish part of the nation"; the VNV was politically excluded. Following the usual Nazi policy, the most radical and servile followers gained the most. All this, however, was rendered meaningless by the fact that in September 1944, Belgium was liberated by Allied forces and the Belgian democratic state was restored. The supporters of the National Socialist occupation were convicted by military courts, but not one important political leader was executed.

Soon after the war the extreme-right tendency was able to reinstitute itself (in a version adjusted to the democratic context), because the Catholic Party (for electoral and political motives) pursued a weak policy with regard to the mainly Flemish nationalistic collaborators of the VNV. An undertow of postwar Flemish nationalism continued to defend the antidemocratic concepts of the prewar and wartime period. That is one of the explanations for the revival of extreme-right Flemish nationalism during the 1980s. In 2004, the extreme-right party Vlaams Blok got 24.1 percent of the Flemish vote.

Bruno De Wever

See Also: ANTI-SEMITISM; CATHOLIC CHURCH, THE; CLERCQ, GUSTAVE ("STAF") DE; DEGRELLE, LEON; DIKSMUIDE; FARMERS; GERMANY; HITLER ADOLF; HOORNAERT, PAUL; *LEBENSRAUM;* MAN, HENDRIK/HENRI DE; NATIONALISM; NAZISM; NETHERLANDS, THE; PANGERMANISM; POLITICAL CATHOLICISM; POSTWAR FASCISM; RACIAL DOCTRINE; REXISM; SEVEREN, GEORGES ("JORIS") VAN; SS, THE; TOTALITARIANISM; WAR VETERANS; WORLD WAR I; WORLD WAR II

References
Buchanan, Tom, and Martin Conway, eds. 1996. *Political Catholicism in Europe, 1918–1965.* Oxford: Clarendon.
Conway, M. 1993. *Collaboration in Belgium: Léon Degrelle and the Rexist Movement 1940–1944,* New Haven: Yale University Press.
De Wever, B. 1994. *Greep naar de macht. Vlaams-nationalisme en Nieuwe Orde. Het VNV 1933–1945,* Tielt: Lannoo.

BENN, GOTTFRIED (1886–1956)

One of the most important German poets of the twentieth century, whose essayistic work revealed his anti-individualistic, antidemocratic, and antihumanitarian sentiments on historico-philosophical grounds. In 1933, as acting dean of the Section for Literature of the Prussian Academy of Arts, Benn demanded that the members of the academy sign a declaration of loyalty to the new National Socialist administration. Benn, an admirer of Marinetti, declared himself a supporter of the Fuehrer principle, calling for the "breeding" of a new "race" and for the putative synthesis of art and power in Italian Fascism. Even after he was declared to be "degenerate" in 1936, Benn understood his art as an appropriate supplement to National Socialist ideology. Benn justified his political misjudgments as based on his autonomous amoral concept of art in his 1950 autobiography *Doppelleben* (*Double Life*).

Susanne Pocai

See Also: ART; DEGENERACY; DEMOCRACY; FUTURISM; INDIVIDUALISM; LEADER CULT, THE; MARINETTI, FILIPPO TOMMASO; NAZISM; RACIAL DOCTRINE; VITALISM

References
Alter, Reinhard. 1976. *Gottfried Benn: The Artist and Politics (1910–1934)*. Frankfurt: Peter Lang.
Benn, Gottfried. 1950. *Doppelleben: zwei Selbstdarstellungen*. Munich: Limes.
Ray, Susan. 2003. *Beyond Nihilism: Gottfried Benn's Postmodernist Poetics*. Oxford: Lang.

BENOIST, ALAIN DE (born 1943)

Leading postwar French extreme right-wing intellectual who is a graduate of the faculty of law and letters in the Sorbonne. De Benoist has made many journalistic and intellectual contributions to extreme-right publications under a variety of pseudonyms. He is best known, however, as one of the key figures in the French New Right movement GRECE. He was a co-founder of the main tribune of GRECE, *Nouvelle Ecole*, in February/March 1968, becoming its chief editor in 1969; he also wrote editorials for the GRECE journal, *Eléments*, from 1963 (under the pseudonym of Robert de Herte), and from 1988 he edited the journal *Krisis*. De Benoist is also the author of a number of political and philosophical works. He has moved away from fascism in more recent years.

Steve Bastow

See Also: EUROPE; EUROPEAN NEW RIGHT, THE; EUROPEANIST FASCISM/RADICAL RIGHT, THE; EVOLA, JULIUS; FRANCE; GRAMSCI, ANTONIO; GRECE; POSTWAR FASCISM

References
Camus, Jean-Yves. 1998. *L'extrême droite aujourd'hui*. Toulouse: Milan.
Griffin, R. 2000a. "Plus ça change! The Fascist Pedigree of the Nouvelle Droite." Pp. 217–252 in *The Development of the Radical Right in France*, edited by E. Arnold. London: Macmillan.
———. 2000b. "Interregnum or Endgame? The Radical Right in the 'Post-fascist' Era." *Journal of Political Ideologies* 5, no. 2: 163–178.

BERAN, RUDOLF (1887–1954)

Czech right-wing politician of the interwar period. During the first Czechoslovak Republic, Beran was an important figure in the Agrarian Party, which formed one of the pillars of the pluralistic system. Beran was one of the prominent members of the right-wing faction in the party, and in 1935 he was elected party leader. He favored cooperation between Czechoslovakia and the Sudeten Germans and with Nazi Germany. In 1938, after the Munich Pact, Beran became party leader of the new right-wing Party of National Unification and prime minister of the authoritarian second Czechoslovak Republic. His administration pursued anti-Semitic and anti-Gypsy measures. After the Nazi occupation, in March 1939, Beran became for one month prime minister of the first government in the Protectorate of Bohemia and Moravia. He tried to defend a certain degree of Czech autonomy. In 1941 he was arrested by the Germans but was released in 1943. After the war he was sentenced to twenty years in prison, where he died in 1954.

Miroslav Mares

See Also: ANTI-SEMITISM; APPEASEMENT; CZECHOSLOVAKIA; GERMANY; HITLER, ADOLF; MUNICH AGREEMENT/PACT, THE; NAZISM; ROMA AND SINTI, THE; SLOVAKIA; SUDETENLAND, THE; WORLD WAR II

References
Mastny, V. 1971. *The Czechs under Nazi Rule.* New York: Columbia University Press.
Rataj, Jan. 1999. *O autoritativní národní stát.* Praha: Nakladatelství univerzity Karlovy.
Sugar, P. F., ed. 1971. *Native Fascism in the Successor States, 1918–1945.* Santa Barbara, CA: ABC-CLIO Press.
Tomás˘ek, Dus˘an, and Jan Kvacek. 1999. *Obûalována je vláda.* Praha: Themis.

Although the Nazis invested a great deal in promoting the 1936 Berlin Olympics as a showcase for the regime and its ideology, superlative black American athlete Jesse Owens made their claims about "Aryan" superiority look ridiculous by his prowess. (Bettmann/Corbis)

BERLIN OLYMPICS, THE

International sporting event that Hitler presented to the world as a showcase for the achievements and the glories of the Nazi regime. The eleventh Olympiad, held in Berlin in 1936, had actually been awarded in 1933 to the German capital, before Hitler's accession to power, and at first the Nazis denounced it as "a festival dominated by Jews." But Hitler did a volte-face and decided to use the Olympics as a public relations opportunity for his regime. There was a three-week moratorium on the anti-Semitic campaign, and Richard Strauss and Carl Orff were commissioned to compose music for the occasion, while artists worked on massive illustrative paintings and statues. For the first time a relay of runners carried the Olympic flame from Greece to Germany, and from the German border all the way to Berlin the roads were lined with children waving Nazi flags, creating, for the benefit of the press, a strong impression of a happy citizenry enthusiastic for the Nazi regime. The opening ceremony provided the opportunity for Hitler to parade with 40,000 SA men while a choir of 3,000 sang Nazi songs. Although shot-putter Hans Woelke won the first gold medal of the games for Germany, subsequently public attention and adulation shifted to the black U.S. sprinter Jessie Owens, who won four gold medals, somewhat tarnishing the luster of supposed Aryan superiority.

Cyprian Blamires

See Also: ANTI-SEMITISM; ARCHITECTURE; ART; ARYANISM; HITLER, ADOLF; MUSIC (GERMANY); NAZISM; PROPAGANDA; RACISM; SPORT

References
Bachrach, Susan D. *The Nazi Olympics: Berlin 1936.* New York: Little, Brown.
Krüger, Arnd, William Murray, and W. J. Murray, eds. 1972. *The Nazi Olympics: Sport, Politics and Appeasement in the 1930's.* Urbana: University of Illinois Press.
Mandell, R. D. 1972. *The Nazi Olympics.* London: Souvenir Press.

BHAGAVADGITA, THE

Title of Hindu Scripture meaning *The Song of the Lord;* Alfred Rosenberg, Jakob Wilhelm Hauer, Walter Wüst, and other SS intellectuals incorporated its metaphysics of battle and deed into their version of Nazism, which influenced Himmler and the SS. Indeed, Himmler defended his lethal decisions and his detachment from their consequences with words spoken by Lord Krishna (*Krsna*) to the warrior Arjuna. To Nazis with this kind of interest, the *Bhagavadgita* conjoined the holy with the bellicose. Thus Hauer talks about *männertrotzige Kriege* ("wars of male defiance") that, rather than obeying universalistic moral prescriptions, fuse mystic and warrior, making faith the ultimate sanction of war. The *Bhagavadgita* is a philosophical dialogue between Krishna and Arjuna on the occasion of a looming civil war that requires of the warrior that he kill people related to him. The warrior is faced with the conflict between his duty to fight for honor and empire and the guilt that he will inevitably incur because he must kill those of his own blood. Arjuna learns from Krishna that the conjunction of duty and guilt places the warrior's deed beyond good and evil. Guilt is an inevitable accompaniment of many necessary human actions. "As is stated in the XVIII. Chapter of the *Bhagavadgita:* Everything done by the human being is afflicted with guilt (*sadosa*), like fire with smoke."

Karla Poewe

See Also: ARYANISM; DECADENCE; HAUER, JAKOB WILHELM; HIMMLER, HEINRICH; MYSTICISM; NAZISM; ROSENBERG, ALFRED; SS, THE; TIBET; WAR; WARRIOR ETHOS, THE

References

Cecil, Robert. 1972. *Myth of the Master Race.* London: Batsford.

Hale, Christopher. 2003. *Himmler's Crusade: The Nazi Expedition to Find the Origins of the Aryan Race.* Hoboken, NJ: John Wiley.

Hauer, J. W. 1932. *Indiens Kampf um das Reich.* Stuttgart: Kohlhammer.

———. 1934. *Eine indo-arische Metaphysik des Kampfes und der Tat: Die Bhagavadgita in neuer Sicht.* Stuttgart: Kohlhammer.

Padfield, Peter. 1990. *Himmler Reichsführer SS.* London: Papermac.

Whisker, James B. 1983. *Social, Political, and Religious Thought of Alfred Rosenberg: An Interpretive Essay.* Washington, DC: University Press of America.

BIANCHI, MICHELE: *See* FASCIST PARTY, THE

BIOLOGY: *See* EUGENICS; HEALTH; SCIENCE; SOCIAL DARWINISM

BIRTH CONTROL: *See* DEMOGRAPHIC POLICY; FAMILY, THE; RACIAL DOC-

TRINE; SEXUALITY; SOCIAL DARWINISM

BLACK HUNDREDS, THE: *See* ORTHODOX CHURCHES, THE; RUSSIA; STALIN, IOSIF VISSARIONOVICH

BLACK METAL

Musical genre favored by young neo-Nazis today, though it is less popular than "White Noise." Black Metal is characterized by its "minimalist form, fast guitar riffs, hammering drums and unintelligible vocals" (Cayton 1999). Descended from death metal, it is overtly racist and usually explicitly National Socialist in its politics, with bands present in most European countries and North America; the most notable examples are Absurd (Germany), Burzum (Poland), Blood Axis (United States), and Kristalnacht (France). Some of those associated with Black Metal bands have been convicted of church-burning, violence, and murder.

John Pollard

See Also: NAZISM; NEO-NAZISM; ROCK MUSIC; SKINHEAD FASCISM; WHITE NOISE

Reference

Cayton, C. 1999. "Black Metal Unmasked." *Searchlight* no. 288 (June): 13–17.

BLACKSHIRTS: *See* GREAT BRITAIN; ITALY; *SQUADRISMO*

BLANCHOT, MAURICE (1907–2003)

Celebrated French journalist and literary critic and forebear of poststructuralism who was also a (dissident) sympathizer with Maurras; in the 1930s he attacked republicanism and the Rights of Man and contributed to many far-right reviews. In March 1937 he was one of a far-right group who were arrested for incitement to murder—the targets having been left-wing prime minister Léon Blum and the communist Maurice Thorez. It has been said that Blanchot incarnated the "fascist spirit" of the era. Under the Vichy regime he wrote articles for the Petainist *Journal des débats* and lent his support to *Jeune France,* a Vichy cultural organization.

Cyprian Blamires

See Also: ABSTRACTION; FRANCE; FRENCH REVOLUTION, THE; MAURRAS, CHARLES; PETAIN, MARSHAL HENRI PHILIPPE; VICHY

Reference
Wolin, Richard. 2004. *The Seduction of Unreason: The Intellectual Romance with Fascism from Nietzsche to Postmodernism.* Princeton: Princeton University Press.

BLITZKRIEG

A completely new concept of military attack whose stunning power at the start of World War II seemed to symbolize the merciless unstoppability of the Nazi advance, their advanced military technology, and their superlative strategic thinking. Abandoning the trench warfare of the previous global conflict, the Blitzkrieg tactic involved destroying the enemy air force while it was still on the ground by assault from the air, bombing enemy transports, lines of communication, and troop concentrations, while light mechanized forces advanced with the heavier tanks in the rear. The term has since become synonymous with the idea of sustained, all-out, brutally aggressive attack.

Cyprian Blamires

See Also: GERMANY; HITLER, ADOLF; LUFTWAFFE, THE; TECHNOLOGY; WORLD WAR II

Reference
Delaney, J. 1996. *The Blitzkrieg Campaigns: Germany's "Lightning War" Strategy in Action.* London: Arms and Armour.

BLOOD

A term that had an important status in Nazi ideology and that drew on a long tradition of racial thinking,

particularly in the Germanic and Anglo-Saxon worlds. Purity of blood was associated with racial vigor and race purity. The interplay between the rapidly developing science of serology and blood as myth were complex. In the nineteenth century, ideas of purity of blood and the "mixing" of bloods crossed physiological with cultural thinking. Gobineau spoke of blood in a cultural and linguistic sense. The physiological sciences assisted in racial classification. Blood groups were linked to racial types. This classification was pioneered by a Polish physiologist, Ludwik Hirszfeld, in Salonika in 1917. The linkage of ethnicity and blood group gave rise to a new methodology in anthropology, and from the 1920s large-scale surveys of blood groups were carried out. Julius Bernstein, a mathematician at Goettingen, made important contributions to the statistics of blood groups.

The German radical Right became increasingly interested in blood group studies and lobbied to exclude Jewish scientists from them. The right-wing publisher Julius Lehmann published a journal, the *Zeitschrift für Rassenphysiologie,* in 1928 as part of the endeavor to promote racial surveys by means of blood group study. The Nazi activist Walther Darré in 1929 popularized the ideology of *Blut und Boden*—"blood and soil"—as a program for rejuvenating the German peasantry and attracting rural support for the NSDAP. The Nuremberg Laws of 1935 were phrased in terms of blood purity. These sought to exclude marriage and all forms of sexual and social contact between Germans and Jews. Nazi race theorists—notably Lothar Tirala in Nuremberg—believed that sexual intercourse of a Jew with a German corrupted both the German and their offspring. These concerns with racial purity reached a culmination with the Nazi measures of racial screening in the occupied East. Racial experts attempted to identify residual Germanic elements among the Slavs. Not only Jews but also Roma were defined by the Nazis as having inferior blood and as meriting total eradication. Other "races," such as Slavs, were also defined as inferior and subjected to exterminatory measures. Medical expertise was essential to maintain the fitness of higher races by eliminating the mentally ill and the severely disabled, and preventing reproduction among carriers of inherited diseases.

Scientists saw serological studies as important in immunology. Experiments were made in concentration camps, injecting infected blood in hopes of producing immunity to typhus. Malaria studies in Germany and Italy gave much attention to parasites in the blood. During World War II blood group research developed for the purposes of transfusion. Auschwitz prisoners were forced to give blood in immense quantities. The SS had blood groupings tattooed on their upper arm. The Kaiser Wilhelm Institutes undertook blood protein research in association with Mengele at Auschwitz. The extent to which the scientists analyzing the blood at the institutes were aware of its provenance remains a matter of conjecture and debate today.

Paul Weindling

See Also: ANTHROPOLOGY; ANTI-SEMITISM; ARYANISM; AUSCHWITZ; BLOOD AND SOIL; CONCENTRATION CAMPS; DARRE, RICHARD WALTHER; EUGENICS; EUTHANASIA; GOBINEAU, COMTE JOSEPH ARTHUR DE; HEALTH; MEDICINE; MENGELE, JOSEF; NAZISM; RACIAL DOCTRINE; ROMA AND SINTI, THE; RURALISM; SCIENCE; SLAVS, THE (AND GERMANY); SS, THE; UNIVERSITIES; *UNTERMENSCHEN*

Reference
Weindling, Paul. 1989. *Health, Race and German Politics between National Unification and Nazism, 1870–1945.* Cambridge: Cambridge University Press.

BLOOD AND HONOR: *See* SKINHEAD FASCISM

BLOOD AND SOIL (*BLUT UND BODEN*)

A fundamental element in the belief system of some Nazi ideologues who preached a return to a rural way of life and the maintenance of the purity of the "Nordic" or "Aryan" race, often found in association with the veneration of Germanic divinities and an anti-Christian and especially anti-Catholic stance. The point of departure for blood and soil ideology was a critical attitude toward industrialization, liberalism, materialism, social democracy, and democratic demands—indeed, toward much of modernity as such. Linked to this was a lament over a postulated general cultural decline resulting from such social developments. A return to a rural way of life was proposed as a means to social renewal. The rural way of life was to lead to the development of virtues and character-qualities that had allegedly been lost through civilization. A supposedly higher "Nordic" or "Aryan" type of man was to be bred through selection. The reproduc-

tion of persons who did not correspond to the ideas of the representatives of the blood-and-soil ideology—such as individuals with physical or mental handicaps, the so-called asocials, homosexual men, persons of the Jewish faith and Jewish origins, Sinti and Roma, and others—was to be restricted as much as possible. After World War I the actual murder of members of this only vaguely defined circle of persons was increasingly on the agenda. A close association arose between the blood-and-soil ideology and Social Darwinistic, eugenicist, and anti-Semitic thinking. The idea of a "healthy" people emerging from the peasantry was closely bound up with the demand for a corporatist society. The "new aristocracy of blood and soil" (the title of a book by the National Socialist Rural Affairs Minister Walther Darré) was to form the leadership elite of the renewed state system, and it would be constantly augmented from the ranks of persons "steeled in the rural struggle for existence." Representatives of the blood-and-soil ideology in Germany often propagated expansionist goals. New space for rural settlements was to be created in Eastern and Southeastern Europe. The Slav populace was regarded as inferior, and there was a plan for its enslavement or expulsion.

Blood-and-soil ideology was by no means exclusive to Germany or to National Socialist groupings. Knut Hamsun, Norwegian novelist and Nobel Prize winner for literature, is one of the best-known representatives of a blood and soil ideology. Other renewal movements that were very far from Nazism also called for a return to nature and to the virtues associated with peasant life. What was distinctive about Nazi blood-and-soil ideologues was their emphasis on breeding and the idea of an "Aryan race" postulated as superior.

Although blood-and-soil ideology was part of the National Socialist program, the realization of its social goals—a corporative society, a "new nobility," a return to peasant values—was not seriously pursued after the access to power of Hitler and the NSDAP, and the blood-and-soil ideologues around Darré were quite soon marginalized. However, their ideas were to some extent reflected in the work of the race and settlement office of the SS, which took an active part in the expulsion, expropriation, and settlement policies in the conquered territories of Eastern Europe. The war against Poland and the Soviet Union came under the premise of conquering living space in the East. The murder of the Eastern European Jews and the Polish elites and the mass deportation of Poles, Ukrainians, and other Eastern Europeans for forced labor to Germany were part of the desired ethnic "new order" in Europe, although, of course, the recruitment of forced laborers also had a pragmatic motive at a time of acute labor shortage. The murder of the Jews, Slavs, Sinti, and Roma as declared enemies and subhumans and persons deemed "unworthy to live" can be seen as an implementation of blood-and-soil ideology, along with the pursuit of "research" in racial hygiene, but there was only a very limited implementation of the breeding idea.

Among the practical measures that resulted from the blood-and-soil ideology were the Law for the New Ordering of Peasant Property Relations of 12 May 1933. This contains the following statement: "The indissoluble connection of blood and soil is the essential presupposition for the healthy life of a people." The Reich Ancestral Estate Law of 29 September 1933 limited succession to male descendants and forbade the division of the land of so-called "ancestral estates."

In keeping with their general lack of interest in racial theories, the Italian Fascists were not receptive to blood-and-soil ideology, but they did have their own brand of ruralism and nostalgia for a "healthier" preindustrial lifestyle.

Michael Schäbitz (translated by Cyprian Blamires)

See Also: ANTI-SEMITISM; ARISTOCRACY; ARTAMAN LEAGUE, THE; ARYANISM; ASOCIALS; BLOOD; CIVILIZATION; DARRE, RICHARD WALTHER; DECADENCE; DEMOCRACY; ELITE THEORY; EUGENICS; FORCED LABOR; HAMSUN, KNUT; HIMMLER, HEINRICH; HOMOSEXUALITY; *LEBEN-SRAUM*; LIBERALISM; MATERIALISM; NAZISM; NEW ORDER, THE; NORDIC SOUL, THE; PALINGENETIC MYTH; RACIAL DOCTRINE; ROMA AND SINTI, THE; RURALISM; SLAVS, THE (AND GERMANY); SS, THE; *UNTERMENSCHEN*

References

Bramwell, A. 1985. *Blood and Soil: Richard Walther Darré and Hitler's "Green Party."* Bourne End: Kensal.

Klemperer, Victor. 2000. *Language of the Third Reich.* Trans. Martin Brady. London: Athlone.

BLUT UND BODEN: *See* BLOOD AND SOIL

BODY, THE CULT OF THE

The model of the "new man" to whose emergence the fascist revolution was dedicated was not the knightly champion of the weak of Christian myth, or the polymath humanist of Renaissance fame, or the Confucian wise man, or the Romantic poet, but the warrior. It was inevitable, therefore, that fascism planned to do everything it could to encourage the physical health and fitness of the people. Fascist youth movements in Italy and Germany encouraged their members to participate in sporting activities and to enjoy walking and hiking in the countryside. Mussolini himself was not above being photographed bare-chested and apparently participating in physical activity. This is no doubt one of the numerous instances where fascism picked up on contemporary trends, for walking and hiking had been growing in popularity since the end of the nineteenth century. In the German-speaking world in particular, there was also a cult of nudity in some circles. In fact, fascism put itself at the head of a contemporary cultural movement that saw clothing becoming increasingly less formal and constricting, especially for women. After World War I voluminous dresses gave way to knee-length skirts, and women began to reveal much more of their bodies at the beach (where they had previously gone into the sea voluminously clothed) and in sporting activities like tennis, where bulky clothing was obviously an impediment. Men likewise took to shorts for sporting activities like football. This was yet another area where fascism, far from being reactionary, was in fact at the forefront of modernity. The German university guide for 1936 showed a file of young men four abreast, stretching back far into the distance: they are all bare-chested and wearing only shorts and shoes. Admittedly this was the year of the Berlin Olympics, but it would have been unimaginable in pre–World War I days.

As a movement that prided itself in being "young" and representative of all the most progressive and forward-thinking trends of the day, fascism naturally profiled young and beautiful bodies in its propaganda. That applied not just to young men but also to young girls. Fascists were out to create a "new order," and that required all the physical and mental energy and fitness that only the young possessed. In the case of Nazism there was an additional reason for the cult of the body, for Nazi ideologues propagated the notion of Aryan superiority, which was understood not just as a superiority in intelligence but also as a physical superiority. Membership in the elite SS required a certain minimum physique, not simply because it was a crack fighting force but also because it was meant to be the very embodiment of the superiority of the Aryan race. A superiority in the soul was in fact believed to be manifested in physical beauty and physique. The Jew was considered to manifest his twisted soul by the caricatural physical ugliness that he was alleged to display and that cartoonists liked to play on mercilessly. Eugenics was the Nazi answer to the threat of physical degeneracy, which might arrive should alien, non-Aryan, and therefore inferior elements contaminate pure Aryan stock. But in this they were following a trend of the day, since eugenics was widely fashionable in the 1930s far beyond fascist circles.

Cyprian Blamires

See Also: ANTI-SEMITISM; ARYANISM; BERLIN OLYMPICS, THE; BLOOD; DECADENCE; DEGENERACY; EUGENICS; FASCIST PARTY, THE; LEISURE; NAZISM; NEW MAN, THE; PROGRESS; RACIAL DOCTRINE; REVOLUTION; SOUL; SPORT; SS, THE; *WANDERVÖGEL*, THE; WARRIOR ETHOS, THE; YOUTH

References

Mangan, J. A. 1999. *Shaping the Superman: Fascist Body as Political Icon—Aryan Fascism*. London: Frank Cass.
———, ed. 2000. *Superman Supreme: Fascist Body as Political Icon—Global Fascism*. London: Frank Cass.
Mosse, G. L. 1996. *The Image of Man: The Creation of Modern Masculinity*. Oxford: Oxford University Press.

BOLIVIA

Many members of the very large German community in Bolivia adhered to National Socialism in 1933, and NSDAP local groups began to be formed in the country in 1934. Leading Nazi propagandists such as General Hans Kundt and SA chief Ernst Roehm, who was exiled to the country from 1928 to 1930, worked as military advisers to the Bolivian government. In 1937 a falangist party (Falange Socialista Boliviana; FSB) was founded by Oscar Unzaga de la Vega. It espoused a corporatist ideology, called for an "organic democracy" and "constructive" socialism, and favored the slogan "Solidarity, Discipline, Hierarchy, Responsibility, Authority." Although it was opposed in the following years by successive governments, it always had access to money and political influence.

The Bolivian National Revolutionary Party (Movimiento Nacionalista Revolucionario; MNR), established in 1941, took over European fascist ideas including anti-Semitism. The MNR was an extreme nationalist and anti-imperialist party advocating state interventionism and nationalization of the mines. Originally supported above all by young officers sympathetic to fascist ideologies, it aimed to be a party of national integration and made use of mass propaganda

methods. After 1946 it distanced itself, however, from its fascist beginnings. In the elections in 1951 the MNR was the strongest party, but it was kept out of power and launched a coup on 9 April 1952 with the support of miners and reformist officers. It embarked on land reforms but was cautious in regard to the promised nationalization of the mines. On 9 November 1964 a coup brought General René Barrientos (1919–1969) to power and marked the beginning of the regime of the generals, which lasted up to 1982. Barrientos relied on an alliance of the military with the peasantry, reacting brutally to socialist movements supported by the guerrilla activities of Ernesto Che Guevara. After the death of Barrientos there was a series of rapidly changing regimes, while the MNR and the falangist FSB came together to form a right populist front with the FPN (Frente Popular Nacionalista).

On 23 August 1971 a coup brought General Hugo Banzer Suárez (1926–2002) to power; his slogan was "Order, Peace, Work." Suárez's military dictatorship undoubtedly had fascist features. He suppressed all opposition by execution and torture (up to 1978, at least 200 men were murdered and 15,000 imprisoned on political grounds). He consolidated the power of the army and built a powerful secret police with advice from former SS officers. Under Banzer's regime, the Gestapo chief and "Butcher of Lyons," Klaus Barbie, had a spectacular career. Barbie got to Bolivia in 1951 with the help of the U.S. secret services and took citizenship in 1957 under the name of Klaus Altmann. He was unmasked in the 1960s and France demanded his extradition in 1972, but General Banzer refused. Barbie was the only senior SS officer who was able to continue his work after the war, advising the Bolivian regime in secret police matters. He was not extradited to France until 1983.

After coup attempts by the extreme Right, Banzer replaced the existing military-civil regime with a purely military dictatorship and abolished parties and unions. In 1975 he entered a close alliance with Chile's military dictator Augusto Pinochet. His plan to settle 30,000 white settler families from the now independent Zimbabwe in Bolivia encountered stiff resistance from the Bolivian people. At the end of 1977 the mineworkers and their families rebelled, and about 1,000 men embarked on a hunger strike to force the release of political prisoners. Banzer was abandoned by the United States, and on 21 July 1978 he resigned as dictator.

The elections that followed led to widespread unrest under the fragmented parties of right and left. Banzer entered with his own right-wing party, National Democratic Action (Acción Democrática

Nacionalista; ADN), which had right populist traits, but in 1993 he made an electoral pact with the Social Democrats. From July 1980 to August 1981, Bolivia was ruled by the bloodiest regime so far, that of General Luis Garcia Meza, with systematic resort to torture by the secret police and the employment of death squads. Government chiefs were involved in the cocaine trade, and the regime was often referred to as "Cocaine Fascism." Continuing instability and corruption eventually brought General Hugo Banzer back to power as president from 1997 to 2001 with his ADN, but he gave up power in August 2001 on grounds of ill health.

Markus Hattstein
(translated by Cyprian Blamires)

See Also: ANTI-SEMITISM; AUTHORITARIANISM; BARBIE, KLAUS; CHILE; CORPORATISM; DEMOCRACY; DICTATORSHIP; FALANGE; GESTAPO, THE; MILITARY DICTATORSHIP; NATIONALISM; NATIONALIZATION; NAZISM; ORGANICISM; PINOCHET UGARTE, GENERAL AUGUSTO; PROPAGANDA; REVOLUTION; RHODESIA; SOCIALISM; SS, THE

References
Alexander, R. J. 1982. *Bolivia: Past, Present, and Future of Its Politics.* New York: Praeger.
Klein, H. S. 2003. *A Concise History of Bolivia.* Cambridge: Cambridge University Press.

BOLSHEVISM

A major factor in Hitler's rise to power was fear, among political elites as well as German society at large, of "Bolshevism." In common parlance in the English-speaking world, Bolshevism was often referred to as "the red peril" (while the perceived Asiatic menace, in particular of Communist China, was known as "the yellow peril"). Also, *Bolshevism* became an abusive term for describing ideas associated with the Soviet Russians and their disciples, not just among fascists but in the population at large as well, and it gave rise to the expression "bolshie," used of a person who is considered obstructive and rebellious.

The Russian term *bol'shevizm*, literally "majority-ism," emerged during the Second Congress of the Russian Social-Democratic Labor Party in London in 1903, when a radical faction led by Vladimir Lenin (1870–1924) won the majority in a vote and started to call itself *bol'sheviki* ("majorityites"). Although the moderate forces within the RSDLP subsequently often collected majorities, they were henceforth called *men'sheviki* ("minorityites"). Whereas, in 1905–1906, an imminent split of the RSDLP was eventually prevented by restoration of party unity, a similar conflict of the two factions in 1912 led to the emergence of two distinct parties. In April 1917, the Bolsheviks formalized the split by calling themselves RSLDP (Bolsheviks). In 1918, they renamed themselves Russian Communist Party (Bolsheviks). The name All-Union Communist Party (Bolsheviks) was used from 1925 until 1934, when the title Communist Party of the Soviet Union (Bolsheviks) was introduced. In 1952, the appendix, (Bolsheviks), was dropped.

Scholarly interpretations of the Soviet experience have used the term *Bolshevism* with three conceptualizations. First: Following Lenin's own claims and the official Soviet doctrine, it is seen as representing one—namely, the crucial—variety of Marxism. Bolshevism, also called Marxism-Leninism, is perceived as the result of a consistent application of Marxist theoretical principles to Russian political reality, if not practical politics, in general. Second: Following the critique of Lenin by left-wing intellectuals of his time, Bolshevism has been interpreted as a fundamental revision or betrayal of classical Marxism. Here, Bolshevism appears as a form of secular fundamentalism that misuses egalitarian and scientific pretensions to underpin an exclusive concept of politics and repressive political institutions. Third: Following historical interpretations that see the Soviet period as a constituent part of Russian national history, a third approach stretches the meaning of the term *Bolshevism* to signify a general pathology in Russian political thought that had been present before the emergence of the Bolshevik Party, and traces of which can be found in the political thinking of post-Soviet Russia's economic reformers. *Bolshevism* here means a radical approach to modernization in which rapid economic reform and social engineering by an unaccountable government are accompanied by suppression of political pluralism, surplus extraction from the population, and other repressive measures that may include state terrorism.

The rise of Bolshevism in the early twentieth century was intimately linked to the emergence and political success of both the Italian Fascist and German Nazi movements. Under the influence of Georges Sorel, a branch of Italian socialism developed into National Syndicalism, which became a principal component of Italian Fascism. In spite of Bolshevism's and fascism's different attitudes to, above all, private property and nationalism, both fascists and antifascists acknowledged common sources and resulting similarities between Bolshevism and fascism, including their revolutionary ideology, their elitism, their disdain for bourgeois values, and their totalitarian ambition. Notwithstanding such affinities, fascism rose to power after World War I on a radically anti-Marxist platform that addressed the dread, among the upper and middle classes, of a communist revolution. The shared anti-Marxism of the old establishment and fascism constituted, apart from other common denominators, such as nationalism or sexism, a major precondition for their cooperation throughout Mussolini's rule, as well as for temporary alliances between conservative and fascist groupings across Europe during the interwar period.

While Italian Fascism's relationship to Bolshevism was ambivalent, Nazism had few affinities with socialist revisionism and has often been identified with anti-Bolshevism. The German philosopher of history and pioneer of comparative fascist studies Ernst Nolte radicalized this view to a theory amounting to a partial apology for Nazism. The cruelty and annihilation policies of the Nazis were, according to Nolte, paradoxically informed at one and the same time by their horror of Bolshevism and by their copying of the Bolsheviks. While general "extremism theory" does not claim a "causal nexus" between the Gulag and Auschwitz, as Nolte does, it establishes a close relationship between right- and left-wing extremism in seeing them not only as radically opposed but also as in vital need of, or even fundamentally similar to, each other.

Although these interpretations have been disputed, a number of features of Bolshevism and Nazism/Fascism did show striking similarities, including their revolutionary action and proletarian nation theories, leadership principles, one-party dictatorships, and party-armies. In some cases Hitler publicly acknowledged his debt to the Bolsheviks when, for instance, proposing to make Munich "the Moscow of our movement." Whether or to what degree the Red Guards or early Soviet concentration camps constituted necessary models for similar institutions created later by the Nazis has, however, been a matter of debate.

Although a reduction of Nazism to anti-Marxism, as has been proposed by Nolte, is misleading, pronouncement of radical anticommunist slogans was both a major electoral campaign strategy of various fascist movements and a coherent expression of fascist anti-universalism. As Europe was shaken by news of the Bolshevik regime's consolidation, mass crimes, world-hegemonic ambitions, and intrusion into foreign communist parties via the Comintern, fascist militant anti-Marxism gained acceptance in many

countries. More often than not, fascist anti-Bolshevism was linked to anti-Semitism within theories of "Judeo-Bolshevism," seeing the relatively high percentage of assimilated Jews in the early Bolshevik Party leadership and first Soviet governments as proof of a Jewish plot. Paradoxically, conspiracy theories of the Nazis and other fascist movements linked "Jewish Bolshevism" in the Soviet Union to "Jewish finance capital" in the West.

Notwithstanding Hitler's pronounced anti-Bolshevism, a significant minority of early Nazi leaders, including the Strasser brothers and Joseph Goebbels, voiced qualified pro-Bolshevik views in the mid-1920s. Later such inclinations gave way to Nazism's sharpening of its profile as Germany's most radically anticommunist movement—a tendency that, in view of emerging Stalinism and its increasing influence on the German Communist Party, contributed to the NSDAP's electoral success. It also informed the civil war–like situation in Germany in the early 1930s, when militias of the Nazis, communists, social democrats, and other political forces were engaged in frequent street fighting. Although anti-Bolshevism constituted a major factor in Nazi ideology, propaganda, and activities, it was, at least in Hitler's worldview, a concept subordinated to radical anti-Semitism. Within the latter, Marxism, Christianity, and liberalism all appeared as inventions of the Jews.

In some interpretations, finally, Bolshevism, especially in its Stalinist transmutation, is seen as belonging to the family of fascist ideologies. This conceptualization implies that Russian socialism underwent, in the 1930s to the 1950s, a transition that, in some ways, followed the revision of West European socialism initiated by Sorel and others in the late nineteenth century, and that eventually led to the emergence of certain French, Italian, and other varieties of fascism.

Whereas the transformation of Russian Bolshevism had to remain veiled in the Soviet period, abrogation of universalism and celebration of nationalism became manifest in the reformulation of the agenda of the post-Soviet Communist Party of the Russian Federation undertaken, above all, by its leader and major ideologue, Gennadii Ziuganov (born 1944). Post-Soviet Russian socialist revisionism did not, however, lead to a fascistization of the Russian "communist" movement. Rather, Ziuganov's agenda, sometimes labeled National Bolshevism, expresses a specifically Russian variety of ultraconservatism that idealizes the "achievements" of the Soviet regime, especially under Stalin, and has a largely positive attitude to the czarist period, following nineteenth-century Russian political thinkers in identifying the "Russian Idea" with socialist principles. This form of nonfascist ultranationalism sees, in distinction to orthodox Marxism, continuity between the prerevolutionary, Soviet, and post-Soviet periods, and is open to alliance with fascist forces. It claims that the Russian people—or "healthy forces" within them—follow an alternative civilizational path, a sustainable form of development in which modernization takes place without the disrupting effects of individualism, globalization, social division, loss of traditional identities, and sexual emancipation.

Andreas Umland

See Also: ANTI-COMINTERN PACT, THE; ANTI-SEMITISM; AUSCHWITZ; BOURGEOISIE, THE; CHRISTIANITY; COMINTERN, THE; CONCENTRATION CAMPS; CONSPIRACY THEORIES; ELITE THEORY; FASCIST PARTY, THE; GLOBALIZATION; GOEBBELS, PAUL JOSEPH; HITLER, ADOLF; HITLER-STALIN PACT, THE; INDIVIDUALISM; LEADER CULT, THE; MARXISM; MATERIALISM; MUSSOLINI, BENITO ANDREA; NATIONAL BOLSHEVISM; NATIONALISM; NAZISM; PALINGENETIC MYTH; PARAMILITARISM; POSTWAR FASCISM; REVOLUTION; RUSSIA; SEXUALITY; SOCIALISM; SOREL, GEORGES; SOVIET UNION, THE; STALIN, IOSIF VISSARIONOVICH; STRASSER BROTHERS, THE; SYNDICALISM; TOTALITARIANISM; WORLD WAR II

References

Furet, Francois, and Ernst Nolte. 2002. *Fascism and Communism.* Trans. Katherine Golsan. Lincoln: University of Nebraska Press.

Gregor, A. James. 2000. *The Faces of Janus: Marxism and Fascism in the Twentieth Century.* New Haven: Yale University Press.

Lovell, David W. 1984. *From Marx to Lenin: An Evaluation of Marx's Responsibility for Soviet Authoritarianism.* Cambridge: Cambridge University Press.

Medish, Vadim, ed. 1997. *My Russia: The Political Autobiography of Gennady Zyuganov.* Armonk, NY: M. E. Sharpe.

Nolte, Ernst. 1987. *Der europäische Bürgerkrieg 1917–1945: Nationalsozialismus und Bolschewismus.* Frankfurt am Main: Propyläen-Verlag.

Ree, Erik van. 2000. "Nationalist Elements in the Work of Marx and Engels: A Critical Survey." *MEGA-Studien* 7, no. 1: 25–49.

Sternhell, Zeev, with Mario Sznajder and Maia Asheri. 1994. *The Birth of Fascist Ideology: From Cultural Rebellion to Political Revolution.* Princeton: Princeton University Press.

Ulam, Adam Bruno. 1998. *The Bolsheviks: The Intellectual and Political History of the Triumph of Communism in Russia.* Cambridge: Harvard University Press.

BONAPARTISM: *See* **CAESARISM**

BONHOEFFER, DIETRICH (1906–1945)

German theologian and pastor and member of the Protestant Confessing Church movement. Bonhoeffer joined the political conspiracy to overthrow the Nazi regime and was executed on 9 April 1945 in the Flossenbürg Concentration Camp. Bonhoeffer's opposition to Nazism was shaped by his family (many of whom were strong supporters of the Weimar republic), by his theological perspectives, and by his experiences abroad, particularly in the ecumenical movement. During the 1920s ecumenical leaders were already alarmed by fascist trends in Germany and elsewhere in Europe, particularly by the ideological co-option of religion embodied in nationalistic, ethnically defined religious movements like the German Christians. Bonhoeffer was an early critic of the *völkisch* church advocated by German Protestant nationalists, speaking out at an ecumenical meeting in 1932 against the racialized theology of Emanuel Hirsch and Paul Althaus. He was also influenced by his time in the United States in 1930 and 1931 as an exchange student at Union Theological Seminary, New York. He became interested in the African-American experience of racism and in the labor movement, and gained a new appreciation for the importance of civil liberties. In the early months of the Nazi regime he drew direct connections between his U.S. experience and what he was seeing in Nazi Germany, writing the U.S. theologian Reinhold Niebuhr on one occasion that Germany needed a civil liberties union.

In February 1933 he gave a radio address on the "Fuehrer principle" that was a direct attack on the authoritarian model of leadership symbolized by Adolf Hitler; broadcasting authorities took Bonhoeffer off the air in the midst of his remarks. In April 1933, his essay "The Church Faces the Jewish Question" raised the possibility of church resistance against state authorities who had ceased to exercise power legitimately. Bonhoeffer had emerged as an early and outspoken critic of Nazi policies and of the pro-Nazi German Christian movement. Throughout the 1930s, however, his primary focus was the role and identity of the Protestant church under the new political circumstances. He represented the radical wing of the Confessing Church in calling for a church that would remain independent of

Nazi ideology, and he devoted much of his ministry to training and supporting Confessing Church candidates for the ministry. By the late 1930s, Bonhoeffer had become politically active in the German resistance, under the influence of his brother-in-law Hans von Dohnanyi, who worked with the German military intelligence (*Abwehr*) office led by Admiral Wilhelm Canaris. Bonhoeffer acted as a courier, carrying resistance documents abroad via his ecumenical contacts. His writings during the resistance period focused on the ethical dilemmas faced by people under totalitarianism, particularly the unique ethical demands of resistance. His resistance experience also shaped his thinking about the church and the future of religion. In the decades since his death, Bonhoeffer has become a symbol of religious resistance against oppression, and his writings have inspired Christian political activists throughout the world.

Victoria Barnett

See Also: ANTIFASCISM; CANARIS, ADMIRAL WILHELM; CHRISTIANITY; CONCENTRATION CAMPS; CONFESSING CHURCH, THE; GERMAN CHRISTIANS, THE; GERMANY; HITLER, ADOLF; JULY PLOT, THE; LEADER CULT, THE; LIBERALISM (THEOLOGY); LUTHERAN CHURCHES, THE; NAZISM; NIEMOELLER, MARTIN; PROTESTANTISM; RACISM; RELIGION; THEOLOGY; TOTALITARIANISM; *VOLK, VÖLKISCH;* WEIMAR REPUBLIC, THE

References

Bethge, Eberhard. 2000. *Dietrich Bonhoeffer: A Biography.* Rev. ed. Ed. Victoria Barnett. Minneapolis, MN: Fortress.
Bonhoeffer, Dietrich. 1997. *Letters and Papers from Prison.* Enl. ed. Ed. Eberhard Bethge. New York: Simon and Schuster.
Kelly, Geoffrey B., and F. Burton Nelson. 2003. *The Cost of Moral Leadership: The Spirituality of Dietrich Bonhoeffer.* Grand Rapids, MI: Wm. B. Eerdmans.

BONO, EMILIO DE (1866–1944)

A key leader in the Italian Fascist regime, De Bono, a career soldier, was decorated for his courage in action in World War I. He was appointed one of the quadrumvirs who organized the March on Rome, and when Mussolini came to power he became director general of public security and then the first commander of the Fascist militia. He was especially valued by the regime for his connections with members of the Italian royal family. De Bono was accused of complic-

ity in the Matteotti murder but acquitted. In September 1929 he was made minister of the colonies, and in that role he played an important part in Italian government policy toward Ethiopia, which he was keen to invade. He was responsible for all the preparations for the Ethiopian war and led the invasion forces into the country on 3 October 1935. Mussolini was dissatisfied by his conduct of hostilities, and he was replaced by Badoglio. De Bono gradually lost faith in Mussolini, and at the Grand Council meeting of 25 July 1943 he voted for Il Duce's deposition. In January 1944 he was executed by the restored Mussolini regime for this treachery.

Cyprian Blamires

See Also: BADOGLIO, PIETRO; ETHIOPIA; FASCIST PARTY, THE; GRAND COUNCIL OF FASCISM, THE; ITALY; MARCH ON ROME, THE; MATTEOTTI, GIACOMO; MUSSOLINI, BENITO ANDREA; QUADRUMVIRS, THE; WORLD WAR I

References

Cannistraro, Philip V. 1982. *Historical Dictionary of Fascist Italy.* Westport, CT: Greenwood.
De Grand, A. 1982. *Italian Fascism: Its Origins and Development.* Lincoln: University of Nebraska Press.

BOOKS, THE BURNING OF THE

An event that has gone down in history as an early symbol of the deeply antihumanistic, philistine, and tyrannical nature of Nazi doctrine. Appointed Reich propaganda minister in 1933, Goebbels embarked on a policy of bringing the arts into line with Nazi goals. He encouraged German students to strip their libraries of "un-German" books and burn them. As its contribution to this campaign, the German Student Association called for a nationwide action against the Un-German Spirit, which was to culminate in a purging of "un-German" books by fire. Local chapters of the association were to be responsible for publicizing this program. The association produced twelve "theses" (a word that was deliberately reminiscent of the Theses of Martin Luther, generally considered to have been the opening shots in the German Reformation) on the need to "purify" the national language and culture of "alien" influences. Placards announcing the theses were posted, and these called for the universities to become focuses for German nationalism. On the night of 11 May of that year, a special ceremonial

The public ritual bonfires of "corrupt" books encouraged by the new Nazi regime in Germany in 1933 symbolized the "purification" required to seal the rebirth of the German people. (National Archives)

bookburning was held in Berlin to the accompaniment of SA and SS band music and a torchlight parade. At least 20,000 books were brought by members of right-wing student organizations from the library of the Wilhelm Humboldt University and other collections and were thrown into a huge bonfire in front of the university while Goebbels made an enthusiastic speech. Particularly singled out for destruction were books written by Jews, socialists, and liberals, and they included works by Marx, Freud, Einstein, Proust, H. G. Wells, Thomas Mann, Heine, Sinclair Lewis, Erich Maria Remarque, Hemingway, and even Helen Keller. This Berlin event was broadcast live across Germany. The same symbolic ritual was repeated in university towns across Germany, in some places on other evenings.

These symbolic ritual "cleansings" excited a shocked reaction from the world's news media. In the United States the significance of what had happened was widely understood, and there were demonstrations and protests in several U.S. cities. The celebrated journalist Walter Lippmann wrote that "there is a government in Germany which means to teach its people that their salvation lies in violence." The burning of the books is an illustration of the brilliant propagandist mentality of Goebbels, who understood that such visual illustrations of Nazi policy and principles said as much to the German people and to political opponents of the regime as any legal enactment.

Cyprian Blamires

See Also: ANTI-SEMITISM; BAEUMLER, ALFRED; DEGENERACY; FREUD, SIGMUND; GERMANNESS; GOEBBELS, (PAUL) JOSEPH; LIBERALISM; LUTHER, MARTIN; MARXISM; NATIONALISM; NAZISM; PROPAGANDA; SA, THE; SOCIALISM; SS, THE; UNIVERSITIES

References

Bosmajian, Haig. 2005. *Burning Books.* Jefferson, NC: McFarland.

Reuth, Ralf G. 1995. *Goebbels: The Life of Joseph Goebbels, the Mephistophelean Genius of Nazi Propaganda.* London: Constable and Robinson.

BORMANN, MARTIN
(1900–1945)

A close friend of Hitler, from May 1941 leader of the party chancellery and from April 1943 "secretary to the Fuehrer." After World War I, Bormann was involved with different radical right organizations and associations. In 1924 he took part in a lynching and was condemned to a year's imprisonment. After his entry into the NSDAP in 1927 his career in the party began. In 1928 he was active in the party head office in Munich. After the rise to power of Hitler and the NSDAP, he advanced in July 1933 to the position of chief of staff with Hitler's deputy in the party, Rudolf Hess. In October 1933 he was promoted to the rank of a Reich leader of the NSDAP. With the "Adolf-Hitler-Contribution to the German Economy" organized by Bormann in 1933, which brought money from employers into the party coffers, he demonstrated (not for the first time) his skills with financial affairs. In 1933, Hitler entrusted him with the administration of his own finances, and that brought him access to the Reich chancellor and to the close circle around him.

The powers of Hess's staff, and later those of the party chancellery, were never clearly set out and were constantly extended. Its principal task was to implement the will of the party over the state apparatus. This meant participation in legislative activity, a deliberate assertion of influence over appointments, and frequent interventions on the state and party political levels. After Hess's flight to England in May 1941, Bormann was appointed to succeed him. His department had the title of Party Chancellery and he himself the authority of a Reich minister, but his actual power went beyond his formal positions in the party and state apparatus. He has often been ascribed the role of actual deputy to Hitler—though that must be nuanced—and he was certainly one of the most influential individuals in the regime. This found expression in his subsequent appointment in April 1943 as "secretary to the Fuehrer." Factors that assisted him in his rise to the position of gray eminence of the National Socialist state and confidant of Hitler were his administrative and financial abilities, his unscrupulousness and intriguing, and his unconditional loyalty to Hitler. He remained at Hitler's side right up to the latter's suicide, and he pursued to the end—though with decreasing success—the implementation of Hitler's lunatic orders, including the destruction of German's remaining infrastructure.

Bormann pursued the aims and the ideology of the NSDAP with the utmost brutality. He pushed through the exclusion of the Christian churches from public life, favored extremely harsh treatment of the Slav population in the territories occupied by German troops, and an intensification of the anti-Semitic measures of the Nazi state. Bormann's ultimate fate remained unclear for a long time. In October 1946 the International War Crimes Tribunal in Nuremberg condemned him to death in absentia. In spite of frequent reports that Bormann had survived, the search for him proved fruitless. In 1972 the state prosecutor at Frankfurt came to the conclusion that a body found in that year in Berlin was unquestionably his. It is likely that at the beginning of May 1945, Bormann was killed in an attempt to escape the encirclement of Berlin. Doubts have however been repeatedly expressed as to this version, and a shadow of uncertainty over his final end still lingers.

Michael Schäbitz
(translated by Cyprian Blamires)

See Also: ANTI-SEMITISM; CHRISTIANITY; GERMANY; HESS, RUDOLF; HITLER, ADOLF; NAZISM; NUREMBERG TRIALS, THE; SLAVS, THE (AND GERMANY); WORLD WAR II

References
Lang, Jochen von. 1979. *The Secretary: The Man Who Manipulated Hitler.* New York: Random House.
McGovern, J. 1968. *Martin Bormann.* London: Barker.
Whiting, Charles. 1996. *The Hunt for Martin Bormann: The Truth.* Barnsley: Pen and Sword.

BÖSZÖRMÉNY, ZOLTAN

Founder of the agrarian-based Hungarian National Socialist Workers' Party (Nemzeti Szocialista Magyar Munkáspárt) and its newspaper, the *National Socialist.* Party members wore brown shirts together with the swastika. His party was renamed the Hungarian National Socialist Workers' Party Scythe Cross Peoples' Movement (Nemzeti Szocialista Magyar Munkáspárt Kaszáskereszt Böszörmény népmozgalom). The new symbol was based on two crossed scythes supporting a skull, with a sword and an eagle on top. The colors were the national red-white-green. Membership was highly hierarchical and secretive, with new members forced to take an oath—sometimes with a coffin or a skull in presence. Members admitted were called storm troopers, and Böszörmény was referred to as the Great Leader (*Vezér*). His party attempted to enter official politics by running in twelve different districts during the 1935 national election. However, none of the candidates—not even the Great Leader himself—were elected.

Following this defeat, Böszörmény's extreme ideas led him to a futile attempt to overthrow the government in 1936 by organizing a wholesale uprising. It was a botched coup that ended with him and his followers in court and with the disbanding of the Scythe Cross Party. Böszörmény was allowed to escape to Germany, and between 1938 and 1940 he lived under the protection of the German political police; he was later returned to Hungary, where he was arrested and jailed. The date of his birth is not known, nor any details as to the end of his life.

László Kürti

See Also: ARROW CROSS, THE; CULTS OF DEATH; GERMANY; HUNGARY; LEADER CULT, THE; NAZISM; SWASTIKA, THE; WORLD WAR II

References
Nagy-Talavera, N. 1970. *The Green Shirts and Others*. Stanford: Stanford University Press.
Rogger, Hans, and Eugen Weber. 1965. *The European Right: A Historical Profile*. London: Weidenfeld and Nicholson.
Sugar, P. F., ed. 1971. *Native Fascism in the Successor States*. Santa Barbara, CA: ABC-CLIO Press.
Szakács, Kálmán. 1963. *Kaszáskeresztesek*. Budapest: Kossuth.

BOTTAI, GIUSEPPE (1895–1959)

Italian Fascist journalist and politician, elected to parliament in 1921 after war service. In 1923, Bottai founded the periodical *Critica fascista* (1923–1943),

which represented the views of those who took the regime's ideology and corporatist aspirations seriously. After 1926, as undersecretary at the Ministry of Corporations, he helped to draft the Fascist Charter of Labor and served as minister of corporations from 1929 to 1932. Later he became minister of national education (1936–1943). During the 1930s he supported the reformist aspirations of younger fascists and backed more innovative and modernist trends in art and architecture through his work at the Ministry of National Education. However, he enthusiastically applied the racial and anti-Semitic legislation of 1938 and 1939 in the schools. An opponent of Italy's alliance with Nazi Germany and entry into World War II, he voted on the Fascist Grand Council to remove Mussolini on 25 July 1943.

Alexander de Grand

See Also: ANTI-SEMITISM; ARCHITECTURE; ART; AXIS, THE; CORPORATISM; FASCIST PARTY, THE; GRAND COUNCIL OF FASCISM, THE; ITALY; MUSSOLINI, BENITO ANDREA; RACIAL DOCTRINE; WORLD WAR II

References
Cannistraro, Philip V. 1982. *Historical Dictionary of Fascist Italy*. Westport, CT: Greenwood.
De Grand, Alexander. 1978. *Bottai e la cultura fascista*. Bari: Laterza.

BOULANGISM

French political ideology associated with a movement focusing on General Georges Boulanger (1837–1891), who became minister of war in the French government in 1886. He created a personality cult, sought a mass following, and combined a radical, action-based extreme nationalist doctrine with progressive socioeconomic proposals and antiparliamentary rhetoric. Some historians have consequently branded his movement "pre-fascist."

Cyprian Blamires

See Also: CAESARISM; FRANCE; LEADER CULT, THE; NATIONALISM; PARLIAMENTARISM; PROTOFASCISM

Reference
Irvine, W. D. 1989. *The Boulanger Affair Reconsidered: Royalism, Boulangism, and the Origins of the Radical Right in France*. Oxford: Oxford University Press.

BOURGEOISIE, THE

Mussolini was not afraid to praise the "petty bourgeoisie" of small and middle peasants. He more rarely spoke, though, of an urban petty-bourgeoisie or bourgeoisie, either in praise or condemnation. The term *bourgeois* was employed occasionally by himself and other fascist ideologues as a term of abuse, referring to individuals or their mentality. In this context, it conveyed notions of crassness, materialistic values, cowardice, and the inability to comprehend the heroic ideal of the fascist "warrior." The bourgeois preferred his own comfort to the battle for the regeneration of the nation. This kind of contempt for bourgeois values was something that fascists shared with their opponents on the Left, and indeed it was a commonplace of nineteenth-century art and literature—for example, in the novels of Balzac, from which Marx said he had learned a great deal. For fascists as for the communists, the bourgeois mentality was supremely incarnated in the hated creeds of liberalism, individualism, and parliamentarism.

In the interwar years, a number of socialists identified fascism as a tool of the existing order. In 1924, the Comintern defined fascism as "the instrument of the big bourgeoisie for fighting the proletariat." In 1924, Stalin characterized fascism as "the bourgeoisie's fighting organization." In 1931, Manuilsky claimed that fascism "grows organically out of bourgeois democracy." Four years later, Dimitrov analyzed the phenomenon as "a form of class domination [by] the bourgeoisie" (Beetham 1983, 153ff.). Such formulas drew on Marx's distinction between the workers and the owners of capital. They have since fallen out of favor. First, they are seen to minimize the capacity of fascists to organize independently on the basis of their own demands. Second, they underestimate the conflicts between different blocs of capitalist interests.

In the period before the fascist seizure of power in Germany and Italy, the leaders of the far Right debated the future relationship between the fascist parties and the existing economic rulers. The leading fascist politicians knew that they had to choose between the interests of their supporters and those of the wealthy. Once they had taken power, the conditions of the workers would either rise or fall. Fascist unions would have to choose whose interests they represented. If public services were to improve, someone would have to pay for the changes. Understanding the logic of these choices,

the leaders of the Italian and German fascist parties recognized in advance that they would have to rule in alliance with the generals, the businessmen, and the leading civil servants. Long before fascist movements took power, they began to make contacts with the ruling class. Hitler's famous 1932 speech to the Düsseldorf industry club belongs to this period.

Both in Italy and Germany, the members of the capitalist class were faced with their own choice of whether to accept fascism or to confront it. Different fractions of capital chose different options. The Italian Confederation for Industry backed Mussolini only after his seizure of power. In Germany, there were some prominent businessmen who supported Hitler's party from the early days. As early as 1922, Hitler's backers included publishers, steel magnates, and the industrialists Henry Ford and Fritz Thyssen. One important factor lying behind the National Socialist breakthrough in the 1930 elections was a pact with the leading German media magnate Alfred Hugenberg. Other units of capital preferred a quieter solution to the crisis. When the economy was at its strongest, fascist methods often appeared barbaric. Yet as recession took hold, many bosses concluded that they had no other option but to crush their workers.

In opposition, fascist parties had promised to rule in the interests of the entire nation. The actual beneficiaries did not include the workers, who suffered from falling real wages, rising prices, the dissolution of the unions, and an increase in working hours. In many factories the rate of work intensified. When people complained, they were liable to be taken away by the secret police. Rural groups also suffered under fascism, as did small employers, whose numbers fell sharply under both regimes. The relationship between fascism and the bourgeoisie was complex. In early 1920s Italy and early 1930s Germany, there were very few signs of tension between industrialists and the new governments. Quite to the contrary, many businessmen were happy to see the fascists destroying the institutions of the organized working class. Yet fascism did not simply obey the laws of capitalist rationality. The longer that fascism remained in power, the greater were the tensions. There was no economic logic, for example, in killing skilled Jewish metal workers, who might otherwise have built the arms for the German war effort. Moreover, World War II was catastrophic for both Italian and German business.

David Renton

See Also: BOLSHEVISM; CAPITALISM; COMINTERN, THE; ECONOMICS; FARMERS; FASCIST PARTY, THE; FORD,

HENRY; GERMANY; HOLOCAUST, THE; HUGENBERG, AL-
FRED VON; INDIVIDUALISM; INDUSTRY; ITALY; LIBERAL-
ISM; MATERIALISM; MUSSOLINI, BENITO ANDREA;
NAZISM; PALINGENETIC MYTH; PARLIAMENTARISM; SO-
CIALISM; STALIN, IOSIF VISSARIONOVICH; THYSSEN,
FRITZ; TRADES UNIONS; WARRIOR ETHOS, THE

References
Adler, Franklin Hugh. 1995. *Italian Industrialists from Liberalism to Fascism: The Political Development of the Industrial Bourgeoisie, 1906–1934.* Cambridge: Cambridge University Press.
Beetham, D. 1983. *Marxists in the Face of Fascism: Writings on Fascism from the Inter-War Period.* Manchester: Manchester University Press.
Gluckstein, D. 1999. *The Nazis, Capitalism and the Working Class.* London: Bookmarks.
Mason, T. 1993. *Social Policy in the Third Reich: The Working Class and the National Community.* Oxford: Berg.

BRASILLACH, ROBERT (1909–1945)

Key literary fascist in 1930s France, contributing from 1931 to *Je suis partout* (which he directed from 1937 on) and Thierry Maulnier's *Combat,* in addition to acting as a literary critic for *Action Française.* Mobilized during the war on the French side, he returned from captivity in April 1941 and subsequently resumed his activities as editor of *Je suis partout.* Although he became increasingly disillusioned with Nazism as the war progressed—he wrote his last article for *Je suis partout* on 27 August 1943—that did not bring an end to his literary endeavors on the far Right; he moved, rather, to the journal *Révolution nationale,* run by Drieu la Rochelle's former secretary, Lucien Combelle. He was arrested after the war, then tried and sentenced to death for treason.

Steve Bastow

See Also: ACTION FRANÇAISE; DRIEU LA ROCHELLE, PIERRE; FRANCE; FRENCH REVOLUTION, THE; NATIONALISM

References
Soucy, R. 1995. *French Fascism: The Second Wave, 1933–1939.* New Haven: Yale University Press.
Verdès-Leroux, Jeannine. 2000. "The Intellectual Extreme Right in the 1930s." Pp. 119–132 in *The Development of the Radical Right in France,* edited by E. Arnold. London: Macmillan.

BRAZIL

Brazil produced one of the largest fascist organizations in South America—Acão Integralista Brasileira (Brazilian Integralist Action; AIB)—often referred to as the Integralistas. AIB formed in 1932 when several smaller right-wing forces joined together under the leadership of Plínio Salgado. It emerged in a time of political upheaval and economic crisis. The Depression had hit Brazil hard, causing the price of coffee, its major export, to plummet. In response to the economic and political turmoil that ensued, Getúlio Vargas assumed the presidency of Brazil and effectively ended the Old Republic and the rule of the landed oligarchy. The climate of political and economic uncertainty that ensued afforded the AIB the political space it needed to organize. Taking advantage of this opportunity, AIB became the first "nonproscribed national and popular party in Brazil." (Deutsch 1999, p. 248). AIB organized support at the municipal, state, and national levels and developed a mass base among Brazilians. It reached out to workers and promised them that they would obtain social justice in the future Integralista state. It supported workers for two reasons: (1) to undermine the appeal of the Communist Party, which led many of the unions and had successfully organized workers; and (2) because it believed that workers, as Brazilians, should be incorporated into its nationalist and corporatist plans. By 1936, AIB had roughly 200,000 members, 20 percent of whom were women.

Inspired by the ideas of Italian Fascism, AIB was nationalistic, anticommunist, and anti-Jewish. AIB had three primary goals: (1) to form an Integral state; (2) to establish a corporatist government; and (3) to centralize the nation. It considered itself a revolutionary force because it rejected conservatism and "embraced a dynamic and total view of continued material and spiritual renovation." Unlike many other fascist organizations, AIB was racially tolerant and included some members of African and indigenous ancestry.

Like its Italian counterparts, the AIB understood the importance of symbols and rituals to solidify people's identification with the group. Every year local chapters of the AIB commemorated the "Night of the Silent Drums" and paid tribute to fallen Integralistas. The annual ceremony began at 11:00 P.M. with the singing of the Integralista hymn and ended at midnight with three minutes of silence. The ritual served to bind the scattered chapters together into one national party and reaffirm members' sense of their own history. Although the AIB encouraged women to join the movement, it maintained distinct roles and images for men and women. Women joined a female group called the Blusas Verdes (Green Blouses), while men formed the Camisas Verdes (Green Shirts). The uniformity of the color indicated a shared organizational affiliation, while the distinct names reflected a gender coding that mirrored the organization's vision of men's and women's separate roles in society and politics. AIB women maintained the groups' charity organizations and helped the poor. Nevertheless, their involvement in the militant fascist organization placed them in a more confrontational situation, one that demanded some modifications to their "traditional" gender roles. On at least one occasion, they stood guard as their (male) leader spoke and jeering leftists threatened to attack. Despite their more masculine attire and willingness to confront an angry crowd of men, these women worked to preserve established notions of gender. When they paraded they wore floral bouquets to soften and feminize their appearance, and they set up classes to instruct women in cooking, sewing, home economics, civility, and childcare.

Much of its leadership, including Plínio Salgado, believed that the party could achieve power through electoral victories. AIB participated in municipal, state, and national elections, and many of its candidates won seats. Unwilling to fully depend on legal means to obtain power, however, the AIB occasionally resorted to violence and engaged in street fights with the Left, some of which resulted in deaths on both sides. The fascist organization mistakenly believed that it operated with Vargas's full support and erroneously expected him to rely on the Integralistas as his party after he came to power. Instead, Vargas staged a coup in 1937 and, once he was firmly established in power, suppressed all political parties, including AIB. In May 1938 members of the AIB, in conjunction with some members of the navy, attacked the presidential palace and other government institutions. Their attempted coup failed and led to the arrest of 1,500 people, some of whom served jail terms while others, including Plínio Salgado, went into exile. Government repression effectively weakened the Integralistas, which, to all intents and purposes, ceased to exist.

Although AIB no longer functioned, some of its ideas and members continued to play an important role in Brazilian politics. Vargas presided over the Estado Novo (New State) from 1937 to 1945, which implemented some of the corporatist ideas promulgated by

AIB, such as the subordination of the working class to the state. It also sponsored the conservative gender ideas that the Integralistas favored, such as the definition of woman as mother. Confronted by the growing power of the Left and the reforms instituted by the João Goulart government (1962–1964), some Integralistas supported the 1964 coup that overthrew his government. Salgado joined ARENA (National Renovating Alliance), the more promilitary of the two parties approved by the military government set up following the coup, as did other AIB members.

Margaret Power

See Also: INTRODUCTION; ANTI-SEMITISM; CONSERVATISM; CORPORATISM; *ESTADO NOVO;* FASCIST PARTY, THE; INTEGRAL NATIONALISM; ITALY; MUSSOLINI, BENITO ANDREA; NATIONALISM; PALINGENETIC MYTH; REVOLUTION; SALGADO, PLÍNIO; STYLE; SYMBOLS; VARGAS, GETULIO DORNELLES; WALL STREET CRASH, THE; WOMEN

References
Deutsch, Sandra McGee. 1999. *Las Derechas: The Extreme Right in Argentina, Brazil, and Chile, 1980–1939.* Stanford: Stanford University Press.
Payne, Leigh A. 2000. *Uncivil Movements: The Armed Right Wing and Democracy in Latin America.* Baltimore: Johns Hopkins University Press.
Skidmore, Thomas. 1967. *Politics in Brazil, 1930–1964: An Experiment in Democracy.* London: Oxford University Press

BRITISH FASCISTI/ BRITISH FASCISTS, THE

The first British movement to identify itself openly as a fascist party, founded by Rotha Lintorn-Orman in 1923 as the British Fascisti and renamed British Fascists in 1924. Prominent individuals who lent their support to the birth of the party were Lord Garvagh, its first president, and his successor, Brigadier Robert Blakeney, along with other senior services personnel including the Earl of Glasgow, Colonel Sir Charles Burn MP. Arthur Hardinge, Fellow of All Souls and former ambassador to Spain, became party treasurer in 1926. The British Fascisti was set up as a paramilitary organization; it included an infantry section whose members were expected to confront socialist agitators on the streets. There were divisional and district commanders to supervise the different units. At headquarters there was a grand council to act as the decision-making body. To some extent this mirrored the militaristic styles of organization found in movements like the Boys' Brigade or the Salvation Army, but the parallels with Italian Fascism are clear. Although there was no uniform initially, by 1927 a blue shirt with dark trousers or skirt and blue hat had been adopted. The consensus of scholarly opinion is that the "fascism" of the movement lay more in its trappings than in its ideology, which is generally reckoned to have been a form of ultrapatriotic conservatism. But its historic position as the first concrete outward sign of a desire to emulate Mussolini and his Fascist movement in Britain gives it some significance, as does the fact that it was founded by a woman, who indeed ensured that there was a high degree of feminine involvement in the party. The scholarly consensus here is that while Lintorn-Orman had anything but a radical feminist agenda, she did harness feminist activism in the name of a radical nationalism.

Cyprian Blamires

See Also: CONSERVATISM; FASCIST PARTY, THE; GREAT BRITAIN; LINTORN-ORMAN, ROTHA; PARAMILITARISM; STYLE; WOMEN

Reference
Linehan, Thomas. 2000. *British Fascism 1918–1939: Parties, Ideology, and Culture.* Manchester: Manchester University Press.

BRITISH NATIONAL PARTY, THE

A racial fascist party founded in 1982 in the United Kingdom by former National Front chairman John Tyndall. After nearly a decade in the political wilderness, in 1993 it won a council seat in Tower Hamlets, East London, though it was lost the following year. Nick Griffin, who assumed the chairmanship in 1999, provided a fresh impetus through his attempts to "modernize" the party. Following race riots across northern England in 2001 and a barrage of anti-asylum hysteria from the press, the BNP won a string of local election victories in the Midlands and northern England between 2002 and 2003.

Graham Macklin

See Also: GREAT BRITAIN; GRIFFIN, NICHOLAS; IMMIGRATION; NATIONAL FRONT (UK); POSTWAR FASCISM; RACISM; TYNDALL, JOHN

References
Eatwell, Roger. 1998. "Britain: The BNP and the Problem of Legitimacy." Pp. 143–156 in *The New Politics of the Right,* edited by Hans-George Betz and Stefan Immerfall. London: Macmillan.
———. 2000. "The Extreme Right and British Exceptionalism: The Primacy of Politics." Pp. 172–192 in *The Politics of the Extreme Right: From the Margins to the Mainstream,* edited by Paul Hainsworth. London: Pinter.

BRITISH UNION OF FASCISTS, THE: *See* GREAT BRITAIN

BROEDERBOND, THE

Masonic-type organization founded around 1918 in South Africa to protect and promote the Afrikaner People and their culture. The Broederbond (Afrikaner Brotherhood) originated before 1910 within the student debating society Jong Suid Afrika. Initially membership was open, but physical attacks by opponents caused them to become a secret society in 1921. In 1925, the leaders went to Potchefstroom University College to ask for help. A complete reorganization along Christian-National lines followed. For the next thirty years Potchefstroom academics supported by like-minded Calvinists dominated the Broederbond, which created a host of cultural organizations including the Federasie van Afrikaanse Kultuurvereniginge (Federation of Afrikaner Cultural Organizations), the Volkskas (People's Bank), trades unions, and popular publications. The Broederbond tried to distance itself from fascist and Social Darwinist sympathizers with Hitler during World War II, but its Calvinist language was not always easy to distinguish from white supremacist racial rhetoric. During the 1950s, Prime Minister Henrik Verwoerd (1901–1966) wrested control of the Broederbond from the Calvinists, causing a bitter internal feud. According to the opposition press, the Broederbond was a nefarious secret society controlling the government. To many Afrikaners it was a Robin Hood–type organization that helped farmers fend off bankruptcy during droughts and bought shoes for the children of poor families. In 1989 the Broederbond polled its members, who decided that now was the time to release Nelson Mandela, abandon apartheid, and chart a new course for South Africa.

Irving Hexham

See Also: CONSERVATISM; HITLER, ADOLF; RACIAL DOCTRINE; SOCIAL DARWINISM; SOUTH AFRICA; WORLD WAR II

References
Bloomberg, Charles. 1989. *The Afrikaner Broederbond.* Bloomington: Indiana University Press.
Vatcher, William Henry, Jr. 1965. *White Laager: The Rise of Afrikaner Nationalism.* London: Pall Mall.

BROWNSHIRTS: *See SA*

BRÜNING, HEINRICH (1885–1970)

Chancellor of Germany from 1930 to 1932 and a key figure in the rise to power of Adolf Hitler. Brüning came to the chancellorship as a member of the Center Party at a time of economic crisis. He could not persuade the Reichstag to accept his financial medicine, and in July 1930 he dissolved it. Instead of increasing his support, as he had hoped, the new parliamentary membership produced by the resulting elections contained increased numbers of Nazis and communists. Brüning resorted to rule by presidential decree. Eventually, dissension between himself and President Hindenburg led to his dismissal from the chancellorship in May 1932. After Hitler took power at the beginning of 1933, Brüning tried to persuade Hitler's Nationalist allies to join the Center Party in forcing through modifications to the Enabling Act, so as to preserve civil liberties, but the Nationalists refused; the act, the foundation of the dictatorial powers assumed by the Nazi regime, was passed. The following year Brüning fled to the United States, where he became a Harvard professor.

Cyprian Blamires

See Also: CENTER PARTY, THE; ENABLING ACT, THE; GERMANY; HINDENBURG, PAUL VON BENECKENDORFF UND VON; HITLER, ADOLF; NAZISM; WEIMAR REPUBLIC, THE

Reference
Patch, J. 1998. *Heinrich Brüning and the Dissolution of the Weimar Republic.* Cambridge: Cambridge University Press.

BUCARD, MARCEL (1895–1946)

Involved in numerous French extreme-right movements between the wars before taking the helm of the fascist movement Parti Franciste, Bucard was born into a petit-bourgeois family. He had seemed destined for an ecclesiastical career but moved into politics after fighting in World War I. He unsuccessfully stood as an MP for the right-wing Union Nationale et Républicaine in 1924, before disillusionment with parliamentary politics saw him join Valois's Faisceau. He next became involved in the extreme-right newspaper *L'Ami du Peuple,* backed by the perfume millionaire François Coty, for whom he acted as a link with the Croix-de-Feu. In 1932, Bucard co-founded the Milice Socialiste Nationale, and on 29 September 1933 he founded Le Francisme, subsequently renamed the Parti Franciste. This was dissolved by the government on 18 June 1936, but reconstituted as the Parti Unitaire Français d'Action Socialiste et Nationale (PUF). Bucard revived the Parti Franciste following the Armistice, becoming an active collaborator, and was one of the founders of the Légion des Volontaires Français (LVF). Arrested on 30 June 1945 in Merano in Italy, he was tried the following February and condemned to death.

Steve Bastow

See Also: FINANCE; FRANCE; LA ROCQUE DE SEVERAC, FRANÇOIS, COMTE DE; NATIONALISM; SOCIALISM; VALOIS, GEORGES; WORLD WAR I

References
Deneil, A. 1979. *Bucard et le francisme.* Paris: Editions Jean Picollec.
Soucy, R. 1995. *French Fascism: The Second Wave, 1933–1939.* New Haven: Yale University Press.

BUDDHISM

Buddhism was used to various ends by Nazi propagandists and SS researchers calling themselves National Socialist scientists. Propagandists like Johannes von Leers saw it as an "active and courageous" religion. According to him, Gautama Buddha, an Aryan, faced down suffering, decay, and death by conquering human greed for life and wealth, thereby witnessing to a very non-Jewish spirit. Jakob Wilhelm Hauer saw the world in terms of a fundamental clash between two faith-worlds (*Glaubenswelten*), the Near-Eastern Semitic and the Indo-Germanic. Buddhism was part of the Indo-Germanic faith world that he hoped would once and for all triumph over "Jewish" Christianity. The Nazi Buddhist scholar Georg Grimm (1868–1945) hoped that Europe would be freed once and for all of Jewish mythology. The holy religions returning home, as it were, from Asia were falling on fertile soil in Nazi Germany.

SS researchers saw Buddhism from two perspectives. First, Buddhist and Sanskrit scholars at universities or the Ahnenerbe Research Institute of the SS attempted to prove the Aryan origins of the Buddha-doctrine. Second, they intended to research what value and teachings the practices of Shakyamuni (Gautama Sidartha) might have for the founding of a new National Socialist religion. Since the swastika was also an important symbol for Buddhists, it was used by German Buddhists before World War I, and Karl Gjellerup's best-selling book *Der Pilgrim Kamanita,* published in 1913, had a swastika on its cover. The book was an inspiration for Himmler. Himmler's theory informed the research of Ahnenerbe scholars. Favoring monocausal explanations, he argued that Germanic culture originated on the island of Atlantis, colonized the world, and left traces of a buried holy Aryan world religion, of which Buddhism was a part, in Asia. SS scholars like Ernst Schäfer and Bruno Beger were expected to find proof of the Aryan world religion in the remote mountains of Tibet. While the lamaism of Tibet that Schäfer and Beger discovered did not conform to the SS notion of a warrior religion, and also created conflict with the Ludendorffs, who saw lamaism as part of a world conspiracy of occultists to conquer the mind of Europe, it soon enchanted SS men. After all, Schäfer's Ph.D. advisor, Hans F. K. Günther, claimed that Tibet's aristocrats were connected to the higher European race; the lamaistic Buddhist bureaucracy became an example to the SS order, and lama death-rituals prepared SS researchers for their future work in the death camps.

Karla Poewe

See Also: AHNENERBE; ANTHROPOLOGY; ANTI-SEMITISM; ARYANISM; GOEBBELS, MAGDA; GÜNTHER, HANS

FRIEDRICH KARL; HAUER, JAKOB WILHELM; HIMMLER, HEINRICH; LUDENDORFF, ERICH; LUDENDORFF, MATHILDE; OCCULTISM; SS, THE; SWASTIKA, THE; TIBET; WARRIOR ETHOS, THE

References

Hale, Christopher. 2003. *Himmler's Crusade.* Hoboken, NJ: John Wiley and Son.
Kater, Michael H. 2001. *Das "Ahnenerbe" der SS 1933–1945.* München: R. Oldenbourg.

BUF: *See* GREAT BRITAIN

BULGARIA

Fascist parties and organizations never became a mass movement in Bulgaria, but between 1934 and 1944 the country showed a pronounced sympathy for the Axis. In the late nineteenth century a majority of the Bulgarian elite were pro-German. The "Greater Bulgaria" reestablished in March 1878 on the lines of the medieval Bulgarian empire after liberation from Turkish rule did not last long. In July 1878 (the Berlin Congress) Bulgaria had to cede a large part of Macedonia to Serbia and Greece and Süddobrudscha to Romania, which was confirmed after the Balkan War of 1913. Rightwing conservative and nationalistic circles continued to nurture hopes of recovering those territories ("Revision Policy"), and the entente with Germany and the Axis after 1934 was chiefly to serve that purpose. In World War I, Bulgaria came in on the side of Germany and Austria for the same reason, and in 1915/1916 occupied Macedonia and Süddobrudscha, only to lose them again in 1918/1919.

In October 1918, Czar Boris III (1894–1943) came to the throne, and he was to play a key role in the rapprochement with the Axis. In the years after 1919, conservative regimes came to power with the chief aim of opposing communism. From 1923 to 1926 the rightwing extremist Alexander Cankov (1879–1948) was president, a militant anticommunist who in 1934 founded the National Social Movement (Sgovor) as a general disparate fascist movement of right-wing renegades from the bourgeois parties. His followers were known as "Cankovists." In 1932, Christo Kuntschev also founded a Bulgarian pendant to the NSDAP, the

NSBRP, which, however, fragmented and faded. From 1929 there were intensive trade contacts between Bulgaria and Germany, and Cankovists and right-wing Bulgarian officers were courted by Italy and the German Reich in 1933.

Czar Boris made overtures to Germany and was received by Hitler in Berlin as his first foreign state visitor on 1 March 1934. After the collapse of the military regime of Georgiev (May 1934–January 1935), the czar took over the government provisionally on 22 January and then definitively on 21 April 1935. The personal government of the czar showed a mixture of authoritarian-conservative, fascist, and monarchistic traits and is therefore differently assessed; while in the West it was considered a "royal dictatorship," in Marxist history it is described as "monarcho-fascism." After the prohibition of parties decreed in June 1934, the czar also dissolved the Cankovist organization and the parafascist officers' association of "Legionaries," but on the other hand in 1936 took Cankovists on board as ministers in the government. Following a state visit to Bulgaria by Hermann Goering and other senior Nazi officials in May 1935, there were increasingly intensive contacts between the German and Bulgarian governments. In 1937, Bulgaria began to receive substantial credits from the German Reich for the funding of an armaments program.

After Bulgaria had played an active mediatorial role between Germany and the Western powers in 1938 during the Sudeten crisis and at the Munich talks, Germany and Italy put the czar under massive pressure to come into the Axis. However, Czar Boris wanted to pursue a policy of neutrality and also to pressure the Axis powers to recognize Bulgarian revisionist aims—especially as on 9 February 1934 the neighboring states of Yugoslavia, Greece, Romania, and Turkey had concluded the "Balkan Pact" for the rejection of Bulgarian demands. Bulgaria was careful to be actively involved in the Hitler-Stalin Pact of August 1939, not wishing to be squeezed between those two powerful regimes.

After the outbreak of World War II, it became increasingly difficult for Bulgaria to stick to her original policy of neutrality. In February 1940 the czar made the weak philo-German scholar Bogdan Filov (1883–1945) president. In return for German mediation of the Treaty of Craiova (7 September 1940), in which Romania ceded Süddobrudscha according to the 1913 borders to Bulgaria, she agreed to mold her domestic policy to German wishes. On 23 January 1941,

Czar Boris brought in the Law for the Protection of the Nation, which was a copy of the Nuremberg race laws against the Jews, who constituted only about 1 percent of the population (that is, 50,000 persons). As a result of that law, around 20,000 Jews were "moved" from Sofia to the provinces up to July 1943, but the deportation to the death camps that the Germans were demanding was resisted by the czar and by all circles of the population. After massive pressure from the Axis Powers, Bulgaria came into the Three Power Pact with Germany, Italy, and Japan on 1 March 1941. The German invasion of the Soviet Union on 1 June 1941 was, however, so unpopular in Bulgaria that the Germans did not dare to put Bulgarian divisions into the battle against Russia. Sympathy for Germany among the populace rapidly decreased, and the government avoided breaking off diplomatic contact with the Soviet Union. However, German troops needed Bulgaria as an operational base against the USSR; in return for her "loyalty to the alliance," Bulgaria received Macedonia and Thrace from the Germans in 1941. Her hopes of occupying the territory of Salonika were, however, blocked by Italy.

Pro-Russian opinion in the populace led to a growth in the illegal Communist Party and to Partisan activity. German military officials demanded a stronger intervention by the Filov regime, which thereupon set up a "state gendarmerie" for fighting the partisans in January 1943. Czar Boris III died on 28 August 1943; his son Simeon II was still a child, so a three-man regency council ruled in his place, including Bogdan Filov and Prince Kyrill (1895–1945), brother to Czar Boris and friendly to the Germans. He had taken part in a failed coup in 1936 with the Cankovists. But now the trend of the war was clearly in favor of the Soviet Union. Under pressure both from the German military and the communist partisans, Filov realized that (as a consequence of the Prohibition of Parties in 1934) he lacked mass support. With the aid of fascist legionaries and Germanophile forces he created the Bulgarian National Association in the summer of 1943.

Ivan Bagrjanov, made president in June 1944, sought to distance himself prudently from Germany and to avoid an open breach with the USSR. As Romania changed sides, seeing the way the wind of war was blowing, Bulgaria declared her neutrality on 23 August 1944 and announced that she was withdrawing from the war. In spite of that, on 8 September 1944, Soviet troops entered Bulgaria; Bulgaria now declared war on

Germany. Bogdan Filov and Prince Kyrill were condemned to death by a "people's court" and executed in February 1945.

Markus Hattstein
(translated by Cyprian Blamires)

See Also: ANTI-SEMITISM; AXIS, THE; BARBAROSSA, OPERATION; CZECHOSLOVAKIA; CONCENTRATION CAMPS; GERMANY; GOERING, HERMANN; HITLER, ADOLF; HITLER-STALIN PACT, THE; HOLOCAUST, THE; ITALY; MARXIST THEORIES OF FASCISM; MONARCHY; NATIONALISM; NAZISM; NUREMBERG LAWS, THE; ROMANIA; SOVIET UNION, THE; WORLD WAR I; WORLD WAR II; YUGOSLAVIA

References
Miller, M. 1975. *Bulgaria during the Second World War.* Stanford: Stanford University Press.
Oliver, H. 1998. *We Were Saved: How the Jews in Bulgaria Were Kept from the Death Camps.* Sofia: Sofia.
Sugar, P. 1971. *Native Fascism in the Successor States, 1918–1945.* Santa Barbara, CA: ABC-CLIO Press.

BURNING OF THE BOOKS, THE:
See BOOKS, BURNING OF THE
BUSINESS: *See* BANKS; ECONOMICS; INDUSTRY; U.S. CORPORATIONS

BUTLER, RICHARD GIRNT (1918–2004)

Known as "Pastor" or "Reverend" Butler, for nearly thirty years one of the best-known representatives of the U.S. white supremacist, anti-Semitic far Right. Born in Colorado in 1918, he studied aeronautical engineering before doing war service with the U.S. Armed Forces. He became acquainted with other white supremacists while working for Lockheed in southern California. After serving as national director of the Christian Defense League for ten years, Butler moved to Idaho with his congregation, which became Aryan Nations with the aim of forming a "national racial state." Breakaways left Butler isolated, but at his death he retained a strong profile on the far Right.

Cyprian Blamires

See Also: ANTI-SEMITISM; ARYAN NATIONS; POSTWAR FASCISM; RACIAL DOCTRINE; UNITED STATES, THE (POSTWAR); WHITE SUPREMACISM

References
Dobratz, B. 2000. *The White Separatist Movement in the United States: "White Power, White Pride!"* London: Johns Hopkins University Press.

CABLE STREET, THE BATTLE OF

This set-piece confrontation between fascists, antifascists, and the Metropolitan Police took place in London on 4 October 1936, just as the Civil War was breaking out in Spain. Oswald Mosley's British Union of Fascists (BUF) had recently recovered from a previous setback, the clashes at Olympia in 1934. The BUF recruited a number of working-class racists in London's East End. Following the BUF's decision to hold a march through the area, antifascists responded by blocking the route. The police attempted to force a way through but were repulsed. Cable Street was later used, in the 1940s and 1970s, as a mobilizing symbol of successful antifascist protest.

David Renton

See Also: ANTIFASCISM; BRITISH FASCISTS/BRITISH FASCISTS, THE; GREAT BRITAIN; MOSLEY, SIR OSWALD; SPANISH CIVIL WAR, THE

References
Cable Street Group. 1995. *The Battle of Cable Street 1936.* London: Cable Street Group.
Thurlow, R. 1998. *Fascism in Britain: From Oswald Mosley's Blackshirts to the National Front.* New York: I. B. Taurus.

CAESARISM

Term employed by Gramsci, Thalheimer, and others to identify contemporary fascisms in Germany and Italy as modernized versions of Bonapartism (the authoritarian political ideology associated with Napoleon Bonaparte and the Emperor Napoleon III—dictatorship appealing to mass support). Mussolini claimed to have introduced a "Third Italian Civilization" after the Roman Empire and the Renaissance. The militaristic and expansionistic spirit of the Romans was evidently close to the self-image of the Italian Fascists themselves. Three days before the March on Rome, Mussolini lectured his supporters on the role played by war in giving birth to the Roman spirit. In art and literature, the supporters of the fascist regime repeatedly compared Mussolini's court to the glories of Rome. Similar models were found in Germany, where Oswald Spengler argued that the only alternative to the decline of the West was national rebirth, directed by new "legions of Caesar."

The parallels between modern and ancient Rome also influenced the theories of fascism's opponents. One of the first sustained critics to write about fascism was the Italian communist Antonio Gramsci. He drew on the writings of Karl Marx and in particular on

Marx's concept of "Bonapartism." Gramsci employed the synonym "Caesarism" to distinguish fascism as an Italian version of Bonapartism. Karl Marx's analysis had appeared in *The Eighteenth Brumaire of Louis Bonaparte* (1852). That pamphlet showed how a small minority movement could take power. Napoleon's nephew began his career as an adventurer with the support of just a few intellectuals and members of the urban poor. He was able to defeat his rivals in a coup and declare himself emperor, taking the title Napoleon III. Marx blamed Bonaparte's victory on the malaise of two grander forces in French society, the working class and the bourgeoisie. Forced into open conflict in 1848, neither had overwhelmed the other. Instead, their mutual exhaustion had opened the way for Bonapartism. It was a form of class society in which the previous ruling class continued to dominate the economy, but its preferred representatives did not administer the state.

Seventy-five years later, Antonio Gramsci sought to explain the victory of Fascism in Italy from detention in a Fascist jail. He suggested that Mussolini's support had drawn on social layers similar to those who had followed Bonaparte, the "famished" urban poor, supplemented by a "subversive" class of rural peasants who were willing to back any revolution, left or right. Fascism was an independent party that ruled in the interests of capital. It was also a system of personal rule. Caesarism was a "situation" in which "the forces of conflict balance each other in a catastrophic manner." The same notions of equilibrium that Marx had detected in 1852, Gramsci found in early 1920s Italy. The advance of the workers' movement during the revolutionary years of 1919–1921 had been enough to weaken the previous rulers, but not to topple them.

Antonio Gramsci's theories were similar to those of a German Marxist, August Thalheimer, also writing around 1930. Thalheimer compared fascism to Bonapartism. There were additional points he made, however, that help to fill out Gramsci's analysis. The first was his observation that fascism appeared eighty years after Napoleon III. In other words, it depended in part on the sclerosis of the system, the replacement of free trade by a system of trusts and monopolies. A second point he made was that Louis Napoleon had modeled his secret society on those of his rivals on the small French insurrectionary Left. By contrast, Mussolini's and Hitler's model was the totalitarian Soviet Communist Party. The fascist conception of the power of the state was much grander and more dangerous than Bonaparte's.

David Renton

See Also: BOULANGISM; FASCIST PARTY, THE; GERMANY; GRAMSCI, ANTONIO; HITLER, ADOLF; ITALY; LEADER CULT, THE; MARCH ON ROME, THE; MARXIST THEORIES OF FASCISM; MUSSOLINI, BENITO ANDREA; ROME; WAR

References
Baehr, Peter, and Melvin Richter, eds. 2004. *Dictatorship in History and Theory: Bonapartism, Caesarism, and Totalitarianism.* Washington, DC: German Historical Institute.
Beetham, D. 1983. *Marxists in the Face of Fascism: Writings on Fascism from the Inter-War Period.* Manchester: Manchester University Press.
Gramsci, A. 1976. *Selections from the Prison Notebooks.* London: Lawrence and Wishart.
Marx, K., and F. Engels. 1979. *Collected Works.* Vol. 11. London: Lawrence and Wishart.

CALENDAR, THE FASCIST

As a movement deeply bound up with the attempt to overcome national or racial decadence and create a "new man," fascism has always tended to generate a powerful longing for the renewal of historical time in its most fervent supporters, particularly in the interwar period, when a profound structural crisis affected the entire world of Western modernity. Once installed in power, Italian Fascism devoted considerable energy to the development of an elaborate "political religion," to induce in Italians the subjective sense of living through a temporal revolution. For example, it has been calculated that between 1922 and 1944 the citizens of Verona could have participated in 727 "events" (or, on average, one every ten days), including celebrations, symposia, commemorations, demonstrations, and inaugurations designed to lift them out of the decadence of pre-Fascist time and weld them into the regenerated "national community." As a result, the private time of committed Fascists became regularly transcended by the suprapersonal time of the reborn Italy.

An essential part of this process was played by the institution of a new calendar, which was intercalated with the Christian religious year of major feasts, holy days, and saint days and which overlaid the secular calendar introduced as part of the civic religion of liberal Italy. Thus 23 March, Youth Day, commemorated the founding of the Fasci; 21 April, Labor Day, the founding of Rome; 24 May, Empire Day, the entry of Italy into World War I; 20 September, Italian Unity, the incorporation of Rome into the Kingdom of Italy; 28

October, the Fascist Revolution, the March on Rome. In 1931 the regime even introduced a "Fascist Epiphany," which in Milan included a "Christmas Day's" distribution of gifts in the name of Mussolini to be known as the "Duce's Christmas." When Saturday became a holiday for most workers, it was promptly dubbed the "Fascist Saturday." The outstanding example of this attempt to turn calendar time into an instrument of fascistization, however, was the superimposition over the Gregorian time-scheme of a specifically Fascist one. The year 1922, that of the March on Rome, became year I of the Fascist era, and all official publications were dated in terms both of Anno Domini and of the years that had passed since the first stage in Mussolini's "conquest of the state." In this way Italians were encouraged to feel that it had betokened not just a change of administration but also the inauguration of a new era in the history of an "eternal" Italian civilization.

In its fundamental conception of historical time Fascism was deeply akin to Hitler's regime, which, after seizing power in 1933, also instituted an elaborate political religion as part of its bid to found a "thousand-year Reich" (a millennial concept that points to a deep metaphysical urge to transcend "ordinary" historical time). Events such as the yearly Nuremberg rallies and the Berlin Olympics were transformed into huge liturgical celebrations of the phoenixlike resurrection of Germany from the ashes of the Weimar Republic and the fulfillment of her "Aryan" destiny. The Nazi calendar involved the "makeover" of the 1 May feast of the coming of spring, already appropriated by Marxism to mark International Labor Day, so that it celebrated German Labor Day instead. Hitler's birthday and the date of his accession to the chancellorship became major holy days in the sacralization of the state. Inevitably the regime also poured considerable energy into commemorating the failed putsch of November 1923. Its centerpiece was an elaborate choreographed ritual, part operatic pageant, part religious ceremony, that turned the steps of the Feldherrnhalle in Munich's Odeonplatz—built as a memorial to the martyrs of the *Kampfzeit* ("time of struggle"—that is, before Nazism came to power)—into an "altar" and transformed the hall itself into a temple to the new Reich. Within National Socialist myth, 9 November 1923 thus became a turning point at which the old era of decadence and "Jewish" hegemony was overthrown and a new glorious chapter in the story of Germany's destiny inaugurated.

Roger Griffin

See Also: INTRODUCTION; "ANTI-" DIMENSION OF FASCISM, THE; ANTI-SEMITISM; ARCHITECTURE; ARYANISM; BERLIN OLYMPICS, THE; CHRISTIANITY; DECADENCE; FASCIO, THE; FASCIST PARTY, THE; GOEBBELS, (PAUL) JOSEPH; HITLER, ADOLF; MARCH ON ROME, THE; MUNICH (BEER-HALL) PUTSCH, THE; MUSSOLINI, BENITO ANDREA; MYTH; NEW MAN, THE; NATIONALISM; NAZISM; NUREMBERG RALLIES, THE; PALINGENETIC MYTH; PROPAGANDA; RACIAL DOCTRINE; RELIGION; REVOLUTION; SCHIRACH, BALDUR VON; SCHÖNERER, GEORG RITTER VON; SYMBOLS; TOTALITARIANISM; TRADITIONALISM; *VOLKSGEMEINSCHAFT,* THE

References

Berezin, M. 1997. *Making the Fascist Self.* Ithaca: Cornell.

Berghaus, G. 1996. "The Ritual Core of Fascist Theatre: An Anthropological Perspective." In *Fascism and Theatre,* edited by G. Berghaus. Oxford: Berghahn (reprinted in Griffin, R., and M. Feldman, eds. 2003. *Fascism.* Critical Concepts in Political Science, vol. 3, pp. 71–98. London: Routledge).

Boyd Whyte, I. 1995. "Berlin, 1 May 1936." In *Art and Power: Europe under the Dictators 1930–1945.* London: Hayward Gallery (reprinted in Griffin, R., and M. Feldman, eds. 2003. *Fascism.* Critical Concepts in Political Science, vol. 3, pp. 292–306. London: Routledge).

Fenn, R. 1997. *The End of Time.* London: Society for the Promotion of Christian Knowledge.

Gentile, E. 2000. "The Sacralisation of Politics: Definitions, Interpretations and Reflections on the Question of Secular Religion and Totalitarianism." *Totalitarian Movements and Political Religion* 1, no. 1 (reprinted in Griffin, R., and M. Feldman, eds. 2003. *Fascism.* Critical Concepts in Political Science, vol. 3, pp. 39–70. London: Routledge).

Vondung, K. 1979. "Spiritual Revolution and Magic: Speculation and Political Action in National Socialism." *Modern Age* 23, part 4: 391–402 (reprinted in Griffin, R., and M. Feldman, eds. 2003. *Fascism.* Critical Concepts in Political Science, vol. 3, pp. 251–263. London: Routledge).

CALVO SOTELO, JOSÉ (1893–1936)

Spanish finance minister under the Miguel Primo de Rivera dictatorship (1923–1930) and a determined, violent opponent of the Second Republic (1931–1936). Editor of the intellectual, authoritarian right-wing journal *Acción Española* and leader of the elitist monarchist cause of the exiled Alfonso XIII, he became increasingly influenced by fascism—a tag that he happily embraced on occasion. During the spring of 1936, Calvo Sotelo's public attacks on the republic grew ever more virulent. His assassination by socialist assault guards on 13 July 1936 finally clinched the involvement in the military revolt of a number of prevaricating officers, including Francisco Franco.

Sid Lowe

See Also: FALANGE; FRANCO Y BAHAMONDE, GENERAL FRANCISCO; SPAIN; SPANISH CIVIL WAR, THE

References
Artiles, Jenaro. 1976. *They Had to Die: New Light on the Deaths of Calvo Sotelo, Sanjurjo, and Mola in the Spanish Civil War.* Mexico City: B. Costa-Amic.
Carr, R. 2001. *Modern Spain, 1875–1980.* Oxford: Oxford University Press.

CAMBODIA: *See* KAMPUCHEA

CANADA

Fascism in Canada is complex. There have been hundreds of overlapping organizations, many short-lived, with leading fascists moving between organizations, and Canadian fascism has had its own unique character, with special regional variations. Canadian fascists have been world leaders in such areas as Holocaust denial. Canadian fascism began in the 1920s with the Ku Klux Klan particularly prominent. Klans emphasized different scapegoats in different provinces, with the French most targeted in Saskatchewan, for example, and Asians most targeted in British Columbia. The Klan was especially popular in the western province of Saskatchewan. In the 1920s, Klan membership in Saskatchewan was between 20,000 and 40,000, and many elected officials were Klansmen.

In 1920s Quebec, other fascist organizations were more prominent; fascism was pronouncedly anti-Semitic, and it was linked to Quebec separatism. The earliest influential Quebec figure was the father of Quebec separatism, Father Lionel Grouxl. Grouxl called for the birth of a new Quebec tied to land, religion (Roman Catholic), and language (French). Correspondingly, he blamed Jews for current problems and organized a boycott of Jewish merchants and goods, the *achat chez nous* ("buy from our own") movement. A leading figure in that movement was journalist Adrian Arcand—father of Canadian Fascism. The most prominent fascist leader of the time, Arcand gave Canadian Fascism its distinctly Nazi orientation. Arcand was not a separatist but a Canadian nationalist who spearheaded a Nazi movement that extended into English Canada. He broadcast his messages via three newspapers that he edited, and he founded the National Socialist Christian Party. Allied federally with the Tories, the National Socialist Christian Party helped to elect the federal Tories and received funding from them. Another significant fascist party in the 1930s was the Canadian Nationalist Party, led by William Whittaker and dedicated to creating a corporatist state. On 5 June 1934 approximately a hundred of Whittaker's Brownshirts appeared heavily armed in the streets of Winnipeg.

Anti-Semitism and Nazism were an accepted part of Canadian society before World War II. Mainstream newspapers frequently carried anti-Semitic articles. Signs in Toronto restaurants prohibited Jews and dogs from entering. In Toronto as well as other Ontario cities, there was a proliferation of Nazi gangs known as "swastika clubs." On 16 August 1933, members of one such gang unfurled a huge swastika flag, thereby sparking the Christie Pits Riot, the largest riot in Toronto history. Anti-Semitism and openness to Nazism is reflected in government policy of the time. In 1937, Liberal Prime Minister McKenzie King developed a trade deal with Hitler. Correspondingly, Britain looked to Canada to host the second international conference on refugees precisely because Canada could be counted on to take a tough line on Jewish refugees. Come World War II, leading fascists were imprisoned. Nonetheless, after the war, Canada was second only to Argentina in the number of fleeing Nazis that it admitted. Throughout the decades, many were employed as anticommunist spies. Correspondingly, until 1948, Jews remained the European refugees least favored by Canadian immigration.

Fascism was at a very low ebb in the 1950s. In the mid-1960s and 1970s, a limited revival began, largely centered in Toronto. Significant in that regard are the Canadian Nazi Party, headed by John Beattie, and the Western Guard, led by Don Andrews and John Ross Taylor. During the late 1970s, the government set up federal and provincial human rights commissions. Since then, the human rights apparatus has frequently been used successfully to curb fascist activity. The first of the fascists to be curtailed by it, Western Guard leader John Ross Taylor, was jailed in 1979 for failure to comply with a tribunal order to desist from broadcasting hate messages on the Guard's hateline (a phone number which, when called, allows the user access to a propagandist message). A far more substantial fascist

German-Canadian Ernst Zundel, a central figure in the modern Holocaust Denial movement. (AP Photo/Thomas Kienzle)

upsurge began in the 1980s and continued into the late 1990s. Important organizations during that period include the Aryan Nations, the Church of the Creator, the Nationalist Party, the Canadian Knights of the Ku Klux Klan, and the Northern Hammerskins. Of particular note is the Heritage Front, founded in 1989 and initially led by Wolfgang Droege. An umbrella group that unites the radical Right, the front networks with fascist groups of all persuasions. During its heyday in the early 1990s the front patrolled specific streets, promoted white power concerts, and marched on Parliament Hill, declaring parliamentarians traitors. Organizations centered around white power music also thrived in that era, with George Burdi, for example, founding Resistance Records, the largest white power music business in North America.

Throughout this period, Canadian and international fascism has been particularly affected by one figure living in Toronto—Ernst Zundel, a landed immigrant from Germany. A disciple of Arcand, Zundel set up Samisdat Publishing in Toronto in the 1960s. Samisdat Publishing is dedicated to the dissemination of Holocaust denial material. Zundel was jailed after being convicted of spreading false news but was released when the Supreme Court struck down the false news statute. The Zundel trials brought together leading Holocaust deniers from around the world. They also gave birth to the *Leuchter Report* (a forensic analysis of gas chamber remnants). Despite fundamental flaws, this report has become a fascist classic and is quoted throughout the Internet. Zundel remains at the hub of international Holocaust denial. The enormity of his influence became clear in 1991 when the West German authorities identified Zundel as one of the six major exporters of Holocaust denial material to Germany. With the turn of the century, there was a minor upsurge in fascism, with Heritage Front again more active. Zundel's status, on the other hand, became more fraught. In 2002 the Canadian Human Rights Commission ruled that material on the Zundelsite (webpage) violates the Canadian Human Rights Act. Correspondingly, in 2003 the minister of immigration issued a security certificate declaring Zundel a national security risk.

Bonnie Burstow

See Also: ANTI-SEMITISM; ARYAN NATIONS; CATHOLIC CHURCH, THE; CORPORATISM; HOLOCAUST DENIAL; KU KLUX KLAN, THE; NAZISM; NEO-NAZISM; PARLIAMENTARISM; POSTWAR FASCISM; ROCK MUSIC; SWASTIKA, THE; WHITE NOISE; WHITE SUPREMACISM

References
Burstow, Bonnie. 2003. "Surviving and Thriving by Becoming More 'Groupuscular.'" *Patterns of Prejudice* 37, no. 4: 415–428.
Kinsella, Warren. 1994. *Web of Hate.* Toronto: HarperCollins.
Lipstadt, Deborah. 1994. *Denying the Holocaust.* New York: Penguin.

CANARIS, ADMIRAL WILHELM (1887–1945)

One of the most prominent military men to be executed in connection with the July Plot against Hitler, even though he did not support it. Canaris joined the Imperial Navy in 1905 and started working for the secret service during World War I. He took part in the antidemocratic Kapp putsch; his anticommunism and his rejection of the Weimar Republic and the Versailles Treaty made him join forces with the Nazis. Having entered the fleet command in 1920, he participated in the illegal arming of the German armed forces. Holding the rank of an admiral, he became head of the German secret service in 1935. His office played a part in the faked attack on the Gleiwitz station that was used by the Nazi leadership to justify propagandistically the invasion of Poland. On account of shortcomings in performing his duty (especially massive exposure of secret agents), Canaris was deprived of power in February 1944. His attitude toward the political opposition is still a topic of debate. He had contacts with top representatives of the opposition inside the military as early as 1938 and rejected some of Hitler's measures, but his reservations did not stop him from doing his work; he did not approve the July plot. Nevertheless he was arrested as a supporter and shot on 9 April 1945 in the concentration camp in Flossenbürg.

Fabian Virchow

See Also: GERMANY; JULY PLOT, THE; KAPP PUTSCH, THE; KREISAU CIRCLE, THE; NAZISM; WEIMAR REPUBLIC; WORLD WAR I; WORLD WAR II

References
Brissaud, André. 1973. *Canaris: The Biography of Admiral Canaris, Chief of German Military Intelligence in the Second World War.* London: Weidenfeld and Nicholson.
Manvell, Roger. 1969. *The Canaris Conspiracy: The Secret Resistance to Hitler in the German Army.* New York: McKay.

CAPITALISM

Fascists rarely spoke of capitalism as a system. To do so would have been to risk accepting the political outlook of the Left. Yet fascists frequently denounced injustices that others typically blamed on capital. Mussolini complained of the tendency that capitalism exhibited to become impersonal. The famous Twenty-Five Points adopted as a party program by the German National Socialists in February 1920 included references to the state's obligation to provide work for its citizens, the abolition of incomes unearned by work, the reduction of interest rates, the nationalization of trusts, profit-sharing in large industrial enterprises, the dismantling of large department stores and their leasing to small traders, and the abolition of ground rent and of speculation in land.

Insofar as fascist spokesmen recognized capitalism as a system and called for its reform, their most consistent point was a rejection of trading and banking—which they dubbed "finance"—and a preference for industry. Some of this argument was taken over from varieties of parliamentary socialism. Thus the British fascist Oswald Mosley was able to move seamlessly from a period before 1930 as a left-wing Labor advocate of full employment to a later period when he preached a right-wing fascist critique of "finance," now blamed loosely on the Jews. Other economic influences on Mosley's supporters included the parallel theories of social credit and the Italian model of the corporate state. Meanwhile French fascists fulminated against the laissez-faire spirit of the Liberal state; the corollary of war economies was a general increase in state spending.

Many of the adversaries of interwar fascism argued that this barbaric movement had been able to emerge only as a result of certain flaws inherent in the capitalist system itself. One antifascist, Max Horkheimer, wrote: "Whoever does not want to speak of capitalism should be equally silent on fascism" (Renton 1999, 101). It was argued that fascism had based itself on certain features of life that recurred under capitalism, such as the division of the world into nation-states, the tendency of the economic order to go into crisis, and the hostility of large employers to working-class organization. Yet in recent years a number of writers, including some Marxists, have argued that fascism was not merely or even primarily a reflection of market economic conditions. This debate has been most polarized in the consideration of the causes of the Holocaust.

We can list briefly some of the background factors that were said to have linked fascism to capitalism. One of the most important pillars of fascist ideology was extreme nationalism, but xenophobia made no sense in a precapitalist world. The rise of a global system of nation-states was linked to the emergence of the world market. By doing away with the previous patchworks of overlapping fiefdoms, the emergence of the state made the spread of industry possible. Without capitalism there would have been neither nations nor nationalism. Capitalism was also said to have provided the economic background to fascism. The rise of this movement depended on collective feelings of injustice and anger. So long as millions continued to go hungry, while a few rich men prospered, the potential for social crisis would continue. In the actual history of the 1920s and 1930s, two economic processes had been of still more direct importance. One was the global deflation of the mid-1920s, most acute in Germany. The other was the catastrophic recession following the 1929 Wall Street Crash. Fascism thrived on the subsequent mood of despair. Capitalists were also blamed for having financed the far Right. Fascism was linked to the antiproletarian instincts of the owners of the greatest industries. Such magnates as Thyssen, Hugenberg, or the U.S. car boss Henry Ford—who also funded Hitler—believed that their whole world was under attack from militant unions. They gave generous donations to the various fascist parties. They also agitated within the capitalist class for more fascistic solutions to the economic crisis.

Two further points were developed by interwar antifascists. One was the argument that the capitalist system had gone through different periods of growth. In the nineteenth century, for example, when the system was thriving and the economy growing rapidly in almost every country, the most characteristic face of politics was liberalism. In the slump of the 1930s, by contrast, politics came to be dominated by fascism and war. Another insight was that all around Europe, both fascist and nonfascist states responded to the Depression by employing similar economic schemes. Projects of forced labor were introduced to set the unemployed back at work. Tariffs were employed, in France and Britain as well as Italy and Germany. The relationship between private capital and the state shifted in favor of the state.

David Renton

See Also: ANTI-SEMITISM; AUTARKY; BANKS, THE; BOLSHEVISM; CORPORATISM; ECONOMICS; EMPLOYMENT; FINANCE; FORD, HENRY; HITLER, ADOLF; HOLOCAUST, THE; HUGENBERG, ALFRED VON; INDUSTRY; LIBERALISM; MARXIST THEORIES OF FASCISM; MOSLEY, SIR OSWALD; MUSSOLINI, BENITO ANDREA; NATIONALISM; NATIONALIZATION; NAZISM; STATE, THE; THYSSEN, FRITZ; TRADES UNIONS; WALL STREET CRASH, THE; WORK; XENOPHOBIA

References
Bracher, K. D. 1971. *The German Dictatorship: The Structure and Effects of National Socialism.* Harmondsworth: Penguin.
Broszat, M. 1981. *The Hitler State: The Foundation of the Internal Structures of the Third Reich.* London: Longman.
Gluckstein, D. 1999. *The Nazis, Capitalism and the Working Class.* London: Bookmarks.
Mason, T. 1993. *Social Policy in the Third Reich: The Working Class and the National Community.* Oxford: Berg.
———. 1995. *Nazism, Fascism, and the Working Class.* Cambridge: Cambridge University Press.
Renton, D. 1999. *Fascism, Theory and Practice.* London: Pluto.
Traverso, E. 1999. *Understanding the Nazi Genocide: Marxism after Auschwitz.* London: Pluto.
Leon, A. 1970. *The Jewish Question: A Marxist Interpretation.* New York: Pathfinder.

CAPORETTO

Catastrophic World War I Italian military defeat at the hands of the Austro-Hungarian forces in the autumn of 1917, frequently exploited by Mussolini in his propaganda as a symbol of failure and treachery that exposed the shamefulness of the Italian political and military establishment. This defeat inflicted deep wounds on the national psyche and has been described as "Italy's Golgotha."

Cyprian Blamires

See Also: AUSTRO-HUNGARIAN EMPIRE/HABSBURG EMPIRE, THE; ITALY; MUSSOLINI, BENITO ANDREA; PAPACY, THE; SECULARIZATION; WORLD WAR I

References
Morselli, M. 2000. *Caporetto, 1917: Victory or Defeat?* London: Frank Cass.

CARLYLE, THOMAS (1795–1881)

Scottish historian and essayist whose belief in the power of heroic individuals to transform history, penetrating critique of British society, and admiration for the Germanic spirit proved highly congenial to Nazi ideologues. Carlyle was in fact one of the most significant and radical conservative thinkers of the nineteenth century. Born in a remote rural locality, he studied in Edinburgh and went on to work as a teacher until his success enabled him to live by his writing and he settled in London. In 1865 he became lord rector of the University of Edinburgh. Carlyle was marked both by radical Scottish Puritanism and by German Idealism (Kant, Fichte, Schiller, and Goethe), and he steeped himself in German literature from his early years. From the start he constructed a polarity between the "sacrificial seriousness" of the Germans and the "superficial, pleasure-seeking" English. In his *Signs of the Times* (1829, initially published anonymously), he lamented the gulf between the astounding material achievements of the machine age and the characterless and weak-willed mediocrity of modern man.

The public influence of Carlyle as political theorist began with his essay on Chartism. He called for strong government intervention, as against the prevailing spirit of laissez-faire that abandoned the poor to their fate and neglected the social question, and he spoke of the "right of the common man" to leadership by a far-seeing statesman as "the most unquestionable and most natural" of all human rights. Carlyle criticized the emerging mass democracy, claiming that the crowd always needed decisive leadership, but he also criticized the aristocracy for having given itself up to comfortable living and for clinging to its privileges. He attacked the liberal middle class for their boundless faith in progress, their capitalistic and utilitarian striving for profit, and their egoism, which were so completely opposed to the truly heroic spirit. For all his conservatism, Carlyle had

strong and undisguised sympathies with social revolutionary solutions.

In *Past and Present* (1843), Carlyle's language took on a threatening and prophetic tone when he contrasted medieval life in the cloister with a present marked by "decadence." In *Occasional Discourse on the Nigger Question* (1849), his thought also acquired a racist tinge when he spoke of the unfitness of the blacks to rule themselves and argued for a modern form of slavery and imperialism.

Particularly influential on Mussolini and Hitler were Carlyle's theories on history, which he expounded in *The French Revolution* (3 vols., 1837), *On Heroes and Hero Worship* (1841), and his *History of Frederick the Great* (6 vols., 1858–1865). He saw all historical development as deriving from towering individuals—heroes and geniuses; he claimed that the mass of men need a hero and leader figure to tell them how to live and to provide them with a role model. For Carlyle (as later for Hitler) all history was a work of "Providence" that rewarded the worthy and capable, even when they had to subjugate the world by fire and sword.

Markus Hattstein (translated by Cyprian Blamires)

See Also: ARISTOCRACY; CAPITALISM; CONSERVATISM; DECADENCE; DEMOCRACY; ELITE THEORY; FREDERICK II, THE GREAT; GERMANNESS; HERO, THE CULT OF THE; HITLER, ADOLF; LEADER CULT, THE; MODERNITY; MUSSOLINI, BENITO ANDREA; NAZISM; PROGRESS; RACISM; REVOLUTION; UTILITARIANISM; WARRIOR ETHOS, THE

References
Heffer, Simon. 1995. *Moral Desperado: A Life of Thomas Carlyle.* London: Weidenfeld and Nicholson.
Kaplan, Fred. 1983. *Thomas Carlyle: A Biography.* Cambridge: Cambridge University Press.
Vanden Bossche, C. 1991. *Carlyle and the Search for Authority.* Columbus: Ohio State University Press.

CARREL, ALEXIS (1873–1944)

French-born U.S. doctor and researcher, Nobel Prize winner, and admirer of Hitler whose best-seller *Man, the Unknown* (1935) brought him worldwide fame for his frank advocacy of eugenics and concern for race hygiene. Carrel was a researcher for many years at the Rockefeller Institute for medical research in New York. When he reached the statutory retirement age of sixty-five he asked for an exemption, but it was refused, whereupon he accused the institute's Jewish members of forcing him out; in fact, there were no Jews on the board of scientific directors. Carrel was a close friend of Hitler admirer and anti-Semite Charles Lindbergh. In 1941, Carrel went to Paris on the advice of Lindbergh and obtained financial backing from the Vichy leader Marshal Pétain to set up a Foundation for the Study of Human Problems that was to advance the implementation of his eugenic principles. After the Liberation he was accused of collaboration with the Nazis but died of a heart attack before he could be tried.

Cyprian Blamires

See Also: ANTI-SEMITISM; EUGENICS; FRANCE; HITLER, ADOLF; LINDBERGH, CHARLES AUGUSTUS; NAZISM; PETAIN, MARSHAL HENRI PHILIPPE; RACIAL DOCTRINE; VICHY

References
Carrel, Alexis. 1948 (1935). *Man, the Unknown.* West Drayton: Penguin.
Wallace, Max. 2003. *The American Axis.* New York: St. Martins Griffin.

CARTO, WILLIS (born 1926)

Founder in 1955 of Liberty Lobby, considered by some to be the most influential right-wing extremist propaganda organization currently in existence in the United States. He receives little publicity, as he avoids the spotlight. He has a history of association with anti-Semitic and pro-Nazi periodicals and publishing. An offshoot of Liberty Lobby is the Institute for Historical Review, which Carto founded in 1979 to disseminate Holocaust denial. In 2001, Carto relinquished control of Liberty Lobby.

Cyprian Blamires

See Also: ANTI-SEMITISM; HOLOCAUST DENIAL; INSTITUTE FOR HISTORICAL REVIEW, THE; NEO-NAZISM; POSTWAR FASCISM; UNITED STATES, THE (POSTWAR); WHITE SUPREMACISM

References
Dobratz, B. 2000. *The White Separatist Movement in the United States: "White Power, White Pride!"* London: Johns Hopkins University Press.
Durham, M. 2000. *The Christian Right: The Far Right and the Boundaries of American Conservatism.* Manchester: Manchester University Press.

CATHOLIC ACTION: *See* CATHOLIC CHURCH, THE; PAPACY, THE; PIUS XI, POPE; POLITICAL CATHOLICISM

CATHOLIC CHURCH, THE

Any examination of the relationship between the Catholic Church and fascism necessarily consists of three strands: (1) those fascist movements that were themselves Catholic in inspiration or in tendency; (2) the attitudes of the general Catholic public in the Western democracies toward international fascism; and (3) the activities of the Vatican and of the Catholic hierarchy in individual countries during the fascist era. These strands naturally interweave at times. But what emerges is that there *was* such a thing as "Catholic fascism," which evidenced itself in a number of national movements. Great sections of the general Catholic public in such countries as Britain and France showed considerable enthusiasm for what has been termed "Mediterranean fascism," with many of them nevertheless baulking at what they saw as "pagan" Nazism. Certain Catholic bishops and archbishops, in various countries before and during World War II, did acquiesce in fascist brutalities (while others distinguished themselves by their protests); the Vatican, starting from its usual foreign policy standpoint of negotiating concordats to safeguard Catholic interests, reached a high point of opposition to Nazism in the late 1930s under Pius XI with the encyclical *Mit brennender Sorge,* after which, under Pius XII, its actions (or inaction) have led to considerable controversy.

Among the movements in the late nineteenth century and the early twentieth century that have been seen as "protofascist," there were a number that had a considerable Catholic following. This is particularly true of the French "radical Right" movement Action Française, founded in 1898, which has at times been described as "better placed within the reactionary right-wing tradition," even though it had "affinities with fascism" (Eatwell 1995, 19); another view, however, holds that Action Française was closely related to what was to become fascism, and that in the interwar period, after the emergence of Italian Fascism, it was itself aware of that relationship. Be that as it may, the Catholic strain has been a constant in the French radical Right.

When Italian Fascism came into existence immediately after World War I, it was essentially a secular movement, one of its main characteristics being strong hostility toward the Catholic Church. Increasingly, however, after Mussolini's advent to power in 1922, he began to see that open conflict with Catholicism would be damaging and could lose him too much support. His eventual ideal seems to have been "peaceful coexistence"; that was helped by the pro-Fascist attitudes of a number of churchmen, while even those who were not necessarily enthusiastic took a similar view of the need to compromise. These attitudes on both sides led to the Lateran Pacts of 1929, which were vitally important both for the Catholic Church and for Fascism. They resolved church-state relations, which had remained in abeyance ever since the occupation of Rome in 1870, the main elements being (1) a treaty recognizing the independence and sovereignty of the Holy See and creating the State of the Vatican City; (2) a concordat defining the civil relations between the government and the Church within Italy ("free Church in free State"); and (3) financial compensation to the Holy See for its losses in 1870. These pacts brought great benefits to the Church, in that it became the established church in Italy and also achieved political status as an independent state. But they were even more important for Mussolini, in that they gave his regime formal recognition and greater support within a significant section of the Italian population, while ensuring that the clergy were forbidden to take part in politics and that bishops swore allegiance to the Italian state. At the same time, they presented Italian Fascism to international opinion as a responsible and respectable regime.

One incidental by-product was the impetus that was given to support for Fascist Italy among the Catholic populations of the Western democracies, who seemed to believe that what was essentially a pragmatic piece of political maneuvering was in fact a proof of the essentially "Catholic" nature of the Italian regime. What many such observers failed to note were the increasingly tense relations between Fascism and the Church in Italy in the immediate aftermath of the Lateran Pacts, culminating in Pius XI's 1931 encyclical *Non abbiamo bisogno,* which retaliated to the Fascist Party's attacks on the youth movement Catholic Action and condemned "a regime based on an ideology which clearly resolves itself into a pagan worship of the State."

With the rise of antidemocratic forces and the spread of dictatorial regimes in Europe in the 1930s, and with the new conviction that these were all part of a new "international Fascism," a number of movements in various countries presented a close combination of Catholicism and fascism. This was, of course, true mainly of predominantly Catholic countries such as Spain, Portugal, and Ireland, or countries such as Belgium with a strong Catholic community. The Rexist movement in Belgium, for example, was headed by Léon Degrelle, a product of the Catholic University of Louvain and former editor of the *Cahiers de la Jeunesse Catholique (Journal of Catholic Youth).* This movement, stemming from the journal *Rex* (a name based on Christ's title *Christus Rex,* Christ the King), was Catholic, anticapitalist, and anticommunist. Sympathetic observers in other countries saw Degrelle as a charismatic figurehead for a new Fascist surge.

Even in a country like Ireland, where the fascist "Blueshirts" movement was comparatively small and ineffective, the same syndrome was to be found. As early as the late 1920s, Professor Walter Starkie had been seeing fascism as the opportunity for a "spiritual awakening" of Ireland that would avoid the "selfish individualism and agnosticism" that underlay most modern political theory. Eoin O'Duffy, the leader of the Blueshirts, went further. He saw the Blueshirts' mission as that of leading Ireland out of its difficulties by setting up "the only Christian system of government which will work successfully in the modern world"—that is, corporatism. Their main work would be to "inspire our people with a consciousness of the great destiny of Ireland as a Christian state," and to rekindle the spirit of the old Irish missionaries who had saved Christianity in the Dark Ages, by holding themselves ready to stem the tide of communism and materialism that was engulfing modern Europe (Griffin 1995, 182–184).

In Portugal, Salazar's *Estado Novo* ("New State") has sometimes been described as conservative rather than fascist, but there are more similarities than differences between it and the more extreme fascist movement, the National Syndicalists (which has often been contrasted with Salazar's government). The policies of both of them stem directly from the prewar Integralist movement, a prime example of "pre-fascism" of the Action Française type. Indeed, it has been pointed out that those most disposed to learn from and emulate Italian and Nazi models in Portugal had all "been grounded in the teachings and intellectual style of *Integralismo*" (H. Martins in Woolf 1968). One of the moving forces behind Integralism and also behind Salazar's doctrines was Catholicism, and the *Estado Novo* was established on traditional Catholic principles, the process culminating with the Concordat of 1940.

As for Franco's Spain, one of the major planks in Nationalist propaganda during the Civil War had been the idea of a "crusade" against those who would destroy the Church. Franco too has often been seen as a "conservative reactionary" rather than a fascist. But there is no doubt that contemporary observers saw his regime as a natural ally of the Italian and German regimes, and he seems to have considered himself and his followers as belonging to the same international movement as Italian Fascism and German Nazism, while showing, as did those movements, specific national characteristics. The Spanish Church (apart from the priests in the Basque province, who showed that it was possible for Catholics to rally to the Republican side) strongly supported Franco's cause in the Civil War; that, and the accounts of Republican atrocities against priests, nuns, and churches, led many Catholics in other countries to believe implicitly in the "crusade" propaganda, and to mobilize help for the Franco side. This view was reinforced by the Spanish hierarchy's letter "to the bishops of the whole world," which claimed that the insurrection and the resultant civil war were theologically just in that they aimed to save the principles of religion, that the National movement was a vast family in which the citizen could attain his total development, and that the Basque priests were to be reproved for not having listened to the voice of the Church.

One must not, of course, make exclusive generalizations about Catholic attitudes to the Spanish Civil War. In France, alongside the many who shared the poet Paul Claudel's view, as expressed in his poem "To the Spanish Martyrs," that what was at stake was the very future of the Church in a country that had been one of the bastions of the faith, there were also writers such as Georges Bernanos, Jacques Maritain, François Mauriac, and the group associated with the journal *Sept,* who deplored such Catholic commitment to what they believed to be an unworthy cause. It remains true, nevertheless, that there was a large majority of French Catholics who saw Franco's cause as a worthy one.

In Britain, support for Franco extended from the aristocratic Catholicism of recusant society to the working-class Catholicism of the inner cities. Many prominent Catholics joined The Friends of National Spain, which held many public meetings throughout the United Kingdom. An FNS meeting in Perth, for example, expressed "heartfelt sympathy with fellow Christians in Spain who are suffering such prolonged martyrdom" and declared a conviction that "there will be no peace in Spain or the Western Mediterranean until the forces of anarchy, tyranny and Communism are crushed." The Archbishop of Westminster formed a Spanish committee to consider measures of humanitarian help to the Nationalist side. It consisted of such prominent figures as Lord Fitzalan of Derwent and

Lord Howard of Penrith. Evelyn Waugh's future sister-in-law, Gabriel Herbert, was typical of the young Catholics who supported its aims; she became an ambulance driver for Franco's troops. The kind of rhetoric that underlay such commitment can be found in the unpublished diary of one aristocratic British enthusiast: "Got the glorious news about 2 p.m. that the Carlists had occupied Barcelona! *Viva Requetes!* And so God in his infinite goodness has caused his Son to triumph again in Spain to the confusion and ruin of Red Anti-Christ. *Viva Franco! Arriba Espana!"*

There was also ample evidence of support for Franco's cause in British working-class Catholicism. This was so strong and widespread that "the Labour Party, aware that many Catholic workers actively opposed the Spanish Republic, feared it might lose the Catholic vote if it appeared too vigorously pro-Republican" (Srebrnik 1995). In the East End of London, the tepidity of the strong Irish Catholic element within the local Labor Party in relation to antifascism was what made so many Jews join the Communist Party.

Apart from the question of the Spanish Civil War, there was also a strong element of support for "Mediterranean fascism" in general among French and British Catholics, who indiscriminately placed Mussolini, Salazar, and Franco in the same category. That could in some cases even extend to other "Catholic fascist" movements such as Rexism; the Catholic leader of the Welsh Nationalist movement, Saunders Lewis, for example, could almost in the same breath praise Salazar, "one of the two or three greatest statesmen of Europe to-day," and Degrelle, seen as spokesman of large numbers of his fellow countrymen (*The Welsh Nationalist,* September and October 1936).

Nazism, however, presented a completely different problem. Admirers of Mussolini such as Douglas Jerrold, and Sir Charles Petrie recoiled at the "barbarism" both of Nazi methods and Nazi beliefs. Mussolini, after all, had seemed, not only to his enthusiastic supporters but also to the public at large, a respectable member of the European family of nations. Jerrold attacked Nazi anti-Semitism while continuing in his support for Mussolini. Petrie saw Italian-style Fascism as standing "for the family, for religion, and for discipline," whereas Nazism, "the old Prussianism in a new form," applied eugenic tests to the relations of the sexes, was trying to make religion a department of state, and preferred emotionalism to self-control (*Saturday Review,* 20 May 1933). Similarly, in France, Henri Massis, a fervent Catholic admirer of Mussolini, Franco, and Salazar, felt that Hitler was wrongly associated with Italian Fascism, whose "noble, elevated virtues" were the contrary of

Nazism's "doctrines of force, of violence" (Massis 1939). Much of the French Catholic press, which had been so favorable to Mussolini and Franco, denounced the "false gods" of Nazism, particularly after the papal encyclical of 1937, *Mit brennender Sorge.*

Meanwhile, what were the Vatican's attitudes to these matters? As far as Spain was concerned, in 1937 the Vatican formally recognized Franco's side in the Civil War as the official government of Spain. This meant that any Catholic who took the Republican side was a rebel against the pope. On the question of Germany, however, the Vatican's policies were much more hesitant. Throughout the interwar period, one of the Vatican's great concerns had been to regularize the Church's position in individual countries by a series of concordats. The Lateran Treaties with Italy had fitted into that context, based on the traditional aims of Vatican diplomacy, which were to live with regimes, even those most contrary to the principles of the Church, rather than to oppose them. When the Nazis came to power in 1933, therefore, it was hardly surprising that the Vatican should have set about negotiating a concordat to safeguard the position of the Church within Germany. What its negotiators failed to see, at this stage, was that the subsequent actions of the Nazi regime were to change completely the context in which such agreements had been negotiated in the past. The concordat was negotiated on behalf of Pope Pius XI by his secretary of state, Cardinal Pacelli, the future Pius XII, and signed on 20 July 1933. Pacelli, as papal nuncio to Germany for thirteen years from 1917, had throughout the 1920s been renegotiating with the German states their individual concordats, which had until then accorded German Catholics considerable autonomy from the Vatican. He hoped thereby to solidify papal power. He also hoped eventually to negotiate a concordat with the whole German nation. It was ironic that the opportunity for this should finally have occurred when the new, despotic regime had taken power—but, as with the Lateran Treaties, it was seen as a move providing advantages to both sides. The Church was able thereby to solidify its power among German Catholics, but at the same time hoped it could safeguard the German Catholic minority against persecution or encroachments on its freedom of conscience. The Nazis ensured thereby that the Church in Germany, which up to then had taken some part in opposing the rise of Nazism, would no longer have any significant opposition role, as bishops had to pronounce an oath of loyalty to the state, and clergy were prohibited from belonging to, or working for, political parties.

In any event, it was Hitler who gained all the advantages. On the one hand he used the concordat, and on the other he ignored its provisions. By the mid-1930s he had instituted show trials of clergy and a concerted drive to convert Catholics to the new Nazi faith. The Church was concerned not to present too stark a choice for German Catholics, for fear that, in the fervently nationalistic mood of the time, they might choose the secular faith. This meant that the Church played a far less oppositional role in the Third Reich than the Protestant Confessing Church. On the other hand, the Catholic public was far less inclined to support Nazism. Although support from the Nazis came from all social groups, "they achieved their best support in Protestant areas. . . . [T]he industrial workers were under-represented among their supporters and members, as were Catholics" (Cheles, Ferguson, and Vaughan 1995). Meanwhile, the Nazis were putting even more pressure on the Catholics. A drive against religious separateness in the school system and the exertion of pressure on parents to transfer their children to interdenominational schools was the last straw for the Vatican authorities. Pius XI produced a powerful encyclical in 1937 entitled *Mit brennender Sorge* (*With Burning Concern*). Written in German, it was addressed directly to German Catholics. In it the pope denounced the Nazi attitude toward the concordat. They had "sowed the seed of distrust, unrest, hatred, defamation, of a determined hostility overt or veiled, against Christ and his Church." Infidelity to Christ was seen by the Nazi leaders as "a signal and meritorious act of loyalty to the modern State." The Church wished sincerely for a true peace between Church and State in Germany, but would defend its rights and its freedom if necessary. It has been pointed out that this encyclical, while being a powerful indictment of Nazism, was so on the basis purely of Nazism's attitudes to the Catholic Church, rather than that of the regime's other activities. It has been claimed, however, that Pius XI was planning to produce another encyclical about racism and anti-Semitism, entitled *The Unity of Human Races,* that the text had actually been prepared, and that only his death in February 1939 had prevented its publication.

The former cardinal Pacelli succeeded Pius XI as Pius XII. Pacelli had in fact been the main compiler of *Mit brennender Sorge* for Pius XI, so much might have been hoped of him as an opponent of the Nazi regime. It soon became clear, however, that he was, as a former Vatican diplomat, committed to the traditional methods of the Vatican secretariat: caution, and a preference for negotiation rather than confrontation. Coupled with that, he was an even more violent opponent of communism than his predecessor and cautious about anything that might tip the balance of forces in Europe toward the Left. Pius XII's record, both before and during World War II, has been a subject of considerable debate. On the one hand, his silence in the face of the Nazi treatment of the Jews has been condemned; on the other, much has been made of behind-the-scenes activities on his part that showed a concern to wield influence to the best of his ability, within the limits that he had set himself.

During World War II, the record of the Catholic Church in the various occupied territories, and those allied to the Reich, was a varied one. At one extreme there were the vicious activities of the Ustasha under Ante Pavelić in Croatia, which was installed by the Germans as an independent state in 1941. The Ustasha was a Catholic nationalistic movement violently opposed to the Orthodox Serbs with whom they had been part of prewar Yugoslavia. Under their rule about 600,000 Serbs, Jews, and Gypsies were massacred, and thousands of Serbs were forcibly converted to Catholicism. A number of Catholic priests took a leading part in such Ustasha activities. Throughout the war the Vatican was in full diplomatic relations with Croatia and had a papal nuncio in the capital, Zagreb. Although full details of the Ustasha activities were known, they were never condemned by the Church.

Monsignor Tiso's regime in Slovakia, which was declared independent under German protection in March 1939, was a different matter. Although the Slovak Popular Party, of which Tiso was leader, was a Catholic party, Tiso's Catholicism was subordinate in importance to his Slovak nationalism. Tiso's party's activities can in no way be compared to those of the government of Croatia, but, like most governments of puppet states, it has come under considerable criticism for acquiescence in the deportation of Jews as the war proceeded. Tiso's own role in this has always been seen as an ambiguous one. He had, however, definitely prepared anti-Semitic legislation as early as late 1938, and laws excluding Jews from the professions and the university were in force by August 1939. But he voiced public criticism of the deportations, which were stopped despite heavy German opposition, from October 1942 to October 1944.

Vichy France is a good example of a puppet state in which the reactions of the local hierarchy were extremely varied. A majority of bishops and clergy welcomed the advent of the Pétain government immediately after the German invasion of 1940, seeing it as the first Christian government in France since 1870 and an opportunity to revive Christian values in a society that had been ruled for too long by the godless Third Republic. Support for Vichy did not, however, necessarily imply acceptance of the German occupier, and many French Catholics began by late 1940 to feel considerable unease at the anti-Semitic policies of Vichy, unease that turned to alarm when the German authorities commenced the deportations of 1942. The attitudes of the cardinals and archbishops ranged from the strongly pro-Nazi Cardinal Baudrillart, who blessed the Frenchmen who went to fight for Germany on the Eastern Front as "the crusaders of the twentieth century," to Cardinal Gerlier of Lyon and Archbishop Saliège of Toulouse, who protested in 1942 against the Jewish deportations and called on Catholics to shelter and hide Jews. The refugee networks set up as a result, mainly by the religious orders, saved thousands of Jewish children, while many Catholic families sheltered individual Jews. The activities of individual Catholics in all the occupied countries were similarly varied.

The war itself changed the perceptions of most Catholics, and in the succeeding years the Vatican has completely revised its attitudes. In those places where "neofascist" movements have gradually emerged, Catholic support or participation has been no greater, and usually less, than that of other sections of society. While the political pronouncements of the "breakaway" traditionalist Archbishop Lefèvre were naively reminiscent of the rhetoric of Action Française, the party that appeared most to resemble that prewar movement, Le Pen's Front National, seems to have attracted mainly nonpracticing Catholics to its cause. And despite its nostalgic evocation of the "Catholic Right" of the prewar era, it is interesting to note that its electoral propaganda by now appears to contain almost no religious content. The same is true of extreme-right movements within other Catholic countries, such as Austria.

Richard Griffiths

See Also: ACTION FRANÇAISE; ANTIFASCISM; ANTI-SEMITISM; AUSTRIA; BELGIUM; CENTER PARTY, THE; CHAMBERLAIN, HOUSTON STEWART; CHRISTIANITY; CONFESSING CHURCH, THE; CONSERVATISM; CORPORATISM; CROATIA; DEGRELLE, LEON; *ESTADO NOVO;* FASCIST PARTY, THE; FRANCO Y BAHAMONDE, GENERAL FRANCISCO; FRANCOISM; GERMANY; GREAT BRITAIN; HITLER, ADOLF; INTEGRAL NATIONALISM; IRELAND; ITALY; LE PEN, JEAN-MARIE; LUTHERAN CHURCHES, THE; MARXISM; MATERIALISM; MUSSOLINI, BENITO ANDREA; NATIONAL FRONT, THE (FRANCE); NAZISM; O'DUFFY, EOIN; PAPACY, THE; PAVELIĆ, DR. ANTE; PETAIN, MARSHAL HENRI PHILIPPE; PIUS XI, POPE; PIUS XII, POPE; PORTUGAL; POSTWAR FASCISM; PROTESTANTISM AND NAZISM; PROTO-FASCISM; RELIGION; REXISM; ROMA AND SINTI,

THE; SALAZAR, ANTÓNIO DE OLIVEIRA; SALGADO, PLÍNIO; SCHMITT, CARL; SERBS, THE; SLOVAKIA; SPAIN; SPANISH CIVIL WAR, THE; SPANN, OTHMAR; STATE, THE; SYNDICALISM; THEOLOGY; THIRD REICH, THE; TISO, MGR. JOSEF; USTASHA; VICHY; YUGOSLAVIA

References
Anon. 1940. *The Persecution of the Catholic Church in the Third Reich.* London: Burns and Oates.
Blinkhorn, Martin. 1990. *Fascists and Conservatives.* London: Unwin Hyman.
Cheles, Luciano, Ronnie Ferguson, and Michalina Vaughan. 1995. *The Far Right in Western and Eastern Europe.* London: Longman.
Eatwell, Roger. 1995. *Fascism: A History.* London: Chatto and Windus.
Griffin, Roger. 1995. *Fascism.* Oxford: Oxford University Press.
Griffiths, Richard. 2000. *An Intelligent Person's Guide to Fascism.* London: Duckworth.
Grunberger, Richard. 1971. *A Social History of the Third Reich.* London: Weidenfeld and Nicolson.
Halls, W. D. 1995. *Politics, Society and Christianity in Vichy France.* Oxford: Berg.
Massis, Henri. 1939. *Chefs.* Paris: Plon.
Pollard, J. 1985. *The Vatican and Italian Fascism.* London: Macmillan.
Sánchez, José M. 1987. *The Spanish Civil War as a Religious Tragedy.* Notre Dame, IN: University of Notre Dame Press.
Srebrnik, Henry. 1995. *London Jews and British Communism 1939–1945.* London: Vallentine Mitchell.
Thomas, Hugh. 1961. *The Spanish Civil War.* London: Eyre and Spottiswoode.
Walker, Lawrence D. 1970. *Hitler Youth and Catholic Youth 1933–1936: A Study in Totalitarian Conquest.* Washington, DC: Catholic University of America Press.
Woolf, S. J., ed. 1968. *European Fascism.* London: Weidenfeld and Nicholson.

CELINE, LOUIS FERDINAND (1894–1961)

Pseudonym of French doctor and right-wing interwar novelist Louis-Ferdinand Destouches. Céline was a prominent anti-Semite and supporter of fascism. His literary breakthrough came with the novel *Voyage au bout de la nuit (Journey to the End of the Night)* in 1932, which was followed by a number of novels marked by a profound anti-Semitism: *Mort à credit* (1936), *Bagatelles pour un massacre* (1937), *L'Ecole des cadavres* (1938), and *Les beaux draps* (1941). Carroll argues that Céline's work picks up the threads of anti-Semitism from "where Drumont left off, giving a new language and style to anti-Semitism" (Carroll 1995, 180). He played little

active part in politics during the collaboration, but he did contribute numerous pieces for the ultracollaborationist press and was friends with a number of ultracollaborationists. Céline fled France following the Liberation, first to Germany then to Denmark, where he was arrested and imprisoned for a year until February 1947. He returned to France in 1951, following an amnesty.

Steve Bastow

See Also: ANTI-SEMITISM; DRUMONT, EDOUARD ADOLPHE; FRANCE

References
Carroll, D. 1995. *French Literary Fascism.* Princeton: Princeton University Press.
Vitoux, F. 1994. *Céline: A Biography.* New York: Marlow.

CENSORSHIP: *See* BOOKS, THE BURNING OF THE; FRICK, WILHELM; PRESS, THE; RADIO; THEATER

CENTER PARTY, THE

At the end of World War I, the Catholic Center Party (Zentrumspartei; originally founded in 1870 by the Catholics of Germany to defend the rights of the Church) held the balance of power in the German Reich. It advocated recognition of the Weimar constitution, fulfillment of the Treaty of Versailles, better education, and closer relations with the Vatican. The party continued to advance the Church's interests in Germany until Hitler's rise, but by early 1933 he had largely stripped it of power. To the great embarrassment of the Holy See, the party supported the Enabling Act, which gave Hitler essentially unlimited powers, and it briefly considered forming a coalition with the Nazis, just for survival.

In 1933 the Nazis killed several activists in the party, and it was almost eliminated in March of that year. For the next three months the Nazis brutalized the remaining members of the Center Party, as well as other Catholics. On 5 July 1933, two weeks before the concordat between Germany and the Holy See was signed, the membership dissolved in the hope that this would stop the persecution. Pius XI, like all popes since at least Pius X (1903–1914), agreed with removing clergy from direct political involvement. Pius thought that the Church could be more effectively defended with the lay organization Catholic Action than by parliamentary action. Therefore, when the concordat was signed, he agreed to a term barring German priests and bishops from involvement in party politics. Since the only political party left in Germany at this time was the Nazi Party, that provision actually ended up being an asset to the Church. The relevant provision of the concordat said: "[T]he Holy See will prescribe regulations which will prohibit clergymen and members of religious institutes from membership in political parties and from working on their behalf." The supplemental protocol said: "The conduct enjoined upon the pastors and members of religious institutes in Germany does not entail any limitation of the prescribed preaching and interpretation of the dogmatic and moral teachings and principles of the Church."

Despite the removal of Catholic clergy from direct participation in the political process, they were not restricted from making statements that dealt with basic human rights. Moreover, Catholic laypersons were in no way restricted from political activity. The agreement with Germany was very similar in this respect to the Lateran Treaty signed with Italy in 1929 and to instructions given to the French clergy in the mid-1920s. The Church did not agree to restrictions on its right to involve itself in politics whenever "the fundamental rights of man or the salvation of souls requires it." The Catholic clergy were in fact very far from being silenced, and many of them spoke out against the Nazis.

Ronald Rychlak

See Also: BRÜNING, HEINRICH; CATHOLIC CHURCH, THE; ENABLING ACT, THE; GERMANY; HITLER, ADOLF; LATERAN PACTS, THE; MUSSOLINI, BENITO ANDREA; NAZISM; PAPACY, THE; PIUS XI, POPE; POLITICAL CATHOLICISM; WEIMAR REPUBLIC, THE; WORLD WAR I

References
Evans, E. L. 1981. *The German Center Party 1870–1933: A Study in Political Catholicism.* Carbondale: Southern Illinois University Press.
Rychlak, R. J. 2000. *Hitler, the War, and the Pope.* Huntington, IN: Our Sunday Visitor.

CERCLE PROUDHON, THE

Group of French far-right intellectuals who began meeting in December 1911 to promote nationalist an-

tidemocratic thinking. Among the moving spirits behind it were Georges Valois and Charles Maurras. They founded a journal, the *Cahiers du cercle Proudhon,* in January 1912.

Cyprian Blamires

See Also: ACTION FRANÇAISE; FRANCE; MAURRAS, CHARLES; VALOIS, GEORGES

References
Sternhell, Ze'ev. 1978. *La Droite révolutionnaire: Les origines françaises du fascisme 1885–1914.* Paris: Seuil.
Weber, Eugen. 1962. *Action française.* Stanford: Stanford University Press.

CHAMBER OF CORPORATIONS, THE: *See* TRADE UNIONS

CHAMBERLAIN, HOUSTON STEWART (1855–1927)

Son of an English admiral and one of the most important proponents of *völkisch* ideology in general and *völkisch* anti-Semitism in particular. Often described as a spiritual forefather of the Third Reich. From 1888 onward he became increasingly influential within the Bayreuth circle that was centered around the composer Richard Wagner's widow, Cosima, and that constituted one of the key *völkisch* milieux in pre–World War I days. His main work is *Die Grundlagen des neunzehnten Jahrhunderts* (1899; English translation: *The Foundations of the Nineteenth Century,* with introduction by Lord Redesdale).

Chamberlain was born in England in 1855 but suffered from poor health and spent most of his life on the Continent. After marrying the German-born Anna Horst in 1878, he settled in Geneva to take up university studies and graduated in 1881. He immediately started working on his doctoral dissertation, but because of poor health and financial difficulties, the dissertation did not appear until 1896. Initially it had been a study of the mechanics of sap movements in plants, but it developed into an attempt at proving the existence of a vitalist life force. Influenced by Kant, Schopenhauer, and ancient Indian texts, Chamberlain became increasingly convinced that the only plausible explanation for the existence of sap movements was indeed the existence of a vitalist life force. Another consequence of Chamberlain's scientific development was a growing antipositivist conviction that science could not be separated from philosophy, religion, and art but had to be perceived as part of a vitalist whole. This view on science was not uncommon in the last decades of the nineteenth century, but it became increasingly outdated as the century drew to its close.

Chamberlain first came into contact with philosophical Wagnerism in the late 1870s, and before settling in Vienna in 1889 he spent four years in Dresden, during which not only his dedication to the neo-Romantic and *völkisch* Bayreuth spirit became more manifest, but also his anti-Semitism. From the 1890s onward, Chamberlain became an extremely productive writer, authoring numerous books, pamphlets, and articles in favor of the Bayreuth spirit. In Vienna, Chamberlain wrote *Die Grundlagen des neunzehnten Jahrhunderts,* which was meant as the first of three works determining the role of the Aryan race in the past, present, and future, but only the first part of this trilogy was ever finished. In it, he describes world history as a dialectical struggle between the pure Aryan and Jewish races; the rise of world civilizations was seen as the accomplishment of the Aryan race. To Chamberlain, race was not only a biological entity but also a metaphysical force in history, and the Aryan race carried the mark of spirituality and advancement through history. In contrast, the Jews were pictured as materialistic and greedy, and the aim of the Jewish race was, according to Chamberlain, to use conspiratorial methods to destroy the Aryan race and enslave the world under Jewish rule.

Because the Aryan race was perceived as the only race with a religious and spiritual capacity, race and religion became closely intertwined in Chamberlain's thinking, and the creation of a pure "Aryan Christianity" became perhaps the most important vehicle for Aryan resurrection. In his attempt to cleanse Christianity of Jewish and other un-Aryan influences, Chamberlain launched violent attacks not only against Jews and Judaism but also against Catholicism. Chamberlain was also one of the ardent advocates of the myth of the "Aryan Christ," claiming that Jesus must have been Aryan by descent. In this calling for a renewal of the Christian faith, Chamberlain was one of the anticipators of the religious thought of Alfred Rosenberg. In 1908, Chamberlain married Richard Wagner's youngest daughter, Eva, and moved to Bayreuth. During World War I he became a German citizen. From 1916 to his death, in 1927, he was more or less confined to bed, but his reputation as one of Germany's most prominent *völkisch* thinkers and a personal friend of the kaiser brought floods of visitors to his home. Adolf Hitler visited Chamberlain in 1923, and in Hitler Chamberlain saw a messianic figure for the rebirth of the Aryan spirit.

Lena Berggren

See Also: ANTI-SEMITISM; ART; ARYANISM; BAYREUTH; CHRISTIANITY; CONSPIRACY THEORIES; CULTURE (GERMANY); GERMANIC RELIGION, THE; HITLER, ADOLF; LIBERALISM (THEOLOGY); MATERIALISM; MITFORD FAMILY, THE; POSITIVISM; PROTOFASCISM; RACIAL DOCTRINE; ROSENBERG, ALFRED; THEOLOGY; VITALISM; *VOLK, VÖLKISCH;* WAGNER, (WILHELM) RICHARD

References
Field, Geoffrey G. 1981. *Evangelist of Race: The Germanic Vision of Houston Stewart Chamberlain.* New York: Columbia University Press.

CHAMBERLAIN, NEVILLE: *See* APPEASEMENT

CHESTERTON, ARTHUR KENNETH (1896–1973)

Journalist and Shakespearean drama critic of considerable note who had served with distinction during World War I before joining the British Union of Fascists in 1933. Chesterton (second cousin to the celebrated novelist and Catholic polemicist G. K. Chesterton) rose to become Oswald Mosley's director of propaganda, editing both *Action* and *Blackshirt* as well as writing a hagiography of Mosley, *Portrait of a Leader.* He resigned from the BUF in 1937, escaped internment on the outbreak of World War II, and joined the British army. This conferred a measure of respectability upon him, enabling him to emerge in 1954 as chairman of the League of Empire Loyalists, which protested against "colored" immigration and the decline of the British Empire. Through his newsletter *Candour* and his book *The New Unhappy Lords* (1965), Chesterton became a pivotal source of conspiratorial anti-Semitism for the far Right on both sides of the Atlantic. In 1967 the LEL merged with several other organizations to become the National Front. Chesterton was its first chairman, but he died estranged from it.

Graham Macklin

See Also: ANTI-SEMITISM; BRITISH FASCISTS/BRITISH FASCISTS, THE; CONSPIRACY THEORIES; GREAT BRITAIN; MOSLEY, SIR OSWALD; NATIONAL FRONT, THE (UK); WORLD WAR I

References
Baker, David. 1997. *Ideology of Obsession: A. K. Chesterton and British Fascism.* London. I. B. Tauris.

CHILDREN: *See* EDUCATION; EUGENICS; EUTHANASIA; FAMILY, THE; HEALTH; LEISURE; WOMEN; YOUTH

CHILE

The Movimiento Nacional Socialista (National Socialist Movement; Nacis, or MNS) was the first fascist organization in Chile and the most important one during the 1930s. Founded by three Chileans—Francisco Javier Díaz Valderrama, Carlos Keller, and Jorge González von Marées (known as *el jefe,* "the boss")—it drew inspiration from the Nazi program, which Díaz translated into Spanish. Ardently nationalist, the MNS called for the expulsion of communists and foreigners and supported strong governmental values such as order, hierarchy, and social justice. Anti-Jewish sentiment existed within the MNS but did not consistently dominate its discourse as it did that of German Nazis. During the 1930s, the Nacis engaged in attacks on the Left, which responded in kind. Although much of the leadership was upper class, and some of them had German ancestry, most of the supporters were neither of German background nor wealthy. Women joined the male-dominated MNS, which upheld conservative ideas about gender and defined women's role based on their biological destiny to be wives and mothers. Estimates of membership range from 20,000 to 30,000. In 1935 the Nacis and right-wing military officers planned the overthrow of the elected government. The plot failed, and sixty-three Nacis died in the aftermath, a blow that contributed to the defeat of the group.

For the next thirty years fascism as an organized force languished in Chile. Many small extreme-right parties formed, but they were short lived and had few members. In the 1960s, the political situation in Chile moved to the left. In 1966 the small extreme right National Action Party joined the Conservative and Liberal parties, two parties of the right, to form the National Party. Although the party was not fascist, it contained fascist elements within it. In 1970, when Salvador Allende and the leftist Popular Unity coalition won the presidential election, Sergio Onofre Jarpa, a former member of the Naci youth organization, emerged as leader of the National Party.

Patria y Libertad (Fatherland and Liberty), a neofascist organization led by attorney Pablo Rodríguez, formed in 1970 to oppose the Allende government. To that end it blew up electrical towers, engaged in street battles with supporters of the Allende government, took over radio stations, and even raised funds for striking mineworkers. It took its inspiration from Spaniard José Antonio Primo de Rivera but lacked the mass following of the Spanish Falange. A woman's branch formed and participated in public demonstrations, neighborhood organizing, and other antigovernment activities. Considered the armed wing of the National Party, in June 1973 members of Patria y Libertad supported a coup against Allende. When the commander-in-chief of the Chilean military, who was loyal to the elected government, put down the uprising, leaders of the neofascist organization fled the country. A U.S. citizen, Michael Townley, worked with Patria y Libertad. After the military overthrew Allende in 1973, Townley and other members of Patria y Libertad worked with the DINA, the Chilean secret police. Townley and the DINA murdered Chilean Orlando Letelier and North American Ronni Moffit in Washington, DC, in 1976. Members of Patria y Libertad and other groups on the extreme Right welcomed the coup that brought the Pinochet military dictatorship to power. However, as fervent nationalists, they opposed the neoliberal economic policies introduced by the Pinochet dictatorship and distanced themselves from it. Although he was authoritarian and ruled dictatorially, Pinochet's support of neoliberal economic policies and his unwillingness to support national business and industry distinguished him from classic fascists.

Margaret Power

See Also: ANTI-SEMITISM; AUTHORITARIANISM; DICTATORSHIP; ECONOMICS; KELLER, CARLOS; MILITARY DICTATORSHIP; NATIONALISM; NAZISM; PINOCHET UGARTE, GENERAL AUGUSTO; POSTWAR FASCISM; PRIMO DE RIVERA, JOSÉ ANTONIO; SOCIALISM

References

Deutsch, Sandra McGee. 1999. *Las Derechas: The Extreme Right in Argentina, Brazil, and Chile, 1890–1939*. Stanford: Stanford University Press.

Power, Margaret. 2002. *Right-Wing Women in Chile: Feminine Power and the Struggle against Allende, 1964–1973*. University Park: Pennsylvania State University Press.

CHINA

In the 1930s, an allegedly fascist movement flourished for a time within the then-ruling political party, the Chinese Nationalist Party (Kuomintang, KMT, or Guomindang). It was known as the Blue Shirts Society (Lanyi she), but the movement identified itself as the Chinese Renaissance Society (Zhonghua fuxing she) and should for various reasons be classed as "fascistic" rather than "fascist." What precipitated the founding of the society was Japan's invasion of China's northeastern provinces of Manchuria. Convinced that the very survival of China was imperiled, twenty young men—all KMT members and graduates of the Whampoa Military Academy—founded the society on 1 March 1932 in Nanjing in order to "save the nation." The movement was organized as a series of concentric circles. Within the innermost ring was the 300-member "Three People's Principles Earnest Action Society," charged with policy-making. Mass organizations constituted the outermost ring, the largest of which was the Chinese Renaissance Society, with a membership of about 100,000.

The Renaissance movement was animated by a resolve to modernize China through the realization of the ideological program (the Three People's Principles) of Sun Yat-sen, the founder of the KMT. The movement believed that only through an aggressive program of economic and political development could China be saved and revitalized. Economic development would begin with land reform, which included the equalization of land rights, the reallocation of land to the tillers, and collective farms. Rapid industrialization would be promoted through a mixed economy that combined state capital with private initiative. The economic program required a fundamental political restructuring that would begin with the installation of a strong central government that could wield effective authority over the national territory without being compromised by foreign imperialists or domestic rivals—communists and warlords. At the same time, a sense of nationalism would be inculcated among the people, whom Sun had long lamented as resembling "a tray of loose sand." That strong central government would be undertaken by a single party led by a charismatic leader. Authoritarian rule was believed to be necessary because of Japan's invasion. However, single-party rule was conceived to be an emergency and transitional measure, the necessary means toward the ends of national defense, rapid industrialization, and eventual self-government—all of which were consistent with Sun's Three Principles. The Renaissance movement believed that the KMT would be that single party—but only if it reformed itself with a renewal of commitment to Sun's ideology, the purification of corrupt and elitist practices, and the cultivation of grassroots support among the Chinese masses.

In effect, the Chinese Renaissance Society was an effort to reform the KMT by returning the party to Sun's ideology of developmental nationalism. As such, the society was one of many movements and ideologies of delayed industrialization in the nineteenth and twentieth centuries, among which were Meiji Japan, Fascist Italy, and countries that embraced Marxism-Leninism, Kemalism, Gandhiism, and Nasserism. Unlike Italian Fascism, however, the one-party authoritarian rule advocated by both Sun and the Renaissance Society was to be strictly transitional—as the necessary means toward the abiding end of democratic government. Although short-lived, the Renaissance movement counted among its achievements four mass campaigns in the 1930s: the New Life Movement, the National Voluntary Labor Movement, the National Economic Reconstruction Movement, and the National Military Education Movement. In March 1938, in an effort at party unity, the Renaissance Society was dissolved by an Extraordinary National Conference of the KMT and merged with two other intraparty factions to form the Three People's Principles Youth Corps.

If fascism is to be found in China, a better candidate might actually be the post-Maoist People's Republic of China (PRC). Beginning in 1979, the Chinese Communist Party (CCP) under the leadership of Deng Xiaoping undertook significant capitalist reform of the economy, which catapulted China into the rank of a world power. At the same time, though nominally still Marxist, China's ideology became that of developmental irredentist nationalism. The transformation of the PRC into a quasi-fascist state was cemented in July 2001 when the party chief and head of state, Jiang Zemin, proposed that capitalists be admitted into the ranks of the Communist Party.

Maria Chang

See Also: INTRODUCTION; AUTHORITARIANISM; ECONOM-ICS; FASCIST PARTY, THE; INDUSTRY; IRREDENTISM; ITALY; JAPAN; JAPAN AND WORLD WAR II; LEADER CULT, THE; MASSES, THE ROLE OF THE; MODERNITY; NATION-ALISM; REVOLUTION; TECHNOLOGY

References

Chang, Maria Hsia. 1985. *The Chinese Blue Shirt Society: Fascism and Developmental Nationalism.* Berkeley: University of California, Institute of East Asian Studies.

———. 2001. *Return of the Dragon: China's Wounded Nationalism.* Boulder, CO: Westview.

Eastman, Lloyd E. 1974. *The Abortive Revolution: China under Nationalist Rule, 1927–1937.* Cambridge: Harvard University Press.

CHRISTIAN IDENTITY

Small racialized hybrid of Protestantism developed in the United States. There is no central organization or clerical hierarchy, and followers create autonomous local churches or meet in homes. The most virulent groups promote white supremacy and anti-Semitism in an amalgam of authoritarian, totalitarian, and fascistic ideas that a few critics claim comes very close to neo-Nazism. Some Identity groups celebrate Hitler as a prophet. Christian Identity evolved from British Israelism or Anglo-Israelism, which emerged as a movement in the late 1800s with the claim that Protestants in England could trace their bloodline to the twelve tribes of Israel, thus making Anglo-Saxons the inheritors of a special covenant with God. In the United States, this is extended to claim that the real "identity" of Protestants is God's Chosen People, and the United States is thus the Promised Land of biblical prophecy.

Barkun stresses the role of apocalyptic belief and millennial expectation in Christian Identity, and follows the theology through influential ideologues including Wesley Swift, William Potter Gale, Sheldon Emry, Richard Butler, and Pete Peters. This branch of Identity blossomed in the late 1930s and was nurtured by Swift from the late 1940s through the 1960s. Gale developed the belief in a "Manichaean struggle between white, divine, Anglo-Saxon Christians, and Satanic Jews" (Levitas 2002, 81). Rejecting federal officials as corrupted by this evil Jewish conspiracy, Identity writers have denounced the authorities in Washington, D.C., as the Zionist Occupation Government.

While anti-Judaism has periodically played a pernicious role in Christianity for two millennia, Identity has crafted a particularly vicious theory in which the people who call themselves Jews not only are Satanic but also represent a separate genetic seedline from Aryans, who claim direct descent from the loins of the biblical Adam. Kaplan explains that there are various interpretations of how the two seedlines started, with factions claiming that the evil Jews sprang from "the unholy union of Satan with Eve or from the conversion of the barbaric Khazar tribe to Judaism," or some combination of both. Blacks and other people of color are sometimes called pre-Adamic or Mud People to signify their status as not quite the finished human product of God's plan. Jews are portrayed as manipulating Mud People to subvert the cosmic destiny of the Aryan race. Like most millenarian movements, Identity sees an approaching major transformation of society, but Identity envisions it as an apocalyptic race war. Several Identity followers have used this viewpoint to justify attacks on Jews and Jewish institutions, as well as government agents and agencies. Some incidents have culminated in shootouts and murders. An underground antigovernment survivalist movement known as the Posse Comitatus helped spread the message of Christian Identity across the United States in the 1970s and 1980s. Identity pastor Richard Butler founded the Aryan Nations compound in the rural state of Idaho. In the 1980s, Butler attracted hundreds of Identity adherents and organizers to national conferences and campouts. Butler faded as a national leader in Identity, but a new crop of Identity pastors continues to spread the message and vie for visibility and influence.

Chip Berlet

See Also: ANTI-SEMITISM; ARYAN NATIONS; ARYANISM; AUTHORITARIANISM; BUTLER, RICHARD GIRNT; CHRISTIANITY; HITLER, ADOLF; NEO-NAZISM; PROTESTANTISM; RACIAL DOCTRINE; RACISM; SURVIVALISM; TOTALITARIANISM; UNITED STATES, THE (POSTWAR); WHITE SUPREMACISM; ZIONIST OCCUPATION GOVERNMENT, THE

References

Barkun, Michael. 1997. *Religion and the Racist Right: The Origins of the Christian Identity Movement.* Rev. ed. Chapel Hill: University of North Carolina Press.

Kaplan, Jeffrey. 1997. *Radical Religion in America: Millenarian Movements from the Far Right to the Children of Noah.* Syracuse, NY: Syracuse University Press.

Levitas, Daniel. 2002. *The Terrorist Next Door: The Militia Movement and the Radical Right.* New York: Thomas Dunne/St. Martin's.

CHRISTIANITY

Unlike their treatment of the Bolsheviks and Marxist ideologues in general, both Mussolini and Hitler were careful in their public utterances to avoid making provocative statements about the traditional religion of their fellow countrymen. Indeed, it is arguable that this was one of the reasons for their success in achieving power. They presented themselves as defenders of their national traditions against atheistic Bolshevism, the implication being that the Christian religion would be included among those traditions, and this helped to ingratiate them with churchgoers among their constituency, many of whom were understandably terrified by the sight of the murderous Bolshevik crusade against religion and the churches in the Soviet Union. On the other hand, both Mussolini and Hitler made it clear that they intended religion to be restricted to the "religious sphere," and that any attempt by Christians to influence state policy or to resist fascism would be regarded as criminal. Both dictators made concordats with the Catholic Church but did so for the sake of obtaining the kudos of apparent approval from the papacy, which they knew would help to obtain Catholic support for their regimes. Alongside this propagandist maneuvering, which was enough to placate many who wanted to believe in these regimes as bulwarks against communism, went a more or less overt contempt for Christianity. That is clear both in Mussolini's autobiography and in Hitler's *Table Talk:* Hitler despised Protestantism and Catholicism alike. But the fascist dictators were bent on creating a new political religion of their own and would brook no competition from the churches. What distinguished them from the Bolsheviks was that they professed to believe in a spiritual dimension and in ideas like that of the soul and rejected Marxist monism. They detested materialism and did not reject religion out of hand as "the opium of the people" but desired to create—or revive from ancient times, as some Nazis saw it—a national religion such as was anticipated in the eighteenth century by Rousseau. One of the most powerful embodiments of this was their attempt to superimpose new calendars of fascist special memorial days on the existing Christian-based calendar.

Both Hitler and Mussolini disliked the egalitarian and internationalist aspects of Christian doctrine, according to which all are equal in the eyes of God and all persons of whatever nation or color are brothers and sisters. They were deeply influenced by the Social Darwinist ideas of life as a permanent and ineluctable state of struggle, with only the fittest surviving. In the Nazi version of fascism, this was complemented and reinforced by a particular set of assumptions about race based on ideas, widespread in the nineteenth century, about a great and noble Aryan race whose Germanic descendants had fallen into a state of decadence. This idea that civilization had fallen into decay was also a commonplace of the era in the writings of publicists like Spengler, with his famous title *The Decline of the West,* much admired by Mussolini as well as in Germany. Both Italian Fascism and Nazism saw themselves as messianic agents of redemption from decay, sent to save their fellow countryman and the world from the forces of corruption—chiefly meaning materialism in both its Bolshevik and capitalist varieties. For Mussolini that meant the exaltation above traditional Christian virtues of the warrior values of courage, pride, resolve, steeliness, physical prowess, and a readiness to sacrifice oneself for the nation. For the Nazis it meant all that but also something more. For they regarded the chief agents of materialism in the world as the Jews, and they paradoxically saw Jews behind both capitalism and Bolshevism.

The Nazis tapped into a very particular Protestant Germanic view of the past that was embodied in the writings of many publicists from the second half of the nineteenth century into the first half of the twentieth. They took up a traditional Protestant polemic against Catholicism which sprang from the Protestant Reformation idea that they were purifying the Church from centuries of "accretion"—that there was an authentic Gospel in the early days of the Church that needed to be recovered from under centuries of accumulated sediment. In particular, they accused the Catholics of having built up a whole sacramental system that provided believers with salvation cheaply and mechanically; it seemed that all the believer had to do according to this system was to carry out his outward sacramental obligations according to Church rules, and he could expect to go to heaven. The sixteenth-century reformers had believed that they were instead promoting a return to the true "inwardness" of the Gospel, according to which it was the attitude of the believer's heart toward God that was paramount. So they took an ax to the traditional rituals and ceremonies of the Church and cut them back to a basic core that they regarded as the necessary minimum, calling on believers to focus on the state of their souls instead. The sacramental system of medieval Catholicism was condemned by the Reformers not just as a religion of "materialism" and purely outward conformity but also because they believed it to be a revival of "Judaism" in the Church. This was because they believed that the great breakthrough brought about by Christ was precisely the move forward from a Jewish religion of ritual and ceremony—purification rites, the wearing of special garments, verbal repetition of the law, and so forth—in favor of an inward spiritual religion of the heart. On this view, materialism was in fact the main feature of Catholicism and Judaism alike, and the Catholic Church represented the reintrusion into the Church of the Judaism that Jesus had transcended. (The Catholic Church, by contrast, actually taught that both inward disposition and outward ritual performance were necessary and complementary, the gestures of the body expressing—ideally at least—the hoped-for disposition of the heart.) The "turn inward" of the Protestants was intensified by the difficulty that faced them when their movement began to fragment into a variety of sects; they could not claim to be "One Church" as the Catholics clearly could. The Catholic Church remained one outwardly, and the Protestants resorted therefore to the belief in an inward spiritual body of believers who were in fact united in spirit even if at odds in appearance.

Precisely this Protestant theory that identified Catholic and Jewish "materialism" as coming from the same stable appeared in the arguments of protofascist ideologues like Houston Stewart Chamberlain and Alfred Rosenberg. Only now they turned it against the Protestants as well. For these ideologues the whole outward structure of Christianity—including the Protestant church bodies and the liturgies and ceremonies they had retained—was still materialistic, and Luther had not gone far enough. Fatally, he had retained the Old Testament, which was of course a completely Jewish and therefore "materialistic" document. Instead he should have realized that the "inwardness" that Christ was really preaching about was a complete release from the prison of Jewish "materialism." It was an "inwardness" that had no need of ceremonies that recalled Jewish origins. Indeed, Jesus, on this argument, was not even a Jew at all, his Galilean roots betraying the fact that he was really of Aryan stock. These themes were not invented by fascist ideologues; they were commonplace in German liberal theology. So it was that an "Aryanized" version of Christianity was promoted which believed that Jesus had come to preach a Gospel of racial purity and inwardness completely detached from Jewish "materialism." Stripped of its racial convictions it would perhaps resemble something like the UK extreme-radical "Sea of Faith" movement in theology. However, the racial component was crucial to Nazism.

The "internationalist" dimension of Christianity was offensive to fascists as hypernationalists. Again, the Nazis saw it as a reflection of Christianity's continuing bondage to Judaism. Jews were international because of their tribal blood relationships; Christians claimed to belong to an international family of faith united on the ground of a common adherence to Christ, holding that what believers across the globe had in common transcended their allegiance to their nation. That at least was the theory, though it often remained unobserved in practice. For both Italian Fascists and German Nazis the idea that a global belief system could trump national values was anathema. And for the Nazis there was a particular resonance of the idea of an "international" community; once again, they saw in this element of Christianity a reflection of its fondness for Judaism. The logic of all this was that in attacking Jews they knew themselves also to be attacking Christianity, and indeed it is clear from Hitler's *Table Talk* that he planned to deal with the churches after he had dealt with the Jews, when the war was over. In other words, the Holocaust of Jews was but a prelude to the destruction of Christianity, which had sprung from Judaism. In place of Christianity the fascists proposed the religion of consecration to the nation. In Nazism there were also some—including Himmler—who aspired to create a new "Germanic" religion.

Despite the clearly universalist teachings of Christ, which make it difficult to understand how they could be combined with hypernationalism, many attempts have been made to synthesize fascism with Christianity. In the interwar years many Catholics were attracted to the Mussolinian regime by its principles of order, authority, and discipline, and by its emphasis on solidarity. The phenomenon of clerico-fascism was a reflection of this. In most cases it was a matter of the imitation of outward trappings, although certain doctrines particularly identified with Italian Fascism such as corporatism seemed perfectly compatible with Catholicism. With Nazism, Catholicism could have little truck officially or in theory, although there is no doubt that many Catholics had absorbed the traditional hostility to the Jews endemic in European society as a consequence of difficulties regarding the Jews' rejection of the messiahship of Christ. Protestantism had less difficulty with hypernationalism, since it often existed in practice in the form of a state church or within a single-nation frame. Many Protestants too had absorbed traditional anti-Judaism and could not readily distinguish this from the Nazi racial anti-Semitism. (Protestants were not a significant presence in Italy, but in Germany their attitude was of course crucial.) Hence their ability to synthesize Christianity with hypernationalism, as in the German Christian Movement.

In the United States, many fundamentalist movements have drawn on Nazi themes such as Aryanism, anti-Semitism, and racism. The powerful nationalistic element that undergirds U.S. identity has predisposed them to ally the Bible with hypernationalism to create a potent force against a variety of enemies—but especially against blacks and Jews—and they are naturally receptive to conspiracy theories of all kinds. They are often perfectly aware of the continuity of their views with German Nazism. The lines between the vast number of "mainline" Christian groupings that represent "normal" forms of Protestantism and such heretical sects can become blurred. There has also been a small but persistent lobby of extreme Protestants for whom the Vatican was the controlling influence behind interwar fascism in Europe. At the same time there are also American Christian Zionists who fervently support the establishment and consolidation of the state of Israel, seeing it as a fulfillment of biblical prophecy and a necessary step toward the end times.

Cyprian Blamires

See Also: ANTI-SEMITISM; ARYANISM; BOLSHEVISM; CALENDAR, THE FASCIST; CAPITALISM; CATHOLIC CHURCH, THE; CHAMBERLAIN, HOUSTON STEWART; CHRISTIAN IDENTITY; CLERICO-FASCISM; CONSPIRACY THEORIES; CORPORATISM; COSMOPOLITANISM; COSTAMAGNA, CARLO; DINTER, ARTUR; ELITE THEORY; GERMAN CHRISTIANS, THE; GERMAN FAITH MOVEMENT, THE; GERMANIC RELIGION; HIMMLER, HEINRICH; HITLER, ADOLF; HOLOCAUST, THE; LIBERALISM (IN THEOLOGY); LUDENDORFF, MATHILDE; LUTHER, MARTIN; LUTHERAN CHURCHES, THE; MARXISM; MATERIALISM; MUSSOLINI, BENITO ANDREA; NATIONALISM; NEO-NAZISM; NORDIC SOUL, THE; ORTHODOX CHURCHES, THE; PALINGENETIC MYTH; PAPACY, THE; PIUS XI, POPE; PIUS XII, POPE; POLITICAL CATHOLICISM; PROTESTANTISM AND NAZISM; RACIAL DOCTRINE; RELIGION; CATHOLIC CHURCH, THE; ROSENBERG, ALFRED; SCHIRACH, BALDUR VON; SECULARIZATION; SOCIAL DARWINISM; SOUL; SOVIET UNION, THE; THEOLOGY; TOTALITARIANISM; UNITED STATES, THE (PRE-1945); UNITED STATES, THE (POSTWAR); WARRIOR ETHOS, THE; WHITE SUPREMACISM

References

Bergen, Doris. 1996. *Twisted Cross: The German Christian Movement in the Third Reich.* Chapel Hill: University of North Carolina Press.

Blet, Pierre. 1997. *Pius XII and the Second World War.* Leominster: Gracewing.

Blinkhorn, Martin. 1990. *Fascists and Conservatives.* London: Unwin Hyman.

Buchanan, Tom, and Martin Conway, eds. *Political Catholicism in Europe 1918–1965.* Oxford: Oxford University Press.

Cheles, Luciano, Ronnie Ferguson, and Michalina Vaughan. 1995. *The Far Right in Western and Eastern Europe.* London: Longman.

Ericksen, Robert P., and Susannah Heschel, eds. *Betrayal: German Churches and the Holocaust.* Minneapolis: Fortress.

Evans, E. L. 1981. *The German Center Party 1870–1933: A Study in Political Catholicism.* Carbondale: Southern Illinois University Press.

Halls, W. D. 1995. *Politics, Society and Christianity in Vichy France.* Oxford: Berg.

Helmreich, Ernst Christian. 1979. *The German Churches under Hitler: Background, Struggle, and Epilogue.* Detroit: Wayne State University Press.

Ioanid, R. 1990. *The Sword of the Archangel Michael: Fascist Ideology in Romania.* Boulder, CO: Westview: Eastern European Monographs.

Manhattan, Avro. 1986. *The Vatican's Holocaust.* Springfield, MO: Ozark.

Ozment, Steven. 2004. *A Mighty Fortress: A New History of the German People, 100 BC to the Present Moment.* London: Granta.

Paris, Edmond. 1961. *The Vatican against Europe.* London: Wickliffe.

Pollard, J. 1985. *The Vatican and Italian Fascism.* London: Macmillan.

Rychlak, R. J. 2000. *Hitler, the War, and the Pope.* Huntington, IN: Our Sunday Visitor.

Steigmann-Gall, Richard. 2003. *The Holy Reich: Nazi Conceptions of Christianity.* Cambridge: Cambridge University Press.

Wolff, R. J., and J. R. Hoensch, eds. 1987. *Catholics, the State and the European Radical Right.* Boulder, CO: Social Science Monographs.

CHURCHILL, SIR WINSTON LEONARD SPENCER (1874–1965)

Legendary British statesman famed for his spirited leadership of his country in the face of the threat from Nazi Germany. He was born into a family with a highly distinguished pedigree (descendants of the eighteenth-century Duke of Marlborough, one of Britain's most successful generals) and at one of the country's most majestic residences, Blenheim Palace (named after one of the duke's finest victories). His father, Lord Randolph Churchill, was a notable politician and (briefly) Conservative cabinet minister. His mother was Jeannette Jerome, daughter of a New York businessman, and that may have contributed to the establishment of his lasting reputation in the United States and to his close relationship with U.S. President Roosevelt. Churchill's realistic but resolute oratory at the height of World War II was an inspiration not just for the British but also for others across the Commonwealth and indeed in North America. His speeches continue to be quoted as epitomizing the heroic resistance of the British people to the campaign of the German bombers. One sentence is particularly cherished, from a speech, after the end of the Battle of Britain, commenting on the courage and tenacity of the RAF fighter pilots who had to take on the might of the Luftwaffe: "Never in the history of human conflict has so much been owed by so many to so few." He was blunt and uncompromising in his manner of addressing the British people, openly declaring that they could defeat Hitler only with hard work and unstinting self-sacrifice. Churchill was British prime minister from 1940 to 1945 and again from 1951 to 1955.

Cyprian Blamires

See Also: BATTLE OF BRITAIN, THE; COLD WAR, THE; HITLER, ADOLF; LUFTWAFFE, THE; ROOSEVELT, FRANKLIN DELANO; WORLD WAR II

References
Jenkins, R. 2001. *Churchill.* London: Macmillan.
Lukacs, John. 1996. *The Duel: 10 May–31 July 1940: The Eighty-day Struggle between Churchill and Hitler.* New York: Houghton Mifflin.

Count Galeazzo Ciano, Mussolini's son-in-law and for a time his foreign minister, is one of the best-known figures of the Fascist regime outside Italy as a result of the publication of his Diaries. (Hulton Archive/Getty Images)

CIANO, COUNT GALEAZZO (1903–1944)

Journalist who became Mussolini's foreign minister for seven years from June 1936; husband of Edda Mussolini, the Duce's eldest daughter, whom he married in 1930; and one of the personalities involved with Italian Fascism best known outside Italy. That is in part because his published diary of his years as foreign minister have been both a best-seller internationally and a crucial source for historians of the period. He was the son of Italian World War I naval hero Admiral Constanzo Ciano (1876–1939), an early adherent to Fascism who was minister of posts and communications for ten years from 1924, before being elected president of the Chamber of Fasces and Corporations. Before becoming

foreign minister, Galeazzo Ciano had been head of Mussolini's press office (1933) and later minister for press and propaganda (1935). As foreign minister he collaborated in the creation of the Axis between Italy and the Third Reich, but he nonetheless wanted Mussolini to break off the alliance with Germany after the invasion of Poland. He encouraged Mussolini to develop a Balkan policy with the aim of setting boundaries to German power, and in response to the German annexation of Czechoslovakia in 1939 he promoted the invasion of Albania on Good Friday 1939. Fully aware of Italian military weaknesses, he encouraged Mussolini to stay out of the war in September 1939. By early 1940, Ciano's position had weakened because of a widespread conviction that Germany was going to win the war and that therefore Italy needed to be part of it, so as to enjoy some of the spoils. He himself was not uninfluenced by that current of opinion. But after war was declared by Italy, Ciano's influence dwindled, and in February 1943 he was appointed ambassador to the Holy See. He voted in favor of the deposition of Mussolini on 25 July 1943, during the session of the Grand Council of Fascism. Arrested by the Germans, he was tried in Verona and condemned to death for high treason. His wife's efforts to save his life were unavailing.

Alessandro Campi and Cyprian Blamires

See Also: ALBANIA; AXIS, THE; FASCIST PARTY, THE; GRAND COUNCIL OF FASCISM, THE; ITALY; MUSSOLINI, BENITO ANDREA; PAPACY, THE; THIRD REICH, THE; WORLD WAR II

References
Ciano, G. 2002. *Diary, 1937–1943: The Complete, Unabridged Diaries of Count Galeazzo Ciano, Italian Minister of Foreign Affairs, 1936–1943.* London: Phoenix.
Moseley, Ray. 1999. *Mussolini's Shadow: The Double Life of Count Galeazzo Ciano.* New Haven: Yale University Press.

CINEMA, THE: *See* FILM

CIORAN, EMIL (1911–1995)

Romanian philosopher and essayist, nationalist, and sympathizer with the Iron Guard in the interwar years. Cioran was born the son of a Romanian Orthodox priest in Rasinari, Transylvania (today Romania), during the latter days of Hungarian rule. In 1928 he enrolled in the philosophy department of the University of Bucharest, where he absorbed the Romanian form of *Lebensphilosophie* ("philosophy of life"; Romanian: *trairism*) articulated by the mentor of the interwar generation, Professor Nae Ionescu. This intellectual climate laid the basis for Cioran's later thought. In 1934, Cioran published some of his early philosophical reflections under the title *On the Heights of Despair.* Cioran's reading of Schopenhauer, and the chronic state of illness in which he spent his student years, led to a profoundly pessimistic view of mankind and society. Freedom, while a blessing for many, to Cioran seemed "a curse": it put human beings in a situation of forced choice between good and evil, an unbearable burden that could be cast off only through dictatorship.

In 1931, Cioran graduated as a licentiate with a dissertation on Bergson, spending the rest of his life as a freelance student. From 1933 to 1935 he studied at the University of Berlin under Nicolai Hartmann and Ludwig Klages. His observations on the rise of Nazism were the subject of a number of articles published in the press at home. Cioran admired the way in which the Germans were breaking through the fixed "forms" (*Forme*) of their culture. In Hitler he saw the embodiment of German culture fulfilling its own "destiny" (*Schicksal*). Germany was a reminder that only a radical change could awaken the young Romanian nation from the lethargy in which the majority of its citizens, mostly peasants, were still living. Cioran elaborated on this vision for a new Romania in his famous book of 1936, *The Transfiguration of Romania.* Romania's problem, Cioran argued, was that it was still largely a geographical rather than a political entity.

Cioran rejected the commonly held belief that the course of history could make no sudden leaps. He called upon the Romanians to abandon their habit of passively bearing history and to imagine themselves as the beginning of a new history: "Every person willing or called to play a prophetic role in the life of Romania has to convince himself that every gesture, every act, every attitude in this country is an absolute beginning." *The Transfiguration of Romania* combined this typically Russian messianic nationalism with Spengler's cultural theory into a manifesto of a "national revolution." In 1937, Cioran proposed to C. Z. Codreanu the adoption of his book as the program for the guard's future state, an offer that Codreanu declined. In November 1937, Cioran left with a scholarship for Paris, where he spent most of the rest of his life. He later distanced himself from nationalist positions and expressed regret for his connections with the Iron Guard. After the war he became widely known as a philosopher in a pessimistic and frequently aphoristic mode.

Philip Vanhaelemeersch

See Also: CODREANU, CORNELIU ZELEA; DECADENCE; ELIADE, MIRCEA; HITLER, ADOLF; LEGION OF THE ARCHANGEL MICHAEL, THE; NATIONALISM; NAZISM; ORTHODOX CHURCHES, THE; ROMANIA; RUSSIA; SCHOPENHAUER, ARTHUR; SPENGLER, OSWALD

References
Petreu, Marta. 1999. *Un Trecut Deocheat sau "Schimbarea la Fata a României."* Cluj-Napoca: Biblioteca Apostrof (reprinted in English translation: Petreu, Marta. 2005. *An Infamous Past: E. M. Cioran and the Rise of Fascism in Romania.* Chicago: Ivan R. Dee).
Radu, Ioanid. "The Sacralised Politics of the Romanian Iron Guard." *Totalitarian Movements and Political Religions* 5, no. 3 (winter 2004): 419–453.

CIVILIZATION

For many Nazi propagandists, this word represented an alien, anti-German "Western" concept. French writers like Jacques Bainville spoke before World War I of a conflict between superior French *civilisation* and barbaric German *Kultur*. In Germany the word *Zivilisation* was used predominantly as a synonym for the more popular *Kultur* up until the 1880s. Primarily as a result of the negative effects of industrialization, there was a devaluation of the idea of *civilization* through its neglect in general linguistic usage in proportion to that of *culture,* contributed to by philosophers such as Friedrich Nietzsche and Ferdinand Tönnies and philosophizing writers such as Houston Stuart Chamberlain. With World War I and the beginning of Allied propaganda, German criticism of "civilization" was nationalistically charged up to the antithesis of *Kultur* versus *Zivilisation.* "Civilization" was considered in almost all camps as something foreign and plainly anti-German. Although a nationalist, Oswald Spengler was an exception, formally contradicting German war propaganda with his influential definition in which he universalized "civilization" and described it as the inevitable final stage of every culture, and therefore also of German culture. Official National Socialist terminology prescribed by Alfred Rosenberg attempted to revalue the concept of "civilization" in order to counteract the debasement of science and technology, which were subsumed under "civilization." These efforts were not widely accepted, and thus there was a coexistence during the Third Reich of official attempts at revaluation on the one hand and vituperative attacks on "Western" civilization by lesser party members and writers on the other.

The Italian term *civiltà* as the highest material and spiritual expression of social cohabitation is in no way inferior to the French *civilisation* as regards emotionality and messianic fervor. During World War I, *civiltà* became a nationalistic propaganda slogan directed against the German-Austrian enemy's rallying cry of *Kultur.* The Fascists rededicated the traditional *civiltà* as *nuova civiltà,* which they in turn associated with the "total state." *Civiltà* became an instrument for the justification of their expansionist demands, which led to the invasion of Ethiopia in 1935/1936.

Susanne Pocai

See Also: CHAMBERLAIN, HOUSTON STEWART; COLONIALISM; CULTURE; ENLIGHTENMENT, THE; ETHIOPIA; GERMANNESS; IMPERIALISM; MUSSOLINI, BENITO ANDREA; NATIONALISM; NAZISM; NIETZSCHE, FRIEDRICH; NIHILISM; NORDIC SOUL, THE; PROGRESS; ROSENBERG, ALFRED; SCIENCE; SPENGLER, OSWALD; TECHNOLOGY; THIRD REICH, THE

References
Beard, Charles A., and Mary R. Beard. 1948. *The American Spirit: A Study of the Idea of Civilization in the United States.* New York: Macmillan.
Benveniste, Émile. 1953. "Civilisation. Contribution à l'histoire du mot." Pp. 47–54 in *Éventail de l'histoire vivante: Hommage à Lucien Febvre,* edited by Fernand Braudel. Vol. 1. Paris: Colin.
Elias, Norbert. 2000. *The Civilizing Process.* Trans. Edmund Jephcott. Oxford: Blackwell.
Lochore, Reuel Anson. 1935. *History of the Idea of Civilization in France: 1830–1870.* Bonn: Röhrscheid.
Pflaum, Georg Michael. 1961. *Geschichte des Wortes "Zivilisation."* München: Dissertation.

CLASS

Mussolini frequently claimed to advocate a kind of "socialism of the trenches," in which the final victors would be the workers, peasants, or veterans (depending on his audience). But just as important to fascism was its claim that a corporate state could transcend the narrow divisions of economic interest and unite everyone in the service of the nation. Hitler, for example, claimed to have studied propaganda by watching the marches of the revolutionary Left, and the early programs of the NSDAP spoke of the abolition of incomes "unearned by work." Yet in the face of the possibility of winning a middle-class electorate, any hints of working-class politics were soon dropped. In the early postwar years, when many European countries possessed mass communist parties and when trade unions were generally more confident, attempts were made to define a working-class fascist tradition. Dubbed "Strasserism" after Gregor and Otto Strasser, two of Hitler's NSDAP rivals, this movement maintained that true national socialism was the authentic working-class tradition. Strasserism was always a minority current within the postwar Right, for it based itself in a social terrain that was largely hostile. It also exhibited an unusual contempt for the interwar fascist leaders. Strasserism was finally dispatched by the success of different postwar fascist strategies, which have been deliberately agnostic on the question of interwar continuity, but which have copied the cross-class appeal of the 1930s fascist parties.

Faced with the rise of fascism, its enemies claimed that the movement recruited from only narrow classes of people. For Marxists, the most important point was that fascism had failed to win working-class support. Similar ideas then entered academia after 1945. Socialist historians have continued to argue that the proletariat remained largely immune from fascist contagion. Meanwhile, a number of political sociologists developed similar arguments as part of a different project of categorizing radical movements by their social content. More recent historians have suggested that class patterns of political support were quite complex. Among interwar leftists, Giovanni Zibordi linked fascism specifically to small traders and shopkeepers, while Karl Radek described fascism as the "socialism of the petty bourgeoisie." According to Leon Trotsky, "The main army of fascism still consists of the petty bourgeoisie and the new middle classes; the small artisans and shopkeepers of the cities, the petty officials, the employees, the technical personnel, the intelligentsia, the impoverished peasantry" (Sparks 1978, 43).

In the 1950s, the claim that fascism represented a form of middle-class revolt became something of an orthodoxy among political scientists. Renzo de Felice insisted that the petty bourgeoisie had given fascism the fullest support, while Seymour Lipset went even further, arguing that fascism was decisively shaped by that support. In a period of growth the middle class would normally turn to liberalism for its politics, but in a period of decline it would turn instead to fascism. For Lipset, fascism represented the "authoritarian centre," an authentic response to the crisis of middle-class life. In recent years, the trend has been away from class theories of fascism. The "new consensus" understands fascism as an intellectual tradition, characterized by a synthesis of different ideas, including racism and elitism, nationalism and socialism. Roger Griffin argues that "[t]here is nothing in principle which precludes an employed or an unemployed member of the working classes or an aristocrat . . . from being susceptible to fascist myth" (Griffin 1995, 7). A number of more traditional historians have also argued that fascism received wide support, distributed broadly among different social classes. In particular, Conan Fischer has suggested that the German Nazi Party, and especially its paramilitary wings, recruited large numbers of unemployed workers.

David Renton

See Also: INTRODUCTION; AUTHORITARIANISM; BOURGEOISIE, THE; CORPORATISM; ELITE THEORY; MARXISM; MASSES, THE ROLE OF THE; MUSSOLINI, BENITO ANDREA; NATIONALISM; NAZISM; POSTWAR FASCISM; RACISM; SOCIALISM; SOCIOLOGY; STRASSER BROTHERS, THE; TRADES UNIONS; TROTSKY, LEON

References
Beetham, D. 1983. *Marxists in the Face of Fascism: Writings on Fascism from the Interwar Period.* Manchester: Manchester University Press.
Fischer, C. 1995. *The Rise of the Nazis.* Manchester: Manchester University Press.
Griffin, R. 1995. *Fascism.* Oxford: Oxford University Press.
Renton, D. 1999. *Fascism, Theory and Practice.* London: Pluto.
Sparks, C. 1978. "Fascism and the Working Class, part one: The German Experience." *International Socialism Journal* 2: 41–60.

CLAUSEN, FRITS (1893–1947)

Country doctor from southern Jutland, between 1933 and 1944 leader of the Danish National Socialist Workers Party (DNSAP). Clausen never overcame the contradiction inherent in being a Danish fascist and nationalist who imitated the German Nazis when in fact they were the greatest threat to Denmark's national independence. Welcoming the German occupation in 1940, he expected, like Quisling in Norway, to be entrusted with the Nazification of Danish society and Denmark's absorption into a Greater Germanic empire. He was regarded as a traitor by most Danes and as an incompetent by the Germans, who preferred until 1943 to cooperate with the existing Danish government. Discredited in both Danish and German eyes by the DNSAP's miserable showing in the 1943 elections, Clausen was removed as party leader, interned by the Danish government, and died of a heart attack before his trial for treason.

Philip Morgan

See Also: DENMARK; EXPANSIONISM; NATIONALISM; NAZISM; NORWAY; PANGERMANISM; QUISLING, VIDKUN; WORLD WAR II

References
Djursaa, M. 1981. "Who Were the Danish Nazis?" Pp. 237–256 in *Fascism in Europe,* edited by S. J. Woolf. 2d ed. London: Methuen.

CLERCQ, GUSTAVE ("STAF") DE (1884–1942)

Leader of the Flemish National League (Vlaams Nationaal Verbond; VNV) during World War II, an important pro-German movement in the Flemish part of Belgium. Elected to the Belgian parliament in 1919, he agitated for an independent Flanders and the dismantling of Belgium. In 1933 he took the lead of the VNV (founded by himself), a party hostile to the continuance of the Belgian state, which managed to get 15 percent of the votes in the Flemish Belgian election contest of 1939. The VNV was a political party of the authoritarian Right with a fascist faction. De Clercq had connections with Nazi Germany (such as the *Abwehr*). He involved his party in a political and military collaboration with Germany and accepted National Socialism as the party ideology. After his death he was succeeded as VNV leader by Hendrik Elias.

Bruno de Wever

See Also: AUTHORITARIANISM; BELGIUM; DEGRELLE, LEON; GERMANY; HOORNAERT, PAUL; NATIONALISM; NAZISM; PANGERMANISM; REXISM

References

Littlejohn, D. 1972. *The Patriotic Traitors: A History of Collaboration in German-occupied Europe 1940–1945.* London: Heinemann.
Wever, B. de. 1989. *Staf De Clercq.* Brussels: Grammens.
Woolf, S. J., ed. 1981 [1968]. *Fascism in Europe.* London: Methuen.

CLERICO-FASCISM

A term that has different meanings in two different contexts. In the context of Italian history the term was coined by party leader Fr. Luigi Sturzo to describe those politicians who went over from his Catholic Partito Popolare Italiano and supported Mussolini and the Fascists. Fourteen clerico-fascist candidates stood in Mussolini's "big list" in the 1924 general elections, and later formed the Centro Nazionale Italiano as a permanent focus of Catholic political support for Fascism. By the time the CNI had disbanded, it had helped prepare the ground for the agreement between Mussolini and Pope

Pius XI in 1929 and helped save several Catholic-controlled banks. Outside of Italy, the term has been used rather loosely to describe such regimes as the Dollfuss-Schuschnigg "Christian, corporative, and German" state in Austria between 1933 and 1938; Salazar's *Estado Novo* in Portugal; Franco's Spain; and even the Republic of Slovakia, a client state of Nazi Germany between 1939 and 1945. While there were strong Catholic, clerical, and some corporatist elements in all of these regimes, it is doubtful whether they can seriously be described as "fascist," inasmuch as they were not the product of the coming to power of a mass organization with a radical revolutionary ideology based on palingenetic populist ultranationalism.

John Pollard

See Also: INTRODUCTION; AUSTRIA; BELGIUM; CATHOLIC CHURCH, THE; CORPORATISM; CROATIA; DOLLFUSS, ENGELBERT; *ESTADO NOVO;* FALANGE; FASCIST PARTY, THE; FRANCO Y BAHAMONDE, GENERAL FRANCISCO; ITALY; MUSSOLINI, BENITO ANDREA; NATIONALISM; PALINGENETIC MYTH; PIUS XI, POPE; PIUS XII, POPE; POLITICAL CATHOLICISM; PORTUGAL; RELIGION; REVOLUTION; SALAZAR, ANTÓNIO DE OLIVEIRA; SCHUSCHNIGG, KURT; SLOVAKIA; SPAIN; USTASHA

References

Pollard, J. 1990. "Conservative Catholics and Italian Fascism: The Clerico-fascists." Pp. 31–49 In *Fascists and Conservatives: The Radical Right and the Establishment in Twentieth Century Europe*, edited by M. Blinkhorn. London: Unwin Hyman.
Wolff, R. J., and J. R. Hoensch. eds. 1987. *Catholics, the State and the European Radical Right.* Boulder, CO: Social Science Monographs.

CODREANU, CORNELIU ZELEA (1899–1938)

Founder and first leader of the Romanian Legion of the Archangel Michael (often known as the Iron Guard). Codreanu studied law at the university of Iasi (in northwestern Romania, near the Russian border), where he first became involved in anti-Semitic and anticommunist activities. In 1923, Codreanu conspired to murder a number of Jewish bankers and politicians but was arrested before the plan could be carried out. He killed the police prefect of Iasi, a murder for which he was acquitted, and which became the prototype of many more political assassinations by the legion. He was arrested in the night of 16–17 April 1938 and executed on 29–30 November 1938.

Philip Vanhaelemeersch

See Also: LEGION OF THE ARCHANGEL MICHAEL, THE; ORTHODOX CHURCHES, THE; ROMANIA

References
Ioanid, R. 1990. *The Sword of the Archangel Michael: Fascist Ideology in Romania.* Boulder, CO: Westview: Eastern European Monographs.

COLD WAR, THE

Period of international confrontation or stand-off between the nations of the West, generally embodying in some degree the philosophy of capitalism and largely under the leadership of the United States, and the communist world, under the leadership of the USSR and China. It lasted from 1945 until the fall of the Berlin Wall in 1989. British statesman Winston Churchill famously set the tone for the era in his reference to the "iron curtain" that had come down between (communist) Eastern and (liberal) Western Europe after the war, and this rhetorical image became reality with the construction of physical walls to stem emigration from Eastern Europe to the West after 1961. This was the international context for the evolution of postwar fascist movements, which identified completely with the U.S. anticommunist crusade of the era, though not with U.S. liberal capitalism.

Cyprian Blamires

See Also: CAPITALISM; CHURCHILL, SIR WINSTON LEONARD SPENCER; ECONOMICS; POSTWAR FASCISM; UNITED STATES, THE (POSTWAR)

References
Nolte, E. 1982. *Marxism, Fascism, Cold War.* Assen: Van Gorcum.

COLLINS, SEWARD (1899–1952)

U.S. journalist and propagator of fascistic ideas in the interwar years. Born in Syracuse, New York, Collins graduated from the Hill School and Princeton Univer-

sity. Owner of the literary monthly *The Bookman* from 1927 and its editor from 1929, Collins devoted the journal to New Humanism, a philosophy focused on neoclassicism, aristocracy, and Burkean conservatism. In 1933 he converted *The Bookman* into the *American Review,* which was far more eclectic. *The American Review* featured New Humanists like Irving Babbitt and Paul Elmer More, Southern Agrarians like Allen Tate and Robert Penn Warren, Roman Catholic and Anglican neoscholastics like architect Ralph Adams Cram and historian Christopher Dawson, and advocates of the British political philosophy called Distributism like Hilaire Belloc and G. K. Chesterton. He opposed competition, individualism, industrialism, parliamentary government, and, in the words of contributor T. S. Eliot, "free-thinking Jews." Many of the more distinguished contributors dropped off as Collins began to espouse a curious brand of "Park Avenue" fascism, one that had as its essence "the revival of monarchy, property, the guilds, the security of the family and the peasantry, and the ancient ways of European life." He found Mussolini "the most constructive statesman of our age," then endorsed Francisco Franco as the journal ended in 1937. In 1941, Collins served briefly on the editorial board of the militantly anti-interventionist *Scribner's Commentator.*

Justus Doenecke

See Also: ANTI-SEMITISM; CONSERVATISM; DISTRIBUTISM; EGALITARIANISM; FAMILY, THE; FRANCO Y BAHAMONDE, GENERAL FRANCISCO; INDIVIDUALISM; INTERVENTIONISM; MONARCHISM; MUSSOLINI, BENITO ANDREA; PARLIAMENTARISM; RURALISM; TRADITIONALISM; UNITED STATES, THE (PRE-1945)

References
Hoeveler, J. David, Jr. 1999. "American Review." Pp. 235–242 in *The Conservative Press in Twentieth-Century America,* edited by Ronald Lora and William Henry Longton. Westport, CT: Greenwood.
Stone, Albert E., Jr., 1960. "Seward Collins and the *American Review*: Experiment in Pro-Fascism, 1933–37." *American Quarterly* 12 (spring): 3–19.

COLONIALISM

It is difficult to generalize about fascism's attitude to colonialism, given the mosaic of disparate responses to the question by the various movements in interwar Europe. Fascist Italy did subscribe to a colonial agenda, first through the "pacification" of Libya and Somalia (a pacification that involved persecution and mass murder of the indigenous populations), and in 1935 through a colonial war against Ethiopia, whose capital, Addis Ababa, was occupied in May 1936. By contrast, Adolf Hitler, while paying lip service to the demand for the return of German colonies in the context of his revisionist discourse (the Versailles Treaty, with its "Colonial Guilt" clause, had deprived the Reich of its previous colonial possessions), made clear that his territorial priorities lay in a *Lebensraum*-oriented expansion within Europe at the expense of the Soviet Union. In a country with an already extensive colonial network, Oswald Mosley, leader of the British Union of Fascists, propagated the need to maintain (rather than expand) and defend the British Empire against disintegration. In the Iberian peninsula, fascist and parafascist ideologies—the Spanish Falange and Francoism in Spain, *salazarismo* in Portugal—glorified their countries' imperial past as a mobilizing myth of historic national "superiority," but that invocation was firmly rooted in the past, with no political implications for present action.

Even in the case of Fascist Italy—whose championing of colonial expansion was discordant with the bulk of interwar fascist movements and regimes—colonialism was adopted through an intellectually circuitous route. Mussolini presented the need to consolidate and expand the Italian colonial empire through a combination of political, economic, and demographic arguments. His regime's emphasis on the rebirth of modern Italy, his focus on the myth of the "third Rome"—which carried obvious imperial implications—and his determination to elevate the country to the status of a genuine Great Power identified colonial expansion in Africa as an excellent political opportunity without (he mistakenly believed) any direct complications for the stability of the European system. Furthermore, the acquisition of colonial territory would also function as an alternative destination for immigration, thus ensuring that the then constant stream of Italians leaving the country for the United States would be absorbed within the (expanded) national territory and thus remain part of the national economy. Finally, Mussolini's obsession with demographic theories of population growth as evidence of national rebirth (for example, his "strength in numbers" slogan) identified colonies as an area for both resettling excess population and for absorbing the future expected increase in the national population, ensuring at the same time a parallel increase in agricultural resources for the nation.

Thus, it is evident that fascism displayed an inconsistent attitude toward colonialism, with its diverse responses constituting more a reflection of national traditions and ambitions than a normative ideological stance. The fact that fascism emerged as an intellectual and political force in a European context with an already developed (and by then largely questioned) colonial discourse meant that it inherited tendencies already embedded in indigenous nationalism. In those cases where the overriding goal of national rebirth could be served through the invocation of colonialism (politically or simply as a matter of prestige) or economic goals could be fulfilled through expansion overseas, fascist movements or regimes displayed various degrees of colonial enthusiasm. But nothing in fascist ideology prescribed colonialism as a direct priority, and indeed colonialism remained a peripheral element in the fascist experience, even (eventually) in the case of Fascist Italy.

During the difficult transition period of the 1950s, some radical right-wing forces (for example, Poujadists in France) waged a last-ditch battle to defend the colonial past and the status of their countries. The almost total retreat of the European states from the colonial field and into the Continent by the 1960s realigned the attention of fascist movements with fundamentally different notions of national rebirth. A nostalgic colonial imagery continued to be part of the populist regime discourse in Francoist Spain and Salazarist Portugal until the 1970s, but (unlike the interwar period) with little ideological substance and political relevance to wider contemporary political debates.

Aristotle Kallis

See Also: DEMOGRAPHIC POLICY; ETHIOPIA; EXPANSIONISM; FALANGE; FASCIST PARTY, THE; FRANCO Y BAHAMONDE, GENERAL FRANCISCO; FRANCOISM; GREAT BRITAIN; HITLER, ADOLF; IMPERIALISM; ITALY; *LEBENSRAUM;* LIBYA; MOSLEY, SIR OSWALD; MUSSOLINI, BENITO ANDREA; PORTUGAL; POSTWAR FASCISM; POUJADE, PIERRE MARIE RAYMOND; ROME; SALAZAR, ANTÓNIO DE OLIVEIRA; SLAVS, THE (AND GERMANY); VERSAILLES, THE TREATY OF; WORLD WAR II

References
Grimal, Henri. 1965. *Decolonization: The British, French, Dutch and Belgian Empires, 1919–1963.* London: Routledge and Kegan Paul.
Hildebrand, K. 1973. *The Foreign Policy of the Third* Reich. London: Batsford.
Hobsbawm, E. 1987. *The Age of Empire, 1875–1914.* London: Weidenfeld and Nicolson.
Naylor, Philip C. 2000. *France and Algeria: A History of Decolonization and Transformation.* Miami: University of Florida Press.

Segre, C. 1974. *Fourth Shore: The Italian Colonisation of Libya.* Chicago: University of Chicago Press.

Smith, W. 1986. *The Ideological Origins of Nazi Imperialism.* New York: Oxford University Press.

COMBAT 18

Fascist paramilitary organization that emerged from the British National Party in 1992. Led by Paul "Charlie" Sargent, Combat 18 (C18) takes its name from the numerical position in the alphabet of Adolf Hitler's initials. During the 1990s, C18 acquired a fearsome reputation for violence against ethnic minorities, political opponents, and rival fascists, forging close links with various football "firms" and also with Loyalist paramilitaries in Northern Ireland. While it remains active, the group has greatly diminished following Sargent's incarceration for murder, the culmination of an internal feud regarding the future direction of C18 and profits from the lucrative "white noise" scene.

Graham Macklin

See Also: FOOTBALL/SOCCER; GREAT BRITAIN; NEO-NAZISM; POSTWAR FASCISM; RACISM; WHITE NOISE

References
Lowles, Nick. 2001. *White Riot: The Violent Story of Combat 18.* Bury: Milo.

COMINTERN, THE

Established in 1919 following the Bolshevik revolution in the USSR, the Communist International, or Comintern, was the assembly of the world's communist parties: leading Comintern figures recognized earlier than anyone else fascism's potential to become an international force. Indeed, several important Marxist theories of fascism were generated under the aegis of the Comintern. These include a famous 1923 speech by the German socialist Clara Zetkin that characterized Mussolini's party as representing more than terror and violence. Fascism was both a form of antisocialist reaction, she argued, and also an independent agent, a mass movement with deep social roots. By 1929, the

Comintern was associated with the narrow and self-defeating strategy of the German Communists and their argument that the German Socialists were to be feared equally with Hitler's party. Later, Marxist theories of fascism tended to emerge outside or in criticism of the Comintern. The rise of a bureaucracy within Russia, the association of Stalin with "Socialism in One Country," and the increasing use of violence by the Russian state against the people, all served to reduce the interest of the leading Russian communists in the international movement. The Comintern was formally shut down in 1943.

David Renton

See Also: ANTI-COMINTERN PACT, THE; ANTIFASCISM; HITLER, ADOLF; MARXISM; MARXIST THEORIES OF FASCISM; NAZISM; SOCIALISM; SOVIET UNION, THE; STALIN, IOSIF VISSARIONOVICH

References
Hallas, D. 1985. *The Comintern.* London: Bookmarks.
Serge, V. 1963. *Memoirs of a Revolutionary 1901–1941.* Oxford: Oxford University Press.

COMMUNISM: *See* BOLSHEVISM; COMINTERN, THE; MARXISM; SOCIALISM; SOVIET UNION, THE; STALIN, IOSIF VISSARIONOVICH

COMMUNITY

Fascism can be seen as a form of revolutionary nationalism that in all its many permutations seeks to combat the forces of decadence, which it sees as causing the degeneration and breakdown of society. Its ultimate goal as movement and regime is to induce the rebirth of the nation's entire political culture, a project that embraces regenerating not just its power as a state and military force but also its social, moral, and artistic achievements and other signs of society's cohesion and vitality. The aspiration to create a healthy community can thus be seen as a definitional feature of generic fascism, and the fascist utopia constitutes an organic entity to which each individual is bound through the suprapersonal ties of ancestry, culture, and "blood."

Unlike ultraconservatives, however, fascists do not want to restore a lost age but to create a new type of community, fully adapted to the modern age yet firmly rooted "spiritually" in the past and steeped in the allegedly healthy values of the nation or people that prevailed before its decline. It was this vision that Italian Fascism attempted to realize, largely unsuccessfully, through a variety of policies designed to create the new "Fascist Man," and that placed the creation of the morally and genetically healthy *Volksgemeinschaft* at the center of Nazi domestic policies. Both the Italian Fascist and the German Nazi regimes, though for different historical reasons, identified the parliamentary system and the liberal society it purported to serve with everything that fascism abhorred: egotistic individualism, soulless materialism, life-sapping rationalism, identity-eroding cosmopolitanism, class division and factionalism, loss of national solidarity and purpose, and a marginalized role within the arena of international politics. In the Third Reich, the anti-Semitism so central to Nazism's diagnosis of the crisis in Germany generated a pervasive conspiracy theory according to which the nation's very being was threatened by (Jewish) finance capitalism and (Jewish) Bolshevism, operating both internationally and from within. The solution to the national community's weakness in both countries was to establish a single-party state ruled by a leader whose charismatic authority was underpinned by an elaborate program of social engineering designed to mobilize popular enthusiasm for the new order at all levels of society (another point of contrast with conservatism). That involved not just totalitarianism in the negative sense—namely, propaganda, censorship, coercion, and, in the case of the Third Reich, an extensive apparatus of state terror—but also "positively" restructuring the educational system, organizing the economy (in the case of Italy) or culture (in the case of Germany) on corporatist principles, and seeking to harness work, youth, and leisure to the cause of the nation through the creation of mass organizations. Both states introduced social and demographic measures for increasing the population and improving its physical fitness.

Despite the rhetoric of a "new Rome" however, Fascist society retained large elements of pre-Fascist Italy and considerable pockets of diversity and nonconformism. This was partly due to inefficiency and to the intrinsic limits of the state's interference in civil society and existing institutions, but also to the regime's need to co-opt as many currents of spontaneous Italian creativity and productivity as possible (a policy that scholars have termed "hegemonic pluralism"). In the Third Reich the attempt was made to enforce greater harmo-

nization (*Gleichschaltung*) on all spheres of life with the new state, though the new Germany remained far more heterogeneous and "polycentric" in reality than official propaganda claimed. It also set out, with a systematic ruthlessness and "efficiency" unthinkable under Mussolini, to purge the national community of all the alleged enemies of its moral cohesion and racial purity. This is to be attributed to the fact that what set Nazism apart from other fascisms was not its anti-Semitism but its understanding of the bonds of community as the product not just of social and cultural history but also of racial history. German history was reimagined as the history of an "Aryan" people whose purity and inner strength were constantly under threat from inner and outer enemies.

Under Hitler, self-appointed "racial experts" construed "Aryanness," an essentially mythic concept, in scientific and pseudo-scientific ("scientistic") terms, drawing on currents of Social Darwinism and eugenics that were common to all Europeanized societies at the time. The result was an elaborate program of "racial hygiene" involving mass sterilization and "elimination" that became an integral part of the Third Reich's measures to regenerate the "national community." The human consequences were horrific for those considered officially *gemeinschaftsunfähig*—literally, "incapable of forming part of the community." In practice this led to the persecution or extermination of such out-groups as Jews, communists, Roma and Sinta gypsies, homosexuals, the physically and mentally handicapped, Jehovah's Witnesses, and those branded as irremediably "asocial," a loose category that could embrace any form of social behavior deemed to betray lack of commitment to Hitler's "new order."

Fascist Italy and the Third Reich were the only regimes to result from the successful conquest of state power by a fascist movement, and in which it is therefore possible for historians to study what the fascist vision of community meant when put into practice. Despite the genuine fervor generated by the leader cult and the high degree of public consensus that both regimes won as long as their domestic and foreign policies seemed successful, the rapid defascistization of both societies after 1945 suggests that the "new Rome" and *Volksgemeinschaft* remained a chimera, more the product of propaganda and wishful thinking than a realizable goal. Mussolini managed to "nationalize" the mass of Italians to an unprecedented degree as long as the prospect of a European war seemed remote, but not to fascistize them, so that the popular consensus on which he depended had, by the time he was deposed in July 1943, long since melted away. The Nazification of Germany penetrated much further into the fabric and mentality of "ordinary" Germans, but, despite the power of the Fuehrer myth at the height of the Third Reich's power and its persistence to the bitter end, the battle of Stalingrad in the winter of 1942–1943 cruelly exposed the twin myths of Hitler's infallibility and of the inherent superiority of the new German hero who willingly lived and died for his nation whatever the cost.

The theories of several pioneers of modern sociology can shed light on the utopia that the interwar fascists were trying to achieve. In terms of the theories of Ferdinand Tönnies (1855–1936), interwar fascism was an attempt to wipe away the evils of a society based on *Gesellschaft* ("association"), the type of contractual and inherently pluralistic civil society with which the Weimar Republic became so widely identified, and replace it with the values and structures of an organic *Gemeinschaft* (community). If Émile Durkheim's (1858–1917) theory of social cohesion is applied, the domestic policies of the two fascist regimes can be seen as attempts to re-create the bonds of "mechanical solidarity" that he claims existed before they were gradually dissolved by modernization to be replaced by those based on work, personal values, and class (which he somewhat idiosyncratically called the basis of "organic solidarity"). It was the inadequacy of organic solidarity to provide a shared cosmology and collective sense of transcendence that he claimed engendered the experience of profound isolation, meaninglessness, and despair he termed anomie. Fascism can thus be seen as an attempt to put an end to anomie through creating a powerful mythic sense of roots, belonging, homeland, and higher fate enacted within a historical rather than a divine sphere of transcendence. In the context of Max Weber's (1864–1920) interpretation of modernity as the product of rationalization and disenchantment, the driving force of fascism in both Italy and Germany was the goal of regenerating a society debilitated by the decay of "traditional" politics and the ineffectiveness of "legal rational" politics through the power of "charismatic" politics. Simultaneously, it sought to "re-enchant" national life through deliberately exploiting the power of myth, political religion, and aesthetic politics to unite a nation in a common sense of strength and purpose. The intended result was a charismatic community, or what the Nazis called a "community of destiny" (*Schicksalsgemeinschaft*), capable of ushering in a new era of civilization purged of both liberalism and communism, thereby granting a secular immortality to all its members by playing an integral part in a heroic period of the nation's "sacred" history.

One of the features common to the many fascist movements that arose between 1918 and 1945, not just in Europe but also in South Africa, Brazil, and Chile, was that, as in Italy and Germany, the community or nation that it strove to rescue from decadence was broadly identified with the nation-state, even if the project of regeneration sometimes involved irredentist territorial claims, and hence expanding the borders to include all ethnic members of the nation within them. This led some forms of fascism to look back to a Golden Age of the nation's history when the health of the organic community was allegedly manifested in a harmonious relationship between the cultural, artistic, and the political spheres. Thus Italian Fascism instituted a cult of Rome (*Romanità*), the British Union of Fascists idealized England's Elizabethan Age, and the Falange glorified Spain's sixteenth century, the *siglo de oro*.

Since 1945 a number of new varieties of fascism have arisen that no longer identify the reborn community with the existing nation-state. A number of varieties of contemporary fascism—notably the European New Right and Third Positionism—see historical ethnic groups ("ethnies"), such as the reawakened Welsh or Bretons, finding their natural place within a reawakened, "imperial" or "organic" Europe, a vision known as "the Europe of nations" or "the Europe of a hundred flags." This paradoxical concept of community is expressed in the name adopted by one of the more recent extreme right-wing formations, which calls itself the National European Communitarian Party, and which in its ideology blends both fascist and socialist critiques of the new global order. Meanwhile, Universal Nazis all over the world present Hitler's struggle as having been fought against the decadence of communism, materialism, and racial mixing, not just for Germany but also the whole Aryan race, which is now imagined as constituting a global diasporic community of superior beings with battle-fronts against degeneracy in each nation. Some U.S. Nazis, as well as the Afrikaner Werstandsbeweging (AWB) in South Africa, see the only solution to the evils of multiracialism currently being "imposed" by the state government in the creation of separatist homelands for whites only, carved out from the existing nation-state.

Paradoxically, the only "real" fascist community that can exist since the defeat of the Axis powers is the virtual one created by the Worldwide Web of sites devoted to fantasies of racial and cultural regeneration that continue to proliferate. This community is strictly metapolitical and as such is impotent to have any impact on real politics at a systemic level. However, it may continue to provide the ideological fuel for "lone wolves" such as Timothy McVeigh and David Copeland, the

Oklahoma and London bombers, respectively, who operate outside any meaningful community in the sense of healthy interpersonal human relations and a high degree of socialization. Indeed, they may be partly driven to their desperate acts of terrorism precisely by its absence in their lives.

Roger Griffin

See Also: INTRODUCTION; ABSTRACTION; "ANTI-" DIMENSION OF FASCISM, THE; ANTI-SEMITISM; ARYANISM; ASOCIALS; AXIS, THE; BLOOD AND SOIL; BOLSHEVISM; BRAZIL; CAPITALISM; CHILE; CONSERVATISM; CONSPIRACY THEORIES; CORPORATISM; COSMOPOLITANISM; CULTURE; CYBERFASCISM; DECADENCE; DEMOGRAPHIC POLICY; ECONOMICS; EDUCATION; EUGENICS; EUROPE; EUROPEAN NEW RIGHT, THE; EUROPEANIST FASCISM; EXPANSIONISM; FALANGE; GERMANY; *GLEICHSCHALTUNG;* GLOBALIZATION; GREAT BRITAIN; HERO, THE CULT OF THE; HITLER, ADOLF; HOMOSEXUALITY; INDIVIDUALISM; IRREDENTISM; ITALY; LEADER CULT, THE; LEISURE; LIBERALISM; LONDON NAIL BOMBINGS, THE; MASSES, THE ROLE OF THE; MATERIALISM; MCVEIGH, TIMOTHY; MODERNITY; MUSSOLINI, BENITO ANDREA; MYTH; NATIONALISM; NAZISM; NEW MAN, THE; NEW ORDER, THE; NIHILISM; OKLAHOMA BOMBING, THE; ORGANICISM; PALINGENETIC MYTH; PANGERMANISM; PARLIAMENTARISM; PROPAGANDA; RACIAL DOCTRINE; RATIONALISM; RELIGION; REVOLUTION; ROMA AND SINTI, THE; ROME; ROOTLESSNESS; SOCIAL DARWINISM; SOCIOLOGY; SOUTH AFRICA; SPAIN; STALINGRAD; THIRD POSITIONISM; THIRD REICH, THE; TRADITION; UTOPIA, UTOPIANISM; *VOLKSGEMEINSCHAFT,* THE; WEIMAR REPUBLIC, THE; YOUTH

References
Brooker, Paul. 1991. *The Faces of Fraternalism: Nazi Germany, Fascist Italy and Imperial Japan.* Oxford: Clarendon.
Durkheim, E. 1949. *The Division of Labor in Society.* Trans. G. Simpson. Glencoe, IL: Free Press.
Peukert, Detlev J. K. 1989. *Inside Nazi Germany: Conformity, Opposition and Racism in Everyday* Life. Harmondsworth: Penguin.
Toennies, Ferdinand. 1987 [1887]. *Community and Association* (*Gemeinschaft und Gesellschaft*). Michigan: Michigan University Press.
Weber, Max. 1968. *Economy and Society.* Part 2. Trans. Guenther Roth and Claus Wittich. Berkeley: University of California Press.

CONCENTRATION CAMPS

Although they were to be found at various times and in various places—Joseph Goebbels's propaganda noted Britain's policy of repressive internment during the Boer War, for example, and they were also found in the Soviet Union—concentration camps are most frequently associated with the Third Reich in Germany between 1933 and 1945. Under the direction of Nazism, and in particular the SS, during this dozen years an estimated 1.9 million Europeans of virtually all nationalities and demographic groups died in concentration camps; this figure excludes those systematically murdered in extermination centers (like Auschwitz-Birkenau) more squarely associated with events of the Holocaust. Concentration camps and their hundreds of auxiliary satellites were employed for various reasons; suppression of dissent, slave labor, racial (or religious, political, or medical) persecution, and, of course, punishment and death. Indeed, camps played an integral role in campaigns of mass murder undertaken by the Nazis and their allies: nearly half of those incarcerated died through state-directed violence, deprivation, malnutrition, and disease. By the end of World War II, some 10,000 internment locations in Europe held more than 700,000 captive workers, prisoners, and victims; a vast network incorporating varying types of custody (in terms of severity, length of sentence, and category of offense); and opportunities for resistance, escape, and prospects for survival. Inmates' nationalities changed substantially during this period: in 1939 an overwhelming majority of them were German, whereas that group constituted less than 10 percent of the total concentration camp population by 1945.

Emergency decrees published in the wake of the Reichstag fire in late February 1933—less than a month after Hitler had been appointed chancellor of Germany—explicitly authorized "preventative" police actions against political dissidents, especially communists and socialists. Widespread arrests and the subsequent overcrowding of prisons was an important reason behind Heinrich Himmler's announcement of 20 March 1933 that established the former gunpowder factory outside Munich, called Dachau, as the first concentration camp in National Socialist Germany. Camps were soon established across Germany, and by 31 July 1933 camps such as Oranienburg, Sonnenburg, and Osnabrück held 26,789 prisoners in "protective custody." By September 1939, victims were suffering even worse treatment in the camps, which held not only political dissidents but also Jews and "asocials"—notably homosexuals, Roma and Sinti travelers, and Jehovah's Witnesses; they had now come under the supervision of a complex system of control by the SS.

At the height of the Nazi domination of Europe, camps stretched from Natzweiler/Struthof in France to Jasenovac in Croatia, guarded by up to 40,000 special

Inmates of Buchenwald concentration camp a few days after its liberation by American troops. These camps were the embodiment of Nazi theories about the regeneration of the German people through the elimination of "alien" elements. (National Archives)

SS guards or nationalist collaborators. The range of victims extended especially to Polish and Russian nationals during the war, and from 1941 systematic killing operations—ranging from shooting and the application of the so-called Euthanasia Campaign to mass murder by work or gassing—were additionally intended to annihilate European Jewry in concentration camps. Importantly, over 1941 and 1942 concentration camps took on this additional role as facilities intended for the efficient murder and disposal of millions of victims at institutions like Chlemno, Majdanek, and elsewhere; more than 3 million people, the vast majority Jews, died in these locations of industrial murder.

At the same time the camps continued to serve different, although interrelated, functions: as holding camps (Westerbork, Bergen-Belsen, Theresienstadt), extermination camps (Belzec, Sobibor, and Treblinka), and increasingly, forced labor camps (Mauthausen, Ravensbrück, Sachsenhausen). The latter operated largely in support of the German war effort, in partnership with an array of private firms like IG Farben, Krupp, BMW, and Messerschmitt. Profit was nevertheless eclipsed by exploitation, as a severely malnourished and overworked labor force was literally worked to death for wartime German industry. As the tide of war progressively turned against the Axis Powers, camps multiplied all these functions. Conditions deteriorated sharply and numbers of inmates expanded rapidly; for example, the overall total of prisoners rose by some 300,000 (from 224,000) during the year August 1943 to August 1944. Early in 1945 all the camps were closed ahead of advancing Allied armies, and a "death march" of prisoners took place toward central Germany. Although this final action caused the death of another quarter of a million victims, hundreds of thousands nevertheless lived and many survived to testify to the varied functions of Nazi concentration camps, frequently summarized as inflicting upon inmates the experience of hell.

Matt Feldman

See Also: ANTIFASCISM; ANTI-SEMITISM; ARYANISM; ASOCIALS; AUSCHWITZ(-BIRKENAU); AXIS, THE; EUTHANASIA; FORCED LABOR; GOEBBELS, (PAUL) JOSEPH; HIMMLER, HEINRICH; HITLER, ADOLF; HOLOCAUST, THE; HOMOSEXUALITY; IG FARBEN; INDUSTRY; JEHOVAH'S WITNESSES, THE; KRUPP VON BOHLEN UND HALBACH, ALFRIED; MARXISM; MEDICINE; MENGELE, JOSEF; NAZISM; PARAGUAY; PROPAGANDA; RACIAL DOCTRINE; REICHSTAG FIRE, THE; ROMA AND SINTI, THE; SOCIALISM; SS, THE; THIRD REICH, THE; USTASHA; WORLD WAR II

References
Hackett, David A., ed. 1995. *The Buchenwald Report.* Boulder, CO: Westview.
Kogon, Eugon. 1949. *The Theory and Practice of Hell.* New York: Farrar, Straus.
Krausnick, Helmut, and Martin Broszat. 1970. *Anatomy of the SS State.* London: Granada.
Todorov, Tzvetan. 1999. *Facing the Extreme: Moral Life in the Concentration Camps.* London: Phoenix.
Wachsmann, Nikolaus. 2004. *Hitler's Prisons: Legal Terror in Nazi Germany.* London: Yale University Press.

CONDOR LEGION, THE: *See* LUFTWAFFE, THE

CONFESSING (or CONFESSIONAL) CHURCH, THE

Between 1933 and 1945, the movement within German Protestantism that opposed the pro-Nazi "German Christians" and their attempts to create a Reich church. Around one-third of all German Protestant clergy belonged to the Confessing Church at its height in 1934. Confessing parishes were established throughout the country, but the church was strongest in Berlin-Brandenburg and the Prussian regional churches. Founded primarily to oppose the "German Christians" and their attempt to apply Nazi racial legislation to church laws governing membership and the ordination of clergy, the Confessing Church was formally established in May 1934 at the Barmen synod, a national church meeting attended by representatives of all the German regional Protestant churches. Its founding document, the Barmen declaration of faith, was written by the Swiss theologian Karl Barth. It called for a church based upon the Christian confessions that would retain its independence from all worldly ideology. The fifth thesis of the Barmen declaration directly opposed totalitarian control by the state over all aspects of human life, and declared the church to be a counterforce to such control.

The Barmen declaration was unanimously approved by all the church delegates present, who viewed it as a response to attempts by the "German Christians" to control German Protestantism ideologically. This unanimity soon dissolved. Despite their opposition to "German Christian" ideology, most Protestant leaders in 1934 still viewed the National Socialist government positively; for them, the Barmen document was a declaration of church independence from the state and its ideological allies, not a statement of opposition to a totalitarian state. The declaration's radical antitotalitarian potential was embraced by only a few. At the Dahlem synod in October 1934, a radical faction sought to declare the Confessing Church the only true church, a move that could have created a breakaway church. This brought resistance from more moderate church leaders; thereafter, the numbers of active Confessing Christians diminished. Like the "German Christians," the Confessing Church and its members never formally left the German Protestant Church.

Outside Nazi Germany, the Confessing Church attracted support from some Christian leaders who drew parallels between the ideological demands of Nazism on the German churches and the experience of the Russian churches under communism. The issue of church independence from Nazi ideology and state control was indeed the primary concern of the Confessing Church, but its ranks also included some radical members who sought a broader, more outspoken opposition to the Nazi regime, to its dismantling of civil liberties, and to its persecution of the Jews. A few of its members, such as the theologian Dietrich Bonhoeffer, eventually joined the political resistance to overthrow the regime. As the Nazi regime tightened its hold on German society and intensified its persecution of opponents, the radical sectors of the Confessing Church were compelled to go further underground. Many Confessing pastors were arrested, and the church's youth work was the target of particular observation and harassment. In 1937 a decree by Heinrich Himmler banned the Confessing Church's seminaries, forcing seminary training of its pastors to be conducted secretly and illegally. Nonetheless, where Nazi policies did not affect the church directly, there were few instances of active resistance or public protest, and with few exceptions the Confessing Church was silent about the Nazi persecution of the Jews. One exception was the Berlin office of Pastor Heinrich Grüber, which helped some 2,000 Jews (many of them converts to Christianity) to emigrate until the Gestapo closed the office in 1941; all the staff members of the office, including Grüber, were sent to concentration camps.

With the beginning of war in September 1939, the church's situation changed. Most Protestant clergy, including the illegally trained Confessing Church clergy, became soldiers in the *Wehrmacht*. Church criticism of Nazi policies became even more muted, and most Protestant leaders made a point of professing their patriotism. With the defeat of Nazism, the Confessing Church was viewed as one of the few German institutions to have opposed Nazism, and its leaders portrayed their struggle under Nazism as a religious battle against fascist ideology. Nonetheless, most of them sought a quick re-establishment of social peace in postwar Germany, and that led them to oppose the Allied denazification program and similar measures. By the late 1950s, the Confessing Church as a distinct movement had ceased to exist.

Early depictions of the Confessing Church portrayed it as far more heroic than it had actually been. Only with a more critical and detailed examination of the church's record, including the nationalism and anti-Semitism of many of its leaders, did a different portrait come to light. The Confessing Church emerged primarily in opposition to the extremist "German Christian" movement. It remained torn between traditional Protestant nationalism and its desire for church independence from ideological co-option and state control. It opposed the Nazi regime on issues of church independence and on a few moral issues, notably the euthanasia program. Many clergy and lay members helped individual Jews, but the official church chose to remain silent on the issue of the Holocaust. Only in isolated cases did Confessing Christians offer systemic

critiques of the National Socialist system and challenge the legitimacy of the regime; one such exception was Dietrich Bonhoeffer's 1933 essay "The Church Faces the Jewish Question," which raised the issue of potential church resistance against the illegitimate exercise of state authority.

Victoria Barnett

See Also: ANTIFASCISM; ANTI-SEMITISM; BONHOEFFER, DIETRICH; CHRISTIANITY; CONCENTRATION CAMPS; DENAZIFICATION; GERMAN CHRISTIANS, THE; HIMMLER, HEINRICH; HOLOCAUST, THE; LUTHERAN CHURCHES, THE; NATIONALISM; NAZISM; NIEMOELLER, MARTIN; PROTESTANTISM; RACIAL DOCTRINE; RELIGION; THEOLOGY; TOTALITARIANISM; WEHRMACHT, THE; WORLD WAR II; YOUTH

References
Barnett, Victoria. 1992. *For the Soul of the People: Protestant Protest against Nazism.* New York: Oxford University Press.
Gerlach, Wolfgang. 2000. *And the Witnesses Were Silent: The Confessing Church and the Jews.* Lincoln: University of Nebraska Press.
Helmreich, Ernst Christian. 1979. *The German Churches under Hitler: Background, Struggle, and Epilogue.* Detroit: Wayne State University Press.
Hockenos, Matthew D. 2004. *A Church Divided: German Protestants Confront the Nazi Past.* Bloomington: Indiana University Press.
Rittner, Carol, Stephen D. Smith, and Irena Steinfeldt, eds. 2000. *The Holocaust and the Christian World: Reflections on the Past, Challenges for the Future.* London: Kuperard.

CONFESSIONAL CHURCH, THE: *See* CONFESSING CHURCH, THE CONSERVATIVE REVOLUTION: *See* HEIDEGGER, MARTIN; MOHLER, ARMIN; NIHILISM

CONSERVATISM

Many observers have labeled fascism a variant of conservatism, and there are four main reasons for that. First, fascists have invariably shown massive hostility to the Left. Running battles between supporters of Mussolini and Hitler and adherents of the Left were a feature of the early years of fascism, both in Italy and in Germany. The symbolic murder of the socialist parliamentary Matteotti marked a watershed in the development of Mussolini's regime, while in Germany the National Socialists came to power on the back of a powerfully anticommunist program and in an atmosphere of widespread fear of a Bolshevik revolution at home. Second, a fundamental core ingredient of the fascist worldview is hypernationalism, a creed consciously and aggressively developed as a reaction to the internationalism of the Left. This was indeed the essential reason for the hatred that fascists displayed toward the Left: they felt that there was something innately treacherous and weak about internationalism. Mussolini returned from the war to an Italy that he considered to be adrift and rudderless because of the influence of internationalists and pacifists. Both he and Hitler reflected the deep feelings of betrayal felt by the war veterans who came home to a sense that their sacrifices had been a waste of time. They who had fought bravely and suffered atrociously in the trenches had no say in the destiny of their countries, which were guided by politicians who had not fought—and worse, by profiteers who had actually made huge profits out of the war. At a time when their countries were being inwardly divided and crippled by left-wing agitators, there were no strong leaders ready to defend the national interest at all costs. So then, given the traditional spectrum of political thinking in which socialist and communist stood at the opposite pole from conservative, observers naturally located these fascist enemies of the Left with the conservatives. Of course, the rhetoric of the Left itself also viewed matters in that light—the fascists were "conservatives" not least because they had no intention of bringing down the forces of international capitalism nor of liberating the workers of the world from their chains. Not only so, but evidently there was great advantage for the Left in branding conservatives generally as "fascist," a label that if it stuck would blacken them not simply in the eyes of the Left but also in the eyes of centrists or left conservatives.

The third reason why fascism became associated with conservatism was the degree of support that fascists did actually receive from conservative elements. Conservatives of a traditional stamp were naturally delighted to welcome a new force that was pledged to roll back the Bolshevik menace. It was music to their ears. Conservatives were prepared to swallow aspects of fascist ideology that they did not particularly like in order to side with this powerful new ally. The pill was sweetened to the extent that fascism did actually contain some ideological priorities that held an attraction in conservative circles. Their nationalist propaganda, with its pride in the heroic past of Italy and Germany,

seemed to mesh naturally with traditional conservatism. Did not the very root of the term "fascist" refer to the *fasci,* or bundles, that were carried by the lictors of Ancient Rome? And what did the term "Third Reich" mean if not to stress the continuity of German history with the First Reich of the Holy Roman Emperors and the Second Wilhelmine Reich? Likewise their stress on such values as order, the martial virtues, and the preservation of private property. There was so much that seemed to chime with traditional conservative values. There was also a great emphasis in fascist propaganda on the virtues of order, discipline, and hierarchy, which held an obvious appeal to the conservative mind.

A fourth reason why fascism became associated with conservatism is this: historically, some essentially conservative regimes—such as Vichy France, Franco's Spain, Salazar's Portugal, Hungary under Horthy, and Romania under King Carol and General Antonescu—did find it expedient at certain points to take advantage of fascism's dynamism and populist appeal to increase their own popularity by adopting some external trappings of fascism. This has resulted in such regimes frequently being referred to as "fascist." However, it is also true to say that whenever such regimes felt threatened by signs of fascism's growing mass appeal, they moved to emasculate it, as in the case of Spain and Vichy, or crush it, as in the case of Brazil, Chile, Portugal, Hungary, and Romania. But that has not prevented such regimes from having misleadingly acquired the enduring label of "fascist." By contrast, socialist or left-wing leaders have never seen any advantage in openly flirting with fascism, even though their regimes may in reality have shared more or less of fascism's totalitarian features. This is to say that while in certain circumstances conservative politicians or movements have felt able to "look" fascist, the same has never been true for left-wing regimes. Moreover, histories of socialism do not accept "National Socialism" as a variant of socialism, not even bothering to explain why not or to comment on the exclusion.

Superficially, then, it looks as though the assumption on the Left that fascism was just a superheated variety of conservatism might seem to hold water. But the truth is that fascism no more fitted into the traditional category of the Right than it did into that of the Left. Fascism disrupted the comfortable left/right polarity and proposed something entirely new that was in essence a kind of hybrid of right and left. "Revolutionary Conservatism" was the term used by Moeller Van der Bruck; "National Socialism" was the term preferred by Hitler. By the time that the traditional conservatives had finally grasped that neither Hitler nor Mussolini was "one of them," it was already too late. This is illustrated by the July Plot against Hitler's life in 1944, which was planned and executed not by left-wingers or by liberals but by conservatives who felt that Hitler was destroying "their" Germany.

According to the definition of fascism given by Griffin in the Introduction, fascism is a form of revolutionary hypernationalism that assumes an existing state of decadence needing to be remedied. There are two elements here that are incompatible with conservatism as traditionally understood. First, the term *revolutionary.* No traditional conservative approach to politics can assimilate the term *revolution* in the way that fascists understood it: that is, a violent revolution achieved by force. Conservatism has always been essentially hostile to that kind of revolution, although there were currents (protofascist and others) in the decades before the appearance of Nazism that did attempt to propose a rapprochement of the two concepts; in the United Kingdom, the term *Thatcherite revolution* has become common currency. But these are benign understandings of the concept that assume a democratic or at least consensual change, not a violent one. Second, there is the question of the remedy for the decadence. Whereas the traditional conservative thinks in terms of restoring the best of the past, the "new man" of fascism is an unprecedented phenomenon, a new creature of a new world, a utopian figure that neatly parallels the utopian new man envisaged by communist propagandists. There is no way of bending the mind-set of an Edmund Burke, a Disraeli, a Joseph de Maistre, a Russell Kirk, a Ronald Reagan, or a George Bush so that it can fit into that particular box.

The term *National Socialist* tells us all we need to know. Fascism was nationalistic, and therefore it did not belong to the Left. But it was also "socialist," or, in Italy, corporatist, which is equally anti-individualist, so that it could not be bracketed with the Right. In other words, fascism was something new and unprecedented; it straddled the old political divide, and perhaps that was one reason why it caught so much of Europe off guard between the wars. One of the most unexpected and confusing aspects of fascism to the onlooker was its appeal to the masses, whom it managed in Germany and Italy at least to wean away from the Left, who had previously looked upon the masses as their own dedicated fiefdom. This was an unprecedented phenomenon to which the Left did not know how to respond.

Cyprian Blamires

See Also: INTRODUCTION; ANTIFASCISM; ANTONESCU, GENERAL ION; ART; BRAZIL; CHILE; CORPORATISM; COS-MOPOLITANISM; DECADENCE; FRANCO Y BAHAMONDE, GENERAL FRANCISCO; FRANCOISM; HERO, THE CULT OF THE; HITLER, ADOLF; HOLY ROMAN EMPIRE, THE; HORTHY DE NAGYBÁNYA, MIKLÓS; HUNGARY; INDIVIDUALISM; INTERNATIONALISM; ITALY; JULY PLOT, THE; MARXISM; MARXIST THEORIES OF FASCISM; MASSES, THE ROLE OF THE; MODERNISM; MODERNITY; MOELLER VAN DEN BRUCK, ARTHUR; MUSSOLINI, BENITO ANDREA; NATIONALISM; NAZISM; NEW MAN, THE; PARAFASCISM; PORTUGAL; PROTOFASCISM; REVOLUTION; ROMANIA; ROME; SALAZAR, ANTÓNIO DE OLIVEIRA; SOCIALISM; SPAIN; THIRD REICH, THE; THIRD WAY, THE; TOTALITARIANISM; TRADITIONALISM; UTOPIA, UTOPIANISM; VICHY; WAR VETERANS; WARRIOR ETHOS, THE

References
Blinkhorn, M., ed. 1990. *Fascists and Conservatives: The Radical Right and the Establishment in Twentieth Century Europe.* London: Unwin Hyman.
Griffin, R. 1991. *The Nature of Fascism.* London: Routledge.
Payne, S. 1995. *A History of Fascism 1914–1945.* London: University College London Press.

CONSPIRACY THEORIES

A belief in conspiracy theories is an important feature of a large variety of extreme-right movements (though it is by no means limited to them). The most notorious example is undoubtedly the belief of the Nazis in a Jewish world conspiracy, and the combination of conspiracy theories with anti-Semitism has often featured in the discourse of extreme-right parties. The conspiracy theories of extreme-right movements include, however, a much vaster panoply of would-be conspirators. Organizations accused of conspiracies may include the United Nations (in the case of the Militiamen in the United States), Freemasonry, the Catholic Church (an object of particular suspicion on the part of Protestant fundamentalist groups), or the Trilateral Commission (an international organization of private citizens whose avowed aim is to discuss the common challenges and leadership responsibilities of the democratic industrialized areas of the world).

Extreme-right conspiracy theories have their origins in counter-revolutionary explanations of the French Revolution, and in particular in the book written by the abbé Barruel, *Mémoires pour servir à l'histoire du jacobinisme,* first published in 1797. According to Barruel, the French Revolution was the outcome of a conspiracy of philosophers against religion, of Freemasons against the French monarchy, and of the Illuminati (a German group related to Freemasonry, forbidden in 1785, mainly because of its secretive nature and its allegedly nefarious political activities in Bavaria) against the social order. The obsession of many extreme-right movements with Freemasonry—a combination of hostility mixed with fascination—derives from this book. The long-gone Illuminati still play a role in contemporary conspiracy theories, especially for U.S. fundamentalist Christian groups. (They have sprung to prominence again in recent times as a result of featuring prominently in the best-selling book and accompanying film, *The Da Vinci Code*.) Barruel set out what has often been the basic characteristic of extreme-right conspiracy theories: a narrative of how secret elites conspire to subvert the social order. They thus combine populism with a defense of the social order as threatened by specific groups. Anti-Semitism could easily be integrated in such a perspective, and Jews—not present in Barruel's volume—soon appeared in nineteenth-century counter-revolutionary conspiracy theories. With the Russian Revolution of 1917, communists became an additional partner in these alleged worldwide conspiracies.

Conspiracy theories inspired by a conservative and counter-revolutionary background seem to have undergone an additional evolution during the nineteenth century. Reflecting the competitive Social Darwinist dynamics of international relations that came to the foreground in the late nineteenth century, they became outspokenly nationalist. The groups accused of conspiracies were more and more described as cosmopolitan elites allied to foreign powers. Such theories of the betrayal of the nation abounded in the period following World War I and formed a basic feature of extreme-right discourse in Germany. Versions of such conspiracy theories were, however, articulated in many European countries. Because of their international contacts, Jews and Freemasons have always been particularly prone to become the scapegoats of such theories, and Jews and Freemasons were in fact accused by both camps of having betrayed their nation during World War I. However, extreme-right conspiracy theories have tended to display an outspoken and exclusivist nationalism rarely found in conspiracy theories from other ideological backgrounds.

Contemporary versions of conspiracy theories as proposed by extreme-right movements are less concerned with the revolutionary subversion of the social order. The demise of communism after 1989 is reflected in a decline of its role in these theories. They nevertheless are very much concerned with the threat to the social order posed by outsiders. This may take

the form of updated versions of classic themes of conspiracy theories: for example, the role of Freemasons as seen by some extreme-right movements in Russia, who brand them "enemies of the nation." Freemasons and Jews now tend, however, to play a less prominent role in such theories than in the past. Contemporary conspiracy theories may focus instead on denouncing organizations symbolizing the threat of "cosmopolitanism," such as the United Nations. Such theories can integrate other groups perceived to be enemies of the nation. Discreet international groupings of economic and political elites, such as the Trilateral Commission or the Bilderberg Group (an international annual meeting of European and North American leaders whose discussions are conducted behind closed doors—though their meeting locations, lists of participants, and agendas are public knowledge), are particularly apt candidates for this role. Contemporary versions of extreme-right conspiracy theories at the same time display a continuity with traditional themes and introduce new elements. Reflecting the centrality of the issue of immigration in extreme-right propaganda, European extreme-right movements phrase their conspiracy theories in the language of a clash of civilizations. Profiting from the post-9/11 political climate, they denounce Islamic conspiracies. They may combine that focus with more traditional features of conspiracy theories. The Lega Nord in Italy, for example, explains immigration as the result of a conspiracy of the United States and Islam against Europe (and European cultural particularities), with the complicity of the Italian Left and Catholic organizations that allegedly favor immigration.

Conspiracy theories enjoy a particular popularity within the panoply of groups on the extreme-right fringes of the political scene of the United States. The worldview of Militiamen, white supremacists, Identity Christians, or conservative groups like the John Birch Society is strongly marked by a belief in conspiracy theories against the American people and its Constitution. These generally decentralized groups have produced a huge variety of such theories, but they have in common the denunciation of international groups and organizations (which may include the United Nations and the Trilateral Commission, or the Jews) that are accused of dominating the federal government for the purpose of subverting the U.S. Constitution and of enslaving the American people. Such theories are frequently based on an eschatological vision of history with its roots in fundamentalist Christianity.

Michel Huysseune

See Also: ANTI-SEMITISM; CATHOLIC CHURCH, THE; CHRISTIAN IDENTITY; COSMOPOLITANISM; COUNTER-REVOLUTION; FREEMASONRY/FREEMASONS, THE; FRENCH REVOLUTION, THE; IMMIGRATION; NATIONALISM; NAZISM; ORTHODOX CHURCHES, THE; POSTWAR FASCISM; *PROTOCOLS OF THE ELDERS OF ZION, THE; RUSSIA*; SOCIAL DARWINISM; SOVIET UNION, THE; TRADITIONALISM; UNITED NATIONS, THE; UNITED STATES, THE (POSTWAR); WEBSTER, NESTA; ZIONIST OCCUPATION GOVERNMENT, THE

References
Cohn, N. 1967. *Warrant for Genocide: The Myth of a Jewish World-Conspiracy and the Protocols of the Elders of Zion.* London: Eyre and Spottiswoode.
Fenster, M. 1999. *Conspiracy Theories: Secrecy and Power in American Culture.* Minneapolis: University of Minnesota Press.
Taguieff, P.-A. 2005. *La Foire aux illuminés: Esotérisme, théorie du complot, extrémisme.* Paris: Fayard.

CONSUMERISM: See ECOLOGY; ECONOMICS; GLOBALIZATION
CONTRACEPTION: See DEMOGRAPHIC POLICY; FAMILY, THE; HEALTH; SEXUALITY; WOMEN

CORFU

A Greek island with considerable strategic importance, the object of Mussolini's first act of foreign aggression, in August 1923. Four Italians who were part of an international commission to delimit Albania's frontiers were murdered on Greek territory near the border. Mussolini demanded reparations from the Greek government, which refused. Mussolini occupied the island after first bombarding the island's fortress from the sea, but there were refugees sheltering in it of whom sixteen were killed; worldwide anger was such that Greece referred the matter to the League of Nations. However, it was the Conference of Ambassadors that resolved the matter, persuading the Greeks to offer an indemnity to Italy in return for the evacuation of Corfu, which duly took place at the end of the following month.

Cyprian Blamires

See Also: ALBANIA; GREECE; ITALY; LEAGUE OF NATIONS, THE; MUSSOLINI, BENITO ANDREA

References
Barros, James. 1966. *The Corfu Incident of 1923: Mussolini and the League of Nations.* Princeton: Princeton University Press.
Burgwyn, H. J. 1997. *Italian Foreign Policy in the Interwar Period, 1918–1940.* Westport, CT: Greenwood.

CORPORATISM

In theory, corporatism (often called "corporativism") is a system of organizing the economy in such a way that representatives of capital and labor, together with representatives of the state, work together in sectoral "corporations" to promote harmonious labor relations and to maximize production in the national interest. Italian Fascism laid particular claim to having developed the theory and practice of corporatism, and it is often seen as being the most characteristic of its policies. The "corporate state" is thus the putative realization of that theory, but it should be said that in the Italian case the concept of the "corporate state" is sometimes used to describe Fascist economic policies more broadly.

The origins of corporatism lie in the writings of pre–World War I Italian nationalists like Enrico Corradini, Alfredo Rocco, and Luigi Federzoni. They sought to create institutions that would make it possible for Italy to escape the chronic industrial unrest and class conflict of the early 1900s and mobilize the nation's efforts against external enemies in wars of expansion. Another ideological source was the prewar revolutionary syndicalism of later Fascists like Edmondo Rossoni. The experience of World War I, in which the war effort was essentially sustained by collaboration between industrialists, the military, and the state, with trade union activity placed under strict controls, was arguably another inspiration for the corporatist institutions that were developed in the mid-1920s. By 1916, *Il Popolo D'Italia*, Mussolini's daily newspaper, was calling itself the "organ of soldiers and producers," a reflection of the conversion of Rossoni and others from revolutionary to "national syndicalism."

The beginnings of the Fascist corporate state may be traced back to the Palazzo Vidoni Pact of October 1925, in which Olivetti, on behalf of Confindustria, the main Italian employers' organization, and Rossoni, on behalf of the Fascist trade unions, recognized each other as the sole representatives of Italy's industrial employers and employees, respectively, thus effectively spelling the doom of the non-Fascist trade unions, Socialist and Catholic alike.

A year later, Rocco as minister of justice had the opportunity to translate his prewar ideas into practice by means of the Labor and Anti-Strike Law, which formalized the Palazzo Vidoni Pact arrangements, made both strikes and lock-outs illegal, and set up labor tribunals to deal with employer-employee disputes. The non-Fascist unions had been dissolved by the end of 1926, but they were not the only victims of Rocco's legislation; so too was Rossoni's vision of strong and free trade Fascist unionism inside the Fascist state. The year 1927 saw the promulgation of a Charter of Labor, setting out workers' rights and duties and implementing the labor tribunals. In 1924 a Ministry of Corporations was set up, and through the 1930s the whole of the economy and the professions were progressively organized into twenty-two corporations according to sector, culminating in the transformation of the National Council of Corporations and lower house of the Italian Parliament into a "Chamber of Fasces and Corporations," which represented Italy's economic forces and the Fascist movement rather than constituting the political representation of the population.

Despite the rather elaborate facade, the "corporate state" was largely a sham. The representatives of employees in a given sector were rarely employees themselves, just party nominees; as Tannenbaum has pointed out, "Fascist Italy had complete control over the labor force but very little control of the nation's economic structure" (Tannenbaum 1973, 100). By the time of the war, even some Fascist leaders themselves had become extremely critical of an economic system in which corruption and confusion were rife, and which had signally failed to meet the needs of war. Nevertheless, corporatism had its benefits for Fascism: one of the few safety valves for criticism of the regime was provided by an ongoing debate about the nature of the corporate state led by Ugo Ogetti, a proponent of left-wing corporatism. Mussolini constantly trumpeted the benefits of Italy's "third way" between capitalism in crisis and the horrors of "socialism in one country"—the Soviet Union. At first sight, Fascist corporatism bore a strong resemblance to those visions of corporatism that, in the spirit of the medieval guild organization of masters and workers, bulked large in the Catholic Social Teaching enunciated in the papal encyclicals *Rerum Novarum* of 1891 and, more pertinently, *Quadragesimo Anno* forty years later. In the latter, Pius XI was critical of the Fascist version of corporatism, but that did not prevent authoritarian Catholics in Austria, Portugal, and Spain from seeking to emulate it—at least in some labor and social organizations.

Yet the other major fascist regime, Nazi Germany, never took corporatism seriously. The obvious reason was the absence of a corporatist strand of thought in either National Socialism or its precursors. The only economic institution that the Nazi *Gleichschaltung* created that was corporatist in nature was the Reichsnahrstand (literally, the "Reich Nutrition Estate"), a vertical organization of the agricultural and food-processing industries that owed its existence to the Nazis' concern not to repeat the experience of World War I, when the Allied blockade and resulting food shortages had undermined the German war effort. No other truly corporatist institutions were established by Hitler, who was content with the destruction of free trade unions and the regimentation of the workers in the DAF, the German Labor Front. The creation of the DAF entailed the destruction of one of the most powerful labor movements in Europe and satisfied the employers, who were now bosses in their own workplaces. The Nazi dictatorship's relations with the employers, most especially the industrialists, had its ups and downs, but the Nazis had no difficulty working with them as long as they accepted increasing economic regulation and planning by the state in return for the survival of private capitalism.

Corporatist ideas appeared in the programs of most interwar fascist movements, including Oswald Mosley's British Union of Fascists, but never really survived the collapse of Italian Fascism and the fact that in Mussolini's restored Fascist regime—the Salò Republic—the official program largely abandoned corporatist institutions in favor of an Italian form of "National Socialism" that was a sign of a self-conscious attempt to revert to the policies of early Fascism.

John Pollard

See Also: INTRODUCTION; AUSTRIA; CAPITALISM; CATHOLIC CHURCH, THE; CORRADINI, ENRICO; ECONOMICS; EMPLOYMENT; FASCIST PARTY, THE; FEDERZONI, LUIGI; FRANCOISM; *GLEICHSCHALTUNG;* INDUSTRY; LABOR FRONT, THE; LAW; MOSLEY, SIR OSWALD; MUSSOLINI, BENITO ANDREA; NATIONALIZATION; NAZISM; PERONISM; PIUS XI, POPE; POLITICAL CATHOLICISM; PORTUGAL; ROCCO, ALFREDO; SALÒ REPUBLIC, THE; SOCIALISM; SOVIET UNION, THE; SPAIN; SPANN, OTHMAR; STATE, THE; SYNDICALISM; THIRD WAY, THE; TRADE UNIONS; WORLD WAR I

References
Cannistraro, P. V. 1982. *Historical Dictionary of Fascist Italy.* Westport, CT: Greenwood.
Overy, R. 1994. *War and the Economy in the Third Reich.* Oxford: Oxford University Press.
Pollard, J. F. 1998. *The Fascist Experience in Italy.* London: Routledge.
Tannenbaum, E. 1973. *Fascism in Italy: Society and Culture, 1922–1945.* London: Allen Lane.

CORRADINI, ENRICO
(1865–1931)

Author, journalist, and propagandist for imperialist expansion. With Giuseppe Prezzolini and Giovanni Papini he edited the nationalist periodical *Il Regno* from 1903 until 1906; in 1910 he founded the Italian Nationalist Association. Corradini made two important contributions to Fascist theory. He argued that Italy as a poor proletarian nation had a right to colonial expansion, and that she could not afford to disperse her energies in domestic class struggle. During World War I he again called for the suppression of class struggle and parliamentary wrangling, in favor of the solidarity of productive Italy. Corradini supported the merger of the Italian Nationalist Association with the Fascist Party in 1923 and was appointed to the Italian Senate.

Alex de Grand

See Also: CLASS; COLONIALISM; CORPORATISM; EXPANSIONISM; FASCIST PARTY, THE; IMPERIALISM; ITALY; PARLIAMENTARISM; PRODUCTIVISM

References
De Grand, A. J. 1978. *The Italian Nationalist Association and the Rise of Fascism in Italy.* Lincoln: University of Nebraska Press.

COSMOPOLITANISM

Term of abuse in the vocabulary of fascist ideologues both of German Nazi and Italian Fascist inspiration, for whom it represented the obverse of the hypernationalism to which they were devoted. In their thinking, "cosmopolitanist" creeds were those that stressed international connections and belongingness to a global community transcending national borders; to a nationalist, the "cosmopolitan" could not be trusted because his loyalty was to something wider than his own nation. Similar terms of abuse in the vocabulary of fascist rhetoric were "universalism" or "internationalism." The modern origins of contempt for "cosmopolitanism" can be traced back to the rise of Protestantism at the Reformation, which coincided with the rise of the idea of nationhood. Martin Luther not only pioneered a breakaway from Rome; in so doing he also fostered incipient nationalism, giving a huge impetus to the use of the vernacular German as opposed to the universal Latin of the Catholic Church. The Catholic Church was a supremely "cosmopolitan" body in the sense that it was a global movement that promoted the same creed in all countries while subjecting local churches to an international head, the papacy.

In practice, the term *cosmopolitan* was applied by interwar fascists chiefly to Marxists, Freemasons, and Jews. In Nazi thinking, Marxism and Freemasonry were themselves part of an international Jewish conspiracy, so that "cosmopolitan" often meant "Jewish." For Mussolini and his followers, the Italian Fascist creed did not include the anti-Semitic strain that was so central to Nazism (though it was incorporated late on, partly under pressure from Germany). The term *cosmopolitan* also carried an overtone of decadence in fascist thinking, and it was sometimes allied with the term *metropolitan* as suggesting the seductions of the big cities with their night clubs, American jazz music, and generally looser morals. In Italy deliberate (unsuccessful) attempts were made in the interwar years to discourage migration from rural areas to the cities for this reason.

In postwar fascism in Europe, there has been something of a turn away from hostility to internationalism in revulsion against the excesses of interwar nationalism, and attempts have been made to construct an internationalist fascism that will embody the best of European values; the "enemy" now has become the immigrant, in particular the black or Asiatic member of the community in question. On the other hand, some extreme-right movements in the United States in particular see the hand of conspiracy in international organizations like the United Nations.

Cyprian Blamires

See Also: ABSTRACTION; AMERICANIZATION; "ANTI-" DIMENSION OF FASCISM, THE; ANTI-SEMITISM; CATHOLIC CHURCH, THE; CHRISTIANITY; CONSPIRACY THEORIES; DECADENCE; DREYFUS CASE, THE; DRUMONT, EDOUARD; EGALITARIANISM; EUROPEAN NEW RIGHT, THE; EUROPEANIST FASCISM/RADICAL RIGHT, THE; FASCIST PARTY, THE; FREEMASONRY/FREEMASONS, THE; HITLER, ADOLF; IMMIGRATION; JESUITS, THE; LUTHER, MARTIN; NATIONALISM; MARXISM; MUSSOLINI, BENITO ANDREA; POSTWAR FASCISM; RATIONALISM; ROOTLESSNESS; RURALISM; SOCIALISM; TRADITIONALISM

References
Griffin, R. 1991. *The Nature of Fascism.* London: Routledge
Mussolini, Benito. 2006. *My Autobiography: With "The Political and Social Doctrine of Fascism."* Mineola, NY: Dover.
Payne, S. 1995. *A History of Fascism 1914–1945.* London: University College London Press.

COSTAMAGNA, CARLO
(1881–1965)

Italian Fascist ideologue and anti-Semite who retained a commitment to Roman Catholicism. Born near Savona, Costamagna became a judge, and, after the March on Rome, he was asked by Mussolini to work on a Fascist remodeling of the Italian constitution. Later he was involved in the drafting of corporatist legislation and became professor of corporative law at the University of Ferrara, as well as editor of *Lo Stato* (*The State*). His view of the Fascist trade unions and corporations was quite narrowly defined, arguing that they were chiefly to be regarded as instruments of state control, opposing the claim of other Fascist ideologues that the unions should have a crucial role in the reorganization of society. He rejected the actualism promoted by Gentile and argued that Italian Fascism was indebted to the traditions of Italian civilization and also to Roman Catholicism. He attacked the Jews as a threat to the "spiritual integrity" of Europe.

Cyprian Blamires

See Also: ACTUALISM; ANTI-SEMITISM; CATHOLIC CHURCH, THE; CHRISTIANITY; CORPORATISM; FASCIST PARTY, THE; GENTILE, GIOVANNI; LAW; MARCH ON ROME, THE; ROME; STATE, THE; TRADES UNIONS; TRADITIONALISM

Reference
Gregor, A. J. 2005. *Mussolini's Intellectuals: Fascist Social and Political Thought.* Oxford: Oxford University Press.

COUGHLIN, Fr. CHARLES EDWARD (1891–1979)

Canadian Catholic priest and radio broadcaster favorable to the Nazis and from the late 1930s overtly anti-Semitic. Born and educated in Ontario, Father Coughlin first became famous because of his radio broadcasts from his parish in Royal Oak, Michigan, a suburb of Detroit. Although he initially endorsed the New Deal, by mid-1935 he had split with Franklin Roosevelt. His National Union for Social Justice, founded the previous year, combined such concrete proposals as the abolition of a Federal Reserve Board with such vague ones as "a

just, living, annual wage" for all citizens. In 1936 he was the mainstay behind the abortive Union Party, whose program stressed inflation, generous old-age pensions, and income redistribution. By 1938 he exhibited an overt anti-Semitism, which first appeared in his weekly *Social Justice* and gradually in his radio sermons as well. That year he published an edition of *The Protocols of the Elders of Zion,* defended various Nazi actions, and accused the Jews of financing the Bolshevik Revolution. In 1939 he fostered a small paramilitary organization, the Christian Front, which engaged in violent acts against Jews. Once World War II broke out, Coughlin blamed the conflict on "Jewish International bankers," who "own or control the world." In 1942, on the orders of his ecclesiastical superiors, he ended all political activity, restricting himself thenceforth strictly to parish work.

Justus Doenecke

See Also: ANTI-SEMITISM; CATHOLIC CHURCH, THE; CONSPIRACY THEORIES; PARAMILITARISM; *PROTOCOLS OF THE ELDERS OF ZION, THE*; RADIO; ROOSEVELT, FRANKLIN DELANO; UNITED STATES, THE (PRE-1945)

References
Brinkley, Alan. 1982. *Voices of Protest: Huey Long, Father Coughlin, and the Great Depression.* New York: Knopf.
Marcus, Sheldon. 1973. *Father Coughlin: The Tumultuous Life of the Priest of the Little Flower.* Boston: Little, Brown.
Warren, Donald. *Radio Priest: Charles Coughlin, The Father of Hate Radio.* New York: Free Press.

COUNTER-REVOLUTION

One of the most characteristic claims of the fascist tradition has been that theirs is an authentically revolutionary movement. Once in power, fascism would transcend the miseries of day-to-day life. Poverty and alienation are blamed on "the old parties." Where it took control of the state, fascism claimed to have liberated the nation. Mussolini's March on Rome and the violent scenes witnessed in Germany in the spring of 1933 were accorded the status of "national revolutions." Mussolini spoke of "the profound transformation which Fascism has brought about, not only in the material lives of the Italian people, but in their spirit." Fascism had achieved "the transition from one type of civilization to another" (Griffin 1995, 72–73). According to Goebbels, "[T]he revolution we have carried out is a total one. It has embraced all areas of public life and transformed them from below. It has completely changed and recast the relationship of people to each other, to the State, and to life itself." Its main victory, he went on to argue, had been to rescue the threatened German people (ibid., 134).

Yet while fascism often adverted to its revolutionary heritage, a number of fascist spokesmen also made the claim that fascism was a form of counter-revolution. That idea took two forms. In its "soft" variety, fascists argued only that theirs was the true revolution, while the rival movements of the Left only played games. One smear that Hitler employed to denigrate the communists of post–World War I Germany was that, faced with the opportunity to seize power in 1918–1919, they had not dared to confront the state. On the big demonstrations, the revolutionaries would not even walk on the grass. A second, "harder" argument was that fascism was opposed not merely to the self-deceived revolutionists of 1918 but also to the very process of revolution itself, going back to France in 1789. Asvero Gravelli of the Italian Fascist journal *Antieuropa* maintained that, whereas the French Revolution had stood for liberalism and democracy, fascism stood for "the concept of hierarchy, the participation of the whole people in the life of the State, social justice through the equitable distribution of rights and duties, the injection of morality into public life, the prestige of the family, the moral interpretation of the ideas of order, authority and freedom" (ibid., 67). Similar ideas were taken up in France by the royalist supporters of Charles Maurras and Action Française, and even by self-declared republicans, including François de la Rocque of the Croix de Feu. For both Maurras and La Rocque, the French Revolution was synonymous with democracy and "decadence." La Rocque argued that the crowd, abandoned to itself, became an uncontrollable and chaotic force. What was needed was government by an enlightened aristocracy.

Would it be more accurate to lay the stress on the revolutionary or on the counter-revolutionary aspects of fascism? Various historians have taken their lead from different aspects of the fascist self-image. David Schoenbaum argues that German fascism did result in a transformation of status structures. The fascist state was aware of its own unwillingness to deliver profound economic or social change. It responded to this gap by attempting a revolution in expectation. Fascist art exalted muscular workers. At least in aesthetic terms, such subaltern groups could feel that "their" culture had captured the state. Yet Schoenbaum's ideas have proved controversial. As Donny Gluckstein has argued, fascism was experienced in terms of increased hours and inten-

sity of work, static pay, and food shortages. The mundane reality of most people's lives remained similar to what it had been before, or even worse: social inequalities remained entrenched, and the exploitation of the poor continued. In this bleak context, it seems strange to speak of a fascist "social revolution." Fascism may have projected some alternative future, but that was never conceived of as a more generous society. Far from being a utopia, it was in fact a more hierarchical society than before. The fascists defended their ideal among themselves with the boast that at least their enemies would suffer.

Fascism was certainly "counter-revolutionary" in the limited sense that fascist parties emerged in response to a period of mass protest when communist revolution seemed possible. In Italy, many of the gangs that joined Mussolini's Fascio had begun as strike-breakers. In Germany, the cadres of fascism were recruited from the Freikorps, a milieu of officers and middle-class youth mobilized by the state to prevent insurrection.

David Renton

See Also: INTRODUCTION; ACTION FRANÇAISE; COMMUNISM; CONSERVATISM; COSMOPOLITANISM; DECADENCE; DEMOCRACY; FAMILY, THE; FREIKORPS, THE; FRENCH REVOLUTION, THE; GOEBBELS, (PAUL) JOSEPH; LA ROCQUE DE SEVERAC, FRANÇOIS COMTE DE; LIBERALISM; MARCH ON ROME, THE; MARXIST THEORIES OF FASCISM; MASSES, THE ROLE OF THE; MAURRAS, CHARLES; MUSSOLINI, BENITO ANDREA; REVOLUTION; SOCIALISM; TRADITIONALISM

References

Davies, Peter. 2002. *The Extreme Right in France, 1789 to the Present.* London: Routledge.
Gluckstein, D. 1999. *The Nazis, Capitalism and the Working Class.* London: Bookmarks.
Griffin, R. 1995. *Fascism.* Oxford: Oxford University Press.
Kershaw, I. 1985. *The Nazi Dictatorship.* London: Edward Arnold.
Schoenbaum, D. 1998. *Hitler's Social Revolution: Class and Status in Nazi Germany 1933–1939.* London: Norton.
Soucy, R. 1995. *French Fascism: The Second Wave 1933–1939.* New Haven: Yale University Press.

COVENTRY

English Midlands city that was subjected to a devastating air-raid by the Luftwaffe involving nearly 450 bombers on 15 November 1940. At the heart of this great manufacturing center was a celebrated medieval cathedral which was destroyed (along with about 70,000 homes) in the raid. German propaganda afterward threatened that the Luftwaffe would *coventrieren* ("treat the same as Coventry") other British cities. The massively destructive Allied bombing raid on the beautiful and historic German city of Dresden in February 1945, leading to a firestorm and huge loss of civilian lives, has been regarded by some as motivated at least in part by a desire for revenge. Dresden was undefended and was full of refugees at that point in the war. After the war Coventry Cathedral was rebuilt and made the focus of reconciliation, initially between Britain and Germany, later in relation to international conflicts in general. In 2005 the dedication of the rebuilt Frauenkirche in Dresden set the seal on the postwar strategy of reconciliation.

Cyprian Blamires

See Also: LUFTWAFFE, THE; WORLD WAR II

References
Hodgkinson, George. 1981. *Coventry and the Movement for World Peace. Writings and speeches 1971–1975.* Coventry: Chapelfields.
Longmate, N. 1976. *Air Raid: Bombing of Coventry 1940.* London: Hutchinson.

CROATIA

Croatian nationalist extremism is personified in the aspiration for a Greater Croatian state, the idealization of peasant and patriarchal values, a rejection of so-called Easternness, and a hatred of Serbs. Croatian right-wing extremism has evolved through three historical phases: extreme Croatian nationalism as espoused by the nineteenth-century politician Josip Frank; the fascism of the Ustasha movement, and the contemporary right-wing extremism of the Tudjman regime. Modern Croatian nationalism started with Ante Starcevic, founder of the Croatian Party of Rights (HSP), who is often called the father of Croatian nationalism. Originally a believer in South Slav unity, he became disillusioned with that idea and embraced nationalist ideals. Starcevic believed in an independent Greater Croatian state that would include Bosnia-Hercegovina; he declared Muslims to be the purest of Croats. By contrast, he denied the existence of Serbs in Bosnia and Croatia completely, declaring that many "Serbian" historical figures had, in fact, been Croatian. He refused to accept the

term "Serb" or any expressions of "Serbianness"—for example, the Cyrillic alphabet—in Croatia. He believed that the Serbs of Croatia and Bosnia were Orthodox Croats, and his political ally Eugen Kvaternik proposed the creation of a Croatian Orthodox Church to separate Serbs from their "false" identity. When Serbs insisted on a separate identity, Starcevic labeled them "Slavoserbs," a term that implied they were people of a slave origin and "impure" blood. In 1895 a more radical rival to the HSP, the Pure Party of Rights, was established by Josip Frank. Although it was loyal to the Habsburg Empire and did not agitate for independence, its hatred of Serbs was far more extreme and its newspapers called openly for their destruction. Its supporters (called Frankists) regularly participated in violent anti-Serb activities, instigating anti-Serb pogroms in 1902 and in 1908 raising a legionary force to persecute rebellious Bosnian Serbs. Its members also committed atrocities against Bosnian Serbs as part of Austrian military units during World War I. Five days after the declaration of the Yugoslav state in 1918, Frankist army officers launched a counter-revolution in Zagreb. After its defeat, many Frankists moved abroad, and a unit of "Croatian legionaries" was formed.

In interwar Croatia, Frankist influence was strongest at Zagreb University and middle-class areas of Zagreb, but otherwise the new party representing the Frankists, the Croatian Party of Rights, did not have much support. After the assassination of Croatian peasant leader Stjepan Radic in 1929, the Frankists turned to terrorism with the creation of the Ustasha movement. During the 1930s, as the political situation in Yugoslavia worsened, the ideology of extreme nationalism became more attractive to ordinary Croatians; in addition to having activists abroad, the Ustasha movement also had the support of some of the Croatian population. During the 1930s, many Croatian educational and cultural institutions were infiltrated and taken over by Frankists. Parts of the Catholic Church and the Croatian Peasant party also became strongly nationalistic. The creation of a semi-independent Croatian state in 1939 did little to alter nationalist feeling, and many Croatians welcomed with jubilation the creation of an independent Croatia.

With the collapse of the Yugoslav state in 1991, Croatia became an independent state again. However, with independence came right-wing extremism. The new president of Croatia, Franjo Tudjman, advocated ultra-nationalist policies. He proposed that veteran Ustasha officials in exile abroad be given government positions and that squares in Zagreb and other cities be renamed after pro-Ustasha writers. At his instigation, new nationalist histories sought to downplay the Ustasha genocide; simultaneously, a demonization campaign was begun against native Serbs, who were portrayed as a separatist menace and a Trojan horse for a Greater Serbia. The Croatian authorities also made ominous noises about the "over-representation" of Serbs in public life. After the outbreak of hostilities between the Serb-dominated Yugoslav army and the Croatian government, intercommunal violence erupted. However, some political leaders waiting in the wings were even more extreme than Tudjman and his Croatian Democratic Union. Dobroslav Paraga's Croatian Party of Rights (HSP) was the largest of a number of ultra-nationalist parties that emerged in the 1990s. It articulated the view that Serbs in Croatia did not exist, that Bosnia was a part of Croatia, and that Muslims were ethnically Croats; it proposed the establishment of a Croatian Orthodox Church. It also created its own paramilitary wing, the Croatian Defence Force, which was implicated in the ethnic cleansing and persecution of Croatian Serbs. The rising popularity of Paraga and his party led to his arrest and eventual replacement as head of his party. Paraga ultimately reconsidered his ultra-nationalist views, and his new party, HSP—1861, articulated a moderate form of Croatian nationalism that opposed the persecution of Serbs and other non-Croatians in Croatia and even sought an alliance with the main Serb political party. However, the extremism of the ruling party did not moderate, and in 1994–1995 hundreds of thousands of Serbs were murdered or expelled from Croatia.

Following the death of Tudjman in 2000, his HDZ was defeated and replaced by a reformist coalition. Despite coming to power vowing to move Croatia away from its nationalist past, it disappointed many Croatians. Its cooperation with the War Crimes Tribunal was deeply unpopular and, in any case, piecemeal. Moreover, little progress was made toward the return of Serb refugees. Faced with a deteriorating economy and continuing problems with the War Crimes Tribunal in The Hague, in 2003 the electorate returned the HDZ to power in coalition with a party that had made its electoral breakthrough in those elections: the nationalist Croatian Party of Rights.

Rory Yeomans

See Also: AUSTRO-HUNGARIAN EMPIRE/HABSBURG EMPIRE, THE; CATHOLIC CHURCH, THE; NATIONALISM; ORTHODOX CHURCHES, THE; PARAMILITARISM; POLITICAL CATHOLICISM; RACIAL DOCTRINE; SERBS, THE; SLAVS, THE (AND ITALY); USTASHA, WORLD WAR II; YUGOSLAVIA

References

Gross, Mirjana. 1979–1980. "Croatian National Integrational Ideologies from the End of Illyrianism to the Creation of Yugoslavia." *Austrian History Yearbook* 15–16: 3–33.

Irvine, Jill A. 1995. "Nationalism and the Extreme Right in the Former Yugoslavia." Pp. 145–173 in *The Far-Right in Western and Eastern Europe,* edited by Luciano Cheles, Ronnie Ferguson, and Michalina Vaughan. London: Longman.

———. 1997. "Ultranationalist Ideology and State-Building in Croatia, 1990–1996." *Problems of Post-Communism* 44, no. 4 (July–August): 30–43.

CROCE, BENEDETTO (1866–1952)

Italian philosopher, historian, literary critic, and senator, Croce came to symbolize a liberal and cultural antifascism that won him many admirers. He consistently offered moral and financial support to other antifascists, actions that were closely and continuously scrutinized by the authorities who, nevertheless, tolerated his presence.

Croce emerged as a major public figure in Italy in the early twentieth century with a humanist philosophy excoriating the transcendental categories of religion and positivist science. His widely influential philosophy of "immanence" highlighted the freely creative role of individuals in history. With this broadly liberal-inspired outlook he aimed to reconcile humanity's "spiritual" need for meaning and purpose—or "faith"—with the practical contingencies of everyday life. In addition to the volumes of his *Filosofia dello spirito,* he publicized his ideas in his review *La Critica,* coedited with Giovanni Gentile.

Croce's philosophy originally separated politics from ethics, largely accepting the instrumental character of political life, from which he tended to remain aloof. He was deeply skeptical of democratic politics and suspicious of political movements that attributed an ethical role for the state. He remained neutral regarding Italy's role in World War I but was briefly education minister in its aftermath. Like other moderately conservative liberals, Croce initially welcomed Fascism as a return to order. Although he disliked its aggressive style, rather naively he saw it as having value in restoring the authority of liberal institutions. Following Matteotti's murder in 1924, however, he

Benedetto Croce was Italy's most celebrated intellectual of the interwar era; his public opposition to the Fascist regime, (for example in his "Manifesto of Anti-Fascist Intellectuals") was tolerated by Mussolini. (Library of Congress)

became a persistent critic of the regime and permanently broke off his friendship with Gentile (by then a member of the Fascist Party). He responded to Gentile's "Manifesto of Fascist Intellectuals" by writing the "Manifesto of Anti-Fascist Intellectuals." He also altered his philosophy to highlight his support for the liberal ideals of the Risorgimento and their benign effect on political life, implying a closer relation between politics and ethics than suggested earlier; before all party opposition was banned, he formally joined the Liberal Party. Never an active member of the resistance or proponent of physical violence against the regime—being elderly and, in any case, believing such activities unlikely to be successful—Croce resided in Italy throughout the Fascist period and continued to write, speak, edit *La Critica,* and defend the idea of liberalism as a kind of religion.

Croce understood Fascism to be a moral illness, a temporary retreat from Europe's liberal heritage into irrationalism. Unlike many of those active in the resistance, he did not conceive of it as a consequence of deeper structural problems in the Italian state. After the regime's collapse, he argued that Fascism had constituted merely a "parenthesis" in Italian history and advised, unsuccessfully as it turned out, a return to pre-Fascist liberal institutions.

James Martin

See Also: ANTIFASCISM; FASCIST PARTY, THE; GENTILE, GIOVANNI; ITALY; LIBERALISM; MANIFESTO OF FASCIST INTELLECTUALS, THE; MATTEOTTI, GIACOMO; *RISORGIMENTO,* THE

References
Rizzi, Fabio Fernando. 2003. *Benedetto Croce and Italian Fascism.* Toronto: University of Toronto Press.
Roberts, David D. 1987. *Benedetto Croce and the Uses of Historicism.* Berkeley: University of California Press.

CULTS OF DEATH

At the Wewelsburg Castle headquarters of the SS, Himmler developed a complex set of rituals around the idea of reconnecting with German ancestors who would then become the vanguard in the nation's rebirth; the elite's distinctive death's head insignia, symbolizing both the desire to kill and a willingness to be killed, played with a deeper semiotic of death than mainstream Nazi propaganda. Further, the initiation rituals for the SS elites, such as having to dig a hole in the ground in eighty seconds to avoid being crushed by an oncoming tank, went beyond normal army training and were pursued to inculcate a heightened awareness of their own death in the recruits, in order to strengthen their fighting abilities by forcing them to accept the potential of their demise for the "higher" cause.

Among the interwar fascisms, it was, however, the Romanian Iron Guard that generated the most developed cult of death, with its notorious death squads. Central to its ideology were legionary songs, with lines that celebrated death and ran thus: "Death, only legionary death/Is a gladsome wedding for us/The legionary dies singing/The legionary sings dying," and "Legionaries do not fear/That you will die too young/For to die is to be reborn/And are born to die."

The scene on the USS Bunker Hill *shortly after it was hit by two Japanese kamikaze (suicide bombers) attacks in May 1945. Although kamikaze was a native and not a European tradition, it had definite similarities to the interwar fascist cults of death. (National Archives)*

Further, like Himmler's ideology, which incorporated aspects of Germanic religion to infuse the SS with a metaphysical dynamic, Codreanu did likewise by drawing on Romanian Orthodox Christianity to develop a language in which, to his radicalized audience, he convincingly argued that national rebirth could result from individual death. Significantly, followers of the Iron Guard took up these fantasies—such as Ion Moța, who fought in Spain with the intention of being killed to become a martyr to the cause, or the Guardists who descended upon Bucharest when the movement was suppressed by Antonescu in January 1941 and who, while carrying out a vicious pogrom in the Jewish quarter, walked into hails of bullets singing Orthodox hymns with bells ringing whenever one of their number fell— thereby crossing the line between a rhetorical use of the

language of self-sacrifice and entering into a genuine cult of death.

Spanish military figures such as General Milan Astray also developed military cults of death during the Spanish Civil War, and the grave of José Antonio Primo de Rivera became an object of cultist fascination among many Spanish fascists. Japan likewise developed a cult of death in the form of its famous Kamikaze pilots. The emperor cult of wartime Japan was clearly powerful enough to activate a genuine sense of "higher" purpose that allowed individuals to rationalize their own deaths as part of a wider process of becoming of the Japanese Empire on the world stage. One pilot recorded in a letter that his sacrifice was in order to "let this beautiful Japan keep growing." Another letter, written by a pilot called Isao, recorded: "We are sixteen warriors manning the bombers. May our death be as sudden and clean as the shattering of crystal: Isao soaring into the sky of the southern seas. It is our glorious mission to die as the shields of His Majesty. Cherry blossoms glisten as they open and fall" (Griffin 2003).

Paul Jackson

See Also: INTRODUCTION; ANTONESCU, GENERAL ION; CODREANU, CORNELIU ZELEA; GERMANIC RELIGION; HIMMLER, HEINRICH; JAPAN; LEGION OF THE ARCHANGEL MICHAEL, THE; MOŢA, ION I.; ORTHODOX CHURCHES, THE; PALINGENETIC MYTH; PRIMO DE RIVERA, JOSÉ ANTONIO; SECULARIZATION; SPANISH CIVIL WAR, THE; SS, THE

References

Campbell, Joseph. 1993. *The Hero with a Thousand Faces.* London: Fontana.

Griffin, Roger. 2003. "Shattering Crystals": The Role of "Dream Time" in Extreme Right-wing Political Violence," *Terrorism and Political Violence* 15, no. 1 (spring): 57–96.

Inoguchi, Rikihei, Tadashi Nakajima, and Roger Pineau. 1985. *The Divine Wind: Japan's Kamikaze Force in World War II.* New York: Bantam.

Nagy-Talavera, N. 1970. *The Greenshirts and Others.* Princeton: Princeton University Press.

CULTURE (Germany)

A key term in the vocabulary of interwar fascist propagandists. Particularly from the late nineteenth century, the substance of the German concept of culture developed frequently in conflict with the concept of "civilization." In general linguistic usage, "civilization" was often associated with the material: it was considered to be superficial, soulless, utilitarian, and leveling. In contrast to this, the emotional and moral was adjudged to the consistently positively connoted *Kultur* of the intellectual-artistic element in society. In the transition from the nineteenth to the twentieth century in Germany, the culture-civilization antithesis was taken up first and foremost by conservatives. In an indirect reference to Nietzsche, Leopold Ziegler proposed a view of *Kultur* that made it highly elitist and opposed to any type of equality and democracy. Ziegler diagnosed his epoch as having a maximum of "civilization" but a minimum of "culture."

German philosophy had a formative impact on the deepening of the culture-civilization antithesis. Almost thirty years before Spengler, Ferdinand Tönnies described civilization as the depraved successor to a culture destroyed by the class struggle, in *Gesellschaft und Gemeinschaft (Community and Society)* in 1887. For Friedrich Nietzsche it was in the nature of culture to be both more full of life and decidedly apolitical. His definition of *Kultur* strongly inspired German literature (Thomas Mann) and philosophy (Oswald Spengler) and made a lasting impression across borders reaching as far as Russian symbolism. Houston Stewart Chamberlain claimed, in *Die Grundlagen des neunzehnten Jahrhunderts* (1899), that only certain races are capable of culture—that is, of art, religion, and ethics. Chamberlain's *national* interpretation of culture and his devaluation of civilization as mere convenience were to be portentous for the decades to come.

At the beginning of the twentieth century, *Kultur* was increasingly instrumentalized for national purposes. At the founding convention of the German Association of German Scholars in 1912, Johann G. Sprengel argued that a "higher" culture was constituted solely through "blood." With the outbreak of World War I the writer Thomas Mann, the political economist Werner Sombart, and philosophers such as Ernst Troeltsch and Paul Natorp were protagonists of the campaign against "Western" *Zivilisation* in the name of *Kultur*. Mann hypostatized the antithesis of civilization and culture as the contrast between intellect and nature, politics and morality; for him the Germans were per se an apolitical, unrevolutionary race, whose culture had an inherent dislike of democracy and parliamentarism. Sombart's perception of German culture was closely related to his anticapitalist, fundamentally anti-Semitic instincts, which found an outlet in his 1915 anti-English war propaganda *Händler und Helden*. Sombart's psychology of peoples denounced the English as acquisitive materialists, whose colonial spirit served only to disguise their intellectual poverty. German *Kultur,* on the other hand, Sombart associated with "heroism" and antiutilitarian selflessness. In *Der Geist der deutschen Kultur* (1915), Troeltsch associates German *Kultur* with the tradition of romantic irrationalism, which is deeply contradictory to the assumed rationalist character of French civilization.

Deeply impressed by Nietzsche's vitalism, Oswald Spengler understood *Kultur* in *Der Untergang des Abendlandes* (1918/1922) as an organism that passes through an inventive phase of childhood and youth, before the creative powers slowly ebb in manhood. While he regarded this creative, vital phase as *Kultur,* Spengler refers to the aging, death-marked stage of decay as *Zivilisation,* the irrevocable destiny of every culture in his eyes. Spengler was clearly strongly influenced by the ethnologist Leo Frobenius's organicist culture theory: Frobenius held the view two decades before Spengler that the cultural process is not subject to the human will.

Kultur was interpreted as *national* in the prescribed National Socialist terminology—as opposed to internationalistic, metropolitan *Zivilisation.* Adolf Hitler always preferred *Kultur* to *Zivilisation* in the various editions of *Mein Kampf.* The prerequisite for all real culture was for Hitler the attitude that set common interest before personal interest. The Jews, in contrast, had only a pseudo-culture, made up of commodities originally belonging to other races that had already corrupted in their hands. But Hitler used the terms *culture* and *civilization* synonymously from the 1930s.

Susanne Pocai

See Also: ANTI-SEMITISM; ARYANISM; BLOOD; CAPITALISM; CHAMBERLAIN, HOUSTON STEWART; CIVILIZATION; COSMOPOLITANISM; DEMOCRACY; ELITISM; HERO, THE CULT OF THE; HITLER, ADOLF; MATERIALISM; *MEIN KAMPF;* NATIONALISM; NAZISM; NIETZSCHE, FRIEDRICH; NIHILISM; ORGANICISM; PARLIAMENTARISM; RACIAL DOCTRINE; RATIONALISM; ROOTLESSNESS; ROSENBERG, ALFRED; SOUL; SPENGLER, OSWALD; UTILITARIANISM; VITALISM

References

Bénéton, Philippe. 1975. *Histoire de mots: Culture et civilisation.* Paris: Presses de la Fondation nationale des sciences politiques.
Fisch, Jörg. 1992. "Zivilisation, Kultur." Pp. 679–774 in *Geschichtliche Grundbegriffe: Historisches Lexikon zur politisch-sozialen Sprache in Deutschland,* edited by Otto Brunner, Werner Conze, and Reinhart Koselleck. Vol. 7. Stuttgart: Klett-Cotta.
Kroeber, Alfred Louis, and Clyde Kluckhohn. 1952. *Culture: A Critical Review of Concepts and Definitions.* Cambridge, MA: Peabody Museum.
Sprachwissenschaftliches Colloquium (Bonn), ed. 1967. *Europäische Schlüsselwörter. Wortvergleichende und wortgeschichtliche Studien.* Vol. 3: *Kultur und Zivilisation.* München: Max Hueber.
Williams, Raymond. 1961. *Culture and Society: 1780–1950.* Harmondsworth, Middlesex: Penguin.

CULTURE (Italy)

Fascism aimed to remake Italy and used culture—in the form of ritual, symbols, and spectacle (an "aestheticized politics")—in the service of this project of regeneration. On the one hand, intellectuals like Giovanni Gentile sought to renew elite or "high" culture by fusing Italy's artistic and cultural patrimony with the principles of Fascist ideology. On the other, the regime tried to reform or change "low" culture—that is, popular culture—through means such as the Fascist Institutes of Culture, created in 1924. Working through the *dopolavoro,* or Fascist after-work leisure organizations, the Fascist Institutes of Culture and the National Committee for Popular Traditions tended to identify popular culture with folk customs. These groups organized and sometimes revived popular celebrations, such as local patron saints' days and agricultural work festivals. The regime thus paradoxically encouraged forms of local or regional cultural identification (the so-called *piccole patrie*) in the service of a larger national identity. In the 1930s, Fascist Party Secretary Achille Starace promoted rural customs and traditions, locating the national character of *il popolo* ("the people") in the countryside. Starace's 1938 "reform of custom" sought to eliminate decadent bourgeois culture. Proponents of the rural or *Strapaese* movement in literature favorably contrasted the countryside to the city, now seen as the site of sterility, degeneration, and decay. This privileging of the countryside went against a long-standing valorization in the Italian peninsula of the *urbs* as the site of *civiltà* (civilization and civility).

During the Fascist period, the idea of Italian civilization—which in its medieval origins had denoted a broad, inclusive understanding of Italianate culture—became wed to an ideology of nationalism and imperial expansion. Folklorists and ethnographers thus served the regime by searching in territories like Dalmatia and Libya for "survivals" of Roman/Latin culture, whose existence then justified the "return" of those areas to Italy.

Pamela Balling

See Also: INTRODUCTION; ART; CIVILIZATION; DECADENCE; DEGENERACY; ELITISM; GENTILE, GIOVANNI; LEISURE; NATIONALISM; PALINGENETIC MYTH; ROME; RURALISM/RURALIZATION (ITALY); STARACE, ACHILLE

References

De Grazia, Victoria. 1992. *How Fascism Ruled Women: Italy, 1922–1945.* Berkeley: University of California Press.
———. 2002. *The Culture of Consent: Mass Organization of Leisure in Fascist Italy.* Cambridge: Cambridge University Press.
Gabaccia, Donna. 2000. *Italy's Many Diasporas.* Seattle: University of Washington Press.
Horn, David. 1994. *Social Bodies: Science, Reproduction, and Italian Modernity.* Princeton: Princeton University Press.
Simeone, William E. 1978. "Fascists and Folklorists in Italy." *Journal of American Folklore,* 91, no. 359: 543–557.

CYBERFASCISM

The Internet offers a wealth of opportunities for the far Right. Thousands of extremist websites now proliferate because of the affordability of web authoring packages. These have enabled even the most isolated and impoverished extremist to jettison samizdat publishing and limited distribution networks, replacing them with professional, multimedia technology that can globally project a sophisticated and "respectable" image, crucial for those seeking electoral success. Such a medium also offers the advantage of easy manipulation according to the target audience, particularly the youthful and disaffected, though paradoxically the evidence suggests that this is the socioeconomic group least likely to have access to the Internet. Extremists use the Internet as a means of disseminating ideological tracts and virulently racist material, downloadable flyers, Internet radio programs, details of demonstrations, publications, contact addresses, e-group discussion forums, mailing lists (often with tens of thousands of adherents), and even Aryan dating pages as a means of both recruiting and fostering communal cohesion among often disparate activists.

The potential for on-line recruitment (and commercial gain) is considerably enhanced by groups like Resistance Records, owned by the National Alliance, which offers free downloadable sound files and MP3s of merchandise unlikely to be found in mainstream shops, particularly the "white noise" music CDs. Thus virtual immersion in the "white noise" scene serves as a prelude to actual immersion and thereafter membership in fascist parties themselves. However, the growing availability of music-sharing technology could render this previously lucrative venture increasingly redundant. The Internet is also utilized to incite violence. Websites such as Red Watch list the names, addresses, and photographs of political opponents, setting them up for intimidation and worse by "lone wolf" activists who, like the London nail bomber, can easily download bomb-making instructions from elsewhere on the web. This virtual activism compensates for the numerical weakness of the far Right by fostering among geographically isolated activists an inflated sense of belonging to a global and vigorous "cyber-community," a virtual cocoon shielded from antifascist opposition in the "real world," though this also has the potential disadvantage of removing activism into the ethereal realm and thereby neutering its actual effect. However, one particularly distinct advantage of the Internet, especially for activists in Germany, where Holocaust denial is illegal, is its ability to bypass national laws by simply hosting websites on Internet service providers (ISP) outside their national borders, where similarly strict laws do not apply. E-mail technology also provides an effective, and—with the aid of encryption technology—relatively secure means of communication that protects activists from surveillance and prosecution.

Graham Macklin

See Also: ARYANISM; COMMUNITY; HOLOCAUST DENIAL; LONDON NAIL BOMBINGS, THE; NEO-NAZISM; POSTWAR FASCISM; RACISM; WHITE NOISE

References

Copsey, Nigel. 2003. "Extremism on the Net: The Extreme Right and the Value of the Internet." Pp. 218–233 in *Political Parties and the Internet,* edited by R. Gibson, P. Nixon, and S. Ward. London: Routledge.

Eatwell, Roger. 1996. "Surfing the Great White Wave: The Internet, Extremism and the Problem of Control." *Patterns of Prejudice,* 30, no. 1: 61–71.

CZECHOSLOVAKIA

Czechoslovakia was created out of historically Czech lands (Bohemia, Moravia, part of Silesia), Slovakia, and Carpatho-Ukraine in 1918, after the fall of the Austro-Hungarian monarchy. Up to 1938, Czechoslovakia was a multinational political democracy. Parts of major non-Czech minorities (especially German) rejected the existence of Czechoslovakia as a nation-state. Their nationalism led to the foundation of ethnic movements with authoritarian, fascist, and Nazi orientations. However, there were also right-wing tendencies within existing Czech parties. Some of the Czech right-wing democratic parties had small factions that tended toward fascism. This was typical of the National Democratic Party, Agrarian Party, and Czechoslovak People's Party. There were also smaller rightist authoritarian parties (sometimes with associated paramilitary organizations). Some of them established (together with the National Democrats) the National Unification Party in the mid-1930s. In elections in 1935, they won 5.6 percent of the votes.

Czech fascist movements had emerged at the beginning of the 1920s, inspired by Italian Fascism. Their program and ideology included anticommunism, anti-

Semitism, anti-pangermanism, panslavism, and corporatism. Part of the movement was also Catholic-oriented. Some fascist groups in Moravia supported Moravian regionalism. In 1926 the National Community of Fascists (NOF) was created from these groups under the leadership of General Radola Gajda. An attempted coup in 1933 (the capture of barracks in Brno-Židenice) was a failure. The paramilitary organizations of the NOF were called Junák and Obrana. Electoral results for Czech fascists were not significant.

Sudeten German irredentism constituted a more dangerous security threat for Czechoslovak democracy (the Sudetenland was an area in the west of the country with a largely German-speaking population). Inside the Sudeten German movement there were streams loyal to Czechoslovakia, but as early as 1930 some Sudeten Germans demanded the unification of Sudetenland with neighboring Germany. The political representative of those demands was the Sudeten German Party (with 15.2 percent of the votes in 1935 elections) under the leadership of Konrad Henlein, massively supported by Nazi Germany. This party also had a paramilitary organization, Freiwilliger Schutzdienst. Almost all the members of this organization revolted against Czechoslovakia in September 1938, but Czech troops restored order, and many of the FS members emigrated. In Germany they set up the Sudetendeutsches Freikorps. There were also problems with fascism inside other nationalist movements in interwar Czechoslovakia. Many Slovaks rejected the idea of a unified Czechoslovak nation and wanted an autonomous Slovakia. The political representative of that attitude was Hlinka's Slovak People's Party, inspired by Mussolini's Fascism (for example, the paramilitary organization Rodobrana). Fascist and right-authoritarian orientation also became significant for the Hungarian irredentist movement in Slovakia, Polish irredentists in Silesia, and Carpatho-Ukrainian nationalists. In Czechoslovakia there were also fascist organizations of Russian and Ukrainian immigrants.

German pressure on Czechoslovakia to permit the secession of Sudetenland to Germany culminated in 1938, when, as a result of the Munich Agreement, Czechoslovakia was forced to cede this part of its territory to Germany. The Sudeten German Party ended its activity, and its members mostly joined the NSDAP. Slovakia and Carpatho-Ukraine became autonomous, while parts of Czechoslovakia were occupied by Hungary and Poland. Slovakia began building an authoritarian regime, and militant Slovak nationalists founded a paramilitary organization called the Hlinka Guard. In the Czech lands a right-wing authoritarian system was established with two parties—the governmental Party of National Unity and the opposition National Party of Labor. Rudolf Beran became prime minister. Paradoxically, there was fascist opposition to this regime, an organization known as Vlajka (Flag), which among other things carried out terrorist attacks against Jews.

Slovakia declared its independence on 14 March 1939. German troops occupied the rest of the Czech lands on 14 and 15 March 1939. Carpatho-Ukraine was occupied by Hungary, and Hitler's Germany established the Protectorate of Bohemia and Moravia. An attempt by some Moravian nationalists to annex the south of Moravia to Slovakia in March 1939, or to establish an Independent Moravia as part of the Reich, was not successful. The Protectorate of Bohemia and Moravia was formally autonomous and had its state organs (president, government, a small governmental army), but real power was in the hands of the *Reichsprotektor,* and from 1943 of the German state minister of Bohemia and Moravia (Karl Hermann Frank).

During the years 1939 to 1941 some Czech Protectorate politicians (including Prime Minister Alois Eliáš) tried to resist the German occupation, but the Nazi occupying forces liquidated those people and only collaborationists loyal to Germany were appointed state officials (the symbol of Czech collaboration was Minister Emanuel Moravec). Traditional Czech fascists protested against the official representation of the protectorate, demanding more influence. That attitude was typical of Vlajka. Up until 1945 the Germans rejected the requests made by Czech and Moravian collaborationists to establish a Czech SS-Division to fight against the Allies (SS-Division Böhmen und Mähren consisted exclusively of Sudeten Germans). A small military unit inside the structures of the Waffen-SS called Svatováclavská dobrovolnická rota (St. Wenceslas's Volunteer Column) was founded only in March 1945. Czech antifascist patriots destroyed this unit totally during the uprising in May 1945.

Slovakia became a satellite of Nazi Germany in 1939. Some scholars have called this right-wing authoritarian regime clerico-fascism, because many Catholic clerics held prominent state posts. Catholic priest Jozef Tiso became president of Slovakia. Slovak troops fought together with German troops against Poland and the Soviet Union. On 29 August 1944 antifascist Slovaks rose up against the Germans and the collaborationist regime, but the uprising was defeated. Some Slovak fascists fought brutally against partisans and civilians up to the end of the war.

After the war, Czechoslovakia was reunified. Carpatho-Ukraine was incorporated into the Ukrainian Soviet Republic, and Sudeten Germans were transferred to Germany and Austria. The communists had monopolized political power in 1948. There existed only small illegal fascist or Nazi groups after the war. Some Slovak and Czech fascists immigrated to Western countries. In the 1980s militant youth groups inspired by Nazism (Totenkopf, Werwolf) appeared in Czech areas. After the fall of communism in 1989, some Slovak separatists tried to use the heritage of the Slovak fascist state in their political propaganda. In the Czech lands, some right-wing extremists accepted the ideology of interwar fascism and protectorate collaboration. One stream of skinhead subculture became pan-Aryan Nazi in orientation, the other stream became anti-German Czech nationalist. Czechoslovakia ended its existence on 31 December 1992.

Miroslav Mares

See Also: ANTI-SEMITISM; ARYANISM; AUSTRO-HUNGARIAN EMPIRE/HABSBURG EMPIRE, THE; BERAN, RUDOLF; CLERICO-FASCISM; FRANK, KARL HERMANN; GAJDA, GENERAL RADOLA; HENLEIN, KONRAD; HEYDRICH, REINHARD; HUNGARY; IRREDENTISM; MUNICH PACT, THE; NATIONALISM; NAZISM; PANGERMANISM; PARAMILITARISM; POSTWAR FASCISM; SKINHEAD FASCISM; SLAVS, THE (AND GERMANY); SLOVAKIA; SUDETENLAND, THE; TISO, MGR. JOSEF

References

Kelly, David D. 1995. *The Czech Fascist Movement 1922–1942.* New York: Columbia University Press.

Mastny, V. 1971. *The Czechs under Nazi Rule.* Columbia: Columbia University Press.

Pasák, Tomáš. 1999. *Český fašismus 1922–1945 a kolaborace 1939–1945.* Praha: +Práh.

Polišenský, Josef Vincent. 1991. *History of Czechoslovakia in Outline.* Prague: Bohemia International.

D-DAY LANDINGS, THE

Massed invasion of France by Allied forces commencing on 6 June 1944 (D-Day), also known as the "Normandy Landings." D-Day marked the beginning of the end for the Nazi occupation of Continental Europe. Fifty-nine naval convoys of British and U.S. naval vessels comprising more than 2,000 transports and 700 warships launched the invasion forces onto the Normandy coast, supported by airborne units. At the end of the first day more than 150,000 soldiers had been landed.

Cyprian Blamires

See Also: GERMANY; HITLER, ADOLF; WORLD WAR II

References
Kemp, Anthony. 1994. *D-Day: The Normandy Landings and the Liberation of Europe.* London: Thames and Hudson.

DALMATIA

Area in the northwest of the Balkan peninsula, formerly part of the Austro-Hungarian Empire, with a racially and linguistically mixed population; source of interethnic conflict and subject of irredentist claims by Italian nationalists and their Fascist successors.

Cyprian Blamires

See Also: D'ANNUNZIO, GABRIELE; FIUME; IRREDENTISM; ITALY; SLAVS, THE (AND ITALY)

D'ANNUNZIO, GABRIELE (1863–1938)

Celebrated Italian poet, writer, and dramatist, but also soldier, aviator, political activist, and man of action, whose ideas anticipated Mussolinian Fascism in many respects. He was born in Pescara, where, in 1879, he published his first collection of poems, entitled *Primo vere.* Influenced by the late Romantic aesthetic of "decadentism" and by Nietzsche's doctrine of the Superman, he moved to Rome, where he began an intense period of artistic and social activity. It was during this period in Rome that some of his most famous novels came out: *Il piacere* (1889), *L'Innocente* (1892), *Il trionfo della morte* (1894), *La vergine delle rocce* (1899), *Il fuoco* (1900).

Politically, D'Annunzio espoused generically nationalist and conservative positions at the start of his career. In the summer of 1897 he won a parliamentary seat on the ticket of a party of the Left. During the electoral campaign he made a celebrated campaign speech in which he criticized socialism and adopted Darwinian tones in defense of private property, lauding a heroic-aristocratic vision of the social order. On account of his aesthetic interests and his eccentric posing, he became known as the "Member for Beauty." Very soon, however, he distanced himself from the liberal and reactionary Right, to move to radical revolutionary positions that were to a large extent those of Italian Fascism. His literary work was imbued with a political vision that was very critical of parliamentary democracy but was also hostile to social conservatism and the privileges of the economic oligarchy, which, in his judgment, ruled Italy. In the novel *Le vergini delle rocce,* for example, he attacked the great families of the Roman aristocracy, who he believed had betrayed the aesthetic and political duties of their rank and had followed the cult of money, business, and financial speculation. In the work *Il fuoco,* however, the protagonist, Stelio Effrena, was presented as a skillful orator, a "national prophet" who aspires to dominate the masses by the power of his charisma. In the theatrical drama *La Nave* the imperialistic policies of Venice are exalted in politico-mythological terms as a model of political power for united Italy.

In reality D'Annunzio was a dandy, an aesthete uneasy among professional politicians, a restless figure destined to waver between right and left, between reaction and revolution. To the compromises of parliamentary life he much preferred action and the "grand gesture." World War I was his great opportunity; it enabled him finally to adopt the image of the "soldier poet," the "armed aesthete." At the outbreak of the conflict he volunteered to serve even though he was already in his fifties, and he distinguished himself by some courageous propagandistic enterprises that had a profound impact on Italian public opinion, such as his 700-mile round-trip flight with nine planes to drop propaganda leaflets on Vienna.

Once the war was over, D'Annunzio took troops to occupy the city of Fiume and prevent the Allies from ceding it to Yugoslavia; he claimed it as Italian. It is to D'Annunzio in Fiume that should be attributed the birth of the pararreligious ritual type of politics that would be a feature of Fascist politics-as-spectacle a few years later: the Roman salute, the dialogue from the balcony with the crowd, the cult of the dead, the war cry *eia eia alalà.* But with the Fiume episode he also sealed his role as anticipator of the Fascist revolution from the ideological point of view, as is demonstrated in particular by the constitution he launched in Fiume on 30 August 1920, whose syndicalist and corporatist proposals would be taken over almost lock, stock, and barrel by early Fascism.

In the two years that preceded the March on Rome and the victory of Fascism, the popularity of d'Annunzio in Italy was greater than that of almost any other political leader, Mussolini included. But his lack of pragmatic spirit and political realism prevented him from capitalizing politically on the broad consensus of support that he enjoyed in the country, especially among the young and among former servicemen. In 1924, with Fascism now firmly in power, D'Annunzio withdrew to private life in Gardone Riviera, in a sumptuous residence called the Vittoriale degli Italiani. It was a kind of museum for the celebration of war and victory. For the rest of his life he lived in a splendid isolation, always officially lauded by Mussolini, who never missed any opportunity to recall how much Fascism owed to D'Annunzio. A typical example of this was the decision to establish at public expense in 1926 the National Institute for the publication of the complete works of the poet and "commandant"—the only figure who in his day could really have blocked Mussolini and become the head of Fascism and of Italy in the Duce's stead.

Alessandro Campi
(translated by Cyprian Blamires)

See Also: ARISTOCRACY; CONSERVATISM; CORPORATISM; COUNTER-REVOLUTION; DEMOCRACY; FASCIST PARTY, THE; FIUME; HERO, THE CULT OF THE; ITALY; MARCH ON ROME, THE; MUSSOLINI, BENITO ANDREA; NIETZSCHE, FRIEDRICH; PARLIAMENTARISM; PROTOFASCISM; REVOLUTION; SALUTES; SOCIAL DARWINISM; STYLE; SYNDICALISM; WAR; WARRIOR ETHOS, THE; WORLD WAR I

References
Bonadeo, A. 1995. *D'Annunzio and the Great War.* Madison, NJ: Fairleigh Dickinson University Press.
Ledeen, M. 2002. *D'Annunzio: The First Duce.* London: Transaction.

DANZIG/GDANSK: See POLAND AND NAZI GERMANY
DAP: *See* DREXLER, ANTON; NAZISM

DARRE, RICHARD WALTHER (1895–1953)

Minister of agriculture in the Third Reich, leader of the SS Rasse- und Siedlungshauptamt (1931–1938) and of the Reich Farmers Movement, and coiner of the term *Blut und Boden*, Darré was born in Argentina and trained in agriculture and breeding. His first visit to Germany was in 1905. In 1914 he volunteered for the German army and was awarded the Iron Cross. A member of the Freikorps in 1918, he joined the *Stahlhelm* in 1922. In 1926–1927 he published fourteen articles on breeding. He became a member of the NSDAP in 1930. In books like *Neuadel aus Blut und Boden* (1930) he called for the recognition of a new German nobility, drawn from among the farmers. He was dismissed from his post in 1942 and charged with corruption.

Göran Dahl

See Also: ARISTOCRACY; BLOOD AND SOIL; FARMERS; FREIKORPS, THE; RURALISM; STAHLHELM

References

Bramwell, A. 1985. *Blood and Soil: Richard Walther Darré and Hitler's "Green Party."* Bourne End: Kensal.

DAWES PLAN, THE: *See* REPARATIONS

DEAT, MARCEL (1894–1955)

French journalist and political activist who collaborated with the Nazis, Déat was a much-decorated soldier from World War I who operated within the reformist faction of the French Socialist Party up until 1933, when he was ejected from it. The Parti Socialiste de France–Union Jean Jaurès (PSdF), which he subsequently formed, propagated a third way *planiste* political program. In the years before World War II, Déat increasingly organized his political actions around the theme of avoiding a war with Germany, and he was elected MP for Angoulême in 1939 on a pacifist agenda. Supporting full powers for Pétain in June 1940 and collaboration with Germany, Déat unsuccessfully agitated for a one-party state at Vichy. Failure led him to leave Vichy for Paris, where he became chief editor of the newspaper *L'Oeuvre,* which vigorously attacked Vichy for its lack of commitment to collaborationism. In February 1941, Déat co-founded the ultracollaborationist Rassemblement National Populaire with Eugène Deloncle, former leader of the Cagoulards ("Hooded Men"), a fanatically anticommunist far-right group responsible for a failed coup attempt against the French government in 1937. Déat was appointed minister of work and national solidarity on 17 March 1944. He fled Paris during the Liberation, eventually taking refuge in a convent in Turin under the name Leroux and converting to Catholicism.

Steve Bastow

See Also: FRANCE; FRENCH REVOLUTION, THE; NAZISM; PACIFISM; PETAIN, MARSHAL HENRI PHILIPPE; VICHY

References

Bastow, S. 2000. "Inter-War French Fascism and the Neo-socialism of Marcel Deat." Pp. 38–51 in *Discourse Theory and Political Analysis,* edited by D. Howarth. Manchester: Manchester University Press.
White, D. S. 1992. *Lost Comrades: Socialists of the Front Generation 1918–1945.* Cambridge: Harvard University Press.

DEATH, CULTS OF: *See* CULTS OF DEATH
DEATH CAMPS: *See* CONCENTRATION CAMPS; USTASHA

DECADENCE

A belief in the degenerate state of contemporary society (and often of the modern world in general) is an essential premise for fascism's utopia of national regeneration and rebirth, which experts in comparative fascist studies increasingly see as the ultimate rationale for the radicalness of its revolutionary assault on the status quo. The decline and fall from seemingly unassailable political, economic, and cultural power of Egypt, Greece, Rome, and Byzantium haunted the imaginations of broad sections of the European intelligentsia in the late nineteenth century; many were convinced that the enormous scientific, industrial, and material progress of the Western world had occurred at the cost of the spiritual values and visionary grasp of the ultimate purpose or mystery of existence, without which all civilizations eventually collapse. The obsession with decadence could take two contrasting forms. In the first, the decline was perceived as inexorable, the West's spiritual resources shrivelling to the point at which a more vital race of barbarians might put it out of its misery of growing dissolution and anarchy, a diagnosis that induced terminal "cultural pessimism." In the second, the current crisis presaged a new phase of civilization based on a revitalizing vision of reality that would enable morality and the social order to be regenerated, a presentiment that induced the paradoxical mood of "palingenetic" cultural pessimism—that is, pessimism about the viability of the present combined with an unshakable belief in an imminent transformation and rebirth. This second response to decadence has an affinity with the many premodern cosmological myths that conceive historical time to be not linear but cyclic, passing from a golden age to an age of depravity and back to a new creation, often after a major cataclysm has wiped out a world become dissolute. The Hindu cyclic scheme of creation and destruction according to which the whole of humanity is now ensnared in the *kali yuga,* or black age, is an outstanding product of this epic narrative of decay and rebirth being projected onto the historical process, and it is one that directly influenced the elaborate philosophy of Julius Evola, one of the most influential ideologues of postwar fascism.

Despite profound differences in the content of their work, Richard Wagner, Émile Zola, William Morris, Friedrich Nietzsche, Fëdor Dostoevsky, and Leo Tolstoy are all emblematic of the rejection by many creative thinkers of the official cult of progress based on technological and material advance, and engaged in the quest for a total cultural revolution based on a renewed metaphysical vision. This drive for palingenesis, the sense that the breakdown of contemporary reality may be ushering in a new one, is arguably central to all modernism and is clearly expressed in the architectural utopianism of such figures as Walter Gropius and Charles Le Corbusier. An important permutation of this pattern is the "political modernism" that arises when thinkers focus on the need for a new political order to enable the nation, or "the West," to save itself from the decadent process that is now engulfing it. In France, Georges Sorel, and in Germany, Julius Langbehn, Arthur Moeller van den Bruck, and the many

völkisch writers who aspired to bring about a "new Germany" are examples of figures who saw the cultural crisis of the day as the birth pangs of a new sociopolitical reality appropriate to the modern age.

Considered against that background, fascism emerges clearly as a form of political modernism, based not on a pessimistic sense of decadence but on a palingenetic diagnosis of the state of the nation and the West as a whole. While historians have naturally tended to focus on the social and political expression of fascism's struggle to regenerate society, a deeper insight into its ideological and psychological dynamics is afforded by the study of a number of figures who, at least for a time, were attracted to, or even drawn into active support of, fascist movements by their concern to put an end to the decadence of the age: W. B. Yeats, Louis-Ferdinand Céline, Drieu la Rochelle, A. K. Chesterton, Giovanni Papini, Filippo Marinetti, Gabriele D'Annunzio, Julius Evola, Oswald Spengler, Ernst Jünger, Gottfried Benn, and Martin Heidegger are among the better known examples of this pattern. Perhaps the most significant exemplar, however, is the Romanian writer Emil Cioran, who in the aftermath of World War II wrote a stream of essays in impeccable French forensically exploring the decadence of the modern world and the dissolution at the very heart of human existence. However, this arch-pessimism is to be seen in dialectical relation to the fact that before the war he had been a staunch supporter of the Romanian Iron Guard and had devoted his considerable poetic gift to celebrating its bid to put an end to the process of decay that was allegedly destroying his country. It was only after events had dashed his hopes in the new Romania and Europe announced by its leader Corneliu Codreanu that his optimism turned to terminal "cultural pessimism."

The theme of national and societal decadence and its imminent or ultimate reversal under fascism arguably provides the key to the inner coherence and continuity of fascist ideology, despite the bewildering range of component ideas that constitute its ideology in any one instance. In the interwar period the threats to the nation identified by fascists could include the growth of communism; the weakness of liberalism; the proliferation of materialism, cosmopolitanism, and aesthetic modernism; the blurring of "natural" gender roles; miscegenation; and symptoms of racial degeneracy. Since 1945 further signs for fascists of the encroaching decadence are the rise of multiculturalism, globalization, consumerism, the Americanization of society, and the looming ecological crisis. However, it would be a fallacy to assume that there is unity among fascists, either about the causes of decadence or their cure. Fascism has espoused antiurbanism as well as a belief in a powerful, urbanized technocracy, and incorporated mainstream secular and scientific currents of thought as well as ones drawing on occultism, paganism, or Christian beliefs tailored to the cause of national rebirth. Its nationalism has ranged from cultural and historical varieties to ones imbued with eugenic and Social Darwinian ideas of race, its concepts of revolution from versions celebrating violence and war to others stressing the need for achieving "cultural hegemony" as the premise to political change.

In the cultural sphere fascism has adopted a wide range of aesthetics, and should not be equated with antimodernism as such. It should also be noted that the Nazi campaign to expunge modernism from art was for the fascist mind-set not a manifestation of decadence but a ritual act of purging intended to make way for the appearance of a new art reflecting the healthy values of the regenerated national community. Even if fascism has often been portrayed in films as the product of moral decay, fascists have always seen themselves as defending the West against its onslaught.

Roger Griffin

See Also: INTRODUCTION; AMERICANIZATION; ART; BENN, GOTTFRIED; CÉLINE, LOUIS-FERDINAND; CHESTERTON, A K; CIORAN, EMIL; CODREANU, CORNELIU ZELEA; COSMOPOLITANISM; D'ANNUNZIO, GABRIELE; DECADENCE; DRIEU LA ROCHELLE, PIERRE; ECOLOGY; EUGENICS; EVOLA, JULIUS; GLOBALIZATION; HEIDEGGER, MARTIN; JÜNGER, ERNST; LANGBEHN, JULIUS; LIBERALISM; MARINETTI, FILIPPO; MODERNISM; MOELLER VAN DEN BRUCK, ARTHUR; MODERNITY; MYTH; NATIONALISM; NAZISM; NEW MAN, THE; NIETZSCHE, FRIEDRICH; NIHILISM; OCCULTISM; PALINGENETIC MYTH; PAPINI, GIOVANNI; POSTWAR FASCISM; RACIAL DOCTRINE; REVOLUTION; ROMANIA; ROME; SCIENCE; SOCIAL DARWINISM; SOREL, GEORGES; SPENGLER, OSWALD; TECHNOLOGY; UTOPIA, UTOPIANISM; WAGNER, (WILHELM) RICHARD; YEATS, WILLIAM BUTLER

References

Pick, D. 1989. *Faces of Degeneration: A European Disorder, c. 1848–1918.* Cambridge: Cambridge University Press.

Starrs, R. 1994. *Deadly Dialectics: Yukio Mishima.* Folkestone: Curzon (reprinted, pp. 249–266, in R. Griffin and Matt Feldman, eds. 2003. *Fascism.* Critical Concepts in Politics Series, vol. 1. London: Routledge).

Stern, F. 1961. *The Politics of Cultural Despair.* Berkeley: University of California Press.

Sternhell, Z. 1976. "Fascist Ideology." Pp. 325–406 in *Fascism: A Reader's Guide: Analyses Interpretations, Bibliography,* edited by W. Laqueur. London: Wildwood House (reprinted, pp. 81–141, in R. Griffin and M. Feldman, eds. 2003. *Fascism.* Critical Concepts in Political Science, vol. 3. London: Routledge).

DEGENERACY

A common term in the vocabulary of the global interwar eugenics movement and a key term in Nazi racial doctrine. The chief jurist of Nazism, Hans Frank, defined it as the condition of being excluded from "the normal 'genus' of the decent nation." He claimed that it resulted from racial mixing, as when a "decent representative of his race" has children by a person of inferior racial stock. The Nazis believed that this theory had been scientifically proven. They rated in the category of "inferior stock" not simply members of certain races—above all the Jews and the Slavs, Sinti and Roma—but also persons whose criminal or simply unconventional behavior branded them as "aliens" in the body of the German people and therefore as incapable of contributing to the health of society: for example, "asocials" and homosexuals. The Nazis considered it not just desirable but also a definite duty for the sake of the health of the German people to eliminate the damaging sexual congress that produced the "degenerates," and to enslave or to destroy the individuals who resulted from that congress. They attempted to eliminate the racial mixing through legislation and through punishment of those guilty, and they set out to deal with the degenerate results of such congress through imprisonment, enslavement, or simple annihilation.

Among the forms of behavior that the Nazis believed harmful to the health and well-being of the German people were all those that did not conform to the Nazi viewpoint on morality. This applied moreover not simply to ordinary moral conduct but also to artistic creations. Degeneracy, in other words, could be manifested in a book or a picture. The famous "burning of the books" at the instigation of Goebbels gave a dramatic illustration not simply to Germans but also to the whole world of the strength of Nazi contempt for "degenerate" books and their authors. The concept was also applied to the world of music, and concert programs were "cleansed" of degenerate scores. At the same time, the notorious Exhibition of Degenerate Art displayed to the world Nazi disgust at various forms of "degenerate" artistic modernism. In this they were of course echoing the classic pretension of totalitarian regimes to pass judgment on the whole of culture, which was also a feature of Soviet communism, which preached contempt for "bourgeois" art and promoted a particular artistic style as appropriate for a socialist regime. But this aspect of Nazism set it apart on the other hand from Mussolini's Italy, where the Futurists were enthusiastic supporters of the Fascist movement (at least in its earlier days). The "degeneracy" theory is one of a number of areas in which Nazism differed substantially from Italian Fascism on account of the biological racial doctrine, which did not form part of the fundamental Italian Fascist outlook.

Cyprian Blamires

See Also: ANTHROPOLOGY; ANTI-SEMITISM; ART; ASOCIALS; BOOKS, THE BURNING OF THE; CONCENTRATION CAMPS; FRANK, HANS; FUTURISM; GOEBBELS, PAUL JOSEPH; HEALTH; HOLOCAUST, THE; HOMOSEXUALITY; ITALY; MARINETTI, FILIPPO TOMMASO; MEDICINE; MUSIC (GERMANY); MUSSOLINI, BENITO ANDREA; NAZISM; RACIAL DOCTRINE; ROMA AND SINTI; SLAVS, THE (AND GERMANY); SOCIAL DARWINISM; TOTALITARIANISM

References
Chamberlin, E. J., and S. L. Gilman, eds. 1985. *Degeneration: The Dark Side of Progress.* New York: Columbia University Press.
Pick, D. 1989. *Faces of Degeneration: A European Disorder, c. 1848–1918.* Cambridge: Cambridge University Press.

DEGENERATE ART: *See* ART

DEGRELLE, LEON (1906–1994)

Leader of the Belgian Rex movement, which collaborated with the Nazis during World War II. Degrelle's early career was closely tied to the world of Catholicism. In 1929, Degrelle became editor of the publication of the largest Belgian Catholic youth organization, L'Action Catholique de la Jeunesse Belge (ACJB). The following year he became director of its publishing house, Christus Rex. Degrelle used Rex to try to radicalize the Catholic Party. His failure to achieve this led him to put Rex forward as an independent force in the May 1936 general elections, in which they won twenty-one seats on a program of authoritarian political reform. Rexism became increasingly influenced by fascism as the 1930s went on, a transformation paralleled by declining electoral appeal. After the German invasion in 1940, Degrelle advocated a peace settlement with Nazism, moving to a position of explicit

pro-Nazism by January 1941. He subsequently volunteered for the Légion Wallonie, joining the fighting on the Eastern Front and seeking to use the LW as the vehicle for the National Socialist revolution in Wallonia. Condemned to death after the Liberation, Degrelle escaped to Spain, where he was granted Spanish citizenship and continued his political activities

Steve Bastow

See Also: AUTHORITARIANISM; BELGIUM; CATHOLIC CHURCH, THE; POLITICAL CATHOLICISM; REXISM; WORLD WAR II

References
Conway, M. 1993. *Collaboration in Belgium: Léon Degrelle and the Rexist Movement.* New Haven: Yale University Press.
Payne, S. 1995. *A History of Fascism 1914–1945.* London: University College London Press.
Rees, P. 1990. *Biographical Dictionary of the Extreme Right since 1890.* Hemel Hempstead: Harvester Wheatsheaf.

DEMOCRACY

"Fascism denies that the majority, through the mere fact of being a majority, can rule human societies" (*Enciclopedia italiana,* entry "Fascism"). This denial, penned under the name of Mussolini, was related to the rejection of egalitarianism common to Italian Fascism and Nazism, which, by contrast, affirmed "the irremediable, fruitful and beneficent inequality of men, who cannot be levelled by such a mechanical and extrinsic fact as universal suffrage" (ibid.). However, the same article suggests that there is a way that the term "democracy" can be understood which is compatible with Fascism—namely, when it is understood as "organized, centralized, authoritarian democracy." Fascists deny that they are against "democracy" as such, only the liberal, individualist version of it that has become the touchstone or criterion for judging the others. In this respect they resemble the Bolsheviks, who claimed to be building a "true" democracy through "workers' councils" rather than through the representative parliamentary systems favored in the classic democratic regimes of Europe and the United States. Hitler and Mussolini both excoriated democracy as understood in the liberal parliamentary tradition as being one of the elements of contemporary decadence. For Mussolini it was the parliamentary system, with its party squabbles and endless talking, that sapped the energies and purpose of the Italian nation; for Hitler it was the democratic Weimar Republic that symbolized a failed social and political order that was tainted by the treachery which had brought to an end a war that Germany had not lost militarily.

What the fascists did was to substitute populism for democracy, setting out to win mass support and to endear the regime to the masses through their involvement in huge public political rituals and spectacles. The Nuremberg Rallies were clearly planned to bond the masses emotionally to the regime through theatrical staging that encouraged a sense of solidarity and elicited a sense of wonder at the power of a renascent Germany. This strategy aimed at winning over the hearts and imaginations of the masses, rather than at offering them any opportunity for deliberative participation in policy or engaging their intelligence in the political process. Particularly in the case of the Nazis (and to a lesser extent with the Italian Fascists), this process was further intensified by the deliberate inculcation of personal devotion to the Leader through propaganda and visual imagery. His image was professionally and powerfully "promoted" (especially to children and to the young), as the advertising world would say today. The truth is that emotional identification with "their" leader (through the universal imposition of the *Heil Hitler!* greeting, for example) proved a more successful means of consolidating Hitler's power than any ballot box could have done. Mussolini too promoted a leader cult, but that was not solely a fascist phenomenon; it was exploited with equal effect in communist regimes.

A key role in the enlistment of popular sympathies was played by the enrollment of different sectors of society in mass movements—especially the youth, but also women. These gave opportunities for sporting and outdoor activities and the development of friendships and socialization. What was different from liberal democracies here was, of course, the element of coercion—these were not volunteer movements but enforced expressions of national solidarity. Essentially, Germany under the Nazis and Italy under Mussolini were set up on a kind of military model where priority was given to the virtues of discipline and solidarity, with citizens knowing their place and trained to serve the purposes of a militant nationalist crusade. Hitler expressed great respect for men of the people, saying that he would much rather have a good street brawler on his side than half a dozen fine talkers or intellectuals. So successful was he at winning over the hearts of the German people that they fought to the last gasp for him, and the only serious threat to his supremacy came

with the July Plot in 1944, a conspiracy promoted by conservative elite elements who felt that he was destroying "their" Germany.

Cyprian Blamires

See Also: ABSTRACTION; ARENDT, HANNAH; BOLSHEVISM; DECADENCE; EGALITARIANISM; ELITISM; FASCIST PARTY, THE; HITLER, ADOLF; INDIVIDUALISM; JULY PLOT, THE; LEADER CULT, THE; LEISURE; LIBERALISM; MASSES, THE ROLE OF THE; MILITARISM; MUSSOLINI, BENITO ANDREA; NATIONALISM; NOVEMBER CRIMINALS/*NOVEMBERBRECHER*, THE; NUREMBERG RALLIES, THE; PARLIAMENTARISM; PROPAGANDA; RELIGION; TOTALITARIANISM; WEIMAR REPUBLIC, THE; YOUTH

References

Fieschi, Catherine. 2004. *Fascism, Populism and the French Fifth Republic: In the Shadow of Democracy.* Manchester: Manchester University Press.
Griffin, R. 1991. *The Nature of Fascism.* London: Routledge.
Payne, S. 1995. *A History of Fascism 1914–1945.* London: University College London Press.
Sontheimer, Kurt. 1978. *Antidemokratisches Denken in der Weimarer Republik.* München: Deutsche Taschenbuch.

DEMOGRAPHIC POLICY

Interwar fascism had a great interest in the physical fitness and fertility of the population. A buoyant birthrate was deemed an index of national vitality and power. Although these concerns date from the turn of the century, the fascist state saw demographic programs as part of the aims of modernization and rejuvenation. Nazi demographers assisted by census techniques collected medical, health, and welfare data. Data on diseases and crime were analyzed, and states organized central registries. Hamburg had a Central Health Passport Archive, and Thuringia had an Office for Racial Welfare to centralize and analyze the statistics. They used the new technology of Hollerith punch cards. These techniques assisted them in their concerns regarding the racial makeup of the Reich, enabling them to calculate the numbers of Jews in the population, how many had emigrated, and the location of those that remained. They also calculated how many full, half-, and quarter-Jews still lived in the Reich. The SS demographer Richard Korherr's statistical conclusions about numbers of Jews in the occupied territories assisted Adolf Eichmann with the implementation of the Final Solution. In 1943, Korherr calculated for Himmler and Hitler how many Jews had been killed, country by country. Similar techniques were applied to identify social deviants and for the genocidal measures against the Roma. In the occupied territories, notably The Netherlands, census techniques were used in the deportation of Jews to the concentration and death camps of the East.

Both Nazi Germany and Fascist Italy pursued contradictory policies toward women as workers and as child producers. Neither state resolved these contradictions as women took an increasing role in the war economy. The demographer Corrado Gini devised a cyclical theory of population and took a leading role in Italian Fascist demography. He devised a system of fiscal incentives to raise the birth rate. These included bachelor taxes. An extensive system of maternal and infant welfare provisions underpinned Fascist demography. Gini had direct access to Mussolini, who studied demographic bulletins, and demographic growth was regarded as vital to sustaining Italy's status as a Great Power. Model communities were founded as part of rural settlement programs, such as Fertilia in Sardinia.

Paul Weindling

See Also: ANTI-SEMITISM; CONCENTRATION CAMPS; EICHMANN, ADOLF; EUGENICS; FAMILY, THE; FASCIST PARTY, THE; HEALTH; HIMMLER, HEINRICH; HITLER, ADOLF; HOLOCAUST, THE; MEDICINE; RACIAL DOCTRINE; ROMA AND SINTI; RURALISM; SEXUALITY; SS, THE; WELFARE; WOMEN

References
Black, E. 2001. *IBM and the Holocaust.* New York: Three Rivers.
Goetz, Aly, and Karl-Heinz Roth. 1984. *Die restlose Erfassung, Volkszählen, Identifzieren, Aussondern im Nationalsozialismus.* Berlin: Rotbuch.
Ipsen, C. 1996. *Dictating Demography: The Problem of Population in Fascist Italy.* Cambridge: Cambridge University Press.
Seltzer, W. 1998. "Population Statistics, the Holocaust, and the Nuremberg Trials." *Population and Development Review* 24: 511–552.
Weindling, P. 1989. *Health, Race and German Politics between National Unification and Nazism.* Cambridge: Cambridge University Press.

DENAZIFICATION

At the conferences of Yalta in February 1945 and Potsdam in July and August of that same year, the three main Allies—Britain, the United States, and the Soviet Union—decided that all members of the Nazi Party in Germany should be removed from public office to facilitate the development of a democratic Germany. In the following months, about 95,000 implicated persons were interned in the U.S. zone of occupation, 67,000 in the Soviet zone, and 64,000 in the British zone. France, although not represented at Yalta and Potsdam, interned about 19,000 persons in her zone. The Nuremberg Trials dealt with the most senior National Socialists. It soon became clear, however, that the four Allies were operating on very different criteria in their denazification policy. U.S. policy followed a line between re-educating the German population and the need for punitive action based on the assumption that Germans had a collective guilt for the crimes committed in their name. Britain was more pragmatic in her approach, since her zone included the heavily industrialized—and thus severely destroyed—Ruhr Valley. Denazification often came second to reconstruction. France was very lax in her denazification attempt, even employing individuals from other zones who had lost their positions. The Soviet Union soon became more interested in the nationalization of industry and the collectivization of her zone, thus allowing former Nazi Party members to retain office if they joined the re-established Communist Party.

In October 1946, the Allies decided to coordinate the denazification policy more closely. A questionnaire was drawn up for all Germans to fill in, to assess their involvement with National Socialism. Since it was up to the individuals to prove their innocence, the questionnaire soon became a symbol of arbitrariness. In the spring of 1947, the Allies decided to leave the execution of the denazification program to the Germans. With the onset of the Cold War, denazification began to lose its significance. The Soviet Union unilaterally ended denazification in her zone in March 1948. In the three Western zones, re-education and rebuilding soon became a priority. Between 1950 and 1954, West German legislators passed a number of laws that effectively concluded denazification in the three Western zones, which had become the Federal Republic of Germany (FRG) in 1949. Under the Occupation Statute, the three Western Allies had retained certain powers of intervention in the affairs of the Federal Republic. In 1953, Britain arrested a number of former Nazis, including Werner Naumann, a former state secretary under Joseph Goebbels. The group was accused of trying to infiltrate the Liberal Party (FDP) in North Rhine-Westphalia. The "Naumann Affair" was the final act of the Allies' denazification policy.

Christoph H. Müller

See Also: COLD WAR, THE; FRANCE; GERMANY; GOEBBELS, (PAUL) JOSEPH; GREAT BRITAIN; NAZISM; NEO-NAZISM; NUREMBERG TRIALS, THE; POSTWAR FASCISM; WORLD WAR II

References
Smith, Arthur L. 1996. *The War for the German Mind: Re-educating Hitler's Soldiers.* Oxford: Berghahn.
Tent, James F. 1982. *Mission on the Rhine: Reeducation and Denazification in American-Occupied Germany.* Chicago: University of Chicago Press.
Wheeler-Bennett, John W., and Anthony James Nicholls. 1972. *The Semblance of Peace: The Political Settlement after the Second World War.* London: Macmillan.

DENMARK

Fascism in the Italian mold inspired a few groups in Denmark that openly sported the symbol of the fasces in the early 1920s and proclaimed Benito Mussolini to be the model of a modern politician. However, they soon petered out, as did many of the small antiparliamentary leagues formed by dissatisfied members of the national-conservative and liberal-rural parties. Leaving aside a number of established right-wing intellectuals among leading novelists, academics, and journalists, who attempted to discredit the legitimacy of democracy and parliamentarism, the political system in Denmark was characterized by a high degree of consensus. A series of Nazi parties did, however, appear during the 1930s. The first party, the biggest and the most influential, not least in the first year of the German occupation of Denmark (1940–1945), was Danmarks National Socialistiske Arbejderparti (Danish National Socialist Worker's Party), formed in 1930. The party, usually abbreviated to DNSAP, was in its very name and ideology strongly influenced by the German National Socialist Worker's Party (NSDAP) under the leadership of Adolf Hitler. Apart from a heavy leaning on Danish prehistoric myths and a strong display of nationalism, the first program drafted by DNSAP was an almost literal translation of the twenty-five points listed in the German NSDAP's program, and the Danish Nazis also acquired their symbols and militaristic activities from their German role-model. But unlike its German counterpart, Danish Nazism was unable to command the support of more than a fraction of the electorate. At its best DNSAP gained 1.8 percent of the total vote at the 1939 national election, which translated into three mandates at the

Copenhagen headquarters of the Danish National Socialist Workers' Party. Much influenced by the German NSDAP, it was never able to have the same popular impact. (Library of Congress)

National Assembly. At that time DNSAP counted approximately 5,000 members, a number that steadily progressed during the war, reaching 20,000 at its peak in 1943. The party recruited its core membership from rural districts as well as the urban lower middle class, but with the advent of the war the membership base grew broader, with the working class being the largest social grouping in the party. In Danish politics the DNSAP was mostly isolated, although toward the late 1930s the party flirted briefly with the Agricultural Party, which was also represented in the national parliament. Like their fellow Nazis in other European countries, Danish Nazis regarded liberalism and communism as a synonym for all the "evils" that had disrupted the highly acclaimed unity between race, state, and nation. Only a direct overthrow—preferably by referendum—would put an end to what the Nazis perceived as the damage of democratic equality, Bolshevism, capitalism with its exploitative nature, modernism in the arts with its extreme stylistic experiments, and U.S. popular culture. Other Nazi parties, often overtly critical of the

DNSAP, which they denounced for being too soft on racial issues, tried to compete with the bigger party, but they were unable to exercise any role. Denmark was a country with many Nazi parties—a number of which did not last long, often consisting of activists who knew each other beforehand—but only a limited number of Nazis.

During the occupation, the DNSAP sought influence with the German occupiers, but, notwithstanding lofty promises from Berlin during the first months of the occupation to install the DNSAP as the new Danish government, the Danish Nazis did not acquire the power they hoped for; they were soon treated as an inconvenience rather than a useful aide. Apart from mobilizing a squadron of volunteers to fight along the Waffen SS on the Eastern Front, the Danish Nazis remained insignificant during the war. After the liberation of Denmark in May 1945, the Nazi parties were not—unlike in several other formerly occupied countries—made illegal, nor was it prohibited to be a member of a Nazi party. Today there is only one small Nazi party, Dansk National Socialistisk Bevægelse (Danish National Socialist Movement), which has made several unsuccessful runs at local elections without winning any seats.

Adam Holm

See Also: AMERICANIZATION; BOLSHEVISM; CLAUSEN, FRITS; DEMOCRACY; EGALITARIANISM; FASCIO, THE; HITLER, ADOLF; LIBERALISM; MARXISM; MODERNISM; MUSSOLINI, BENITO ANDREA; NAZISM; PARLIAMENTARISM; RACIAL DOCTRINE; SYMBOLS; WAFFEN SS, THE; WORLD WAR II

References

Djursaa, M. 1981. "Who Were the Danish Nazis?" Pp. 237–256 in *Fascism in Europe,* edited by S. J. Woolf. 2d ed. London: Methuen. Holm, A. 2001. "'Opposing the Past'— Danish Radical Conservatism and Right-Wing Authoritarianism in the Inter-War Years." In *International Fascism 1919–1945,* edited by R. Mallet. London: Frank Cass.

DENNIS, LAWRENCE (1893–1977)

U.S. advocate of fascist-style reforms in the interwar years. Born in Atlanta, Dennis received his formal education at Phillips Exeter academy and Harvard University. In 1930 he began attacking the overseas activities of U.S. investment banking in the *Nation* and the *New Republic,* and the question put by the title of his book, *Is Capitalism Doomed?* (1932), was answered with a resounding "yes." By 1934, as editor of a right-wing tabloid, *The Awakener,* he was attacking the "halfway" measures of the New Deal.

His "fascist" reputation, however, came with *The Coming American Fascism* (1936), in which he declared that capitalist expansion had ended with the frontier and that the U.S. government had little to offer but war and welfare spending. His ideology was similar to fascism in that it combined a one-party state with strident nationalism, continental autarky, and centralized economic controls that molded private ownership to public will—in short, a truly corporatist and organic society transcending localized interests. His politics, which lacked any racist dimension, centered on the twin poles of economic corporatism and rigid isolationism.

In February 1939, Dennis became coeditor of a mimeographed bulletin, the *Weekly Foreign Letter,* and in mid-March 1940 he became the sole author. Receiving $1,200 from the German embassy, the newsletter was far more strident than most other non-interventionist journals. Although circulation remained at only a few hundred, it reached certain leading anti-interventionists, many of whom were far more in the political mainstream than Dennis himself. His book *The Dynamics of War and Revolution* (1940) claimed that wars of conquest were inevitable, and envisioned a world divided into power zones dominated, respectively, by the United States, Japan, the Soviet Union, Germany, and Great Britain. In 1944 he was tried for sedition, an event covered in his book *A Trial on Trial: The Great Sedition Trial of 1944* (with Maximilian St. George, 1944), but within two years all charges were dropped. One of his celebrated contemporaries whom he attempted to influence was the world-famous aviator Charles Lindbergh, who was also well known for his sympathetic attitude toward Hitler.

Justus Doenecke

See Also: AUTARKY; CAPITALISM; CORPORATISM; ECONOMICS; HITLER, ADOLF; INTERVENTIONISM; LINDBERGH, CHARLES; ORGANICISM; RACISM; ROOSEVELT, PRESIDENT FRANKLIN DELANO; UNITED STATES, THE (PRE-1945); WAR

References

Doenecke, Justus D. 1972. "Lawrence Dennis: Revisionist of the Cold War." *Wisconsin Magazine of History* 55 (summer): 275–286.

———. 1999. "The Weekly Foreign Letter." Pp. 283–294 in *The Conservative Press in Twentieth-Century America*, edited by Ronald Lora and William Henry Longton. Westport, CT: Greenwood.

Wallace, Max. 2003. *The American Axis: Henry Ford, Charles Lindbergh, and the Rise of the Third Reich*. New York: St. Martin's Griffin.

DEPRESSION, THE GREAT: *See* WALL STREET CRASH, THE
DEUTSCHHEIT: See GERMANNESS

DEUTSCHLAND ERWACHE! ("GERMANY AWAKE!")

Nazi slogan much favored by Hitler, used as the title of a popular song. It sometimes occurred in combination with the slogan *Juda verrecke!* ("Perish Judah!"), and its thrust was that Germany needed to awake to the "Jewish menace" that was destroying it from within.

Cyprian Blamires

See Also: ANTI-SEMITISM; ECKART, JOHANN DIETRICH; GERMANNESS; HITLER, ADOLF; NAZISM

DICTATORSHIP

Often treated as synonymous with fascism, and in this respect it is similar to the word *authoritarianism.* But theorists of totalitarianism like Arendt recognized early on that this feature of fascist practice was far from unique. Dictatorships can exist in the context of many different creeds, and the interwar fascist dictatorships of Mussolini and Hitler were in a sense but the mirror image of that of Stalin. Many other communist leaders, most spectacularly Chairman Mao of China, have ruled dictatorially, and a number of South American countries have had a rich experience of this kind of government. The truly distinctive marks of fascism do not lie in the undoubtedly dictatorial nature of the regimes of

Hitler and Mussolini, nor in fascism's cult of the leader—also common in nonfascist dictatorships—but in its hypernationalist revolutionary zeal for a total renewal of societies believed to be mired in decadence. In the sphere of theory, a writer like Carl Schmitt could defend the idea that the preservation of social order requires that "dictatorial" powers be entrusted to a strong leader without accepting these core ideas of fascism.

Cyprian Blamires

See Also: INTRODUCTION; ARENDT, HANNAH; AUTHORITARIANISM; HITLER, ADOLF; LEADER CULT, THE; MILITARY DICTATORSHIP; MUSSOLINI, BENITO ANDREA; NATIONALISM; SCHMITT, CARL; STALIN, IOSIF VISSARIONOVICH; TOTALITARIANISM

References
Baehr, Peter, and Melvin Richter, eds. 2004. *Dictatorship in History and Theory: Bonapartism, Caesarism, and Totalitarianism*. Washington, DC: German Historical Institute.

Lee, S. 2000. *European Dictatorships, 1918–45*. London: Routledge.

Linz, J. 2000. *Totalitarian and Authoritarian Regimes*. London: Lynne Rienner.

DIEDERICHS, EUGEN (1867–1930)

German publisher, promoter of the Youth Movement, and reformer whose organicist notions of community made him receptive to right-conservative, prefascist influences. The cultural pessimism of Diederich's critique was directed against the driving forces of modern civil society: against rationalism and political liberalism—admittedly without his deriving an authoritarian theory of the state from it. Hence the authors promoted by the publishing house he founded in 1896 and the newspaper *Die Tat*, which he took over in 1912, included social democrats and socialists.

Susanne Pocai

See Also: AUTHORITARIANISM; COMMUNITY; CONSERVATISM; LIBERALISM; NAZISM; ORGANICISM; PROTOFASCISM; RATIONALISM; STATE, THE

References
Stark, Gary D. 1981. *Entrepreneurs of Ideology: Neoconservative Publishers in Germany: 1890–1933*. Chapel Hill: University of North Carolina Press.

DIKSMUIDE

Small Belgian town in which annual gatherings of Flemish nationalists have taken place for many years, for a time in the 1980s and 1990s boosted by attendance of neo-Nazis from other European countries. The so-called Yzerbedevaart was initially organized (1927) in commemoration of the Flemish soldiers who had been killed on the Yzer front during World War I. In the course of time it has become a gathering of several Flemish nationalist and far-right parties and organizations, including the Vlaams Blok. Along with the rally around the huge stone memorial, Yzertoren, that attracted up to 50,000 people in its golden age, there are marches by uniformed columns through the town, political meetings, and stalls selling nationalist paraphernalia.

Fabian Virchow

See Also: BELGIUM; NEO-NAZISM; POSTWAR FASCISM; VLAAMS BLOK; WORLD WAR I

References
Brink, Rinke van den. 1996. *L'internationale de la haine: Paroles d'extrême droit: Belgique, France, Italie.* Bruxelles: Pire.
Mudde, Cas. 2002. *The Ideology of the Extreme Right.* Manchester: Manchester University Press.

DINTER, ARTUR (1876–1948)

Völkisch religious writer who exercised an influence on Hitler. After completing studies in philosophy and science he became a schoolmaster (1905–1908), then a stage manager at different German theaters. In 1914 he did military service, and in 1916 he was badly wounded; in 1917 he published his *völkisch* work *Die Sunde wider das Blut (The Sin against Blood).* In 1919 he was one of the founders of the Völkisch Schutz- und Trutzbund, and after the banning of the NSDAP in 1924 he founded the Grossdeutschen Volksgemeinschaft in Thuringia. In April 1925 he became a member of the NSDAP (member no. 5) and Gauleiter of Thuringia (until 30 September 1927). In 1928 he became a member of the Reichsleitung of the NSDAP. Dinter was a very radical representative of *völkisch* religion and strove for the "restoration of the pure teach-

ing of the Savior" through the proclamation of a "properly" Germanic Christian creed, which was to free Christian teaching from "Jewishness." In 1927 he founded the Geistchristliche Religionsgemeinschaft and launched bitter attacks on the churches. That brought him into increasing conflict with Hitler, with whom he engaged in a power struggle that he lost; on 11 October 1928 he was thrown out of the NSDAP. His requests for readmission were rejected in 1933 and 1937, and in 1939 he was also ejected from the Reichsschrifttumskammer.

Markus Hattstein
(translated by Cyprian Blamires)

See Also: ANTI-SEMITISM; ARYANISM; GERMAN CHRISTIANS, THE; NAZISM; *VOLK, VÖLKISCH;* WAR VETERANS; WORLD WAR I

References
Steigmann-Gall, R. 2003. *The Holy Reich: Nazi Conceptions of Christianity, 1919–1945.* Cambridge: Cambridge University Press.

DISABILITY: *See* EUGENICS; EUTHANASIA; HEALTH

DISTRIBUTISM

Distributism (also known as distributionism or distributivism) is a political and economic theory offering a "third way" between the twin "materialistic" poles of capitalism and communism through the institution of a decentralized, pastoral economic system. Based on the medieval guild system, distributism eschewed socialist collectivism and industrial trade unionism in favor of traditional family values, individualism, self-sufficiency, ruralism, and private property, all within a microeconomic framework. Such an idyllic system of localized, craft-based communities is thus often seen by many as a panacea for the degeneration of Western civilization supposedly wrought by the advent of the Industrial Revolution and the rise of capitalism. Such ideas, though not of course inherently fascist, have, however, exerted a strong influence on those fascist ideologues seeking to exploit concerns about globalization and immigration. One of its more infamous proponents has been Nick Griffin, current leader of the British National Party. In the 1980s, Griffin was a leading activist in the National Front during its period of "revolutionary" ideological ferment. Grouped around the ideological fountainhead of *Nationalism Today,* Griffin and his cohorts invoked a plethora of marginal thinkers and traditions in an attempt to divine a radical "English" nationalism. In this context distributism served as the inspiration for wistful musings on the possibility of self-sufficient, "racially pure" settlements that Griffin, as a member of the International Third Position (ITP), actually attempted to put into practice in a rural enclave in France during the early 1990s.

The origins of distributism can be traced back to the Greek philosophers, though its most famous modern exponents were the Edwardian Catholic literary figures G. K. Chesterton (1874–1936) and Hilaire Belloc (1870–1953). Their ideas on the subject of the distribution of wealth and the sanctity of property found their fullest exposition in Belloc's *The Servile State* (1912) and *The Restoration of Property* (1930), and G. K. Chesterton's *The Outline of Sanity* (1926), as well as in the pages of *G. K.'s Weekly.* Both Chesterton and Belloc were voluble anti-Semites, and their hostility and ergo that of distributism toward the financial institutions of capitalism and "usury" have often prefaced the drift of its adherents toward crude anti-Semitic stereotypes born of the conspiratorial belief that Judaism and capitalism are synonymous. The distributist beliefs of the Chesterton-Belloc circle survived after World War II through newsletters, several of which dovetailed into the National Front, founded in 1967 by A. K. Chesterton, the second cousin of G. K. Chesterton, though distributism remained essentially dormant until revived in the 1980s. Its present-day advocates do, however, include Catholics and other supporters who have nothing to do with fascist doctrines.

Graham Macklin

See Also: ANTI-SEMITISM; BOLSHEVISM; BRITISH NATIONAL PARTY, THE; CAPITALISM; CHESTERTON, ARTHUR KENNETH; CONSPIRACY THEORIES; DECADENCE; ECONOMICS; FAMILY, THE; GLOBALIZATION; GREAT BRITAIN; GRIFFIN, NICHOLAS; IMMIGRATION; INDIVIDUALISM; MARXISM; MATERIALISM; NATIONAL FRONT (UK); NATIONALISM; RURALISM; SOCIALISM; THIRD POSITIONISM

References
Belloc, Hilaire. 1912. *The Servile State.* London: T. N. Foulis.
———. 1936. *The Restoration of Property.* New York: Sheed and Ward.
Chesterton, Gilbert Keith. 1926. *The Outline of Sanity.* London: Methuen.
English Nationalist Movement. 1995. *Distributism: A Summary of Revolutionary Nationalist Economics.* London: Rising.

DIVORCE: *See* FAMILY, THE; SEXUALITY

DMOWSKI, ROMAN (1864–1939)

Chief ideologue and leader of the Polish nationalist movement known as Endecja (National Democracy), which emerged in the late nineteenth century. Endecja subscribed to an increasingly exclusivist ethnic definition of Polish identity, marked by a strong degree of anti-Semitism. Dmowski tried to emulate Italian Fascism by setting up the extraparliamentary Greater Poland Camp (Oboz Wielkiej Polski; OWP) in 1926. The OWP was banned by the authorities between 1932 and 1933.

Rafal Pankowski

See Also: ANTI-SEMITISM; FASCIST PARTY, THE; ITALY; MUSSOLINI, BENITO ANDREA; NATIONALISM; PIASECKI, BOLESLAW; PILSUDSKI, MARSHAL JOZEF; POLAND

References
Polonsky, Antony. 1984. "Roman Dmowski and Italian Fascism." Pp. 130–146 in *Ideas into Politics: Aspects of European History 1880–1950,* edited by Roger Bullen, Hartmut Pogge von Strandtmann, and Antony Polonsky. London: Croom Helm.

DOCTORS: *See* HEALTH; MEDICINE

DOENITZ, ADMIRAL KARL (1891–1980)

Named by Hitler as his successor in the last days of World War II, he held the position of Fuehrer of the Reich for twenty-three days in May 1945. Born in Grünau bei Berlin, Doenitz served in the submarine fleet in the navy during World War I, from 1916 to 1918. He stood out among high officers in the navy for his enthusiastic adherence to National Socialism and in

1939 was appointed by Hitler to head the U-boat service. He developed the tactics used by U-boats in the war on Allied shipping and in 1943 became supreme commander of the navy. After Hitler named him as his successor, Doenitz set up a government in Schleswig-Holstein but was captured by the British on 23 May 1945. At the Nuremberg Trials he was sentenced to ten years' imprisonment and was released in 1956.

Cyprian Blamires

See Also: HITLER, ADOLF; NAZISM; NUREMBERG TRIALS, THE; WAR VETERANS; WORLD WAR I; WORLD WAR II

Reference
Padfield, P. 1984. *Doenitz: The Last Fuehrer.* London: Gollancz.

DOLCHSTOSS, THE: *See* NOVEMBER CRIMINALS, THE

DOLLFUSS, ENGELBERT (1892–1934)

Chancellor of Austria from 1932 to 1934. A Christian Social Party member, Dollfuss earned a reputation as a rural reformer in the Peasants' League and Lower Austrian Chamber of Agriculture, and as minister of agriculture and forestry. As chancellor he allied with Benito Mussolini and the fascist Heimwehr in Austria, attempting to steer the country on a course between Nazism and socialism under the aegis of an authoritarian one-party state under the Fatherland Front. That precarious balancing act ended with his assassination in a failed putsch carried out by the Austrian Nazi Party on 25 July 1934.

Laura Gellott

See Also: AUSTRIA; CLERICO-FASCISM; HEIMWEHR, THE; MUSSOLINI, BENITO ANDREA; NAZISM; SCHUSCHNIGG, KURT VON

References
Bischof, G., A. Pelinka, and A. Lassner, eds. 2003. *The Dollfuss/Schuschnigg Era in Austria: A Reassessment.* New Brunswick, NJ: Transaction.
Brook-Shepard, G. 1961. *Dollfuss.* London: Macmillan.

DONALDSON, IAN STUART: *See* SKINHEAD FASCISM; SKREWDRIVER
***DOPOLAVORO:* *See* LEISURE**

DORGERES, HENRY (1897–1985)

French peasant activist and journalist, for a time in the 1930s (1933–1934) avowedly fascist. As editor of farmers' weeklies in Brittany, Dorgères (born Henri D'Halluin) gained a following by opposing social security (1929). His Défense paysanne movement mobilized depression-stricken farmers, mostly in northwestern France. Its *Chemises vertes* ("Greenshirts") took action against farm foreclosures and striking farm workers. Dorgères proclaimed a nationalist, corporatist, ruralist, antiparliamentarian, and anti-Semitic worldview. For serving as propagandist for Vichy's Peasant Corporation, Dorgères lost his civic rights (1946), a sentence commuted for purported resistance activities. Elected to parliament as a Poujadist (1956–1958), he later campaigned for a French Algeria.

Robert O. Paxton

See Also: ANTI-SEMITISM; CORPORATISM; FARMERS; FRANCE; NATIONALISM; PARLIAMENTARISM; POUJADE, PIERRE MARIE RAYMOND; RURALISM; VICHY

Reference
Paxton, Robert O. 1997. *French Peasant Fascism.* New York: Oxford.

DORIOT, JACQUES (1898–1945)

Interwar leader of the "left-wing fascist" Parti Populaire Français (PPF) and a former high-ranking member of the French Communist Party (PCF), who had been seen by some as the next PCF leader. That prospect was brought to an end by his agitation for a united front against fascism, which saw him expelled from the party. In 1936, Doriot formed the PPF, which called for reform of the republic, notably through a strengthening of executive power and the introduction of some form of corporatism. The predominant ideological element, however, was anticommunism. The party was the largest extreme-right mass party of the interwar period (it claimed to have 300,000 members in 1938, though at least one scholar has doubted that it ever exceeded 50,000 to 60,000 members, with around 15,000 active militants). Initially supportive of Pétain during the war and appointed to the National Council in Vichy, Doriot soon became a partisan of ultracollaboration. Doriot was the first leader to propose the Légion des Volontaires Français (LVF), and he went himself to fight on the Eastern Front during the war.

Steve Bastow

See Also: CORPORATISM; FARMERS; FRANCE; FRENCH REVO-
   LUTION, THE; MARXISM; PETAIN, MARSHAL HENRI
   PHILIPPE; SOCIALISM; VICHY

References
Soucy, R. 1995. *French Fascism: The Second Wave, 1933–1939.*
   New Haven: Yale University Press.
Verdès-Leroux, Jeannine. 2000. "The Intellectual Extreme
   Right in the 1930s." Pp. 119–132 in *The Development of the
   Radical Right in France,* edited by E. Arnold. London:
   Macmillan.

DRANG NACH OSTEN ("DRIVE TO THE EAST"), THE

Hitler's expression for the Reich policy of conquering Slav territories to the East of Germany in order to satisfy Germany's supposed need for more *Lebensraum*—"living space." In *Mein Kampf,* whose fourteenth chapter is dedicated to "Eastward orientation," Hitler argued that an increase in her living space was essential if Germany were to rise to the status of world power; the only place where "new territories" could be found was in Russia, so *Ostpolitik* ("Eastern policy") actually meant "the acquisition of the necessary soil for the German people." This acquisition of territory in the East, which Hitler saw as his "historic mission," along with the annihilation of the Jews, formed a favorite theme of his speeches and monologues. He associated a racist ideology of the "inferiority" of the Slavs with the economic concept of a ruthless exploitation of the resources of Eastern Europe. The peoples of the East must be set to work: "Slavdom is a born mass of slaves

that cry for a master"; since the Slavs "were not destined to a life of their own," they must be "Germanized." In the context of his "European territorial ordering," the brutal achievement of which he entrusted to Himmler and the SS in 1942, Hitler planned the settlement of 100 million persons of German origin in the East. According to the plans made by Hitler and Himmler, the "persons of German origin" settling in Russia were to "organize" the native Slav populace into an army of slaves and servants.

Markus Hattstein
(translated by Cyprian Blamires)

See Also: ANTI-SEMITISM; BARBAROSSA, OPERATION;
   HITLER, ADOLF; HOLOCAUST, THE; *LEBENSRAUM; MEIN
   KAMPF;* NAZISM; SLAVS, THE (AND GERMANY); SOVIET
   UNION, THE; SS, THE; WORLD WAR II

References
Leitz, C. 2004. *Nazi Foreign Policy, 1933–1941: The Road to
   Global War.* London: Routledge.
Meyer, Henry Cord. 1996. *Drang nach osten: Fortunes of a
   Slogan-concept in German-Slavic Relations, 1849–1990.*
   Berne: Peter Lang.

DRESDEN: *See* **COVENTRY**

DREXLER, ANTON (1884–1942)

Founder of a nationalist German workers' party (1918) known as the Committee of Independent Workmen, which he merged with a larger one called the Political Workers' Circle in 1919 to form the Deutsche Arbeiterpartei (German Workers' Party; DAP); Adolf Hitler became member no. 7 of this party in 1919. Drexler was a locksmith and toolmaker from Munich; he regarded himself as a champion of the workers but was hostile to the Marxism of the trade unions. Drexler was a believer in conspiracy theories that scapegoated Jews, capitalists, and Freemasons as the enemies of simple German working folk. Hitler soon became chairman of the DAP, which he merged into the NSDAP, with the uninspiring and gentle Drexler sidelined as honorary chairman. Drexler was sent to prison after the Munich Beerhall putsch. He left the NSDAP in 1923 and was elected to the Bavarian Parliament the following year. He took no interest in Nazism and distanced himself from Hitler from then on.

Cyprian Blamires

See Also: ANTI-SEMITISM; CAPITALISM; CONSPIRACY THEORIES; FREEMASONRY/FREEMASONS, THE; HITLER, ADOLF; MARXISM; MUNICH PUTSCH, THE; NATIONALISM; NAZISM; PROTO-FASCISM

References
Bessel, R. 1993. *Germany after the First World War.* Oxford: Clarendon.
Kershaw, Ian. *Hitler, 1889–1936: Hubris.* London: Allen Lane.

DREYFUS CASE, THE

A seminal event in the history of modern European anti-Semitism and of the modern Right in France. A (false) accusation of treachery made against a Jewish officer in the French army focused the hostility of defenders of a traditional image of Catholic, monarchical France on a perceived trend toward a Jewish "takeover" of the nation. Captain Alfred Dreyfus (1859–1935) was accused of high treason in October 1894; shortly afterward he was condemned to life imprisonment on the basis of forged evidence and deported to Devil's Island in French Guyana. He was accused of having betrayed military secrets to Germany. Doubts about the guilt of Dreyfus and about the fairness of the procedure against him, and debates about a reopening of the case, split French society down the middle into pro- and contra-Dreyfus parties. The pro-Dreyfus faction consisted of the defenders of the republic founded on the rule of law, while the anti-Dreyfusards represented monarchist and anti-Semitic positions. In actual fact, the guilty party was the French major Charles Ferdinand Walsin-Esterhazy, who was spying for the Germans for financial reasons, but he was protected by the French general staff, who were convinced of Dreyfus's guilt; Walsin-Esterhazy was acquitted before a court-martial at the beginning of 1898 on the basis of an expert graphological report. In reaction to this acquittal, the writer Emile Zola published his famous open letter to the French president entitled *J'accuse,* in which he attacked the court-martial, the War Ministry, and the general staff.

Even though it was known that the evidence against Dreyfus was fabricated, an appeal in 1899 led to a sec-

ond conviction, to ten years' imprisonment. Shortly afterward, however, Dreyfus was pardoned by the French president, though without being completely rehabilitated. His rehabilitation and his return to military service did not take place until the quashing of the appeal verdict in 1906. The years of the Dreyfus case featured numerous dramatic revelations and surprising turns of events, regime crises, resignations of ministers, and putsch attempts that kept the French public agog. Demonstrations and duels were the order of the day. The Dreyfus Affair led indirectly to a reform of the French army and the eventual separation of church and state in that country. At the height of the drama of the court case, French anti-Semites formed into various groupings, such as the French Anti-Semitic League, and denunciation of the Jews as aliens and "a race destructive of the nation" were often combined with a critique of the democratic system in France. There were repeated anti-Jewish acts of violence and anti-Semitic demonstrations, both in Paris and in the provinces.

The Dreyfus Affair also impacted on the development of Zionism. Theodor Herzl was the Paris correspondent of the Vienna newspaper *Neue Freie Presse* at the time of the trial in December 1894. The sight of the open displays of hatred against the Jews at this time fueled his conviction that the 'Jewish question' could only be resolved by the creation of a Jewish state. Two years later he published his *Der Judenstaat. Versuch einer modernen Lösung der Judenfrage,* which was the founding manifesto of the Zionist movement.

Michael Schäbitz (translated by Cyprian Blamires)

See Also: ACTION FRANÇAISE; ANTI-SEMITISM; DEMOCRACY; DRUMONT, EDOUARD ADOLPHE; FRANCE; MAURRAS, CHARLES; PROTO-FASCISM; ZIONISM

References
Bredin, Jean-Denis. 1987. *The Affair: The Case of Alfred Dreyfus.* London: Sidgwick and Jackson.
Chapman, G. 1972. *The Dreyfus Trials.* London: Batsford.
Snyder, L. L. 1972. *The Dreyfus Case: A Documentary History.* New Brunswick, NJ: Rutgers University Press.

DRIEU LA ROCHELLE, PIERRE (1893–1945)

French novelist and political essayist who became a key figure in French literary fascism. His concern with the need to overcome the decadence of modern life underpinned his adoption of a variety of doctrinal views, but from 1934 on, he declared himself a fascist and published his *Socialisme fasciste.* He was an active member of Doriot's PPF from 1936 to 1938, contributing to the party newspaper, *L'Emancipation Nationale.* During that period he also contributed to *Je Suis Partout.* He left the PPF in November 1938 over its support for the Munich Agreement, but he remained a fascist. In 1942 he rejoined the PPF, and in 1943–1944 he edited Lucien Combelle's *La Révolution Nationale.* He committed suicide on 15 March 1945.

Steve Bastow

See Also: DECADENCE; DORIOT, JACQUES; EUROFASCISM; EUROPE; FRANCE; MUNICH PACT, THE; SOCIALISM

References
Carroll, D. 1995. *French Literary Fascism.* Princeton: Princeton University Press.
Soucy, Robert. 1979. *Fascist Intellectual: Drieu La Rochelle.* Berkeley: University of California Press.

DRUMONT, EDOUARD ADOLPHE (1844–1917)

Leading figure of nineteenth-century French anti-Semitism, who wrote a range of books and pamphlets, the most notable of which was the raging success *La France juive* (1886), which was reprinted more than two hundred times. Drumont drew on both religious anti-Semitism and the anti-Semitism propagated in socialist circles to produce a new nationalistic and populist anti-Semitic synthesis going beyond a purely religious dimension. Following in the footsteps of Alfonse Toussenel and his *Les Juifs rois de l'époque: Histoire de la féodalité financière,* first published in 1840, Drumont tied the Jews in to the activities of big capital, which rode roughshod over small business interests, and propounded a racial nationalism that excluded Jewishness from the characteristics of Frenchness. In the stock language of polemicists against financial speculators, as already employed by Toussenel, he claimed that Jewish fortunes were not an embodiment of the results of hard work but the symbols of the power of a dominant race. Carroll argues that the book, "provided an enormous literary storehouse of figures and stories for others to refer to, col-

lecting and embellishing on the 'historical evidence' linking the Jew to . . . the material destruction and spiritual decadence of France" (Carroll 1995, 174) in all aspects of French social, economic, political, and religious life. "Everything comes from the Jew," argued Drumont, and "everything returns to the Jew" (Drumont, *La France juive,* cited in Girardet 1983, 143). The Jew was presented as a parasite—because he was in essence, by nature, irremediably non-French and not assimilable to Frenchness—that was invading the healthy body that was France. The key to the revival of French grandeur was the elimination of the Jew, who must be dealt with just like any other parasitical micro-organism. Such ideas were reproduced in other works by Drumont, such as *Le testament d'un anti-sémite* (1891) and *La fin d'un monde,* and in the daily paper he produced from April 1892, *La libre parole,* for which Girardet claims print runs of 200,000 within months of first publication. Drumont's publications and political activities formed, claims Sternhell, the conceptual framework of French anti-Semitism, running from the formation of the Ligue national antisémitique française of 1889 (co-founded by Drumont with the slogan "France for the French") through to World War I, and exerted a decisive influence upon the work of such figures as Barrès and Maurras.

Steve Bastow

See Also: ACTION FRANÇAISE; ANTI-SEMITISM; BARRES, MAURICE; DECADENCE; DREYFUS CASE, THE; FRANCE; MAURRAS, CHARLES; NATIONALISM; PROTO-FASCISM; RACIAL DOCTRINE

References
Busi, F. 1986. *Drumont: The Pope of Anti-Semitism.* Lanham, MD: University Press of America.
Carroll, D. 1995. *French Literary Fascism.* Princeton: Princeton University Press.
Girardet, R. 1983. *Le nationalisme français. Anthologie 1870–1914.* Paris: Editions du Seuil.
Sternhell, Z. 1978. *Le Droit révolutionaire. Les origines françaises du fascisme.* Paris: Editions du Seuil.
Wilson, Stephen. 1982. *Ideology and Experience: Anti-Semitism in France at the Time of the Dreyfus Affair.* Oxford: Littman Library of Jewish Civilization.
Winock, Michel. *Nationalism, Anti-semitism, and Fascism in France.* Trans. Jane Marie Todd. Stanford: Stanford University Press.

DUCE, THE: *See* MUSSOLINI, BENITO ANDREA AMILCARE

DUGIN, ALEKSANDR GEL'EVICH (born 1962)

Russia's most prolific propagator of "neo-Eurasianism." Inspired by, among others, the "Conservative Revolution" and the New Right, neo-Eurasians believe in an age-old conflict between individualistic Atlanticist sea powers and traditionalistic Eurasian land powers. A widely read adept of mysticism, Dugin was also a co-founder of the National Bolshevik Party in 1994 and the Eurasia Party in March 2002. However, his primary role has been that of a political theorist and head of the productive publishing house Arktogeya (Northern Land).

Andreas Umland

See Also: EUROPEAN NEW RIGHT, THE; INDIVIDUALISM; MYSTICISM; NATIONAL BOLSHEVISM; NATIONALISM; POSTWAR FASCISM; RUSSIA

Reference
Ingram, Alan. 2001. "Alexander Dugin: Geopolitics and Neo-Fascism in Post-Soviet Russia." *Political Geography* 20, no. 8: 1029–1051.

DÜHRING, (KARL) EUGEN (1833–1921)

Well-known representative of positivism in Wilhelmine, Germany and prophet of anti-Semitism. From 1864 to 1877 Dühring was lecturer in philosophy and national economy at Berlin University. His ideas were the object of a celebrated critique by Friedrich Engels. In his *Die Judenfrage als Racen-, Sitten- und Culturfrage* of November 1880, he preached a radical racial anti-Semitism, accusing the Jews of exploiting and damaging the peoples among whom they lived, and tracing this back to an unalterable "race character." Dühring called for the revocation of the emancipation of the Jews. He also discussed social isolation, internment, and even deportation as possible "solutions" for the "Jewish question," which he claimed was a "life-or-death matter for modern peoples."

Michael Schäbitz
(translated by Cyprian Blamires)

See Also: ANTI-SEMITISM; NAZISM; NIETZSCHE, FRIEDRICH; PROTO-FASCISM; RACIAL DOCTRINE

References
Dühring, Eugen. 1997. *Eugen Dühring on the Jews.* Uckfield: Historical Review.
Engels, Friedrich. 1984. *Anti-Dühring: Herr Eugen Dühring's Revolution in Science.* Chicago: Charles H. Kerr.

DUKE, DAVID (born 1950)

Well-known U.S. white supremacist and anti-Semitic and racial nationalist. He spread his ideas with the help of a smooth photogenic public image and coded rhetoric that stressed "White Rights." Beginning in high school, Duke moved through various Ku Klux Klan, neo-Nazi, and racist organizations, eventually becoming a Louisiana Ku Klux Klan leader, or "Grand Wizard." Duke later attempted to sanitize his views, and in 1979 he established the National Association for the Advancement of White People. In 1989 he was elected as a Republican to the Louisiana House of Representatives. Duke lost a 1991 governor's race, but garnered 55 percent of the white votes.

Chip Berlet

See Also: ANTI-SEMITISM; KU KLUX KLAN; NEO-NAZISM; RACISM; UNITED STATES, THE (POSTWAR); WHITE SUPREMACISM

References
Bridges, Tyler. 1994. *The Rise of David Duke.* Jackson: University Press of Mississippi.
Duke, David. 1998. *My Awakening: A Path to Racial Understanding.* Covington, LA: Free Speech.
Rose, Douglas, ed. 1992. *The Emergence of David Duke and the Politics of Race.* Chapel Hill: University of North Carolina Press.
Zatarain, Michael. 1990. *David Duke: Evolution of a Klansman.* Gretna, LA: Pelican.

DUNKIRK

Port in northern France from which nearly 340,000 members of the British Expeditionary Force, forced back to the Atlantic Coast by the advance of a German force 750,000 strong, were dramatically rescued—

against all expectations—by a huge combined flotilla of British naval vessels and private craft of every description between 31 May and 4 June 1940. The evacuation of the troops from the beaches took place under aerial assault from the Luftwaffe and the event gave rise to the expression "the Dunkirk spirit," to denote courageous resolve in the teeth of enormous odds—particularly as shown by volunteers working together. It has become part of the mythology of resistance to fascism in the English-speaking world.

Cyprian Blamires

See Also: ANTIFASCISM; BLITZKRIEG; LUFTWAFFE, THE; WORLD WAR II

Reference
Lord, Walter. 1998. *The Miracle of Dunkirk.* Ware: Wordsworth.

ECKART, JOHANN DIETRICH (1868–1923)

German nationalist, anti-Semitic theorist, influential mentor of Adolf Hitler, financier, and editor of the *Völkischer Beobachter.* From 1918, Eckart published *Auf Gut Deutsch,* a journal fostering radical nationalism. From 1919, he brought the fledgling Deutsche Arbeiterpartei (German Workers' Party; DAP) funding and high-level introductions for Hitler. Eckart and Hitler devised the first DAP program, combining nationalist, anticapitalist, and anti-Semitic appeals. From 1920, Eckart financed and then later edited the *Völkischer Beobachter,* promoting the Fuehrer cult. His poem "Feuerjo!" (1921), ending with *"Deutschland, erwache!"*, became the famous Nazi Party *Sturmlied;* the slogan adorning the marching banners at the Nuremberg rallies. Eckart's anti-Semitism was rooted in a gnostic, Manichaean type of mysticism. He and Hitler spent hours discussing art, philosophy, and the role of the Jews in world history, as recorded in Eckart's *Der Bolschewismus von Moses bis Lenin* (1924). In a unique tribute, Hitler openly acknowledged Eckart's influence in his dedication of *Mein Kampf* and other memorials in the Nazi Party headquarters in Munich. Eckart has been called "the spiritual father of National Socialism."

Nicholas Goodrick-Clarke

See Also: ANTI-SEMITISM; ART; CAPITALISM; *DEUTSCHLAND ERWACHE!;* DREXLER, ANTON; HITLER, ADOLF; LEADER CULT, THE; *MEIN KAMPF;* MYSTICISM; NATIONALISM; NAZISM; LEADER CULT, THE; PRESS, THE

References

Engelman, Ralph Max. 1971. "Dietrich Eckart and the Genesis of Nazism." Ph.D. dissertation, Washington University, St. Louis.

Lane, Barbara Miller, and Leila J. Rupp. 1978. *Nazi Ideology before 1933.* Manchester: Manchester University Press.

ECKHART, "MEISTER" JOHANN (1260–1327)

One of the most celebrated mystical writers of the later Middle Ages, promoted by some Nazi ideologues as a medieval pioneer of a uniquely German spiritual way. Eckhart, who joined the Dominican Order at a young age, studied in Paris and Cologne and later taught in Paris. His attempts to put mystical experience into words gave to some an impression of heterodoxy, and he was under investigation by the ecclesiastical authorities when he died. After his death, the pope condemned twenty-eight of his propositions. Alfred Rosenberg exploited Eckhart for *völkisch*-racist thought, blithely ripping quotations from the thinker out of context and transforming him into "a "Germanic freedom-fighter" and "theoretician of blood." He claimed that Eckhart's "little spark of the soul" (in Eckhart, the "uncreated in the soul") was equivalent to "the concept of Nordic honor and freedom." Eckhart, "the greatest apostle of the Nordic west," was thus the "born-again Germanic man"; by proclaiming the "equivalence of the soul to God," he became the forerunner of a Germanic will to freedom against enslavement to the Roman Church. According to Rosenberg, Eckhart emphasized "greatness of soul" against "the Jewish idea of man as the servant of God" and the "enslavement of man's soul" inherent in the doctrine of the ecclesial means of grace: "Thus Eckhart showed himself to be the creator of a new religion which had freed itself from Jewish-oriental and Roman influence." Against the "Roman-Jesuit tradition," Eckhart stressed the "godlikeness of the human soul" and thus propagated "the Nordic thought of self-realization." By picking and choosing quotations from Eckhart's sermons, Rosenberg managed to turn him into a pioneer campaigner for racial purity and race consciousness; in Eckhart was found "the myth and religion of the blood." "[In] Meister Eckhart the Nordic soul came fully to consciousness of itself for the first time." This blatant attempt to promote a celebrated Catholic mystic as a forefather of Nazism provoked polemical replies from both Protestant and Catholic theologians. Chief among those who sought to give a more balanced view of Eckhart were Alois Dempf (1934), Käte Oltmann (1935), Heinrich Bornkamm (1936), and Heinrich Ebeling (1941), who put his thought back into the context of late medieval mysticism.

Markus Hattstein
(translated by Cyprian Blamires)

See Also: ANTI-SEMITISM; CATHOLIC CHURCH, THE; CHRISTIANITY; GERMAN CHRISTIANS, THE; GERMANNESS (*DEUTSCHHEIT*); JESUITS, THE; LUTHER, MARTIN; MYSTICISM; NAZISM; NORDIC SOUL, THE; RACIAL DOCTRINE; ROSENBERG, ALFRED; THEOLOGY; *VOLK, VÖLKISCH*

References

Cecil, Robert. 1972. *Myth of the Master Race: Alfred Rosenberg and Nazi Ideology.* London: Batsford.
Clark, J. M. 1949. *The Great German Mystics: Eckhart, Tauler and Suso.* Oxford: Blackwell.
Whisker, James B. 1990. *The Philosophy of Alfred Rosenberg.* Newport Beach, CA: Noontide.
Woods, R. 1990. *Eckhart's Way.* Collegeville, MN: Liturgical Press.

ECOFASCISM: See ECOLOGY

ECOLOGY

Although usually associated with newer forms of left-wing politics and social movements, ecological thought also has a distinctive right-wing variant that intersects with fascism and neofascism. Like many of their left-wing counterparts, political ecologists of the extreme Right suggest that global capitalism and a culture of consumerism have led to an environmental crisis characterized by massive destruction of the natural world. Similarly, too, both argue that the roots of this environmental crisis are to be found in the ways in which modern humans (especially those in the West) conceptualize their place in nature and carry out practices based on such understandings. Finally, both draw upon concepts and models of modern ecological science to frame their political-ecological worldview and to argue for particular solutions. Yet the left- and right-wing varieties of ecological thought part ways dramatically over the theoretical conclusions that can be drawn from these assumptions, as well as the practical solutions needed to halt the crisis.

According to what can be called "right-wing ecology," different human cultures are shaped by unique geographic and environmental features. If we take seriously the claim—one offered by most political ecologists—that human beings should not be considered "above" nature but rather embedded within it (humans being "plain members of the biotic community" in the U.S. environmentalist Aldo Leopold's famous phrase), then a true ecological politics, according to the radical right-wing view, must strive to protect natural diversity in all its dimensions, both the natural diversity of the nonhuman world and the natural diversity of human cultures. Proponents of right-wing ecology therefore argue that, just as a consistent environmentalism defends the unique integrity of a particular ecosystem by excluding non-native and foreign species, so too should it protect cultural diversity by keeping each culture pure through the exclusion of the alien or the foreign. A true and "deep" political ecology must safeguard the plants, animals, and human cultures distinctive to a particular ecosystem or region from the forces of global capitalism, cultural homogenization, and social and physical eradication.

Although proponents of a right-wing ecology can be found in many movements and parties of the extreme Right today, its most prominent supporters and articulate spokesmen are German; its roots can be found in the development of a "New Right" in the late 1970s. Inspired by the French Nouvelle Droite, the German New Right sought to chart a new organizational and ideological course after declining political fortunes led to its fragmentation by the early 1970s. Arguing along Gramscian grounds that its task was to achieve "cultural hegemony," Green representatives of the New Right sought to marry a rediscovered concern for nature to the traditional ultranationalism and racism of the extreme Right. Among their theoretical innovations was the notion of "ethno-pluralism," the doctrine that although no ethnic group or nation can be considered superior to another, differences between cultures, traditions, or ways of life are intractable and should be "respected."

In the late 1970s activists of the New Right joined the environmental and antinuclear movements and even took over some local Green Party organizations—exercising some influence both on more traditional conservatives within the environmental movements and on new organizations of the extreme Right—before they were expelled or left voluntarily. To the former belonged such figures as the German environmental activist, former conservative MP, and best-selling author Herbert Gruhl, who founded two organizations after he left the Greens in 1981 (the Ecological-Democratic Party and The Independent Ecologists of Germany) that soon came to articulate right-wing ecological ideas. To the latter belonged the Republikaner, a new party of the extreme Right that performed well in a series of European and state elections in the 1990s before disappearing into electoral obscurity.

Of course, in many ways modern right-wing ecology simply reflects an updated and reconstituted right-wing nature discourse that first emerged in late nineteenth- and early twentieth-century Germany and that found institutional representation in the conservative wing of the Heimat ("homeland protection") movement. Inspired by the blending of environmental protection policies with right-wing politics characteristic of the founder of the science of ecology, Ernst Haeckel, successive chairmen of the German Federation for the Protection of the Homeland (DBH), the main Heimat organization—that is, Ernst Rudorff, Paul Schultze-Naumburg, and Werner Lindner—all argued that human "rootedness" in a particular landscape and cultural-national tradition is part and parcel of a consistent *Umweltschutz* ("protection of the environment"). Therefore, environmental protection should seek to protect not only ecosystems in all their particularity from alien species and botanical homogeneity but also cultures, nations, and "peoples" from

cross-cultural pollution. The extreme nationalist and *völkisch* ideology of the mainstream of the Heimat movement also found expression among the Nazis—for example, with Nazi agricultural minister Richard Walther Darré and with the director of Prussia's state conservation agency, Walter Schoenichen. Schoenichen is particularly interesting in that, like many contemporary Greens, he suggested that simply tinkering with the industrial system—a moderate "environmentalism," in other words—is an insufficient response to environmental challenges. Instead, he argued that what was needed was no less than a new environmental theory and practice that would be informed by the idea that nature should be preserved in all of its *Eigenart* ("individuality")—including, of course, individual cultures and "peoples"—from a homogenizing "one-world" culture. Laws limiting industrial development, protecting wetlands, promoting reforestation, outlawing cruelty to animals and hunting, and creating nature reserves—all of which were passed under the Nazi regime—seemed to Schoenichen to herald a new age of living in accord with "nature," rather than against it.

Jonathan Olsen

See Also: ANIMALS; CAPITALISM; CULTURE; DARRÉ, RICHARD WALTHER; ECONOMICS; EUROPEAN NEW RIGHT, THE; GERMANY; GLOBALIZATION; GRAMSCI, ANTONIO; NATIONALISM; NATURE; NAZISM; POSTWAR FASCISM; ROOTLESSNESS; SOCIAL DARWINISM; *VOLK, VÖLKISCH*

References

Gasman, Daniel. 1971. *The Scientific Origins of National Socialism: Social Darwinism in Ernst Haeckel and the German Monist League.* New York: American Elsevier.

Olsen, Jonathan. 1999. *Nature and Nationalism: Right-Wing Ecology and the Politics of Identity in Contemporary Germany.* New York: St.Martin's/Palgrave.

Statham, Alison. 1997. "Ecology and the German Right." Pp. 125–138 in *Green Thought in German Culture: Historical and Contemporary Perspectives,* edited by Colin Riordan. Cardiff: University of Wales Press.

ECONOMICS

Confronted with the bourgeois "brandishing his contracts and his statistics, 2 + 2 makes . . . NOUGHT, the fascist barbarian replies, smashing his face in" (Sternhell 1979, 357). As these words of Georges Valois, leader of Le Faisceau (French fascist movement of the 1920s), make clear, interwar fascism had little time or respect for "economics." Fascists denied that what happened in the economy was the motor of historical and social change; they wanted their "revolution" to be understood not as a fundamental change in socioeconomic relations but rather as a "spiritual" revolution, a transformation of consciousness, a moral regeneration of individuals in a collective, national context. Their antibourgeois rhetoric was directed primarily not at middle-class wealth or the middle class as a socioeconomic category but at the "bourgeois" mentality that was the outcome of people devoting their energies exclusively to the acquisition and enjoyment of material wealth—an outlook, presumably, to be found in all levels of society. They wanted to blow away what they condemned as the rational, calculating, materialistic, cautious, sedentary, and selfishly individualistic values of "bourgeois" society and create in their place a new "civilization" of the "new fascist man"—vital, virile, self-sacrificing, living heroically and dangerously. Fascism's ideological asceticism and contempt for the easy life is so out of tune with the spread of consumerism and material prosperity based on rapid economic growth and development in post–World War II Europe that it may provide one of the reasons for the relative marginalization of fascist movements and ideas since 1945.

But if fascist ideology gave no space conceptually to "economics," interwar fascist movements and regimes had a clear sense of the place and function of the economy, which they derived from their core political ideas, hypernationalism, and the "totalitarian" state as the embodiment and instrument of the nation and national power. Put simply, the job of the economy and of economic policy in a fascist polity was to provide the economic resources and muscle for a strong nation. The fascist view of the "primacy of politics" over economics, of the state driving the economy, not the economy the state, was exemplified by Hitler in his memorandum launching the so-called Four Year Plan for the economy in 1936. He first observed that politics in Germany meant only one thing, "the securing of all the spiritual and other prerequisites for the self-assertion of our nation," and then went on to state that "finance and the economy, economic leaders and theories, . . . all owe unqualified service in this struggle for the self-assertion of our nation" (Noakes and Pridham 2000, 89).

Fascism's economic goals were, then, defined by its nationalism, and the ultimate aim was autarky or national economic self-sufficiency. Achieving autarky was bound to involve economic protectionism and an arti-

ficial distortion of the normal patterns of international trade and of capitalist economies, requiring, in turn, that essential lever of fascist "economics," state control and regulation of the national economy. The target of autarky assumed that international relations were perpetually conflictual and competitive, and that the nation needed to be economically independent if it were to survive and progress in a hostile international environment. Both the Italian Fascist and the German Nazi regimes made autarky official policy and saw its realization as an essential preparation for expansionist wars. Autarky was, and is, probably unrealizable for any country—even for interwar Germany, and certainly for interwar Italy, which did not have sufficient indigenous sources of essential energy supplies and raw materials to provide the economic capacity for Great Power politics. As a result, autarky became an end as well as a means for both fascist regimes, a justification for and the intended outcome of wars of imperialist expansion.

Autarky, and the economic protectionism that makes it possible, remained the economic goal of post-1945 neofascist movements, though the goal was framed in a way adapted to wartime and postwar global realities and circumstances. Neofascism's anti-immigration stance is, in part, projected as the defense of the jobs and livelihood of "national" workers. Although some European neofascist movements initially opposed the European Union on autarkic economic grounds, many now couch autarky in European rather than national terms, rephrasing the rhetoric and justifications of the wartime Nazi New Order in conquered and occupied Europe, which envisaged a continental European autarkic zone set against other rival continental blocs. Today's post–Cold War European neofascists oppose globalization and the global economic and cultural hegemony of the United States in the name of a "multiethnic" world and a European "nation," much as their predecessors of the Cold War period saw "Europe" as a "Third Force" in a bipolar world dominated by the U.S. and Soviet "empires."

This fascist "Third Force" stance in international politics was premised on an analogous "Third Way" ideological alignment of domestic politics. Interwar, wartime, and post-1945 fascist movements rejected (on the grounds of their "corrosive materialism") the capitalist and communist ideologies and political and economic systems embodied in the United States and the USSR. They saw themselves as neither capitalist nor communist, claiming instead to offer a solution to the problems of managing modern "mass" societies that lay between capitalism and communism. The domestic "Third Way" was usually "corporatist" or "national syndicalist," or propounded of some related form of economic regulation. Corporatism was, and is, a body of ideas that envisages a socioeconomic and political system based on the representation of people according to their economic and productive function in society, in sectoral organizations (corporations) that harmonize the interests of workers, managers, and the state. A corporately organized economy, based as it is on collaboration between classes and the various groups involved in the productive process, would put an end to counterproductive class conflict and help to maximize national economic production. The high degree of state control of the corporations, which were really seen as a means of state control of the economy rather than as self-administering alliances of "producers," was what distinguished fascist corporatism from its democratic and Catholic versions. Corporatism, or its equivalent, was one of the main planks in the programs of fascist movements in both the interwar and post-1945 periods, and it is one of the clearest lines of continuity between prewar and postwar fascism. From the 1970s, however, neofascists have taken up environmentalism with far more emphasis than did interwar fascists, as a contemporary expression of fascism's hostility to international capitalism and the consumeristic and materialistic mentality that it has generated throughout the world. The call of many contemporary neofascist movements for policies likely to encourage rural repopulation by small family farms brings together fascism's demographic, autarkic, and ecological concerns. And since the countryside is viewed primarily as a "quality of life" issue, this confirms the long-standing fascist contempt for "economics," or, rather, the idea that modern man can live by "economics" alone.

There are still differing opinions as to whether interwar fascism was intrinsically anticapitalist. Its visceral antisocialism certainly serves and defends capitalist interests; both historical fascist regimes were founded on the permanent suppression of independent working-class organizations; and the thrusting, risk-taking, dynamic capitalist entrepreneur was close to embodying the fascist ethos of will, initiative, and action, and often glorified by fascists as a result. Again, fascism, in the words of the Italian Fascist 1927 Charter of Labor, "regards private initiative in the field of production as the most useful and efficient instrument for furthering the interests of the nation" (Delzell 1970, 120); as the Spanish Falange program of 1937 said, it recognizes "private property as a legitimate means for achieving individual, family and social goals" (ibid.). But fascists were, and are, hostile to "finance capital," "plutocracy," and "the power of money," preferring the industrial en-

trepreneur to the money-dealing banker and financier. They made the distinction because the industrialist was "productive" and manufactured things that enhanced national power, while the financier made nothing, except money gained by speculating on the production of others, and was "international" rather than "national," servicing and being serviced by international money markets. Jews have been uniformly portrayed by fascists as anonymous, stateless, and parasitical financiers and speculators. In that characteristically fascist way of combining all the nation's "international" enemies in a sole agency, fascists invented the "plutocratic-Bolshevik" conspiracy whereby both the "gold" and "red" internationalisms were orchestrated against the nation and the national interest by Jews.

Fascist economic policies certainly anticipated the state takeover and even nationalization of key economic sectors, including the banking system, energy, and transport; private capitalists did feel threatened by corporatism, and by any whiff of economic "planning," because they feared that they would have to transfer to the state decisions on what and how they produced. The point was that fascists wanted to ensure that the economy served the national purpose, as defined by them, and were prepared to intervene in the running and management of the national economy in pursuit of that goal. The experience and practice of the two historical fascist regimes, in Italy and Germany, showed that private business survived and prospered where and when it met or synchronized with the fascist goals for the economy; where and when it did not, or could not, the state intervened and became the entrepreneur in place of private capital.

The Italian Fascist regime's main economic agency in the 1930s was the Institute for Industrial Reconstruction (IRI), a giant state firm or holding company. Initially set up as a kind of hospital for ailing industries during the Great Depression, with the state using public money to buy the shares of failing private industries, IRI was made a permanent body in 1937, having the power to take over private firms seen as vital to autarky and war production and to run the now largely publicly owned heavy industrial sector. IRI's subsidiary companies were, however, still structured and managed as private firms. The agencies of the Nazi Four Year Plan Office, with the same goal of directing the economy toward autarky and rearmament, had the same private and public mix, recruiting personnel indiscriminately among Nazi party men, civil servants, armed forces officers, private industrialists, and managers to the vast cartels responsible for price controls and the allocation of labor, materials, and currency in key economic sectors. In a classic demonstration of the fascist primacy of politics over economics, the Four Year Plan Office's response to the German steel industry's reluctance to use lower quality and uneconomic German ore in place of imported ore was to bypass private industry altogether, constructing their own giant steel factory, which used German raw materials and to which was directed as a priority state investment, orders, and scarce supplies of labor.

Philip Morgan

See Also: INTRODUCTION; ANTI-SEMITISM; AUTARKY; BANKS, THE; BOLSHEVISM; BOURGEOISIE, THE; CAPITAL-ISM; CLASS; COLD WAR, THE; CORPORATISM; COS-MOPOLITANISM; DEMOGRAPHIC POLICY; ECOLOGY; EU-ROPE; FALANGE; FINANCE; GERMANY; GLOBALIZATION; IMMIGRATION; INDUSTRY; ITALY; MARXIST THEORIES OF FASCISM; MATERIALISM; NATIONALISM; NATIONALIZA-TION; NAZISM; NEW MAN, THE; PALINGENETIC MYTH; PLUTOCRACY; POSTWAR FASCISM; PRODUCTIVISM; REVO-LUTION; SOCIALISM; SPAIN; STATE, THE; SYNDICALISM; THIRD WAY, THE; TOTALITARIANISM; TRADE; VALOIS, GEORGES; WARRIOR ETHOS, THE

References

Barkai, Avraham. 1990. *Nazi Economics: Ideology, Theory, and Practice.* Oxford: Berg.
Delzell, Charles F., ed. 1970. *Mediterranean Fascism 1919–1945: Selected Documents.* London: Macmillan.
Kershaw, Ian. 1993. *The Nazi Dictatorship: Problems and Perspectives of Interpretation.* 3d ed. London: Arnold.
Mason, Tim. 1968. "The Primacy of Politics: Politics and Economics in National Socialist Germany." Pp. 165–195 in *The Nature of Fascism,* edited by Stuart J. Woolf. London: Weidenfeld and Nicolson.
Morgan, Philip. 2002. *Fascism in Europe, 1919–1945.* London: Routledge.
Noakes, Jeremy, and Geoffrey Pridham, eds. 2000. *A Documentary Reader: Nazism, 1919–1945.* Vol. 2: *State, Economy and Society 1933–1939.* Exeter: Exeter University Press.
Payne, Stanley. 1995. *A History of Fascism, 1919–1945.* London: UCL.
Roberts, David D. 1979. *The Syndicalist Tradition and Italian Fascism.* Chapel Hill: University of North Carolina Press.
Sternhell, Zeev. 1979. "Fascist Ideology." Pp. 325–406 in *Fascism: A Reader's Guide: Analyses, Interpretations, Bibliography,* edited by Walter Laqueur. Harmondsworth: Penguin.

ECUADOR

A derivative of fascism in Ecuador was the concept *Hispanidad* or *Hispanismo,* promulgated in the 1930s by the Ecuadorian intellectual César Arroyo. Arroyo's ideas were used and expanded upon by Jorge Luna Yepes, who became the leader of Acción Revoucionaria Nacionalista Ecuatoriana (ARNE), the highly nationalistic quasi-falangist party formed in 1942 after Ecuador's disastrous war with Peru. One purpose of ARNE was to promote *Hispanidad,* the idea that the Spanish cultural heritage represented the best values for the future of Ecuador and had to be defended against the forces of communism and socialism. ARNE also rejected *indigenismo,* the philosophy that Ecuador had been part of a great Indian civilization, the revival of which was essential for a prosperous and glorious future. Therefore, the Ecuadorian proponents of *Hispanidad* argued that Indians must adopt Western ways to the complete exclusion of their past traditions. That included speaking Spanish, wearing European dress, and the assumption of other aspects of a Hispanic identity. Ecuador could not advance as a modern society until this acculturation process was complete and the entire population had accepted Hispanic values. Not surprisingly, ARNE's strong emphasis on *Hispanidad* meant that it was very sympathetic to Francisco Franco's regime in Spain. While it was originally a small, clandestine party, ARNE achieved a measure of influence in Ecuadorian politics in the 1950s. It supported the candidacy of Ecuador's famous populist caudillo José María Velasco Ibarra, who won the presidency in 1952. Velasco used the *arnistas* and provided them a measure of temporary respect, but the party soon parted ways with the erratic politician. In 1968, ARNE ran Jorge Crespo Toral as its presidential candidate. Despite an energetic campaign and the candidate's personal flair, Crespo Toral and ARNE received a mere 4 percent of the total vote. By the late 1980s, ARNE was no longer an active party in Ecuador.

George Lauderbaugh

See Also: FALANGE; FRANCO Y BAHAMONDE, GENERAL FRANCISCO; MARXISM; NATIONALISM; SOCIALISM; SPAIN

Reference

Martz, John D. 1972. *Ecuador: Conflicting Political Culture and the Quest for Progress.* Boston: Allyn and Bacon.

EDELWEISS PIRATES, THE

Groups of German (mainly working-class) teenagers opposed to Nazism and to the Hitler Youth. Twelve of them were hanged in Cologne in November 1944.

Cyprian Blamires

See Also: ANTIFASCISM; WHITE ROSE; YOUTH

EDUCATION

For the interwar fascists, the goal of education was not the development of free, inquiring, rational minds, nor the opportunity for individuals' fulfillment and advancement, but rather the shaping of a people in their primary duties to nation and state. They were concerned to "educate" the "whole" man and to determine how people behaved in all facets of their lives. Fascism's "totalitarian" idea of education meant reaching and "educating" people not just in schools but also outside the school and university system. The Italian Fascist 1939 School Charter spoke of the periods for scholastic and "political" education coinciding, the schools and the Fascist youth and student university organizations together forming "a single instrument of Fascist education." The "scholastic service" of Italians was meant to start at the age of four and was jointly provided by schools and the youth organizations both in and out of school time until the age of fourteen. But it lasted until the age of twenty-one, way beyond the compulsory schooling age, with the later years being spent wholly in the orbit of the Fascist youth organizations, from where the young person would be expected to graduate into the regime's adult organizations, including the Fascist Party itself. The fascist "totalitarian" view of education was bound to bring fascism into conflict with other providers of education, understood in its broadest sense—that is, the organized religions and the family.

One of the first measures of Mussolini's government in Italy was the educational reform of 1923, introduced by the new minister of education, Giovanni Gentile. The reform was not distinctively Fascist, but it contained much to please the Catholic Church with its reintroduction of religious education in state secondary schools; it was equally pleasing for already established middle-class professional elites, with its restriction of access to a traditional classics and philosophy secondary school curriculum, which, in turn, guarded entry to the universities. Fascist educational reform came with the formal erection of the first-ever "totalitarian" state in the mid to late 1920s. During the 1930s, both the Italian Fascist and German Nazi regimes moved on broadly similar trajectories to change the educational system. Under both regimes there were attempts to "fascistize" the curriculum, teaching methods, and teaching staff in the elementary and secondary state schools and, to a lesser extent, in the universities. New

official textbooks appeared in the late 1930s, the most significant "nationalizing" curriculum changes occurring in history, language, economics, and political science; in Nazi Germany, the teaching of biology was orientated to the regime's racial and demographic policies and intentions. University courses were influenced to a lesser degree, though new content was given to some political science programs in Fascist Italy, with a focus on corporatism; the Nazi German regime introduced new courses in race and genetics, and racked up the race and eugenics content in medicine.

In both regimes, sport and athletic activity were given more time and emphasis in the school curriculum, which became a wedge for further fascist encroachment on the normal school routine, since sport in schools was often taken by instructors from the youth organizations. In Nazi Germany, "doing" sport was a requirement for moving up the school and moving from elementary to secondary education. The enhanced status of sport in the schools reflected the fascist elevation of physical activity and well-being over intellectual activity and achievement. It also signaled the "fascist values" that the regimes intended to inculcate in young people, which were those of the soldier and warrior. So the "values" to be instilled were discipline, obedience, physical strength, and the will to use it, a sense of selfless service to the community, and "national" comradeship combined with ruthlessness and initiative—a "getting things done" mentality. Since this education of the "new fascist man" involved making him feel part of the "national community" and willing to serve it, greater emphasis was placed on learning by "experience" and by "doing," rather than by "thinking" and the transfer of knowledge. This was one reason why the Italian Fascist 1939 School Charter wanted to give schooling a more practical and vocational bent by planning new technical, rural, and craft schools, and intending to introduce manual labor into school programs at all levels. More important, this was also why fascists thought that a "fascist" education was best imparted by membership and participation in the activities of party and youth organizations, many of which took place away from home and school and their influences. Both regimes set up elite colleges with the specific purpose of forming the future fascist leadership cadres, and these, significantly, were contracted out to the Fascist and Nazi parties and youth organizations.

The political reliability of the teaching profession was secured by various means. Teachers had to join the party-run monopoly professional association, which was meant to monitor and indoctrinate its members; candidates for appointment and promotion were vetted for their "political" credentials; male elementary school teachers were expected to double up as youth organization leaders and instructors; and the curricula of teacher training colleges were "fascistized" and recruitment to them controlled.

Philip Morgan

See Also: INTRODUCTION; ABSTRACTION; BODY, THE CULT OF THE; CATHOLIC CHURCH, THE; CORPORATISM; DEMOGRAPHIC POLICY; ELITE THEORY; EUGENICS; FASCIST PARTY, THE; GENTILE, GIOVANNI; GERMANY; ITALY; LEISURE; MEDICINE; MUSSOLINI, BENITO ANDREA; NATIONALISM; NAZISM; NEW MAN, THE; RACIAL DOCTRINE; RELIGION; SPORT; TOTALITARIANISM; UNIVERSITIES; *VOLKSGEMEINSCHAFT,* THE; WARRIOR ETHOS, THE; YOUTH

References

Delzell, Charles F., ed. 1970. *Mediteranean Fascism, 1919–1945: Selected Documents.* London: Macmillan.

Noakes, Jeremy, and Geoffrey Pridham, eds. 2000. *A Documentary Reader: Nazism, 1919–1945.* Vol. 2: *State, Economy and Society, 1933–1939.* Exeter: Exeter University Press.

Tannenbaum, Edward R. 1973. *Fascism in Italy: Society and Culture, 1922–1945.* London: Allen Lane.

EGALITARIANISM

A term of abuse in the vocabulary of interwar and postwar fascism. Both Italian Fascism and German Nazism adhered to the Aristotelian conviction, amplified by the modern elite theorists, that the human race is divided by nature into sheep and shepherds. They built on the postrevolutionary traditionalist attack on the egalitarian extremes practiced in the French Revolution to advocate an unashamed embrace of hierarchy, which was an important term in their vocabulary. It was not for nothing that when Mussolini chose to found a review (together with Margherita Sarfatti) that was to be a vehicle for the Fascist message in Italy, he called it *Gerarchia (Hierarchy).* Like many youth organizations that grew up in the Victorian era in Britain—the Scouts and Guides, the Boys and Girls Brigades, the Salvation Army—the interwar fascist regimes in Italy and Germany adopted a military model, aiming to construct a utopia in which there was a hierarchy of leadership from the Duce or Fuehrer downward. This was facilitated to some extent by their early connections with paramilitarism. Mus-

solini's chiefs were called *gerarchi*—that is, "hierarchs." At the same time they enthusiastically adopted the Social Darwinian thesis of survival of the fittest, which left very little room for egalitarianism. Leadership in society was for those who could outfight and outwit the others. The elite were the fittest, the strongest, the most heroic, the most productive, and, even more than that, those most fervently possessed with the national idea. Fighting qualities were of service only if used in the service of the nation. Egalitarianism belonged in the trash can along with pacifism, Christian universalism, socialism, Bolshevism, and the rest.

Cyprian Blamires

See Also: ABSTRACTION; ARISTOCRACY; COSMOPOLITANISM; ELITE THEORY; FASCIST PARTY, THE; GERMANY; ITALY; HERO, THE CULT OF THE; LEADER CULT, THE; MICHELS, ROBERTO; MOSCA, GAETANO; MUSSOLINI, BENITO ANDREA; NATIONALISM; PARAMILITARISM; PARETO, VILFREDO; PRODUCTIVISM; SARFATTI-GRASSINI, MARGHERITA; SOCIAL DARWINISM; TRADITIONALISM; UNIVERSALISM; UTOPIA; WARRIOR ETHOS, THE

References

Cannistraro, Philip V., and Brian R. Sullivan. 1993. *Il Duce's Other Woman: The Untold Story of Margherita Sarfatti, Benito Mussolini's Jewish Mistress, and How She Helped Him Come to Power.* New York: William Morrow.

Cohen, Carl. 1972. *Communism, Fascism, Democracy: The Theoretical Foundations.* New York: Random House.

De Felice, R., and M. Ledeen. 1976. *Fascism: An Informal Introduction to Its Theory and Practice.* New Brunswick, NJ: Transaction.

Paxton, R. O. 2005. *The Anatomy of Fascism.* London: Penguin.

EHRE ("HONOR")

A primary concept in the vocabulary of Nazism. Alfred Rosenberg speaks of it as the "beginning and end of all our thinking and acting." It was believed by many Nazi ideologues, following on the preaching of nineteenth-century race theorists, to be the characteristic quality of the Aryan or Nordic races, and indeed the origins of the term *Aryan* were tied up to the German word *Ehre.* In the vocabulary of anti-Semitism it was a quality emphatically denied to the Jews, who were considered to have no concept of honor whatever; they were, by contrast, motivated at all times by materialism, which may be considered the opposite quality to honor in much Nazi thinking. This materialism was by extension also considered to be characteristic of the Catholic Church, which had assimilated the "materialism" of the Old Testament religion, an affair of rituals and outward displays. It was argued that the Jew St. Paul had effectively distorted the "spiritual" teachings of the Galilean non-Jew Jesus, so as to turn them into a mere continuation of Judaism, replete with a new set of outward rituals and ceremonies (the Mass and the sacraments and veneration of images and statues, and so forth). The alternative, it was held, might have been something completely new in history, a truly spiritual and inward doctrine focusing on noble, virile, manly, warrior virtues, as opposed to the "groveling" penitence and "subservience" supposedly inculcated by the Catholic Church. Pro-Nazi ideologues claimed that the first person to understand this properly was Martin Luther, although in the Middle Ages the mystic Meister Eckhart was said to have had some inkling of it. In this view, however, although Luther managed to break free of Rome, he never comprehended the need to break free of Jewish "materialism" as well, maintaining a modified sacramental system and remaining in thrall to the Jewish Scriptures. Hence, although by breaking from Rome he pioneered German nationalism and in that sense could be considered a precursor of the Nazis, it was not until the rise of race theory in the nineteenth century that the concept of honor as distinctively fundamental to the Aryans and hence to their German descendants could be understood and theorized.

Honor was believed by Nazi ideologues to distinguish the Germans not only from the Jews but also from the British and Americans, who were considered to have been corrupted by Jewish influence and by philosophies like utilitarianism into a crassly materialistic view of life (echoes of Napoleon's famous comment about the British, that they were "a nation of shopkeepers"). Such thinking was already to be found in the nineteenth century in the writings of Carlyle, a Scottish writer who saw the Germans as having a much nobler sense of life than his British compatriots. It was also to be found in the operas and the writings of composer Richard Wagner, whose works, music, and philosophy of life Hitler idolized. Hitler and many of his colleagues believed themselves to be obligated to rescue their fellow Germans from the same corrupting influences, which they considered a threat to the German soul, a threat that had been made all the more real by the catastrophe of World War I. It was in the name of this image of themselves as bearers of a noble tradition of honor going back millennia to their Aryan forebears that Hitler and many of his fellow Nazis conducted a merciless crusade of destruction against the Jews—the bearers of the "virus" of materialism—and a campaign of persecution against the Catholic Church.

The notion of honor was often connected to that of *Treue* ("loyalty/faithfulness/reliability/integrity"), as symbolized in the slogan that Hitler gave to members of the SS—*SS-Mann, deine Ehre heisst Treue* ("SS member, your honor means loyalty/faithfulness/reliability"). It was embodied in the fascination of Himmler and others with ideas of reviving the Orders of the Teutonic Knights. But the medieval knightly goal of ("groveling") service to God, the Church, and the defenseless was to be replaced by a proud motivation of service to German honor. The concept of "honor" was inextricably bound up with the idea of blood for many Nazi ideologues, for the obvious reason that they believed in racial theories that ascribed qualities to particular races, and in particular superior qualities to the Aryan and therefore the German race. This connection was revived in neo-Nazism, for example in *Blood and Honour,* the title of the magazine and music cult associated with the British neo-Nazi Ian Stuart Donaldson.

Although there was not an identical cult of honor in Italian Fascism, there are strong parallels in the idea held by Mussolini and some of his followers that they were engaged on a crusade for manly, virile, warrior values against weak, effeminate, debilitating creeds like liberalism and pacifism. There was also a similar dislike for Christianity, insofar as it fostered conduct characterized by a spirit of humility, penitence, and meekness. It seems that both Italian Fascism and Nazism were penetrated by Nietzschean contempt for Christian morality.

Cyprian Blamires

See Also: ANTI-SEMITISM; ARYANISM; BLOOD; BLOOD AND SOIL; CARLYLE, THOMAS; CATHOLIC CHURCH, THE; CHRISTIANITY; DECADENCE; ECKHART, "MEISTER" JOHANN; HIMMLER, HEINRICH; HITLER, ADOLF; LIBERALISM; LUTHER, MARTIN; MATERIALISM; MUSSOLINI, BENITO ANDREA; NATIONALISM; NAZISM; NEO-NAZISM; NIETZSCHE, FRIEDRICH; NORDIC SOUL, THE; PACIFISM; RACIAL DOCTRINE; RELIGION; ROSENBERG, ALFRED; SKREWDRIVER; SS, THE; UTILITARIANISM; WAGNER, (WILHELM) RICHARD; WARRIOR ETHOS, THE

References

Burleigh, M., and W. Wippermann. 1991. *The Racial State: Germany 1933–1945.* Cambridge: Cambridge University Press.

Cecil, Robert. 1972. *The Myth of the Master Race: Alfred Rosenberg and Nazi Ideology.* London: Batsford.

Mosse, G. L. 1966. *The Crisis of German Ideology.* London: Weidenfeld and Nicolson.

Whisker, James B. 1990. *The Philosophy of Alfred Rosenberg: Origins of the National Socialist Myth.* Costa Mesa, CA: Noontide.

A key player in the implementation of the Holocaust, Adolf Eichmann became a focus of worldwide attention when put on trial by an Israeli court for his wartime actions in 1961. Hannah Arendt's published reflections on Eichmann and his crimes made her internationally known. (Library of Congress)

EICHMANN, OTTO ADOLF (1906–1962)

The inspiration for Hannah Arendt's phrase "the banality of evil," Adolf Eichmann was both a nondescript bureaucrat and principal engineer of the Holocaust as the head of the Gestapo Jewish section. As Reinhard Heydrich's assistant, Eichmann coordinated the systematic deportation of European Jewry, drafted the minutes of the Wannsee Conference, and played an essential role in the logistics and implementation of the Holocaust. Despite having mounted a legal defense that he was only following orders, Eichmann was hanged on 31 May 1962 for crimes against the Jewish people and crimes against humanity, the only individual to have received a death sentence in an Israeli court.

Working as a traveling salesman during much of the Weimar Republic, Eichmann joined the Nazi Party in 1932, the SS in 1933, and moved to the newly created SD in 1934, where he remained undistinguished as a

Nazi bureaucrat prior to the *Anschluss* of Austria. After he was posted to Vienna in 1938 to assist in the forced emigration of Jews to Palestine, Eichmann's notorious efficiency and administrative skills were noticed by Heinrich Himmler's deputy, Reinhard Heydrich. Touted as an expert on the "Jewish Question," Eichmann worked through Heydrich's RSHA (Reich Security Main Office) and was responsible for the Department of Jewish Affairs. From that powerful position Eichmann devised forced migration plans for Jews, organized deportations, and ultimately advocated genocide through slave labor and extermination by gas in designated concentration camps.

Following World War II, Eichmann escaped from Germany to Argentina, where he lived in secrecy until discovered in 1960 and apprehended by Israeli intelligence agents. In the most significant war crimes trial since the Nuremberg Trials, Eichmann was arraigned in Israel, accused of four types of crime: Crimes against the Jewish Nation, Crimes against Humanity, War Crimes, and Membership in an Illegal Organization (especially the SS). The ensuing prosecution marshaled vast evidence on the machinery of the Holocaust, and the judgment emphasized Eichmann's enthusiasm and central role in the planning and execution of the "final solution," particularly in regard to the extermination of Hungarian Jewry in 1944. When the sentence was handed down in 1961, Eichmann affirmed Israeli charges in terms of both the Holocaust's existence and his participation in it: "I am prepared to hang myself in public in order that all the anti-Semites in the world should have the terrible character of these events emphasized to them. I know that I face the death sentence. I am not asking for mercy because I am not deserving of it" (War Papers, Part 86, p. 3).

Matt Feldman

See Also: ANTI-SEMITISM; *ANSCHLUSS*, THE; ARENDT, HANNAH; AUSTRIA; CONCENTRATION CAMPS; GESTAPO, THE; HEYDRICH, REINHARD; HIMMLER, HEINRICH; HOLOCAUST, THE; NAZISM; NUREMBERG TRIALS, THE; PALESTINE; SD, THE; SS, THE; WANNSEE CONFERENCE, THE; WEIMAR REPUBLIC, THE

References

Arendt, Hannah. 1994. *Eichmann in Jerusalem: A Report on the Banality of Evil.* London: Penguin.
Gray, Randal (ed.). 1978. *The War Papers—Part 86: The Eichmann/Bormann Dossier.* Liverpool: Peter Way and Marshall Cavendish.

EINSATZGRUPPEN, EINSATZKOMMANDOS: See HOLOCAUST, THE; SS, THE

EL ALAMEIN

Legendary confrontation between Allied troops in North Africa under General Bernard Montgomery and the German Afrika Korps under General Erwin Rommel, a turning point in World War II in the autumn of 1942. The German defeat led to the removal of Axis forces from North Africa and blocked any possibility of a relief from the south of the beleaguered German forces at Stalingrad.

Cyprian Blamires

See Also: GERMANY; HITLER, ADOLF; LIBYA; STALINGRAD; WORLD WAR II

Reference
Barr, N. 2005. *Pendulum of War: Three Battles at El Alemein.* London: Pimlico.

ELIADE, MIRCEA (1907–1986)

Celebrated Romanian historian of religion, essayist, novelist, and onetime member of the Iron Guard. Eliade entered the University of Bucharest as a student in philosophy in 1925, a period of great intellectual and moral disorientation in Romania. He played an important role in the quest of young Romanians for a substitute for the old ideals of their parents. In 1927 the leading Bucharest daily, *The Word,* published a series of articles by Eliade entitled the "Spiritual Itinerary." Those articles opened up the generation issue in Romania, and launched Eliade as the spokesman of the so-called new generation. From 1929 to 1931, Eliade studied Indian languages and religions in Calcutta. His articles on India, sent from there and published in the Romanian press, were widely read. Back in Romania, Eliade participated in the famous "Criterion" public talks. These talks were an attempt by the new generation to instill some cosmopolitanism into Romanian intellectual life. Talks were held on contemporary problems, but also on Mussolini and Lenin. The overwhelming success of the talks, and the—for Romania—unprecedentedly liberal spirit that characterized them, aroused suspicion among the authorities. The

Criterion group was forced to continue its activities in private, and eventually ceased to exist.

In December 1933, prime minister Duca ordered the complete elimination of Codreanu's fascist Iron Guard. Hundreds of people suspected of links with the Iron Guard were arrested. The brutality with which these arrests took place deeply impressed the young Eliade. He felt attracted to the Iron Guard because he believed that the religious fervor of Codreanu's followers proved that the Romanians—despite their highly ritualized form of Orthodox Christianity—were not as "unreligious" as some critics believed. The establishment of a royal dictatorship in 1938 was followed by another campaign against supporters of the Iron Guard. Eliade was arrested and sent to a concentration camp for guardists.

During World War II, Eliade served as the Romanian cultural attache, first in London, later in Lisbon. On 12 February 1941, Eliade's adaptation of the classical play *Iphigeneia* was staged in Bucharest. In 1943, he published a long commentary on the Romanian folk legend of Master Manole. Both texts extolled death as a legitimate road to salvation, an idea that reflected the Iron Guard's cult of death and violence. While it is certain that Eliade was a member of the Guardist Axa group in Bucharest, there is much disagreement over the exact nature of his involvement in the movement.

Philip Vanhaelemeersch

See Also: CODREANU, CORNELIU ZELEA; CULTS OF DEATH; IRON GUARD, THE; LEGION OF THE ARCHANGEL MICHAEL, THE; MUSSOLINI, BENITO ANDREA; ORTHODOX CHURCHES, THE; ROMANIA

Reference
Ricketts, Mac Linscott. 1988. *Mircea Eliade: The Romanian Roots 1907–1945.* New York: Columbia University Press.

ELITE THEORY

A trend in sociopolitical thinking (sometimes also known as "elitism") that became influential toward the end of the nineteenth century and that had a particular impact on fascist thinking. The most celebrated names associated with this current of thought were Nietzsche, Michels, Mosca, Pareto, and Sorel. Partly in reaction to developing egalitarian movements and to the veneration of the proletariat in Marxism, these thinkers recurred to an earlier tradition of thought that can be traced back through Machiavelli down to antiquity, according to which it is an iron law of life or nature that small groups will tend to gain control of the leadership of communities and societies. For some with positivist inclinations, such as Pareto, this theory formed part of a scientific approach to sociology and remained purely a question of acknowledged facts. But in interwar fascism the belief in the inevitable ascendancy of elites became an article of pride, and this ascendancy was considered to be wholly desirable.

Cyprian Blamires

See Also: ARISTOCRACY; EGALITARIANISM; HERO, THE CULT OF THE; MARXISM; MICHELS, ROBERTO; MOSCA, GAETANO; NIETZSCHE, FRIEDRICH; PARETO, VILFREDO; POSITIVISM; SOCIOLOGY; SOREL, GEORGES

References
Albertoni, E. A. 1987. *Mosca and the Theory of Elitism.* Oxford: Basil Blackwell.
Finocchiaro, Maurice A. 1999. *Beyond Right and Left: Democratic Elitism in Mosca and Gramsci.* New Haven: Yale University Press.
Hughes, S. H. 1979. *Consciousness and Society: The Reorientation of European Social Thought, 1880–1930.* Brighton: Harvester.
Nye, R. A. 1977. *The Anti-Democratic Sources of Elite Theory: Pareto, Mosca, Michels.* London: Sage.

ELITES: *See* ELITE THEORY
ELITISM: *See* ELITE THEORY

EMPLOYMENT

Austrian far-right politician Jörg Haider won international notoriety for praising Adolf Hitler's "orderly employment" policy. This employment policy was in fact an important part of Hitler's overall political strategy. An early Nazi manifesto declared: "We demand that the state be charged first with providing the opportunity for a livelihood and way of life for the citizens. If it is impossible to sustain the total population of the state, then the members of foreign nations (noncitizens) are to be expelled from the Reich. . . . The first obligation of every citizen must be to work both spiritually and physically." On the other hand, if working people were to become part of the Nazi project and support its aims, they had to be placated and won over.

Hitler understood that workers had simple, basic aspirations: they wanted to work and they wanted to have a reasonable standard of living. So he made promises, and the main promise he made to the working class was that employment levels would be high, while the dreaded dole queue would become a thing of the past.

The most important policy in this context was the construction of the autobahns. The number of workers thought to have been employed on that work by 1936 came to between 4 and 5 percent of the 6,000,000 people registered as unemployed in 1933. There is also a sense in which Hitler's public works programs were about restoring dignity and belief to the unemployed, and glorifying the concept of manual labor. That is why, in some contexts, shovels and spades replaced guns and rifles as symbols of Nazi rule. There has, however, been a tendency to exaggerate the scale of the motorway construction project. The statistics above suggest that it was a significant aspect of Nazi employment policy, but in no way did it alone solve the unemployment problem. It should also be noted that the workers who gained employment on the motorways were subjected to terrible conditions of work—their pay was poor, and their accommodation sometimes almost subhuman.

The corollary of the drive toward full (male) employment was a rather reactionary attitude toward women as workers. Nazi ideology had assigned to women the role of mothers—in effect, guardians of the future. This means that they were discouraged from taking up employment, sometimes coerced into not doing so. The Nazis introduced marriage loans that were conditional on prospective brides giving up employment, and those women who had four or more children were rewarded with the bestowal of the Honor Cross of the German Mother. In Italy, fascist propaganda also prioritized motherhood, and it was only the advent of the war that prevented the regime from reducing the number of women in many sectors of the economy to a mere 10 percent. On the other hand, Mussolini's movement initially called for women to be given the vote, and as late as 1925, Mussolini was addressing his followers on the need to recognize that women could no longer be excluded from work or political involvement. In Germany under the Nazis women remained a major part of the workforce, while before coming to power the Nazi Party was so worried about losing women's votes that in 1932 it even denied any intention of removing women from employment.

Groups that have been branded neofascist in the postwar era have also used the issues of employment and unemployment to bang the drum for policies of exclusion and xenophobia. In simplistic terms, many far-right politicians have made a connection between immigration and unemployment. It has been a basic, unsophisticated tactic, but also an effective one in trying to garner popularity and support.

P. J. Davies

See Also: AUTOBAHNS, THE; FAMILY, THE; HAIDER, JÖRG; HITLER, ADOLF; IMMIGRATION; INDUSTRY; ITALY; LABOR FRONT, THE; LABOR SERVICE, THE; MUSSOLINI, BENITO ANDREA; NATIONALISM; NAZISM; POSTWAR FASCISM; SEXUALITY; STATE, THE; SS, THE; WALL STREET CRASH, THE; WOMEN; WORK; XENOPHOBIA

References
Barkai, A. 1994. *Nazi Economics: Ideology, Theory and Policy.* Oxford: Berg.
Burleigh, M. 2000. *The Third Reich: A New History.* London: Macmillan.
Silverman, D. P. 1998. *Hitler's Economy: Nazi Work Creation Programmes 1933–36.* London: Harvard University Press.
Willson, P. R. 1993. *The Clockwork Factory: Women and Work in Fascist Italy.* Oxford: Clarendon.
Zamagni, G. 1993. *The Economic History of Italy, 1860–1990.* Oxford: Clarendon.

ENABLING ACT (*ERMÄCHTIGUNGSGESETZ*), THE

The legal foundation of the dictatorial powers assumed by the Nazi regime from 1933, powers that enabled the Nazi leadership to impose their will on Germany. A series of articles transferred legislation from the Reichstag to the government, endowed the administration with complete freedom to introduce alterations to the constitution, stripped the president of the right to draft laws and handed it over to the chancellor, and opened the way for the government to have complete freedom of action in foreign affairs. From that point on the Reichstag was reduced to a sham, and between 1933 and 1939 it met on only a dozen occasions. The act was passed on 23 March 1933 by a majority of 441 to 84; the lack of opposition resulted from factors such as the exclusion of the communists, the deployment of SA men at the debate, and the reluctance of the Catholic Center Party to vote against. Monsignor Kaas, leader of the party, had been won over by Hitler, who had promised a concordat with the Vatican and a letter to the pope that would provide guarantees of civil liberties. Such a letter was never sent.

Cyprian Blamires

See Also: BRÜNING, HEINRICH; CATHOLIC CHURCH, THE; CENTER PARTY, THE; GERMANY; HITLER, ADOLF; NAZISM; PIUS XI, POPE; SA, THE

References
Burleigh, M. 2000. *The Third Reich: A New History.* London: Macmillan.
Fischer, K. P. 1995. *Nazi Germany: A New History.* London: Constable.

ENCICLOPEDIA ITALIANA, THE

Among the initiatives launched by the Italian Fascist regime in the cultural arena, the *Enciclopedia italiana,* edited and to a large extent inspired by the philosopher Giovanni Gentile—theoretician of actualism and the "ethical state"—was without doubt the most ambitious and the most important. The work was first planned in 1919 by a group of businessmen in the heat of the nationalist fervor that accompanied the victorious conclusion to World War I, a fervor that was later appropriated by Fascism after its rise to power. Italy was a country that had achieved political unity relatively late (though she possessed a long tradition of cultural unity), and the vision of the originators of this project was to endow her with a great national encyclopedia, a popular editorial instrument making possible the gathering together and presentation to the world of the whole range of diverse expressions of Italian culture. Thanks to this encyclopedic work, Italy would make up lost political and civil ground with respect to other European nations and recover her ancient cultural prestige.

Considerable financial investment and organizational effort were necessary to carry through such an extensive politico-cultural undertaking. After the failure of the original project, as proposed in 1922 by the publisher Angelo Fortunato Formìggini through the Fondazione Leonardo, an agreement was reached on 3 January 1925 between the publisher Calogero Tumminelli and the textile industrialist Giovanni Treccani to set up an establishment that would oversee the publication of the *Enciclopedia italiana di scienze, lettere e arti.* In the prospectus that announced its program and objectives, published on 26 June of that same year, there was an emphasis on its political independence and on the rigorously scholarly nature of the enterprise, which was slated to involve the collaboration of 1,410 contributors under the editorship of Giovanni Gentile. Conceived along the lines of the *Encyclopedia Britan-*

nica and published in thirty-six volumes between 1929 and 1937, with an initial print run of 25,000 for each volume, the *Enciclopedia italiana* actually drew on contributions from 3,272 collaborators, with a predominance of humanities topics over those of a technical-scientific nature. Financial difficulties resulting from the expansion of the scope of the work beyond its original projections ultimately made it necessary to set up a public consortium directly controlled and financed by the state, which thus became the proprietor and publisher of the work.

Gentile's plan was that the *Enciclopedia* should not be a work of political-ideological propaganda, but a great national project involving all the diverse components and expressions of Italian culture—even those hostile to Fascism, or remote from it. Hence his appeal to all Italian intellectuals and academics to offer their scholarly collaboration to the undertaking: an appeal that many welcomed, though it was at the same time vigorously rejected by certain individual public figures such as the liberal economist Luigi Einaudi and the idealist philosopher Benedetto Croce; along with a few other men of culture, they refused to let themselves be involved in a project that fell under the shadow of Mussolini and his regime. The truth is that, in spite of Gentile's desire to present it as a politically independent undertaking, many of the entries in the *Enciclopedia*—above all those of a historical-political and political-juridical nature—were strongly marked by a Fascist or broadly authoritarian-nationalist slant. Alongside the famous article on "Fascism" of 1932 (signed by Mussolini, but almost wholly composed by Giovanni Gentile), we need mention only entries such as "Corporation," "Democracy," "Dictatorship," "Political Economy," "Italy," and "Nationalism," and the contributions by key intellectuals of the regime, such as Felice Battaglia, Carlo Costamagna, Ugo Spirito, and Gioacchino Volpe, and its leading political apologists—Italo Balbo, Luigi Federzoni, and Arturo Marpicati. From this point of view it is fair to regard the *Enciclopedia italiana* as an instrument of cultural policy that helped to consolidate support from sympathetic intellectuals for Mussolinian politics and to root the regime in a context of Italian national history. However, unlike the other great editorial undertaking of the Fascist regime, the four volumes of the *Dizionario di politica* published in 1940, this one was not simply an expression of Fascist ideological totalitarianism, as has sometimes been maintained. Rather, it manifests a relative cultural pluralism—witness not just the substantial contributions provided by prestigious antifascist intellectuals (in some cases of Jewish origin) but above

all the influence exercised on the work in its totality by a culture of Catholic inspiration, well represented by the Jesuit Pietro Tacchi Venturi. Especially after the Concordat between the Italian state and the Holy See in 1929, the presence in the *Enciclopedia* of Catholic themes, principles, and authors became preponderant, and that is one explanation for the repeated complaints made to Gentile by more radical elements in Fascist culture who considered the *Enciclopedia* excessively ecumenical in its choice of authors and insufficiently loyal to the official positions of the regime, from the point of view of doctrinal content.

The *Enciclopedia italiana* was one of the most durable works of the regime. It continued to prosper even after the fall of the dictatorship. After the work was reprinted in 1949 without alteration, appendix volumes continued to be published at intervals. Even today the Istituto della Enciclopedia italiana retains a high profile on the Italian cultural scene. Despite the fact that so many of the entries in the *Enciclopedia* are still the ones written in the 1930s under Gentile's editorship, it continues to be considered a work of major intellectual and scientific importance. From the point of view of historical judgment, this enduring legacy raises a question: to what extent can the *Enciclopedia italiana* be considered overall a cultural product of Fascism, and as such unacceptable (at least in theory) in a historico-cultural context that is different from the one in which it was conceived and completed? One way of answering this question would be to say that, while it is true that the *Enciclopedia italiana* undoubtedly reflects the ideological influence of Fascism, it is also true that it was a great testbed for the entire Italian academic culture of the era and, more generally, for the whole of Italy. In the words of the historian Gabriele Turi, it was the "mirror of the nation," in which Italy reflected all of her history: a history that in the first half of the twentieth century included the Mussolinian dictatorship but that did not coincide wholly with Fascism. This explains why the *Enciclopedia italiana* has been able to survive, with the necessary revisions, not just the death of its editor, Giovanni Gentile, but also the end of the Fascist regime that encouraged and supported it so enthusiastically.

Alessandro Campi
(translated by Cyprian Blamires)

See Also: ANTI-FASCISM; BALBO, ITALO; CATHOLIC CHURCH, THE; CORPORATISM; COSTAMAGNA, CARLO; CROCE, BENEDETTO; CULTURE; DEMOCRACY; FASCIST PARTY, THE; FEDERZONI, LUIGI; GENTILE, GIOVANNI; ITALY; MUSSOLINI, BENITO ANDREA; NATIONALISM; PAPACY, THE; SPIRITO, UGO; VOLPE, GIOACCHINO

References
Stone, M. 1998. *The Patron State: Culture and Politics in Fascist Italy.* Princeton: Princeton University Press.
Tannenbaum, E. R. 1972. *Fascism in Italy: Italian Society and Culture 1922–1945.* London: Allen Lane.

References
Macartney, C. A. 1957. *October Fifteenth.* Edinburgh: Edinburgh University Press.
Rogger, H., and E. Weber. 1966. *The European Right: A Historical Profile.* Berkeley: University of California Press.

ENDRE, LÁSZLÓ (1895–1946)

Openly anti-Semitic Hungarian interwar politician. Endre came from a wealthy rural background and started his political career as an army officer, becoming a loyal supporter of Horthy in crushing the Council of the Republic in 1919. First he was a mayor in Gödöllo, then later was appointed to the chief governor position of Gödöllo district in 1923. He was an active member of the leaderships of MOVE, the Double Cross Blood Association, the Association of Awakening Hungarians, and the Etelköz Association. Endre's name appears among those of the military officers who served Prónay in 1921, an extremely bloody paramilitary group involved with the killing of communists and social democrats throughout the countryside. During the spring of 1937, Endre was influential in creating the Party for Socialist Racial Defense, which was fused with Szálasi's Party of National Will later that year. In September 1937, Endre was elevated to the prestigious position of lieutenant governor of Pest County, a move that forced him to quit his party. As a chief public officer, he enforced the implementation of anti-Jewish laws. His eccentric racialism, life style, and cruel ideas were attributed to his syphilitic condition and insanity. In April 1944 he was made state secretary for the Ministry of Internal Affairs. According to some sources, by that time he had considerable money secreted in Swiss bank accounts. He became a close confidant of Eichmann and was entrusted with the organizational matters of ghettoization and deportation of the Jews. Together with the chief of the gendarmerie, Baky, and the minister of internal affairs, Jaross, he achieved this task so rapidly that within two months more than 500,000 people—almost 90 percent of the entire Jewish population of the countryside—had disappeared. He was hanged early in 1946 for crimes against humanity.

László Kürti

See Also: ANTI-SEMITISM; ARROW CROSS, THE; EICHMANN, OTTO ADOLF; GHETTOS; HORTHY DE NAGYBÁNYA, MIK-LÓS; HUNGARY; PARAMILITARISM; SZÁLASI, FERENC

ENGDAHL, PER: *See* SWEDEN
ENGLAND: *See* GREAT BRITAIN

ENLIGHTENMENT, THE

Fascism is often characterized—and indeed, fascist propagandists have often presented themselves—as hostile to liberalism and the Enlightenment. Yet while rejecting many Enlightenment values, such as egalitarianism, internationalism, liberalism, and rationalism, fascists drew upon Enlightenment thought to create their own revolutionary doctrines. In doing so they used liberalism and other Enlightenment ideas to destroy the old order as a step toward the establishment of the fascist new order. The ambiguity that clouds fascist discussions of the Enlightenment is seen most clearly in the reaction of German National Socialists toward their own history. On the one hand they wanted to condemn the Enlightenment, and with it the French Revolution, as expressions of a capitalistic Jewish conspiracy linked to Freemasonry. On the other, they sought justification for their military adventurism in the campaigns of Frederick the Great. Yet Frederick was a Freemason and Enlightenment monarch who in many ways typified the Age of Reason.

Superficially similar to conservative critiques of the Enlightenment associated with such figures as the Irishman Edmund Burke (1729–1797), the Dutchman Guillaume Groen van Prinsterer (1801–1876), the German Friedrich Julius Stahl (1802–1861), and the counter-revolutionary Traditionalists, the approach of interwar fascist propagandists was in fact fundamentally different. From the conservatives the fascists borrowed their critique of rationalist epistemological reductionism. But instead of asserting a more complex epistemology that recognizes rationality alongside other ways of knowing, fascists rejected all rationality in terms of various forms of intuitive knowledge. Similarly, while the conservatives wished to replace revolutionary justice and views of law with a historically based constitutional model, fascists like the jurist Carl Schmitt developed new judicial forms based on situational law that look to a leader as the source of all wisdom.

The influential protofascist writer Houston Stewart Chamberlain had a huge impact on interwar fascist thinking, and he was implicitly hostile to the Enlightenment, even though he paid it little direct attention. His works were read in Italy, where he influenced popular writers like Julius Evola, although Benito Mussolini is on record as having said that he thought Chamberlain's influence in Italy would be limited. His works were also read in Romania. Chamberlain concentrates on attacking materialism and reshapes the works of Enlightenment philosophers like John Locke and Immanuel Kant, whom he respected, in terms of their roots in Teutonic thought, from which he believed they deviated. According to him, the world is divided between two great world systems— that of the Teutons and that of the Jews. The former produce all that is good, the latter all that furthers their own limited ends through the encouragement of egalitarianism, internationalism, liberalism, materialism, and, by implication, the Enlightenment. Chamberlain's hostility to Enlightenment thought is clearly laid out in his *Arische Weltanschauung* (1905), in which he attempts to find the roots of Western thought in Indian philosophies that predate the Greeks. Indian philosophy, he claims, is aristocratic and possible only when distinct racial conditions and the right form of education combine. As such it is the opposite of all forms of universalism. Therefore, rejecting universalism, Europeans must return to an Indo-European purity of thought that will embrace organic thinking and transcend concerns about logical contradictions. Logic, from Aristotle to John Stuart Mill, is a dead end that must be avoided to discover the truth of internal knowledge. All knowledge, all thinking, he claims, is based on faith; acknowledging this is the genius of the Aryan.

Chamberlain's disciple Alfred Rosenberg takes a similar approach in his *Der Mythus des 20. Jahrhunderts.* Rather than concentrate his attack on the Enlightenment, however, Rosenberg attacks its manifestations, which allows him to praise "the political nobility of Frederick the Great," Kant, and other Enlightenment thinkers as he fits them into his overarching scheme. For him it is not the abstract historical period of the Enlightenment that is evil but the manifestations of Semitic ideas expressed in egalitarianism, capitalism, liberalism, universalism, and the imperialism of Jewish-Christianity. For Rosenberg, Enlightenment thinkers provide National Socialists with the tools they need to destroy Christianity and traditional Western philosophy. Liberalism and other Enlightenment ideas break up the settled order of traditional philosophy, with its reliance on logic. Therefore they can be used in the battle to create a new order that embraces a revolutionary worldview that is organic in character and particular in its racial manifestation.

For some southern Europeans the Enlightenment becomes an expression of Protestantism and of a hostility to tradition that they reject. While figures like Vilfredo Pareto, Giovanni Gentile, Gaetano Mosca, Benito Mussolini, and others embrace tradition, it is "tradition" in the abstract. It is a tradition created by their own mythological understanding, not a specific historical tradition that might limit their freedom of action. For fascist intellectuals the Enlightenment stands in opposition to the organic nature of a 'true' tradition. What they mean by this is a mythological, primal "tradition" that allows them to reject existing aristocracies in favor of their own new aristocracy. Existing ruling elites are to be destroyed through revolutionary action to make way for a new elite selected on the principle of the survival of the fittest. Paradoxically, we can see that this act of destruction actually draws upon Enlightenment values to destroy the old but then goes on to reject those values in favor of new ones based upon the ever-evolving new society in which the 'new man' of fascism will become the ruling elite.

Irving Hexham

See Also: INTRODUCTION; ABSTRACTION; ANTI-SEMITISM; ARISTOCRACY; ARYANISM; CAPITALISM; CHAMBERLAIN, HOUSTON STEWART; CHRISTIANITY; CONSPIRACY THEORIES; COSMOPOLITANISM; EGALITARIANISM; ELITE THEORY; EVOLA, JULIUS; FREDERICK II, THE GREAT; FREEMASONRY/FREEMASONS, THE; FRENCH REVOLUTION, THE; GENTILE, GIOVANNI; GERMANNESS (*DEUTSCHHEIT*); LAW; LIBERALISM; MATERIALISM; MOSCA, GAETANO; MUSSOLINI, BENITO ANDREA; NAZISM; NEW MAN, THE; NEW ORDER, THE; NORDIC SOUL, THE; ORGANICISM; PARETO, VILFREDO; RACIAL DOCTRINE; RATIONALISM; REVOLUTION; ROMANIA; ROSENBERG, ALFRED; SCHMITT, CARL; SOCIAL DARWINISM; TRADITIONALISM; *WELTANSCHAUUNG*/WORLD-VIEW

References
Berlin, I. 2000. *The Roots of Romanticism: The A.W. Mellon Lectures in the Fine Arts, 1965.* London: Pimlico.
Cassirer, E. 1979. *The Philosophy of the Enlightenment.* Princeton: Princeton University Press.
Gay, P. 1996. *The Enlightenment: An Interpretation.* London: W. W. Norton.

Griffin, R. 1991. *The Nature of Fascism.* London: Routledge.

Mosse, G. L. 1999. *The Fascist Revolution: Towards a General Theory of Fascism.* New York: H. Fertig.

Payne, S. 1995. *A History of Fascism 1914–1945.* London: University College London Press.

ENVIRONMENT, THE: *See* ECOLOGY; ECONOMICS; GLOBALIZATION; NATURE

ESTADO NOVO ("NEW STATE")

I. PORTUGAL

Name given to Portugal in 1933 to suggest that the ethos of the country under the Prime Minister/ Dictator Salazar was a modernizing one along fascistic lines (not to be confused with the same term used in Brazil, 1937–1945). The "new state" also provided itself with a paramilitary organization (the Legião Portuguesa) and a national youth organization (Mocidade Portuguesa), as well as a secret police force (PIDE) backed up by special tribunals. The adoption of other externals of Italian Fascism, such as state propaganda, censorship, political rituals, and a leader cult, could not conceal the real nature of Salazar's philosophy, a blend of social Catholicism with integral nationalism à la Maurras. The dictator showed his true colors when he crushed the genuinely fascist-type coup of Rolão Preto in 1935.

Cyprian Blamires

See Also: CATHOLIC CHURCH, THE; CLERICO-FASCISM; INTEGRAL NATIONALISM; MAURRAS, CHARLES; MODERNITY; PARAMILITARISM; POLITICAL CATHOLICISM; PORTUGAL; ROLÃO PRETO, FRANCISCO; SALAZAR, ANTÓNIO DE OLIVEIRA; YOUTH

Reference
Gallagher, T. 1983. *Portugal: A Twentieth-Century Interpretation.* Manchester: Manchester University Press.

II. Brazil: *See* BRAZIL

ESTONIA

A potential fascist threat emerged in Estonia in 1932, when the League of Veterans of the Estonian War of Independence (Eesti Vabadussõjalaste Liit), popularly known as the Vaps movement, became a popular political force. The leaders of the veterans were the lawyer Artur Sirk (1900–1937) and retired General Andres Larka (1879–1943). The global economic depression of the early 1930s increased political tensions and the frequency of cabinet changeovers. In such an atmosphere, the veterans' calls to combat political corruption and establish a strong presidency found resonance. Center-right parties proposed amendments to the constitution creating a presidency in the hope that a strong executive would bring stability. After two successive amendment bills failed in national referenda, the veterans' own proposal for a powerful presidency was approved in October 1933 by 73 percent of voters. In local elections in January 1934, the veterans won in all the major cities. However, on 12 March, before national elections could be held, Prime Minister Konstantin Päts, together with fellow presidential candidate General Johan Laidoner (1884–1953), proclaimed a state of emergency and arrested the leaders of the Veterans' League. The league was declared a danger to public safety. Although claiming to save democracy from the threat of fascism, Päts then proceeded to erect his own authoritarian regime. In 1935, veterans' leaders, with the help of Finnish sympathizers, plotted to overthrow the government, but the conspiracy was uncovered and the plotters incarcerated. Sirk died in Luxembourg in 1937, apparently a suicide. In 1937, Päts proclaimed a new constitution, under which he was elected the first president in 1938. Päts, the Estonian elite, and most of the leaders of the veterans were deported to, and died in, Soviet gulags after the annexation of the country by the USSR in 1940. Hjalmar Mäe, the former veterans' propaganda chief, served as the head of the Estonian self-administration under the Nazi occupation, 1941–1944.

Andres Kasekamp

See Also: FINLAND; NAZISM; PÄTS, KONSTANTIN; SOVIET UNION, THE; VAPS; WALL STREET CRASH, THE

References
Kasekamp, Andres. 2000. *The Radical Right in Interwar Estonia.* London: Macmillan.

Haile Selassie, Emperor of Ethiopia from 1930, who escaped to England after the Italian invasion of his country and was restored to the throne in 1941 by the British. The failure of the League of Nations to deal with Italian aggression was one of many symptoms of its weakness. Mussolini was set on creating a new "Roman Empire." (Library of Congress)

———. 2003. "Extreme Right Parties in Contemporary Estonia." *Patterns of Prejudice* 37, no. 4.

Parming, Tönu. 1975. *The Collapse of Liberal Democracy and the Rise of Authoritarianism in Estonia.* London: Sage.

ETHIOPIA

Following in the footsteps of the liberal Italian state, which had already acquired colonial possessions in neighboring Eritrea and (divided) Somaliland, Mussolini saw Ethiopia as a coveted prize for the country's newfound imperial "destiny." His colonial aspirations were reinforced by the fact that in an earlier invasion, in 1896, Italian troops had been crushed by the Ethiopian forces in Adowa, which remained in the Italian memory as an instance of painful national humiliation. By orchestrating a full-scale invasion of Ethiopia (against the wishes of the Western European powers), Mussolini not only hoped to avenge this defeat but also wanted to consolidate Italy's colonial empire in East Africa, turning the Mediterranean into a new *mare nostrum* by controlling access to Suez.

The invasion (which had been in preparation since the early 1930s) started on 3 October 1935 and caused an immediate international outcry. The emperor of Ethiopia, Haile Selassie, was able to rally his forces and—for a short period—raise serious questions as to the capacity of the Italian forces to conquer the country. At the same time, the League of Nations imposed an economic embargo on Italy that excluded, however, the crucial commodity of oil—thereby wasting the only opportunity for forcing Fascist Italy to reconsider its aggressive foreign policy or to bring its campaign to its knees. Eventually, a renewed Italian operational command and a wave of reinforcements in the spring of 1936 sealed the fate of Ethiopia: vastly outnumbered and not helped by the ineffective international reaction, the country was officially declared part of the Italian *impero* on 10 May 1936, five days after Italian troops entered its capital, Addis Ababa. Emperor Selassie had fled the country a week earlier. His passionate plea to the assembly of the League of Nations in Geneva on 30 June generated a great deal of sympathy but little practical support. Italy had by then amalgamated its three bordering colonial possessions (Somaliland, Eritrea, and Ethiopia) into a single administrative unit (Italian East Africa) with a single new constitution. A little later, Britain and France cynically recognized the Italian conquest of Ethiopia as a fait accompli.

Although independent Ethiopia existed no more, Italian control over the whole of the country was precarious, or even partial. Local tribes continued to fight against the occupying forces, seriously disrupting Italian plans for the reorganization of the country. That, however, did not stop Mussolini from using Ethiopia as a testing ground for many of his subsequent ideological projects. One of them pertained to the introduction of a special set of racial/biological laws, aiming at an apartheid-like separation of the "white" from the indigenous population. As early as June 1936 the idea that "the Fascist empire must not be an empire of half-castes" was officially put forward in Italy. Less than a year later physical contact between the two groups was strictly prohibited and punished, in order to avoid the alleged biological danger of "racial" miscegenation, when a relevant royal decree was put into effect. "Half-castes" were subsequently deprived of full citizenship status. It is believed that the racial experiments in the Italian East Africa deepened Mussolini's fondness for biological theories of "race" and prepared the ground for the introduction of the 1938 anti-Semitic legislation in mainland Italy. However, there is plainly a great difference between racial discrimination against blacks, which was practiced all over the white world and could hardly be said to be a marker of fascism, and the murderous biological anti-Semitism propounded by the Nazis and adopted wherever their creed was taken up or imitated.

Ethiopia remained under tentative Italian control until 1940–1941. Immediately upon Italy's entry into World War II, Haile Selassie moved back to Africa and attempted to coordinate the resistance of Ethiopian tribes against the colonial occupier, in close cooperation with Britain. As Italy's fortunes in the war declined after 1941, so did its control over Italian East Africa, paving the way for Ethiopia's liberation and renewed independence.

Aristotle Kallis

See Also: ANTI-SEMITISM; COLONIALISM; FASCIST PARTY, THE; ITALY; LEAGUE OF NATIONS, THE; MUSSOLINI, BENITO ANDREA; NAZISM; RACIAL DOCTRINE; RACISM; ROME; WORLD WAR II

References

Baer, G. 1967. *The Coming of the Italo-Ethiopian War.* Cambridge: Harvard University Press.
Northedge, F. S. 1988. *The League of Nations: Its Life and Times, 1920–1946.* Leicester: Leicester University Press.
Sbacchi, A. 1985. *Ethiopia under Mussolini: Fascism and the Colonial Experience.* London: Zed.

EUGENICS (Germany and Europe other than Italy)

Eugenics played an important role in the policies of Nazism. The term was originally introduced by Victorian statistician and anthropologist Francis Galton in 1883 to denote the new science of improving the qualities of a race. An alternative term was *racial hygiene,* or *Rassenhygiene,* coined by a young German physician, Alfred Ploetz, in 1895. *Rassenhygiene* linked two rising sciences—anthropology and hygiene—with the idea that the germs of mental illness and deviant behavior could be cleansed and eradicated from the germplasm or hereditary substance. Ploetz founded a Society for Racial Hygiene in 1905. Ploetz's idea was that the physician should be responsible to the race rather than to the sick individual. The racial hygiene strategy was predicated on the view that society was an organism and that the biological fitness of the nation was at stake. Eugenicists sought to restore the fitness of the population to its primal vigor: in this broadly organicist sense, it was Social Darwinist. In its early stages the eugenics movement attracted Jews and socialists as a program of biologically based reform. Aryan enthusiasts such as the members of the Gobineau Society in Germany converged with eugenics, but their myths and concern with blood purity meant that the rationales were distinct.

Victorian statistician and anthopologist Francis Galton, inventor of the term eugenics *as the science of improving the qualities of a race; Nazi racial policies were an attempt to apply this science in practice. (Library of Congress)*

During the 1920s the Nazis racialized eugenic plans to exclude the unfit and promote the birth of groups of high eugenic quality. Originally a utopian socialist, Ploetz gravitated toward the political Right, eventually joining the Nazi Party in 1937. The right-wing publisher Julius Lehmann published numerous eugenic works, including (from 1920) the *Archiv für Rassen- und Gesellschaftsbiologie,* and the Nordic racial tracts of Hans Günther. While Hitler was imprisoned in Landsberg, Lehmann presented him with a copy of the textbook on human genetics and heredity by the botanist Erwin Baur, the anthropologist Eugen Fischer, and the human geneticist Fritz Lenz. The Weimar welfare state implemented a range of positive, welfare-oriented eugenic measures, and there were similar eugenic schemes in Austria. Hitler took up various themes, such as sterilization and the damage to the nation's hereditary stock through sexually transmitted disease. But he preferred the nationalist mythology of blood purity to the scien-

tific complexities of human genetics. Lenz held the first teaching post in racial hygiene in Munich from 1923. By 1929 he believed that the Nazis offered the best chance for realizing the racial hygiene program. As Nazism sought to broaden its appeal to the professional middle classes, eugenics became more prominent in its propaganda. There was a strong convergence between eugenics and Nazism, but at no time did Nazism achieve a monopoly and full control over scientific racism.

In 1933 the *Gleichschaltung* of the Racial Hygiene Society meant exclusion of Catholics, socialists, and Jews, and its membership rapidly grew to fifty-six local groups in 1936 with 3,700 members. The Nazis gave increased resources to racial hygiene, although not every university had an institute or full professor in the subject. The Kaiser Wilhelm Institute for Anthropology, founded in 1927, provided training courses for SS doctors. The Kaiser Wilhelm Institute for Anthropology under Eugen Fischer and (from 1941) Otmar von Verschuer supported Nazi racial policy. Institute members adjudicated on questions of racial identity and sterilization. Verschuer had two assistants in Auschwitz, Liebau and Mengele. The anthropologist Wolfgang Abel was an SS officer. Although the biologist Hans Nachtsheim held no position in the NSDAP, he collaborated with the SS sanatorium Hohenlychen and conducted pressure chamber experiments on epileptic children. His research on convulsions in carefully bred strains of rabbits had direct applicability to neurology and sterilization policy. As the war went on animals were in short supply, but persons deemed racial subhumans—such as Jews and Roma, and especially children—were unscrupulously exploited for human experiments. Nazi social policy can be seen in eugenic terms, but there were contested areas, as when Lenz clashed with Himmler over the biological value of illegitimate children. Himmler supported the *Lebensborn* homes—an SS organization that provided maternity homes for unmarried mothers, with children forcibly seized from the occupied East to Germanize them. (The idea promoted in some quarters that the *Lebensborn* homes were human stud farms where SS officers could have polygamous relationships is a myth.)

The Munich psychiatrist Ernst Rüdin had campaigned for a sterilization law from the early 1900s. He played a key role in drafting the sterilization law that came into force in July 1933. It was profoundly influenced by psychiatric genetics. Sterilization was required for nine supposedly inherited diseases: hereditary feeblemindedness, schizophrenia, manic depression, hereditary epilepsy, Huntington's chorea, hereditary blindness and deafness, hereditary malformations, and severe alcoholism. Although according to the text of the law race was not in itself grounds for sterilization, in practice some of the sterilization courts proceeded harshly against Jews. Unlike euthanasia, the first phase of sterilizations were carried out under an enacted law (passed in July 1933), even though the sterilization courts did not always respect legal niceties in proceedings against Jews. In 1937 the Nazi Physicians League's leaders agitated in a covert and demonstrably illegal manner for vindictively sterilizing the half-caste Rhineland children (whose fathers were black French occupation troops following World War I). This action was supported by the veteran racial anthropologist Eugen Fischer, who became involved in racial propaganda for Rosenberg's Ostministerium and adjudicated on cases of racial ancestry. After 1945, Fischer escaped any war crimes prosecutions.

The implementation of sterilization was different in different regional contexts. In all there were approximately 450,000 victims of sterilization, excluding victims in annexed Austria. Additionally, children of mixed racial origins were targeted for sterilization. X-ray sterilization was used on a large-scale but still experimental basis in the concentration camps between 1941 and 1945, with thousands of victims.

Public health measures were placed on eugenic lines. Rüdin conducted widespread surveys on records of psychiatric institutions, criminality, and death registers to identify the hereditarily sick. The Rockefeller Foundation had committed itself to support racial surveys in Germany from 1930 to 1935, and German eugenicists established strong links with U.S. advocates of immigration controls and sterilization. Among the victims of the German sterilization campaign were an estimated 5,000 deaths from complications. Some categories of 'undesirables', such as the mixed-race Rhineland children, were illegally sterilized. X-ray sterilization was brutally applied to many thousands of racial victims during the war. The Nazis also incarcerated an estimated 15,000 homosexuals, and some 5,000 were killed. At least 10,000 "asocials" were murdered, although exactly how many is still not known. The number of Roma killed by the Nazis is thought to amount to 250,000.

Eugenicists saw the Nazi takeover as an opportunity to expand their power, and they felt angry when challenged by Nazi Party activists. Some racial hygienists, such as Eugen Fischer and Otmar von Verschuer, maintained their position by becoming increasingly compliant toward the Nazi Party apparatus. Party activists like Reich Medical Fuehrer Gerhard Wagner claimed that

the sterilization law was insufficiently racial, and pressure built up for killing the eugenically undesirable. Rüdin felt that he was brushed aside by the racial experts of the SS. The SS found support at certain universities, such as Jena and Strasbourg. The SS-Ahnenerbe combined studies of human prehistory with gruesome human experiments and exerted strong influence on universities. Medical researchers in Munich had links to the concentration camp in Dachau, in Berlin to Ravensbrück and Sachsenhausen, in Jena to Buchenwald, and in Hamburg to Neuengamme. Within the SS, divergent medical factions supporting "geomedicine" as opposed to racial anthropology clashed. Anthropologists such as Otto Reche and Heberer combined academic positions with being SS officers. Despite SS incursions into the universities and its influence in the new "Reich" universities of Strasburg and Posen, its power over academic life was never complete. Many nonparty and non-SS academics pursued racial research agendas, so that resisting the SS did not necessarily mean opposition to racial policy.

Nazi health propaganda encouraged people of good eugenic breeding stock to have at least three children. The idea was that health offices would register the birth of the unfit. Marriage certificates involved tests to make sure that no one who had a sexually transmitted disease or who was carrying a genetic disease, was allowed to marry. The Reich Health Office imposed severe measures against the Roma. Robert Ritter directed measures of registration and psychological evaluation of Roma. He was supported in this work by psychologists and racial anthropologists. Their observations were followed by incarceration of Roma in concentration camps, notably Auschwitz, where Mengele continued observations on Roma families.

Lenz supported the establishment of a racial office to monitor the health of the SS. Between 1933 and 1945, Lenz was director of the Institute for Racial Hygiene at the University of Berlin and departmental director at the Kaiser Wilhelm Institute for Anthropology. The screening of SS marriage applications arose from the concerns of the Reich Peasant Fuehrer Walther Darré to have a hereditarily healthy population settled in the rural East. Poppendick's work as the senior physician in the office between 1941 and the autumn of 1944 was oriented to the hereditary health of the SS and of their intended marriage partners, and the encouragement of "child-rich" families. There were SS villages near to Berlin, and he claimed that his medical work ran parallel to genealogical and statistical studies. The SS schemes were paralleled by measures for the Romanian Iron Guard and Hungarian Arrow Cross.

Nazi race experts planned racial transfers to areas in Eastern Europe once they had been cleared of racial undesirables. This involved a vast program of screening and assessing groups for their racial value. In Poland and what had been Czechoslovakia, the *Volksdeutsche* (those of Germanic racial stock) were identified and given privileges. Some ethnic Germans were to be repatriated to rejuvenate their German roots, while other groups, such as those from the South Tyrol, were to be sent to populate new homesteads in the East. The SS envisaged a belt of warrior peasants who would defend the nation against Bolshevism. After the war there were only limited dismissals and arrests of the eugenicists. Mengele escaped Germany; other eugenicists, such as Lenz and Nachtsheim, were rapidly reappointed, and Verschuer endured only a few years' break in his career. Efforts to prosecute the perpetrators of sterilization failed. The Nuremberg Trials made a serious effort to confront the issues of eugenics and genocide—for example, the selection of the mentally ill for killing in the euthanasia centers and X-ray sterilization. There were numerous acquittals by conservative judges. Eugenics became the family policy of the Federal Republic. Compensation for victims of sterilization was resisted by the Federal Republic, and eventually only meager amounts were paid out when it was proved that sterilization was part of Nazi race policies. Compensation has remained limited for medical victims of National Socialism, and accurate figures on the number of victims of sterilization, euthanasia, and human experiments have yet to be attained.

There were noted eugenic movements in Hungary, Romania, and Vichy France. As in Germany, these initiatives drew on prior traditions of thought on race and heredity, and on positive eugenic ideas of "puericulture." The stress was on measures to raise the birth rate, and the idealization of motherhood as a racial duty. The aim (as in Germany) was to revive primal racial vigor and to rejuvenate society. But the means were more moderate, and sterilization was limited to Nazi Germany, some Swiss cantons, and Scandinavia. The most ambitious scheme was an institute for the study of man under the physiologist Alexis Carrel in France under German occupation. The eugenic input into French demography remains controversial.

Paul Weindling

See Also: AHNENERBE; ANTHROPOLOGY; ANTI-SEMITISM; ARROW CROSS, THE; ARYANISM; ASOCIALS; AUSCHWITZ; BLOOD; BLOOD AND SOIL; BOLSHEVISM; CARREL, ALEXIS; CONCENTRATION CAMPS; CZECHOSLOVAKIA; DARRE, RICHARD WALTHER; DEMOGRAPHIC POLICY; EUTHANASIA; FAMILY, THE; FRANCE; *GLEICHSCHALTUNG;* GÜN-THER, HANS FRIEDRICH KARL; HEALTH; HIMMLER, HEINRICH; HITLER, ADOLF; HOLOCAUST, THE; HOMOSEXUALITY; IMMIGRATION; IRON GUARD, THE; MEDICINE; MENGELE, JOSEF; NATIONALISM; NAZISM; NORDIC SOUL, THE; ORGANICISM; POLAND; PSYCHOLOGY; RACIAL DOCTRINE; ROMA AND SINTI, THE; RURALISM; SCIENCE; SEXUALITY; SOCIAL DARWINISM; SS, THE; UNIVERSITIES; *UNTERMENSCHEN;* VICHY; WARRIOR ETHOS, THE; WEIMAR REPUBLIC, THE; WORLD WAR II

References

Weindling, P. 1989. *Health, Race and German Politics between National Unification and Nazism, 1870–1945.* Cambridge: Cambridge University Press.
———. 2000. *Epidemics and Genocide in Eastern Europe, 1890–1945.* Oxford: Oxford University Press.
———. 2004. *Nazi Medicine and the Nuremberg Trials: From Medical War Crimes to Informed Consent.* Basingstoke: Palgrave-Macmillan.

EUGENICS (Italy)

The Italian Fascists' eugenics program was, by contrast to Nazi Germany, limited and moderate. Their eugenic efforts concentrated on improving racial health and on increasing the population, rather than removing from the gene pool any individuals or groups considered inferior. Founded in 1913, the Italian Committee for the Study of Eugenics generally opposed the "negative" measures suggested by its foreign counterparts. Some Italian eugenicists supported such measures but did not believe that they could be achieved in Italy, because of the Catholic Church's influence and the population's general conservatism. Most eugenicists supported the new Fascist regime and were rewarded with political or academic appointments. For example, Corrado Gini became head of ISTAT, the central statistics institute, and played an important role in leading the demographic campaign.

Despite their concerns about hereditary disease and infirmity, the Fascists took no active steps to prevent so-called undesirables from marrying and reproducing. There were two key reasons for this. Firstly, the Vatican was implacably opposed to eugenics. Pope Pius XI's 1930 encyclical *Casti Connubii* utterly condemned contraception, abortion, forcible sterilization, and any state interference in an individual's freedom to marry and have children. Secondly, the demographic campaign—Mussolini's "battle for births"—very much emphasized quantity over quality. The Fascist desire for empire and expansion required a much larger population base, and the regime did not wish to limit the breeding stock. The Italian Fascists were much less fixated than were the Nazis on creating perfect racial specimens. Nevertheless, Fascist propaganda contained an ongoing theme of racial hygiene. The term *bonifica* ("reclamation") was used to signify the need to cleanse or purify the population. Signs of decay and degeneration identified in the national body included individualistic behavior such as family planning, and "social diseases" such as syphilis, tuberculosis, and alcoholism.

Social medicine journals of the Fascist period contain numerous articles regarding eugenics. Many of the authors advocated the introduction of a compulsory premarital medical examination. Despite this lobbying, such a measure was not implemented. By 1941, the sterilization of those with hereditary mental or physical conditions was being discussed in the regime's journal *La Difesa della Razza*. However, it never became government policy.

Meredith Carew

See Also: CATHOLIC CHURCH, THE; DEGENERACY; DEMOGRAPHIC POLICY; EUTHANASIA; FAMILY, THE; FASCIST PARTY, THE; GERMANY; HEALTH; ITALY; MEDICINE; MUSSOLINI, BENITO ANDREA; NAZISM; PIUS XI, POPE; PSYCHOLOGY; RACISM; SEXUALITY; SOCIAL DARWINISM; WOMEN

References
Gillette, Aaron. 2002. *Racial Theories in Fascist Italy.* London: Routledge.
Horn, David. 1994. *Social Bodies: Science, Reproduction, and Italian Modernity.* Princeton: Princeton University Press.
Ipsen, Carl. 1996. *Dictating Demography: The Problem of Population in Fascist Italy.* Cambridge: Cambridge University Press.

EUGENICS (U.S.A.)

More than twenty U.S. states had enacted forced sterilization and segregation laws together with marriage restrictions before World War II, with California the heartland of the movement. The Carnegie Institution, the Rockefeller Foundation, and the Harriman railroad fortune financed eugenics research in universities including Stanford, Yale, Harvard, and Princeton, where scientists followed race theory and sought data to prove it. Stanford president David Starr Jordan claimed in his 1902 work *Blood of a Nation* that human qualities and talents are passed down through the blood. The Rockefeller Foundation helped found the German eugenics program, including the one that Mengele worked on before going to Auschwitz.

The leaders of the eugenics movement believed that only blonde, blue-eyed Nordic types were worthy of procreating, while those deemed weak and inferior should have their reproductive capacity destroyed. In a 1911 report sponsored by the Carnegie Foundation a number of practical means were proposed for "cutting off the defective germplasm in the human population," including euthanasia. An applied eugenics textbook published in 1918 recommended the execution of those deemed racially unfit in a "lethal chamber," or gas chamber. Various institutions for the insane practiced euthanasia techniques on their inmates. California sterilized nearly 10,000 individuals in the first ten years after introducing eugenics legislation.

In an infamous Supreme Court decision of 1927, Justice Oliver Wendell Holmes declared in favor of preventing "those who are manifestly unfit from continuing their kind." Holmes's statement was quoted by Nuremberg Trial defendants in their defense. California eugenicists published booklets idealizing sterilization and circulated them to German officials and scientists. Carnegie Institution eugenic scientists had close links with Nazi eugenicists, and Hitler is known to have studied U.S. eugenics laws; in a letter to U.S. prophet of eugenics Madison Grant, he called Grant's book *The Passing of the Great Race* his "bible." In 1934, California eugenics leader C. M. Goethe visited Germany, where sterilizations had risen to more than 5,000 each month. He congratulated a U.S. colleague that his work had played a major part in shaping the opinions of those promoting the program. "Everywhere I sensed that their opinions have been tremendously stimulated by American thought."

Cyprian Blamires

See Also: AUSCHWITZ; BLOOD; DEGENERACY; EUTHANASIA; HITLER, ADOLF; MEDICINE; NAZISM; RACIAL DOCTRINE; MENGELE, JOSEF; NUREMBERG TRIALS, THE; RACIAL DOCTRINE; SOCIAL DARWINISM; UNITED STATES, THE (PRE-1945)

References
Black, E. 2003. *War against the Weak: Eugenics and America's Campaign to Create a Master Race.* London: Four Walls Eight Windows.
Grant, Madison. 1916. *The Passing of the Great Race: The Racial Basis of European History.* New York: Charles Scribner's Sons.
Kühl, Stefan. 1994. *The Nazi Connection: Eugenics, American Racism, and German National Socialism.* New York: Oxford University Press.

Starr Jordan, David. 1902. *The Blood of the Nation: A Study of the Decay of the Race through the Survival of the Unfit.* Boston: American Unitarian Association.

Stern, A. 2005. *Eugenic Nation: Faults and Frontiers of Better Breeding in Modern America.* London: University of California Press.

EUROFASCISM

A postwar revisionist, fascist intellectual movement that emphasizes the vital importance of a pan-European alternative to fascism's discredited ultranationalist agenda. Although only informally structured as a branch of fascist ideology, Eurofascism established its position in the immediate postwar period, drawing together existing Europeanists and forming the basis for future ideological development within the radical right. The roots of this movement can, however, be traced to the thought of fascist Europeanists and internationalists in the interwar period. Although overwhelmed by the fervor of fascist ultranationalism at this time, the work of fascist intellectuals such as Julius Evola and Pierre Drieu la Rochelle provided a basis for later development toward Europeanism. In the immediate postwar period, fascists seeking an alternative to the disastrous divisiveness of ultranationalism returned to the idea of Europe—a Europe united to defend a common culture and civilization.

In essence, the themes of conspiracy, crisis, and cultural decadence so prevalent in Eurofascist ideology are derived directly from orthodox interwar fascism. Eurofascism is, however, distinct in its attempt to conceive a truly postnational form of European government. At an international fascist conference held in Malmö, Sweden, in 1951, the newly formed European Social Movement (ESM) proposed a radical agenda for pan-European organization, including supranational control of the economy and armed forces by a European fascist government. Eurofascist ideologues were divided, though, over the importance of the racial question in their reformulated program. For many, the vital concern was with maintaining European political, economic, and cultural integrity, rather than insisting upon a (spurious) definition of biological community. Others, however, adhered more closely to the ideological tradition of Nazism, which led to an almost immediate split within the ESM and the formation of the neo-Nazi Nouvel Ordre Européen (New European Order).

The increased acceptance and even popularity of Europeanist ideas within postwar fascist circles was very much a reflection of the perceived threat to European integrity posed by U.S. liberal materialism and Soviet communism. Following U.S. involvement in Europe through the implementation of the Marshall Plan and the effective Soviet annexation of parts of Eastern Europe, revisionist fascists keenly felt that the continent was in urgent need of self-protection. A highly defensive and protectionist geopolitical outlook is thus a fundamental feature of Eurofascist ideology. The shift toward postnational thinking by fascists, and the influential contributions of figures such as Evola and Mosley, closely mirrored the development of liberal Europeanism in the early 1950s, both movements having responded to the same geopolitical and economic stimuli. Eurofascism, though, remained deeply illiberal and antidemocratic in its outlook and supranational aspirations.

Stephen Goward

See Also: INTRODUCTION; BOLSHEVISM; CIVILIZATION; CONSPIRACY THEORIES; CULTURE; DECADENCE; DEMOCRACY; DRIEU LA ROCHELLE, PIERRE; EUROPE; EUROPEAN NEW RIGHT, THE; EUROPEANIST FASCISM/RADICAL RIGHT, THE; EVOLA, JULIUS; INTERNATIONAL FASCISM; INTERNATIONAL FASCIST CONGRESSES, THE; LIBERALISM; MARXISM; MATERIALISM; MOSLEY, SIR OSWALD; NATIONALISM; NAZISM; NEO-NAZISM; POSTWAR FASCISM; RACIAL DOCTRINE

References
Ferraresi, F. 1987. "Julius Evola: Tradition, Reaction and the Radical Right." *European Journal of Sociology* 28.

Griffin, R., ed. 1995. *Fascism.* Oxford: Oxford University Press.

Sheehan, T. 1981. "Myth and Violence: The Fascism of Julius Evola and Alain de Benoist." *Social Research* 48, no.1.

EUROPE

The appearance of a broader, European concept of community in fascist thought went hand in hand with the strategic alliance of fascist and right-wing authoritarian states throughout the 1930s. Over the course of a decade, Italy was joined by Germany, Austria, Spain, and Portugal in an increasingly significant, if loose, ideological community. The involvement of fighters from Germany and Italy alongside the rebels in the Spanish Civil War confirmed a form of international solidarity between European fascist and right-wing authoritarian states, much as it did for international volunteers from the Left. In the interwar period, though, real fascist Europeanism (that is, truly attempting to detach itself from a national perspective) was relatively rare; the most notable exceptions were found in the work of the Europeanist fascist Pierre Drieu La Rochelle and the Italian thinker Julius Evola. Of those, the latter has been particularly influential in the development of a neofascist consensus on Europe. What sets these figures apart is that they discussed distinctly postnational forms of a fascist Europe; in Drieu's case it was a passionate plea for a fascist European alternative to the internationalism offered by liberalism and communism.

By contrast, most other discussions of Europe had a definitely national edge. During the interwar period, and more intensively so during the period of occupation, the concept of Europe became attached to a number of pan-regional projects. Each of these had a distinct view of some form of fascist Europe; while the views often overlapped, they tended to reflect expressly national origins. These pan-regional projects frequently referred in some way to the term *Europe,* but without any real commitment to a postnational system of European government. Nazi Germany, as the most powerful fascist nation in the late 1930s and throughout the early years of World War II, dominated with its vision of a Greater Germanic Empire. In turn, as they conquered, Nazi intellectuals began to talk more and more in terms of Europe's, as well as Germany's, future. Indeed, such was the strength of Nazi rhetoric that the salvation of Europe, led by a German vanguard, became the duty of all true Europeans. This had, of course, much to do with Germany's aims to stabilize its occupation and reduce local opposition. Whatever the true purpose, though, the result of the period of occupation was the intensification of visions of a Nazi Europe, which in turn attracted new adherents in the occupied territories. Local collaborators often sought to present their national defeat as part of a European Nazi liberation, increasingly identifying their own nation within the framework of a New European Order. That was particularly true of the Dutch Nazi Mussert and the Belgian Rexist leader Degrelle. However, the Nazi leadership was often not very interested in cooperating with these local nationalist leaders in the occupied territories.

Several senior figures within the Nazi hierarchy became involved in formulating policies for the Reich on Europe. Rosenberg, von Ribbentrop, Daitz, Goebbels, and Himmler wrote and spoke at length on the subject of a reconstituted Europe, with Germany as its firmly guiding power. Daitz described in detail the economic

reorganization of Europe in terms not unfamiliar to a protectionist interpretation of the modern European Union. Von Ribbentrop presented a diplomatic approach to Europe's future, in the evolving tradition of European international relations. Rosenberg's vision of Europe was described much more clearly in racial terms, drawing on a mythical construct of Aryanism. Himmler was similarly obsessed with European blood-community and saw the ranks of the SS and Waffen-SS as a higher caste of Nordic Europeans. Nazi visions of a united Europe spawned their own imitations. In Norway, Quisling imagined a pan-Nordic alliance of fascist states. In Hungary, Szálasi was inspired by German Nazism to describe a Magyar empire of the East. What is significant in each of these pro-Nazi visions is that the concept of Europe is different. While each pan-regionalist project made reference to Europe, there was much variation as to its substantive content and effective administration.

The Italian perspective on Europe at this time was problematic, not least because it offered a credible alternative to progressive "Germanization." Nazi discussions on Europe were divided over the position of Latin peoples: while Italy was an important ally, its people did not fit the superficial Aryan profile offered by Nazi ideologues. However, as self-professed heirs to the imperial legacy of Rome, Mussolini's Fascists felt that they could claim legitimacy for themselves as the originators of a European transformation. As fascism took hold and developed in Germany and elsewhere, Mussolini presented this as confirmation that Italy was leading a European revolution in the civilizing tradition of imperial Rome. At Montreux in 1934, Mussolini organized a conference to discuss the creation of a firmly international association of fascist states. Hitler, however, refused to be drawn into any such commitment.

The discussion of Europe in fascist ideology prior to 1945 was a mixture of sincerity and opportunism. Fundamentally, fascism was a deeply nationalist ideology, so that all thinking on an international level included important provisos. The forms of European thinking that did emerge during the late 1930s and early 1940s, apart from certain notable exceptions, were implicitly imperialistic, no matter how elaborately that was disguised by the rhetoric of a European historical community. When the war was over and fascism defeated, it became clear that real internationalism had been an illusion. Moreover, it was increasingly concluded by many regrouping ideologues and activists that fascism's principal failure had been its inability to create a solid postnational system on the continent. It was this process of evaluation that formed the basis for new conceptual discussions of Europe and the reorientation of significant numbers of fascists away from the cult of the nation and toward a pan-European alternative. The historical context of neofascist Europeanism was significantly affected by geopolitical changes occurring within the first decade or so following the war. With the shift in Soviet influence westward to include much of Eastern Europe and the rapid escalation of Cold War tensions, Europe became ever more tightly caught between what was perceived as the threatening grip of the United States and that of the Soviet Union. At the same time, liberal European governments were engaged in creating a postnational structure that would evolve to become the modern European Union. At this stage many Europeanists, both fascist and liberal, concluded that the era of the nation-state was ending, and that a collective pan-European form of government was urgently required. This was the rationale of the architects of the liberal European project: Monnet, Schumann, and Spinelli. It was also the conclusion that led the disparate ranks of some sixteen national fascist movements to form the European Social Movement at Malmö in 1951, with a radically postnational agenda. The foundation of the ESM signified a shift in fascist ideology, reflecting the harsh experience of defeat and the realization that the geopolitical environment was dramatically altered.

By no means all surviving fascists and subsequent neofascists subscribed to the inter- or supranational dimension, but a significant number did, forming the basis for new types of radical-right thinking. Under the influence of Evola in particular, New Right and Eurofascist ideologues began to reconstruct their vision of the salvation of Europe from an explicitly postnational position. These new variations on the theme of fascist Europeanism are, in a sense, disembodied—that is, they are effectively contained within a metapolitical discussion, detached from any significant proactive structure. That is a consequence of the collapse of fascism as a strategic force and the need for revisionist forms of radical-right ideology to discover fresh intellectual territory, untainted by the horrific excesses of Nazi imperialism. The central theme of postwar radical-right Europeanism is resistance to cultural decay, and specifically to the incursion of the materialist ideologies of U.S. liberal-capitalism and (previously) Soviet communism (echoing the theme explored in Oswald Spengler's seminal 1920s text *The Decline of the West*). Movements such as GRECE, influenced by the French intellectual Alain de Benoist, or the *Scorpion* publication, edited by Michael Walker, provide a platform for this type of radical cultural politics.

Although the conditions that resulted in the emergence of postwar radical-right Europeanism are in many ways comparable to those that brought about the foundation of the liberal European Communities in the 1950s, the ideological thrust in each case is markedly different. One of the principal criticisms of the modern European Union made by ideologues of the Europeanist radical Right is that it is based upon material considerations, lacking a deeper spiritual or cultural attachment to the European "homeland" (what Heidegger described as a "rootedness" in historical space). The revised radical-right vision of a united Europe has tended to emphasize the interconnectedness and solidarity of European cultural nations, rather than the strategic connectivity of conventional nation-states. This emphasis brings to the fore ancient cultural identities, often neglected or suppressed within broader liberal national identities based upon civic constitutionalism (for example, the Basques, Bretons, Catalans, Welsh, and so forth). Ideologues of the Europeanist radical Right reject the perceived homogeneity of civic internationalism, and by extension the liberal supranationalism of the European Union, in defense of cultural diversity. One of the more perverse features of this ideological position has been the use made by illiberal Europeanist ideologues of the discourse of minority rights. Thus an implicitly chauvinistic set of ideas has claimed the language of cultural tolerance and diversity, defending the "Europe of a Hundred Flags" against the faceless uniformity of Western liberal-materialism.

Stephen Goward

See Also: INTRODUCTION; ARYANISM; AUSTRIA; BELGIUM; BENOIST, ALAIN DE; COLD WAR, THE; COSMOPOLITANISM; DECADENCE; DEGRELLE, LEON; DRIEU LA ROCHELLE, PIERRE; EUROFASCISM; EUROPEAN NEW RIGHT, THE; EUROPEANIST FASCISM/RADICAL RIGHT, THE; EVOLA, JULIUS; EXPANSIONISM; GERMANY; GOEBBELS, (PAUL) JOSEPH; GRECE; HEIDEGGER, MARTIN; HIMMLER, HEINRICH; HUNGARY; IMPERIALISM; INTERNATIONAL FASCISM; INTERNATIONAL FASCIST CONGRESSES, THE; ITALY; LIBERALISM; MATERIALISM; MUSSERT, ANTON ADRIAAN; MUSSOLINI, BENITO ANDREA; NATIONALISM; NAZISM; NETHERLANDS, THE; NEW EUROPEAN ORDER, THE; NORDIC SOUL, THE; NORWAY; PANGERMANISM; POSTWAR FASCISM; QUISLING, VIDKUN; RIBBENTROP, JOACHIM VON; ROOTLESSNESS; ROME; ROSENBERG, ALFRED; SPAIN; SPANISH CIVIL WAR, THE; SPENGLER, OSWALD; SS, THE; SZÁLASI, FERENC; WAFFEN SS, THE; WORLD WAR II

References
Griffin, R. 1994. *Europe for the Europeans: Fascist Myths of the European New Order 1922–1992.* Oxford: Oxford Brookes University, Humanities Research Centre.

www.brookes.ac.uk/schools/artsandhumanities/history/griffin/europ
    efas.pdf
Herzstein, R. E. 1982. *When Nazi Dreams Come True.* London:
    Abacus.
Holmes, D. R. 2000. *Integral Europe.* Princeton: Princeton
    University Press.
Lipgens, W., ed. 1985. *Documents in the History of European
    Integration.* Berlin: Walter de Gruyter.
Morgan, P. 2003. *Fascism in Europe, 1919–1945.* London:
    Routledge.

EUROPEAN NEW RIGHT, THE

Born around the time of the May 1968 wave of political unrest sweeping industrialized countries, the European New Right (ENR), or Nouvelle Droite (ND), is composed of clusters of think tanks, cultural institutes, and journals formed initially in France and later throughout Europe. Its intellectuals are mainly editors, writers, liberal professionals, academics, and professors of various disciplines, such as politics, history, sociology, psychology, anthropology, sociobiology, literature, cinema, and art. Although with roots in the ultranationalist and neofascist political milieux, ENR intellectuals now claim to be one of the few remaining cultural or political forces (along with the Greens) that challenges liberal democracy and triumphalist global capitalism. Its contemporary theoreticians are heavily influenced by the ideals of the New Left and emulate the example of the 1968 revolutionaries who claimed that they would create a more humane and spiritualized postliberal social order. ENR intellectuals are currently scattered throughout most Western and numerous Central and East European nations. Furthermore, ENR intellectuals could even be found attempting to spread their ideas and cultural influence in the post-communist, post–Cold War confusion and chaos of Russia in the 1990s.

The ENR is a cultural and political "school of thought." Contemporary ENR intellectuals such as Alain de Benoist and Charles Champetier of France, Michael Walker of England, Marco Tarchi of Italy, Pierre Krebs of Germany, and Robert Steuckers of Belgium generally share a long-term, right-wing metapolitical strategy akin to that of the Italian Marxist thinker Antonio Gramsci. This right-wing Gramscianism is designed to awaken certain individuals—namely, intellectual, political, and economic elites—to new ways of seeing and being, to change hearts and minds,

and to gain support for alternative, counterhegemonic conceptions of the world. For Gramsci, like the ENR, the precondition for all successful revolutions in history has first been a revolt against both the dominant spirit and cultural apparatus of the age. This nonviolent, metapolitical stance is directed primarily at societal elites and intellectuals, rather than the masses, and has been a practical and tactical choice conditioned by the negative historical associations of the Right in the public mind since World War II—particularly the legacies of Italian Fascism and Nazism. In the case of the French New Right, the choice of focusing on the cultural, metapolitical realm was also influenced by the bitter debacle of the revolutionary Right's ill-fated attempt to maintain *Algérie française* and the eventual decolonization of Algeria, which began in 1962. The ENR's metapolitical orientation also differentiated it from ultranationalist political parties and violent, extraparliamentary right-wing movements.

The ENR's intense valorization of both anti-egalitarianism and the "right to difference" of all local cultures and regions around the globe (what Martin Lee has dubbed "cultural ethnopluralism"), is a set of themes frequently adverted to in ENR journals, books, articles, and conferences. Both anti-egalitarianism and the "right to difference" are seen by ENR thinkers as almost natural, God-given absolutes. For the ENR, the "right to difference" of individuals and communities must constantly be nourished and promoted in order to allow all world cultures to maintain their uniqueness and distinctiveness against what is viewed as the gray, drab, lifeless, and leveling materialism and egalitarianism of liberal and socialist doctrines. The latter two ideologies, seen as rooted in Judeo-Christian biblical monotheism, are viewed as "totalitarian" and "intolerant." For the ENR, liberalism and socialism are full of missionarylike zeal because they allegedly originate from a culturally insensitive and universalistic belief in one God that respects neither Europe's polytheistic, pagan past nor the differing values and cultural standards of other peoples around the world. In the postcommunist Europe of the 1990s, liberalism and the United States, viewed as the liberal nation of the world par excellence, have become the ENR's dominant enemies. The ENR argues that both the United States and liberal ideology seek to accelerate an insidious, hypermaterialist, and "soft totalitarian" capitalist worldview and ignore the richness of the world's cultural diversity and organic principles of community and solidarity. The ENR insists that the liberal capitalist worldview is egoistic and that it essentially views the entire planet as one large, vulgar supermarket in which all cultures and nations fall under the homogenizing prey of the profit principle and the spell of ethnocentric, cultural Westernization.

The ENR is centered around its intellectual mentor, Alain de Benoist of France. De Benoist was one of the founders of Groupement de recherche et d'étude pour la civilisation européenne (GRECE; Group for Research and Studies on European Civilization). GRECE was founded in 1968 and is the leading Nouvelle Droite cultural institute and publishing house in continental Europe. If his 1978 prize from l'Académie française is an indication, de Benoist is undoubtedly the most sophisticated and lucid of the ENR intellectuals. A major figure who helped to boost de Benoist's status in France in its heyday in the late 1970s was the founder of the French daily *Le Figaro,* Louis Pauwels. Pauwels coined the term *New Right* in 1977, near the height of the ENR's mass media exposure in France. Pauwels sought to distinguish between Old and New Right, and to rid the Right of its "irrational" anti-Semitism. The ENR again came to public prominence in France in 1993, after the Left sought to resurrect the notion that the ENR was a type of sinister new fascism pretending to be a left-wing movement.

Undoubtedly, ENR intellectuals have influenced the style and discourse of extreme-right-wing and neofascist political parties, such as France's Front National, the German Republikaner, and the Italian Movimento Sociale Italiano-Alleanze Nazionale (MSI-AN), although many of its principal theorists have distanced themselves from what they view as the "vulgar," populist, extreme-right and neofascist political groupings. In the early 1980s, a number of prominent ENR theorists, including the former GRECE secretary-general Pierre Vial, joined Jean-Marie Le Pen's anti-immigrant National Front. Despite internal divisions between the ENR and extreme-right-wing political parties, most contemporary extreme-right-wing political or neofascist political parties have mirrored the ENR's metapolitical orientation, or focus on the cultural terrain of political contestation. The Right, the ENR believed, had to outflank the Left on the cultural terrain in order to gain political respectability and success. Like the ENR, the political parties on the far Right also deny any association with the extreme Right or fascist labels, but instead focus on the so-called novelty of the New Right. In addition, like ENR thinkers, the extreme-right and neofascist political groupings attempt to distance themselves from overt forms of anti-Semitism and affinity for the symbolism of the discredited fascist and Nazi past. Finally, the ENR's formulation of the ambiguous notion of the cultural

"right to difference" has been picked up by extreme-right and neofascist political parties in order to legitimize their ultranationalist, chauvinist, and anti-immigrant stances.

While ENR thinkers themselves have vehemently denied the association and label of fascism, they simultaneously continue to pay homage to a pantheon of "conservative revolutionary" authors such as Oswald Spengler and Ernst Jünger, as well as other writers, including revolutionary leftists and syndicalists, who provided inspiration for Italian Fascism or German Nazism. These include Vilfredo Pareto, Julius Evola, Georges Sorel, Gustave Le Bon, and Lenin. Many major contemporary ENR intellectuals, particularly Alain de Benoist, Michael Walker, and Marco Tarchi, began their careers as figures connected with right-wing extremism or neofascism. In France, de Benoist was involved in extreme nationalist and pan-European revolutionary-right student politics in the 1960s; Michael Walker was formerly a (British) National Front organizer for central London; and Marco Tarchi became disillusioned with the Italian neofascist political party named the MSI (the Italian Social Movement; renamed the Alleanza Nazionale, or National Alliance).

Aware of the Right's historical lessons from the experiences of fascism and decolonization, these ENR thinkers have attempted gradually to rehabilitate the cultural and political legacies of the non-Nazi revolutionary Right. In the mid-1970s and again in the early 1990s, the ENR gained some support among the European intelligentsia. A number of cultural and political trends tended to give ENR intellectuals more public exposure and credibility. In the first place, the star of the Left rose so high after World War II because Fascism and Nazism were thoroughly discredited and associated with the Right. However, the Left's Stalinistic excesses in Eastern Europe and the far Left's perceived intellectual and cultural hegemony and dogmatism in continental Europe (for example, the slavishly pro-Soviet, Stalinist historical record of the French Communist Party and many prominent European intellectuals) made the cultural and political revival of the Right almost inevitable. Second, the crumbling of the Communist states in Eastern Europe after 1989 left an ideological vacuum that ENR intellectuals could tap into. Finally, unlike the Anglo-American world, continental Europe has deep ideological and historical affinities for a particular brand of antiliberal, anticapitalist Right. The ENR is seriously indebted to that revolutionary right-wing intellectual tradition, whether it is the writings of the nineteenth-century French counter-revolutionary Joseph de Maistre, the German jurist Carl Schmitt, or the "Marcuse" of the Italian postwar radical Right, Julius Evola.

In spite of new opportunities presented by the changing political landscape, there has been a persistent trend to marginalize ENR intellectuals in public life, especially in France. The prevailing journalistic view has been that ENR intellectuals were rehashing pernicious fascist and Nazi ideas from the past. Furthermore, the ENR's own postmodern denunciation of many intellectual and political cliques and fads of the age made the cultural and intellectual elite very uncomfortable. Its appropriation of quasi-leftist ideas and anti-Western, anti-Christian pagan orientation tended to threaten liberal and socialist cultural and political elites, the ultranationalist Catholic Right, and the neoliberal Right. However, the ENR's ideological synthesis of revolutionary right-wing and New Left ideas and traditions gave the ENR a sense of constant intellectual vigor and energy that could not be fully ignored by even its harshest critics.

ENR thinkers denied the "fascist" label applied to them by their opponents and flaunted an aura of intellectual, cultural, and political tolerance based on a supposedly eclectic, heterogeneous body of thought without a common platform or dogmatic interpretation of the world. ENR political thought has been influenced by radically different sources: from the "conservative revolution" to ecologism, from the New Left to federalism, and from paganism and feminism to scientism. These diverse influences and their "novel" positions—such as feminism, paganism, federalism, pro–Third World solidarity, anti-imperialism, antitotalitarianism, antiracism, and the valorization of "difference"—have been the product of several facelifts between the late 1960s and 1990s. The ENR's "open" attitude toward issues once dominated by the Left and its use of authors concerned with deep existential and spiritual questions—including Friedrich Nietzsche, Julius Evola, Arthur Koestler, and J. R. R. Tolkien—even appealed to the subjective aspirations of a particular segment of European youth in the early 1980s and 1990s. In the world of today many of the ENR's primary concerns now reflect those of the New Left, born in the wake of the U.S. anti–Vietnam War movement in the 1960s. This ENR intellectual overhaul and opening to the Left has led the most reputable scholar of the ENR phenomenon, Pierre-André Taguieff, to suggest that the French Nouvelle Droite journal *Krisis* now falls outside the orbit of right-wing extremism or neofascist taxonomic categories. In response to Taguieff, most experts on the subject suggest

that even *Krisis,* the ENR's most avowedly leftist journal, is itself a mixture of revolutionary Right and New Left influences and themes. In reality, the entire ENR worldview is an ideological synthesis of the revolutionary Right and New Left positions.

The ENR's harshest critics argue that its esoteric, aristocratic elitism and violent revolt against Enlightenment-driven reason and progress, positivism, materialism, capitalism, communism, egalitarianism, universalism, and liberal parliamentarism were all menacingly echoed in this century by many fascist ideologues. These critics also point out that the ENR's attempt to transcend categories like left and right was also common to European fascist theoreticians of the past, whether George Valois in France, Giovanni Gentile in Italy, or Primo De Rivera in Spain. In the new millennium, ENR theorists still have cultural ties to the right-wing conservative revolutionary heritage of the past, as well as to a number of left-wing, syncretic, and postmodern influences, especially the dominant influence of the New Left. In ENR journals of the 1990s, the revolutionary-right themes of the past—namely, the aristocratic conception of life, the military ethic of honor and courage, the "internal empire of the spirit," the search for primordial common cultural origins, and the powerful attachment to myths—mingle in uneasy coexistence with more recent New Left, federalist, ecological, and democratizing impulses. The ENR, then, is a right-wing movement that would not have been possible without a post–World War II reflection about the nature of historical fascism and the revolutionary Right, on the one hand, and the events of May 1968, the phenomenon of the New Left, and the influence of the Left in general, on the other.

Tamir Bar-On

See Also: INTRODUCTION; AMERICANIZATION; ANTI-SEMITISM; ARISTOCRACY; BENOIST, ALAIN DE; CAPITALISM; CHRISTIANITY; COLD WAR, THE; COSMOPOLITANISM; DEMOCRACY; ECOLOGY; EGALITARIANISM; *EHRE* (HONOR); ELITE THEORY; ENLIGHTENMENT, THE; EUROPE; EVOLA, JULIUS; FASCIST PARTY, THE; FEMINISM; FRANCE; GENTILE, GIOVANNI; GLOBALIZATION; GRAMSCI, ANTONIO; GRECE; IMPERIALISM; JÜNGER, ERNST; LE BON, GUSTAVE; LE PEN, JEAN-MARIE; LIBERALISM; MATERIALISM; MOVIMENTO SOCIALE ITALIANO, THE; NATIONAL FRONT, THE (FRANCE); NATIONAL FRONT, THE (UK); NATIONALISM; NAZISM; ORGANICISM; PARETO, VILFREDO; PARLIAMENTARISM; POSITIVISM; POSTWAR FASCISM; PRIMO DE RIVERA, JOSÉ ANTONIO; PROGRESS; REVOLUTION; RUSSIA; SCHMITT, CARL; SOCIALISM; SOREL, GEORGES; SPAIN; SPENGLER, OSWALD; SYNDICALISM; THIRD WAY, THE; TOLKIEN, JOHN RONALD REUEL; TRADITIONALISM; VALOIS, GEORGES; WARRIOR ETHOS, THE

References

Bourseiller, C. 1991. *Extrême droite: L'enquête.* Paris: F. Bourin.

Cheles, L., R. Ferguson, and M. Vaughan, eds. 1991. *Neo-Fascism in Europe.* London: Longman.

Griffin, R. 1991. *The Nature of Fascism.* London: Routledge.

———. 2000a. "Plus ça change! The Fascist Pedigree of the Nouvelle Droite." Pp. 217–252 in *The Development of the Radical Right in France,* edited by E. Arnold. London: Macmillan.

———. 2000b "Interregnum or Endgame? The Radical Right in the 'Post-fascist' Era." *Journal of Political Ideologies* 5, no. 2: 163–178.

Harris, G. 1990. *The Dark Side of Europe: The Extreme Right Today.* Edinburgh: Edinburgh University Press.

EUROPEANIST FASCISM/ RADICAL RIGHT, THE

An ideological current or variant of mainstream postwar fascist nationalism, seeking a form of cultural or racial community at a pan-European level. Europeanist fascists, perceiving threats to their common civilization (particularly in the form of U.S. liberal capitalism and, previously, Soviet communism, have sought to present fascist internationalism as an ideological alternative, and a fascistized European federation as a bulwark against the decadence of the West. The sense of impending cultural and political crisis across Europe in the early twentieth century spawned both nationalist visions of popular rebirth and more far-reaching, though less influential, pan-continental utopias. Explicitly Europeanist, postnational thought was relatively uncommon during the interwar period—unsurprisingly, given the intensity of nationalist rhetoric in the 1930s. Notable examples are found in the work of Pierre Drieu La Rochelle and Julius Evola, the latter having exerted a strong intellectual influence over the development of postwar Eurofascism and the New Right.

The real growth of fascist and radical-right Europeanism has occurred in the postwar period. Following what was regarded by many as the failure of national fascism during and after the war, alternative guises were sought for a cultural radicalism that would defend Europe against looming threats. At this time both Evola and the British fascist Mosley actively supported some form of fascist supranationalism. In the early 1950s, Europeanist Fascist and Nazi movements, such as the European Social Movement and the Nouvel Ordre Euro-

péen (1951), provided the revised radical right with a new orientation. This reflected a will toward international cooperation between neofascists and neo-Nazis echoed by the French fascist Maurice Bardèche in the early 1960s. Continuing and extending the development of postnational thinking on the radical Right, the Groupe de Recherche et d'Etudes pour la Civilization Européenne (GRECE) was formed in 1968. The group brings together ideologues of Europeanist cultural radicalism and displays the intellectual influence of Evola and Heidegger. Thinkers from this New Right background have furthered their European ideas, in particular to adapt to the post–Cold War, post-immigration environment. New Right ideology offers itself as a defense against the "rootless" cosmopolitanism of multicultural Europe, and as a champion of indigenous European identities and ethnic groups. Ideologues such as Alain de Benoist use a form of ironic cultural differentiation as a basis for rejecting the "Other" from European society, and for constructing a mythic understanding of the unity of the indigenous European community.

Stephen Goward

See Also: INTRODUCTION; AMERICANIZATION; BARDÈCHE, MAURICE; BENOIST, ALAIN DE; BOLSHEVISM; COLD WAR, THE; COMMUNITY; COSMOPOLITANISM; DECADENCE; DRIEU LA ROCHELLE, PIERRE; EUROFASCISM; EUROPE; EUROPEAN NEW RIGHT, THE; EVOLA, JULIUS; GRECE; HEIDEGGER, MARTIN; IMMIGRATION; MOSLEY, SIR OSWALD; MULTICULTURALISM; NATIONALISM; NEO-NAZISM; PALINGENETIC MYTH; POSTWAR FASCISM; ROOTLESSNESS; UTOPIA, UTOPIANISM

References

Cheles, L., R. Ferguson, and M. Vaughan, eds. 1991. *Neo-Fascism in Europe.* London: Longman.

Griffin, R. 1994. *Europe for the Europeans: Fascist Myths of the European New Order 1922–1992.* Oxford: Humanities Research Centre, Oxford Brookes University. *www.brookes.ac.uk/schools/artsandhumanities/history/griffin/europefas.pdf*

Mosse, G. L. 1979. *International Fascism: New Thoughts and New Approaches.* London: Sage.

EUTHANASIA

Nazism transformed the meaning of *euthanasia,* which originally meant assisting a terminally ill individual with a painless death. But even before Nazism came to power, through the writings of authors like jurist Karl Binding and psychiatrist Alfred Hoche in the 1920s, the term had begun to be applied to the proposed killing of "lives without value." Alexis Carrel, the Rockefeller Institute of Medical Research scion who returned to France to build up medical research in Vichy, combined the advocacy of euthanasia of this kind with that of sterilization in his best-selling *l'Homme cet inconnu,* while at the same time condemning democracy. In 1935, Hitler told Gerhard Wagner, the Reich physician, that he would implement euthanasia at the start of the war.

Hitler publicly called for the introduction of a policy of ending lives that were burdensome to society at a Nuremberg rally. Preparations for such killings began in the mid-1930s with surveys of patients held in psychiatric hospitals, and there is evidence of a debate in medical circles around Hitler. Hitler's personal physician, Karl Brandt, cited the petition of parents of a severely disabled child to the Fuehrer, requesting that their severely handicapped newborn baby be killed. This created the impression that, in their implementation of euthanasia, Nazi leaders were responding to a popular wish, and Brandt dated the incident to 1938. The medical historian Udo Benzenhöfer has established that child "K" was named Gerhard Herbert Kretzschmar and was born on 20 February 1939. In July of that year Hitler sent Brandt to visit the child, who was in the "care" of the Leipzig professor of pediatrics Werner Catel. Baby Kretzschmar died later that month. After the outbreak of war in 1939 the Fuehrer wrote that he had entrusted Karl Brandt and the administrator Philippe Bouhler with the implementation of euthanasia, and backdated the decree to the start of the war. Brandt supported the use of carbon monoxide gas chambers (causing a slow and painful death) but otherwise was not actively involved in reaching decisions on individual patients. The numbers killed in the initial phase, code named T-4 (after the administrative office at Tiergartenstrasse 4), came to 95,000. The killings were ordered on the basis of medical records sent to the clandestine panel of adjudicating psychiatrists in Berlin.

In 1941 came condemnation from the Roman Catholic bishop of Münster, Clemens von Galen, and some public opposition, particularly from distressed relatives. This resulted in an official halt to the implementation of the policy. Euthanasia personnel, including physicians and technicians, were transferred to the Aktion Reinhardt, which built and ran the extermination camps of Belzec, Sobibor, and Treblinka. Euthanasia continued unabated in the concentration camps, where prisoners were selected for killing in so-called special children's wards and other clinical locations.

Physicians assisted by nurses killed by starvation, injection, and the administration of deadly drugs. The groups killed included newborn babies, children, the mentally disturbed, and the infirm. Some victims were killed merely for challenging the staff in institutions, although they were in good health, and others were not the so-called 'incurables' of Nazi theory. Some physicians killed because of the scientific interest of the "cases." Identifying those killed shows that networks of referral meant that there was widespread complicity of physicians and nurses in euthanasia. At the same time, other physicians made efforts to keep potential victims out of the euthanasia apparatus. Doctor and author Hellmuth Unger prepared a film script to elicit public sympathy. Unger was a press officer for the Nazi Doctors League and author of a novel promoting euthanasia—*Sendung und Gewissen.* He glorified the medical researcher as empowered to take liberties with life.

Large numbers of patients were killed in Poland and the occupied Soviet Union. The deaths encompassed children's euthanasia between October 1939 and April 1945, with some 5,000 child deaths; the T-4 program of special killing centers between early 1940 and August 1941, when 70,273 adults and juveniles were killed; and the program code named 14-f–13 from April 1941 to 1944, with approximately 50,000 concentration camp prisoners killed. The killings of prisoners of war and forced workers from the East were identified as a distinct phase of euthanasia. The *Aktion Brandt* to clear hospital beds from August 1943 to the end of 1944 coincided with renewed intensification of euthanasia killings, which continued throughout the war.

A high excess wartime mortality has been identified in France, but whether the patient deaths in question came about through hunger and willful neglect and whether mistreatment increased is a matter of controversy. One estimate is of approximately 40,000 French victims. After the war a series of trials were conducted against the perpetrators of euthanasia in Austria and Poland. There were numerous acquittals and a concerted shielding of those responsible. The German Psychiatric Association claimed falsely in the 1950s that its members opposed euthanasia. The case against Karl Gross, a neuroanatomist in Austria who dissected the brains of many child victims of euthanasia in Vienna, was thwarted by his plea of mental incapacity.

Paul Weindling

See Also: AUSTRIA; CARREL, ALEXIS; CONCENTRATION CAMPS; EUGENICS; FORCED LABOR; FRANCE; GALEN, CARDINAL CLEMENS AUGUST VON; HEALTH; HITLER, ADOLF; HOLOCAUST, THE; MEDICINE; NAZISM; NUREMBERG RALLIES, THE; POLAND; PSYCHIATRY; VICHY

References

Benzenhöfer, Udo. 1998. "'Kindereuthanasie' im Dritten Reich: Der Fall 'Kind Knauer.'" *Deutsches Ärzteblatt* 95, Ausgabe 19, Seite A-1187/B-987/C-923.

Burleigh, M. 1995. *Death and Deliverance: "Euthanasia" in Germany 1900–1945*. Cambridge: Cambridge University Press.

Friedlander, H. 1995. *The Origins of Nazi Genocide: From Euthanasia to the Final Solution*. Chapel Hill: University of North Carolina Press.

Weindling, P. 1989. *Health, Race and German Politics between National Unification and Nazism, 1870–1945*. Cambridge: Cambridge University Press.

EVOLA, JULIUS (1898–1974)

Memorialized at the time of his death by Italian Social Movement leader Giorgio Almirante as "our Marcuse, only better," Evola was a major influence through his writings on Italy's most brutal and revolutionary neo-Fascists in the three decades following the end of World War II. Leaders of such violent neo-Fascist bands as the New Order, National Vanguard, and National Front found in his philosophy a rationale for seeking to topple Italy's "corrupt and bourgeois" democratic system. From an aristocratic Roman background, Evola was a relatively marginal figure during the years of Mussolini's dictatorship. He admired elements in Fascist doctrine but found that in practice it contained too much cheap populist demagoguery for his taste. Instead, Evola expressed admiration for the Romanian Iron Guard, especially its "legionnaire" spirit and *conducator* Corneliu Cordreanu, while criticizing Italian Fascism from the Right.

A member of what Gertrude Stein referred to as a "lost generation" of young people who fought in and were deeply affected by World War I, Evola was initially attracted to the avant-garde Dada movement that emerged from that conflict. He composed poetry and recited it in cafes to the accompaniment of music by Bartok, Satie, and Schoenberg. He also painted in the Dadaist manner and displayed his works in galleries in Rome, Milan, Lausanne, and Berlin. However, in 1922, Evola abandoned the avant-garde and gave up poetry and painting for philosophy, a subject that would consume the rest of his life. An admirer of Nietzsche and the writers who came to be identified with the German *Konservative Revolution*, Evola embarked on a study of Oriental ideas involving magic, mysticism, and the occult. He was taken especially by the ideas of the French Orientalist René Guénon. The chief result of these studies was Evola's major philosophical work, *La Rivolta contra il mondo moderno* (1934). In this profoundly pessimistic volume Evola stressed the decadent nature of the modern world resulting from the replacement of higher spiritual values by crass materialistic ones. Evola linked the rise of the latter to various other modern evils, such as egalitarianism, democracy, liberalism, and socialism. By contrast to these modern ideas and practices, Evola called attention to the pagan civilizations of Greece (Sparta especially) and early Rome, with their celebrations of the virile, manly values of the warrior. Modern decadence, he believed, was an outgrowth of the humanism associated with the Renaissance, the Reformation, and, above all, the French Revolution, which tore down tradition and natural human hierarchies. Communism and capitalism were the twin evils stemming from this replacement of the spiritual by the material.

During the 1930s, Evola became an editor for the Fascist journal *Regime Fascista*, a publication sponsored by Roberto Farinacci, one of the few figures in the Mussolini dictatorship attracted to Nazism. Evola's relationship with *Regime Fascista* lasted until the collapse of the dictatorship itself in 1943. In that period he wrote a number of works, one of which, the *Sintesi di dottrina della razza* 1941), expressed his views about the destructive role of Jews in the Western world. Jews, or "the Jewish spirit," represented virtually everything that Evola had come to despise about modernity: the worship of mammon, money, and commerce. Further, Jews by their nature were compelled to spread these values wherever they resided and, in consequence, accelerate the decline of their hosts. Unsurprisingly then, Evola had much kinder things to say about Hitler than Mussolini. In fact, except for brief periods, Evola spent the last years of the war in Berlin and Vienna (where he was injured during an Allied bombing raid) working for the Nazi regime. It was also during this period that he began to hold up the Waffen-SS as a basis for optimism for those who had come to despair about the modern world. Evola saw this elite Nazi military force as the revival of a pagan warrior elite that drew volunteers from a number of European countries who were willing to sacrifice themselves in behalf of an already lost cause.

Following the war Evola returned to Italy, a country whose liberation by British and U.S. forces he regarded as an unmitigated disaster. The liberation meant, he believed, that Italy would almost surely follow the decadent path of Western liberal development. In fact, the two largest political parties to emerge in the country were the Christian Democrats and the Communists. To most observers the two forces appeared as bitter enemies, but not to Evola. He considered them to be two sides of the same coin. Christian Democrats and Communists represented alternative forms of the same decadent materialism, the former capitalist, the latter collectivist. He supported neither Coca-Cola nor Marx. The one political force in postwar Italy in which Evola saw some hope, at least for a while, was the neo-Fascist Italian Social Movement (MSI). Although he was never willing to join the MSI, he became, in effect, the movement's guru or, better, the oracle for its most radical and violent elements. At first these elements, largely young Fascist veterans of the Italian Social Republic's armed forces, formed a faction of *evoliani* within the MSI. They responded to his writings in the MSI journal *La Rivolta Ideale* and his 1950 pamphlet *Orientamenti,* which stressed the possibility of a new "European man" who would embrace aristocratic values and who could lead the continent away from its subordination to U.S. and Soviet interests.

When in 1956 control of the MSI passed into the hands of conservatives—those interested in participating in an anticommunist alliance with monarchists and right-wing Christian Democrats—most of Evola's followers left the movement and created their own, more explicitly antidemocratic groups. The New Order and the National Vanguard were the most prominent. The former, whose symbol, twin lightning bolts, and motto, "Duty Is Our Honor," were borrowed from the Nazi SS, and the latter, whose leader, Stefano Delle Chiaie, defined his group as possessing the "legionnaire spirit," played central roles in waging campaigns of antileftist violence in Rome, Milan, and other cities throughout the late 1960s and much of the 1970s. In addition, members of these and other neo-Fascist bands were accused of colluding with right-wing elements within Italy's police and national security establishments to covertly carry out a series of terrorist bombings in public places—for example, at the National Agricultural Bank in Piazza Fontana in Milan in December 1969, in the hope that the Italian public would hold the Left responsible and tolerate a coup d'etat aimed at repressing it.

In two texts, *Men Standing among the Ruins* (1953) and *To Ride the Tiger* (1961), Evola offered guidance to idealistic young neo-Fascists who hoped to live a higher, more spiritual life and, at the same time, participate in the rebirth of their country. The state, Evola asserted, represented the dominating masculine principle

in human life. Control it and everything else would follow. Conventional party politicians were weak and cowardly, incapable of protecting the nation against communist subversion and the decay brought on by capitalist individualism. An elite of heroes or "differentiated men" was necessary to seize control of the state and do what was necessary. In abstract terms, Evola offered a rationale, many of his admirers believed, for a violent seizure of power in Italy. No such seizure occurred, but even after his death in 1974, Evola's views continued to influence still younger generations of neo-fascists in Italy and, more recently, France and beyond.

Leonard Weinberg

See Also: INTRODUCTION; ALMIRANTE, GIORGIO; AMERICANIZATION; ANTI-SEMITISM; ARISTOCRACY; BOLSHEVISM; CAPITALISM; CODREANU, CORNELIU ZELEA; DECADENCE; DEMOCRACY; DICTATORSHIP; EGALITARIANISM; EUROFASCISM; EUROPE; EUROPEAN NEW RIGHT, THE; EUROPEANIST FASCISM/RADICAL RIGHT, THE; FARINNACCI, ROBERTO; FASCIST PARTY, THE; FRANCE; FRENCH REVOLUTION, THE; GRECE; HITLER, ADOLF; INDIVIDUALISM; IRON GUARD, THE; ITALY; LIBERALISM; MARXISM; MATERIALISM; MODERNITY; MOVIMENTO SOCIALE ITALIANO, THE; MUSSOLINI, BENITO ANDREA; NAZISM; NEW MAN, THE; NIETZSCHE, FRIEDRICH; OCCULTISM; PALINGENETIC MYTH; POSTWAR FASCISM; SOCIALISM; SS, THE; TENSION, THE STRATEGY OF; TOLKIEN, JOHN RONALD REUEL; WAFFEN SS, THE; WARRIOR ETHOS, THE; WORLD WAR I

References

Drake, Richard. 1989. *The Revolutionary Mystique and Terrorism in Contemporary Italy.* Bloomington: Indiana University Press.
Ferraresi, Franco. 1996. *Threats to Democracy: The Radical Right in Italy after the War.* Princeton: Princeton University Press.

EX-SERVICEMEN: *See* WAR VETERANS

EXPANSIONISM

One of the features common to many interwar fascist movements was the idea that their existing territory belonged to a (semimythical) larger racial entity that either had existed in the long-distant past or that had never existed at all, other than as a model of what "should" be in the minds of particular (mostly modern) ideologues. This led to aspirations to "re-create" the entities in question by force, a policy of so-called expansionism. This type of policy was different from traditional colonialism, in which the project was to acquire new territories in other parts of the globe, and also from imperialism, which could be applied to any kind of planned acquisition of additional territories—although in common parlance the term *expansionism* would be applied to both colonialism and imperialism. Expansionist thinking was not peculiar to fascists but was propounded in various versions in different countries in the century before the appearance of fascism by the so-called pan movements—for example, Pan-Arabism and Pan-Slavism. The most influential type as far as Nazism was concerned was Pangermanism, a movement long predating the foundation of the Nazi Party in Germany. Pangermanists believed in the creation of some kind of Germanic national entity bringing together German speakers or those of German racial stock under one national roof. Hitler promoted the Pangermanist agenda as a central plank of his foreign policy. Once in power, Italian Fascism took as its model the Roman Empire and vigorously promoted the notion of *Romanità* ("Romanness"). A book published in England had the title *Mussolini's Roman Empire*. In this case the expansionism was not about bringing together ethnic Italians or Italian-speakers (although that sometimes played a role, as with territories to the east of Trieste), but about recreating a past era of Italian greatness. The same idea was found in Albania, with the fascist advocacy of "a greater Albania," and similarly in Croatia, Finland, and Hungary, where it was called "Hungarism." In truth this kind of expansionism was a form of ultranationalism that focused on the idea of a common race or language as the bond of a nation, rather than on that of shared civil and political rights, which had dominated nationalism in its liberal form since the French Revolution. In retrospect we can see that the Pangermanist ideal was indeed nothing more than a continuation and extension of the movement that had led to a "united" Germany in the nineteenth century. Failure to grasp this properly has led some historians not to recognize the core of hypernationalism common to different interwar fascisms.

Cyprian Blamires

See Also: INTRODUCTION; ALBANIA; ARYANISM; COLONIALISM; CROATIA; FINLAND; FRENCH REVOLUTION, THE; GERMANY; HITLER, ADOLF; HOLY ROMAN EMPIRE, THE; HUNGARY; IMPERIALISM; IRREDENTISM; MIDDLE EAST, THE; MUSSOLINI, BENITO ANDREA; NATIONALISM; NAZISM; NEW AGE, THE; PANGERMANISM; ROME

References
Garratt, G. T. 1938. *Mussolini's Roman Empire*. Harmondsworth: Penguin.
Griffin, R. 1991. *The Nature of Fascism*. London: Routledge.
Kallis, A. 2000. *Fascist Ideology: Territory and Expansionism in Italy and Germany, 1922–1945*. London: Taylor and Francis.
Mack Smith, D. 1979. *Mussolini's Roman Empire*. Harmondsworth: Penguin.
Snyder, Louis L. 1984. *Macro-nationalisms: A History of the Pan-Movements*. Westport, CT: Greenwood.

EXTERMINATION CAMPS: *See* CONCENTRATION CAMPS

EYSENCK, HANS JÜRGEN (1916–1997)

Controversial and well-known British psychologist who discussed the psychology of fascism and who suggested that there were racial differences in intelligence. Eysenck claimed that fascists and communists possessed similarly "tough-minded" personalities, although other psychologists contested his analysis of the relevant data. In the 1970s, Eysenck received widespread publicity when, on the basis of results from IQ tests, he argued that blacks were on average genetically less intelligent than whites. Critics disputed his conclusions and claimed that Eysenck was giving support to racist ideas. Certainly fascist groups at the time asserted that Eysenck's work supported their beliefs. During this period, Eysenck was interviewed—and recruited as editorial advisor—by some racist publications.

Michael Billig

See Also: PSYCHOLOGY; RACIAL DOCTRINE; RACISM

Reference
Eysenck, H. J. 1990. *Rebel with a Cause: The Autobiography of H. J. Eysenck*. London: W. H. Allen.

FAISCEAU, LE: See **FRANCE; FRENCH REVOLUTION, THE; VALOIS, GEORGES**

FALANGE

Allegedly fascist but in reality authoritarian conservative movement in Spain, first founded in 1933. In March 1931, Ramiro Ledesma Ramos established the weekly *La Conquista del Estado,* in which he expounded his national-syndicalist theory, synthesized in the unification of economic forces and the elimination of class war. In June 1931, Onésimo Redondo created the Juntas Castellanas de Actuación Hispánica, which in October fused with the group that had gathered around Ledesma; thus there arose a new grouping called Juntas Ofensivas Nacional Sindicalistas (JONS) whose symbology would later pass in its totality into Falange—namely, the yoke, the arrows, and the cries of *España, una, grande y libre!* ("Spain, Unified, Great and Free!) and *Arriba España!* ("Long Live Spain!).

On 29 October 1933, José Antonio Primo de Rivera y Sáenz de Heredia founded Falange Española in the Comedy Theatre in Madrid. Present at the foundational act were Ruiz de Alda and García Valdecasas, who had formed the Agrupación al Servicio de la República. Ideologically it proclaimed itself antiliberal, anti-Marxist, nationalist, and totalitarian, and it picked up on the heritage of earlier violent youth movements such as the Juventudes Mauristas or the Legionarios de Albiñana. It called for the elimination of the political parties and their replacement by an organic political representation of "family, municipality and union." With the intention of widening the bases of the grouping, José Antonio set up conversations with Ledesma that concluded with an agreement made in February 1934, by which the Falange fused with JONS to create Falange Española de las JONS, at the head of it being José Antonio, Ruiz de Alda, and Ledesma Ramos.

FE de la JONS became the shock force of the Right, and the monarchical party Renovación Española gave it financial backing for a few months until the refusal of FE to integrate unconditionally into the groups on the Right. In October 1934, following a proposal by Ledesma, Primo de Rivera became the sole supreme head of Falange. One month later the twenty-seven points of FE de las JONS were published, whose redaction was to a great extent the work of Ledesma. In these we find allusions to the nationalization of the banks and to the noninterference of the Church in affairs of state, which contributed to the abandonment of Falange by the marquis de la Eliseda, the main supplier of funds; his departure gave rise to a serious financial problem which resulted in a further and deeper crisis that ended with the expulsion of Ledesma in January 1935.

The discomfiture of Falange at the elections of February 1936 was brutal, to the point that Primo de Rivera lost his seat. From that moment members of the youth wings of the monarchical party Renovación Española and the Juventudes de Acción Popular, disenchanted with Gil Robles, began to find their way into FE. At the same time the violent attitude of its militias increased, and on 11 March 1936 there was an assault on the socialist professor Jiménez de Asúa; three days later Falange was outlawed, and José Antonio, without a seat and therefore without parliamentary immunity, was incarcerated in the Model Prison in Madrid until he was moved in June to Alicante Prison. There is no doubt about the involvement and complicity of Falange in Franco's military uprising of July 1936.

In April 1937, with José Antonio executed, Franco decreed the dissolution of the political parties. Immediately afterward the Falange Español Tradicionalista y de las JONS was formed on Franco's initiative by representatives of very different ideologies united only by their proclaimed and resolute antiliberalism and anti-Marxism. The idea was to create a single party comprising all those who had supported Franco's uprising. At this period Falange was politically very active under the leadership of Manuel Hedilla Larrey, who had temporarily taken it over after the execution of José Antonio; Hedilla wanted to seize the reins of power, and with the help of his supporters he managed to get himself designated national chief. After a bloody battle between the antagonistic groups within Falange, Franco signed the decree of unification on 19 April 1937. Franco made himself head of the armed forces, of the state, and of the single party. The sole authorized political party (for the ensuing thirty-eight years) was now Falange Español Tradicionalista de las JONS, later transformed into Movimiento Nacional.

However, between 1939 and 1941 Falangist-type conspiracies did not cease, as a protest against the line that the dictatorship of Franco was adopting—a line that conflicted with the initial policies that had motivated the support of Falange for the uprising. On the other hand, many Falangists were perfectly integrated into the structure of the administration and had created solid interests for themselves that they wanted to protect; the only group to remain active was the one led by Ezquer, Ofensiva de Recobro Nacional Sindicalista, which did not manage to provoke anything more than minor skirmishes. But serious confrontations between Carlists and Falangists in Begoña in August 1942 resulted in a rapid and definitive military reaction on the part of the government to take total control of the remains of Falange.

The law of 17 July 1942 created a parliamentary body for the Francoist state; up to that moment the role had been fulfilled by the National Council of the Falange Español Tradicionalista de las JONS, a corporative organ of deliberative character that assembled to listen to the caudillo or to the secretary general of the Movimiento. Until the promulgation of the principles of the Movimiento in 1958, the official doctrine was the twenty-six points of Falange, whose statutes had acquired force of law after the decree signed in August 1937. This recommended indoctrination of children and young people (in schools, youth organizations, and union organizations), together with programs of social action. Where women were concerned, the Female Section (with Pilar Primo de Rivera at its head) opted to reduce the ideological content, venerating motherhood and conventional roles and reinforcing the traditional national-Spanish heritage through women.

Falange lived on, but it lacked internal unity. Already before the death of Franco there were three different tendencies: "rightist" (Raimundo Fernández Cuesta), "centrist" (Márquez and Jato, allied to the Círculos Doctrinales José Antonio), and "leftist" (authentic Falange with the followers of Hedilla). Other groups on the extreme Right (Fuerza Nueva, Círculos Doctrinales Ruiz de Alda, Asociación Juvenil Octubre) considered themselves to be depositories of the intellectual heritage of the original Falange. Falange was dissolved in 1977, and after that there was a proliferation of neo-Falangist groupuscules, at odds with each other and having barely any more impact than the 20 November gatherings to commemorate the anniversary of the deaths of Franco and José Antonio.

Marta Ruiz Jiménez (translated by Cyprian Blamires)

See Also: AUTHORITARIANISM; CLASS; CONSERVATISM; CORPORATISM; FAMILY, THE; FERNÁNDEZ CUESTA, RAIMUNDO; FRANCO Y BAHAMONDE, GENERAL FRANCISCO; FRANCOISM; LIBERALISM; MARXISM; NATIONALISM; ORGANICISM; PRIMO DE RIVERA, JOSÉ ANTONIO; SPAIN; SPANISH CIVIL WAR, THE; SYNDICALISM; TRADE UNIONS; WOMEN; YOUTH

References
Ellwood, Sheelagh M. 1988. *Spanish Fascism in the Franco Era: Falange Española de Las Jons, 1936–1976.* Basingstoke: Palgrave Macmillan.
Payne, Stanley G. 1965. *Falange: A History of Spanish Fascism.* Stanford: Stanford University Press.
Richmond, Kathleen. 2003. *Women and Spanish Fascism: The Women's Section of the Falange, 1934–1959.* London: Routledge.

FALANGE (2): *See* **PHALANGE**

FAMILY, THE

Past and contemporary fascists invariably link the question of the family to wider demographic concerns involving the very survival and standing of the nation. An expanding population, dependent on family formation and the performance of its reproductive and child-nurturing responsibilities, was and is regarded by fascists as both an indicator and a source of national power and security in an unstable and competitive international scene. In the same vein, the defense of the family is often also connected to the defense of the race and racial purity. National decline was and is perceived as a matter of the nonwhite races breeding uncontrollably, while the birth rates of the white races stagnate and fall, and of the miscegenation likely to arise in white race countries containing significant racially "alien" minorities, whether Jews or black and Asian immigrants. These fears of mixed-race relationships reflect assumptions about the role of women as—literally—reproducers of the race, a role best performed and preserved in the family.

Whereas both conservative and liberal conceptions of the family view it as a "natural" and private institution that exists outside state jurisdiction, fascists continue to regard it as primarily a social and national institution, to be controlled by and for the state acting in the nation's interest. Sexual relations and conduct are not seen as a matter of private morality and choice, or of personal and individual fulfillment, but as a matter for state intervention and state policy. In producing and raising more children of good racial quality and "nationalist" outlook, women do their "national" duty in service of state and race. So, for fascists, abortion remains what it was for the Italian Fascist regime in the 1930s, a "crime against the state," condemned not so much in prolife terms of taking an innocent individual life as for debilitating the nation and distorting women's "natural" female and family role.

In practice, then, it is important to locate the family policies of the two historical fascist regimes in Italy and Germany in those regimes' wider "totalitarian" aspirations and claims to be creating a new "fascistized" society, in which the boundaries between state and society and private and public morality and conduct characteristic of a liberal polity were no longer respected. Certainly, both regimes paid a great deal of attention to the family, which consistently informed and, indeed, drove their social and economic policies throughout the 1930s. The Italian Fascist and German Nazi regimes aimed to stem and reverse falling birth rates, by then a general phenomenon in the "developed" world, which, in their view, diluted national power and inhibited the realization of plans for imperialist conquest and expansion. Any number of more or less coordinated pro-natalist measures were taken to encourage early marriage and large families, from improved provision of mother and child welfare to several kinds of fiscal benefits and incentives, including marriage loans for which repayment fell as the number of children in the family rose, family allowances, and tax breaks for husbands who had large families. Preference in appointment to, and promotion in, public employment was given to married as opposed to unmarried men. There were deliberate attempts to limit paid female employment and to return women exclusively to the home, a policy that had another rationale in the Great Depression but that was later undermined by the regimes' expansion of industries geared to autarky and war production. Abortion was made illegal, as were the promotion of and access to other forms of birth control. The Nazi regime, true to its central racial ideology, also introduced negative natalist measures that aimed at racial selection and improvement, including compulsory sterilization and a ban on the marriage of the "congenitally unfit."

Because fertility decline was particularly associated with urban employment and urban living, both fascist regimes glorified and promoted the life and way of life of the fertile, hard-working peasant family, the repository of "national" values and the guarantee of the nation's future. They took significant, if usually ineffective, measures both to prevent the drift of people from countryside to town and to enhance the attractiveness of staying on the land; in Nazi Germany, that was by attempting to provide security of tenure for small farmers, in Fascist Italy by ambitious projects of land reclamation for internal agricultural resettlement. These positive and negative natalist measures did not, and probably could not, generate the intended lasting improvement in birth rates. Also, intended or not, the regimes' own "totalitarian" organizing drive tended to undermine their own idealized family and gender roles, and might well have contributed to the dissolution of the nuclear and patriarchal family structure. By attempting to involve young people and mold them as "fascists" in their "totalitarian" youth organizations, the fascist regimes effectively interposed themselves between children and their parents and took on for themselves the educative and formative functions of the family. Quite literally, family harmony, parental authority, and even any kind of dialogue within the family were likely to have been damaged not only by "normal" teenage rebelliousness and generational conflict but also by the time spent away from the family of both fathers and children on activities sponsored and controlled by the regimes' organizations. That was especially the case when the youth camps aimed to inculcate a "fascist" ruthlessness, will to action, and loyalty to a wider community than the family: the nation.

Although, in line with their martial and virile "values," both fascist regimes devoted less energy to organizing women than men, women were included in the general totalitarian mobilization of society. The very fact of being organized at all outside the home opened up access to a range of new opportunities and activities for many women. Even if those new horizons were only at the level of selling the produce of "autarkic" kitchen "farms" on the market, or visiting the nearest big town as a member of the local women's fascist organization, the totalitarian mobilization of women would have worked against rather than for the creation of the passive, dutiful, housebound wife and mother. Fascism's totalitarian pretensions were, and are, bound to transform the traditional forms of family life and gendering of roles.

Philip Morgan

See Also: INTRODUCTION; ANTI-SEMITISM; AUTARKY; DECADENCE; DEMOGRAPHIC POLICY; ECONOMICS; EDUCATION; EUGENICS; EMPLOYMENT; FARMERS; GERMANY; HEALTH; HOMOSEXUALITY; IMMIGRATION; ITALY; MEDICINE; NATIONALISM; RACIAL DOCTRINE; RURALISM; SEXUALITY; STATE, THE; TOTALITARIANISM; WALL STREET CRASH, THE; WARRIOR ETHOS, THE; WELFARE; WOMEN; YOUTH

References
Cheles, Luciano, Ronnie Ferguson, and Michalina Vaughan, eds. 1991. *Neo-Fascism in Europe.* London: Longman.
De Grazia, Victoria. 1991. *How Fascism Ruled Women: Italy, 1922–1945.* Berkeley.: University of California Press.
Koonz, Claudia. 1987. *Mothers in the Fatherland: Women, the Family and Nazi Policies.* London: Cape.
Pine, Lisa. 1997. *Nazi Family Policy, 1933–1945.* London: Berg.

FARINACCI, ROBERTO (1892–1945)

Exponent of *squadrismo* and of the most intransigent style of Fascism in interwar Italy. After an early period of militancy in the socialist camp, Farinacci joined with the nationalists in arguing for Italian intervention in World War I. In 1919 he gave his support to the Fasci di combattimento and distinguished himself by his activism and his organizational capacities. His extreme ideological radicalism led him into frequent clashes with Mussolini. Secretary general of the Fascist Party from 1925 to 1926, director of the daily *Il Regime fascista,* toward the end of the 1930s he became a fanatical supporter of the racial laws and the alliance with Nazi Germany. He was, in fact, the only major Italian Fascist ideologue at the heart of Mussolini's administration who was attracted to Nazism. He took part in the life of the Salò Republic but without holding any political or administrative position. Captured by the "partisans," he was shot on 28 April 1945.

Alessandro Campi
(translated by Cyprian Blamires)

See Also: FASCIST PARTY, THE; GERMANY; INTERVENTIONISM; ITALY; MUSSOLINI, BENITO ANDREA; NAZISM; RACIAL DOCTRINE; SALÒ REPUBLIC, THE; *SQUADRISMO*

Reference
Fornari, H. 1971. *Mussolini's Gadfly.* Nashville, TN: Vanderbilt.

FARMERS

An essential ingredient in fascist success was the support of small property owners. Where fascist parties failed in their efforts to mobilize small property owners, they never built a national and mass-based following. While all fascist parties tried to win over the small property owners, many failed because they were unable to develop and disseminate a coherent program addressing the material interests of that group, or found the path to mobilizing them blocked by other political parties perceived to be the defenders of their interests. Interestingly, the political Left played a crucial role in determining the outcome of fascist mobilization efforts. Where the Left took up the defense of small property, new parties could not establish a foothold.

ITALY

Italian Fascism could not have succeeded as it did without first securing a foothold in the farming regions of north-central Italy. The Fascists did not come to power as the result of an electoral victory—they received only one-tenth of the national vote in 1921. However, the party's political impact was quite dramatic, given that it was a political newcomer. It gained nearly one-fourth of the popular votes in several provinces. The provinces in which Fascism had the greatest electoral success were all primarily agricultural. By 1921, Italian sharecroppers and laborers wanted to climb the social ladder toward land ownership, and they began to search for a political party that would allow them to achieve that long-range goal. The Italian Fascist Party had made clear its opposition to agrarian socialism and land collectivization. The Fascist Party first offered an agrarian program in early 1921. During the first half of 1921, articles appeared in the Fascist press proclaiming "land to the peasants," "to every peasant the entire fruit of his sacred labor," and "we want the land to belong not to the state but to the cultivator." The Fascist Party proposed to transform agricultural laborers into sharecroppers, sharecroppers into tenant farmers, and eventually all three into landowners. To accomplish these transformations, the Fascists promised to reopen the land market. They would convince large landowners to transfer land to the Fascist land office, which would then allocate or sell the land to interested cultivators, who would have a specified time period in which to pay off their debts. Unlike the socialists, the Italian Fascists addressed the aspirations of those who wanted land, as well as those of landowners who wanted more.

The Fascists' major hurdle was to convince large landowners to place their land on the market, or agree to lease it. The Fascists won over many large landholders by defending the economic importance of large commercial farming, and by convincing the owners of large farms that a larger and stronger class of sharecroppers, tenants, and small owners would provide a buffer between the large landowners and the socialist labor unions; also, it would greatly reduce the socialist threat of class revolution. However, the Fascists did not treat all landlords alike. They defended large-scale commercial farms whose owners directly supervised their estates but vigorously opposed the system of latifundia characterized by absentee landlords, which the Fascists considered contrary to farming's social purpose of direct involvement of the cultivator, economic profitability, and strengthening the national community.

GERMANY

The Nazi Party's initial electoral breakthrough occurred in the German countryside, which may have contributed substantially to the party's ultimate electoral successes in 1932. The NSDAP's ability to establish a foothold among German farmers was greatly enhanced by the Left's ideological dogmatism. The German Left forfeited the potential backing of many farmers who could never feel comfortable in a party that, in attacking private property, rejected the farmer's dream of social advancement. The SPD (Social Democratic Party) had many strikes against it as a prospective choice of Germany's rural community. Not least among the albatrosses that hung around the party's neck were its Marxist legacy of antagonism toward private property, its favoritism toward the industrial working class, and its consistent attacks on protective tariffs for agriculture. Several scholars have referred to rural Germany as the fountainhead of Nazism. The literature on the Nazi Party's rural program highlights a disjuncture between the pre-1928 period and the post-1928 period, leaving the impression that the Nazis, to take advantage of the agrarian crisis, did not discover the rural community until 1928. This literature, I believe, has overstressed the degree to which 1928 signals a turnabout in the NSDAP's rural program. Rather, I argue that farming issues preoccupied the NSDAP from the party's inception in 1920, and that the party's post-1928 pronouncements on these matters were generally consistent with the party's earlier positions. The NSDAP's long-standing attention to the concerns of the rural community—the redistribution of vacant land, idle estates, and state-owned land to the landless, support of productive (profit from one's own labor) capitalism, and protection against unproductive or loan capitalism—gradually and successfully allowed it to stake out its space between the parties of the Left, Center, and Right.

The 1930 NSDAP Agrarian Program stands as the party's major pronouncement on agricultural matters before 1933. The Agrarian Program appeared in the *Völkischer Beobachter* on 6 March 1930. The program embodied both specific proposals to improve the agricultural situation in Germany and an ideological statement praising the virtues of the Nordic or Aryan race. Many of the proposals contained in the Agrarian Program were not new; the NSDAP, the DNVP, and various agricultural regional groups had voiced them earlier. However, the NSDAP displayed innovation in the manner in which these proposals were combined into a single coherent program and were linked to the party's general economic and social strategy. Furthermore, the program contained some novel and politically shrewd suggestions on inheritance and resettlement. In Germany's predominantly Catholic Rhineland and southwest, partible inheritance (division of the land among the heirs) had progressed further than elsewhere in Germany. The Nazis argued that this made the farmer susceptible to the threat of the world market and capitalistic speculation. The NSDAP proposed a Law of Hereditary Entailment, allowing only the eldest child to inherit land. This legislation was designed to prevent the fragmentation of the farm, to ensure that Germany's farmland remained in the hands of pure Germans, to guarantee that farms specified as hereditary-entailed continued in the same family in perpetuity, and to limit the bank foreclosures that had driven thousands of farmers from their hearths.

Closely linked to the NSDAP's inheritance proposals were the party's pronouncements on resettlement. Realizing that the elimination of partible inheritance would produce a sea of disinherited heirs, the party sought to entice them with new land in the East. The NSDAP resettlement policy called for the establishment of large-scale settlements along the Eastern frontier, comprising primarily disinherited farmers' sons and aspiring landowners. Here the Nazis claimed that the state had the obligation to seize land that large estate owners failed to farm themselves, and that the recipients of these farms would receive hereditary leaseholds. Arguing that the creation of farms alone was insufficient for economic viability, the Nazis called for the establishment of rural cities alongside the new farms to provide farmers with local markets for their produce, as well as easy access to required nonagricultural commodities.

The 1930 Agrarian Program held out a consistent promise of a better economic future. The program discussed the need to improve the lot of agricultural laborers by raising them to the status of farmer. That would become possible through the resettlement program, whose objective was also to stem the flight of these laborers from the land and to reduce the demand for imported agricultural labor. Additionally, the resettlement program offered the hope of a brighter future to the noninheriting sons of farmers. In many of the economically depressed farming regions, older farmers did not have enough cash to pay off their younger, noninheriting sons, which was the tradition in Germany's impartible inheritance regions. By promising to set aside land in eastern Germany for the disinherited, the Nazi program offered both parents and children an appealing exit from their dilemma. Farmers in Catholic farming communities, whose interests were consistent with the NSDAP's positions on private property, tariffs, credit, foreclosure, and governmental subsidies, nevertheless objected to the party's inheritance proposals, which would force them to abandon the practice of partible inheritance. Moreover, farmers residing in Catholic communities had a viable alternative to the Nazi Party. The agricultural positions of the Catholic Center Party and its ally, the Bavarian People's Party, mirrored the NSDAP's positions; what is more, the Center Party promoted the interests of the Catholic Church in Germany, making it a better choice than the Nazi Party for many Catholic Germans.

BELGIUM AND FRANCE

In the 1936 Belgian legislative elections, fascists—Rexists and Flemish nationalists—stunned the Belgian electorate by winning 37 of 202 parliamentary seats. This feat was remarkable, since the newly founded Rexist movement (which won 31 parliamentary seats) had no party organization or prior legislative experience. At the heart of the Rexist program was a call for a corporate state modeled on Fascist Italy. According to Léon Degrelle, corporatism was the best means to overcome the chaos of class struggle. The Rexist corporate state would be authoritarian and fully imbued with Christian values. The Rexists were opposed to big business; they blamed the major financial institutions for the worldwide economic depression and the impoverishment of small- and medium-scale family-run businesses. But they were not opposed to private property or to capitalism, and they demanded that the state aid small- and medium-size businesses and farms. In particular, they called for more accessible agricultural credit and restrictions on large agrobusinesses. Among the competing political parties, the Rexists most strongly favored the family-owned farm.

Many of France's interwar fascist movements tried to mobilize France's farming community but ran into the formidable presence of the French Left. Henry Dorgères called for a dictatorship with the peasantry on top. His program was limited to attacks on government bureaucrats, communism, fiscal controls on small indebted tenant farmers and the promotion of strong family values, and fascist corporatism. By Hazo's account, the movement found its greatest backing in the areas of Chateaubriant, Redon, and Presqu'île Guérandaise (parts of the departments of Loire-Inférieure and Ile-et-Vilaine). These areas are, not surprisingly, strongholds of medium-scale tenant farming. Founded in 1928, the Croix de Feu had the largest popular following during the interwar period. In autumn 1935 the movement launched a campaign to penetrate France's rural constituencies, promising to restore to the land the spiritual value that had been corrupted by international capital, parasitical political committees, and revolutionaries. In spite of these efforts the movement's leader, Colonel La Rocque, was well aware of his movement's difficulty in attracting rural adherents. Doriot's PPF (Parti Populaire Français) attempted to attract French farming support in 1937 and 1938. Doriot stressed a rebirth of a strong peasantry, denounced the decline in French fertility levels and excessive urbanization, and called for a return to the provinces. Doriot appealed to the landowning peasantry for support by attacking agricultural laborers' claims for higher wages and by promising that the PPF favored the creation of new credit facilities for smallholders and assistance to smallholders to enable them to specialize in products of quality and to expand their markets in France's colonies.

It appears that fascist parties in Belgium, Italy, and Germany succeeded in establishing substantial popular support from smallholding farmers. In France, by contrast, the socialist Left was perceived, interestingly, as the major defender of the right of small private property. Where fascist parties and movements gained a solid foothold in the countryside, they typically attracted adherents by advocating the direct involvement of the cultivator in the farming enterprise, the redistribution of idle lands and vacant estates, the social mobility of smallholders, the strengthening of the national community, and defense of the rights of small property ownership.

William I. Brustein

See Also: ARYANISM; BELGIUM; BOLSHEVISM; CAPITALISM; CATHOLIC CHURCH, THE; CENTER PARTY, THE; CORPORATISM; DARRE, RICHARD WALTHER; DEGRELLE, LEON; DEMOGRAPHIC POLICY; DORGERES, HENRY; DORIOT, JACQUES; *DRANG NACH OSTEN* ("DRIVE TO THE EAST"), THE; ECONOMICS; FAMILY, THE; FASCIST PARTY, THE; FRANCE; HITLER, ADOLF; INDUSTRY; ITALY; GERMANY; LA ROCQUE DE SEVERAC, FRANÇOIS, COMTE DE; MARXISM; NAZISM; NORDIC SOUL, THE; REVOLUTION; REXISM; RURALISM; SOCIALISM; *VÖLKISCHER BEOBACHTER,* THE; *VOLKSGEMEINSCHAFT,* THE

References
Brustein, William I. 1996. *The Logic of Evil: The Social Origins of the Nazi Party, 1925 to 1933.* New Haven: Yale University Press.
Brustein, William I., and Marit Berntson. 1999. "Interwar Fascist Popularity in Europe and the Default of the Left." *European Sociological Review* 15, no. 2: 25–44.
Cardoza, Anthony L. 1982. *Agrarian Elites and Italian Fascism: The Province of Bologna, 1901–1926.* Princeton: Princeton University Press.
Corner, Paul. 1975. *Fascism in Ferrara 1915–1925.* London: Oxford University Press.
Etienne, J. M. 1968. *Le Mouvement Rexiste jusqu'en 1940.* Paris: Colin.
Linz, Juan. 1976. "Some Notes toward a Comparative Study of Fascism in Sociological Historical Perspective." Pp. 3–121 in *Fascism: A Reader's Guide,* edited by W. Laqueur. Berkeley: University of California Press.
Luebbert, G. M. 1991. *Liberalism, Fascism, or Social Democracy: Social Classes and the Political Origins of Regimes in Interwar Europe.* New York: Oxford University Press.
Noakes, J. 1971. *The Nazi Party in Lower Saxony, 1921–1933.* London: Oxford University Press.
Pridham, Geoffrey. 1973. *Hitler's Rise to Power: The Nazi Movement in Bavaria, 1923–1933.* New York: Harper and Row.
Soucy, Robert. 1995. *French Fascism: The Second Wave 1933–1939.* New Haven: Yale University Press.

FASCI DI COMBATTIMENTO: *See* FASCIO, THE

FASCIO, THE

Bundle of rods or sticks, bound together with an ax, that the Roman lictor used as a symbol of authority. The first major political movement to adopt the name, the Sicilian Fasci of the 1890s, was an early socialist organization. In the years before World War I numerous *fasci operai,* or "worker groups," were formed. In March 1919, when Mussolini formed the first *fascio di combattimento,* or "combat group," the term meant almost nothing. The very ambiguity of the name was perfect for a movement that had yet to define itself. In 1926 the bound rods accompanied by the ax became the official and ubiquitous symbol of the new Fascist state. It conveyed unity and strength, as well as a clear reference to ancient Rome. In 1939 the Italian parliament was renamed the Chamber of Fasces and Corporations.

Alex de Grand

See Also: ITALY; MUSSOLINI, BENITO ANDREA; ROME; SYMBOLS

Reference
Falasca-Zamponi, S. 1997. *Fascist Spectacle: The Aesthetics of Power in Mussolini's Italy.* Berkeley: University of California Press.

FASCIST PARTY (PARTITO NAZIONALE FASCISTA; PNF), THE

The National Fascist Party (PNF) was the political organization that governed in Italy from 1922 to 1943 and implemented an experiment in totalitarian domination.

FROM THE ANTIPARTY MOVEMENT TO THE MILITIA PARTY

The PNF was constituted in November 1921, following the transformation into a party of the movement of the Fasci di combattimento, formed on 23 March 1919 on the initiative of Benito Mussolini with a program that was republican, antistatist, and anticlerical. Mussolini's movement, which called itself "antiparty"—that is, a temporary libertarian association—was not successful. At the beginning of 1920, in the whole of Italy there were only thirty-seven Fasci and fewer than a thousand members, almost all of them in the north of Italy. For that reason Mussolini decided to abandon the program of 1919 and to present Fascism as the defender of the nation, of the productive bourgeoisie, and of the middle classes. At the end of 1920 the Fascist movement effectively became the principal protagonist of antiproletarian bourgeois reaction. Organized into armed squads (*squadrismo*) subsidized mainly by the agrarian bourgeoisie, the Fascists carried out a systematic terrorist program to destroy the political, economic, and social organizations of the Socialist Party where those were strongest—that is, in the Po Valley, in Tuscany, and in Puglia. Equally violent was the activity of Fascist *squadrismo* in the areas bordering

on Yugoslavia against the hostile parties and the Slav population. Membership rose from 20,165 in December 1920 to 187,588 in May 1921, and to more than 200,000 two months later. In May 1921, Fascism took part in the elections and won thirty-five seats in the parliament.

This new Fascism was substantially identifiable with *squadrismo* and was an aggregate of various "provincial fascisms" that had developed locally on their own impulse and not through an initiative of Mussolini's—hence they did not feel any obligation to bow to the authority of the founder of the Fascio. After having approved a so-called pacification pact with the Socialist Party (3 August 1921), Mussolini put forward a plan to organize the Fascists into a party so as to give unity to the new movement and subject it to his own control. He aimed to transform the movement into a sort of "party of labor," as he himself defined it, for the middle classes, by putting a brake on *squadrismo* violence. But the majority of the leaders of the "provincial fascisms" rebelled against Mussolini, rejecting the pacification pact and Mussolini's claim that he merited obedience as the *duce* of Fascism. At this period, in fact, Mussolini was not yet recognized by the mass of the Fascists as a charismatic leader, nor did he officially have the role of principal leader of the Fascist movement. The conflict between Mussolini and the *squadrismo* chiefs was very bitter, and it was exacerbated in the Third National Congress of Fasci (Rome, 7–10 November 1921), at which the constitution of the "National Fascist Party" was agreed upon. Mussolini succeeded in getting acceptance for the proposal to transform the movement into a party, but the heads of the "provincial Fascisms" brought about the rejection of the pacification pact and the maintenance of the armed organization of *squadrismo,* as was established by the statute of the PNF approved in December 1921. That statute laid down the principle of the electivity of posts by the local and national membership in the organization of the internal hierarchy. Mussolini was recognized as Il Duce—that is, as political guide of Fascism, but officially he remained one of the members of the PNF directorate; Michele Bianchi was elected to the post of secretary general of the PNF. Bianchi was one of the founders of the Fasci, a Calabrian former socialist and revolutionary syndicalist who guided the Fascist Party through to the conquest of power. In October of the following year a framework for the "Fascist Militia" was published that definitively sanctioned the complete symbiosis between political organization and armed organization of the PNF.

The Fascist Party was born as a political organization of a new genre—a militia party—and as such it remained unaltered up to its disappearance from the political scene twenty-four years later. The PNF was a militia party not simply because it had its own armed force but also because its organization, its political culture, its ideology, and its way of life were derived from *squadrismo. Squadrismo* was not just a method of violent action but also a mode of conceiving and practicing politics; it was inspired by the military model and by experience of war, and it was characterized by the claim to have a monopoly on patriotism, by the exaltation of violence as the instrument of political regeneration, and by hatred for political opponents, branded "internal enemies" of the nation. Activism remained a fundamental component of the Fascist Party, which always considered itself to be a "movement" and a "militia," and which saw political militancy as a total dedication founded on faith in the absolute primacy of the nation, on the communitarian feeling of comradeship, on the virile ethic of the battlefield, and on the principle of military hierarchy.

The political culture of the PNF was "anti-ideological" in the sense that it despised rationalistic, theoretical conceptions and exalted mythical thought as an expression of the collective consciousness and as a factor in the mobilization of the masses. Its ideology was represented aesthetically by the myths, rituals, and symbols of a new political style that conferred on Fascism the character of an exclusive lay religion, integralist and intolerant. The Fascists openly proclaimed their will to become the new ruling class, for they considered themselves the new aristocracy, an aristocracy of young people who in the trenches had conquered the right to command. This myth of youth was another fundamental component of the Fascist Party. From its birth, the Fascist Party claimed to be superior to all the other parties and to the liberal state. Although despising bourgeois society as materialistic and individualistic, the Fascist Party upheld the leading role of the productive bourgeoisie and the necessity for collaboration between the classes (corporatism), with the goal of intensifying national production (productivism) so as to be able to achieve a foreign policy of power and imperial expansion. The myth of empire as expressed in the exaltation and cult of Rome (*Romanità*) was present in the ideology of the Fascist Party from the beginning, even when it still lacked a precise program for Fascist foreign policy with clearly defined objectives other than the vague goal of redeeming the "mutilated victory"—a goal formulated in generally revisionist statements against the order fixed by the Versailles Treaty.

THE CONQUEST OF POWER

In 1922, with more than 200,000 members, an armed militia, women's and youth associations, and Fascist syndical organizations numbering around half a million members, the PNF had become the strongest political organization in the country. The fact that all of the other parties were in crisis owing to their internal divisions or to the continual assaults to which they were subjected by *squadrismo* opened the door to a Fascist conquest of power. The success of the Fascist Party was, however, not solely the fruit of violence and the political ability of a demagogue who was able to exploit the fears of the bourgeoisie against Bolshevism. In reality, the Fascist Party conquered power and imposed the transformation of the state during a period in which—on the admission of Mussolini himself—to speak of a Bolshevik threat in Italy was nonsense. The Fascist Party not only urged the defense of the economic and social order based on private property but also aimed to realize its own political and cultural revolution through the destruction of the liberal regime and the construction of a new state; this was to be conceived according to the principles and values of a new integralist and palingenetic ideology that, by its very nature, did not admit either in theory or in practice of coexistence with other ideologies and parties. Democracy, as Mussolini said in August 1922, "had completed its task."

The PNF conquered power with a tactic that combined terrorist action with political maneuvering. The March on Rome of 27–28 October 1922—that is, the insurrectional mobilization of the Fascist *squadre*—was not simply a dramatic coup but the culminating moment in a terroristic campaign pursued since the spring of that year both against opposing parties and representatives of the government; whole cities and regions were occupied by thousands of *squadristi* who openly defied the authority of the liberal state. The *squadrista* insurrection in many cities of northern and central Italy and its occupation of governmental buildings, prefectures, barracks, post offices, and railway stations would certainly have been defeated in a confrontation with the regular army. But it generated confusion at the highest level in the state, while Mussolini negotiated his rise to power with the representatives of the liberal regime and the economic world. In this way the Fascist Party obtained the maximum of success with the minimum of risk. The king gave Mussolini the task of forming the new government, which won the trust of the chamber and the senate, but that did not diminish the gravity of what had happened with the March on Rome. For the first time in the history of the European liberal democracies, parliamentary government had been entrusted to the leader of a militia party who repudiated the values of liberal democracy and proclaimed his revolutionary intention of transforming the state in an antidemocratic direction. From that point of view the March on Rome may be considered historically as the first step toward the destruction of the liberal state and the establishment of the Fascist state.

The conquest of power also provoked a serious but temporary crisis at the top of the Fascist Party on account of rivalries between Fascist leaders in the rush to grab public offices, as well as the appearance on the victors' bandwagon of thousands of new members, numbering more than 800,000 by the end of 1923. Between 1923 and 1924 there were also squabbles between various factions of dissident and autonomous Fascists, and especially between the "revisionist" Fascists responsible for the demilitarization of the PNF and the "integralist" Fascists who exalted the role of the party militia and wanted to continue the "Fascist revolution" to the point of total conquest of power and the construction of a new and integrally Fascist state. Mussolini decided to strip the Fascist Party of any sort of autonomy and subject it to his directives. In December 1922 the leadership of the PNF was entrusted to a new supreme organ, the Grand Council of Fascism, composed of the leaders of the party and the Fascist members of the government, with Mussolini as president. *Squadrismo* was legalized on 14 January 1923 with the institution of the voluntary militia for national security, incorporating the *squadre* under the direct command of the head of government. These measures were not enough to discipline the party, however, nor to put a brake on the illicit activities of the *squadristi* chiefs (the *ras,* as the antifascists called them), who continued to rule the roost in the provinces, imposing their will even on the representatives of the government. The crisis provoked by the assassination of the Socialist deputy Giacomo Matteotti on 10 June 1924, carried out by *squadristi* who acted on the orders of close collaborators of Mussolini, gave back the initiative to the integralist Fascists—that is, to the *squadrismo* chiefs, who coerced Il Duce into making a move for total conquest of the monopoly of political power by the PNF at the end of 1924.

THE PARTY IN THE FASCIST STATE

With Mussolini's speech to the Chamber of 3 January 1925, the Fascist Party formally initiated the "legislative revolution" for the destruction of the liberal regime

and the construction of the totalitarian state. In February of the same year, Roberto Farinacci, the principal leader of integralist Fascism, was appointed by the Grand Council as the new secretary of the PNF. Within a few months he succeeded in reconstituting unity and discipline within the party, and he was among the main authors of an intransigent policy to eliminate political opposition definitively and establish a one-party regime. Farinacci had his own idea of a totalitarian party, believing that it must retain its autonomy with respect to the government, and placing the secretary of the PNF, as "head of the party," on the same level as Mussolini—that is, as "head of government" in a dyarchy that was in fact unacceptable to Il Duce. In March 1926, when the authoritarian reforms had concentrated executive power in the hands of Mussolini, Il Duce dismissed Farinacci, and the Grand Council replaced him with Augusto Turati. Turati was also an exponent of integralist Fascism, but one more prepared to support Mussolinian policy in the phase of the transformation of the state into a one-party regime. Turati remained in his post until October 1930 and played a key role in completing the reorganization of the party, conducting a massive purge of corrupt and rebellious elements. This was continued by his successor, Giovanni Giuriati (October 1930 to December 1931), and facilitated the insertion of the PNF into the new regime. A new statute (8 October 1926) abolished internal democracy, and the PNF was definitively subjected to the orders of Il Duce. Successive statutes (1929, 1932, and 1938) perfected the new character of the PNF, which became fully a civil militia under the orders of the *duce* and the servant of the Fascist state. In 1927, Mussolini declared that in the Fascist regime the party was subordinate to the state, as in the provinces the federal secretary was subordinate to the prefect. In fact, contrary to what many scholars still maintain, seeing this as the "political liquidation" of the PNF in the Fascist regime, the subordination of party to state, was merely a rhetorical fiction, for the confusion and symbiosis between state and party became an essential facet of the Fascist regime. This symbiosis became evident in the ambiguous duality of the role of Mussolini as both head of government and head of the PNF. Behind the facade of the regime's monolithic unity, conflicts between party and traditional institutions continued up to the end, and even Mussolini either did not want, or was not able, to avoid them (he may even have encouraged them). For example, the rivalry between prefects and federal secretaries continued, and federal secretaries were never stated to be subordinate to prefects in any of the statutes of the PNF. The federal secretary depended directly on the secretary of the party, and he had powers and functions in his own territory analogous to those that the secretary of the PNF had in the national arena.

During the years of the regime the party was the chief artificer of the totalitarian experiment gradually set in motion after 1925 at a progressively increasing pace. During the secretaryships of Turati, of Giovanni Giurati, and especially of Achille Starace, from December 1931 to November 1939, the party was constantly widening the sphere of its power in state and society.

THE EXPANSION STRATEGY OF THE PNF

The most important manifestations of this PNF "expansion strategy" were the annexations carried out to the detriment of other institutions of the regime, such as the Opera Nazionale Dopolavoro, the most powerful instrument for penetrating the masses, which was incorporated into the PNF in 1932. The other important annexation was the conquest of the monopoly over the education of the new generations that Starace managed to complete in 1937, withdrawing the Opera nazionale Balilla from the aegis of the Ministry of National Education and establishing a single youth organization for anyone from six to twenty-one, the Gioventù italiana del Littorio, which was dependent on the secretary of the PNF. Following the directives of Mussolini, Starace developed the totalitarian organization of the party by bringing millions of men and women of every age into a system of collective life, with the aim of developing a new type of Italian, a "New Man" and a "New Woman." In conformity with its original political culture, the party had a predominant role in the development of Fascist ideology as a political religion, in the celebration of the cult of Il Duce, and in the dogmatic and fideistic indoctrination of the masses through a dense and ever-expanding network of symbols and rites. The party did not hesitate to provoke conflicts with the Church, as happened in 1931 and 1938, in order to claim the monopoly of the education of the young in the principles and values of the Fascist religion.

The presence of the PNF in society became more and more invasive and obsessive; the daily publication of "regulations" told Italians how to live according to the rules and the forms of the new "Fascist Way." Membership in the PNF became a mandatory requirement for all public civil and military employees, so that only PNF members enjoyed "full citizenship." Any Fascist expelled from the PNF was outlawed from public

life. At the end of the secretaryship of Starace (November 1939), the PNF numbered more than 21 million Italians, men and women from six years of age upward, in its numerous political and social subdivisions. This enormous organization ramified from the center to the periphery through provincial federations, the Fasci di combattimento, and the local groups.

TOWARD THE CONQUEST OF THE STATE

With regard to the chamber of deputies and the senate, the "expansion strategy" of the PNF followed different tactics in each case. The definitive fascistization of the chamber of deputies was completed with the political elections of 1929, which eliminated the few surviving non-Fascist deputies elected in 1924. The initiative of the PNF was then crucial in the abolition of the chamber of deputies in 1939 and the establishment of the Chamber of Fasci and Corporations, a move that signaled the death of the principle of parliamentary representation. The new chamber was a direct emanation of the Fascist Party and the corporations. In regard to the senate, whose members were appointed for life by the king on the recommendation of the head of government, the PNF followed a tactic of progressive fascistization via the nomination of new Fascist senators and the activity of an internal association of Fascist senators, the National Fascist Union of the Senate (UNFS), which recruited numerous new members from among the senators nominated prior to the time of Fascism. The fascistization of the senate was to a large extent complete by the early 1930s, with only a few dozen anti-Fascist or non-Fascist senators remaining, and those completely marginalized from the legislative activity of an assembly stripped of autonomy and placed under the control of the Fascist Party through the UNFS.

A new and vaster territory for the expansion of the power of the PNF in society and state were the public bodies, the so-called parallel bureaucracy in a wide range of sectors: from agriculture to welfare, from culture to tourism, from industry to public works, from commerce to transport. There was a huge proliferation of these bodies during the years of the regime; whereas 102 public bodies were created between 1901 and 1921, between 1922 and 1943 353 new public bodies appeared, for the most part controlled by members of the Fascist Party. But the "expansion strategy" of the PNF did not enjoy the kind of immediate success in all the sectors of the traditional state that the more integralist Fascists would have wished. The armed forces, for example, conserved an internal autonomy of administration, though they remained subject to the orders of Mussolini as head of the PNF, who almost always reserved the military departments for himself as head of the government, so that the military was far from immune from party influence.

In the phase of the acceleration of the totalitarian experiment after 1936, the PNF was either the promoter or held the leading role in the racist policy, in anti-Semitic propaganda, and in the antibourgeois campaign for the reform of customs and the intensification of the revolution in the social arena as well. The PNF was moreover committed to the transformation of the constitutional order, leading to a more powerful role and function for the party in the state. In 1937 the secretary of the PNF had the post and functions of a minister. With the new statute of 1938 the PNF was officially declared the only party, taking on as specific tasks "the defense and strengthening of the Fascist revolution and the political education of Italians." In 1941 the new secretary of the PNF, Adelchi Serena, succeeded Ettore Muti (November 1939 to November 1940) and introduced new reforms that subsequently further reinforced the role and power of the party in the state. In the same year the Fascist Party prepared a plan for the reform of the state involving the definitive constitutional affirmation of the primacy of the party as the "driving force of the state." This reform proposed making the Interior and Popular Culture Ministry directly dependent on the Fascist Party, eliminating the dualism between prefect and provincial party secretary with the appointment of a single representative of the party for each province, and officially recognizing the secretary of the party as the highest officer of the Fascist regime after Il Duce. This reform of the state was blocked by Serena's resignation in December 1941 and by the appointment as PNF secretary of a twenty-seven-year-old, Aldo Vidussoni, fresh from the university organizations of the party and completely incompetent to guide the complex machine of the PNF in the difficult years of World War II.

CRISIS AND END OF THE FASCIST PARTY

As the years passed the PNF developed into an enormous bureaucratic apparatus associated with militaristic training and pedagogical propaganda, and it came to be largely discredited in the eyes of the public. It is difficult to say how deeply this totalitarian organization affected the collective consciousness of the Italians, which had been molded and controlled by the PNF.

The fact that in time the party became the single political dimension within which it was possible to exercise some kind of active form of participation, whether individual or collective, in the life of the state is hugely significant. In 1942, one year before the end of the Fascist regime, 27,375,696 Italians, 61 percent of the population—men, women, and children from the age of six years—were involved in the PNF and dependent organizations. One year later, notwithstanding the crisis provoked by the war, the party organization was still growing.

When military defeats undermined the Mussolinian dictatorship and brought it crashing down, a disorderly succession of secretaries (the last being Carlo Scorza, former *squadrista* and exponent of intransigent Fascism, appointed in April 1943) merely compounded an already disastrous crisis. The entire structure of the regime crumbled immediately after 25 July 1943, when Il Duce, disowned by the majority of the chiefs of the Grand Council, was stripped of his powers by the king and arrested. On 2 August 1943 the National Fascist Party was abolished by the new government of Marshal Pietro Badoglio. A few months later, with the constitution of the new Fascist state, the Italian Social Republic, Mussolini tried to reconstitute the Fascist Party, entrusting it to the leadership of Alessandro Pavolini. Composed now of the most totalitarian, intransigent, and violent elements in *squadrismo* and the Fascist regime, plus young people who had been molded by the organizations of the Fascist Party, the new Republican Fascist Party (PFR) redoubled its militarization efforts, establishing the Black Brigades for the war against the partisans of the Resistance; in its program, as approved by the Congress of Verona (14 November 1943), it reprised the antibourgeois and anticapitalist themes that had emerged in the last years of the regime. The PFR made even more of the irrational and mystical themes that were typical of the militia party, such as the ethic of sacrifice, the sense of honor, the warrior spirit, and the cult of violence. It also returned with redoubled enthusiasm to the persecution of the Jews: from 1943 to 1945 more than 7,000 Jews were deported from the territory of the Salò Republic, and of those only 610 came back from the death camps. The victory of the Allies and Resistance forces signaled the end for the PFR on 25 April 1945. The constitution of the Italian Republic as approved in 1947 forbade the re-establishment of the Fascist Party.

Emilio Gentile
(translated by Cyprian Blamires)

References

Cassels, A. 1969. *Fascist Italy.* London: Routledge.

De Grand, A. 2000. *Italian Fascism: Its Origins and Development.* London: University of Nebraska Press.

Gentile, E. 1996. *The Sacralization of Politics in Fascist Italy.* London: Harvard University Press.

Griffin, R. 1991. *The Nature of Fascism.* London: Routledge.

Lyttelton, A. 1973. *The Seizure of Power: Fascism in Italy, 1919–1929.* London: Weidenfeld and Nicholson.

Lyttelton, A., ed. 1973. *Italian Fascisms from Pareto to Gentile.* London: Jonathan Cape.

Payne, S. 1995. *A History of Fascism 1914–1945.* London: University College London Press.

Tannenbaum, E. R. 1972. *The Fascist Experience: Italian Society and Culture 1922–45.* New York: Basic.

FAULHABER, CARDINAL MICHAEL VON (1869–1952)

Leading German Catholic opponent of Hitlerism and anti-Semitism. He was ordained to the priesthood on 1 August 1892 and undertook pastoral work and research in the diocese of Würzburg. He served as chaplain and vicar rector in Rome from 1896 to 1898. He taught Sacred Scripture in Strasbourg before becoming bishop of Speyer in 1911. Faulhaber was appointed archbishop of Munich-Freising in 1917. Four years later he was made a cardinal. When Nuncio Pacelli wrote to Rome in 1923 complaining about the Nazi persecution of Catholics, he noted that the attacks "were especially focused" on the "learned and zealous" Michael Cardinal Faulhaber, who "had denounced the persecutions against the Jews."

In 1934, the year after Hitler came to power, Faulhaber published a book that defended the principles of racial tolerance and called for the people of Germany to respect the Jewish religion. In 1933, Cardinal Faulhaber wrote Secretary of State Pacelli, describing the persecution of the Jews as "unjust and painful." In 1935, Nazis called for him to be killed. In February 1936, Nazi police confiscated and destroyed one of his sermons. This happened twice again the following year. In August 1938, the Nazis ransacked his office. During the riots of *Kristallnacht* (9–10 November 1938), Faulhaber provided a truck for the chief rabbi of Munich to salvage religious objects from his synagogue before it was destroyed. He then gave a speech that resulted in a uniformed Nazi detachment arriving at his residence. They shouted, "Take the traitor to Dachau!" and shattered window frames and shutters. In May 1939, demonstrations against Faulhaber took place throughout Bavaria, and posters were hung saying: "Away with Faulhaber, the friend of the Jews and the agent of Moscow." After the war began, Faulhaber gave an address that resulted in a British newspaper headline reading: "Cardinal Faulhaber Indicts Hitlerism." Martin Niemoeller, a noted German Protestant leader who spent seven years in concentration camps for his opposition to Hitler and the Nazis, said that Faulhaber's sermons showed him "to be a great and courageous man." In his 1945 memorandum to General William Donovan, Fabian von Schlabrendorff praised Faulhaber for stating his opposition to the Nazis and influencing other Catholics to do the same. Schlabrendorff reported that "decisive credit" for the Catholic opposition to Nazism "ought to be given to Cardinal von Faulhaber from Munich . . . whose personal sermons branded Nazism as the enemy of Christendom." After the war, Rabbi Stephen S. Wise, the leading U.S. voice for the Jewish cause, called Faulhaber "a true Christian prelate" who "had lifted his fearless voice" in defense of the Jews.

Ronald Rychlak

References

McCaffrey, R. A., trans. 2003. *The Persecution of the Catholic Church in the Third Reich: Facts and Documents Translated from the German.* Fort Collins, CO: Pelican.

Rychlak, R. J. 2000. *Hitler, the War, and the Pope.* Huntington, IN: Our Sunday Visitor.
Volk, L., ed. 1975–1978. *Akten Kardinal Michael von Faulhaber, 1917–1945.* Mainz: Matthias-Grünewald-Verlag.

FEDER, GOTTFRIED (1883–1941)

Feder belonged to the pioneers of German National Socialism and the left wing of the NSDAP, with ideas of organic democracy and a controlled economy. Born in Würzburg, he studied engineering in Berlin and Zürich. During World War I he developed a hatred of banks and bankers. He published a short manifesto on this, demonstrating his anti-capitalism and anti-Semitism. He was one of the founders of the DAP, which later became the NSDAP. Together with Hitler and others he wrote the first version of the twenty-five points listed in the German NSDAP's program. After the Night of the Long Knives, Feder withdrew from politics and worked as a university teacher.

Göran Dahl

See Also: CAPITALISM; DEMOCRACY; DREXLER, ANTON; ECONOMICS; HITLER, ADOLF; NAZISM; NIGHT OF THE LONG KNIVES, THE; ORGANICISM

References
Stachura, P. D. 1978. *The Shaping of the Nazi State.* London: Croom Helm.
Wagener, O. 1985. *Hitler: Memoirs of a Confidant.* Edited by H. A. Turner. New Haven: Yale University Press.

FEDERZONI, LUIGI (1878–1967)

A founder of the Italian Nationalist Association on 5 December 1910 and its political leader until the merger with the Fascist Party in 1923. Federzoni was elected to parliament in 1914, served as colonial minister (1922–1924) and then as interior minister (1924–1926). A monarchist and authoritarian conservative, Federzoni favored the state bureaucracy over the Fascist Party as the driving force of the Fascist dictatorship. Subsequently he became president of the Italian Senate (1929–1939) and of the Italian Royal Academy (1939–1943). He voted to remove Mussolini at the meeting of the Fascist Grand Council of 25 July 1943.

Alex de Grand

See Also: CONSERVATISM; FASCIST PARTY, THE; GRAND COUNCIL OF FASCISM, THE; ITALY; MONARCHISM; MUSSOLINI, BENITO ANDREA; NATIONALISM

Reference
De Grand, A. 1978. *The Italian Nationalist Association and the Rise of Fascism in Italy.* London: University of Nebraska Press.

FEMINISM

Speaking in 1934, Hitler declared that women's revolt had brought about a situation that went against nature. The slogan of women's emancipation, he held, was "the product of Jewish intellect." Mussolini likewise declared himself opposed to feminism, arguing that "[w]omen must obey. . . . [In] a state like ours they ought not to count." Neofascism has been equally hostile to feminism's re-emergence in the late 1960s. Thus for the British National Party, women should reject feminism and recognize again the importance of their traditional role; while the National Circle of Women of Europe, affiliated to the French National Front, has declared that, whereas feminism stood for a "pseudo-liberation," it sought to conserve the natural harmony between the sexes.

Just as fascists have opposed feminism, feminists have opposed fascism. In the early 1930s they were among those who opposed the rise of Hitler, while later in the decade the feminist Six Point Group was part of the British Section of the Women's Committee against War and Fascism. Opposition continued later in the century, with feminist campaigns against fascism in Britain, France, and other countries.

But the relationship between fascism and feminism is less than straightforward. In part, it has been argued, there was a degree of continuity between feminism and fascism in countries in which the latter took power. In Italy some feminists became supporters of the new regime, claiming that where foreign doctrines were individualist, "Latin feminism" recognized women's duty to the nation. In Germany, Claudia Koonz has suggested, the belief common among the feminists of the time that women and men should be equal but different was continued in the contention of Nazi women that women's sphere would encompass not only the home but also much of public life, including welfare and education. In Britain, too, some feminists were drawn to fascism. One, Norah Elam, argued that the British Union of Fascists was the continuation of the prewar suffragette movement in which she had been active. Two other former suffragettes joined the BUF, but, where one, Mary Allen, remained a supporter of its leader, Sir Oswald Mosley, into the postwar period, the other, Mary Richardson, broke with the movement, denouncing it as betraying its claims to support women's equality. Amid internal tensions, the BUF argued that feminists were mistaken in thinking that fascism would treat women merely as the breeders of cannon fodder. On the contrary, it claimed, fascism would recognize women's equality within employment and the state. In the same period, in Germany, a racist women's publication, *Die Deutsche Kämpferin,* accused the new regime of failing to accept women's equality within the *Volk.*

Arguments like these have continued since World War II. During the 1980s, for instance, a U.S. Nazi publication claimed that the view that feminism was being used to divide the white race was "fundamentally un–National Socialist," while in Britain, *Nationalism Today,* the magazine of one of the factions of the National Front, published an article contending that while feminism was under Jewish control, "nationalists" should champion white women's rights to equal pay and freedom from sexual harassment.

Martin Durham

See Also: ANTI-SEMITISM; BRITISH NATIONAL PARTY, THE; DEMOGRAPHIC POLICY; EDUCATION; EMPLOYMENT; FAMILY, THE; GERMANY; HITLER, ADOLF; INDIVIDUALISM; ITALY; MOSLEY, SIR OSWALD; MUSSOLINI, BENITO ANDREA; NATIONAL FRONT, THE (FRANCE); POSTWAR FASCISM; RACISM; SARFATTI-GRASSINI, MARGHERITA; SCHOLTZ-KLINK, GERTRUD; SEXUALITY; TOTALITARIANISM; UNITED STATES, THE (POSTWAR); *VOLK, VÖLKISCH;* WARRIOR ETHOS, THE; WELFARE; WOMEN

References
De Grazia, Victoria. 1992. *How Fascism Ruled Women: Italy 1922–1945,* Berkeley: University of California Press.
Douglas, R. M. 1999. *Feminist Freikorps: The British Voluntary Women Police, 1914–1940.* Westport, CT: Praeger.
Koonz, Claudia. 1987. *Mothers in the Fatherland: Women, the Family, and Nazi Politics.* London: Jonathan Cape.
Linville, Susan E. 1998. *Feminism, Film, Fascism: Women's Auto/Biographical Film in Postwar Germany.* Austin: University of Texas Press.

FERNÁNDEZ CUESTA, RAIMUNDO (1897–1992)

A senior member of the early Falange Espanola, Fernández Cuesta played a significant role within the Franco regime. Secretary general of FET y de las JONS, the Franco regime's single party, he was minister of agriculture between January 1938 and August 1939, returning to the government in 1951. "Since the rising of 18 July, the Falange has only one decisive aim: obedience to Franco. . . . [We] did, we do and we continue to do whatever Franco wants," he said (Ellwood 1987, 126). After the dictator's death he refounded FE de las JONS, an avowedly nostalgic pro-Franco party.

Sid Lowe

See Also: FALANGE; FRANCO Y BAHAMONDE, GENERAL FRANCISCO; FRANCOISM; SPAIN; SPANISH CIVIL WAR, THE

Reference
Ellwood, S. M. 1987. *Spanish Fascism in the Franco Era: Falange Espanola y de las JONS, 1936–1976.* Basingstoke: Palgrave Macmillan.

FESTETICS, COUNT SÁNDOR (1882–1956)

Hungarian interwar MP and leader of the Hungarian National Socialist Party. He was the nephew of one of the wealthiest landowners in Hungary. In 1918 he served as minister of defense and did not become involved in far-right political movements until the 1930s. He was involved in the creation of a National Socialist "Directorate" in 1934, but he was subsequently expelled from it on the grounds that he was not anti-Semitic enough. He was elected an MP for the Hungarian National Socialist Party in 1935 but became an independent extreme-right deputy after having been removed from the party leadership, eventually allying himself to the Hungarian National Socialist Party–Hungarist Movement. Festetics subsequently retired from politics for good in 1939.

Cyprian Blamires

See Also: ANTI-SEMITISM; HUNGARY; NAZISM

References

Macartney, C. A. 1961. *October Fifteenth*. Edinburgh: Edinburgh University Press.

Nagy-Talavera, N. M. 1970. *The Green Shirts and Others*. Stanford: Stanford University Press.

FILM

Film had a central role in the cultural policies and propaganda campaigns of both Fascist Italy and National Socialist Germany. Although radio was arguably the primary channel of mass information and indoctrination for the duration of these dictatorships, the cinema was the mass medium with the most popular appeal. Documentary films and newsreels had the task of disseminating propaganda about both domestic and foreign events, although both regimes made space for ostensibly "nonpolitical" documentary films. Feature films had a more complex agenda. Both Italian Fascist and German National Socialist officials intended to exploit the ability of commercial cinema to influence and instruct under the guise of entertainment. Within the film production and censorship bureaucracies that these regimes created in the 1930s, the relationships between propaganda and art, ideology, and entertainment were continually debated.

The Italian Fascists and German National Socialists were not alone in those years in attempting to harness the suggestive powers of documentary and feature film for political intent. Democracies had made use of moving images since World War I to shape public perception and create specific political constituencies. Yet the ambitions of fascist regimes were on a far greater scale. Both Italian Fascism and German National Socialism aimed not only to transform the political and social order by creating new antiliberal, antileft, hypernationalistic regimes but also to realize what the historian Emilio Gentile has termed an "anthropological revolution," one that sought to remake the national body and national character by purging it of all supposedly "decadent" and "degenerate" influences. Both Hitler and Mussolini placed new technologies of information, collective mobilization, and reproduction at the service of the state to realize that goal. The place of cinema under these dictatorships may be understood within this framework: it was to facilitate nothing less than the collective transformation of mentalities, morals, and ways of life. Yet for both regimes, film proved to be a double-edged sword. Although fascist movies were to model the looks, speech, and behavior of the members of the new autarkic nation, they were highly influenced by Hollywood and other international film cultures. Coproductions, migrations due to politics, the need to train technicians in new technologies, and the practice of making several "national" versions of one movie simultaneously generated a very international industry culture that ran counter to the protectionist impulses of the 1930s. Thus, although both Fascist Italy and National Socialist Germany attempted to develop national film styles to compete with Hollywood, and encouraged filmmakers to cast recognizably "national" faces, their movies communicated the very kind of cosmopolitan glamour that these regimes had pledged to defeat. Both Italian and German films of this era may be seen as a series of experiments toward the goal of making movies that entertained and absorbed the spectator even as they promoted the results of national revolution and rebirth.

In Italy, as in Germany, the true star of mass spectacle and culture was the dictator, and it is not surprising that Mussolini was the first protagonist of many of the early documentaries and newsreels produced by the Istituto LUCE, which Il Duce founded within a year of assuming power. Yet Mussolini's lack of interest in reviving the Italian feature film industry after its World War I devastation left things in the hands of private entrepreneurs, whose primary aim was often to make money by importing U.S. films. Formal government subsidies for Italian commercial films did not begin until 1931, and a government-controlled film bureaucracy came only with the 1934 founding of the Fascist General Directorate for Cinematography (Direzione Generale di Cinematografia). Headed by Luigi Freddi, it oversaw all film planning, patronage, and censorship, and it served as the model for the Direccíon General de Teatro y Cine in Franco's Spain. The Center for Experimental Cinematography was created the next year to train the future cadres of the new national industry, and 1937 saw the establishment of the state-run Cinecittà studio.

Of the more than 700 films made during the more than twenty years of Italian fascist rule, only about twenty might be considered to be works of clear propaganda. Commercial and aesthetic concerns created a preference for works of subtle rather than open persuasion among many officials, film professionals, and critics. This should not be taken to mean that the regime did not inspire Italians. An overview of Fascist-era movies would reveal a high degree of correlation between their thematic content and that of the regime's various "campaigns"—from the populism of the early 1930s, to the colonial enterprises of the mid-1930s, to the war films and highly stylized adaptations of national literary classics of 1940 to 1943. Indeed, the vast majority of Italian filmmakers remained in Italy for the duration of the regime, either supporting the regime outright or agreeing to the compromises that were necessary to practice their craft.

Mussolini's regime had been in place for eleven years when Hitler came to power in January 1933, and Joseph Goebbels and other National Socialist officials paid attention to the results of Italy's experiments in mass cultural organizing. One difference was the immediate action that the Germans took to impose political controls on the film industry. The Reich Film Chamber (*Reichsfilmkammer*) was established in July 1933 under the aegis of Goebbel's Ministry of Public Enlightenment and Propaganda. It had censorship and production planning responsibilities, and spearheaded a drive to nationalize the German film industry that would not be fully realized until the war years. A Film Credit Bank (*Filmkreditbank*) created in June of that year offered credit to German producers; this patronage measure proved effective in securing cooperation with the new regime, but it did not prevent the flight of dozens of film professionals from Hitler's Germany to European and Hollywood studios. Unlike the Italian Fascists, the National Socialists inherited a successful film industry, headed by the major German film production company, Universum-Film-Aktiengesellschaft (UFA), which dated from World War I. During the Weimar Republic (1918–1933), UFA had spearheaded the building of a national film culture founded on the promotion of expressionism as an alternative to the dominant Hollywood styles. Although the expressionist film style would be denigrated during Hitler's rule, the vision of a uniquely "national" cinema that would signal Germanness, even as it conquered markets abroad, remained during National Socialism—as did the worries about the pernicious influence of wildly popular U.S. films. Indeed, UFA was transformed in 1936–1937 into a state-protected entity to further facilitate protectionist measures, and it was placed entirely under state authority as part of a vast holding-company (Ufa-Film GmbH) in 1942.

Like Freddi, Goebbels believed that ideological messages had to be subtle in the commercial cinema. Of the more than 1,000 feature films made during Hitler's rule, only about 150 are considered to be directly propagandistic. Open propaganda was the province of instructional films, feature-length documentaries—such as National Socialism's most famous film, *Triumph of the Will,* made by Leni Riefenstahl in 1934—newsreels, and *Staatsauftragsfilme* (feature films commissioned and financed by the government). As in Fascist Italy, entertainment films borrowed as much from Hollywood and other film cultures as they did from German national filmmaking traditions. Star worship (of both German and U.S. actors and actresses) was a central component of National Socialist popular culture, and the fantasies of consumer and romantic fulfillment that marked many Hitler-era feature films were not so alien from those projected in the films of 1930s democracies.

Yet National Socialist films do have distinguishing characteristics. They emphasize the recuperation of a sense of wholeness and authenticity in contemporary life, and they promote a sense of belonging to a distinct national community. Whether of the comedic or melodramatic genres, they impart the totalitarian mandates of self-sacrifice, social discipline, and, especially during the war years, the duty of identifying internal and external enemies who threatened the purity of the German *Volk* and its right to expansion. As with many Italian Fascist films, it is not difficult to see how they contributed to the larger social and ideological agendas that guided the dictatorship's development.

Ruth Ben-Ghiat

See Also: AMERICANIZATION; ART; AUTARKY; COLONIALISM; COMMUNITY; COSMOPOLITANISM; DECADENCE; DEGENERACY; FASCIST PARTY, THE; FRANCO Y BAHAMONDE, GENERAL FRANCISCO; FRANCOISM; GERMANNESS (*DEUTSCHHEIT*); GERMANY; GOEBBELS, (PAUL) JOSEPH; HITLER, ADOLF; ITALY; LIBERALISM; MUSSOLINI, BENITO ANDREA; NATIONALISM; NAZISM; PALINGENETIC MYTH; PROPAGANDA; RELIGION; REVOLUTION; RIEFENSTAHL, LENI; SPAIN; TOTALITARIANISM; *TRIUMPH OF THE WILL; VOLK, VÖLKISCH; VOLKSGEMEINSCHAFT,* THE

References
Hake, Sabine. 2001. *Popular Cinema of the Third Reich.* Austin: University of Texas Press.
Hay, James. 1987. *Popular Film Culture in Fascist Italy.* Bloomington: University of Indiana Press.
Landy, Marcia. 1986. *Fascism in Film: The Italian Commercial Cinema, 1931–1943.* Princeton: Princeton University Press.
Reich, Jacqueline, and Piero Garofalo, eds. 2002. *Re-Viewing Fascism: Italian Cinema, 1922–1943.* Bloomington: University of Indiana Press.
Rentschler, Eric. 1996. *The Ministry of Illusion: Nazi Cinema and Its Afterlife.* Cambridge: Harvard University Press.
Welch, David. 1983. *Propaganda and the German Cinema 1933–1945.* Oxford: Clarendon.

FINAL SOLUTION, THE: *See* HOLOCAUST, THE

FINANCE

The sources of finance for fascist movements have been taken as an indication of the true nature of fascism and of the economic interests that were served by fascism. "Who pays?" was what Italian socialists derisively asked of their former comrade, Benito Mussolini, in late 1914, when he was expelled from the Socialist Party for his prowar stance and set up his own daily newspaper, *Il Popolo d'Italia*. The answer was secret funding by the French government and money from some Italian industrialists, both of whom wanted Italy to intervene in World War I on the side of France and Britain. It was this kind of transaction that enabled socialist opponents of fascism and Marxist historians to dismiss fascism as the "agent" of the economic interests of the dominant capitalist classes; Marxists claimed that such interests financed fascist movements because of their hostility to socialism and the social and political gains of the organized working class, and their willingness to use violence against the perceived threat of socialist revolution. A few fascist movements could, at least initially, rely on the personal and family wealth of their founders and leaders—for example, the British Union of Fascists, set up in 1932 by the aristocratic Sir Oswald Mosley. A few became large enough in size to be effectively self-financing. That was the case with the German Nazi Party, which soon became a mass party that lived on many relatively small donations and subscriptions from members and supporters. To survive financially, the Nazi Party did not actually depend on the financial support that it attracted and courted from businessmen's lobbies and associations.

Most other European interwar fascist movements were funded by industrialists, businessmen, and financiers as a party militia to defend them and the "country" against socialism. Sometimes the funding came from individual businessmen, such as the wealthy parfumier François Coty, who seemed determined to invest his business fortune in financing extreme nationalist leagues and movements in interwar France, and whose large gift of money enabled Marcel Bucard, a long-standing member and organizer of several of these leagues, to set up his own fascist movement, Francisme, in 1933. More usually, though, money was given collectively by organized sectional interest groups, such as the lobby of local industrialists and small urban retailers formed in the major central Italian city of Bologna in 1920 that funded the city Fascio to protect property and order during the postwar period of strikes and popular agitation; the longer-established provincial large commercial farmers' associations that directly financed and equipped armed Fascist squads to terrorize socialism out of existence in the countryside of north and central Italy from late 1920; and Redressement Français (French Recovery), a business pressure group formed in 1926 to lobby politicians and parliament in behalf of oil, automobile, and power-generating companies, and which funded the first French fascist movement, Le Faisceau. Some interwar fascist movements also came to depend on subsidies from the Italian Fascist and German Nazi regimes in the 1930s.

These sources of funding for fascist movements self-evidently raised questions about their political independence and made them easy targets for their political opponents. Financing by the two fascist regimes allowed them to be portrayed as the "fifth columns" of aggressive foreign powers and as a threat to national independence and security, a fact that undermined fascist movements' self-image as their countries' only true national and nationalist political force. Financing by businessmen made fascist movements appear little more than violent antisocialism and the mouthpiece of their financial backers. The French fascist movement of the 1920s, Le Faisceau, disintegrated under the weight of this dilemma, its leader, Georges Valois, eventually deciding that he could not risk compromising his political program as the price for securing the financing to keep the movement afloat.

In post-1945 Germany and Italy, neofascist movements have benefited from and come to rely upon systems of public subsidies for political parties, created presumably to end the parties' compromising dependence on private and sectional interest funding. In the case of the MSI, this system rescued the movement financially, since as one of the postwar parties permanently excluded from the orbit of government, it was unable to enjoy and exercise the patronage and favors that came to parties which did form governments and insert themselves into public bodies and institutions. Some Western European postwar neofascist movements have, at various times, funded themselves by criminal activities, either directly by robbing banks or indirectly by receiving the proceeds of international drug trafficking channeled to them by organized crime, including the Mafia. Some have received funding from the Gaddafi regime in Libya and from pro-Iranian Iraqi exiles in Western Europe (on the basis of their anti-Semitic and anti-Zionist positions). Most contemporary neofascist movements, however, continue to rely on self-generated income, membership subscriptions and donations, and profits on the sale of tapes, records, CDs, T-shirts, badges, newspapers, and books, sometimes supplemented by subsidies from individual secret donors. The costs of running a neofascist group or disseminating fascist ideas are, anyway, being reduced by the communications revolution, with extensive use of the Internet, and by the internationalization and cross-fertilization of contemporary groups, who borrow and recycle each other's information and material, a development that is itself a product of the ease of communication across cyber-space.

Philip Morgan

See Also: ANTI-SEMITISM; BOURGEOISIE, THE; BUCARD, MARCEL; CAPITALISM; CYBERFASCISM; FASCIO, THE; FRANCE; GERMANY; GREAT BRITAIN; ITALY; LIBYA; MARXISM; MARXIST THEORIES OF FASCISM; MOSLEY, SIR OSWALD; MOVIMENTO SOCIALE ITALIANO; MUSSOLINI, BENITO ANDREA; POSTWAR FASCISM; QADHAFI (GADDHAFI), MU'AMMAR; SOCIALISM; THYSSEN, FRITZ; VALOIS, GEORGES

References

Cannistraro, Philip V., and Brian R. Sullivan. 1993. *Il Duce's Other Woman: The Untold Story of Margherita Sarfatti, Benito Mussolini's Jewish Mistress, and How She Helped Him Come to Power.* New York: William Morrow.
Eglau, Hans Otto. 2003. *Fritz Thyssen: Hitlers Gönner und Geisel.* München: Siedler Verlag.
Leopold, John A. 1977. *Alfred Hugenberg: The Radical Nationalist Campaign against the Weimar Republic.* New Haven: Yale University Press.
Turner, H. A. 1985. *German Big Business and the Rise of Hitler.* Oxford: Oxford University Press.
Warburg, Sidney. 1983. *Hitler's Secret Backers: The Financial Sources of National Socialism.* Phoenix, AZ: Research Publications.

FINLAND

Fascism in interwar Finland was shaped by the legacy of the Civil War of 1917–1918 between "Whites" and "Reds." The extreme Right sought to "complete" the White victory. In 1929 farmers in the town of Lapua launched a movement to combat communist agitation that soon gained the backing of conservative and business interests. The government attempted to appease the Lapua movement and turned a blind eye to its campaign of physical intimidation against its opponents on the Left. By mobilizing broad popular support, Lapua pressured parliament to adopt anticommunist legislation. However, success emboldened Lapua's leaders to flout the law and seek greater influence. Lapua's support of conservative statesman P. E. Svinhufvud ensured his election to the presidency in 1931, but it was his resoluteness in the face of an ill-planned Lapuan uprising, supported by local civil guard units in Mäntsälä in February 1932, that led to the banning of the movement. A few months later the Isänmaalinen kansanliike (IKL; Patriotic People's Movement) was founded to continue propagating Lapua's goals. While Lapua was purely a reactionary movement, IKL developed characteristics typical of fascist parties. It adopted paramilitary attributes, such as a uniform consisting of a black shirt with a blue tie, and championed "Finnicization"—that is, minimizing the influence of the Swedish minority. Although IKL gained a parliamentary representation of fourteen deputies, it lacked Lapua's impact. In contrast to the broad bourgeois front mobilized by Lapua, IKL was marginalized by the establishment. A central plank in IKL's program was unifying Eastern Karelia (part of the USSR) with Finland—an idea propagated by the Academic Karelia Society (AKS), a nationalist student society influential among the educated classes during the interwar period. When Finland allied itself with Germany against the Soviet Union in 1941, IKL was given a cabinet post and the "Greater Finland" ideal gained approval. In 1944 the Finns sued for peace, and the Soviets dictated the terms of the armistice, which included the liquidation of all organizations deemed "fascist." In the conditions of the Cold War, the emergence of an extreme-right party was precluded, though the Finnish Rural Party under the charismatic leadership of Veikko Vennamo functioned as the populist protest party of the Right. In 1995 it changed its name to the True Finns and won three seats in the 2003 parliamentary elections.

Andres Kasekamp

See Also: INTRODUCTION; COLD WAR, THE; EXPANSIONISM; FARMERS; GERMANY; LAPUA; NATIONALISM; PARAMILITARISM; RURALISM; SOVIET UNION, THE

References

Alapuro, Risto. 1980. "Mass Support for Fascism in Finland." In *Who Were the Fascists: Social Roots of European Fascism,* edited by Stein Ugelvik Larsen, Bernt Hagtvet, and Jan Petter Myklebust. Bergen: Universitetsforlaget.

Karvonen, Lauri. 1988. *From White to Blue and Black: Finnish Fascism in the Interwar Period.* Commentationes Scientarum Socialium 36. Helsinki: University of Helsinki Press.

Rintala, Martin. 1962. *Three Generations: The Extreme Right Wing in Finnish Politics.* Bloomington: Indiana University Press.

FIUME

Adriatic port 70 miles southeast of Trieste (modern Rijeka in Croatia), flashpoint for Italian nationalist irredentism, occupied by the nationalist adventurer Gabriele D'Annunzio in September 1919. The city had been under many different rulers down the centuries, including Austria and Croatia and latterly, Hungary. By 1910 an influx of Italian immigrants had brought their numbers to 22,488 (compared with 13,351 Slavs plus Hungarians, Germans, and others). On 23 October 1918, Croat troops seized Fiume, but in November of that year Italian and Serbian troops took over a dual sovereignty, with an Italian naval presence in the harbor. The Serbian troops were then replaced by an Inter-Allied force, while the victorious powers put the topic on the agenda of the Paris Peace Conference. In 1919, Italy demanded to annex Fiume, even though the secret treaty of London of 1915, which contained Italy's terms for entering the war, had not mentioned Fiume. The grounds for the demand were that Italians were in a majority in the city. The peace conference saw arguments between President Woodrow Wilson of the United States and Italy over the fate of Fiume and North Dalmatia. Wilson insisted that Yugoslavia needed a port and that the Adriatic coast, being overwhelmingly Slavic, should be assigned to Yugoslavia.

The Italian delegation at the peace conference walked out when Wilson made this demand, and Mussolini and D'Annunzio both demanded that the Italian government occupy the city by force. Italian public opinion was with them. The peace conference, however, supported Wilson's intransigence and continued to deliberate without Italy, so that the delegation had to return in humiliation on 5 May 1919. Negotiations dragged on through the summer. At the end of August the Allies decided to cut down the strength of the Italian garrison and assign policing duties to a "neutral" (mainly British) force. The failure

While in occupation of Fiume with his "private army," celebrated Italian World War I hero, politician, and writer, Gabriele D'Annunzio pioneered or popularized certain elements of the style and political thinking later associated with Italian Fascism and Nazism. (The Great War in Gravure: the New York Times Portfolio of the War, The New York Times Co., 1917)

of the Italian negotiators at the conference to make headway intensified a widespread Italian perception that their government was too weak to resolve problems created by the war.

At the beginning of 1919, D'Annunzio, Italy's most celebrated war hero, had seized control of the movement claiming Fiume and Dalmatia for Italy. In June of that year he published a warning that he was ready to seize Fiume by force if the negotiations failed. During the summer Mussolini and D'Annunzio met for the first time (Mussolini's mistress, Margherita Sarfatti, had known the poet for many years). On 12 September, with the arrival of the new police force imminent, D'Annunzio led 2,000 Italian troops into the city. The force included Arditi and soldiers who had deserted to join the invasion. That evening he appeared on the balcony of the governor's palace and called for the support of the citizens, arguing that Fiume was the embodiment of what Italy had fought for in the war. He finished with a proclamation that the city was thenceforth annexed to Italy. By the end of October further desertions from the Italian army had boosted the occupation force to around 8,500, and enthusiastic support came from all over Italy.

D'Annunzio appointed as his propaganda director a war veteran called Francisco Giunta. At the beginning of 1920 Giunta was also made head of the Trieste Fascio by the Fascist Central Committee. Trieste became a crucial point of contact between Mussolini's supporters and those of D'Annunzio. Giunta created a number of Fascist squads. The hinterland of Istria included numerous Slovenes, and Giunta and Mussolini claimed that the squads had been formed to combat Slovene separatists and their Bolshevik allies. In the summer of 1920 the squads burned down Slovene association buildings and then the offices of socialist groupings.

In September 1920, D'Annunzio proclaimed a constitution for Fiume that created corporations set up so as to represent citizens in accord with their occupations or economic interests. Mussolini supported D'Annunzio publicly by publishing articles in praise of him, while at the same time secretly negotiating with Italian Prime Minister Giolitti to abstain from any action should an invasion of Fiume be undertaken by the Italian government. D'Annunzio lost the support of many conservatively minded Italians because he allowed the citizens to indulge in excessively hedonistic lifestyles. He even invented his own religious Holy Days. Meanwhile, the Treaty of Rapallo of 12 November 1920 enacted that Fiume should become a free state. At the end of that year Italian government forces attacked the city and D'Annunzio retired to Lake Garda. In January 1924 the Fascist government formalized Italian annexation of the city, which became part of Yugoslavia in 1945.

Cyprian Blamires

See Also: CORPORATISM; CROATIA; DALMATIA; D'ANNUNZIO, GABRIELE; FASCIST PARTY, THE; IRREDENTISM; ITALY; MUSSOLINI, BENITO ANDREA; SARFATTI-GRASSINI, MARGHERITA; SLAVS, THE (AND ITALY); *SQUADRISMO;* VERSAILLES, THE TREATY OF; WORLD WAR I; YUGOSLAVIA

References
Cannistraro, Philip V., and Brian R. Sullivan. 1993. *Il Duce's Other Woman: The Untold Story of Margherita Sarfatti, Benito Mussolini's Jewish Mistress, and How She Helped Him Come to Power.* New York: William Morrow.
Ledeen, M. 1977. *The First Duce: D'Annunzio at Fiume.* London: Johns Hopkins University Press.
Woodhouse, J. R., ed. 2001. *Gabriele D'Annunzio: Defiant Archangel.* Oxford: Oxford University Press.

FOOTBALL/SOCCER

In Italy the Fascist youth corps, the Balilla, and the Dopolavoro recreational organization coordinated local footballing activities, while the Comitato Olimpico Nazionale Italiano restructured the Italian Football Federation. In 1926 the professional game was institutionalized, and by 1929 the first national league had been established. Rhetoric highlighted training and performance as a demonstration of militaristic Fascist strength, but more visible were the architectural projects that led to the construction or modernization of football stadia in cities such as Milan (1926), Bologna (1927), Rome (1930), Naples (1932), Florence (1933), and Turin (1933).

Government policy did not always manage to conceal obvious conflicts and contradictions. In the first of several incidents, Fascist *squadristi* supporting Bologna invaded the pitch in a game against Genoa in 1925. A nationalist ban on signing foreign players was bypassed by making exceptions for those born abroad of Italian parents. (Five Latin Americans in that category played in the national team.) These apparent incongruities could take nothing away from Bologna's European victories or the success of the national team under its coach Vittorio Pozzo. When the World Cup was held in Italy in 1934, the home team won, its on-pitch violence unpunished by some questionable refereeing. Although the victors received the *Coppa del Duce* in addition to the World Cup itself, the tournament was not as consciously propagandistic as Hitler's Berlin Olympics, in which an Italian universities squad won the football gold. Despite hostile crowds Italy also won the 1938 World Cup in France, famously playing in black shirts for their quarter-final match.

Germany could not rival such success. Felix Linnemann, president of the German Football Federation, was a reliable supporter of Nazi policy, but this did not mean that German football was thoroughly nazified. The SA had their own team, and the sport was played within Kraft durch Freude and the Hitler Youth, yet football remained essentially amateur in Germany, even if the Nazis tolerated the payments made by a few clubs. Moreover, the elimination of Jews and leftists from clubs and a ban on workers' and then on Christian teams considerably reduced the level of popular participation. A central reason why German football never developed into a potent propaganda weapon was the status of the national team. Under trainers Otto

Nerz and, from 1938, Sepp Herberger, Germany had a tendency to lose on unsuitable occasions. In the first game Hitler saw, against Norway in the Berlin Olympics, they went under 2–0. Austria defeated Germany 2–0 in a game in 1938 designed to celebrate the *Anschluss*. (After that Austrian players were incorporated into the German squad; Austria would not have a national team again until after the war.) In the same year Germany was eliminated by Switzerland in the first round of the World Cup. Nazi reprisals could be extreme: in 1942, after Dynamo Kiev beat a Luftwaffe team, the Ukrainian players were sent to a concentration camp. By contrast, the games Germany lost against England in London (1935) and Berlin (1938) were in fact diplomatic triumphs for the Nazis – particularly the 1938 Berlin game, notable for the sight of the English team giving the Nazi salute in the capital of the Reich—a propaganda coup for Hitler.

In Spain football came under Falangist and military control after the victory of General Franco, although it quickly evolved into a site for regional opposition to the centralist regime. Eventually the authorities viewed the sport as a form of political demobilization, but during World War II the Spanish national team took part in games with the Axis powers, raising their hands in the obligatory fascist salute before matches, just like their German and Italian colleagues.

Almost all countries in Europe have their share of football hooligans who are attached to current neo-Nazi and racist groups. In Italy, Inter Milan, Lazio, and Bergamo are among the teams infiltrated, while Real Madrid (with its Ultrasur following) and FC Barcelona (and its Boixos Nois) feature prominently in racist violence. Paris St. Germain attracts racist fans, as does the Hungarian team Ferencváros. The English group Combat 18 is associated with Chelsea and has succeeded in causing disruption when the national team is playing. In the 1990s a survey found that 20 percent of German fans felt close to neo-Nazis.

John London

See Also: ANSCHLUSS, THE; ANTI-SEMITISM; AUSTRIA; AXIS, THE; BERLIN OLYMPICS, THE; BODY, THE CULT OF THE; COMBAT 18; CONCENTRATION CAMPS; FALANGE; FASCIST PARTY, THE; FRANCO Y BAHAMONDE, GENERAL FRANCISCO; GERMANY; ITALY; LEISURE; LUFTWAFFE, THE; MILITARISM; NATIONALISM; NAZISM; NEO-NAZISM; POSTWAR FASCISM; PROPAGANDA; RACISM; SA, THE; SALUTES; SPAIN; SPORT; SQUADRISTI, THE; WARRIOR ETHOS, THE; YOUTH

References
Fernández Santander, Carlos. 1990. *El fútbol durante la guerra civil y el franquismo.* Madrid: San Martín.
Fischer, Gerhard, and Ulrich Lindner. 1999. *Stürmer für Hitler: vom Zusammenspiel zwischen Fußball und Nationalsozialismus.* Göttingen: Die Werkstatt.
Martin, Simon. 2004. *Football and Fascism: The National Game under Mussolini.* Oxford: Berg.
Riordan, J., and P. Arnaud, eds. 1998. *Sport and International Politics: The Impact of Fascism and Communism on Sport.* London: Spon.

FORCED LABOR

The National Socialist regime subjected different groups of its own people and the peoples of the occupied states to forced labor as a means of bolstering its political and economic dominance. The forms and intensities of the force employed varied according to the value that the relevant groups had in the National Socialist hierarchy of races. Among the forced laborers were above all Jews, the inmates of the concentration camps and other places of imprisonment, civilian workers who had been brought from the Occupied Territories to the German Reich, prisoners of war, and persons who had to work for German ends outside the Reich. Alongside the forced labor to which after 1938 a considerable portion of the population of the Reich was subjected, the situation of the forced laborers was distinguished by a higher measure of deprivation of legal cover and shortage of foodstuffs than was the case for the German people at large.

The number of Jews in slave labor in the German Reich—especially in the armaments industry—topped the 50,000 mark in the summer of 1941. But even employment in the armaments industry, so important for the war effort, offered no real protection to them from deportation to ghettos or death camps. By the summer of 1943 virtually all Jewish slave laborers had been deported from Germany. The forced labor for Jews in the territories occupied by Germany began in October 1939 with the imposition of forced labor on the Polish Jews in the General Gouvernement. By the end of 1940 at least 700,000 Jews were working in ghettos or camps under the harshest conditions, doing forced labor for the Germans. With the beginning of the systematic "final solution" at the end of the year 1941, employment in armaments-related work became for Jewish slave laborers a direct matter of survival. But for the most part, however, it meant simply a delay of their death sentence.

Inmates from the Buchenwald concentration camp at work on a German railroad: forced labor played a significant part in the German wartime economy. (United States Holocaust Memorial Museum)

In the early days of the Nazi concentration camps forced labor served above all for the breaking of the prisoners' feeling of self-respect. From 1938 at the latest, the SS began—with the founding of their own economic enterprises—to use prison labor also for the realization of economic goals. With the shortage of labor becoming increasingly acute in the war economy, in late summer 1942 the systematic exploitation of prison labor for the armament industry developed, something that had been happening only occasionally prior to that. The SS made available concentration camp inmates as loan workers on a large scale to private armaments companies such as HASAG, IG Farben, Daimler Benz, and many others. In the spring of 1944 shortages of labor in mining for the armaments industry became so acute that 100,000 Hungarian Jews were deported as concentration camp inmates for forced labor in the Reich. Especially in the last months of the war, the survival chances of these prison workers sank to a mini-

mum. After 1940, some 10,000 foreign and German inmates of special police camps or work camps, who had been guilty of infringements of "work discipline," spent short periods working under conditions similar to those of the concentration camp inmates. After the summer of 1944 more than 90 percent of prisoners in the justice system found themselves involved in the war economy, partly outside the prison walls.

Even before the outbreak of the war, labor shortages in the German Reich had occasionally made necessary the recruitment of foreign labor. After the war began, the occupied territories, in spite of the racist-ideological prejudice against the importation of foreigners into the Reich, were immediately used as a reservoir of labor for German industry and agriculture. Alongside those whose recruitment was not entirely without a voluntary element, there followed recruitment of labor especially in occupied Eastern Europe by conscription and sometimes by manhunts involving brutal violence. There was a clear intensification and brutalization in the practice of recruitment in the occupied territories after the Thuringian Gauleiter Fritz Sauckel was put in charge of labor recruitment in March 1942. A greater part of the labor deported from the occupied territories consisted of women and young persons. Their treatment in the German Reich varied very much according to their "racial origin" and foreign policy considerations. The National Socialists distinguished between workers of Germanic origin, who were formally put on a level close to that of German workers, and workers from alien peoples, who were to be accommodated only in camps and who were at the mercy of further discrimination. For workers from Poland and the Soviet Union there was a special severely discriminatory decree passed that provided for obligatory marking and limited their freedom and mobility considerably. Even for most of the foreigners who had initially signed up voluntarily on a limited contract, return to their homes was forbidden after October 1942. By the late summer of 1944 nearly 6 million foreign civilians were working in the German Reich.

Soon after the invasion of Poland, the German war economy began to exploit the labor of prisoners of war. The employment of prisoners of war was permitted according to the human rights provisions of the Geneva Convention of 1929, as long as it followed principles of humanity and did not stand in direct relationship to war activities. While these guidelines were widely applied to the treatment of Anglo-American prisoners of war, they were infringed in respect of the use of French, Belgian, and Serbian prisoners of war. In the case of Polish, Soviet, and (after 1943) Italian prisoners of war, the human rights provisos were completely ignored. The Nazi leadership first agreed to the employment of Soviet prisoners of war in the autumn of 1941. Up to February 1942, some 2 million of the 3.35 million Red Army soldiers taken prisoner were murdered or died in the concentration camps of the Wehrmacht. From February 1942 to the end of the war, around 1.3 million Soviet prisoners of war died—for the most part in labor service. Overall, more than 57 percent of the 5.9 million Red Army soldiers who were in German imprisonment during the war perished.

The total number of slave laborers employed during the war in the German Reich (inclusive of the annexed territories) is estimated at about 12 to 13 million. Only in the year 2000, after decades of protracted struggle, did a significant proportion of the survivors receive compensation, with the establishment of a foundation—Erinnerung, Verantwortung und Zukunft (Mem-

ory, Responsibility and Future)—funded by contributions from numerous businesses.

It is impossible to calculate more precisely at the present time the number of those who worked as slave laborers for the German conquerors beyond the borders of the Reich. Among them were Jewish and non-Jewish concentration camp inmates and parts of the civilian population of the occupied lands, who under different degrees of compulsion served German administrations, companies, and institutions like the Todt organization, the railways, or the Wehrmacht. Especially in Eastern Europe, the conditions of existence of these persons were at the most not better, and often worse, than the conditions of existence of forced laborers in the Reich. Some were resettled in work camps, but the majority were able to remain in their homes.

Hans-Christoph Seidel
(translated by Cyprian Blamires)

See Also: ANTI-SEMITISM; BARBAROSSA, OPERATION; CONCENTRATION CAMPS; FARMERS; *GENERAL GOUVERNEMENT*/GENERAL GOVERNMENT, THE; GHETTOS; HOLOCAUST, THE; IG FARBEN; INDUSTRY; MEDICINE; NAZISM; PARAGUAY; POLAND; RACISM; SLAVS THE (AND GERMANY); SOVIET UNION, THE; SS, THE; U.S. CORPORATIONS; VOLKSWAGEN; WAR; WEHRMACHT, THE; WOMEN; WORLD WAR II; YOUTH

References
Allen, M. T. 2004. *Hitler's Slave Lords: The Business of Forced Labour in Occupied Europe.* Stroud: Tempus.
Ferencz, Benjamin B. 1979. *Less than Slaves: Jewish Forced Labour and the Quest for Compensation.* Cambridge: Harvard University Press.
Herbert, Ulrich. 1997. *Hitler's Foreign Workers: Enforced Labor in Germany under the Third Reich.* Cambridge: Cambridge University Press.
Spoerer, Mark, and Jochen Fleischhauer. 2002. "Forced Laborers in Nazi Germany: Categories, Numbers and Survivors." *Journal of Interdisciplinary History* 33: 169–204.

FORD, HENRY
(1863–1947)

Leading U.S. car manufacturer and anti-Semite in the interwar years, admired and decorated by Hitler. Ford was born and educated at Springwells (now Greenfield) Township, Michigan. Although he left school at age sixteen and worked for years as a mechanic, in 1903 he founded the Ford Motor Company, soon famous for its innovations in advertising, mass marketing, assembly-line production, high minimum wage, and reduced work week. After failing at various political ventures, which included personal efforts to end World War I and a race for the U.S. Senate, in 1919, Ford launched a weekly magazine, the *Dearborn Independent*. In it he endorsed such traditionally reformist causes as temperance, women's rights, and the League of Nations while attacking big business and Wall Street. Beginning in the spring of 1920, however, and continuing through the beginning of 1922, Ford espoused a vehement anti-Semitism. His editor, William J. Cameron, was a lay preacher who believed that the Anglo-Saxons were the true children of Israel. His private secretary, Ernest Liebold, served as special "investigator" of Jewish influences. Ford published not only the *Protocols of the Elders of Zion* but also a work entitled *The International Jew*, the latter widely translated and circulated throughout the world. In his writings Jews were blamed for a whole series of events, including the assassination of Lincoln, the launching of World War I, and the success of the Bolshevik Revolution. More mundane "offenses" included jazz music, short skirts, and rolled-down stockings for women. By 1923 the journal's circulation was approaching half a million. Four years later, however, Ford terminated the magazine after a major lawsuit and apologized to the Jews for his negative comments. Adolf Hitler had long been a strong admirer of Ford, praising him in *Mein Kampf*. By 1933 the Nazis had published twenty-nine editions of *The International Jew*, and in 1938 Hitler bestowed the Grand Cross of the Supreme Order of the German Eagle on the auto manufacturer. In 1938, Ford suffered a stroke so severe that his mental capacities deteriorated. When World War II broke out in Europe, Ford publicly blamed the conflict on "greedy financial groups" and privately saw Jewish conspiracy at work. The German subsidiary of his Ford corporation played a crucial role in manufacturing vehicles and armaments for the Nazi war effort.

Justus Doenecke

See Also: ANTI-SEMITISM; BOLSHEVISM; CONSPIRACY THEORIES; HITLER, ADOLF; LEAGUE OF NATIONS, THE; *MEIN KAMPF*; *PROTOCOLS OF THE ELDERS OF ZION, THE*; U.S. CORPORATIONS; WORLD WAR I

References

Baldwin, Neil. 2001. *Henry Ford and the Jews: The Mass Production of Hate*. New York: Public Affairs.

Lacey, Robert. 1986. *Ford: The Men and the Machine*. Boston: Little, Brown.

Ribuffo, Leo P. 1992. "Henry Ford and The International Jew." Pp. 70–105. in *Right Center Left: Essays in American History*, edited by Leo P. Ribuffo. New Brunswick, NJ: Rutgers University Press.

Wallace, Max. 2003. *The American Axis: Henry Ford, Charles Lindbergh, and the Rise of the Third Reich*. New York: St. Martin's.

FÖRSTER-NIETZSCHE, ELISABETH (1846–1935)

Sister of Friedrich Nietzsche, enthusiastic disseminator of his works, and admirer of Nazism, for which she claimed her brother as a prophet. Her husband, Bernhard Förster, was a fanatical anti-Semite, and together they settled in Paraguay in 1886 with a handful of other families to found Nueva Germania, which was, in a chillingly prophetic anticipation of the Nazi enterprise, to be a racially pure Aryan colony from which all Jewish "taint" would be excluded. Her philosopher brother made no secret of his contempt for the extreme nationalism and anti-Semitism of the couple. Both Bernhard and Elisabeth were devotees of Richard Wagner, whose circle had nurtured and encouraged their thinking, but Friedrich Nietzsche had found that aspect of Wagnerism increasingly repellent after his initial admiration for the composer had worn off. Elisabeth returned to Germany after the project had run into difficulties and her husband had committed suicide in 1889, and she nursed her brother during the final years of his life, after he had succumbed to insanity. She set up the Nietzsche Archive in the house in which he spent his last years in Weimar, and she developed an editing and publishing center dedicated to the dissemination of the philosopher's writings.

Benito Mussolini professed himself an admirer of Friedrich Nietzsche: in 1908 he wrote that the German philosopher "had the most congenial mind of the last quarter of the nineteenth century," and he claimed that it was Nietzsche who had "cured" him of his classic socialism. When Mussolini came to power in 1922, Elisabeth wrote to congratulate him, and a warm correspondence ensued. In 1928, in her capacity as chairman of the Nietzsche Archive, she gave an address in praise of Il Duce. Writing at this time to the Italian ambassador to Germany, she claimed that her brother would have been proud of the great leader of Italy, "who offers mankind the happy chance of salvation." She assumed that Mussolini had rediscovered the true Nietzschean values. The dictator fully reciprocated her devotion to the spirit of her brother. Elisabeth even arranged to have a play written by Mussolini about Napoleon performed in German at the Weimar National Theater in 1932. Hitler was present and personally gifted her with a bouquet of red roses.

Elisabeth became a devotee of Hitler, whom she referred to as "our wonderful Chancellor" and "a splendid gift from heaven," and she was instrumental in encouraging the idea that Nazism was somehow the fulfillment of her brother's vision—grafting onto his thought anti-Semitic and extreme nationalist ideas for which he had actually expressed antipathy in his lifetime, and making a cult of his memory. Hitler in turn professed himself an admirer of Nietzsche. In 1934 he allocated Elisabeth an honorary monthly stipend in recognition of her services to the Reich. Hitler was present in person at her funeral, along with a Nazi guard of honor. The association of Nietzsche with Nazism brought the philosopher's name into disrepute for several decades.

Cyprian Blamires

See Also: ANTI-SEMITISM; ARYANISM; BAEUMLER, ALFRED; MUSSOLINI, BENITO ANDREA; NATIONALISM; NIETZSCHE, FRIEDRICH; NUEVA GERMANIA; WAGNER, (WILHELM) RICHARD

References

Diethe, Carol. 2003. *Nietzsche's Sister and the Will to Power: A Biography of Elisabeth Förster-Nietzsche*. Chicago: University of Illinois Press.
MacIntyre, Ben. 1992. *Forgotten Fatherland: The Search for Elisabeth Nietzsche*. New York: Farrar, Strauss, and Giroux.
Peters, H. F. 1977. *Zarathustra's Sister: The Case of Elisabeth and Friedrich Nietzsche*. New York: Markus Wiener.

FORTUYN, PIM: *See* NETHERLANDS, THE FOUR-YEAR PLAN, THE: *See* INDUSTRY

FRANCE

Whether authentic fascism developed in France, and, if so, how influential it became, is intensely debated. Many French scholars argue that a strong republican tradition made France "allergic" to fascism. They maintain that whereas some fascist movements and in-

tellectuals existed in France, these were "shallow copies," a coat of "Roman whitewash" splashed onto a home-grown Bonapartist tradition rather than a "true French fascism" (Rémond 1969, 281, 293). Others believe that France was the "real birthplace of fascism" (Sternhell 1994, 4). Indeed, Sternhell considers that it is by studying interwar France, where fascism "impregnated" political culture in a pure form uncompromised by the exercise of power, that one "is able to understand the true significance of fascism in general" (Sternhell 1986, 270).

Fascism faced genuine obstacles in France. When it first appeared in the wreckage and turmoil following World War I, France was a victor nation. Moreover, French patriotism was inextricably tied to the highest moment of French world influence: the universal lessons the French people offered in 1789 by opening the Bastille prison and by issuing the Declaration of the Rights of Man, followed by the conquest of much of Europe by Napoleon Bonaparte, whose rule, however dictatorial, never renounced all the rationalizing, egalitarian, and universalist legacies of the French Revolution. The defeat of Napoleon by European monarchies in 1815 could not turn the clock back forever; the French overthrew three more monarchs in the nineteenth century before their country became, in 1875, the first Great Power governed as a republic. Nevertheless, there was always another France. Many French monarchists and authoritarian nationalists never accepted a parliamentary republic as appropriate for *la grande nation* ("the great nation"). Already before 1914 several incidents had combined antirepublican authoritarian nationalism with popular enthusiasm in France in an unprecedented way that looks in retrospect like a preview of fascism. From 1887 to 1889, General Georges Boulanger, a patriot hero with vague plans for constitutional revision, attracted both labor and monarchist support in multiple electoral campaigns against an allegedly corrupt republic. Later, in the passionate quarrel over the wrongful imprisonment of Captain Alfred Dreyfus for espionage (1896–1906), anti-Dreyfusards linked popular pro-army, pro-Church, and anti-Semitic emotions with authoritarian nationalism. The anti-Dreyfus campaign shifted French nationalism from its French revolutionary origins to the right. By 1914, a new nationalist populism had come into being in France. It drew not only upon the popular patriotism of several nationalist "leagues" but also upon a new cult of will and action expressed by intellectuals like Georges Sorel. The most important organized expression of French anti-Dreyfusard nationalism by 1914 was Charles Maurras's newspaper and movement, Action française. Maurras's mixture of monarchism and Catholicism with popular xenophobia and resentment of international business, along with the belligerency of the young Camelots du roi, who sold *Action Française* in the street and battled leftists, has been pronounced authentically fascist by the philosopher Ernst Nolte, though most consider it at most a precursor, intermediary between reaction and fascism.

The period between the two world wars saw the greatest development of fascist or fascistic movements in France. As the euphoria of the 1918 victory dissipated, the Third Republic coped badly with three simultaneous threats: social revolution (France had the largest communist party in Europe); economic depression; and German revival. With parliament splintered both on the Left (communists vs. parliamentary socialists) and on the Right (parliamentary conservatives vs. antisystem rightists), and with the center (radicals) voting left on constitutional issues and right on socioeconomic ones, no solid majority was available to cope effectively with any of these threats. France had forty-one governments, some of them tarnished by corruption, between 1918 and 1939. Aggressive far-right movements arose whenever the Left gained. When a center-left coalition, the Cartel des Gauches, won the 1924 parliamentary election, Georges Valois, a Maurrassien who had already tried in 1911 to attract workers to the nationalist cause in the Cercle Proudhon, founded the Faisceau (1925), whose name (the "Bundle," or *Fascio*) and ideas derived directly from Mussolini. Pierre Taittinger, a champagne magnate, responded to the reburial in 1924 of socialist leader Jaurès in the Pantheon by forming the more traditionally nationalist Jeunesses Patriotes (Patriotic Youth). Catholic opinion, too, offended by the Cartel's militant secularism, moved rightward with General Noel Currières de Castelnau's Fédération nationale catholique (1925).

Signs of French decline multiplied in the 1930s. The Depression bit, and Hitler successfully dismantled the 1918 peace settlement without a shot. The French birth rate failed even to maintain a stable population, and the average age rose. As the Third Republic's center-left majority (renewed in 1932) became implicated in covering up fraud (the Stavisky Affair), the discontent of the "other France" grew more violent. In the absence of any prospect of uniting fragmented French conservatives in an effective equivalent of Britain's Tories, a new crop of right-wing "leagues" (they rejected the word *party*) blossomed: Jean Renaud's Solidarité française (1933), Bucard's Le Francisme (1933), both financed by the cosmetics industrialist François Coty,

and the Croix de feu (1927, expanded after 1931), along with splinter groups. The principal veterans' associations, enraged by the "lost peace," also espoused authoritarian nationalism. The peak of "league" activism in 1930s France was massive street demonstrations before the chamber of deputies on 6 February 1934 by militants of the Croix de Feu, Solidarité française, Action française, the Jeunesses patriotes, as well as several veterans' movements. Fifteen people were killed and dozens injured. Jittery republicans believed that a "March on Paris" had begun, though no evidence confirms that a coup was planned or that the participating leagues could agree on a single leader. Both the parliamentary republic and the capitalist market worked badly in the mid-1930s and were widely criticized; not all of their critics were fascists.

Although the leagues were strong enough to topple a French government in February 1934, they were not strong enough to install one of their leaders in power. In the period of intense polarization that followed the February riots, the Left drew more votes. The Popular Front coalition (socialists, radicals, and communists) won elections in May 1936. Prime Minister Léon Blum banned paramilitary leagues in June, something that Chancellor Heinrich Brüning had failed to do in Germany six years earlier. The Popular Front's victory had been narrow, however, and the sight of a Jew like Blum as premier, supported by communist votes, aroused the Right to a paroxysm of indignation. Reaction to the Popular Front produced Doriot's Parti populaire français (1936), Colonel François de La Rocque's Parti social français, based on the banned Croix de feu, and Eugène Deloncle's conspiratorial Comité secret d'action révolutionnaire, or Cagoule (French for "hood"). The Cagoule prepared to eliminate communists from the civil service and military and assassinated Italian antifascist refugees in France at the request of Mussolini before being closed down by the police (1937).

Sternhell concluded that fascism "impregnated" the language and attitudes of French public life in the 1930s (Sternhell 1986, 29, 209, 293). Undeniably, fascism became fashionable then among many younger intellectuals, who contrasted its youth, vigor, and excitement with the graying, tired republic. Novelists Robert Brasillach, Pierre Drieu la Rochelle, and Céline, and reviews like *Je Suis Partout* made scorn for the republic intellectually chic. Most French and some foreign critics of Sternhell consider that he makes his "fascist" category far too broad by including a wide range of conservative and authoritarian critics of French parliamentary inefficacy and corruption, and they find his conclusions excessive.

No one denies the label of fascist to Valois's Faisceau, Bucard's Francisme, Renaud's Solidarité française, and Doriot's Parti populaire français between the wars. These enrolled only a few thousand members, however, except for the PPF, which claimed 300,000 members in 1938. A more plausible figure is 60,000, of whom about 15,000 were really active. The PPF had a genuine popular following in Doriot's fief of Saint-Denis (a working-class Paris suburb), where some of his original working-class clientele followed him from communism to fascism, making the PPF easily the most proletarian of the French far-right movements. Marseilles had a PPF mayor (Simon Sabiani), and the party had a mass following in Algiers, along with some intellectual and industrial backers. The one far-right movement that achieved mass catch-all party status between 1936 and 1940 was La Rocque's Parti Social Français (PSF). Any assessment of fascism in France turns on it. If the PSF was fascist, fascism was powerful in 1930s France; if not, fascism remained marginal. La Rocque, an army officer of monarchist background, assumed control in 1931 of the Croix de Feu (CdF), an association of veterans decorated under fire. He opened it to nonveterans and committed it to political activism. He denounced the weakness and corruption of parliament, warned against the Bolshevik threat, and advocated a strong executive capable of vigorous repression of internal and external enemies. His paramilitary Dispos (from the French word for "ready") conducted militaristic automobile rallies (1933–1934) that mobilized secretly for "D-Day" and "H-Hour" in apparent preparation for opposing communist insurrection by force. The CdF's fascist reputation was fortified by participation in the February 1934 demonstrations. La Rocque kept his forces apart, however, and disbanded them when disorder began. While CdF folklore highlighted clashes with communists, La Rocque cultivated a public impression of discipline and order rather than disorderly street violence. Almost uniquely on the French Right, he rejected anti-Semitism and even recruited some patriotic Jews (though his Alsatian and Algerian branches were anti-Semitic). Although La Rocque admired Mussolini (except for what he saw as excessive statism), he retained the anti-Germanism of most French nationalists.

Colonel de La Rocque's replacement for the banned CdF in 1936, the Parti social français (PSF), abandoned paramilitary rallies and turned to elections (not incompatible with fascism, as Hitler and Mussolini showed). He emphasized national reconciliation and socioeconomic justice under a strong but elected leader. The PSF grew rapidly. Some interpret this growth as

public ratification of the PSF's moderation, a judgment reinforced by the departure of disappointed hard-liners for Doriot's PPF and harsh criticisms from the Right of La Rocque as "soft." Others believe that the PSF carried moderate conservatives rightward in their fear of the Popular Front. Some scholars, mostly non-French, have concluded that both La Rocque's first movement (the CdF) and his second (the PSF) were fascist. Important differences, however, between the CdF, with its paramilitary exercises and its apparent readiness to supplant state authority, and the explicitly legalitarian PSF persuade others to split their vote: the former was fascist, the latter not. The PSF, with its unverifiable million-plus members, was the largest party in France on the eve of World War II and the first real mass cross-class party in France. It recruited eight to ten deputies elected under other labels in 1936, and won two more seats in by-elections (1937–1939), but since the national election of 1940 never took place, La Rocque's expectation of a hundred deputies could never be tested.

Fascism's success among French farmers is a significant issue, since both Mussolini and Hitler won their first mass following in the countryside, and since France was still half rural. French farmers, already losing out, resentful of organized labor and urban elites, and devastated by the 1930s price collapse, were ready for extreme solutions. Henry Dorgères's Défense paysanne was the most important extreme-right farmers' movement in the 1930s. But was it authentically fascist? Dorgères openly praised Fascist Italy in 1933 and 1934 (though he later declared it to have been too statist), and he adopted elements of fascist style: colored shirts, inflamed oratory, nationalism, corporatism, xenophobia, and anti-Semitism. His Greenshirts were ready to use violence against farm foreclosures, striking farm workers, and price-cutting middlemen. On the other hand, while Dorgères skillfully aroused farmers' anger, he tended to see urban shopkeepers as enemies and thus failed to build the true "catch-all" party of fully developed fascisms. The size of Défense paysanne is hard to gauge. Dorgères was capable of gathering the largest crowds ever assembled in French country towns. Outside moments of peak excitement, however, his movement was skeletal—farmers, after all, had to go home and work their fields. Dorgères's two largest weeklies (he had several others, as well as a monthly) had a peak circulation of about 50,000 in 1934. Dorgères's movement was also limited to Catholic and conservative Brittany, Normandy, the Channel coast, and a few spots in the Loire Valley. Much of southern and southwestern France remained closed to the

Greenshirts by long-standing peasant attachment to the traditions of the French Revolution, which had given them full title to their little plots. The Communist Party successfully channeled peasant rage away from fascism in traditionally left-leaning regions. Here the French Republican tradition apparently did impede fascism.

Other factors that limited rural fascism in France were the readiness of the French state to repress agrarian strikes (unlike the situation in Italy in 1920–1921), and the entrenched social power of the conservative farm organizations. They organized successful cooperatives and supplied essential services, while the Greenshirts offered only a vent for anger. The crucial turning point arrived in 1937, when Jacques Le Roy Ladurie, president of the powerful French Farmers' Federation (Fédération nationale des exploitants agricoles; FNEA), who had earlier helped Dorgères arouse rural crowds, decided that it would be more efficacious to construct a farmers' lobby capable of influencing state administration from within.

The Depression, for all its ravages, was less severe in France than in more industrially concentrated Britain and Germany. The Third Republic, despite its lurching, never suffered deadlock or total paralysis. Mainstream conservatives did not feel sufficiently threatened in the 1930s to need fascist help. Finally, no single federator emerged to dominate the small army of rival French fascist *chefs,* most of whom preferred intransigent doctrinal "purity" to the kind of deal-making with conservatives that Mussolini and Hitler practiced. As France regained some calm and stability in 1938–1939 under an energetic center-left prime minister, Edouard Daladier, all the far-right movements except the most moderate one, La Rocque's PSF, lost ground. Growth of the Axis threat against France discredited those who appeared to support France's main enemies—another obstacle to fascism in France. The PPF offended some nationalists when Doriot approved the Munich Agreements granting Czech territory to Hitler in September 1938.

Inasmuch as France was a satisfied nation, more concerned to keep its possessions than to expand, but at the same time still traumatized by the bloodletting of World War I, the French far Right found itself in the odd position in the late 1930s of rejecting "Stalin's war" against Hitler and abandoning its traditional terrain of national defense to the antifascist Left. Some French fascist intellectuals openly scorned French patriotism. After 1940 they threw in their lot with Hitler and advocated the submersion of petty French national identity within a grand European fascism (for example,

Déat, Drieu La Rochelle). This rejection of nationalism and expansionist militarism by some sectors of the French far Right after 1938 sets them apart from mainstream fascism. After the defeat of 1940, it was the traditional Right, rather than the fascist Right, that established and ran the collaborationist Vichy government. The defeat of May–June 1940 so discredited the Third French Republic that the French National Assembly voted full powers on 10 July 1940 to an eighty-four-year-old World War I hero, Marshal Philippe Pétain, who had been the most prominent advocate in June of giving up the fight. Pétain set up a provisional capital at Vichy, in the unoccupied south, and governed through authoritarian personal rule supported by the traditional French state services, the economic and social establishment, the military, and the Roman Catholic Church. There was no single party or obligatory youth movement (the Church opposed them). The closest equivalent to a Vichy official party was the veterans' organization, the Légion française des combattants, and the closest to a youth movement was six months of obligatory service for young men in rural camps under paternalist military leadership, the Chantiers de jeunesse. Pétain collaborated with the Nazi authorities in hopes of earning a suitable place in the new German-dominated Europe, which he was convinced was permanent.

Hitler himself preferred to keep Vichy out of the hands of the French fascists. France was the German army's most valuable conquest. Since French neutrality, products, and manpower were indispensable assets for the Reich war machine, Hitler was not about to endanger them by handing the administration of France to one of the petty squabbling fascist chieflings. He kept a number of them available on the Nazi payroll in Paris, however, in case he needed to pressure Pétain with a rival. The most important were Doriot's PPF and the former socialist Marcel Déat's Rassemblement national populaire, which acquired sizable followings. The main role that Hitler gave home-grown fascists in occupied countries was to recruit local volunteers to freeze and die on the Russian front. Doriot and the Belgian Degrelle were the only European fascist leaders to fight in person in German uniform on the Eastern Front. Doriot accompanied some 6,000 other Frenchmen in the semiofficial Légion des volontaires contre le bolshevisme. Only in the last days of the war, when the tide had turned and the conservative notables who had earlier supported Vichy drew back, and when Vichy became transformed into a police state in its fight against the Resistance, did parallel institutions appear—the Milice, or supplementary police; the "special sections" in the judiciary; the Police for Jewish Affairs—and figures close to fascism, such as Déat and Joseph Darnand, obtained office.

For a generation after the Liberation of 1945, the French extreme Right was discredited by association with Nazi and Italian occupation. It had not vanished, however, and movements that show some kinship with fascism persisted. First came survivor movements: the unreconstructed partisans of the anticommunist, anti-American "New Europe" promised by Hitler, and the resentful victims of the postwar purge. Maurice Bardèche, brother-in-law of the executed fascist novelist Robert Brasillach, spoke for them in his 1961 essay "Qu'est-ce que le fascisme?" ("What Is Fascism?"). As the survivors died out, a new extreme-right generation emerged around new themes reflecting the special problems of the postwar Fourth Republic: the loss of Great Power status, the influence of communism among intellectuals, and defense of the white "Occident" against Third World immigrants and revolutionaries. Jeune Nation (begun in 1950), led by Jacques and Pierre Sidos and mobilizing several thousand followers (often students), painted its Celtic cross on walls, mounted physical attacks on the Left, and called for authority, order, and hierarchy.

The losers in France's spectacular economic boom after the 1950s provided more troops for the extreme Right. Struggling shopkeepers and peasants flocked to the UDCA of Pierre Poujade, which peaked at 2,500,000 votes (11.5 percent) in January 1956. The UDCA scorned parliamentary weakness and was occasionally anti-Semitic, but it lacked all the external insignia and most of the authoritarian, corporatist, and expansionist program of classical fascism. It was mostly a pressure group for aid to those left behind by modernization. Loss of empire was the greatest postwar trauma. France lost first Indochina and then Algeria in nonstop colonial wars (1945–1962), an ordeal unmatched by any other colonial power. Anger at decolonization crested with Algerian independence in 1962. Diehards, organized in movements like the OAS (Organisation armée secrète) and MP-13, tried to sabotage the peace, overthrow the republic, and establish an anticommunist military dictatorship.

Charles De Gaulle's Fifth Republic (1958) undermined this generation of far-right activists by providing substitute foci for French national pride: a nuclear bomb, rapid economic growth, and international prestige through an activist foreign policy. Gaullism provided at last the broad, catch-call conservative party that France had lacked. Tiny factions like Occident (1964) and Ordre nouveau (1970–1973) fought each other on streets and campuses for a dwindling antisystem right clientele. Immigration, economic stagnation, and socialism in power (François Mitterrand, 1981–1994) gave the French far Right a new lease on life after 1980. Whereas previous immigrants (with the significant exception of Jews fleeing Russian pogroms in the 1880s) had been Europeans, now they came from Africa and the Caribbean. Many were Muslims who rejected assimilation. When times were good, their labor was needed, but when the postwar boom ended and unemployment reappeared, resentment rose. In addition, many French people resented immigrants for diluting French culture and blamed them for urban decay and delinquency.

The main beneficiary was the Front National (FN), founded in 1972. Gradually taken in hand by a veteran of colonial wars, Jean-Marie Le Pen, the FN won the biggest following of any far-right party since World War II in the 1984 European parliament elections (11 percent) and the 1986 French parliamentary election (10 percent, 35 seats). The FN attracted unemployed and disillusioned former communists as well as traditional rightists, and, with the decline of communism, became the principal beneficiary of protest voting. It capitalized on the resentments of ordinary French people troubled by petty crime, unemployment, and the loss of French prestige in the world. Although Le Pen sometimes let slip an anti-Semitic remark, it was primarily anti-Muslim feelings that fueled his movement rather than anti-Semitism, in decline in France since the end of World War II (even after the cooling of French relations with Israel after the 1967 war).

In the first round of the April 2002 presidential elections, Le Pen came in second, with 19 percent of the vote, but this fluke reflected the Left's divisions. In the second round he was limited to the same 15 percent as throughout the previous decade. Nevertheless, the FN had some success bending the national agenda in its direction. It also managed to root itself in some French cities with declining industrial employment and large immigrant populations, especially along the Mediterranean coast and in eastern France. There it elected mayors and city councilmen and acquired enough local electoral muscle to persuade some mainline conservatives to accept it as a normal partner in electoral coalitions against the Left. The FN exhibited some, but not all, of the features of classical fascism. It echoed fascism in its cult of action, of leadership, and of "law and order," as well as in a xenophobia verging on racism. It lacked other basic features of fascism, however: state economic control, for it wanted economic liberty; military expansionism; and fundamental rejection of the parliamentary republic. Like the PSF in the 1930s, it did best when it muted overt references to classical fascism.

Robert O. Paxton

See Also: INTRODUCTION; ACTION FRANÇAISE; ANTI-SEMITISM; AXIS, THE; BARDÈCHE, MAURICE; BENOIST, ALAIN DE; BLANCHOT, MAURICE; BOLSHEVISM; BOULANGISM; BOURGEOISIE, THE; BRASILLACH, ROBERT; BUCARD, MARCEL; CAESARISM; CATHOLIC CHURCH, THE; CELINE, LOUIS FERDINAND; *CERCLE PROUDHON,* THE; CORPORATISM; CZECHOSLOVAKIA; DÉAT, MARCEL; DORIOT, JACQUES; DREYFUS CASE, THE; DRIEU LA ROCHELLE, PIERRE; DRUMONT, EDOUARD ADOLPHE; ECONOMICS; EUROPE; EUROPEAN NEW RIGHT, THE; EXPANSIONISM; FARMERS; FASCIO, THE; FRENCH REVOLUTION, THE; GRECE; HITLER, ADOLF; IMMIGRATION; INTEGRAL NATIONALISM; LA ROQUE DE SEVERAC, COMTE FRANCOIS DE; LE PEN, JEAN-MARIE; LEADER CULT, THE; MARXISM; MAURRAS, CHARLES; MONARCHISM; MUNICH PACT, THE; MUSSOLINI, BENITO ANDREA; NATIONAL FRONT (FRANCE), THE; NATIONALISM; PETAIN, MARSHAL HENRI PHILIPPE; POSTWAR FASCISM; POUJADE, PIERRE MARIE RAYMOND; REBATET, LUCIEN; SOCIALISM; SOREL, GEORGES; STATE, THE; TRADITIONALISM; VALOIS, GEORGES; VICHY; WALL STREET CRASH, THE; WORLD WAR I; WORLD WAR II; XENOPHOBIA

References

Irvine, William D. "Fascism in France and the Strange Case of the Croix de Feu." *Journal of Modern History* 63 (June 1991): 271–295.

Marcus, Jonathan. 1995. *The National Front and French Politics.* London: Macmillan.

Passmore, Kevin. 1995. "Boy Scoutism for Grown-ups? Paramilitarism in the *Croix de Feu* and the *Parti Social Français.*" *French Historical Studies* 19: 527–557.

———. 1997. *From Liberalism to Fascism: The Right in a French Province, 1928–1939.* Cambridge: Cambridge University Press.

Paxton, Robert O. 1997. *French Peasant Fascism: Henry Dorgères' Greenshirts and the Crises of French Agriculture, 1929–1939.* New York: Oxford University Press.

Rémond, René. 1969. *The Right Wing in France from 1815 to De Gaulle.* Philadelphia: University of Pennsylvania Press.

Soucy, Robert. 1986. *French Fascism, the First Wave, 1924–1933.* New Haven: Yale University Press.

———. 1995. *French Fascism, the Second Wave, 1933–1939.* New Haven: Yale University Press.

Sternhell, Zeev. 1986. *Neither Left nor Right: Fascist Ideology in France.* Berkeley: University of California Press.

———. 1994. *The Birth of Fascist Ideology: From Cultural Rebellion to Political Revolution.* Princeton: Princeton University Press.

Weber, Eugen. 1962. *Action française.* Stanford: Stanford University Press.

———. 1966. "France." In *The European Right,* edited by Hans Rogger and Eugen Weber. Berkeley: University of California Press.

Winock, Michel. 1998. *Nationalism, Anti-Semitism, and Fascism in France.* Stanford: Stanford University Press.

General Francisco Franco came to power in Spain with the aid of Hitler and Mussolini and has often been regarded as the third in a trio of fascist dictators. He kept Spain neutral during World War II, however, and his regime was more authoritarian/traditionalist than fascist. (The Illustrated London News Picture Library)

FRANCO Y BAHAMONDE, GENERAL FRANCISCO (1892–1975)

Dictator of Spain and the nation's sole arbiter at the head of a single party, the army, and a fascistic régime for thirty-six years. The most successful but least well known of Europe's right-wing interwar leaders. Franco lacked charisma, was far from intellectually brilliant, was short and squat, and those who met him invariably commented sarcastically on his femininity. One wrote: "A small man, his hand is like a woman's. . . . [H]is voice is shrill and pitched on a high note which is slightly disconcerting since he speaks very softly—almost in a whisper" (quoted in Preston 1993, 168). That apparent timidity and his natural caution—underpinned, according to some authors, by a feeling of inadequacy and insecurity—undoubtedly aided his survival during nearly four decades, while also hiding his burning ambition. Franco was born in El Ferrol on 4 December 1892, one of five children. His family had a naval history but he joined the army, graduating from the Toledo military academy in 1910. Posted to Morocco, he earned a reputation as a brave soldier, reaching the rank of major in 1917. He was offered the post as second-in-command with the Tercio (Foreign Legion) in October 1920, under the eccentric, one-armed, blind-in-one eye, death-obsessed General José Millán Astray. Franco took over command in 1923.

In October 1923, Franco married Carmen Polo in Oviedo. Throughout the thirty-six years of his dictatorship, he carried the mummified hand of Saint Teresa of Ávila—an ostentatious Catholicism that appears to have stemmed from his pious wife. In 1926, Franco became Europe's youngest general; two years later, he was named commander of Zaragoza's military academy, the closing of which, ordered in July 1931, fueled an intense hostility on his part toward the Republic and Manuel Azaña. The country was by now under a right-wing government, and Franco was called in to put down the 1934 Asturias revolt with the army of Africa, which he did with particular bloodthirstiness, making him a hero among sections of the Right. In 1935 he was made chief of staff at the Ministry of War, losing his post when the Right lost the February 1936 elections. Suspicions over his loyalty led to his relocation to the Canary Islands. Throughout the spring of 1936, Franco prevaricated over joining the plans for a rising against the elected government, earning himself the nickname "Miss Canary Islands 1936" thanks to his coyness. When he did join, he led the vital Army of Africa. Aided by a series of freakily fortuitous deaths, Franco was nominated supreme commander of the nationalist forces and head of state in October 1936, laying the foundations of the Francoist New State.

Although Hitler was an ally, Franco met him only once, in Hendaye on 23 October 1940, where they failed to agree on Spain's entry into the war. Famously, Hitler remarked bitterly: "I'd rather have teeth pulled than go through that again." In his *Table Talk*, Hitler made it clear that he despised Franco for his Catholicism, considering him to be subservient to the priests. As the war turned against the Axis, Franco sought to reinvent himself, but international isolation was the price of a fascist past until the Cold War brought entry into the United Nations in 1950 and then a bases agreement with the United States and a concordat with the Vatican in 1953. In 1969, Franco announced that his successor would be King Juan Carlos.

Sid Lowe

See Also: CATHOLIC CHURCH, THE; CLERICO-FASCISM; COLD WAR, THE; FALANGE; FRANCOISM; HITLER, ADOLF; MILITARY DICTATORSHIP; PRIMO DE RIVERA, JOSÉ ANTONIO; SPAIN; SPANISH CIVIL WAR, THE

References
Fusi, Juan. 1987. *Franco.* Trans. Felipe Fernandez-Armesto. London: HarperCollins.
Preston, Gabrielle A. 2000. *Franco.* London: Weidenfeld and Nicholson.
Preston, Paul. 1993. *Franco: A Biography.* London: Fontana.
Ribeiro de Mensese, Filipe. 2001. *Franco and the Spanish Civil War.* London: Routledge.

FRANCOISM

The political system instituted by General Francisco Franco, dictator of Spain 1936–1975; often branded "fascist" but in fact differing very substantially from the "classic" fascism of Mussolini and Hitler. Francoism was less a coherent political ideology, more a series of pragmatic reactions to a changing political scene, the main aims being the maintenance of Franco's power within Spain and the preservation of Spanish interests in the outside world. As circumstances changed, one or other of the disparate components that made up the ruling party came to the fore, and others became less important. Most generalizations turn out to be invalid, whether they be the Spanish post-Franco characterization of Francoism as having been a form of "fascism," or the delineation, by so many, of Franco's basic political position as having been purely and simply that of a traditional military reactionary.

The picture of Franco as a "conservative" rather than "fascist" figure has always been helped by the fact that the nationalist rebellion in 1936 appears to fit in with a whole Spanish tradition of right-wing military coups from the beginning of the nineteenth century onward, the most recent of which had resulted in the dictatorship of General Miguel Primo de Rivera from 1923 to 1930. Primo de Rivera's 1923 *pronunciamiento* (the forty-third since 1814) expressed many of the ideas that were, in their turn, to bring the military plotters of

1936 to the point of rebellion, speaking as it did of the need to liberate the country from the politicians, "the men who for one reason or another are responsible for the period of misfortune and corruption which began in 1898 and threatens to bring Spain to a tragic and dishonourable end." There was a difference, however. Once Franco had become the leader of the 1936 rebellion, he was only too aware of the problems that would face him after the war. Primo de Rivera's mistake, which Franco was determined not to repeat, had been not to create a political organization that would enable him to govern the country effectively. Franco was aware of the wide variety of political forces that had rallied to the Nationalist cause: Falangists, monarchists, Carlists, Christian Democrats, aristocrats, military men, and Catholics pure and simple. They were all united in the negative aim of what they wanted to get rid of: the left-wing Popular Front Republic that had resulted from the 1936 elections, and the political and social chaos of the previous few years. Yet would they be united in the creation of a new state after the battle?

In April 1937, at the height of the Civil War, Franco created a single party called the Falange Española Tradicionalista y de las JONS (using the names of the two main fascistic movements, but adding the word *traditionalist*). It has sometimes been suggested, by proponents of the "traditionalist" Franco thesis, that he thereby cleverly submerged the fascist-style Falange (weakened in its leadership, partly by the execution of José Antonio Primo de Rivera, the charismatic son of the former dictator) in a vast new party containing all the other nationalist elements. Although there is some truth in that picture, it underestimates Franco's acceptance of the idea of international fascism, of which Spain might be a part, and his pragmatic acceptance of Falangist numerical strength, which had grown so greatly since the outbreak of the war. As Stanley Payne has put it, his goal almost inevitably had to be a "radical and sophisticated state party of at least semi-fascist contours, organized on the basis of the Falange but integrating other Nationalist elements as well" (Payne 1988, 168). Much of the new party was Falangist in tone: the Falangists' blue shirts, red and black flag, and Fascist salute were adopted, as was the slogan *Arriba España;* the Nazi influence was to be found in the slogan *Una Patria, un Estado, un Caudillo;* while in themselves the creation of a single state party, and the elevation of a sole authoritarian figure, the Jefe (the Spanish equivalent of Duce or Fuehrer), to the headship of the state, were very much in line with fascist procedures. In conversation not just with German and Italian representatives but also with more neutral observers, Franco in-

sisted that "the core of the . . . party would be formed by the Falange, which had the soundest program and the greatest following in the country" (Delzell 1970, 288), and that the new unitary party was part of an international movement toward fascism, which by its nature differed from country to country "to the extent that countries and national temperaments vary" (Massis 1939, 150). In a "Call for the Unification of the Fighting Forces," on 18 April 1937, Franco drew a clear distinction between the old-style *pronunciamiento*-driven military Right and new-style fascism, when he described the early twentieth century as being "a period of transition between the *Pronunciamiento* of the nineteenth century and the organic conception of those movements that our present-day world labels 'fascist' or 'nationalist.'"

From all of this we should not necessarily jump to the conclusion that Franco's main aims were "fascist," or that he wholeheartedly espoused the more radical parts of fascist social theory. His Spanish Labor Charter of 1938 was, for example, more paternalistic and regulatory than the "fascist" model. Yet there is no escaping the fact that, in the immediate aftermath of the Civil War and during World War II, "the regime's ideological tone was set by the Falange," and "in the eyes of the outside world, the Falange and Francoism were consubstantial" (Preston 1990, 140). Franco was convinced that Spain was an integral part of the move toward a "new Europe," and that it was essential to associate the country more closely with the German and Italian regimes that were creating it. These were the years, 1939–1942, that have been described as the "fascist temptation" of Franco (Payne 1999, 326), when the Spanish leader was convinced (even though he did not bring Spain into World War II) that the war would create a world dominated by the fascist powers.

By 1943, confidence in the victory of the fascist states had worn thin. Franco's position seemed to many to be perilous, particularly after the fall of Mussolini had shown the fragility of even the most authoritarian rule. Within the ruling party, the "fascist" cause had become less attractive, and the monarchist strain had returned to the fore, with there being also considerable disaffection among the military. Yet, as the war ended, it became clear that any danger to the regime had been illusory. The unwieldy alliance of right-wing interests had too much fear of those forces of the Left that might return if they did not cling together. And Franco's creation of the substructure of a powerful state through the single party had paid off. As the war ended, there was no sign of a collapse of the regime. The chameleon-like nature of Francoism is shown by its adaptation to the postwar situation, in which Spain needed to be acceptable to the conquerors. Food, raw materials, and credit were needed, and they could be supplied only if the country became part of the international economy. Spain could not afford to become a pariah. The regime abandoned most of its fascist trappings, and the Falange had to take a back seat while the Christian Democrats, monarchists, and Carlists who had coexisted with it within the party during its "fascist" stage now came once more to the fore. It is almost certainly post-1945 Francoism that has led many commentators to espouse the theory that Franco was a "traditionalist pure and simple," who had merely used fascism for his own ends up to that time, while cleverly restraining it. Yet as we have seen, that theory does not hold water.

Although the regime remained authoritarian, it produced sops to Western opinion by an appearance of greater democratic procedures, including the use of plebiscites. And in 1947 a new law, the *Ley de Sucesión,* in which Spain was pronounced to be a kingdom, with Franco as its head of state for life, eliminated at a stroke the idea of a fascist state and proclaimed the state's traditionalist legitimacy. By 1951, Franco was able, in a major cabinet reshuffle, to oust most of his remaining Falange ministers. By 1955 he was negotiating with the pretender, Don Juan. Gradually Franco's regime had become accepted in the postwar family of nations, particularly from the late 1940s onward, as the communist threat became clearer and the United States became aware of Spain's strategic uses. In 1952, Spain entered UNESCO, and in 1953, Franco negotiated a treaty with the United States that provided for U.S. bases within Spain. In 1953, too, a Spanish concordat was signed with the Vatican. There came a time for further change, however. By the late 1950s, Franco was faced, on the one hand, by growing tensions within the movement, and on the other by severe problems with the economy. His solution was to create a cabinet of "experts" and technocrats, with major posts going to the Catholic pressure group Opus Dei. Their reforms were successful, and they succeeded in bolstering yet again the authoritarian regime, as industrial production increased and the standard of living rose.

By now Francoism consisted not so much of political activists from its various strands (conservative, fascist, monarchist, Christian Democrat) as of a large number of people whose financial or career stake in the regime's continuance outshone any ideological stance. Franco himself, the authoritarian ruler, was essential to their needs. As Franco grew older, the prospect of his loss led many hesitantly to plan for the future. At the same time, in-fighting between the various strands of the regime, and disaffection among the people, seemed to be pointing to a decline in Francoism's fortunes. In the last stage of Francoism, therefore, from the mid-1960s onward, there developed what has been described as "Moderate Francoism," as reformists tried to direct the regime into more democratic paths. Although the instinct of many Francoists was to desire an unchanged continuation of the authoritarian regime, with the pretender's son Juan Carlos (who had been named as Franco's successor in 1969, and whom many saw as being inexperienced and open to influence) presiding as a puppet over it, the reformists saw the only credible future as lying in a form of democratization, particularly because of the increasing tensions within the regime and opposition to it in large sections of society. They set out to form a link between Francoism and the democratic Left. The first steps toward democratization were taken as early as 1964, with the Law of Associations, and 1966, with a new Press Law. Although the measures thus introduced were limited and cautious (and perceived by some as a sham), the gesture had been made. By the time that Franco died in November 1975, the majority of Francoists had become committed to a middle way, which could in their view save the regime in its present form, under Juan Carlos as king, by making various gestures of a moderate kind toward democratic representation. Only the extreme diehards opposed this strategy. The diehards may have been right in one sense (though their intransigence would probably have caused a return to civil strife). The mistake of the "moderate Francoists" was to believe that Juan Carlos, who had been Franco's protege, was committed to Francoism. As early as 1976, with the creation of the Reform Law, King Juan Carlos swept away the Francoist state.

Richard Griffiths

See Also: INTRODUCTION; CATHOLIC CHURCH, THE; CONSERVATISM; COLD WAR, THE; DECADENCE; FALANGE; FASCIST PARTY, THE; FRANCO Y BAHAMONDE, GENERAL FRANCISCO; HITLER, ADOLF; MONARCHISM; MONARCHY; MUSSOLINI, BENITO ANDREA; NATIONALISM; NAZISM; ORGANICISM; POLITICAL CATHOLICISM; POSTWAR FASCISM; PRIMO DE RIVERA, JOSÉ ANTONIO; SPAIN; SPANISH CIVIL WAR, THE; STATE, THE

References

Delzell, Charles R., ed. 1970. *Mediterranean Fascism 1919–1945.* London: Harper and Row.
Massis, Henri. 1939. *Chefs.* Paris: Plon.
Palomares, Cristina. 2004. *Moderate Francoism and the Slow Journey to the Polls, 1964–1977.* Brighton: Sussex Academic.
Payne, Stanley. 1988. *The Franco Regime, 1936–1975.* Madison, WI: University of Wisconsin Press.

———. 1999. *Fascism in Spain, 1923–1977.* Madison, WI: University of Wisconsin Press.

Preston, Paul. 1990. "Populism and Parasitism: The Falange and the Spanish Establishment, 1939–1975." Pp. 138–156 in *Fascists and Conservatives: The Radical Right and the Establishment in Twentieth-century Europe,* edited by Martin Blinkhorn. London: Unwin Hyman.

———. 1995. *The Politics of Revenge: Fascism and the Military in Twentieth-century Spain.* London: Routledge.

FRANK, ANNE (1929–1945)

Young Jewish girl famed for her posthumously published diary in which she described the experience of hiding with her family from the German occupiers in a secret annex in a former warehouse in Amsterdam. After being discovered by the Gestapo on 4 August 1944, she died in Belsen shortly before the war's end. The diary was translated into many languages and turned into a stage play and film. Today the building where she hid has become a shrine.

Cyprian Blamires

See Also: ANTI-SEMITISM; CONCENTRATION CAMPS; HOLO-CAUST, THE; NETHERLANDS, THE; WORLD WAR II

Reference
Frank, Anne. 1997. *The Diary of a Young Girl.* London: Penguin.

FRANK, HANS (1900–1946)

Legal adviser to the Nazi Party from 1929 and governor-general of occupied Poland from 1939. He was involved in the 1923 Munich Putsch as a storm trooper and in 1926 began to practice as an attorney in Munich. He defended many brownshirts arrested over street fights with communists, and in one of these cases called Hitler as a witness in behalf of a client. Hitler put him in charge of the legal division of the NSDAP, and he represented Hitler in 150 lawsuits. He was also given the task of carrying out research to show that

Hitler himself had no Jewish blood. When Hitler became chancellor, Frank was appointed Bavarian minister of justice, Reich minister of justice, and Reich minister without portfolio. Other positions Frank held included those of Reich leader of the NSDAP and president of the Academy of German Law. As governor-general of Occupied Poland, Frank pursued a policy of destroying the country as a nation and plundering its resources. He also presided over the deportation of Polish Jews to the death camps. On trial at Nuremberg, Frank announced his conversion to Catholicism and penitence and turned on Hitler as betrayer of the German people's trust. But he was condemned to death and hanged.

Cyprian Blamires

See Also: ANTI-SEMITISM; CONCENTRATION CAMPS; *GLEICHSCHALTUNG;* HITLER, ADOLF; HOLOCAUST, THE; LAW; MUNICH PUTSCH, THE; NAZISM; NUREMBERG TRIALS, THE; POLAND; SA, THE; WORLD WAR II

References
Housden, Martyn. 2003. *Hans Frank: Lebensraum and the Holocaust.* Basingstoke: Palgrave Macmillan.

Piotrowski, Stanislaw, ed. 1961. *Hans Frank's Diary.* New York: Wehman.

FRANK, KARL HERMANN (1898–1946)

Sudeten German Nazi politician, a bookseller by profession. Frank was not loyal to Czechoslovakia and inclined to the Sudeten German movement, holding a prominent post in the Sudeten German Party. After the Munich Agreement and the Nazi occupation of the rest of Bohemia and Moravia, he became state secretary of the Protectorate of Bohemia and Moravia (1939–1943) and then German state minister of Bohemia and Moravia (1943–1945). Frank became one of the symbols of the Nazi occupation, power, and terror in the Czech lands (for instance, he was responsible for the destruction of the village of Lidice). After the war Frank was sentenced to death by the Czechoslovak people's court and executed on 22 May 1946.

Miroslav Mares

See Also: CZECHOSLOVAKIA; MUNICH PACT, THE; NAZISM; SUDETENLAND, THE

References

Mastny, Vojtech. 1971. *The Czechs under Nazi Rule.* New York, NY: Columbia University Press.

Smelser, R. M. 1975. *The Sudeten Problem.* Middletown, CT: Wesleyan University Press.

FRANKFURT SCHOOL, THE: *See* PSYCHOLOGY

FREDERICK II, THE GREAT (1712–1786)

King of Prussia and architect of Prussian expansion, one of Hitler's great heroes. Frederick was famous for his involvement with leading figures in the Enlightenment such as Voltaire, but he is remembered above all for having seized Silesia from Austria by force and later for having acquired further territory from Poland. He was considered to be one of the foremost military commanders of the day. In Hitler's office in the new National Socialist Party headquarters, opened in 1931, a painting of the Prussian monarch was there to keep a bust of Mussolini company. At crucial moments in his life Hitler was in the habit of quoting Frederick or of appealing to his example. In January 1924, when Hitler was in prison, he heard the news of Lenin's death and saw it as prophetic of the fall of the Soviet Union, recalling the way in which Frederick the Great had joyfully received the news of the death of the Czarina Elizabeth of Russia in 1762. In 1939 he was in the habit of complaining that Frederick the Great would turn in his grave if he could see the cowardice of the generals of his own day. In 1940 he compared himself, as he contemplated further military advances westward, to the great Prussian monarch planning the first Silesian War. As Hitler contemplated the Allied Offensive after D-Day in the autumn of 1944 and proposed a counteroffensive through the Ardennes—only to be stopped in his tracks by his own generals—he remarked that they had forgotten Frederick the Great, who had defeated enemies twice his strength. How had he done it? By bold attack. As the Allied forces closed in relentlessly on Berlin in the spring of 1945, he had Goebbels read Carlyle's writing on the Prussian monarch to him.

Hitler had tears in his eyes as he heard about Frederick's sudden rise from the abyss with the death of the czarina of Russia.

Cyprian Blamires

See Also: CARLYLE, THOMAS; *DRANG NACH OSTEN* ("DRIVE TO THE EAST"), THE; GOEBBELS, (PAUL) JOSEPH; HITLER, ADOLF; *MEIN KAMPF;* MUSSOLINI, BENITO ANDREA; WORLD WAR II

Reference

Toland, John. 1976. *Adolf Hitler.* New York: Ballantine.

FREEDOM

The Nazis believed themselves to be "freedom fighters," in the sense that they were fighting for Germany to be freed from the chains of the punitive provisions of the Versailles Treaty. The Saar District, for example, continued until 1935 to be administered on the basis of that treaty by the League of Nations, with its highly productive coal mines under French control: this penalty had been imposed on Germany because of the damage done to French coalfields by the Germans in World War I. The Rhineland including Cologne, Düsseldorf, and Bonn had been demilitarized as a result of the treaty conditions until Hitler reoccupied it on 7 March 1936. In addition, the treaty had restricted the size of the German army to 100,000 men, while the demand for financial war reparations laid an intolerable burden on the German economy. Because of all this Hitler and his followers were able to present themselves as liberators who would free Germany from the shackles imposed on them at the end of a war that they claimed had been lost only as a result of treachery. This particular agenda was peculiar to the German Nazis and had nothing to do with the Italian situation. On the other hand, there was another way in which Hitler presented himself as a liberator: that is, of ethnic Germans who were "oppressed" minorities in countries like Czechoslovakia or Poland. Here Mussolini had a similar rhetoric, for there were ethnic Italians living in territories to the east of Trieste under Slav domination; his anticipator D'Annunzio had gone as far as to launch a coup in Fiume in 1919 to "save" the city from being put under Slav domination in the post–World War I settlement.

There was another sense in which German Nazis and Italian Fascists saw themselves as "freedom fighters": they saw themselves as campaigning to free the world from enslavement to various groups. For the Italian Fascists it was the forces of Bolshevism, liberalism, Freemasonry, and "plutocracy." The Nazis were engaged in the same war of liberation, but for them there was a shadowy and pernicious enemy behind these movements manipulating them all—the force of world Jewry. The majority of the fascist or fascistic movements that drew inspiration from German Nazism portrayed themselves as engaged in a crusade to free the world from Jewish domination. Sometimes German Nazi propagandists spoke of the need to overthrow the oppressive forces of Jews *and Jesuits.* The idea behind this rather surprising combination was that these two movements represented the acme of internationalism and were the most intransigent enemies of the hypernationalism which formed the foundation of Nazism. The Jesuits stood out among Catholic movements for their direct dependence on Rome (which meant *in*dependence from both national governments and national church leaderships). But for the individualist meaning of the term *freedom,* familiar in the liberal context, interwar fascists had no time at all. That was because they were committed to a notion that the state and the collectivity came first, the individual only second. The individual had no rights; only the state had rights. It was the vocation of the individual to sacrifice himself and his freedom for the state.

Cyprian Blamires

See Also: INTRODUCTION; ANTI-SEMITISM; BOLSHEVISM; COMMUNITY; CONSPIRACY THEORIES; CZECHOSLOVAKIA; D'ANNUNZIO, GABRIELE; FASCIST PARTY, THE; FIUME; FREEMASONRY/FREEMASONS, THE; GOERING (VON KANTZOW), CARIN; HITLER, ADOLF; INDIVIDUALISM; IRREDENTISM; ITALY; JESUITS, THE; LEAGUE OF NATIONS, THE; LIBERALISM; MARXISM; MARXIST THEORIES OF FASCISM; MUSSOLINI, BENITO ANDREA; NAZISM; NOVEMBER CRIMINALS/*NOVEMBERBRECHER*, THE; PLUTOCRACY; POLAND AND NAZI GERMANY; REPARATIONS; SLAVS, THE; STATE, THE; SUDETENLAND, THE; TOTALITARIANISM; VERSAILLES TREATY, THE; *VOLKSGEMEINSCHAFT,* THE; WORLD WAR I

References

Degrelle, Léon. 1987. *Hitler Century: Hitler—Born at Versailles.* Trans. T. O'Keefe. Newport Beach, CA: Institute of Historical Review.
Haraszti, Eva H. 1983. *The Invaders: Hitler Occupies the Rhineland.* Trans. Z Laszlo. Budapest: Akademiai Kiado.
Henig, Ruth. 1995. *Versailles and After, 1919–1933.* London: Routledge.
Krieger, Leonard. 1973. *The German Idea of Freedom.* Chicago: University of Chicago Press.
Ledeen, Michael A. 1977. *The First Duce: D'Annunzio at Fiume.* London: Johns Hopkins University Press.
Smelser, R. M. 1975. *The Sudeten Problem.* Middletown, CT: Wesleyan University Press.

FREEMASONRY/ FREEMASONS, THE

From the NSDAP to a panoply of contemporary parties, extreme-right movements have frequently expressed their hostility to Freemasonry. Freemasonry often plays an important role in the variety of conspiracy theories articulated by extreme-right parties and their ideologists. The anti-Masonic discourse of extreme-right currents describes Freemasonry as an elite opposed to the "people." While this populist theme is often shared by leftists, the extreme Right combines it with accusations against the alleged or real cosmopolitanism of Freemasonry—an accusation that parallels similar ones voiced against Jews. Because of the international nature of their organization, Freemasons are suspected of having contacts with the enemies of the nation, an issue that was particularly relevant in the early twentieth century with the prevalence of over-heated nationalism. Extreme-right hostility toward Freemasonry has not limited itself to campaigns of denigration. The practice of extreme right parties during the interwar years when in power also included the repression of Freemasonry, whose existence was outlawed. Such repression was practiced by Fascism in Italy, Nazism in Germany, by the Franco regime in Spain, and the Pétain regime in France. Extreme-right groups have, however, frequently displayed at the same time a fascination with Freemasonry, resulting in attempts to infiltrate it or to create similar secret societies.

Freemasonry is a worldwide fraternal organization, a service club that also intends to be a philosophical society. It traditionally abstains from political and religious controversies and has in fact generally been characterized by its conformism and its proestablishment attitude. It originated in Great Britain, where it was founded in 1717. Since then it has spread over the world, although its strongholds remain the Anglo-Saxon world and in a lesser measure Europe and Latin America. Although—or perhaps because—it professed a vague religious creed involving belief in a Supreme Being whom it designated "the Architect of the Universe," Freemasonry frequently encountered hostile reactions from religious groups, and in particular from the Catholic Church. As a consequence, during the nineteenth century in certain predominantly Catholic countries, especially in Europe—France, Belgium,

Italy, Spain, Portugal—it gradually turned more anticlerical. Masonic organizations in those countries abandoned references to a Supreme Being (Belgium in 1871–1872 and France in 1877), which resulted in a schism with Anglo-Saxon Freemasonry not yet overcome. They also became more politically involved and abolished the prohibition on political debates (in Belgium in 1854, to be followed by Freemasons in other Catholic countries). In the second half of the nineteenth century, Freemasonry in these countries was involved in anticlerical politics, including the unification of Italy (which deprived the Catholic Church of its temporal power, thus arousing the Church's hostility to Freemasonry), whose main protagonists, such as Garibaldi, were also prominent Freemasons. In the twentieth century the political role of Freemasonry in these countries gradually subsided, reflecting the diminished weight of anticlericalism in politics.

The far-right critics of Freemasonry drew on the tradition of counter-revolutionary conspiracy theories originating in Abbé Barruel's pamphlet *Mémoires pour servir à l'histoire du jacobinisme* (1797), claiming that the French Revolution was the outcome of a conspiracy of philosophers, Freemasons, and the Illuminati (a Bavarian group related to Freemasonry). During the nineteenth century anti-Masonism was principally propagated by the Catholic Church. Politically, the claims against Freemasonry were activated in the late nineteenth century by the French nationalist Right. The idea of revolutionary Masonic conspiracies also influenced extreme-right writings outside France and Catholic countries. *The Protocols of the Elders of Zion,* produced by the czarist secret services, albeit more concentrated on the role of Jews, nevertheless gave Freemasonry a role in the 'Jewish' conspiracy that the booklet claimed to be divulging. The German adaptation of the *Protocols,* published after World War I, highlighted much more than the Russian original the role of Freemasons, and therefore played an important role in the creation of the myth of the Judeo-Masonic plot (in which communists were also given a prominent place). The vast popularity enjoyed by the *Protocols* between the wars undoubtedly enhanced suspicions about Freemasonry, even in those countries in which it did not play any political role, or where, as in Germany, many of its members were conservative nationalists. During World War II, the Nazis organized anti-Masonic campaigns in all the occupied countries, regardless of the political stance of Freemasonry in those countries.

It should be noted, however, that hostility toward Freemasonry rarely acquired the virulence of anti-Semi-

tism. Italian Fascism was only marginally influenced by this myth. Even Nazism, while outlawing Freemasonry, did not persecute individual Freemasons systematically. The virulence of anti-Masonic campaigns was clearly related to the impact of Catholic anti-Masonry on the extreme Right. In the case of the Franco regime during and after the Spanish Civil War, the brutal persecution of Freemasons no doubt resulted from the presentation of the war as a crusade against the enemies of the Catholic Church. The hostility of the Pétain regime toward Freemasonry stems from a similar cultural background.

The attitude of many contemporary extreme-right currents toward Freemasonry can be traced back to the conspiracy theories cultivated by the extreme Right during the interwar years. No doubt as a result of the diminished political orientation of Freemasonry in those countries in which it was politically very active in earlier periods (for example, France and Belgium), the movement does not play a very prominent role in contemporary extreme-right propaganda. Negative references to Freemasonry persist as an ideological or rhetorical inheritance from the past rather than as a live issue.

Michael Huysseune

See Also: ANTI-SEMITISM; CATHOLIC CHURCH, THE; CONSPIRACY THEORIES; COSMOPOLITANISM; ENLIGHTENMENT, THE; FRANCE; FRANCO Y BAHAMONDE, GENERAL FRANCISCO; FRANCOISM; FRENCH REVOLUTION, THE; GERMANY; ITALY; NATIONALISM; NAZISM; ORTHODOX CHURCHES, THE; PETAIN, MARSHAL HENRI PHILIPPE; *PROTOCOLS OF THE ELDERS OF ZION, THE;* RISORGIMENTO, THE; RUSSIA; SPAIN; TRADITIONALISM; WEBSTER, NESTA; WORLD WAR II

References

Hoyos, A., and B. Brent Morris. 2004. *Freemasonry in Context: History, Ritual, Controversy.* Lanham, MD: Lexington.

Ligou, D., ed. 1998. *Dictionnaire de la franc-maçonnerie.* Paris: PUF.

Neuberger, H. 1980. *Freimaurerei und Nationalsozialismus.* 2 vols. Hamburg: Bauhütten Verlag.

Webster, Nesta. 1994 [1924]. *Secret Societies and Subversive Movements.* Reprint: A & B.

FREIKORPS, THE

Nationalistic paramilitary units put on a formal footing in Germany by Kurt von Schleicher in 1919. Members were demobilized soldiers of lower-middle-class background who had not been absorbed into the Reichswehr, which had been restricted by the terms of the Versailles Treaty to a membership of 100,000. In the beginning (1919–1920), the militaristic and antidemocratic Free Corps, with its membership at 400,000 (as of 1919), mainly fought the Left and supported the German aristocrats in the Baltic States militarily. After their official disbanding in 1920, the Free Corps partly changed to far-right underground organizations responsible for murder and conspiracy.

Fabian Virchow

See Also: HITLER, ADOLF; NATIONALISM; NAZISM; PARAMILITARISM; SCHLEICHER, KURT VON; WEHRMACHT, THE; WEIMAR REPUBLIC, THE

References

Gumbel, Emil Julius.1958. *Statistics of Extremes.* New York: Columbia University Press.
Waite, Robert G. L. 1952. *Vanguard of Nazism: The Free Corps Movement in Postwar Germany 1918–1923.* Cambridge: Harvard University Press.

FRENCH REVOLUTION, THE

Out of the opposition to the French Revolution, modern European conservatism developed, and from conservatism different connecting lines led to fascism. The conservatives opposed the Revolution's democratic ideas, its anticlericalism, and its primacy of reason against tradition. In fascist thinking, the French Revolution was a symbol of materialism, liberalism, Jewry, and Freemasonry, and the polar opposite of its own ideology of national revolution. In the course of the nineteenth and early twentieth centuries, conservatives linked the French Revolution to what they saw as the negative aspects of democracy and mass politics. Gustave Le Bon, an influential theorist of "crowd" behavior, warned that the French Revolution epitomized the irrationality, savagery, and violence of the mob. Some conservatives (along with Marxists and English utilitarians like Jeremy Bentham) decried the universal principles of human rights upon which the Revolution was based. They saw danger in these universal appeals, especially as they promised social equality for Jews and for "inferior" races. The racist thinker and self-appointed aristocrat comte Arthur de Gobineau saw the French Revolution as the over-

whelming of a pure-race "white" aristocracy by the inferior "yellow" mob. Charles Maurras, a classical scholar and militant anti-Semite, who became involved in politics during the Dreyfus Affair and who was a leading figure in the proto-fascist movement Action Française, believed that as a result of the Revolution, France had become dominated by four "confederate Estates": Protestants, Freemasons, Jews, and foreigners. He hoped to destroy these influences and return France to its traditional institutions—particularly the monarchy and Catholicism (a religion that he himself did not actually practice, recommending it instead on sociopolitical grounds as good for the people). Maurras and his movement contributed to the development of attitudes and positions that would later become identified with fascism.

Despite the fact that in general the French Revolution was a target of fascist abuse, there were also ambivalent statements that did not entirely reject it as a model for change. Benito Mussolini regarded the French Revolution as the starting point of a "leftist" (that is, liberal and socialist) era that had come to an end with the ascent of fascism. On 25 February 1922, he wrote in an article in the journal *Gerarchia* that the leftist chain, forged in 1789 and only temporarily interrupted between 1815 and 1848, had reached its apogee in the first two years after World War I. Now it had exhausted its vitality and would give way to a rightist era. In his article "The Doctrine of Fascism," published in the *Enciclopedia Italiana* in June 1932, Il Duce stated that the fascist rejection of socialism, democracy, and liberalism did not mean that the fascists wanted to turn back the clock to the prerevolutionary era; they considered the monarchic absolutism and feudal privileges that the Revolution had abolished to be mere idolatry. But fascism had picked out of the trash of liberal, socialist, and democratic doctrines all those elements that had preserved their vitality. In a speech on the corporative state to the Consiglio Nazionale delle Corporazioni in 1933, Mussolini likewise stressed that the French Revolution had destroyed many medieval remnants such as tolls and compulsory labor and that it had created millions of property owners who still formed the basis of the French nation. The French Revolution had been a cause of the whole nation, not just of a political party.

The German National Socialists saw their seizure of power explicitly as the overcoming of the French Revolution's values. In a 1933 radio speech, Joseph Goebbels stated that the French Revolution would now be wiped out of history. Soon after, Adolf Hitler stated in a private conversation with Hermann

Rauschning that the planned international Nazi Revolution would be the exact counterpart of the French Revolution. The Nazis were particularly disturbed by the completeness of the French Revolution's break with the past. Its repudiation of history seemed to them a logical consequence of the Enlightenment. In Nazi historiography, the French Revolution was depicted as a revolt of Jews and Freemasons (for example, Walter Frank). Moreover, the Nazi ideologist Alfred Rosenberg stated that the Revolution had had as its necessary consequence the establishment of an overbearing influence of women, which he linked to an immoral confusion of sexes and to an overall destruction of the social and political order. The Nazis—like many German nationalists before them—stressed the importance of the so-called *Freiheitskriege* ("wars of liberation") against Napoleonic hegemony between 1813 and 1815 as the overcoming of the French Revolution. In a 1938 lecture, the Nazi historian Erich Botzenhart characterized the French Revolution as a revolution springing from reason, whereas the German uprising of 1813 had been a revolution springing from myth. Parallels between the German defeats of 1806 and 1918, between the Napoleonic *Fremdherrschaft* ("foreign rule") and Weimar Germany under the Treaty of Versailles, and between the wars against Napoleon and Hitler's national revolution, were used to legitimate several elements of Nazi politics. In March 1935, for instance, when universal compulsory military service was reintroduced, the newspaper *Germania* wrote that the soldiers who died fighting Napoleon at the battles of Eylau and Friedland had not been killed for nothing, nor their grandsons in the final battles of 1918: "Tilsit was followed by the uprising of 1813, Versailles is followed by the 16th March 1935!" Some of Hitler's early statements, however, show a certain ambiguity toward the French Revolution: in several speeches of the early 1920s, he contrasted the French Revolution, which he styled "national" and "constructive," favorably with the German Revolution of November 1918. In *Mein Kampf,* he stressed the French Revolution as a model for change that was rooted in the rhetorical strength of the demagogues. The French Revolution as well as Italian Fascism had been successful because they showed a new overall idea. After Hitler's seizure of power, such reflections on revolutionary change were no longer opportune. In summer 1933, SA leader Ernst Roehm, hoping for a second, 'real' national-socialist revolution, looked upon the French armies of the *levée en masse* as a model for a revolutionary Nazi

people's militia. A year later, he and his supporters were liquidated.

The attitudes of French fascists toward the French Revolution were also controversial. Many of them accused the Revolution of having begun a process that culminated in the allegedly corrupt Third Republic (1871–1940), which they failed to overthrow in February 1934. In 1939, the fascist journal *Je suis partout* published a special issue on the French Revolution, dedicated to those who had fought against the Revolution, especially the peasants of the Vendée. But there were also some ambivalent attitudes. Georges Valois, the founder of the fascist organization le Faisceau, saw the Revolution as the beginning of a movement both socialist and nationalist that would be completed by the fascists. The fascist writer Robert Brasillach contemplated the spread of the activist flame first lit in 1789 and indicated how little it had to do with either individual liberty or international peace. Jacques Doriot, a former member of the French Communist Party, which he had left in 1936 to found the fascist Parti Populaire Français, thought that the French Republic would not survive and that a national and social revolution was necessary in order to regain the basis of 1789. After the French defeat in the summer of 1940, the Jacobin Terror was at least momentarily rehabilitated by Marcel Déat, leader of the Rassemblement National Populaire, who—seeking to show the French fascists worthy of being trusted by the Nazis—wrote that, as in Robespierre's times, terror against the sworn enemies of the national revolution had to be the order of the day. However, the authoritarian *Etat français* in the nonoccupied zone under the leadership of Marshal Pétain soon deliberately decreased the Revolution's importance in the official cultural memory. Vichy's *révolution nationale* replaced the revolutionary values *Liberté, Egalité, Fraternité* by the slogan *Patrie, Famille, Travail*. In 1941, the regime offered fifteen Principles of the Community that replaced liberal individualism by a stress on duties, as Vichy's answer to the Declaration of Rights of 1789.

On a less intellectual level, the political culture of the French Revolution was a model for the fascist sacralization of politics. The Revolution had been the starting point of new forms of political organization, new patterns of interpretation, and new political semantics. Especially its mass-mobilizing worship of the nation, of death, and of youth had had great effects on nineteenth-century nationalist movements—not least in Germany and in Italy. This sacralization reached its apogee during the fascist era. After World War II, neofascists and radical-right movements remained hostile to the French Revolution. Jean-Marie Le Pen's Front National, for instance, the strongest radical-right party in contemporary France, quotes in its party program Edmund Burke's criticism of the Revolution's allegedly mechanistic conception of society. It states that the French political and economic elite has been considering society as a field of experimentation since the Revolution and, therefore, adhered to several forms of utopia, like liberalism, socialism, Marxism, Third-Worldism, and globalism.

Christian Koller

See Also: ABSTRACTION; ACTION FRANÇAISE; ANTI-SEMITISM; ARISTOCRACY; BRASILLACH, ROBERT; CONSERVATISM; CONSPIRACY THEORIES; CORPORATISM; COSMOPOLITANISM; DÉAT, MARCEL; DEMOCRACY; DORIOT, JACQUES; DREYFUS CASE, THE; EGALITARIANISM; *ENCICLOPEDIA ITALIANA*, THE; ENLIGHTENMENT, THE; FASCIST PARTY, THE; FRANCE; FREEMASONRY/FREEMASONS, THE; GLOBALIZATION; GOBINEAU, COMTE ARTHUR DE; GOEBBELS, (PAUL) JOSEPH; HITLER, ADOLF; LE BON, GUSTAVE; LE PEN, JEAN-MARIE; LIBERALISM; MARXISM; MARXIST THEORIES OF FASCISM; MATERIALISM; MAURRAS, CHARLES; MECHANISTIC THINKING; *MEIN KAMPF;* MILITARISM; MONARCHISM; MONARCHY; MUSSOLINI, BENITO ANDREA; NATIONAL FRONT, THE (FRANCE); NATIONALISM; NAZISM; NIGHT OF THE LONG KNIVES, THE; ORGANICISM; PETAIN, MARSHAL HENRI PHILIPPE; POSTWAR FASCISM; RACISM; RATIONALISM; RAUSCHNING, HERMANN; RELIGION; ROEHM, ERNST; ROSENBERG, ALFRED; SOCIALISM; STATE, THE; TOTALITARIANISM; TRADITION; TRADITIONALISM; UTOPIA, UTOPIANISM; VALOIS, GEORGES; VERSAILLES, THE TREATY OF; VICHY; WEIMAR REPUBLIC, THE; WOMEN; YOUTH

References
Dann, Otto, and John Dinwiddy, eds. 1988. *Nationalism in the Age of the French Revolution.* London: Hambledon.
Davies, Peter. 2002. *The Extreme Right in France, 1789 to the Present: From de Maistre to Le Pen.* London: Routledge.
Gordon, Bertram M. 1989. "National Movements and the French Revolution: The Justification of the French Revolution in Fascist Italy, Nazi Germany, and Vichy France." Pp. 1662–1670 in *Bicentenaire de la Revolution française 1789–1989: L'Image de la Revolution française,* Vol. III. Paris: Pergamon.
Hobsbawm, Eric J. 1990. *Echoes of the Marseillaise: Two Centuries Look Back on the French Revolution.* New Brunswick: Rutgers University Press.
Hunt, Lynn Avery. 1984. *Politics, Culture, and Class in the French Revolution.* Berkeley: University of California Press.
Mosse, George L. 1989. "Fascism and the French Revolution." *Journal of Contemporary History* 24: 5–26.
———. 1999. *The Fascist Revolution: Toward a General Theory of Fascism.* New York: Howard Fertig.
Soboul, Albert. 1989. *A Short History of the French Revolution: 1789–1799.* Berkeley: University of California Press.

FREUD, SIGMUND (1856–1939)

Founder of psychoanalysis; psychoanalytic ideas have provided the basis for a number of psychological theories of fascism. Freud's own career and personal life were directly affected by the rise of anti-Semitism in Austria and the growth of Nazism. Freud, who was Jewish, spent most of his life in Vienna. He trained as a medical doctor and was drawn to psychiatry, believing that many mental disorders were the product of unconscious sexual desires. When Freud was formulating the basic elements of psychoanalytic theory, the overtly anti-Semitic party of Karl Lueger was governing Vienna. Freud believed that his chances of a career at the University of Vienna were being blocked by anti-Semitism. Although Freud rejected Jewish religious practice, he never renounced his Jewish identity. Most of Freud's early patients and followers were secular Jews like himself. In later life, he would claim that only a Jew could have discovered psychoanalysis. Because Jews were outsiders, they were more likely to be free from the prejudices of what Freud called the "compact majority." When the Nazis came to power in Germany, they denounced psychoanalysis as a "Jewish science," and Freud's books were publicly burned. Freud sought to apply psychoanalytic theory to Jewish history in *Moses and Monotheism* (1939), which was his last book to be published in his lifetime. Freud argued that Moses was actually an Egyptian who had been murdered by Jews. In this book he touched briefly on the irrationality of Christian anti-Semitism and on the pre-Christian roots of Nazism, but he did not develop such ideas. That was left to a later generation of psychoanalytic thinkers. Practicing psychoanalysts like Erich Fromm and Wilhelm Reich, and psychoanalytically influenced social theorists such as Theodor Adorno and Max Horkheimer, were to use Freudian theory to explore how fascist ideology drew upon irrational, unconscious fears.

Michael Billig

See Also: ANTI-SEMITISM; AUSTRIA; BURNING OF THE BOOKS, THE; FROMM, ERICH; JUNG, CARL GUSTAV; LUEGER, KARL; NAZISM; PSYCHOANALYSIS; PSYCHODYNAMICS OF PALINGENETIC MYTH, THE; PSYCHOLOGY; REICH, WILHELM

References
Billig, Michael. 1999. *Freudian Repression.* Cambridge: Cambridge University Press.
Freud, Sigmund. 1999 [1925]. *An Autobiographical Study.* In *Penguin Freud Library,* vol. 15. Harmondsworth: Penguin.
———. 1990 [1939]. *Moses and Monotheism.* In *Penguin Freud Library,* vol. 13. Harmondsworth: Penguin.
Gay, Peter. 1989. *Freud: A Life For Our Time.* New York: Anchor.

FREY, DR. GERHARD
(born 1933)

Chairman of the German extreme-right Deutsche Volksunion (DVU) Party as well as owner of a large publishing house, DSZ-Verlag, and the publisher of the right-wing tabloid National-Zeitung (NZ). Involved in right-wing publishing since the late 1950s, Frey has not only built the largest German extreme-right media empire but has also played a vital part in right-wing politics since the early 1970s. In 1987 the DVU was registered as a party, and in the 1990s it started to have electoral success because of Frey's spending large amounts of his private money on party campaigns. The party landed a huge success in 1998 with 12.9 percent of the vote in the state of Sachsen-Anhalt—a result that the DVU was never able even remotely to repeat. DVU membership has fallen from more than 20,000 in the 1990s to around 12,000 at the time of writing.

Thomas Grumke

See Also: GERMANY; NEO-NAZISM; POSTWAR FASCISM; SCHÖNHUBER, FRANZ

Reference
Stöss, Richard. 1991. *Politics against Democracy: The Extreme Right in West Germany.* Trans. Lindsay Batson. Oxford: Berg.

FRICK, WILHELM
(1877–1946)

Hitler's Reich minister of the interior and a legal expert on whom the Fuehrer placed much reliance. He was born in Alsenz in the Palatinate and studied law at Munich, Göttingen, and Berlin before reading for a doctorate in Heidelberg. He started practicing law in Munich in 1912. He became a close associate of Hitler's in Munich and was one of those put on trial for the Munich Beer-Hall Putsch of 1923. He avoided imprisonment and was elected to the Reichstag as a Nazi Party delegate in 1924. In 1930 he became minister of the interior for Thuringia, and Hitler appointed him Reich minister of the interior soon after becoming chancellor in 1933. During his time in Thuringia, Frick had banned *All Quiet on the Western Front,* an antiwar film that had been passed by the Berlin censors, and he also allowed previously banned National Socialist newspapers to appear again. He created a special chair of social anthropology at the University of Jena for Professor Hans Günther, one of the foremost exponents of Nazi racial theories. He also introduced special ultranationalist prayers into the Thuringian schools. As Reich minister of the interior, Frick ensured that all of the new Reich governors were Nazis; in September 1935 he drew up the Nuremberg Laws, which relegated Jews to second-class citizenship, and in the meantime he was vigorously deporting at least 100,000 individuals to concentration camps. Frick was totally devoted to Hitler and was an expert at cloaking the Fuehrer's actions in legality, arguing that right was what benefited the German people and wrong was what harmed them. At the Nuremberg Trials he was condemned as the one most responsible for bringing Germany under Nazi control, not least through the institution of laws abolishing political parties and trades unions. He was hanged on 16 October 1946.

Cyprian Blamires

See Also: ANTI-SEMITISM; CONCENTRATION CAMPS; FILM; GÜNTHER, HANS FRIEDRICH KARL; HITLER, ADOLF; LAW; MUNICH PUTSCH, THE; NAZISM; NUREMBERG LAWS, THE; NUREMBERG TRIALS, THE; RACIAL DOCTRINE; TRADE UNIONS

References
Neliba, Gunter. 1992. *Wilhelm Frick. Der Legalist des Unrechtsstaates: eine politische Biographie.* Paderborn: Ferdinand Schoningh.
Peterson, E. N. 1969. *The Limits of Hitler's Power.* Princeton: Princeton University Press.

FROMM, ERICH
(1900–1980)

German social psychologist and psychoanalyst who offered a provocative explanation for the psychological roots of fascism. He studied psychology and sociology at the universities of Frankfurt, Munich, and Heidelberg and went on to train as a psychologist at the Berlin Institute of Psychoanalysis. He left Germany in 1933 for the United States. Fromm was later one of the founders of the William Manson Institute of Psychiatry. In *Escape from Freedom* (1941), he suggested that modernity led to alienation, emptiness, and loneliness, because, as Marx had claimed, under capitalism all social relations are market relations. The painful loss of community may lead to a total submission to fascist authority and to a dangerous yearning for an idealized premodern past. Fromm wrote of "the authoritarian social character" that is the energy source responsible for the development of Western capitalism. Common to all authoritarian thinking is the conviction that life is determined by forces outside man's own self, his interest, and his wishes and that the only possible happiness lies in the submission to these forces.

Benjamin Beit-Hallahmi

See Also: ARENDT, HANNAH; AUTHORITARIANISM; CAPITALISM; COMMUNITY; FREUD, SIGMUND; INDIVIDUALISM; MARXISM; MARXIST THEORIES OF FASCISM; NAZISM; PSYCHOANALYSIS; PSYCHOLOGY; REICH, WILHELM; RELIGION; TOTALITARIANISM

References
Fromm, E. 1941. *Escape from Freedom.* New York: Farrar, Rinehart.
———. 1962. *Beyond the Chains of Illusion: My Encounter with Marx and Freud.* New York: Holt and Rinehart.

FRONT NATIONAL: *See* **NATIONAL FRONT (FRANCE)**
***FUEHRERPRINZIP,* THE:** *See* **LEADER CULT, THE**
FUNDAMENTALISM: *See* **CHRISTIAN IDENTITY; CHRISTIANITY; SURVIVALISM**
FUNDING: *See* **FINANCE**

FUNK, WALTHER EMANUEL (1890–1960)

Nazi minister of economics, president of the Reichsbank, and fervent devotee of Hitler, who in his eyes was the only one capable of saving Germany from bankruptcy or from communist revolution. He studied philosophy, law, and economics at the University of Berlin. He was discharged from World War I army service in 1916 on health grounds. A business journalist in the 1920s, Funk became Hitler's personal economics adviser in 1931. After the Nazis took power in 1933, he became government press chief and was also given responsibilities in the area of broadcasting and propaganda. He became minister of economics in 1938 and eventually acquired the responsibility for the financial leadership of the country. According to an agreement he made with Himmler in 1942, valuables and money stolen from Jews murdered in the death camps were to be channeled to the Reichsbank. At the Nuremberg Trials he was sentenced to life imprisonment but was released in 1957 on grounds of ill health.

Cyprian Blamires

See Also: BANKS, THE; BOLSHEVISM; CONCENTRATION CAMPS; ECONOMICS; HITLER, ADOLF; HOLOCAUST, THE; MARXISM; PRESS, THE; PROPAGANDA; RADIO

Reference
Turner, H. A. 1985. *German Big Business and the Rise of Hitler.* Oxford: Oxford University Press.

FUTURISM

Many of the activists in this avant-garde Italian artistic movement were enthusiasts for Mussolinian Fascism and exercised a significant influence on it. Founded in 1909, Futurism had a vast influence on the modernist culture of the early twentieth century in Europe and the world. In Italy, Futurism was also a political movement that gave birth to a Futurist Party in 1918 and that was involved in the birth of the Fasci di combattimento. Some of its supporters went on to contribute to the development of the most modernistic expressions of Fascist aesthetics and cultural policy.

THE FUTURIST POLITICAL POSITION

The establishment of Futurism arose from the publication in *Figaro* on 20 February 1909 of the *Futurist Manifesto* by Marinetti. The new movement aimed to be a revolutionary artistic avant-garde. Futurism sought new forms of aesthetic expression free from

The City Rises, by Futurist painter Umberto Boccioni (1910). The support of many members of the Futurist artistic movement for Italian Fascism is a reminder of its early image as a progressive, avant-garde political movement. (The Museum of Modern Art/Licensed by SCALA/Art Resource, NY)

the cult of the past and talked of a new sense of life exalting modernity as the irreversible process of transformation of the human condition. Futurism desired to be a cultural revolution and, as such, to transform and permeate all aspects of life, not just art, to create the "New Man" of modernity. Consequently, Futurism also had a political position, a confusing mix of anticlericalism, anarchism, patriotism, imperialism, cosmopolitanism, and an exaltation of brutality, violence, and war as essential aspects of modernity. The first Futurist political manifesto was published in 1909, a second in 1911 to exalt the Italian colonial war for the conquest of Libya, and a third appeared in 1913 on the occasion of elections to present the Futurist political program—synthesized in the formula "The word ITALIA must dominate the word LIBERTY." The Futurist political attitude was the expression of an antiauthoritarian modernist nationalism that aimed at modernizing and industrializing Italy through radical political and social reforms. *Italian-*

ism, understood as the exaltation of a new Italian primacy in modern civilization, was always the dominant myth of artistic and political Futurism and was at the origins of the concrete political choices of the greater part of the Futurists.

FROM THE GREAT WAR TO FASCISM: THE FUTURIST POLITICAL PARTY

When the European War broke out in 1914, most of the Futurists, like Umberto Boccioni, Giacomo Balla, Carlo Carrà, Mario Sironi, Antonio Sant'Elia, Ardengo Soffici, and Marinetti himself, were interventionists from the start. They celebrated war for itself as a great destructive and creative event, and staged violent demonstrations calling for the participation of Italy in World War I, which they promoted as the beginning of the "Italian revolution" to create a new state, to regenerate the Italians, and to make Italy a great power.

Many Futurists were volunteers and fighters, and some of them lost their lives at the front.

The Futurist political party was established in September 1918 with its own newspaper, *Roma futurista,* and with a network of *Fasci futuristi* in various Italian cities. On 23 March 1919, Marinetti and other Futurists took part in the foundation of the Fasci di combattimento promoted by Benito Mussolini, and were protagonists in the first violent actions of the Fascist movement against the Socialist Party. The *fascist style,* as a new mentality oriented toward violent political struggle through the medium of small armed groups, the *squadre* (from which *squadrismo* emerged), had many features of Futurist militancy. The Futurist Party, like the Fascist movement in 1919, was republican, democratic, libertarian, nationalist, anticonservative, antisocialist, and anticlerical: one of the points of its program was the "de-Vaticanization" of Italy. The symbiosis between fascism and political Futurism lasted up to the end of May 1920, when a breach occurred as a consequence of the turn to the Right of the fascist movement. Some Futurists became openly antifascist and communist, while others, like Mario Carli and Ferruccio Vecchi, took part in the movement of Gabriele D'Annunzio in Fiume, sympathizing with the Bolshevik revolution and attempting to establish an alliance between Futurists, anarchists, and revolutionary socialists. The political activity of Futurism exhausted itself in the 1920s, along with the fragmentation of the artistic movement; a so-called second Futurism continued the activism in the artistic field in the 1920s, but it lost any originality and autonomy as a movement, and some Futurists converted to aesthetic Formalism and to the cult of a renewed tradition of Italian realism.

FUTURISM AND THE FASCIST REGIME

After Mussolini's rise to power at the end of 1922, many Futurists hooked up with Fascism, with Marinetti at their head, but they did not play any important political role, limiting their activity to the field of art. Their antitraditionalist position was, however, an important component in fascist modernism. The Futurists disputed the field with the Fascist traditionalists, especially in the fields of painting and architecture, and they often had the support of Mussolini. However, the ambivalence of the cultural policy of the Fascist regime, wavering constantly between modernism and classicism, did not allow the Futurists the hegemonic position in the aesthetics and the cultural policy of the

regime that they coveted. Some Futurists, although proclaiming themselves to be loyal and intransigent Fascists, like Marinetti himself, continued to have an anticonformist and iconoclastic attitude, noisily opposing certain fundamental political choices such as the Concordat with the Catholic Church in 1929 or the promulgation of anti-Semitic laws in 1938.

In reality, the totalitarian state that Fascism was constructing was the antithesis of the new state imagined by political Futurism in 1922, just as the "New Man" of Fascism, the "citizen soldier" regimented and educated in the dogmatism of the "Fascist religion," was not in fact the realization of the Futurist ideal of a "New Man"—the "heroic citizen" described in the first Futurist manifestoes as an individual free from any constraint and opposed to all dogmatism. Nonetheless, there remained many elements in common between Fascism and Futurism, like the exaltation of violence, the cult of virility, imperialistic ambition, the bellicose vocation, and also the myth of the leader, which was the preferred subject of many Futurist painters and sculptors. Some Futurists, like Marinetti and Sironi, followed Mussolini right up to the end of the Italian Social Republic.

Emilio Gentile
(translated by Cyprian Blamires)

See Also: INTRODUCTION; ANTICLERICALISM; ARCHITECTURE; ART; BOLSHEVISM; CULTURE; D'ANNUNZIO, GABRIELE; FASCIO, THE; FASCIST PARTY, THE; FREEDOM; INTERVENTIONISM; ITALY; LEADER CULT, THE; LIBERALISM; LIBYA; MARINETTI, FILIPPO TOMMASO; MODERNISM; MODERNITY; MUSSOLINI, BENITO ANDREA; NATIONALISM; NEW MAN, THE; PALINGENETIC MYTH; RELIGION; REVOLUTION; SALÒ REPUBLIC, THE; SARFATTI-GRASSINI, MARGHERITA; SOCIALISM; *SQUADRISMO;* STATE, THE; STYLE; TOTALITARIANISM; WAR; WARRIOR ETHOS, THE; WORLD WAR I

References
Appollionio, V., ed. 1973. *Futurist Manifestos.* New York: Viking.
Berghaus, G. 1996. *Futurism and Politics: Between Anarchist Rebellion and Fascist Reaction, 1909–1944.* Oxford: Berghahn.
Cannistraro, Philip V., and Brian R. Sullivan. 1993. *Il Duce's Other Woman: The Untold Story of Margherita Sarfatti, Benito Mussolini's Jewish Mistress, and How She Helped Him Come to Power.* New York: William Morrow.
Gentile, E. 2003. *The Struggle for Modernity: Nationalism, Futurism and Fascism.* London: Praeger.
Jensen, R. 1995. "Futurism and Fascism." *History Today* 45, no. 11.
Taylor, C. J. 1979. *Futurism: Politics, Painting and Performance.* Ann Arbor, MI: UMI Research.

G

GADDHAFI: *See* QADHAFI (GADDHAFI), MU'AMMAR

GAJDA, GENERAL RADOLA (real name, Rudolf Geidl, 1892–1948)

Leader of the Czech interwar fascist movement. During World War I he fought in the Austro-Hungarian army in Russia and was taken prisoner. Later he was one of the military leaders of the Czech legions during their confrontation with the Bolsheviks in Siberia. In the new Czechoslovak state Gajda became a national hero, was promoted to the rank of general, and held high military posts. After controversial clashes with the Czechoslovakian president, Masaryk, in 1926 he was demoted. In 1927 a new fascist movement in the Czech lands chose Gajda as leader of the National Community of Fascists. He was inspired by Italian Fascism and was anticommunist, anti-Semitic, and pro-German. When German troops occupied Czechoslovakia in March 1939 he pursued a policy of cooperation with the Nazis, but they did not accept him. After the war Gajda was sentenced to two years in prison.

Miroslav Mares

See Also: ANTI-SEMITISM; AUSTRO-HUNGARIAN EMPIRE, THE; BOLSHEVISM; COMMUNISM; CZECHOSLOVAKIA; FASCIST PARTY, THE; GERMANY; ITALY; MARXISM; NAZISM; WORLD WAR II

Reference
Campbell, F. G. 1975. *Confrontation in Central Europe.* Chicago: University of Chicago Press.

GALEN, CARDINAL CLEMENS AUGUST VON (1878–1946)

A patriotic German aristocrat consecrated priest in 1904, appointed bishop of Münster in 1933, and a bitter critic of the Nazis. After initially supporting them in their moves to end unemployment and re-unify Germany, he became a thorn in the flesh of the regime. In 1941 he preached a series of sermons labeling Nazis murderers. Hitler considered having von Galen eliminated but was warned that this would provoke popular unrest. After the war Galen was critical of the treatment of German civilians by the Allies. He died shortly after being appointed cardinal by Pope Pius XII.

Irving Hexham

See Also: ANTIFASCISM; CATHOLIC CHURCH, THE; EMPLOY-
MENT; FAULHABER, CARDINAL MICHAEL VON; HITLER,
ADOLF; NAZISM; PIUS XII, POPE

References
Griech-Polelle, Beth A. 2003. *Bishop von Galen: German
Catholicism and National Socialism.* New Haven: Yale
University Press.
Portmann, Heinrich. 1957. *Cardinal von Galen.* Trans. R. L.
Sedgwick. London: Jarrolds.

GALTON, FRANCIS: *See* EUGENICS; PSYCHOLOGY
GENDER: *See* FEMINISM; SEXUALITY; WOMEN

GENERALGOUVERNEMENT/ GENERAL GOVERNMENT, THE

Official name for the area of Central Poland that the
Nazis placed under a governorship after their invasion
of Poland in 1939. The western provinces of Upper
Silesia, West Prussia, Poznan, and Danzig were simply
annexed to Germany.

Cyprian Blamires

See Also: POLAND AND NAZI GERMANY; WORLD WAR II

GENIUS, THE CULT OF THE: *See* HERO, THE CULT OF THE
GENOCIDE: *See* HOLOCAUST, THE

GENTILE, GIOVANNI (1875–1944)

Unofficial philosophical mentor to Italian Fascism. Although he served Mussolini and the Fascist dictatorship
in a number of capacities (for example, as minister of

public instruction) and was in fact murdered in Florence in 1944 for this service, Gentile was first and foremost a man of ideas. European intellectual historians
remind us that toward the end of the nineteenth century in Western Europe there was a substantial reaction
against positivism and—to the extent it could be identified with this outlook—Marxism as well. Philosophers and social observers informed by philosophical
ideas rebelled against efforts to apply the laws and procedures of the natural sciences to human conduct.
There was even a rebellion, at least to some extent,
against empiricism or the way of knowing reality associated with scientific inquiry. In place of positivist and
empiricist ideas, the critics stressed the role of discre-
tionary human will as the basis of behavior. In regard to
epistemology, such critics emphasized the point that
"reality" is a mix of the physical world outside ourselves
and our subjective perception of it; for many of them
the ideas of Hegel took on a renewed significance.

At the same time as the antipositivist and anti-
Marxist rebellion was underway, various philosophers
also challenged the liberal state, the form of rule apparently preferred by the mainstream political writers
of the era. Individualism, laissez-faire capitalism, parliamentary supremacy, and a minimalist, ethically neutral state were ideas, practices, and institutional
arrangements that they came to regard with contempt.
There was a new current of thought according to
which the state should not be small and neutral but
rather big and pedagogical, playing an essential role in
society and reshaping human beings so that they
might pursue higher goals and objectives than mere
material acquisition. Gentile's philosophy—called actualism, should be understood as emerging from this
antipositivist rebellion and antiliberal mood. The
other element that needs to be introduced is the nation. Gentile was an ardent Italian nationalist whose
writings reflected a desire to see his country's standing
in the world elevated to that of a great power. The
problem, of course, was that Italy and Italians had suffered one setback and humiliation after another over
the preceding centuries. To return Italy to its rightful
place in the world required a maximum exertion of
will. To that end, there was a need for a powerful state,
led by a far-seeing individual, that would be able to
transform not only Italy's external reality but also the
psyche of individual Italians. Human beings were not
by nature atomized individuals but were, instead, social creatures who only realized themselves as members
of a nation. Gentile thus provided the basis and justification for the totalitarian state of the kind that Mussolini sought but never quite achieved.

Italian Giovanni Gentile, advocate of actualism and the only widely-respected philosopher to throw in his lot permanently with an interwar fascist regime. He sponsored a Manifesto of Fascist Intellectuals and was a moving spirit behind the multi-volume Enciclopedia italiana, *a celebration of Italian culture. (Harlingue-Viollet)*

A Sicilian by birth and a precocious student, Gentile was teaching philosophy at the University of Rome when Mussolini came to power at the end of October 1922. Immediately after the Fascist March on Rome, Mussolini (who referred to Gentile as his "teacher") appointed him to his first cabinet post as minister of public instruction, a position he held through 1924. It was also during this period that Gentile became a member of the Fascist Party and, more important, a member of the Grand Council of Fascism. Following these experiences, Gentile served in a variety of posts, largely focused on cultural matters, through the second half of the 1920s and most of the succeeding decade. In these years Gentile was given the responsibility by Mussolini of editing the *Enciclopedia italiana,* a task that came to include writing the first part of the official *Dottrina del Fascismo,* the fundamental exposition of the Fascist state's ideology. Gentile's views, particularly those in-

volving the predominant role of the state in education, brought him into conflict with the Church, which, of course, had its own claims on the attention of Italian youth. So, to the extent that the Fascist regime wished to mollify the Church, its spokesmen began to establish some distance between state policy and Gentile's philosophy. Nonetheless, Gentile remained loyal to Fascism until the end. After King Victor Emmanuel III dismissed Mussolini from power in 1943, effectively bringing the regime to an end, Gentile was one of the few Italian intellectuals who stayed at Il Duce's side. With prompting from the Germans, Mussolini created a neo-Fascist Social Republic (the Salò Republic) in northern Italy—or, in other words, the section of the country that had not as yet been occupied by the advancing Allied armies. Gentile served this new, short-lived regime as the president of the Accademia d'Italia, its foremost cultural institution. On 15 April 1944, less than two months before the liberation of Rome from German occupation, Gentile was shot and killed by anti-Fascist partisans in front of his home in Florence. His body was buried nearby in a vault at the church of Santa Croce, the final resting place for such illustrious Italians as Machiavelli and Galileo.

Leonard Weinberg

See Also: INTRODUCTION; ABSTRACTION; ACTUALISM; CAPITALISM; CATHOLIC CHURCH, THE; CULTURE; EDUCATION; *ENCICLOPEDIA ITALIANA,* THE; ENLIGHTENMENT, THE; FASCIST PARTY, THE; FRENCH REVOLUTION, THE; GRAND COUNCIL OF FASCISM, THE; INDIVIDUALISM; ITALY; LEADER CULT, THE; LIBERALISM; MANIFESTO OF FASCIST INTELLECTUALS, THE; MARCH ON ROME, THE; MARXISM; MATERIALISM; MUSSOLINI, BENITO ANDREA; NATIONALISM; PALINGENETIC MYTH; PARLIAMENTARISM; POSITIVISM; SALÒ REPUBLIC, THE; STATE, THE; TOTALITARIANISM; VICTOR EMMANUEL/VITTORIO EMANUELE III; VITALISM; VOLUNTARISM; *WELTANSCHAUUNG;* YOUTH

References

Gentile, G. 2002. *Origins and Doctrine of Fascism.* New Brunswick, NJ: Transaction.

Gregor, A. James. 2001. *Giovanni Gentile: Philosopher of Fascism.* New Brunswick, NJ: Transaction.

Hughes, S. H. 1961. *Consciousness and Society.* New York: Vintage.

Redner, H. 1997. *Malign Masters: Gentile, Heidegger, Lukacs, Wittgenstein.* London: Macmillan.

GEOPOLITICS: *See* HAUSHOFER, KARL ERNST

GEORGE, STEFAN (1868–1933)

German poet whose antiliberal and *völkisch* philosophy with its anticipation of a new age gained him a wide circle of admirers and approval in Nazi circles. Born 12 July 1868 in Büdesheim (near Bingen), George studied at the gymnasium in Darmstadt. On completing his studies in 1889 he traveled for a year in Europe, visiting London, Italy, and Paris, where he was much attracted to the Symbolist poets, particularly Stéphane Mallarmé. Following three semesters at the University of Berlin, he fell into what became a permanently peripatetic way of life, living with friends in Berlin, Munich, Heidelberg, Basle, Italy, and Paris, publishing his work privately, and maintaining an esoteric Symbolist program wherein pure poetry was understood as revelatory of the mysteries of life, upheld by "a noble few" and "triumphing over torment and transfiguring ecstasy." In *Pilgerfahrten* (1891), he idealized this aesthetic life. A *George-Kreis* ("Circle") quickly arose in which very close friendships were maintained, above all those between George and the young Austrian poet and playwright Hugo von Hofmannsthal (a short but intense relationship), the Germanist and George's strongest supporter, Friedrich Gundolf (from whom he became estranged in 1920), and the young teenager Max Kronberger, whose death at sixteen in 1904 was poeticized by George in terms of Maximin, the ideal of the "spontaneous mind and heroic soul." The Circle included nationalists, republicans, anti-Semites, and Jews. Closely associated with George early in the publication of the periodical *Blätter für die Kunst* (1892–1919) was the poet Karl Wolfskehl, a Jew, attached for a time (as was George in 1923) to the Munich "Kosmiker" who were convinced of the decadence of Western Judeo-Christian culture and pressed for a reinvigoration of the pagan past. Among this circle the philosopher Ludwig Karls saw the greatest hope in primitive Germanic traditions. The most important work of these early years was his *Das Jahr der Seele* (1897).

By 1907 in *Der siebente Ring,* George's earlier aestheticism and its doctrine of art for art's sake developed a political perspective and announced an elitist pedagogical and prophetic role for the poet in opposing contemporary society as decadent, barbarous, and philistine. With the publication of the *Jahrbuch für die geistige Bewegung* (1910–1912), the Circle promulgated its central concerns. In *Der Krieg* (1917), George interpreted World War I as the result of decadence arising out of bourgeois mass culture. Following the war George's popularity increased among young German writers, drawn to his proclamation of a superior cult of youth, high art and beauty, and an elitist ethic of spirit over matter. His *Das neue Reich,* published in 1928 and understood by George more in a spiritual than a practical, political sense, attracted the attention of the National Socialists and other fascist-minded supporters. Both the July Plot conspirator Claus Schenk Graf von Stauffenberg and Joseph Goebbels were members of the George Circle, as were the literary historian Ernst

Robert Curtius and the cultural and political critic Ernst H. Kantorowicz. In 1933, George immigrated to Switzerland, where he died at Minusio near Locarno on 4 December.

The earliest critical work on George tended to be controlled by members of the George Circle, and that pattern continued after World War II, as did the tendency to downplay any links between George and the Circle and the rise of Nazism. The exact relationship between the two is difficult to ascertain. George did express anti-Jewish sentiments, but he supported the Jewish members of the Circle. Certainly when his 1921 poem "Der Dichter in Zeiten der Wirren" was reprinted in 1928, many understood it as a prophetic reference to Adolf Hitler. When the Nazis took power, Goebbels offered him the presidency of a newly established German Academy of Poetry, which George declined, but such an action need not have been because of political opposition on his part to the new powers. It might to some extent have been a result of his consistent distancing of himself from the populace at large. In 1927, for example, he declined the Frankfurt Goethe Prize, eventually accepting it under pressure but without the public honor. His emigration in 1933 was most likely because of his declining health and not for political reasons.

Peter Erb

See Also: ANTI-SEMITISM; ART; CULTURE; DECADENCE; ELITE THEORY; GERMANNESS (*DEUTSCHHEIT*); GERMANY; GOEBBELS, (PAUL) JOSEPH; HITLER, ADOLF; JULY PLOT, THE; LIBERALISM; NATIONALISM; NAZISM; NEW AGE, THE; *VOLK, VÖLKISCH;* WAR; WORLD WAR I

References

Antosik, Stanley J. 1978. *The Question of Elites: An Essay on the Cultural Elitism of Nietzsche, George, and Hesse.* Bern: Peter Lang.

Bennett, Edwin Keppel. 1954. *Stefan George.* Cambridge: Bowes and Bowes.

Frank, Lore, et al. 2000. *Stefan George-Bibliographie 1976–1997: mit Nachträgen bis 1976: auf der Grundlage der Bestände des Stefan George-Archivs in der Württembergischen Landesbibliothek.* Tubingen: Niemeyer.

George, Stefan. 1927–1934. *Gesamt-Ausgabe der Werke: Endgültige Fassung.* 18 vol. in 15. Berlin: Georg Bondi.

Goldsmith, Ulrich Karl. 1959. *Stefan George: A Study of His Early Work.* Boulder: CO University Press.

Marx, Olga, and Ernst Morwitz. 1974. *The Works of Stefan George Rendered into English.* 2d ed. Chapel Hill: University of North Carolina Press.

Metzger, Michael M., and Ericka A. Metzger. 1972. *Stefan George.* New York: Twayne.

Norton, Robert. 2002. *Secret Germany: Stefan George and His Circle.* Ithaca: Cornell University Press.

GERMAN CHRISTIANS, THE

A movement within the German Protestant church during the Nazi era that advocated an "Aryan" church that would conform to the National Socialist political agenda. Emerging from several Protestant *völkisch* movements during the 1920s and early 1930s, the German Christians sought church renewal along ethnic nationalist lines. At its height the movement included about 600,000 members, or about 2 percent of German Protestants. The German Christian movement incorporated a number of aspects typical of fascist thinking: rigid gendering and support for stereotypical gender roles, anti-internationalism, romanticism, a blend of traditional symbols and myths with modern ideology, and a strong emphasis on ethnic identity and separatism.

When Adolf Hitler came to power in January 1933, the German Christians immediately began a drive to make the German Protestant church conform to the new government. After the passage of the first laws banning "non-Aryans" from the civil service, the German Christians pushed for similar laws within the church. Hitler viewed the German Christians as early allies in his aim to nazify all aspects of German life, and publicly supported the group in the July 1933 national Protestant church elections. The German Christians won two-thirds of the vote in these elections, thus gaining power in most regional church governments. They promoted a national Reich church and elected one of their members, Ludwig Müller, to be Reich bishop. In the months that followed, the movement gained strength, culminating in a mass rally in November 1933 at the Sports Palace in Berlin, where the German Christians declared an agenda for the Protestant church that included the elimination of the Old Testament from the Bible and placed the Reich church squarely under Nazi authority.

The Sports Palace rally provoked a backlash among Protestants throughout Germany. Despite their nationalism, most Protestant leaders were theologically conservative. They feared the loss of church independence under Nazism and viewed the German Christians as too ideologically driven. An opposing church group, the Confessing Church, emerged to counter the German Christian agenda, and the German Protestant church found itself in a struggle (the *Kirchenkampf*) between the two groups and church moderates who hoped to avoid a schism. Despite the clear ideological lines that had been drawn, the *Kirchenkampf* was primarily about church independence vs. conformity to the Nazi regime. By the late 1930s, the ranks of the German Christians had dwindled. Nonetheless, they continued to incorporate Nazi ideology into church liturgies and theology, and because of their power in the regional church leadership, they attempted throughout the Third Reich to exclude people considered "non-Aryan" under Nazi racial law and compel the church to conform to state regulations.

The real impact of the movement during the Third Reich may have been to make a "nazified" ideological Christianity appear legitimate. After 1945, most German Christians merged back into mainstream German Protestantism, and many of their leaders eventually found positions in the Lutheran Church.

Victoria Barnett

See Also: ANTI-SEMITISM; ARYANISM; CHRISTIANITY; CONFESSING CHURCH, THE; COSMOPOLITANISM; HITLER, ADOLF; LUTHERAN CHURCHES, THE; MÜLLER, BISHOP LUDWIG; NATIONALISM; NAZISM; PROTESTANTISM; SEXUALITY; THEOLOGY; THIRD REICH, THE; *VOLK, VÖLKISCH*; WOMEN

References

Bergen, Doris. 1996. *Twisted Cross: The German Christian Movement in the Third Reich.* Chapel Hill: University of North Carolina Press.

Ericksen, Robert P., and Susannah Heschel, eds. 1999. *Betrayal: German Churches and the Holocaust.* Minneapolis, MN: Fortress.

Helmreich, Ernst Christian. 1979. *The German Churches under Hitler: Background, Struggle, and Epilogue.* Detroit, MI: Wayne State University Press.

GERMAN-AMERICAN BUND, THE

The German-American Bund (Amerikadeutscher Volksbund) was established in the United States in March 1936, following the demise of an earlier pro-Nazi group, the Friends of the New Germany. Between 1936 and 1939 the Bund—meaning federation—was led by Fritz Kuhn, a German-born, naturalized U.S. citizen who had served as a machine-gunner in the Bavarian infantry in France during World War I. A former member of the Freikorps and a longtime member of the National Socialist German Worker's Party (NSDAP), Kuhn consciously adopted the manner and style of Hitler, seeing himself as an "American Fuehrer." The Bund endeavored to unite all German Americans behind its National Socialist agenda, while at the same time demanding that the United States remain neutral in any forthcoming European conflict. Fervently anti-Semitic and anticommunist, the Bund's first official announcement declared that its purpose was "to combat the Moscow-directed madness of the Red world menace and its Jewish bacillus-carriers" (Grover 2003, 177). Such views were propagated through the Bund's newspaper, *Deutscher Weckruf und Beobachter,* in numerous pamphlets, at marches, camps and rallies, and through its promotion of films such as *The Triumph of the Will* and Hitler's autobiography, *Mein Kampf.* Kuhn also created a Bund youth division modeled on the Hitler Youth, where, in addition to receiving instruction on National Socialist ideology (including how to salute the swastika correctly), children could meet to take part in such activities as folk-singing, traditional dancing, and military drill.

The exact size of the German-American Bund is difficult to determine. Estimates of its membership at the height of its popularity—between 1937 and 1938—range from 6,600 to 50,000, for example. The Bund's largest single public display took place on 20 February 1939, when more than 22,000 people attended its Pro-American Rally and George Washington Birthday Exercises at New York's Madison Square Garden. In a hall bedecked with swastikas, American flags, and an enormous portrait of George Washington, attendees heard Kuhn denounce Franklin D. Roosevelt for being part of a Bolshevik-Jewish conspiracy to undermine the United States: Roosevelt was referred to as "Frank D. Rosenfeld" and the New Deal dismissed as the "Jew Deal." The event was widely covered in the national and international press, and the public outcry was considerable. In addition, an investigation into the Bund's financial activities was launched by New York district attorney Thomas E. Dewey. Although the Bund was the subject of a House Un-American Activities Committee investigation in 1938, it was Dewey's enquiry that proved to be its undoing. Found guilty of embezzlement and forgery, Kuhn was sentenced to a two-and-a-half to five year prison term, and without his leadership the organization became increasingly splintered and ineffective. On 8 December 1941, the day after the Japa-

German-American Bund parade in New York in 1939. This event is a reminder that there was much sympathy for German Nazism (and Italian Fascism) in interwar America. There was little enthusiasm in the U.S. for intervention in World War II until after Pearl Harbor. (Library of Congress)

nese attack on Pearl Harbor, the Bund's executive committee voted unanimously to disband what remained of the movement.

Darren Mulloy

See Also: ANTI-SEMITISM; BOLSHEVISM; HITLER, ADOLF; MARXISM; *MEIN KAMPF;* NAZISM; PEARL HARBOR; ROOSEVELT, FRANKLIN DELANO; SOVIET UNION, THE; SWASTIKA, THE; *TRIUMPH OF THE WILL;* UNITED STATES, THE (PRE-1945); YOUTH

References
Bell, Leland V. 1970. "The Failure of Nazism in America: The German American Bund, 1936–1941." *Political Science Quarterly* 85, no. 4: 585–599.
Canedy, Susan. 1990. *America's Nazis, A Democratic Dilemma: A History of the German American Bund.* Menlo Park, CA: Markgraf.
Diamond, Sander A. 1974. *The Nazi Movement in the United States, 1924–1941.* Ithaca, NY: Cornell University Press.
Grover, Warren. 2003. *Nazis in Newark.* New Brunswick, NJ: Transaction.

GERMAN FAITH MOVEMENT, THE

A religious movement founded in 1933 as an amalgam of earlier movements by J. W. Hauer to replace traditional Christianity with a pagan cult. The rituals attached to birth, marriage, and death were to be de-Christianized, and Christmas was to give way to a pagan solstice festival. Its leaders prohibited nativity plays and carols in schools and attacked the practice of daily prayers in the classroom. By 1936 it had already been marginalized, and it fragmented soon afterward into smaller groupings.

Cyprian Blamires

See Also: ANTI-SEMITISM; ARYANISM; CHRISTIANITY; GERMANIC RELIGION; GERMANNESS (*DEUTSCHHEIT*); GERMANY; HAUER, JAKOB WILHELM; OCCULTISM

Reference
Poewe, K. 2005. *New Religions and the Nazis.* London: Routledge.

GERMANIC RELIGION

Renewed interest in the ideas of a discrete German *Volk* emerged from the traditions of Romanticism, pantheism, and of philosophical idealism that developed during the nineteenth century and that counterpointed the rationality of the Enlightenment. The concept of a distinct German *Volk* signified a people who possessed a "transcendental essence" that was to be found in their mythologies and a "true" appreciation of both their "cosmic" and "natural" surroundings. From this appreciation a connection to a "transcendental essence" would emerge manifesting the true creativity and soul of the nation. The cosmos was understood to possess a "living force" that was directed to the earth, and all true self-fulfillment had to be in tune with that cosmic life force. The symbol of the tree represented this idea. Its roots signified the German peasant's strength and rootedness in history and in the land, while the crown of the tree reached out and captured the cosmic life force. The Jews were specifically seen as the antithesis of a rooted people, not in communion with the cosmic life force. Often they were represented as a snake at the bottom of the tree, challenging the Germanic sense of "rootedness." French and British industrialism and the alienation of the modern city were also seen as the antitheses of the true German *Volk*. This was characterized as "natural" and rural life, and the peasant farming communities of the Middle Ages symbolized the ideal of patriarchal communities that lived in communion with nature and were viewed as an integral part of the land rather than as a human imposition onto it.

In the literature on Germanic religion, the normative importance of Wilhelm Heinrich Riehl's *Land und Leute* was crucial in fleshing out the role of workers not as a modern proletariat but as medieval artisans. Riehl also sketched out a Christianity that was not restricted by theology, but rather emphasized localized piety. Also influential in the development of this ideology during the nineteenth century were Berthold Auerbach's writings of Manichean peasant narratives triumphing over evil, and Jakob Grimm's *Deutsche Mythologie.* However, of primary importance as ideologues of Germanic religion that fed into the Nazi thought systems were Paul de Lagarde and Julius Langbehn. Lagarde conceived of the "nation" as a spiritual essence that had declined and needed major renovations in order once again to reflect the organic, national "inner attitude." He wrote that St. Paul had transformed the simple piety that typified this dynamic "inner attitude" into a sterile theology through codifying religion in Hebrew law. Therefore, Lagarde appealed for a return to an "original" Christianity that was inherently Germanic, and sought to guide the German nation from modernity back to their spiritual essence through a return to the estates of the Middle Ages.

Following on from Lagarde's ideas was Langbehn. He injected into Lagarde's dynamic a mysticism that drew from the theosophical speculation that was in the air at the turn of the twentieth century, and he was especially influenced by Emanuel Swedenborg's theorizations of the extra-sensory world. Again Langbehn saw the Jewish people as the antithesis of the German *Volk*, which was, by definition, rooted in the landscape of the German nation. This was typical of how various appreciations of a discrete "Germanic religion" sought to anthropomorphize the world, or rather northern Germany, in order to protect the idealized German soul. Within such theorizing there was also a tendency to replace Christ with the German *Volk* that was truly in communion with God and the Universe, thereby making possible a dynamic of mystical unity between individual selves, the *Volk,* and the cosmos. Also, the historical Christ was often mutated into a symbol of simplistic moral and pious ideals. Other ideologues of importance in theorizing this dynamic included Moritz von Egidy, Hermann Lietz, Ferdinand Schöll, and Kurt Wilhelmi.

Paul Jackson

See Also: ANTI-SEMITISM; CHRISTIANITY; DECADENCE; ENLIGHTENMENT, THE; GERMANNESS (*DEUTSCHHEIT*); GERMANY; LAGARDE, PAUL DE; LANGBEHN, JULIUS; MATERIALISM; MYSTICISM; NATIONALISM; NATURE; NAZISM; NORDIC SOUL, THE; OCCULTISM; ORGANICISM; RATIONALISM; ROOTLESSNESS; RURALISM; THEOLOGY; VOLK, VÖLKISCH

References
Mosse, G. L. 1966. *The Crisis of German Ideology: Intellectual Origins of the Third Reich.* London: Weidenfeld and Nicholson.
Stern, Fritz. 1974. *The Politics of Cultural Despair: A Study in the Rise of the German Ideology.* Berkeley: University of California Press.

GERMANNESS (*DEUTSCHHEIT*)

A quality considered by many Nazi ideologues as innate to those of German blood—that is, those of German race. In practice, it was often equivalent to "Nordicness." The concept was found most frequently in its adjectival form as *deutsch* ("German/Germanic"). This had nothing to do with political citizenship or the holding of a German passport; it had purely to do with racial purity: a "German" could be a citizen of Czechoslovakia or Austria or Poland, as much as of Germany itself. But German racial purity was believed to go along with certain superior qualities of "soul" and character, so to that extent behavior or a way of thinking or a moral code could be considered "German." Equally it could be considered "un-German," and the term for that was *deutschfremd* ("alien to the German"). This kind of vocabulary was pioneered by the Pangerman movements, and it is of vital importance to an understanding of Nazi thinking. An important term in the vocabulary of "Germanness" was *Herrenvolk,* meaning "master race," as a designation for the Germans. "Germanness," like "Nordicness," had predominantly Protestant undertones, for such an elevation of a particular race could not readily be accommodated to a globalized church that owed allegiance to Rome and the papacy, and the German culture referred to was much more that of Lutheran Prussia than that of Catholic Bavaria. Such theories glorified the partially secularized Protestant culture of Kant and Hegel, Goethe and Schiller. Obviously this had very limited attraction to the Italian Fascists, for their Latin Mediterranean traditions were very different from the German on many levels, and theirs was a powerful autochthonous culture that had no need to borrow from Germany. Mussolini, however, did have an equivalent myth to that of Germanness in *Romanità* ("Romanness"). Moreover, there were parallel phenomena elsewhere—for example, in Hungary, where there was a myth of 'Magyar' superiority.

Cyprian Blamires

See Also: ARYANISM; AUSTRIA; CZECHOSLOVAKIA; EXPANSIONISM; GENTILE, GIOVANNI; GERMANIC RELIGION; GERMANY; GLOBALIZATION; HITLER, ADOLF; HUNGARY; *MEIN KAMPF;* MUSSOLINI, BENITO ANDREA; NAZISM; NORDIC SOUL, THE; PANGERMANISM; PAPACY, THE; POLAND; RACIAL DOCTRINE; ROME

References

Hermand, Jost. 1992. *Old Dreams of a New Reich: Volkish Utopias and National Socialism.* Bloomington: Indiana University Press.
Snyder, Louis L. 1978. *Roots of German Nationalism.* New York: Barnes and Noble.
Stern, Fritz. 1961. *The Politics of Cultural Despair: A Study in the Rise of the Germanic Ideology.* Berkeley: University of California Press.

GERMANY

Although fascism originated in Italy, it was in Germany under Adolf Hitler that the most notorious, powerful, and destructive fascist regime arose in the 1930s, a regime known to history as Nazism. Its origins can be traced back to the previous century. In the aftermath of the French Revolution, Europe saw the rise of various forms of Romantic movement. It began as a mainly cultural reaction to the rationalism of the Enlightenment, exalting the idealism, the myths, and the hopes of a tragic and suffering individual—it was, as the nineteenth century drew to a close, gradually blended in Europe with early liberal values. On German soil, however, these Romantic ideas took a slightly different path. Whereas the sense of pessimism and mystical longing for cathartic rehabilitation remained basically unaltered, the individual was being replaced by *das Volk* (the people) and the nation was assigned holistic and organic qualities. This shift from an idealization of the single individual to an idealization of the nation, one and undivided, meant that "foreign" values were associated with distinctly negative qualities. These "un-German" values were seen as "progressive and liberal" in a bad sense, in that they threatened a traditionalist and protectionist economic system. They were styled by *völkisch* thinkers as "mechanistic, materialistic, and superficial"—consequently violating a "spiritual" and "authentic" Germanic culture. Furthermore, 'foreign' ideas proposed abstract thinking, intellectualism, and rationalism—in contrast to the blessings of "common sense" and of things concrete and tangible, such as the family and the community. Universalistic and egalitarian, such ideas were used in defense of "the rights of man"—in other words, in opposition to "natural hierarchies" that were soon to form the basis for a creed of anti-Semitism and outright racism. Finally, these 'foreign' ideas came to be represented as 'feeble' and 'worn

Celebrated German writer Ernst Jünger, one of a number of authors whose elitist, anti-democratic, and nationalistic rhetoric helped create an ambience favorable to the rise of Nazism. (Sophie Bassouls/Corbis Sygma)

out', seeking to obstruct the young and vigorous ideas of the rising Germanic nation.

These psychological and cultural factors were reinforced by the fact that Germany's bourgeois revolution, as opposed to the "healthy" evolution of Britain and France, remained haphazard and incomplete. The nation exhibited a flawed development—*ein Sonderweg* (a special path). Middle-class constituencies remained embedded in a "preindustrial" and "premodern" worldview. Artisans, white-collar employees, and civil servants clung to antique notions of caste and estate, and, anxious to guard their corporatist privileges and mercantilist traditions, mobilized against the advance of modern capitalism. As the bells of 1900 tolled, the philosophical underpinnings for the coming cataclysm had already therefore sunk deep into the foundation of German society. Other contributory causes of the rise of Nazism were of a more political and practical nature. As a Romantic reaction against a superficial bourgeois existence, movements like *Wandervögel,* which were interested in reviving old Teutonic values as a protest

against industrialization, attracted mainly middle-class teenagers. Although *Wandervögel* were prohibited after 1933, their associations with youth and invigorating country life, marches, and song were systematically exploited by the Hitler regime. Stahlhelm was founded by World War I veterans: German-nationalistic and a stern opponent of 'bourgeois decadence' and the Weimar Republic, the organization often joined forces with the Nazis, especially in the period after 1929. Germany's war reparations imposed by the 1919 Treaty of Versailles amounted to no less than 132 billion gold marks, even today a sum of immense proportions. This "deliberate act of aggression against the Germanic *Volk*" was to become an important ingredient in Hitler's speeches. Another World War I myth on which Hitler drew heavily was that of the legend of the "stab in the back" (*die Dolchstosslegende*), implying that the war on the battlefields was virtually won and that the military had been betrayed by ignorant civilians and feeble-minded bureaucrats, with the sinister figure of "the Jew" lurking behind them.

The major financial crash on Wall Street in 1929 gave the forces of the Right a—possibly decisive—momentum. Unemployment skyrocketed, and the Weimar democrats were subjected to increasing criticism. Correspondingly, calls for forceful leadership grew in proportion, demands from which the charismatic Adolf Hitler was soon to profit. Who then supported Hitler? And for what reason? The National Socialists appealed to those social strata that had suffered considerably during the Great Depression. Especially in the early 1930s, they won acclaim for beating the Great Depression and for curing the massive unemployment. In contrast, Marxist historians point toward the link between the Nazi regime and the ruling classes. Some argue that Hitler's main thrust came from a radicalized, *völkisch* notion of a community, whereby "non-Aryans" and Jews in particular were seen as inferior races. Those of a more republican leaning hold, in contrast, that the rise of Nazism should be sought in the cynical fragmentation of society, in the disintegration of a moderate, civic-minded community. Scholars who stress the *völkisch*, cultural origin of Nazism as opposed to more practical, economic causes often suggest that Hitler had a stronger position among academics than among the working classes. Others, such as Daniel Goldhagen, argue that the anti-Semitic issue was the prime reason for Hitler's support; still others play down its real significance. Hitler biographer Alan Bullock, for example, maintains that Austrians may have supported *Die Anschluss* in 1938 not because of Hitler's anti-Semitism but in spite of it. The issue of free choice versus compulsion keeps attracting attention. At times, it is claimed that Hitler simply managed to force the entire German population to support the regime. To others, the system rested mainly on open support and outright enthusiasm by "willing" soldiers and an eager electorate.

Why, then, did the Germans not consciously choose *not to* support the Nazi regime? Were the German population in general really aware of the unfathomable scale of human suffering caused by Adolf Hitler and his party? Information was disseminated in Europe fairly slowly in 1940. Many Germans throughout the country insisted that they simply did not know what was going on until the end of the war; and besides, the camps were for the most part situated far from major German cities, many of them being in Poland. Documents regarding the early euthanasia program (that is, the killing of those "racially inferior") indicate that the Nazis realized that the German public was far from convinced about the "humanitarian" nature of these measures. On the other hand, it has been argued that the Germans gradually adjusted their values to Nazi values. Some even deny the whole idea that Nazi propaganda was crudely forced onto more than 60 million Germans. On the contrary, it was meant to appeal to them and to match up with everyday German thinking. The idea that the average German was simply ignorant about the whole drama has been subject to considerable critique. After all, the trains to the concentration camps passed through virtually all parts of Germany. Major German industries, such as IG Farben and Siemens, supplied material to the concentration camps. Adolf Hitler himself never shied away from his objectives. Neighbors disappeared, never to return. A vast array of material on the police and the camps and various discriminatory campaigns was regularly published in the press of the day. In brief, the idea of a general unawareness among Germans does not seem convincing.

In the immediate aftermath of 1945, democratic opinion in Germany and abroad felt great distress at the fact that radical rightist values still had an undisputed audience. The German Conservative Party-German Right Party (DKP-DRP) had been formed as early as 1946 by former Nazis. That same year, in one opinion poll, a surprising 48 percent of Germans thought that some races were more fitted to rule than others. After the 1949 Bundestag elections, the Allied system of licensing parties ended. Domestically, the new German government decided to dismantle the denazification program, which was already losing impetus as the Cold War led to changing Allied priorities. This new climate provided the opportunity to create a more truly neo-Nazi party. A remarkable variety of conservative and nationalist groups contested the elections, gaining a total of 10.5 percent of the vote. The Socialist Reich Party (SPR) was founded in October 1949 as a result of a rightist breakaway from the DKP-DRP. That same year, six out of ten Germans thought, on opinion poll evidence, that Nazism was a good idea badly carried out.

Still, in contrast to certain dark forecasts, the 1950s did not witness a further radicalization of the German political landscape, and by the beginning of the 1960s, radical nationalist groups seemed to be slipping into oblivion. One major reason for this was the German economic miracle. In 1964, the Ministry of the Interior's official report on neo-Nazism and radical nationalism put forward further reasons for the electoral collapse of the rightist fringes: the growing awareness of the evils of the past, weak radical leadership, personal differences between the leaders, and a strong tendency toward factionalism that made it difficult for one major organization to emerge.

In 1971, Thies Christophersen set up a publishing house where various neo-Nazi views, such as Holocaust denial, were published. Times were now changing. After a period of shared beliefs and tacit agreement, there were new tendencies toward a political polarization, whereby more pronounced rightist *and* leftist positions each saw their stock rise. German would-be fascist movements were again enjoying a slightly widening electorate. In 1977, the National Socialist Action Front (ANS) was formed. Its leader, twenty-two-year-old Michael Kühnen, offered a strange mixture of charm and brutality, Marxism and Nietzsche. Kühnen's low esteem of homosexuality was surprising, given his own homosexuality and the fact that he himself was to die of an AIDS-related illness in 1991. In 1989 the Republican Party (Die Republikaner) and Franz Schönhuber attracted a spectacular rise in support, not wholly different from that of Jörg Haider's Austrian Freedom Party. The Republican Party, initially set up in 1983, did not openly defend Nazism. Rather, it seemed to advocate a more authoritarian government that would restore order and national pride. Other rightist parties of moderate fame are the Deutsche Volksunion (DVU), led by Gerhard Frey, and the older Nationaldemokratische Partei Deutschlands (NPD).

There were also a number of rightist attacks against civilians. In 1981 a former member of NPD blew himself up while placing a bomb at the 1980 Munich Beer Festival, killing another 12 people and injuring 211. The euphoria after the reunification of BRD and DDR quickly came to a standstill as the early 1990s saw a major wave of neo-Nazi violence sweeping the country, particularly in the so-called "new" *Länder*. In the face of a passive or even encouraging local population and a powerless police, foreign workers and asylum seekers were burned out from their homes by gangs of skinheads in the former DDR city of Hoyerswerda. At Mölln in former West Germany a fire bomb attack killed a Turkish woman with her young granddaughter and niece. Worse still, in Rostock in the late summer of 1992, some 1,000 Nazis attacked immigrants and asylum seekers. The year 1992 alone had witnessed more than 2,500 rightist attacks on foreigners across Germany, 697 cases of arson, and 17 people killed. Statistics at the time showed that these attacks reflected rightist trends among the entire electorate. In 1989, 38 percent of West Germans thought that, but for the persecution of the Jews, Hitler could be counted among the country's top statesmen. Other polls revealed that some 10 to 15 percent of Germans could be classed as anti-Semitic, and that negative stereotypes, such as the belief that Jews are cunning, were increasing.

A rightist trend was also at hand on the German official scene. It was a sign of the times when in 1982 the conservative poet Ernst Jünger was awarded the prestigious Goethe Prize. Even his 1920s writings, hitherto seen as highly problematic because of their indisputable links to fascist aesthetics, were accorded an accolade for their literary and intellectual content. Furthermore, the desire to "normalize" the past was probably the motivation behind Helmut Kohl's controversial decision to invite President Ronald Reagan to attend a ceremony at the Bitburg Military Cemetery to commemorate the fortieth anniversary of the end of World War II: among the graves were those of forty-five members of the Waffen SS. A few years later, in June 1993, the Christian Democrats and Social Democrats jointly decided to remodel Germany's immigration law from the most liberal in Europe into one of the most restrictive. Coming in the immediate aftermath of one of the most severe outbursts of German fascist violence since 1945, the new laws could be seen as an ex post facto endorsement of those attacks. However, to some these measures evidently seemed insufficient, as an arson attack in Solingen later on that same year left five Turkish immigrants dead.

As a final indication of a more rightist tendency, the "historians' debate" (*Historikerstreit*) had wide repercussions regarding what may, and what may not, fall within the borders of fair and legitimate historical analysis. On the surface, the "historians' debate" dealt with three major issues. First, the participants discussed the concept of the singularity of the Holocaust, primarily as opposed to Stalinist atrocities. Second, the discussants argued about the need for today's historians to identify with the German troops during the Nazi period. The liberal critics held that, if an approach of "identification" was to be chosen at all, historians should rather empathize with the prisoners in the concentration camps. Third, the liberal critics assumed that the conservative camp—comprising, among others, Ernst Nolte and Andreas Hillgruber—was part of an overall effort to normalize the representation of the Nazi past and to remove the major conceptual and emotional obstacles to the revival of a politically dubious right-wing German identity.

These recent rightist trends constitute only one aspect of a general polarization of the German political scene. The times since the 1970s have also been characterized by an expanding leftist discussion about the nation's distressing twentieth-century history. Among other things, this "coming to terms with the past" (*Vergangenheitsbewältigung*) has meant a growing awareness of Nazi atrocities and increasing efforts to capture those criminals still on the run. The gradual rise in number of (would-be) Fascist organizations in Germany has also resulted in a proliferation of a corresponding leftist, antifascist, movement within the nation. In addition, cultural depictions of postwar Germany in which the wartime period played a vital role—such as the ambitious television project *Heimat;* critical assessments from a distinctly political perspective of the allegedly apolitical philosopher Martin Heidegger; and, finally, Jewish communities seeking economic compensation for their suffering—all indicated that an era of consensus was coming to an end.

Göran Adamson

See Also: INTRODUCTION; ABSTRACTION; *ANSCHLUSS,* THE; ANTIFASCISM; ANTI-SEMITISM; ARYANISM; AUSCHWITZ (-BIRKENAU); AUSTRIA; BARBAROSSA, OPERATION; BERLIN OLYMPICS, THE; BLITZKRIEG; BODY, THE CULT OF THE; BRÜNING, HEINRICH; CAPITALISM; COLD WAR, THE; COMMUNITY; CONCENTRATION CAMPS; CONSERVATISM; CONSPIRACY THEORIES; CULTURE; DENAZIFICATION; *DRANG NACH OSTEN* ("DRIVE TO THE EAST"), THE; ECONOMICS; EGALITARIANISM; EMPLOYMENT; ENABLING ACT, THE; ENLIGHTENMENT, THE; EUTHANASIA; FAMILY, THE; FARMERS; FASCIST PARTY, THE; FOOTBALL/SOCCER; FRANCO Y BAHAMONDE, GENERAL FRANCISCO; FREDERICK II, THE GREAT; FRENCH REVOLUTION, THE; FREY, DR. GERHARD; GERMANIC RELIGION; GERMANNESS (*DEUTSCHHEIT*); GUERNICA; HAIDER, JOERG; HEIDEGGER, MARTIN; HERO, THE CULT OF THE; *HISTORIKERSTREIT,* THE; HITLER, ADOLF; HOLOCAUST, THE; HOLOCAUST DENIAL; HOMOSEXUALITY; IG FARBEN; IMMIGRATION; INFLATION; ITALY; JÜNGER, ERNST; KÜHNEN, MICHAEL; LEADER CULT, THE; *LEBENSRAUM;* LEISURE; LIBERALISM; MARXISM; MARXIST THEORIES OF FASCISM; MATERIALISM; MECHANISTIC THINKING; MILITARISM; MODERNISM; MODERNITY; MUNICH PACT, THE; NATIONALISM; NAZISM; NEO-NAZISM; NIETZSCHE, FRIEDRICH; NORDIC SOUL, THE; NOVEMBER CRIMINALS/ *NOVEMBERBRECHER,* THE; NUREMBERG; NUREMBERG RALLIES, THE; ORGANICISM; POLAND AND NAZI GERMANY; POSTWAR FASCISM; RACIAL DOCTRINE; RACISM; RATIONALISM; RURALISM; SCHÖNHUBER, FRANZ; SONDERWEG ("SPECIAL PATH"), THE; SPANISH CIVIL WAR, THE; SPORT; SS, THE; STAHLHELM; TECHNOLOGY; TRADITION; UNIVERSITIES; VERSAILLES TREATY, THE; *VOLK, VÖLKISCH; VOLKSGEMEINSCHAFT,* THE; WAFFEN SS, THE; WALL STREET CRASH, THE; *WANDERVÖGEL,* THE; WAR; WAR VETERANS; WARRIOR ETHOS, THE; WEHRMACHT, THE; WEIMAR REPUBLIC, THE; WOMEN; WORLD WAR I; WORLD WAR II; YOUTH

References
Arendt, Hannah. 1979. *The Origins of Totalitarianism.* New York: Harcourt Brace.
Betz, Hans Georg. 1994. *Radical Right-wing Populism in Western Europe.* Basingstoke: Macmillan.
Bullock, Alan. 1961. *Hitler, a Study in Tyranny.* New York: Bantam.
Burleigh, M. 2000. *The Third Reich: A New History.* London: Macmillan.
Cheles, Luciano, et al. 1995. *The Far Right in Western and Eastern Europe.* New York: Longman.
Dahl, Göran. 1999. *Radical Conservatism and the Future of Politics.* London: SAGE.
Eatwell, Roger. 1996. *Fascism: A History.* London: Vintage.
Evans, R. 2003. *The Coming of the Third Reich.* London: Allen Lane.
Farías, Victor. 1989. *Heidegger and Nazism.* Philadelphia: Temple University Press.
Gay, Peter. 1974. *Weimar Culture: The Outsider as Insider.* London: Penguin.
Golsan, Richard J., ed. 1998. *Fascism's Return—Scandal, Revision, and Ideology since 1980.* Lincoln: University of Nebraska Press.
Griffin, Roger. 1991. *The Nature of Fascism.* London: Routledge.
Habermas, Jürgen. 1989. *The New Conservatism: Cultural Criticism and the Historian's Debate.* Cambridge: Polity.
Hainsworth, Paul. 1992. *The Extreme Right in Europe and the USA.* London: Pinter.
Immerfall, Stefan, and Hans Georg Betz, eds. 1998. *The New Politics of the Right: Neo-populists and Movements in Established Democracies.* New York: St. Martin's.
Mommsen, Hans. 1991. *From Weimar to Auschwitz—Essays in German History.* Cambridge: Polity.
Mosse, George. 1999. *The Fascist Revolution: Toward a General Theory of Fascism.* New York: Howard Fertig.
Ott, Hugo. 1993. *Martin Heidegger: A Political Life.* London: Harper Collins.
Ozment, Steven. 2004. *A Mighty Fortress: A New History of the German People.* London: Granta.
Payne, Stanley G. 1997. *A History of Fascism 1914–1945.* London: UCL.
Taggart, Paul. 2000. *Populism: Concepts in the Social Sciences.* Buckingham: Open University Press.

"GERMANY AWAKE!": See *DEUTSCHLAND ERWACHE!*

GESTAPO (*GEHEIME STAATSPOLIZEI*), THE

The secret state police after the NSDAP seized power in 1933, one of the main instruments of organized terror by which the Nazis secured their power in Germany and, during World War II, in the conquered countries. The Gestapo, founded and headed by Hermann Goering in Prussia in 1933, soon came under the influence of Heinrich Himmler, who already directed the SS and who had gained control of the political police departments in other parts of the Reich. In April 1936 he also controlled the Gestapo de jure, and, later that year, merged it with the Kriminalpolizei (Criminal Investigation Police) under the new name of Sicherheitspolizei (abbreviated Sipo, for Security Police). Three years later, the Sipo was joined with the Sicherheitsdienst (abbreviated SD, for Security Service), an intelligence branch of the military, the new institution then called the Reichssicherheitshauptamt (RSHA, Reich Security Central Office) and commanded by Reinhard Heydrich up to the time of his assassination in late May 1942.

Recruited from professional police officers, the Gestapo had the official task of investigating and combating all tendencies said to be dangerous to the state. To implement its goals the Gestapo relied heavily on a measure called *Schutzhaftbefehl* ("protective custody order"), by which they imprisoned people without judicial proceedings, most often in concentration camps, where the prisoners were tortured or murdered. In February 1936 a new legal basis for the Gestapo came into force which declared that such actions were not restricted by judicial review. Beyond the elimination of political opponents, the primary target groups of intimidation and persecution were Jews, Gypsies, and homosexuals.

Even if the number of full-time Gestapo personnel never exceeded 40,000 and the number of informers was limited, it could count on great willingness on the part of party officials and *Volksgenossen* to be involved in denunciation. During World War II the Gestapo played an important role in exerting terror in the countries occupied by the Nazis; especially as part of the Einsatzgruppen of the SS, its members participated in the huge-scale maltreatment and killings of Jews, gypsies, communists, and partisans. The Gestapo was deeply implicated in the attempted extermination of European Jewry, forcing the Jews into ghettos and arresting them to be deported to the extermination camps. As the prospect of defeat loomed ever larger, members of the Gestapo even intensified their murderous activities from the autumn of 1944 in many parts of Germany, and went over to murdering foreign laborers, killing prisoners of war as well as Wehrmacht deserters, and lynching Allied pilots shot down over Germany. At the Nuremberg Trials the entire organization was indicted and convicted of crimes against humanity.

Fabian Virchow

See Also: ANTI-SEMITISM; CONCENTRATION CAMPS; GERMANY; GHETTOS; GOERING, HERMANN; HEYDRICH, REINHARD; HIMMLER, HEINRICH; HOLOCAUST, THE; HOMOSEXUALITY; LAW; NAZISM; NUREMBERG TRIALS; ROMA AND SINTI, THE; SA, THE; SD, THE; SS, THE; WEHRMACHT, THE; WORLD WAR II

References
Aronson, Shlomo. 1969. *Beginnings of the Gestapo System: The Bavarian Model in 1933*. Jerusalem: Israel University Press.
Browder, George C. 1996. *Hitler's Enforcers: The Gestapo and the SS Security Service in the Nazi Revolution*. New York: Oxford University Press.
Gellately, Robert. 1990. *The Gestapo and German Society: Enforcing Racial Policy 1933–1945*. Oxford: Clarendon.
Joshi, Vandana. 2003. *Gender and Power in the Third Reich: Female Denouncers and the Gestapo (1933–45)*. Basingstoke: Palgrave Macmillan.

GHETTOS, THE

The medieval practice of confining Jews to specific areas of towns ("ghettos") was revived by the Nazis as part of their strategy for dealing with "the Jewish problem." In September 1939, Heydrich gave orders that the Jews of newly conquered Poland were to be forced into ghettos in the larger cities. This effective incarceration of Jews was the prelude to the Holocaust and made that project easier, in that it was much simpler to deport to concentration camps whole populations of individuals already clearly identified as Jewish by their address. The first such ghetto was established in Lodz, and subsequently others were set up in various areas of Eastern Europe; the largest and most famous, however, was the Warsaw Ghetto, which was eventually home to 350,000 persons herded behind a brick wall. Conditions in these areas rapidly deteriorated to the point where unemployment, starvation, and deprivation reduced the inmates to a state in which they actually resembled the "subhuman" image that the Nazis had of them. The Warsaw Ghetto also became an enduring symbol of Jewish resistance in the first months of 1943, when the "Jewish Combat Organization" formed by inmates offered armed resistance to deportation. They managed to hold out until May, when the ghetto was finally destroyed. The ghetto phenomenon was not entirely restricted to the world of German Nazism: for example, in Croatia during World War II,

Jewish civilians are marched down a street during the destruction of the Warsaw Ghetto, the most celebrated of the Jewish ghettos established in European cities by the Nazis. Ghettoization facilitated the project of the Holocaust by forcing the Jews into a particular locality from which they could be readily deported to the death camps. (National Archives)

officials of the ruling Ustasha Party similarly drove Serbs (whom they considered racially inferior) into ghettos.

Cyprian Blamires

See Also: ANTI-SEMITISM; CONCENTRATION CAMPS; CROATIA; HOLOCAUST, THE; POLAND AND NAZI GERMANY; SERBS, THE; *UNTERMENSCHEN* ("SUBHUMAN"); USTASHA

References
Dembowski, Peter F. 2005. *Christians in the Warsaw Ghetto: An Epitaph for the Unremembered.* Notre Dame, IN: University of Notre Dame Press.
Fischer, Klaus P. 1998. *The History of an Obsession: German Judeophobia and the Holocaust.* London: Constable.
Grynberg, Michal, ed. 2004. *Words to Outlive Us: Eyewitness Accounts from the Warsaw Ghetto.* Trans. Philip Boehm. Cambridge: Granta.
Gutman, Y. 1982. *Jews of Warsaw, 1939–1943: Ghetto, Underground, Revolt.* Trans. Ina Friedman. Bloomington: Indiana University Press.

GLEICHSCHALTUNG

A key term, meaning "coordination," used by the Nazis to describe the aim of working in the common direction set by German National Socialism as summed up in the slogan "One *Volk,* one Reich, one Fuehrer." It conveys the idea of marching in step and recalls the comradeship of frontline soldiers during World War I. The essential, if contradictory, idea was an imposed pseudo-collegial consensus embracing the entire nation as applied to the attitudes and practices of individuals and groupings such as the Hitler Youth. National Socialists were expected to exercise "inner *Gleichschaltung*" to conform their thoughts and actions to those of the party and Fuehrer. As a political policy it was initiated by Hans Frank to regulate German states, or provinces (*Gleichschaltung der Länder* 31/3 and 7/4 1933). Political parties such as the Communist Party and the SPD were outlawed (28 March and 22 June 1933, respectively) and those that remained were reorganized (14 July 1933). Culture, education, industry, and farming were brought into line with National Socialist objectives. The Protestant churches resisted through what became known as the *Kirchenkampf,* although the majority were drawn into a National Socialist framework.

Irving Hexham

See Also: CONFESSING CHURCH, THE; CULTURE; EDUCATION; FARMERS; FRANK, HANS; GERMANY; INDUSTRY; MILITARISM; NAZISM; RELIGION; TOTALITARIANISM; WAR VETERANS; WARRIOR ETHOS, THE; WORLD WAR I; YOUTH

References

Dow, James R., and Hannjost Lixfeld, eds. 1994. *The Nazification of an Academic Discipline: Folklore in the Third Reich.* Bloomington: Indiana University Press.

Remy, Steven R. 2003. *The Heidelberg Myth: The Nazification and Denazification of a German University.* Cambridge: Harvard University Press.

Schmitz-Berning, Cornelia. 2000. *Vokabular des Nationalsozialismus.* Berlin: Walter de Gruyter.

Taylor, Brandon, and Wilfried van der Will, eds. 1990. *The Nazification of Art: Art, Design, Architecture, Music and Film in the Third Reich.* Winchester, UK: Winchester School of Art.

GLOBALIZATION

Neofascist political parties such as the National Front in France or the Freedom Party in Austria and the European New Right have railed against globalization, Americanization, the European Union (EU) project, immigration, the erosion of homogeneous cultural identities, and the loss of sovereignty of nation states. These radical right-wing, ultranationalist political forces have tended to unite with revolutionary leftists, Maoists, Trotskyites, and anarchists in fighting what they consider the excesses of globalization. Whereas the Left rejects globalization because of the acceleration of neoliberal values and institutions such as the EU and World Bank, the erosion of the welfare state, and the rise in poverty at home and abroad, the fascists, neofascists, and New Right fear globalization because they fear the Americanization of their societies as well as the loss of national or regional cultures.

Interwar fascists similarly loathed globalization, which they labeled with such terms as "cosmopolitanism." In racially based fascist and Nazi literature, the Jew was the epitome of the "rootless cosmopolitan," whereas fascists and Nazis supposedly enjoyed a rootedness in the land of their homogeneous national cultures. Neofascist, ultranationalist, Third Positionist, and New Right tendencies similarly reject globalization and cosmopolitanism, particularly the demise of homogeneous regional or national cultures and the spread of multicultural societies. Hence it is no accident that one branch of the New Right based in Germany has called for homogeneous communities within the context of a heterogeneous community of cultures and nations. The ENR in general views globalization, Americanization, and the Judeo-Christian tradition as the true "totalitarianism" and "fascism."

Globalization has tended to both hinder and assist neofascism around the globe. On the one hand, the presence of immigrants in large numbers in France, Germany, and other European countries has created de facto, functioning multicultural societies. On the other hand, ultranationalist politicians like Jean-Marie Le Pen in France have exploited the fears created by globalization's greater economic and cultural openness to make immigration one of the dominant issues in electoral contests in Western Europe since the mid-1980s. Similarly, neofascist groups from the United States, Germany, Russia, and Italy have used the Internet to recruit followers around the world. A point of growing convergence between neofascists and the radical Left has been the antiglobalization protests from Seattle to Genoa that challenge the demise of democracy and national sovereignty as a result of the implementation of global trade agreements such as the World Trade Organization (WTO) and the impact of institutions such as the World Bank.

While interwar fascists remained rhetorically committed to their respective national myths of regeneration, they cooperated in practice, as in the Axis alliance between Nazi Germany, Fascist Italy, Franco's Spain, and Hirohito's Japan. In the post–World War II period, Anne-Marie Duranton-Crabol has demonstrated some of the cultural links between the French Nouvelle Droite and other ENR chapters. Europeanwide, neo-Nazis meet annually, while the radical Right has an alliance of like-minded political parties in the European Parliament. While insisting on the ideological heterogeneity of the ENR, Duranton-Crabol has also recognized the "multinational" character of GRECE, a key ENR think tank. Ultranationalist political parties have made great gains in an era of greater globalization, but other forces such as the decline of communist and socialist parties have been at work to allow for the rise of ultranationalist political movements. In the 1990s, France's Jean-Marie Le Pen reached the second round of the presidential election; the neofascist (or postfascist?) National Alliance joined the Italian coalition government, and the anti-immigrant Freedom Party achieved the same coalition status in Austria. In the postcommunist period, we witnessed the beginning of transversal and eclectic sorts of political alliances and syntheses that cut across Right and Left with issues such as immigration. Playing on fears associated with globalization, the hegemony of liberal democracy, and a U.S.- or Western-led cultural imperialism propagated by large multinational corporations upon non-Western countries and cultures, neofascist, ultranationalist, and New Right forces have begun to make their impact on the European body politic. As in the interwar era, when a collection of "neither right nor left" political forces helped to usher in the fascist era, today anticapitalist forces both on the radical Right and Left seek to undermine liberal democracy by highlighting the dehumanizing effects of globalization, or the antiliberal, antidemocratic trends of liberal democracies themselves.

Tamir Bar-On

See Also: AMERICANIZATION; AUSTRIA; AUTARKY; AXIS, THE; BOLSHEVISM; CAPITALISM; COSMOPOLITANISM; CULTURE; DEMOCRACY; EUROPE; EUROPEAN NEW RIGHT, THE; EUROPEANIST FASCISM/RADICAL RIGHT, THE; FRANCO Y BAHAMONDE, GENERAL FRANCISCO; GERMANNESS (*DEUTSCHHEIT*); GERMANY; GRECE; HAIDER, JÖRG; HIROHITO, EMPEROR; IMMIGRATION; IMPERIALISM; ITALY; JAPAN; LE PEN, JEAN-MARIE; LIBERALISM; MULTICULTURALISM; NATIONAL FRONT, THE (FRANCE); NATIONALISM; NAZISM; NEO-NAZISM; NIHILISM; PALINGENETIC MYTH; POSTWAR FASCISM; ROOTLESSNESS; RUSSIA; SPAIN; THIRD POSITIONISM; TOTALITARIANISM; TRADE; UNITED STATES, THE (POSTWAR); WORLD WAR II

References

Barber, Benjamin R. 1995. *Jihad versus McWorld: How Globalism and Tribalism Are Reshaping the World.* New York: Ballantine.
Bobbio, Norberto. 1996. *Right and Left: The Significance of a Political Distinction.* London: Polity.
Duranton-Crabol, Anne-Marie. 1988. *Visages de la nouvelle droite: Le GRECE et son histoire.* Paris: Presses de la Fondation nationale des sciences politiques.
Griffin, Roger, ed. 1995. *Fascism.* Oxford: Oxford University Press.
Simmons, Harvey. 1996. *The French National Front: The Extremist Challenge to Democracy.* Boulder, CO: Westview.
Sternhell, Ze'ev, et al. 1994. *The Birth of the Fascist Ideology.* Princeton: Princeton University Press.

GOBINEAU, JOSEPH ARTHUR COMTE DE (1816–1882)

One of the most widely read proponents of Aryan racial theory, highly influential in Germany on the Nazi movement. Born into an impoverished noble family, he was convinced that his family descended from Norman Viking nobility. Throughout his life, Gobineau remained obsessed with heredity and blood. He combined conservative Catholic values and modern influences, notably Hölderlin and Novalis, with their distaste for bourgeois values and a Romantic nostalgia for the Middle Ages. He befriended Richard Wagner, who shared his ideas about race.

The Revolutions of 1848 strengthened Gobineau's conviction of the evil of the values they represented—notably, democracy and national self-determination. This conviction he expressed in his play *Manfredine.* His most celebrated work was the "Essai sur l'inégalité des races humaines" (1853–1855). In this work Gobineau stresses the superiority of the white man, who has a greater intelligence, a higher morality, and a better physical harmony than other races. The predecessors of white European culture were the Aryan peoples of North India. The original Aryans were virtuous, in the sense of Rousseau, in that they were unspoiled and not corrupted. Gobineau believed that all successful civilizations had received help from the white Aryan race. From the original Aryan civilization in India, other true white Aryan civilizations sprang, such as ancient Egypt, Persia, Greece, Rome, and Western Christianity, founded by Germanic tribes.

Paradoxically, Gobineau claimed that white Aryans even founded Chinese civilization, and also the great middle and southern pre-Columbian civilizations. The white Aryans merely dissolved into the indigenous people, leaving behind their great heritage. Great empires invite multicultural and racial intermingling that brings corruption, and that is the cause of their demise. Historical development does not end in civilization but in destruction. Civilization is determined by race. The dilution of blood leads to a loss of control. Gobineau believed that he saw clearly the signs of decay in nineteenth-century Europe as a result of racial mixing. European history must of necessity be a history of war, in which the superior, "purest" peoples conquer the less pure, less vital, and degenerate peoples. It will lead to the end of European civilization and the end of the great white Aryan race.

Philip van Meurs

See Also: AHNENERBE; ANTHROPOLOGY; ANTI-SEMITISM; ARYANISM; BLOOD; BLOOD AND SOIL; BODY, THE CULT OF THE; CHAMBERLAIN, HOUSTON STEWART; DECADENCE; DEGENERACY; DEMOCRACY; GERMANNESS (*DEUTSCHHEIT*); GÜNTHER, HANS FRIEDRICH KARL; NAZISM; NORDIC SOUL, THE; RACIAL DOCTRINE; SCIENCE; SPENGLER, OSWALD; TIBET; UNIVERSITIES; WAGNER, (WILHELM) RICHARD; WHITE SUPREMACISM

References
Biddiss, Michael B. 1970. *Father of Racist Ideology: The Social and Political Thought of Count Gobineau.* London: Weidenfeld and Nicholson.
Gobineau, J. A. 1967. *The Inequality of Human Races.* New York: Howard Fertig.
Herman, A. 1997. *The Idea of Decline in Western History.* New York: The Free Press.

GOEBBELS, (PAUL) JOSEPH (1897–1945)

One of Hitler's closest associates and head of the Nazi propaganda machine. Hitler probably owed his success as much to Goebbels and his propaganda skills as to any other Nazi chief. Goebbels, who grew up in a strict Catholic home, was excluded from military service in World War I because of osteomyelitis. This affliction left him with a crippled foot, which he would later claim to be the result of a war wound, and with an inferiority complex to match. This was made even worse by the fact that he was small in stature, so that he looked the very opposite of the tall, blonde Aryan of Nazi myth. In 1920 he acquired a Ph.D. in literature (on the Romantic movement) after studying in Freiburg, Bonn, Würzburg, Munich, and Heidelberg. He subsequently began to indulge a taste for a Bohemian lifestyle. His record of employment at this period included a stint in a bank, acting as a clerk in the Cologne Stock Exchange, and a position with a publisher. He wrote a novel, *Michael,* in 1923, though it was not published until 1929: it reflects a deeply rooted antibourgeois feeling. After initial contacts with the National Socialist movement in 1924, he became editor of papers like *Völkische Freiheit* (1924), *Der Angriff*

Joseph Goebbels, the driving force behind the hugely innovative, wide-ranging, and effective Nazi propaganda campaigns. He was remarkably successful in 'branding' Nazism as a powerful progressive force that could lift the German people to a new greatness. (Library of Congress)

(1927), and *Das Reich* (1940). Having first sided with the Strasser brothers and expressed suspicion of Hitler, he turned to the dominant Hitler faction in 1926, becoming a slavish adulator of the latter. Goebbels was rewarded with the position of NSDAP-*Gauleiter* of Berlin the same year. He subsequently became one of the most unscrupulous agitators in the Nazi movement, exploiting the worries of the unemployed during the world economic crisis and presenting Hitler as the savior of the German people. His speeches were replete with extreme nationalism and anti-Semitism. In 1929, Hitler made him chief of the NSDAP propaganda apparatus after Goebbels had repeatedly provoked violent clashes with left wingers in working-class areas of Berlin.

Goebbels was responsible for many of the propagandistic innovations that gave the Third Reich such a powerful and imposing reputation. He was responsible for elevating the versifier Horst Wessel to martyr status, despite the latter's ignominious death in a brawl and the feebleness of his doggerel. In *Der Angriff* Goebbels played relentlessly on certain repetitive themes—the November Criminals, the ineptitude of parliamentary government, and the wickedness of the Jews. He composed the Ten Commandments for National Socialists, which amount to a manic call to hypernationalist pride in Germany and her destiny combined with an unashamed exultation in violence. In 1930 he became a deputy in the Reichstag. Upon becoming Reich secretary for public enlightenment and propaganda (March 1933), Goebbels established an extensive propaganda apparatus embracing radio, newsreels, and feature films, and he pushed ahead with a policy of tight control of the news media and the cultural sector: his philosophy could be summed up in the phrase "total propaganda." He was now effectively the "dictator of culture" in all of Germany. His propaganda pamphlets majored in the exploitation of crispness in phrasing and the obsessive use of capital letters, which he probably borrowed from the practice of some contemporary U.S. newspapers.

Goebbels took an active part in the expulsion of antifascist artists and in a wide range of terrorist activities, such as the boycott of Jewish shops on 1 April 1933 and *Kristallnacht*. Later he demanded the deportation of the Jews living in Berlin and indeed called for the extermination of Jews and Gypsies. Goebbels played a prominent role in mobilizing the German population for the expansionist policy that led to open war in 1939. After the defeat of the Wehrmacht at Stalingrad, Goebbels delivered his "Sports Palace speech" in which he demanded "total war." In July 1944 he became the "total war" plenipotentiary and tried to mobilize Germany's very last resources for a final victory. Hitler had once designated him as his successor as chancellor, but by the final period of the war he had been disgraced. Staying with Hitler in a bunker in Berlin right down to the last days of the war, Goebbels killed his family and himself on 1 May 1945.

Fabian Virchow and Cyprian Blamires

See Also: ANTI-SEMITISM; ARYANISM; BOOKS, THE BURNING OF THE; CULTURE; FILM; GERMANY; *GLEICHSCHALTUNG*; HITLER, ADOLF; HOLOCAUST, THE; *KRISTALLNACHT*; NATIONALISM; NAZISM; NIGHT OF THE LONG KNIVES, THE; NOVEMBER CRIMINALS/*NOVEMBERBRECHER*, THE; PROPAGANDA; RADIO; ROMA AND SINTI, THE; STALINGRAD; STRASSER BROTHERS, THE; THIRD REICH, THE; WALL STREET CRASH, THE; WEHRMACHT, THE; WESSEL, HORST; WORLD WAR I; WORLD WAR II

References
Bärsch, Claus-Ekkehard. 2004. *Der junge Goebbels: Erlösung und Vernichtung.* Munich: Fink.
Fetscher, Iring. 1998. *Rede im Berliner Sportpalast 1943: Joseph Goebbels "Wollt ihr den totalen Krieg?"* Hamburg: Europäische Verlagsanstalt.
Herzstein, Robert E. 1986. *The War that Hitler Won: Goebbels and the Nazi Media Campaign.* St. Paul, MN: Paragon House.
Lemmons, Russel. 1994. *Goebbels and Der Angriff.* Lexington: University Press of Kentucky.
Rentschler, Eric. 1996. *Ministry of Illusion: Nazi Cinema and Its Afterlife.* Cambridge: Harvard University Press.
Reuth, Ralf Georg. 1995. *Goebbels: The Life of Joseph Goebbels, the Mephistophelean Genius of Nazi Propaganda.* London: Constable.
Roberts, Jeremy. 2001. *Joseph Goebbels: Nazi Propaganda Minister.* New York: Rosen.

GOEBBELS, MAGDA (1901–1945)

Convert to Nazism after experience of Buddhism and Zionism and wife of Joseph Goebbels; her life is worthy of record not simply because of her marriage to Hitler's brilliant minister of propaganda but also because of the way in which it illustrates the eclectic spiritual path of so many contemporaries. Magda Behrend was the daughter of a maid who married Dr. Oskar Ritschel, a wealthy building engineer, soon after Magda's birth. Ritschel was apparently Magda's biological father. From Ritschel, a nominal Catholic, Magda learned Buddhism. When Magda married the twenty-year-older multimillionaire Günther Quandt, he insisted that she become a Protestant. Magda then engaged in an affair with the passionate young Zionist Chaim Vitaly Arlosoroff, from about 1928 to 1932. During these years she gave herself over to Zionism. In 1930 she met Goebbels, whose radicalism fascinated her, and she soon read and absorbed Rosenberg's *Der Mythus des 20. Jahrhunderts*, Hitler's *Mein Kampf*, and other National Socialist literature. On 19 December 1931 she and Goebbels were married, apparently with the ceremony officiated by a minister belonging to the National Socialist German Christians. Magda's political-religious career—from Catholicism to Buddhism to Protestantism to Zionism to National Socialism—led to absolute moral relativism and cynicism in which she was outdone only by Goebbels himself. It is said that she learned the ability to keep her distance in the presence of adversity from Buddhism, and Buddhist literature apparently accompanied her throughout her life. Having remained loyal to Hitler until his death, Joseph and Magda Goebbels murdered their six children and committed suicide in 1945. Magda's son from her first marriage (Harald Quandt, 1921–1967) survived the war and became an industrialist like his father.

Karla Poewe

See Also: BUDDHISM; CATHOLIC CHURCH, THE; GERMAN CHRISTIANS, THE; GOEBBELS, (PAUL) JOSEPH; HITLER, ADOLF; *MEIN KAMPF;* NAZISM; PROTESTANTISM; ROSENBERG, ALFRED; ZIONISM

References
Ebermayer, Erich, and Hans Roos. 1952. *Gefährtin des Teufels.* Hamburg: Hoffmann und Campe.
Klabunde, Anja. 2003. *Magda Goebbels.* New York: Time Warner.
Sigmund, Anna Maria. 2005. *Die Frauen der Nazis.* München: Wilhelm Heyne Verlag.

Nazi chief Hermann Goering, who spearheaded German rearmament and particularly the creation of Nazi aerial power in the shape of the famed Luftwaffe. (The Illustrated London News Picture Library)

GOERING (von KANTZOW), CARIN (1888–1931)

Carin von Kantzow (née von Fock), Swedish baroness who left her husband to become the first wife of Hermann Goering in 1923. Her family was suspicious of Goering for a time because he had taken to morphine after being injured in the Munich Putsch. When Carin died after a long struggle with tuberculosis in 1931, Goering was devastated, and named his Prussian mansion Carinhall, making it something of a shrine to her memory. A memoir of her life published in 1934 by a relation glamorized her relationship with Goering, whom she saw as a noble and heroic freedom fighter; it was a great publishing success.

Cyprian Blamires

See Also: FREEDOM; GERMANY; GOERING, HERMANN; MUNICH PUTSCH, THE; NAZISM

Reference
Wilamowitz-Moellendorff, Fanny Gräfin von. 1934. *Carin Göring.* Leipzig: Warneck.

GOERING, HERMANN (1893–1946)

The highest-ranking Nazi leader to face the Nuremberg War Crimes Tribunal. The son of a jurist appointed by Bismarck as the first German commissioner in the colony of South-West Africa, Goering was brought up in Bavaria in a semifeudal aristocratic environment and graduated from a cadet school and joined the German air corps in World War I. Highly decorated with the Pour le Mérite, he had the aura of a war hero when hostilities ended, but he joined the ranks of the many war veterans who were deeply embittered by the betrayal of Germany by the "November Criminals" who had "stabbed an undefeated Germany in the back" and un-

dermined the efforts and the sacrifices of her brave sol-
diery. He married Carin von Kantzow, who left her
husband to be with him; her premature death in 1931
was a severe blow to him. At Hitler's behest Goering
became commander of the storm troopers in 1922. He
was injured in Hitler's abortive putsch of 9 November
1923 and had to flee Germany. He returned in 1927,
renewed his contact with Hitler, and after working for a
while as a salesman became one of the very first NS-
DAP members of the national parliament in the
Weimar Republic in 1928. In 1932 he became president of the Reich parliament.

Unlike Goebbels and Himmler, Goering was much
more a man of action than ideologue. He not only
acted as an important intermediary between the NS-
DAP and industrial circles, the aristocracy, and the military leadership, but also became responsible for the
undercover arming of the German air force after 1935.
After the takeover of power by the NSDAP, Goering
became secretary of the interior in the state of Prussia
and head of the police forces. Together with Heinrich
Himmler and Reinhard Heydrich he set up the first
concentration camps, in order to imprison and torture
political opponents. In April 1933 he became head of
the Prussian state. At the end of June 1934 he helped to
murder Ernst Roehm. He acquired a large estate in
Prussia and lived there the life of a wealthy but eccentric country squire, collecting and displaying jewelry
and exotic costumes. Well bred and sophisticated in
his manners, he gave a cultured tone to the Nazi leadership.

On 1 May 1935, Goering became commander of
the German air force and then spearheaded the four-
year plan (1936) that prepared Germany's industrial
base and production capacity comprehensively for war.
Under his patronage the *Reichswerke Hermann Goering*
became one of the biggest industrial conglomerates in
Germany, heavily involved in the plunder of the occupied territories. During the war Goering organized the
theft of artworks throughout Europe. As supreme commander of the German air force he was responsible for
the deployment of the Condor Legion to Spain to support the forces of Franco, for aerial warfare against
Poland and France, and for the first night-bombing
raids on London in September 1940. But his failure to
destroy the Royal Air Force was crucial to the progress
of the war, for it obliged Hitler to abandon his planned
cross-channel invasion of Britain. Goering was an ardent believer in the creation of a German Empire in
Europe and was completely devoted to Hitler, even to
the point of stating that he had no conscience, because
his conscience was Adolf Hitler. The latter admired

him for his coolness and brutal decisiveness, but the
two became increasingly estranged in the last two years
of the war. Goering evaded execution at Nuremberg after the end of the war by committing suicide.

Fabian Virchow

See Also: BATTLE OF BRITAIN, THE; BLITZKRIEG; CONCEN-
TRATION CAMPS; FRANCO Y BAHAMONDE, GENERAL
FRANCISCO; GERMANY; GOERING (VON KANTZOW),
CARIN; HEYDRICH, REINHARD; HIMMLER, HEINRICH;
HITLER, ADOLF; LUFTWAFFE, THE; MUNICH PUTSCH,
THE; NAZISM; NIGHT OF THE LONG KNIVES; NOVEMBER
CRIMINALS/*NOVEMBERBRECHER*, THE; NUREMBERG TRI-
ALS, THE; ROEHM, ERNST; SA, THE; SPANISH CIVIL WAR,
THE; WAR VETERANS; WEIMAR REPUBLIC, THE; WORLD
WAR I; WORLD WAR II

References
Hoyt, Edwin Palmer. 1994. *Angels of Death: Goering's Luftwaffe.*
    New York: Forge.
Manville, Roger, and Heinrich Fraenkel. 2005. *Goering.*
    London: Greenhill.
Martens, Stefan. 1985. *"Erster Paladin des Führers" und
    "Zweiter Mann im Reich."* Paderborn: Schöningh.
Overy, Richard James. 2000. *Goering: The Iron Man.* London:
    Phoenix.

GÖMBÖS, GYULA (1886–1936)

Extreme nationalist World War I veteran and career
military officer, prime minister of Hungary from 1932
to 1936. After World War I he became a key organizer
of the Hungarian National Defense League (MOVE)
and served as a close confidant of Regent Horthy. From
1921 he was one of the chief ideologues of the racist
National Unity Party (NEP), but he can also be credited with having organized one of the first openly racist
and anti-Semitic parties in the country in 1923, the
Hungarian National Independent Race Defenders'
Party (MNFFP). In order to advance in political life, he
quit his party and accepted political positions: from
1929 he served as minister of defense in two governments, and in 1932, with the help of military officers
and wealthy landowners, he became prime minister. In
that position he managed to secure close working relations with Italy and Germany and had a meeting with
Hitler in 1933. He was involved with planning the
murder of French foreign minister L. Barthou, an action that almost cost him his office. He fashioned many

party and state rituals in imitation of those introduced in Italy under Mussolini, inaugurating the practice of exhanging the special greeting "Long Live Our Leader," and he attempted to appeal to all social classes in order "to transform the whole soul of the nation" (Macartney 1957, 116).

László Kürti

See Also: INTRODUCTION; ANTI-SEMITISM; ARROW CROSS, THE; EXPANSIONISM; FASCIST PARTY, THE; GERMANY; *HEIL HITLER!;* HITLER, ADOLF; HORTHY DE NAGYBÁNYA, MIKLÓS; HUNGARY; ITALY; MUSSOLINI, BENITO ANDREA; NATIONALISM; NAZISM; RACIAL DOCTRINE; RELIGION; STYLE; THEATER; WAR VETERANS; WORLD WAR I

Reference
Macartney, C. A. 1957. *October Fifteenth: A History of Modern Hungary, 1929–1945.* Edinburgh: Edinburgh University Press.

GOOSESTEP, THE

A marching mode for parades that originated in the 1600s with the Prussian army and that was adopted by several countries in the twentieth century. It became most closely associated with Hitler's Nazism and its tightly knit, synchronized parading armies. A slightly different version of the goosestep was instituted by Mussolini's regime in 1938 with the name of *passo romano.* The "Roman step" for military parades was considered a symbol of discipline and order—an expression of the military spirit—and Mussolini claimed it had its origins among the ancient Romans.

Angela Falasca-Zamponi

See Also: FASCIST PARTY, THE; HITLER, ADOLF; MILITARISM; MUSSOLINI, BENITO ANDREA; NAZISM; ROME; SYMBOLS; WARRIOR ETHOS, THE

GRAMSCI, ANTONIO (1891–1937)

Interwar Italian Marxist and opponent of Mussolini who produced influential political writings while imprisoned by the Fascist regime. Celebrated as the main

inspirer of postwar "Eurocommunism," Gramsci has also made an impact on postwar fascism. He was born in Sardinia, and after university studies in Turin he participated in a review of socialist culture, *l'Ordine Nuovo.* After visiting Moscow in 1922, he was elected to the chamber of deputies. He was arrested in 1926 and sentenced to twenty years' imprisonment for activities against the state. His *Prison Notebooks* gave him an international reputation as a Marxist philosopher. Gramsci pioneered the concept that political movements need to attain a "cultural hegemony" in society in order to be successful. Contemporary European New Right intellectuals generally share a long-term, right-wing metapolitical strategy akin to that of Gramsci. A right-wing Gramscianism is designed to awaken certain individuals—namely, intellectual, political, and economic elites—to new ways of seeing and being, to change hearts and minds, and to gain support for alternative, counterhegemonic conceptions of the world. For Gramsci, like the ENR, the precondition for all successful revolutions in history has first been a revolt against both the dominant spirit and cultural apparatus of the age. This nonviolent, metapolitical stance is directed primarily at societal elites and intellectuals rather than at the masses and has been a practical and tactical choice on the part of the postwar Right, conditioned by the public's negative historical associations of this political position with the legacies of Italian Fascism and German Nazism. Right-wing Gramscianism in the ENR mold consciously differentiates itself from both the violent, extraparliamentary political movements and parliamentary political parties of the radical, ultranationalist Right.

Tamir Bar-On and Cyprian Blamires

See Also: BENOIST, ALAIN DE; CAESARISM; EUROPEAN NEW RIGHT, THE; EUROPEANIST FASCISM/RADICAL RIGHT, THE; FASCIST PARTY, THE; ITALY; MARXISM; MUSSOLINI, BENITO ANDREA; NAZISM; POSTWAR FASCISM; PROPAGANDA

References
Finocchiaro, Maurice. 1999. *Beyond Right and Left: Democratic Elitism in Mosca and Gramsci.* New Haven: Yale University Press.
Gramsci, Antonio. 1959. *The Modern Prince and Other Writings.* New York: International.
Griffin, Roger, ed. 1995. *Fascism.* Oxford: Oxford University Press.
Levitas, Ruth, ed. 1986. *The Ideology of the New Right.* Cambridge: Polity.
Taguieff, Pierre-André. 1985. "La stratégie culturelle de la nouvelle droite." In *Vous avez dit fascismes?* edited by R. Badinter. Paris: Montalba.

GRAND COUNCIL OF FASCISM, THE

Formed by Mussolini in December 1922 as an essentially consultative political organ; from 1928 it gained a strengthened role as the seat of supreme power in the government. In theory, at least, it was held to be the seat of supreme power in the government; it comprised the top leadership of the Fascist Party, with the prime minister as chairman. It was responsible for choosing the list of candidates for the chamber of deputies and was to be consulted on important governmental business. It was in particular entrusted with the task of selecting Mussolini's successor. On the night of 24–25 July 1943 it did in fact vote to unseat Mussolini, who was then imprisoned but subsequently rescued by the Germans and enabled to set up the short-lived Salò Republic.

Cyprian Blamires

See Also: CIANO, COUNT GALEAZZO; FASCIST PARTY, THE; ITALY; MUSSOLINI, BENITO ANDREA; SALÒ REPUBLIC, THE

GRAND MUFTI OF JERUSALEM, THE: See IRAQ; PALESTINE

GRANDI, DINO (Conte di Mordano, 1895–1988)

Major influence in the formulation of Italian foreign policy as Mussolini's foreign minister from 1929 to 1932 and then ambassador to Great Britain. In 1939 he was appointed by Mussolini as minister of grace and justice and president of the chamber of the Fasci and corporations. He was of all the Fascist leaders the one most opposed to Italy's entering the war on the side of Germany. In collaboration with the monarchy and the conservative establishment, he played a leading role in the fall of Mussolini and the Fascist regime in July 1943.

Alessandro Campi
(translated by Cyprian Blamires)

See Also: CIANO, COUNT GALEAZZO; CORPORATISM; FASCIST PARTY, THE; GERMANY; GRAND COUNCIL OF FASCISM, THE; INVERVENTIONISM; ITALY; MONARCHY; MUSSOLINI, BENITO ANDREA; VICTOR EMMANUEL III/VITTORIO EMANUELE III, KING; WORLD WAR II

References
Cardoza, A. L. 1982. *Agrarian Elites and Italian Fascism.* Princeton: Princeton University Press.
Lyttelton, A. 2004. *The Seizure of Power: Fascism in Italy, 1919–1929.* London: Routledge.

GREAT BRITAIN

Given traditional assumptions regarding fascist masculinity and its retrograde view of women, it is ironic that Britain's first overtly fascist group—the British Fascisti (or "Bloody Fools" as they soon became known)—was founded in May 1923 by a woman, Mrs. Rotha Lintorn-Orman. Her group rapidly attracted several thousand members who engaged in attacks on left-wing newspaper vendors, strike-breaking, and, most notably, the kidnapping of Harry Pollitt, leader of the Communist Party of Great Britain in March 1925 (he was later released). The party then slowly disintegrated, its more able members defecting to other parties, while Lintorn-Ormon drank herself to death. In parallel with the decline of the British Fascisti, Arnold Spencer Leese, a retired veterinary surgeon and world authority on diseases of the one-humped camel, founded the Imperial Fascist League (IFL) in 1929. The IFL was a small racial, nationalist sect wedded to biological Nazism and the conspiratorial anti-Semitism of Nesta Webster and *The Protocols of the Elders of Zion;* the latter book had been kept in print in England since 1919 thanks to Henry Hamilton Beamish, founder of the Britons Publishing Company, an anti-Semitic conveyor belt of "Jew-wise" thought that finally closed its doors in 1983. Although Leese made absolutely no impact on interwar politics, his racial fascism was hugely influential upon the development of post-1945 fascism.

The key figure in the history of British fascism was Sir Oswald Mosley, a political lothario who had crossed the floor from the Conservative Party in 1926 to join Labour over the government's use of "Black and Tan" paramilitaries in Ireland. Mosley was too intolerant and impetuous for the rigors of parliamentary bureaucracy, however. Following the rejection of his

"Mosley memorandum" outlining his solution to the unemployment crisis through Keynsian economics, Mosley resigned from the party in 1931, determined to challenge the ossified "old gangs" of British politics. He went on to found the New Party, and, having made a study of Continental fascism, he modeled its youth movement, NUPA, on Hitler's storm troopers. The electorate comprehensively rejected the New Party at the 1931 general election. That did not deter Mosley, who outlined his ideas for a corporate state in *The Greater Britain;* in October 1932 he founded the British Union of Fascists, which soon absorbed the other fascist parties except for the IFL, which refused, carping from the sidelines that Mosley was a "Kosher fascist" with a Jewish wife.

Like Mussolini, Mosley came from an (atypical) socialist background, though his "left-wing" beliefs were soon rejected in favor of elitist, authoritarian, and anti-Semitic politics, which won the backing of newspaper magnate Lord Rothermere; Rothermere's *Daily Mail* proclaimed in January 1934 "Hurrah for the Blackshirts!" (that is, BUF members known by their distinctive black shirts, in imitation of Mussolini's *squadristi*). By June 1934 membership of the BUF stood at 50,000. Hoping to capitalize on its middle-class support, the BUF held a large meeting in London's Kensington Olympia, but the organized violence of antifascist opponents and the brutality of the blackshirt response—not to mention news of Hitler's "Night of the Long Knives"—succeeded in repelling mainstream opinion, which was appalled by such "un-British" methods. Thereafter, the BUF declined rapidly, its support hinging on the strength of its anti-Semitic invective as it retreated into London's slum-ridden East End. In October 1936, Mosley attempted to lead a march through the East End, only to be stopped by the massed ranks of antifascist opposition and the police. In the wake of the "Battle of Cable Street," the government passed the Public Order Act (1936), which forbade political uniforms and imposed a number of other limitations on the BUF. It also led Mussolini to cease his secret subsidy to the BUF, plunging the party into an acute financial crisis and forcing Mosley to undertake a massive retrenchment that saw many of its most able activists—including John Beckett, William Joyce, and later A. K. Chesterton—being dismissed or resigning from the party. The BUF underwent a brief resurgence in the late 1930s as Mosley opposed a "Jews War" against a Nazi Germany that was approaching its zenith, and to whose fortunes his own fate was now intimately connected.

In May 1940, as France fell to the Nazis, the British state hurriedly interned more than 800 leading fascists—including Mosley—and proscribed the BUF. This simple expedient crushed British fascism and marked a "watershed" in its history. Never again was British fascism representative of a mass movement. Mosley and a hard core of his followers found salvation in their "martyrdom" to "the cause," but for the majority it was the end of the road. This sense of isolation was compounded by popular memories of the "spirit of the Blitz" and a "people's war" against fascism, coupled with mass revulsion at revelations of Nazi genocide, all of which served to place British fascism firmly beyond the pale, forcing its true believers into the political catacombs. After 1945 this embittered and envenomed residue again coalesced around Mosley, who in 1948 formed the Union Movement (UM), the final panel in a triptych of failed political endeavor that soon atrophied, as a result of a high-octane mix of antifascist violence, internal feuding, and media silence. In 1947, Mosley published *The Alternative,* in which he set forth his grandiose geopolitical settlement for postwar Europe, which would stand as a "Third Force" between "Mob" (Russia) and "Money" (the United States). Although it created a brief flurry of interest among the detritus of Continental fascism, it only served to alienate further what little support Mosley had retained among "Britain First" fascists who saw such an ideological inversion as not so much "beyond fascism and democracy" as "beyond comprehension." In 1951, Mosley abandoned England for Ireland and subsequently France, where he died in self-imposed exile in 1980.

But while the Mosleyite tradition of British fascism withered on the vine, the fortunes of British fascism underwent a curious inversion. At a moment when the British government was encouraging emigration from the West Indies and Asia to plug large gaps in the British economy, a new generation of fascist activists came of age, adhering to the biological Nazism of Leese and his dictum "Keep Britain White." This new wave came into its own following the Notting Hill race riots in London in 1958, leading to the racialization of British politics, which had hitherto shied away from openly discussing mass immigration. Poised to capitalize upon this was the League of Empire Loyalists (LEL), founded in 1954 by A. K. Chesterton with money from a wealthy expatriate supporter to protest against "colored" immigration and the "scuttle" of the British Empire. Although the LEL was mocked for its Blimpish exterior, it was responsible for keeping the "Jew-wise" tradition of conspiratorial anti-Semitism alive and served as a crucible for a number of fascist careers, including those of John Bean, Colin Jordan, Martin Webster, and John Tyndall. After leaving the LEL, these activists formed two separate "racial nationalist" groups, the National Labour Party and the White Defence League, which in 1960 merged to form the British National Party, whose racial nationalism, espoused through its journal *Combat,* was influential upon a young Jean-Marie Le Pen. In 1962 the BNP split over Jordan's Nazi histrionics, and he and Tyndall founded the National Socialist Movement (NSM), which achieved notoriety when Jordan declared that "Hitler was right" at a public meeting in Trafalgar Square. Both men were soon jailed for public order offenses, including wearing political uniforms and raising a paramilitary force, the Spearhead group. Shortly after their release the NSM itself split, with Tyndall leaving to form the Greater Britain Movement (GBM), which sought a distinctly "British" form of National Socialism—leading to the caricature of Tyndall as a "John Bull in Jackboots."

In 1967 the LEL, the BNP, and the smaller Racial Preservation Society came together to form the National Front, which, while shunning Jordan, was joined by members of the GBM, including (after a brief hiatus) Tyndall himself. Chesterton resigned as NF chairman in 1971, bitterly disillusioned with the party, as the National Socialist core (which he had allowed to join) began to exert its influence over its politics. The primacy of this faction was symbolized by Tyndall's assumption of the chairmanship in 1972. The foundation of the NF coincided with the infamous "Rivers of Blood" speech by Conservative MP Enoch Powell in April 1968, protesting in the strongest terms what he perceived to be the baleful effects of immigration. For the first time a mainstream British politician had sought to make immigration a political issue. The Conservative prime minister, Edward Heath, dismissed Powell, but his provocative and incendiary speech struck a chord with many. Powell's speech provided a huge fillip for the NF, which switched from trying to entice into its ranks disillusioned Conservatives to trying to win working-class support, marking a revival in its political fortunes. Across the Channel, the small Front National was one of the first to understand the potentialities of its formula for populist racist anti-immigration politics.

In the wake of Powell's speech the NF began to acquire strong levels of local support in East London as well as in Leicester and Bradford (places with a high proportion of Asian immigrants), achieving a considerable crossover of support with the middle-class racism of the Monday Club, a Conservative ginger group vehemently opposed to the "liberal" politics of Heath. In terms of electoral support, however, the NF peaked in 1973, when Martin Webster polled 16 percent in West Bromwich. Despite prophecies that they were on the verge of an electoral breakthrough, NF candidates polled an average of only 3.2 percent in the 1974 general election, leaving the party in the doldrums until a brief resurgence in 1976–1977, following the expulsion of Asians from Malawi and Uganda (many of whom sought a new home in Britain), saw the party poll 199,000 votes in the Greater London council elections. It failed to win a single council seat, however. Unperturbed, during the 1979 general election the NF fielded the largest number of candidates of any insurgent political party since the Labour Party in 1919. Again, the "breakthrough" failed to materialize. On the eve of the poll Margaret Thatcher, leader of the Conservative Party, talked of Britain's being "swamped" with immigrants, signaling that the Conservatives would take a "tough" line on immigration. With the rug pulled from under them, the NF imploded into warring factions and disintegrated as a national entity. In 1982, Tyndall—who had been made a scapegoat for the failure of the NF—founded another BNP, though his overt Nazism ensured its isolation, barring a brief success in 1993 when it elected a solitary councillor to a local council seat in the Isle of Dogs in London, a seat that it soon lost. Perhaps the most notable development of the 1990s was the formation of the BNP stewards group Combat 18, though they soon parted amid bitter animosity to pursue their own course.

Whilst the far Right remained a negligible force in the 1990s (ironically, as Continental fascism was again resurgent), this was a decade of effervescent ideological ferment. Although the BNP remained wedded to National Socialist orthodoxy, the younger cadres of the NF, whose activists included future BNP chairman Nick Griffin, became influenced by Third Position fascism and the "spiritual racism" of Julius Evola, to which they were introduced by a group of fugitive Italian fascists wanted on terrorism charges. The resulting ideological friction ensured that the NF fractured further and was reduced to irrelevancy. Following his dalliance with the "Third Way," Griffin joined the seemingly moribund BNP and in 1999 ousted Tyndall as party chairman, paving the way for its "modernization." This approach gradually began to pay dividends and indeed survived the exposure of the fact that London "nail-bomber" David Copeland was a party member. Although the BNP remains at its core a National Socialist party, the "Nazi" tag has begun to lose its efficacy for antifascist campaigners, as the BNP taps into a deep reservoir of popular hostility toward immigration, leading it to be seen in many quarters as an anti-immigration rather than fascist party—thus aiding Griffin's quest to forge it into a respectable entity.

In 2001 serious rioting occurred in the northern towns of Oldham, Bradford, and Burnley (where there was a combination of a high Asian immigrant population and unemployment resulting from the decline of the textile industry). In the aftermath of these riots (in which members of the far Right actively participated), Griffin stood as a candidate in Oldham during the general election and received 16.4 percent of the vote, the highest percentage polled by a fascist candidate since Martin Webster in 1973. By the end of 2004, against a backdrop of tabloid hysteria about "bogus" asylum seekers and Islamic terrorism, the BNP managed to win a handful of local council seats, particularly in Burnley, where it briefly held the balance of power. In early 2005 Griffin was arrested and charged with incitement to racial hatred following comments he made to an undercover reporter, but he was subsequently acquitted. It remains to be seen if Griffin can succeed where so many other would-be Fuehrers have failed: to take British fascism from the margins to the mainstream.

Graham Macklin

See Also: INTRODUCTION; AMERICANIZATION; ANTIFAS-CISM; ANTI-SEMITISM; AUTHORITARIANISM; BOLSHE-VISM; BRITISH FASCISTI/BRITISH FASCISTS, THE; BRITISH NATIONAL PARTY, THE; CABLE STREET, THE BATTLE OF; CATHOLIC CHURCH, THE; CHESTERTON, ARTHUR KEN-NETH; COMBAT 18; CONSERVATISM; CONSPIRACY THEO-RIES; CORPORATISM; DEMOCRACY; ELITE THEORY; EU-ROPE; EVOLA, JULIUS; FASCIST PARTY, THE; GRIFFIN, NICHOLAS; HITLER, ADOLF; HOLOCAUST, THE; IMMIGRA-TION; INDUSTRY; IRVING, DAVID JOHN CAWDELL; ITALY; JOYCE, WILLIAM; LE PEN, JEAN-MARIE; LEESE, ARNOLD SPENCER; LINTORN-ORMAN, ROTHA; LONDON NAIL BOMBINGS, THE; MITFORD FAMILY, THE; MOSLEY, SIR OSWALD; MUSSOLINI, BENITO ANDREA; NATIONAL FRONT, THE (FRANCE); NATIONAL FRONT, THE (UK); NA-TIONALISM; NAZISM; NIGHT OF THE LONG KNIVES, THE; PARAMILITARISM; PLUTOCRACY; POSTWAR FASCISM; *PRO-TOCOLS OF THE ELDERS OF ZION, THE;* RACIAL DOCTRINE; RACISM; RADIO; SA, THE; SOCIALISM; SOVIET UNION, THE; THIRD POSITIONISM; THIRD WAY, THE; TYNDALL, JOHN; WEBSTER, NESTA; WHITE SUPREMACISM; YOUTH

References

Baker, David. 1996. *Ideology of Obsession: A. K. Chesterton and British Fascism.* London: I.B. Tauris.

Cross, Colin. 1966. *The Fascists in Britain.* London: Barrie and Rockliff.

Dorril, Stephen. 2006. *Blackshirt: Sir Oswald Mosley and British Fascism.* London: Viking.

Linehan, Thomas. 1996. *East End for Mosley.* London: Frank Cass.

Renton, David. 1998. *Fascism and Anti-Fascism in Britain in the 1940s.* London: Macmillan.

Thurlow, Richard. 1998. *Fascism in Britain: From Mosley's Blackshirts to the National Front.* London: I.B. Tauris.

———. 2001. *Fascism in Modern Britain.* Stroud: Sutton Martin. Walker, Martin. 1977. *The National Front.* London: Fontana/Collins.

GRECE

Officially established in Nice, France, in January 1968, the think tank GRECE (Groupement de recherche et d'étude pour la civilisation européenne (Group for Research and Studies on European Civilization) has clear ideological origins in the French radical Right, pro-colonialist, and ultranationalist milieux. Alain de Benoist doyen of the European New Right, or Nouvelle Droite (ND), is a founding and leading member of GRECE. De Benoist has steered GRECE and the ND in general toward a strategy of "right-wing Gram-scianism" that has differentiated them from both the extraparliamentary and parliamentary movements and the political parties of the radical Right. In its heyday in the late 1970s, GRECE was also able to enlist the ideological firepower of prominent intellectuals from around Europe.

Although GRECE originated from an attempt to rehabilitate the radical Right after the horrors of fascism and Nazism, it ultimately modeled itself on left-wing think tanks seeking to reinvigorate socialist doctrines such as the French Club Jean Moulin of the 1960s. GRECE's purpose was the formation of a "community of work and thought" and the establishment of a coherent ideological corpus for the radical Right. From the early 1970s to the early 1980s, the doctrine of GRECE had a major impact on the ideology of the entire Right. The French National Front (FN) was particularly influenced by GRECE's ideas on culture, race, and immigration, although the club's idiosyncratic ideas on religion (it scathingly attacked the Judeo-Christian heritage of the West and supported neopaganism) led the FN as well as the mainstream Right to keep its distance. By contrast, the

Club de l'horloge (Clock Club), an offshoot of GRECE established in 1974 by former members of GRECE, continues to play an extremely important part in the FN and, to a certain extent, in the French Republican Party. The Club de l'horloge has tended to take more orthodox views on religion and to distance itself from the anticapitalist, anti-American, and pro-pagan positions of GRECE.

GRECE has been repeatedly accused of quasi-fascist sympathies by liberals and the Left, which has weakened impact of the allegedly "new" message it was purporting to convey. Beginning in the 1980s and 1990s, it sought to broaden its appeal by playing on themes generally associated with the Left and New Left. Historians and political pundits point out that GRECE's elitist, hierarchical, Indo-European, pro-pagan, Nietzschean, and "neither right nor left" stances were similar to those of the "conservative revolutionaries" and other antiliberal radicals of the interwar period that influenced both the Italian Fascist and the German National Socialist regimes. Yet GRECE claimed that its main goals were to defend European civilization from its primary enemies: globalizing, U.S., hypercapitalist (that is, the Anglo-American New Right), egalitarian, homogenizing, and Judeo-Christian civilization. While GRECE's philocommunism and opening to the Left predated the fall of the Soviet Union in 1991, the European Left mocked these left-wing positions as mere survival strategies of a radical right-wing think tank that remained committed to the decidedly anti-immigrant notion of a Europe of homogeneous communities within the context of a heterogeneous world. Whereas in the 1960s and 1970s GRECE used race and biology to support the "right to difference" of cultures and communities, in the 1980s and 1990s it switched to more subtle cultural arguments in favor of the "right to difference." GRECE's notion of the "right to difference" was ominously picked up by FN leader Jean-Marie Le Pen, who argued into the new millennium for the "right to difference" of the "French French" to close their borders to non-European, Islamic immigrants from North Africa.

Tamir Bar-On

See Also: AMERICANIZATION; BENOIST, ALAIN DE; CAPITALISM; COLONIALISM; ELITE THEORY; EUROPE; EUROPEAN NEW RIGHT, THE; EUROPEANIST FASCISM/RADICAL RIGHT, THE; FRANCE; GLOBALIZATION; GRAMSCI, ANTONIO; IMMIGRATION; LE PEN, JEAN-MARIE; LIBERALISM; NATIONAL FRONT, THE (FRANCE); NATIONALISM; NAZISM; NIETZSCHE, FRIEDRICH; POSTWAR FASCISM; RACISM; THIRD WAY, THE

References

Bar-On, Tamir. 2001. "The Ambiguities of the Nouvelle Droite, 1968–1999." *European Legacy* 6, no. 3, 333–51.

De Benoist, Alain. 1979. *Vu de droite*. Paris: Copernic.

Duranton-Crabol, Anne-Marie. 1988. *Visages de la nouvelle droite: Le GRECE et son histoire*. Paris: Presses de la Fondation nationale des sciences politiques.

Griffin, Roger, ed. 1995. *Fascism*. Oxford: Oxford University Press.

Simmons, Harvey. 1996. *The French National Front: The Extremist Challenge to Democracy*. Boulder, CO: Westview.

Sternhell, Ze'ev, et al. 1994. *The Birth of the Fascist Ideology*. Princeton: Princeton University Press.

Sunic, Tomislav. 1990. *Against Democracy and Equality: The European New Right*. New York: Peter Lang.

Taguieff, Pierre-André. 1994. *Sur la nouvelle droite: jalons d'une analyse*. Paris: Descartes.

GREECE

Greece experienced something like a fascist regime starting in the summer of 1936—and it was less of a single event than the culmination of a trend inherent in the antinomies of the post-1922 period. On 4 August, General Ioannis Metaxas, a rather marginal political figure in the 1920s and 1930s with an ultraconservative royalist background and fascist leanings, put an end to a period of parliamentary rule and ushered in an authoritarian-fascist regime that was named after the date on which the new regime was inaugurated ("Fourth of August"). In the previous decade or so Greece had painfully oscillated between republicanism and constitutional monarchy, liberal and conservative politics, democratic rule and military *pronunziamentos* (successful or abortive). While Greece had been a republic since 1922, the constitutional issue was never fully resolved, with the liberal establishment (represented by Eleftherios Venizelos, who dominated Greek politics until the early 1930s) maintaining a strict antirestoration policy and their conservative rivals steadily moving from an uneasy acceptance of the republic to a mixture of legal and conspiratorial schemes for the return of the exiled royal family. A coup d'etat by the intransigent royalist Kondylis in the autumn of 1935 paved the way for a rigged referendum on the constitutional issue and a dramatic monarchical restoration in November of the same year, thus putting an unceremonious end to the "stillborn republic." The retired General Metaxas, untainted by the political infighting of the previous decade and firmly loyal to the king, was swiftly elevated from political semiobscurity (his party had repeatedly failed to make an impact on pre-1935 Greek politics) first to the position of minister of war and then, in April 1936, to that of caretaker prime minister. While elections were due to take place in early autumn, the palace plotted with Metaxas for the overthrow of the parliamentary system, leading to the declaration of the "Fourth of August" dictatorship.

The regime that Metaxas established until his death in January 1941 gradually accumulated a series of "fascist" elements. The technique of a highly emotive "leadership cult" was imported from Italy and Germany, resulting in an ever-growing glorification of the leader as a powerful legitimizing myth for the dictatorship. At the same time, Metaxas ensured that the new generation of Greeks would be indoctrinated in a decidedly totalitarian manner through the all-pervading nature of his National Youth Organization, EON (Ethniki Organosis Neoleas), which adapted the techniques of the two major fascist regimes to the realities of interwar Greece. His admiration for Salazar and his corporatist *Estado Novo* experiment in Portugal was evident both in his speeches and in many of his political initiatives for social engineering. His disdain for liberalism, his determination not only to break with parliamentary traditions but also to move authoritarian rule in a populist direction by absorbing "fascist" tendencies, his thinly veiled (albeit not always directly imposed) totalitarian schemes, as well as his discourse of national "regeneration" were perfectly in tune with the generic European trends of the period, even if they were evidently less ambitious than the fascist projects pioneered in Fascist Italy and National Socialist Germany.

These and other contradictions (for example, Metaxas's cohabitation with the monarchy, his endorsement of the king's traditionally pro-British foreign policy, and his strongly religious perspective on Greek national "rebirth") have resulted in an inconclusive verdict on whether his regime can fairly be labeled "fascist." Strictly speaking, the Fourth of August phenomenon falls under the category of "parafascist" rule, reflecting the appropriation, imitation, or adaptation of fascist themes in an otherwise conservative-authoritarian context of politics. Although essentially accurate, that description does not mirror Metaxas's departure from his own ultraconservative background and his experiments with substantially more populist forms of modern dictatorship that brought his regime closer to the fascist experience. His emphasis on EON

(which he often referred to as "my EON," as his most significant contribution to Hellenic "regeneration") reflected both a vote of confidence in totalitarian social intervention and an admission that the preconditions for this scheme in interwar Greece had to be created in time. His ideology also emanated from primary myths of Greek nationalism that were largely different from those propagated by Mussolini and Hitler but that at the same time showed a political pragmatism dictated by wider geopolitical considerations: religious identity, a glorification of the country's "Byzantine" past but also an abandonment of the "Megali Idea," and a search for security against Italy's expansionist aspirations in the Mediterranean through alignment with Britain.

In the end, the four and a half years of his rule proved insufficient for the rooting of his Fourth of August political vision. A few months before his death, faced with an Italian ultimatum to accept the occupation of "strategic parts" of Greek territory, Metaxas had courageously opted for war. By the time of his death, the Greek army had expelled Italian troops from Greece and occupied large parts of southern Albania. In an extremely delicate balancing act, Metaxas had struggled to avoid the extension of the conflict through a possible German intervention. With his death the skin-deep "fascistization" of Greek society evaporated and was eclipsed by a new and painful reality of war, occupation by Nazi Germany, and struggle for mere survival.

The failure of the Metaxist project in the long term was revealed by the relative weakness (ideological and political) of the Greek extreme Right in the postwar period. Although Greece by no means enjoyed a stable parliamentary system in the 1950s and 1960s, the period of the "Colonel's Junta" (1967 to 1974) was a painful parenthesis for the country. Crucially, it also constituted a step backward—away from the Metaxist project of fascist social engineering and toward the traditional model of military *pronunziamento*. Since the restoration of democracy, a variety of small extreme right-wing parties and movements have appeared, some of which (for example, Chrissi Avgi) have barely concealed their *fascisant* tendencies. "National regeneration" discourse has witnessed a modest resurgence in the last decade, with further new organizations (such as the neo-orthodox, hypernationalist LAOS) contesting both the intellectual and the political space, albeit with hitherto limited success.

Aristotle Kallis

See Also: INTRODUCTION; ALBANIA; AUTHORITARIANISM; CLERICO-FASCISM; CONSERVATISM; CORFU; CORPO-RATISM; DICTATORSHIP; *ESTADO NOVO* ("NEW STATE"); FASCIST PARTY, THE; GERMANY; HITLER, ADOLF; IMPERIALISM; ITALY; LEADER CULT, THE; LIBERALISM; METAXAS, GENERAL IOANNIS; MILITARY DICTATORSHIP; MONARCHISM; MONARCHY; MUSSOLINI, BENITO ANDREA; MYTH; NATIONALISM; NAZISM; PALINGENETIC MYTH; PARAFASCISM; PARLIAMENTARISM; PORTUGAL; POSTWAR FASCISM; REVOLUTION; SALAZAR, ANTÓNIO DE OLIVEIRA; STYLE; TOTALITARIANISM; WORLD WAR II; YOUTH MOVEMENTS

References
Higham, R., and T. Veremis, eds. 1993. *The Metaxas Dictatorship: Aspects of Greece, 1936–1940.* Athens: Hellenic Foundation for Defence and Foreign Policy and Speros Basil Vryonis Center for the Study of Hellenism.
Kofas, J. 1981. *Authoritarianism in Greece: The Metaxas Regime.* New York: East European Monographs/Columbia University Press.
Mavrogordatos, G. 1983. *Stillborn Republic: Social Coalitions and Party Strategies in Greece,1922–1936.* Berkeley: University of California Press.
Vatikiotis, P. J. 1988. *Popular Autocracy in Greece, 1936–1941: A Political Biography of General Ioannis Metaxas.* London: Frank Cass.

GREY WOLVES: See TURKEY

GRIFFIN, NICHOLAS (born 1959)

Leader of the British National Party. The scion of a wealthy far-right family, Griffin studied law at Cambridge University. Rising through the ranks of the National Front, he emerged as a key exponent of "third position" ideas during the 1980s and was subsequently involved with the International Third Position (ITP). Griffin joined the British National Party in 1995 and in 1998, as editor of *The Rune,* received a nine-month suspended prison sentence for inciting racial hatred. Becoming chairman in 1999, Griffin "modernized" the party, presiding over its modest local council gains in 2002–2003.

Graham Macklin

See Also: BRITISH NATIONAL PARTY, THE; GREAT BRITAIN; NATIONAL FRONT (UK), THE; POSTWAR FASCISM; THIRD POSITIONISM

Reference
Searchlight Magazine, 1980 to present.

GROUPUSCULES

Small groups pursuing political goals outside party politics and the parliamentary system, usually at one of the extremes of the political spectrum; contemporary fascists often operate in such groups, which focus on spreading their propaganda rather than on political action. Their activities are facilitated by the Internet and by other modern means of communication.

Cyprian Blamires

See Also: INTRODUCTION; CYBERFASCISM; POSTWAR FASCISM

References
Griffin, R. 2003. "From Slime Mould to Rhizome: An Introduction to the Groupuscular Right." *Patterns of Prejudice* 37, no. 1: 27–50.

GUERNICA

Basque town in Spain held by forces loyal to the Republic in the first year of the Spanish Civil War, virtually destroyed over three hours of aerial bombardment by some forty-three bombers and fighter planes of the Nazi German Condor Legion (with material assistance from Fascist Italy) on Monday, 26 April 1937. The result was the annihilation of most of the city and many hundreds of, mostly civilian, lives (the highest estimated death toll is 10,000, although the official Basque records from the time are probably a more realistic figure, at 1,650). Anticipating some of the Blitzkrieg tactics later extended during World War II by the Third Reich, the bombing of Guernica is emblematic, insofar as domestic political ideologies and international participation (or refusal thereof) shaped much of the Spanish Civil War. The bombing is memorably rendered in Pablo Picasso's massive (eleven-foot, six-inch by twenty-five-foot, eight-inch) allegorical masterpiece completed by the summer of 1937, *Guernica,* a painting depicting some of the historical precedents and bloody consequences of the attack on the eponymous city. Although the destruction of Guernica was vehemently denied by Nazi Germany, Fascist Italy, and Nationalist Spain—indeed, the bombing was initially blamed on retreating inhabitants of the Euzkadi, or "Basque Country," in northern Spain—it is now clear that the operation was endorsed by the Nationalist leadership, quite probably by General Francisco Franco himself. Having taken over leadership of the anti-Republican forces shortly after hostilities erupted in Spain on 17 July 1936, Franco moved quickly to reduce Republican outposts in the semi-independent Basque region. This was because of Nationalist refusal to countenance Basque autonomy, in addition to the strategic importance of cities like Gijón, Guernica, and Bilbao, with respect to Republican communications as well as arms manufacturing and importation.

Guernica had only limited numbers of Republican defenders and had been previously untouched by the Spanish Civil War, despite heavy fighting in many of the surrounding regions. While airplanes had been used strategically in World War I, and civilian targets had already been bombed in the Spanish Civil War, the combination of both on a previously unrivaled scale meant that, over the course of several hours on a market day, a town of some 6,000 inhabitants could be annihilated virtually without risk to the attackers. Such was the destruction of Guernica that the 4th Navarre Brigade was able to occupy the town virtually unopposed three days after the Condor Legion bombing. Here, too, the psychological effects of targeted aerial bombardment—including massive shells, incendiary bombs, and machine gun strafing—coupled with widespread material and human pulverization, indicated that noncombatants were to be increasingly the victims of technological advances in warfare.

Matt Feldman

See Also: ART; BLITZKRIEG; FASCIST PARTY, THE; FRANCO Y BAHAMONDE, GENERAL FRANCISCO; GERMANY; ITALY; LUFTWAFFE, THE; MODERNITY; NAZISM; SPAIN; SPANISH CIVIL WAR, THE; TECHNOLOGY; THIRD REICH, THE; WAR; WORLD WAR II

References
Arnheim, Rudolf. 1992. *The Genesis of a Painting: Picasso's "Guernica."* Berkeley: University of California Press.
Carr, Raymond. 1993. *The Spanish Tragedy: The Civil War in Perspective.* London: Weidenfeld and Nicolson.
Fraser, Ronald. 1988. *Blood of Spain: The Spanish Civil War 1936–1939.* London: Penguin.
Hensbergen, Gijs van. 2004. *Guernica: The Biography of a Painting.* London: Bloomsbury.
Thomas, Gordon, and Max Morgan-Witts. 1975. *The Day Guernica Died.* London: Hodder and Stoughton.

GÜNTHER, HANS FRIEDRICH KARL (1891–1968)

Leading theorist of the "Nordic Race" ideology. He was born in Freiburg im Breisgau in 1891. The enterprising medical and *völkisch* publisher Julius F. Lehmann recruited Günther for his academic stable to write the *Rassenkunde des deutschen Volkes.* Although the finished work earned praise from the university-based racial hygienists Fritz Lenz and Eugen Fischer, other racial hygienists were concerned as to the scientific accuracy of Günther's anthropology. When Max von Gruber, who held a senior position in Munich racial hygiene, voiced his concerns, Lehmann's response was characteristically robust. He explained that he had not commissioned a textbook of anthropology and racial hygiene but a synthesis to enlighten the German people. It was less a question of science and more an issue of awakening racial consciousness of the Nordic blood running in the veins of every German. Günther's *Rassenkunde* was an outstanding success, and in all an estimated 500,000 copies of Günther's works were sold by 1945. The numerous photographs and reproductions of paintings and skulls established a putative Nordic type, as well as outlining how Germans included a number of distinct racial types. Lehmann published six other books by Günther, such as *Rasse und Stil* in 1926 and *Der nordische Gedanke.* Lehmann published his tract on choosing a spouse for marital happiness and fitness, and he warned that counterselective factors damaged the health of white races. In 1930 he published the deeply anti-Semitic *Rassenkunde des jüdischen Volkes* by Günther, as the counterpart to the racial studies of the German *Volk.* With the election of a National Socialist administration in Thuringia, Günther was appointed professor of racial studies at the University of Jena in 1930. By the later 1930s, Günther felt brushed aside by corporate and industrial interests in the Nazi state, and he withdrew to Freiburg im Breisgau. After the war he continued to publish, claiming—unconvincingly—that he had always been apolitical.

Paul Weindling

See Also: ANTHROPOLOGY; ANTI-SEMITISM; ARYANISM; BLOOD; BLOOD AND SOIL; EUGENICS; GERMANY; GOBINEAU, COMTE ARTHUR DE; HEALTH; NAZISM; NORDIC SOUL, THE; RACIAL DOCTRINE; SCIENCE; SEXUALITY; UNIVERSITIES; *VOLK, VÖLKISCH*

References

Aly, Goetz, Peter Chroust, and Christian Pross. 1994. *Cleansing the Fatherland: Nazi Medicine and Racial Hygiene.* Trans. Belinda Cooper. Baltimore: Johns Hopkins University Press.

Proctor, Robert. 1989. *Racial Hygiene: Medicine under the Nazis.* Cambridge: Harvard University Press.

Stark, G. 1981. *Entrepreneurs of Ideology: Neoconservative Publishers in Germany, 1890–1945.* Chapel Hill: University of North Carolina Press.

Weindling, P. 2002. "The Medical Publisher J.F. Lehmann and Racial Hygiene." In *Die "rechte Nation" und ihr Verleger. Politik und Popularisierung im J.F. Lehmanns Verlag 1890–1979,* edited by S. Stöckel. Berlin: Lehmanns Media.

GYPSIES: *See* ROMA AND SINTI, THE

HAIDER, JÖRG
(born 1950)

Chairman of Austria's Freedom Party (FPÖ) from 1986 to 2000, Jörg Haider is one of the most controversial figures of contemporary Austrian politics. He was born in Bad Goisern (Upper Austria) into a convinced National Socialist family: his father was a member of the Nazi Party, and his mother was active in Hitler's Bund deutscher Mädel. Despite this familial legacy and his numerous provocative statements about National Socialism, it would be wrong simply to consider Haider a neo-Nazi. Actually, his political profile is more complex.

Haider's political career began very early. In 1972 he was elected the leader of the Ring of Freedom Youth (the youth wing of the FPÖ), and in 1974 he joined the party executive. At that time, Haider belonged to the liberal and moderate-leaning wing of the party. Nonetheless, in 1976 he changed his position. Being appointed party secretary in Carinthia, a province dominated by the other (German nationalist) wing of the party, he became a convinced Pangermanist. Climbing the party ladder (deputy in 1979, party chairman of Carinthia in 1983), he progressively gained the support of the radical nationalist members at the federal level and prepared his conquest of the FPÖ leadership. In 1986, he organized a "putsch" during the Innsbruck Congress and was elected chairman of the party. His victory, which was greeted by bursts of *Sieg Heil!*, led to the end of the governmental coalition between the FPÖ and the SPÖ (1983–1986). Under his leadership, the FPÖ became one of the strongest political forces in Austria. That was mainly the result of the implementation of a catch-all strategy: while adopting a populist anti-establishment discourse and a xenophobic and authoritarian program, Haider did not hesitate, during the 1990s, to abandon traditional German nationalist and anticlerical positions to maximize the electoral support of the party. Thanks to this strategy, the FPÖ obtained 26.9 percent of the votes in the 1999 national elections and, the following year, entered into the government, together with the Österreichischer Volks Partei. After that the behavior of Haider, who was elected governor of Carinthia in 1999, became more and more erratic. Resigning from his post as chairman in 2000, he adopted a very critical position toward the FPÖ members of the government, leading the party into a serious internal crisis. This curious attitude, as well as his provocative meetings with Saddam Hussein and his anti-Semitic statements, largely contributed to disconcert the FPÖ electorate. In 2004, the party obtained only 6.1 percent of the votes in the European elections. Now, Haider seems somewhat discredited, both on the Austrian political scene and within his own party, led since 2004 by his sister, Ursula Haubner.

Alexandre Dézé

See Also: ANTICLERICALISM; ANTI-SEMITISM; AUSTRIA; HITLER, ADOLF; HUSSEIN, SADDAM; NATIONALISM; NAZISM; NEO-NAZISM; PANGERMANISM; POSTWAR FASCISM; *SIEG HEIL!*; XENOPHOBIA; YOUTH MOVEMENTS

References
Höbelt, Lothar. 2003. *Defiant Populist: Jörg Haider and the Politics of Austria.* West Lafayette, IN: Purdue University Press.
Wodak, Ruth, and Anton Pelinka, eds. 2001. *The Haider Phenomenon in Austria.* London: Transaction.

HAMSUN, KNUT (born Pederson, Knud, 1859–1952)

Norwegian author, 1920 winner of the Nobel Prize in literature (for *Growth of the Soil,* 1917), and prominent representative of literary modernism, whose published works were marked by racism, anti-Semitism, antifeminism, and a phobia about democracy. Before the publication of *Hunger* (1890), he polemized against the liberation of former slaves in *On the Cultural Life of Modern America* (1889), denying them their personhood. Hamsun's fundamentally racist convictions are also reflected in a number of his literary works, in which he denounced the tolerance of "blacks" as a sign of the moral breakdown of the "white" world. At the same time the picture of the Jew as swindler, crook, and betrayer pervades all of his literary oeuvre. Alongside blacks and Jews, Hamsun's third target is the English, whom he pursued as "degenerate" with phobic energy.

During World War I, Hamsun sided with Germany, thereby provoking a newspaper controversy. In 1935 he published an article about the opponent of Nazism and editor of the newspaper *Die Weltbühne,* Carl von Ossietzky, who had been interned in the Sachsenhausen concentration camp in 1933. In this article Hamsun

The celebrated Norwegian writer Knut Hamsun, a strong supporter of German Nazism. (Library of Congress)

justified the establishment of concentration camps in Germany and opposed Ossietzky's being awarded the Nobel Peace Prize. As a follower of the National Socialists and supporter of Vidkun Quisling's National Unity Party, Hamsun increasingly withdrew from the Norwegian public, in particular from the Norwegian Writer's Association. While his eldest son became a member of the SS and his wife joined Quisling's National Unity Party, Hamsun's regular party membership has never been confirmed, although he wore the party badge on his lapel.

After the Germans invaded Norway in 1940, Hamsun pushed his anti-English agitation still further and called upon his compatriots not to resist the occupying forces. Following a meeting with Joseph Goebbels in 1943, Hamsun presented his host with the Nobel Prize medal that he had been awarded as a token of gratitude. A subsequent meeting with Hitler, however, turned into a fiasco, after Hamsun raised the issue of the brutal regime of the Reich Commissioner for the Occupied Norwegian Territories, Josef Terboven.

Nevertheless, he composed an obituary for Hitler after the collapse of the Third Reich that was published in May 1945.

At the end of the war, Hamsun was placed under house arrest in an old people's home and in the meantime admitted to a psychiatric hospital. In court proceedings for treason in 1947, he was adjudged to be sane and sentenced to a fine. Even in his last book, *On Overgrown Paths* (1949), Hamsun remained true to his political beliefs and to his worship of Hitler. Following a period of boycott his books were reissued in the early 1950s.

Susanne Pocai

See Also: "ANTI-" DIMENSION OF FASCISM, THE; ANTI-SEMITISM; CONCENTRATION CAMPS; DECADENCE; DEGENERACY; DEMOCRACY; FEMINISM; GERMANY; GOEBBELS, (PAUL) JOSEPH; HITLER, ADOLF; MODERNISM; NAZISM; NORWAY; PACIFISM; QUISLING, VIDKUN; RACIAL DOCTRINE; RACISM; SS, THE; THIRD REICH; WORLD WAR II

References
Boyer, Régis, ed. 2002. *Knut Hamsun.* Lausanne: Age d'Homme.
Brennecke, Detlef. 1999. "Knut Hamsun: '. . . der Typ, den der Faschismus voraussetzt.'" Pp. 95–116 in *"Alles nur Kunst?": Knut Hamsun zwischen Ästhetik und Politik,* edited by Raimund Wolfert. Berlin: Berlin Verlag.
Ferguson, Robert. 1987. *Enigma: The Life of Knut Hamsun.* London: Hutchinson.

HANDICAPPED, THE: *See* EUGENICS; EUTHANASIA; HEALTH

HANFSTAENGL, ERNST FRANZ SEDGWICK ("PUTZI") (1887–1975)

Foreign press chief of the German Nazi Party, and a member of Hitler's inner circle before his rise to power. His father was an art dealer and his mother the daughter of a New England family related to Captain John Sedgwick, who was killed in the American Civil War. Hanfstaengl graduated from Harvard University in 1909 and spent the whole period of World War I in the United States. When he returned to Germany he became acquainted with Hitler and gave him an entree into the Munich art world. Hitler took refuge in Hanfstaengl's villa after the Munich Putsch. Hanfstaengl had contacts in England, including the Mitfords. After Hitler came to power in 1933, Hanfstaengl found himself too much of a "moderate" for the new chancellor. By 1937 he was fearful for his life and fled Germany. He acted as a White House advisor during World War II.

Cyprian Blamires

See Also: GERMANY; HITLER, ADOLF; MITFORD FAMILY, THE; NAZISM; WORLD WAR I; WORLD WAR II

Reference
Conradi, Peter. 2005. *Hitler's Piano Player: The Rise and Fall of Ernst Hanfstaengl.* London: Gerald Duckworth.

HAUER, JAKOB WILHELM (1881–1962)

Founder in 1933 of the German Faith Movement (Deutsche Glaubensbewegung), a rival movement to that of the German Christians; both of these movements promoted the idea of a "Germanic" religion. Hauer had been a missionary with the Basle Mission in India between 1906 and 1911, and in 1927 he became a professor in Tübingen and associated himself with Rosenberg's Kampfbund für die deutsche Kultur (Association for the Defense of German Culture). He made himself a specialist in the "Aryan worldview." He became a member of the NSDAP in 1937 and liked to portray the German Faith Movement as the true religious expression of Nazism. He expected members of the movement to work together with Catholics and Protestants. In 1945, Hauer was interned, but he was released in 1949.

Cyprian Blamires

See Also: ARYANISM; CATHOLIC CHURCH, THE; GERMAN CHRISTIANS, THE; GERMAN FAITH MOVEMENT, THE; GERMANIC RELIGION; GERMANNESS (*DEUTSCHHEIT*); NAZISM; NORDIC SOUL, THE; PROTESTANTISM; ROSENBERG, ALFRED

Reference
Poewe, Karin. 2005. *New Religions and the Nazis.* London: Routledge.

HAUSHOFER, KARL ERNST (1869–1946)

Reputed in the 1930s to be "the man behind Hitler" on account of his geopolitical ideas, which undergirded Hitler's foreign policy. Haushofer was born in Munich but spent much of his early professional life in Asia, where he was entrusted with diplomatic missions. After army service in World War I he became professor of geography at the University of Munich in 1921, founding the Institute for Geopolitics there. One of his pupils at the university was Rudolf Hess, who subsequently told Hitler about Haushofer's ideas. Haushofer argued that the British seaborne empire was in decline and that the time had come for a Continental power to take up the baton of world leadership. Germany needed *Lebensraum* and should expand to the East and make the rural areas of Ukraine a counterpart to the industrial heartlands of Germany. However, Haushofer believed that it was important for Hitler to seek friendship with Great Britain. Geopolitics of the kind preached by Haushofer became very fashionable in Nazi Germany. Haushofer's son Albrecht was implicated in the July Plot and shot by the Gestapo, and his father committed suicide two years later.

Cyprian Blamires

See Also: *DRANG NACH OSTEN* ("DRIVE TO THE EAST"), THE; GERMANY; GESTAPO, THE; HESS, RUDOLF; HITLER, ADOLF; IMPERIALISM; JULY PLOT, THE; *LEBENSRAUM*; NAZISM; SLAVS, THE (AND GERMANY); TIBET; WORLD WAR I; WORLD WAR II

References
Leitz, C. 2004. *Nazi Foreign Policy, 1933–1941: The Road to Global War.* London: Routledge.
Tambs, Lewis A., ed. 2002. *An English Translation and Analysis of Major General Karl Ernst Haushofer's "Geopolitics of the Pacific Ocean": Studies on the Relationship between Geography and History.* Trans. Ernst Brehm. Lampeter: Edwin Mellen.

"HAW-HAW, LORD": *See* JOYCE, WILLIAM

HEALTH (Germany)

The value of health was central to Nazi racial propaganda. Ideas of leadership were boosted by the concept of an "iron surgeon" who would ruthlessly cut out any political opposition. Hitler himself favored the careers of SS surgeons like Karl Brandt and Karl Gebhardt, assigning them significant roles within his disintegrating Reich. State power looked to a strong physique, a healthy way of life, and a buoyant birth rate.

Preventive medicine was an important element of racial policy, and, in common with welfare states at the time, the Nazi state encouraged a healthful eating regimen and exercise. But within this agenda, Nazism sought to attain these aims on the basis of selection and destruction of the weak and unfit.

The Nazi state saw efforts to unify health services, notably with the combining of state and municipal health offices. These took a major role in coercive sterilization and in building up databanks on the hereditarily degenerate and on "asocials." The insurance basis of health provision was also subject to central state control, while the German Red Cross was put under the SS. Industrial health services were seen as a means of increasing output and efficiency. A division remained between the state and the NSDAP health offices. Although the Nazi state involved increasing centralization, factionalism meant that Leonardo Conti's efforts as Reich health Fuehrer were thwarted by Hitler, who appointed Karl Brandt as commissar of civilian and military medical services in 1943. Brandt managed to open several emergency hospitals as a response to the bombing of cities, but his powers were limited by his small staff and the rapidly deteriorating military situation. Supplies of pharmaceuticals like Salvarsan began to run short, and Nazi Germany was not as innovative as the Allies in deploying DDT and in the large-scale production of penicillin. The SS sought to exert control over military and civilian health services: Himmler sought to influence medical faculties and public health appointments, but effectively there remained a multiplicity of organizations with overlapping competencies.

Public health came under a succession of forceful Nazis, but it remained an arena of personal and political tension. Racial enthusiasts like the genetically trained Karl Astel in Thuringia studied fertility and sought to weed out "degenerate" groups, such as homosexuals, on the basis of hereditary biological databanks. Arthur Gütt developed public health on a eugenic basis but was regarded as too moderate by racial experts in the Nazi Party. Gerhard Wagner, the Reich physicians' Fuehrer, was critical of Gütt. Their successor, Leonardo Conti, attempted to unify public health and insurance-based services but was unsuccessful. The Reichsgesundheitsamt supported the racialization of medicine. Its director, Hans Reiter, was a noted Nazi activist and a competent bacteriologist. The Health Office supported numerous racial studies. Robert Ritter took a leading role in studies of Sinti and Roma. This involved genealogical studies, psychological and anthropological assessments, and the sending of many to concentration camps. Those sent to the Gypsy camp in Auschwitz were killed.

The anti-Nazi tract *Heil Hunger!* by the refugee physician Martin Gumpert drew attention to the rise of diphtheria, scarlet fever, and maternal mortality in Germany after 1933. The rise of infectious diseases pointed to a worsening position of women and children, the result of the demands of the war economy for women in industry. During the war the incidence of tuberculosis and cancer rose rapidly, and there were major epidemics of typhus because of the mistreatment of racial victims and prisoners of war. Delousing was a feature both of public health practice and of racial ideology, as well as providing a significant technique of genocide. The loosening of moral strictures contributed to a rise in sexually transmitted disease.

Forced laborers suffered atrociously, and pregnant women among them were subjected to forced abortions. The German health care system required slave labor carrying out menial jobs to function. Foreign laborers were even used as teaching objects. Public health under German occupation varied greatly in different countries. On the whole the occupied East (notably Poland and the Soviet Union) fared worse than the West, but all areas of occupation experienced deportations and privations. Nazi values shaped clinical practice. This can be seen in the registration of patients for having congenital diseases.

Paul Weindling

See Also: ANTI-SEMITISM; ASOCIALS; AUSCHWITZ; BLOOD; BLOOD AND SOIL; CONCENTRATION CAMPS; DEGENERACY; DEMOGRAPHIC POLICY; EUGENICS; EUTHANASIA; FAMILY, THE; FORCED LABOR; GERMANY; GHETTOS; HIMMLER, HEINRICH; HITLER, ADOLF; HOLOCAUST, THE; HOMOSEXUALITY; MEDICINE; NAZISM; RACIAL DOCTRINE; ROMA AND SINTI, THE; SEXUALITY; SS, THE; UNIVERSITIES; WELFARE; WOMEN

References
Weindling, P. 1989. *Health, Race and German Politics between National Unification and Nazism, 1870–1945.* Cambridge: Cambridge University Press.
———. 2000. *Epidemics and Genocide in Eastern Europe, 1890–1945.* Oxford: Oxford University Press.
———. 2004. *Nazi Medicine and the Nuremberg Trials: From Medical War Crimes to Informed Consent.* Basingstoke: Palgrave-Macmillan.

HEALTH (Italy)

In the field of public health, as in other areas of social policy, the Fascist regime intervened to a degree unprecedented in united Italy's brief history. The regime attempted to reduce the incidence of the "social diseases," boost the number of children surviving to adulthood, and encourage healthy living. These measures were part of Mussolini's demographic campaign to increase and strengthen the Italian population. Mussolini's government focused its propaganda efforts and funding initiatives primarily on social medicine: transmissible diseases, the care of mothers and infants, addiction to drugs and alcohol, and measures to improve general health. Fascism placed a very strong emphasis on improving maternal welfare and lowering the infant mortality rate. One of the centerpieces of the fascist pronatalist campaign was the Opera Nazionale per la Maternità e l'Infanzia (ONMI). This organization was established in 1925 to coordinate the provision of services for pregnant women, mothers, and young children. Centers were opened in which women could receive free prenatal health care and where classes on childrearing and hygiene were offered; female volunteers also visited mothers at home. ONMI was tasked with a vast set of responsibilities. Unfortunately, it was severely underfunded, and its personnel and services were unevenly distributed. Many local ONMI branches existed only on paper, and southern Italy was particularly poorly served. ONMI undoubtedly provided useful medical and welfare assistance to many women, but it fell far short of the ambitious goals set for it.

Alcoholism and drug abuse were recognized as growing problems. The Fascist approach revolved around increasing the legal restrictions and penalties and committing some alcoholics and drug addicts to institutions. The regime dispensed much advice regarding healthy living. Fascist organizations for both adults and children emphasized sport and physical activity. Experts did debate the wisdom of vigorous exercise for women, but generally they approved. Mussolini portrayed himself as physically fit and strong, and a good example to follow.

Meredith Carew

See Also: BODY, THE CULT OF THE; DEMOGRAPHIC POLICY; EUGENICS; FAMILY, THE; ITALY; MEDICINE; MUSSOLINI, BENITO ANDREA; SEXUALITY; SPORT; WARRIOR ETHOS, THE; WELFARE; WOMEN

References
Gori, Gigliola. 2004. *Italian Fascism and the Female Body: Sport, Submissive Women and Strong Mothers.* London: Routledge.
Quine, Maria Sophia. 2002. *Italy's Social Revolution: Charity and Welfare from Liberalism to Fascism.* Basingstoke: Palgrave.
Whitaker, Elizabeth Dixon. 2000. *Measuring Mamma's Milk: Fascism and the Medicalization of Maternity in Italy.* Ann Arbor: University of Michigan Press.

HEARST, WILLIAM RANDOLPH (1863–1951)

Celebrated U.S. right-wing publisher with a large stable of dailies and magazines as well as radio stations who endorsed the regimes of Mussolini and Hitler. In 1928 he called the Italian dictator a man of "astounding ability." A publisher who intermittently had Winston Churchill, David Lloyd George, and Aristide Briand on his payroll at first felt privileged to add Mussolini as a contributor to his newspapers, even though Il Duce's columns were in fact ghostwritten by his mistress, Margherita Sarfatti. The arrangement ended in 1936, though Hearst had already expressed his irritation four years earlier, when Mussolini endorsed Italian cancellation of war debts to the United States. In 1931 and 1932, Hearst papers gave Hitler a forum in which to denounce the Versailles Treaty, though the German Fuehrer annoyed Hearst by missing deadlines and withholding promised exclusives. Meeting the German dictator in Berlin in 1934, Hearst solidified an arrangement to incorporate German footage in his own newsreel films. According to some Hearst defenders, who wrote their account years later, the publisher pleaded with Hitler to end persecution of the Jews. Soon, however, after his return to the United States, Hearst praised Hitler as one who had restored "character and courage" to Germany.

In 1932, Hearst endorsed the presidential candidacy of Franklin Roosevelt. His Hollywood studio, Cosmopolitan Pictures, released a movie, *Gabriel over the White House,* which suggested that the United States needed a proto-dictatorship. Based on a novel written by a British writer, the film described a president who felt impelled to usurp congressional power, declare martial law, establish a wide-ranging public works program, and impose disarmament on recalcitrant world powers. The newly installed Roosevelt endorsed the film. When World War II broke out in 1939, Hearst was strongly anti-interventionist, though in September 1939 he denounced the claim of aviator Charles A. Lindbergh that American Jews were prominent among those pulling the United States into the conflict. Once the United States entered the war, however, Hearst supported the U.S. effort.

Justus Doenecke

See Also: ANTI-SEMITISM; CHURCHILL, WINSTON LEONARD SPENCER; FILM; HITLER, ADOLF; HOLOCAUST, THE; INTERVENTIONISM; LINDBERGH, CHARLES AUGUSTUS; MUSSOLINI, BENITO ANDREA; ROOSEVELT, FRANKLIN DELANO; SARFATTI-GRASSINI, MARGHERITA; UNITED STATES, THE (PRE-1945); VERSAILLES TREATY, THE; WORLD WAR II

References
Cannistraro, Philip V., and Brian R. Sullivan. 1993. *Il Duce's Other Woman: The Untold Story of Margherita Sarfatti, Benito Mussolini's Jewish Mistress, and How She Helped Him Come to Power.* New York: William Morrow.
Mugridge, Ian. *The View from Xanadu: William Randolph Hearst and United States Foreign Policy.* Montreal: McGill-Queens University Press.
Nasaw, David. 2000. *The Chief: The Life of William Randolph Hearst.* Boston: Houghton Mifflin.
Pizzitola, Louis. 2002. *Hearst over Hollywood: Power, Passion, and Propaganda in the Movies.* New York: Columbia University Press.

HEIDEGGER, MARTIN (1889–1976)

Leading twentieth-century German philosopher and dues-paying member of the NSDAP between 1933 and 1945. Despite his well-documented collusion with the Third Reich between about 1933 and 1935 as an outspoken advocate of Nazi policies and ideology, as well as his role as a leading spokesman in the process of *Gleichschaltung,* Heidegger continued to treat his involvement with Nazism as marginal until his death in 1976. In partial consequence, intense scholarly debate persists regarding the depth, degree, and duration of Heidegger's association with fascist philosophy and Nazi practices. Retaining a central place in contemporary philosophy and academia, Heidegger also continues to be championed by various radical right-wing associations, ranging from the European New Right and Alain de Benoist's GRECE in France to Pierre Krebs's Thule Society in Germany and Troy Southgate's National Revolutionary Faction in England.

Heidegger was born and raised in the "antimodern" Roman Catholic town of Messkirch in Baden, southwest Germany. His formative education and experiences included war service at a weather station near Verdun, growing disenchantment with Catholicism, and sustained philosophical studies leading to increasingly senior academic posts, in addition to important relationships with fellow philosophers Karl Jaspers, Hannah Arendt, and Edmund Husserl. Despite studying under the last-named for a decade prior to the 1927 publication of his breakthrough text *Being and Time,* Heidegger gradually turned against his Jewish mentor as he gravitated toward Nazism. Discussion continues over the contributing roles played by Heidegger's reactionary upbringing, his anti-Semitic wife, Elfride, and the severe socioeconomic crisis in Germany following the Great Depression in 1929—not to mention the extent to which Heidegger's philosophical texts may be said to anticipate an acceptance of Nazism.

In his notoriously difficult philosophical texts, Heidegger may be understood to develop from the phenomenological critiques of Husserl—that is, inquiring into the "essence" of things and metaphysics—toward what Heidegger called an "existential analytic." By the occasion of the publication of Heidegger's celebrated *Being and Time,* in 1927, his derivation of phenomenology was turned toward the concrete structures of individual existence (*Dasein*) as understood through temporality. Crucially, however, the main themes propounded in this work—notably inauthenticity, destiny, resoluteness, and particularly historicity—were soon applied by the philosopher to Germany as a whole, which became in his mind an organic and ethnically based *Dasein* capable of self-renewal through a spiritual revolution. There is no doubt that Heidegger explicitly placed the language of his "existential phenomenology" into the service of the Third Reich. "The National Socialist revolution is bringing about the total transformation of our German *Dasein*"; "[t]here is only the one will to the full *Dasein* of the State. The *Führer* has awakened with will in the entire people and has welded it into one resolve" (Wolin 1993, 50–52). A number of similar statements were made in 1933–1934 by Heidegger in his new position as rector of the University of Freiburg, which dovetailed with his joining of the Nazi Party (party number 3,125,894). Both events were made public in Heidegger's rectoral address on 27 May 1933, a ceremony flanked by Nazi officials and uniformed paramilitaries, indicating his support for the politicization of German universities and national life generally (although he later denied this, as well as any

German philosopher Martin Heidegger, perhaps the most influential philosopher of the postwar era, was for a limited period an open supporter of Nazism. (Bettmann/Corbis)

active support for Nazism, in a 1966 interview with *Der Spiegel*). The period of Heidegger's activism during the formative years of the Third Reich have been variously understood as a naive foray into politics by an "apolitical" intellectual, an attempt to limit Nazi influence in German universities from the inside, a hope to "lead the leaders" of National Socialism with a brand of philosophical fascism, or a genuine acceptance of fascist ideology that converged with Nazism to a greater or lesser extent.

As rector, Heidegger denounced Jewish, pacifistic, or democratic colleagues to the Gestapo—including the previous rector of Freiburg—facilitated the Nazi transition to power in the universities, and applied his philosophical ideas and language to Nazism. However, Heidegger's many supporters also rightly point out that he ceased all activism by 1936 at the latest, as the result of a "turn" in his own philosophy, opposition to the realities of National Socialism, or, following Heidegger's own defense of his actions, upon realizing that Nazism was incapable of accomplishing the "spiritual" mission he had projected onto the regime. In various forms, this apologia regarding his relationship with Nazism was advanced during Heidegger's postwar denazification hearings, his interview with *Der Spiegel,* and in various private communications. For example, in 1948, Heidegger responded to entreaties to explain his political behavior by a former student, Herbert Marcuse, with this justification: "I expected from National Socialism a spiritual renewal of life in its entirety, a reconciliation of social antagonisms and a deliverance of Western *Dasein* from the dangers of communism"; he concluded this letter by equating Nazi crimes against the Jews with atrocities committed by the Russians in East Germany (ibid., 61).

Despite worldwide fame brought about by philosophical tracts such as *Being and Time, An Introduction to Metaphysics, Letter on Humanism, The Question concerning Technology,* and *What Is Called Thinking?,* Heidegger was never able to explain his allegiance to Nazism fully, or to unequivocally demarcate his "political" activities from his "philosophical" explorations during the 1930s and thereafter. Unresolved questions moved again into public view in 1987, following the publication of Victor Farias's *Heidegger et le Nazisme;* the next decade witnessed scores of texts examining this subject from a number of theoretical and empirical perspectives. Many of the continuing debates concern the level of ideological commitment, degree of political acumen, correspondence (or otherwise) of Heidegger's philosophical texts to his political actions, and later strength of dissent that he demonstrated during this twelve-year association with the Third Reich.

Heidegger's later philosophy stressed the concealment and forgetting of "Being"—literally *Dasein,* or "Being there"—which he claimed had been obscured by the "productionist metaphysics" of later Greek Antiquity (especially after Socrates). By this he meant that utility and progress had effectively overcome notions of beauty, spirituality, and authenticity—whether personal or communal. Where his earlier work had approached individual comportment to "Being," Heidegger's later texts inquired into the communal and metaphysical character of "Being's" absence, as well as the invariably negative consequences testifying to such a loss. This led Heidegger into studies of humanism, technology, and types of "thinking" that contributed to the decline of those positive aspects engendered by proximity to "Being." Ultimately, this critique came to rest on poetry—especially that of the German poet Friedrich Hölderlin—as the best medium in which to make sense of the "flight of the gods" while preparing for their return. By opposing

philosophy to poetry, Heidegger's final writings thereby attempted to transgress the very boundaries delimited by post-Platonic philosophy—itself the product of the European "decadence" so antithetical to his thinking and, arguably, actions.

During this period of Heidegger's partial rehabilitation in postwar Germany, a self-confessed fascist named Armin Mohler published his doctoral thesis in 1950, *Die Konservative Revolution in Deutschland.* His designation of Heidegger and other intellectuals such as Ernst Jünger, Carl Schmitt, and Gottfried Benn—all of whom also briefly embraced Nazism in the early 1930s—as the "Trotskyites of the German Revolution" was integral to Mohler's attempt to categorize hundreds of creative artists and intellectuals as "conservative revolutionaries." These individuals, disenchanted with the Weimar Republic and longing for a comprehensive spiritual rebirth in Germany, were viewed by Mohler as nevertheless distinct from, and even hostile to, National Socialism. Consistent with Roger Griffin's heuristic interpretation of fascism in the Introduction to the present work, the "Conservative Revolution" can be understood as a form of "non-Nazi fascism," insofar as both arguably share the same ideological nexus—in particular, the longing for total national renewal—but differ on a range of concrete policies to bring it about, especially with respect to the militarization of society and racial cleansing. In that regard, Heidegger's own protestations against the "ceaseless organizing" and racial "biologism" inherent in the Third Reich illustrates the distinction between "vulgar" Nazism and a more "enlightened" (but equally illiberal) fascist variant advocated by various "conservative revolutionary" thinkers.

Mohler's contribution also clarifies much of the postwar appropriation of Martin Heidegger by Third Positionist, radical right, and neofascist groups. A running theme in these texts emphasizes Mohler's concept of an "interregnum," whereby any breakthrough by fascism is indefinitely deferred, given the ascendancy of liberal democracy and popular revulsion at Nazi "perversions" of fascist ideology. Heidegger's own form of "inner emigration" and metapolitical philosophy following World War II is frequently seized upon in the "battle of ideas" engaging contemporary fascists and continues to be championed in publications such as *The Scorpion, Nouvelle Ecole,* and *Eléments.* Heidegger's emphasis on the "loss of Being" in his later work, especially on Friedrich Hölderlin and the Presocratics, is frequently read by the extreme Right as a retention of spiritual alternatives to the perceived decadence of Western civilization. Thus, while Heidegger's political activities in the 1930s continue to challenge scholars, far-right groups find Heidegger a pioneer in understanding the current "interregnum," or stage of preparation and withdrawal into metapolitics, prior to any possible European spiritual regeneration.

Matt Feldman

See Also: INTRODUCTION; ANTI-SEMITISM; ARENDT, HANNAH; BENN, GOTTFRIED; BENOIST, ALAIN DE; CONSERVATISM; DEMOCRACY; DENAZIFICATION; EUROPEAN NEW RIGHT, THE; EUROPEANIST FASCISM/RADICAL RIGHT; GERMANY; GESTAPO, THE; *GLEICHSCHALTUNG;* GRECE; JÜNGER, ERNST; MILITARISM; MOHLER, ARMIN; NAZISM; ORGANICISM; PACIFISM; PALINGENETIC MYTH; PARAMILITARISM; POSTWAR FASCISM; RACIAL DOCTRINE; REVOLUTION; SCHMITT, CARL; THIRD POSITIONISM; THIRD REICH, THE; UNIVERSITIES (GERMANY); WALL STREET CRASH, THE; WEIMAR REPUBLIC, THE; WORLD WAR II

References

Griffin, Roger, ed. 1995. *Fascism: A Reader's Guide.* Oxford: Oxford University Press.
Heidegger, Martin. 1998. *Pathmarks* [selected writings]. Cambridge: Cambridge University Press.
Ott, Hugo. 1993. *Martin Heidegger: A Political Life.* London: HarperCollins.
Rockmore, Tom. 1992. *On Heidegger's Nazism and Philosophy.* Hemel Hempstead: Harvester Wheatsheaf.
Safranski, Rudiger. 1998. *Martin Heidegger: Between Good and Evil.* London: Harvard University Press.
Wolin, Richard, ed. 1993. *The Heidegger Controversy: A Critical Reader.* London: MIT Press.

HEIL HITLER!

Formula of greeting ("Hail/Long live Hitler!") imposed by law on the German people by the Nazi regime; the traditional formula of greeting had been *Guten Tag!* ("Good day!"). The term *Heil* had customarily been employed in acclamations, and the crowds used it in greeting both Hitler and Ludendorff when they were released from the Landsberg Prison. It was adopted in general use by the Nazis in their rallies from 1925 onward. In the Third Reich adults were made to greet each other with the new formula, and children at school used it at the start of each new lesson. It was accompanied by the celebrated right-arm salute.

Cyprian Blamires

See Also: DEMOCRACY; HITLER, ADOLF; LUDENDORFF, ERICH; MASSES, THE ROLE OF THE; *MEIN KAMPF;* NAZISM; NUREMBERG RALLIES, THE; PROPAGANDA; RELIGION; SALUTES; *SIEG HEIL!;* THIRD REICH, THE; TOTALITARIANISM

Reference

Kershaw, Ian. 2001. *The Hitler Myth: Image and Reality in the Third Reich.* Oxford: Oxford University Press.

HEIMAT: See ECOLOGY

HEIMWEHR ("HOME GUARD"), THE

Austrian initially nationalist paramilitary grouping constituted chiefly by World War I veterans that adopted a quasi-fascist program with the Korneuburg Oath in 1930; this rejected parliamentary democracy along with Marxism and the class struggle and favored dictatorship. It was, however, based on Austrian nationalism rather than on Pangermanism. In the 1930 elections the Heimwehr won eight parliamentary seats, but afterward it succumbed to internal conflicts; many members joined the Nazis. Engelbert Dollfuss absorbed what remained of the Heimwehr into the Fatherland Front in 1934.

Cyprian Blamires

See Also: AUSTRIA; CLASS; DEMOCRACY; DICTATORSHIP; DOLLFUSS, ENGELBERT; KORNEUBURG OATH, THE; MARXISM; NATIONALISM; PANGERMANISM; PARAMILITARISM; PARLIAMENTARISM; WAR VETERANS; WORLD WAR I

Reference

Edmondson, C. E. 1978. *The Heimwehr and Austrian Politics 1918–1936.* Athens: University of Georgia Press.

HENLEIN, KONRAD (1898–1945)

Sudeten German Nazi politician. He was a gymnastics teacher by profession and one of the leaders of the German union of gymnasts. He was opposed to the creation of the independent republic of Czechoslovakia (of which he found himself a citizen), which resulted in 1918 from the dismemberment of the Austro-Hungarian Empire. In 1933 he founded the Sudeten German Home Front; in 1935 it changed its title into the Sudeten German Party. The Sudeten German movement nazified under Henlein's leadership toward the end of the 1930s. This was an important factor in the Munich Agreement in 1938. Henlein became governor of the District of Sudetenland and district leader of the NSDAP. He committed suicide on 10 May 1945, two days after being taken prisoner of war by the Americans.

Miroslav Mares

See Also: AUSTRO-HUNGARIAN EMPIRE/HABSBURG EMPIRE, THE; CZECHOSLOVAKIA; MUNICH AGREEMENT/PACT, THE; NAZISM; SUDETENLAND, THE; VERSAILLES, THE TREATY OF; WORLD WAR II

References
Luza, Radomir. 1964. *The Transfer of the Sudeten Germans: A Study of Czech-German Relations 1933–1962.* London: Routledge and Kegan Paul.
Smelser, R. M. 1975. *The Sudeten Problem.* Middletown, CT: Wesleyan University Press

HERO, THE CULT OF THE

Influenced by writers like Thomas Carlyle, Nietzsche, and Michels, interwar fascists turned away from the Marxist notion of human existence as wholly subject to the iron laws of the historical process, and spoke boldly of the crucial role in history of heroic figures. The two kinds of hero that they had in mind were in the first place the charismatic leader, who was invariably also a fighter, like Frederick Barbarossa or Frederick the Great for the Nazis, or the Roman Caesars for the Italian Fascists; significantly, Mussolini himself actively collaborated in the writing of three historical dramas, on Julius Caesar, Napoleon, and the nineteenth-century hero of Italian unification Cavour. Hitler liked to have Carlyle's biography of Frederick the Great read to him. But they also venerated the towering inventive genius who enabled science to make fresh strides. The Nazis gave huge credence to the notion of the genius as the key to technological advance. In this they were true heirs to the Romantic movement, which had promoted the idea of the "great" artist or thinker as not simply a per-

son with special gifts but also a seer or a prophetic genius whose skills made him a medium of divine inspiration. Both Italian Fascists and German Nazis also followed the Romantic lead in assuming that the hero or genius did not need to live by the rules of ordinary morality or "normal" conduct, which he was able to transcend.

Cyprian Blamires

See Also: BARBAROSSA, FREDERICK, HOLY ROMAN EMPEROR; CARLYLE, THOMAS; FASCIST PARTY, THE; FREDERICK II, THE GREAT; GERMANY; HITLER, ADOLF; ITALY; MARXISM; MICHELS, ROBERTO; NAZISM; NIETZSCHE, FRIEDRICH; ROME; TECHNOLOGY; THEATER; TRADITION; WARRIOR ETHOS, THE

References
Bentley, Eric. 1947. *The Cult of the Superman: A Study of the Idea of the Heroism in Carlyle and Nietzsche, with Notes on Other Hero-worshippers of Modern Times.* London: Robert Hale.
Campbell, Joseph. 1993. *The Hero with a Thousand Faces.* London: Fontana.
Griffin, Roger. 2003. "'Shattering Crystals': The Role of 'Dream Time' in Extreme Right-wing Political Violence." *Terrorism and Political Violence* 15, no. 1 (spring): 57–96.
Mosse, George L. 1990. *Fallen Soldiers: Reshaping the Memory of the World Wars.* New York: Oxford University Press.
———. 1996. *The Image of Man: The Creation of Modern Masculinity.* Oxford: Oxford University Press.

HERRENVOLK ("MASTER RACE"), THE: *See* GERMANNESS (*DEUTSCHHEIT*)

HESS, RUDOLF (1894–1987)

Nazi leader who became famous for his flight to Scotland during World War II with the aim of making peace. Hess joined the antidemocratic Free Corps Epp (1919) and became an early follower of Hitler and of the NSDAP in 1920, later taking part in the attempted coup in 1923. Hess functioned as the private secretary of Hitler and became deputy Fuehrer and the Nazi Party's chief of staff (1933). When he landed in Scotland in May 1941 with the aim of negotiating a separate peace and having British prime minister Winston Churchill dismissed, Hitler pronounced him mad.

After his internment the Nuremberg court found him guilty of planning a war of aggression and conspiracy against world peace, and he therefore received a life sentence. Since his death, neo-Nazis in Germany have organized demonstrations honoring Hess that have attracted as many as 5,000 followers.

Fabian Virchow

See Also: CHURCHILL, SIR WINSTON LEONARD SPENCER; FREIKORPS, THE; GERMANY; HAUSHOFER, KARL ERNST; HITLER, ADOLF; MUNICH (BEER-HALL) PUTSCH, THE; NAZISM; NEO-NAZISM; NUREMBERG TRIALS, THE; *SIEG HEIL!*; WORLD WAR II

References
Manvell, Roger, and Heinrich Fraenkel. 1973. *Hess: A Biography.* New York: Drake.
Paetzold, Karl, and Manfred Weißbecker. 1999. *Rudolf Heß. Der Mann an Hitlers Seite.* Leipzig: Militzke.
Stafford, David. 2002. *Flight from Reality: Rudolf Hess and His Mission to Scotland, 1941.* London: Pimlico.

HEYDRICH, REINHARD (1904–1942)

German Nazi politician, one of the leading figures in the initiation and realization of the Holocaust. Heydrich was born in Halle. He served in the German navy from 1922 to 1930. In 1931 he joined the NSDAP and also embarked on a successful career in the SS. He attained to the rank of *SS-Obergruppenführer.* He became chief of the Sicherheitspolizei (Sipo), chief of the SD, and chief of the Reichssicherheitshauptamt (RSHA). Heydrich was responsible for many of the anti-Jewish measures of the Third Reich, including plans for the "final solution of the Jewish question." On 20 January 1942 he was the main figure at the Wannsee Conference, which played an important role in the realization of the Holocaust. In 1941, Heydrich was designated *ReichsProtector* in the protectorate of Bohemia and Moravia. Heydrich wanted to stabilize the situation in the protectorate, with its important armaments industry. He began to carry out brutal repression against the Czech resistance while at the same time trying to pacify Czech workers with social benefits. The Czech exile government in London, in cooperation with British Special Operations Executive (SOE), sent several Czech agents to the territory of the protectorate of Bohemia

and Moravia. These agents, with the help of the Czech anti-Nazi underground, wounded Heydrich fatally on 27 May 1942 (he died several days later in hospital). This action led to a wave of Nazi terror (including the obliteration of the Czech villages of Lidice and Ležáky). The assassination of Heydrich still plays a dominant role in Czech antifascist traditions. On the other hand, some contemporary Czech neo-Nazis see Heydrich as a symbol of the friendship linking German and Czech pan-Aryan-oriented National Socialists. One small neo-Nazi group called Rytíři slunečního kruhu ("Knights of the Sun Wheel") founded the formalized Cult of Reinhard Heydrich in 2000.

Miroslav Mares

See Also: ANTI-SEMITISM; ARYANISM; CZECHOSLOVAKIA; HOLOCAUST, THE; NAZISM; NEO-NAZISM; SD, THE; SS, THE; THIRD REICH, THE; WANNSEE CONFERENCE, THE; WORLD WAR II

References
Deschner, G. 1981. *Heydrich: The Pursuit of Power.* London: Orbis.
Whiting, C. 1999. *Heydrich: Henchman of Death.* Barnsley: Leo Cooper.

HIERARCHY: *See* EGALITARIANISM

HIMMLER, HEINRICH (1900–1945)

Leading Nazi ideologue who presided over the SS and held other key positions of responsibility in the Nazi regime. After World War I, Himmler became a firm believer in the "stab in the back" theory and became involved in paramilitary activities. After joining the Nazi Party in 1923, Himmler took part in the Munich Beer-Hall Putsch, and he subsequently became propaganda leader of the movement between 1925 and 1930. In 1929, Himmler became the head of Hitler's black-shirted personal bodyguard, the SS, and in 1930 he became the Nazi Reichstag deputy for Weser-Emms. During this time Himmler enlarged the SS, and, along with Reinhard Heydrich, formed the SD. After the Nazis came to power, Himmler became the police president

SS Chief Heinrich Himmler (wearing glasses) inspecting a prisoner of war camp in Russia. A key figure in the Holocaust, Himmler was a leading representative of the mystical/pagan element in Nazism which co-existed with a strong concern for technology and scientific progress. (National Archives)

for Munich in 1933, and by April 1934 he had become head of all German criminal police forces as well the de facto head of the political police force, the Gestapo. The year 1933 also saw Himmler establish the first of the concentration camps, at Dachau. Moreover, because of Himmler's heavy involvement with organizing the purge of 30 June 1934, his personal standing within the Nazi movement received a further massive fillip.

After the outbreak of war in 1939, Himmler's rise continued. Following the invasion of Poland, he was promoted to "Reich commissioner for the strengthen-

ing of Germandom." This gave him overall responsibility for the massive ethnic cleansing programs initiated in that country. Himmler also headed the Waffen-SS, a private army drawn from "Germanic" populations across Europe that, at one point, comprised some thirty-five divisions. The attempted assassination of Hitler in 1944 augmented Himmler's standing as the loyal servant of the Fuehrer. After that he was elevated to "commander-in-chief of the reserve army and the army group Vistula," which fulfilled a lifelong dream of his for military glory that stemmed from his lack of combat experiences during World War I. By this point Himmler was considered to be the natural successor to Hitler, though this final promotion was stymied after the Fuehrer learned of Himmler's attempts to sign a negotiated peace with the Allied powers. Despite being stripped of his party membership, Himmler survived this betrayal. After the fall of the regime Himmler was captured, though he escaped trial by committing suicide on 13 May 1945 while in the custody of the British.

Ideologically, Himmler was a key player in the Nazi regime and sought to use the race question in order to generate a crucial role for the SS. He contributed to Nazi debates on racial breeding and ensured that the SS would be a "racial elite" within the Nazi system. This stemmed from his belief in the superiority of the Nordic blood race, which he was fearful would die out without drastic interventions. Himmler had an obsession with Germanic religion, which he attempted to inculcate within SS ideology. He wanted to generate nothing less than a new religion and "morality" that was inherently "Germanic," that would be steeped in traditions such as "blood and soil," and that from its base at Wewelsburg Castle would worship German ancestors. This neopaganism viewed SS soldiers as the resurrection of Teutonic knights and sought to create a new *Herrenvolk* aristocracy, all of which necessitated the creation of the Greater German Reich, which would place Germany at the heart of a "higher" international order. Himmler backed this ideology with an extreme "might is right" rationale. During the war he viewed himself as fighting a race war against the Slavs of the East in order to re-create the Germanic peasant communities of the Middle Ages. Of the ethnic cleansing programs of the Holocaust, for which as head of the SS he was especially culpable, Himmler famously claimed: "This is a glorious page of our history which has never been and never will be written." A demonstration of the effectiveness of the ideological vision that Himmler contributed to imprinting on the minds of SS men is revealed by their willingness to exceed all moral barriers in the Holocaust.

Paul Jackson

See Also: ANTI-SEMITISM; ARISTOCRACY; ARTAMAN LEAGUE, THE; BLOOD; BLOOD AND SOIL; CONCENTRATION CAMPS; ELITE THEORY; GERMANIC RELIGION; GERMANNESS (*DEUTSCHHEIT*); GERMANY; GESTAPO, THE; HEYDRICH, REINHARD; HITLER, ADOLF; HOLY ROMAN EMPIRE, THE; JULY PLOT, THE; LEADER CULT, THE; LIEBENFELS, JÖRG ADOLF JOSEF LANZ VON; MUNICH (BEER-HALL) PUTSCH, THE; NAZISM; NIGHT OF THE LONG KNIVES, THE; NORDIC SOUL, THE; NOVEMBER CRIMINALS/*NOVEMBERBRECHER*, THE; OCCULTISM; PANGERMANISM; PARAMILITARISM; PROPAGANDA; RACIAL DOCTRINE; RURALISM; SCHÖNERER, GEORG RITTER VON; SD, THE; SLAVS, THE (AND GERMANY); SS, THE; *UNTERMENSCHEN* ("SUBHUMANS"); WAFFEN-SS, THE; WARRIOR ETHOS, THE; WORLD WAR I; WORLD WAR II

References
Ackermann, Josef. 1993. "Heinrich Himmler: *Reichsführer—SS.*" Pp. 98–111 in *The Nazi Elite,* edited by R. Smelser and R. Zitelmann. Basingstoke: Macmillan.

Breitman, Richard. 2004. *The Architect of Genocide: Himmler and the Final Solution.* London: Harvill.

Hale, Christopher. 2004. *Himmler's Crusade.* New York: Bantam.

Lumsden, Robin. 2005. *Himmler's Black Order, 1923–1945.* Stroud: Sutton.

HINDENBURG, PAUL VON BENECKENDORFF UND VON (1847–1934)

Highly popular field marshal in the German army in World War I who in 1925 became president of Germany as the candidate of the parties of the Right. As such he was responsible for the appointment and dismissal of the head of state, the Reich chancellor. Following the massive electoral success of the NSDAP in 1932, the conservative/monarchist-inclined Hindenburg appointed Hitler (though only with some misgivings) as chancellor of a right coalition in January 1933. The idea cherished by Hindenburg that in this way he could curb Hitler and the NSDAP proved to be a fatal misjudgment. Within a few months Hitler had eliminated all political opposition and set up a dictatorship. After Hindenburg's death in 1934, Hitler had a law passed transferring all of the powers of the Reich president to himself.

Michael Schäbitz
(translated by Cyprian Blamires)

See Also: CONSERVATISM; GERMANY; HITLER, ADOLF; NAZISM; WEHRMACHT, THE; WEIMAR REPUBLIC, THE; WORLD WAR I

References
Astore, W. J. 2005. *Hindenburg: Icon of German Militarism.* Washington, DC: Potomac.

Dorpalen, A. 1964. *Hindenburg and the Weimar Republic.* Princeton: Princeton University Press.

HINDUISM: *See BHAGAVADGITA,* THE; DECADENCE; INDIA

HIROHITO, EMPEROR (1901–1989)

The 124th emperor of Japan, who presided over Japanese militarization, entry into the Axis, and the outbreak of hostilities against the United States and the Allies. In March 1921, Hirohito became the first crown prince of Japan to go abroad, touring Western Europe. He acceded to the throne on 25 December 1926. The years after his enthronement saw the rise of a powerful new type of nationalism ("the Imperial Way"), based on the idea that the emperor could be regarded as the living embodiment of Japan and a model of excellence. This ideology held that Japan needed to assert her identity over against the political ideas of the West, whose military-industrial might had provoked a sense of inferiority in the nation. Hirohito played an influential role in the development of Japanese foreign policy up to and including the war years. After the war Hirohito's position was gravely weakened when he was forced by the United States to abandon the traditional imperial claim to divinity in 1946. He never admitted any guilt for Japanese aggression in Manchuria or against the United States at Pearl Harbor. He became "the prime symbol of his people's repression of their wartime past" (Bix 2000, p. 17).

Cyprian Blamires

See Also: INTRODUCTION; AXIS, THE; CULTS OF DEATH; INTERVENTIONISM; JAPAN; JAPAN AND WORLD WAR II; LEADER CULT, THE; MILITARISM; NATIONALISM; PEARL HARBOR

References
Bix, H. 2000. *Hirohito and the Making of Modern Japan.* London: Duckworth.
Brooker, Paul. 1991. *The Faces of Fraternalism: Nazi Germany, Fascist Italy and Imperial Japan.* Oxford: Clarendon.

HISTORICAL REVISIONISM: *See HISTORIKERSTREIT,* THE; HOLOCAUST DENIAL

HISTORIKERSTREIT, THE

The West German "Historians' Dispute" about the singularity of the Holocaust began in earnest in 1986 and lasted for less than a year. The central argument was about whether the crimes committed under Nazi rule were singularly outstanding in their horror, or whether they ought to be seen in context with Stalin's rule of terror. Almost all prominent German historians participated, while foreign historians of Germany mostly abstained. The main protagonists were the historians Ernst Nolte and Michael Stürmer on the one side, and philosopher Jürgen Habermas and historian Hans Mommsen on the other. Nolte had argued in an article for the conservative daily *Frankfurter Allgemeine Zeitung* (FAZ) in June 1986 that the historiography of Nazi Germany needed revision. The crimes committed under Hitler, he argued, ought to be seen in relation to the Soviet Union's genocides. Was not the Gulag Archipelago more original than Auschwitz? he asked. And did not the "class murder" of the Bolsheviks happen before the "race murder" of the Nazis? In embryonic form, Nolte had voiced similar thoughts as early as 1980 (also in the FAZ), where he had called for an interpretation of German history between 1933 and 1945 in the context of the upheavals unleashed by the Industrial Revolution. In July 1986, Habermas answered Nolte's article with a stinging attack on "neo-conservative" historians like Nolte and Stürmer, rejecting the alleged attempt to relativize German crimes through comparison with other genocides. Habermas used the liberal weekly *Die Zeit* as his platform. Ironically, Nolte had been instrumental in the 1960s in overcoming a rather simplistic model of totalitarianism—that is, the attempt to explain Nazism and Stalinism as two sides of the same coin. His critics were quick to point out in the summer of 1986 that he had now resurrected that very model, and they accused him and his followers of trying to whitewash German history by comparison with other barbaric regimes. Although Nolte had initially stated very clearly in 1980 that German historiography did not need revisionism, but merely a revision, he was now accused of attempting a major reinterpretation of German history, rather than just minor adjustments.

In hindsight, the *Historikerstreit* was more a moral and political debate and less a historiographical dispute. Some non-German historians dismiss it as negligible for our understanding of Nazi Germany. It came at a time in West Germany when mainstream conservative politicians were calling for Germany to "step out of the shadow of history"—that is, to begin to understand West Germany as a "normal" Western nation. The *Historikerstreit* did, however, interlink with the historiographical debate about whether Germany had followed a "special path" (*Sonderweg*) toward modernity that might explain the extremely violent upheavals between 1914 and 1945, or whether Germany had instead simply experienced an extreme version of broader European developments.

Christoph H. Müller

See Also: ANTI-SEMITISM; ARENDT, HANNAH; ARYANISM; AUSCHWITZ; BOLSHEVISM; GERMANY; GOBINEAU, COMTE ARTHUR DE; HITLER, ADOLF; HOLOCAUST, THE; HOLOCAUST DENIAL; NAZISM; PROTO-FASCISM; RACIAL DOCTRINE; SOVIET UNION, THE; SONDERWEG ("SPECIAL PATH"), THE; STALIN, IOSIF VISSARIONOVICH; TOTALITARIANISM; TRADITION

References

Knowlton, James, and Truett Cates, trans. 1993. *Forever in the Shadow of Hitler? Original Documents of the "Historikerstreit," the Controversy concerning the Singularity of the Holocaust.* Atlantic Highlands, NJ: Humanities.

Müller, Jan-Werner. 2000. *Another Country: German Intellectuals, Unification and National Identity.* New Haven: Yale University Press.

HISTORY: *See* TRADITION

HITLER, ADOLF (1889–1945)

Leader of the Nazi Party and Reich chancellor between 1933 and 1945. Following the death of President Hindenburg in August 1934, he became sole leader of Ger-

Adolf Hitler receiving flowers on behalf of admirers. The Nazi regime was adept at exploiting the propaganda potential of photo opportunities in the growing world of the mass media in the 1930s. (Bettmann/Corbis)

many. Adolf Hitler was born in Braunau am Inn, Austria, on 20 April 1889. He was the son of a fifty-two-year-old Austrian customs official, Alois Schickelgruber Hitler, and his third wife, a young peasant girl, Klara Poelzl, both from the region of Lower Austria. The young Hitler was hostile to his authoritarian father and strongly devoted to his protective and indulgent mother. He grew up dreaming of an artistic career. After spending four years in the Realschule in Linz, Hitler left school in 1905 at the age of sixteen without taking any final examinations and with a poor school report that drew particular attention to his inadequate command of the German language. In October 1907 he left home for Vienna to seek admission to the Viennese Academy of Fine Arts. Embittered at his rejection by the academy, he returned briefly to Linz after the death of his mother in December 1908. Alone and without an occupation, he left for Vienna again. Living as a virtual "down and out" in the capital, Hitler encountered the demagogic political techniques of Vienna's Christian-Social Party mayor, Karl Lueger, and came into contact with the eccentric racial theories of the defrocked monk Lanz von Liebenfels and his racist journal *Ostara;* also with the Austrian Pangerman leader Georg von Schönerer. From such sources Hitler developed his pathological hatred of Jews and Marxists, liberalism, democracy, and the cosmopolitan Habsburg monarchy.

Isolated and unsuccessful, Hitler left Vienna for Munich in May 1913 at the age of twenty-four to avoid service in the Austrian army. However, when war broke out in August 1914, he enlisted in the Sixteenth Bavarian Infantry Regiment, serving as a dispatch runner. Hitler proved an able and courageous soldier, receiving first the Iron Cross (Second Class) in 1914 and the Iron Cross (First Class) for bravery in 1918, a rare award for a common soldier in the Imperial German Army. However, Hitler was never promoted beyond the rank of lance corporal (1917). Twice wounded, he was badly gassed in October 1918 and spent three months recuperating in Pasewalk Hospital in Pomerania. When the armistice was declared, Hitler was driven to impotent rage by the abortive November 1918 revolution in Germany, as well as by the military defeat. He discovered, however, an outlet for his frustrations in postwar Munich. In the summer of 1919 he had been assigned by the Reichswehr to spy on extremist groups, and it was in this capacity that he was sent to monitor the activities of the nationalist and racist German Workers' Party (Deutsche Arbeiterpartei; DAP), led by the Munich locksmith Anton Drexler. In September 1919 he joined the DAP (which had some twenty to forty members), and, on 16 October, he made his first address to the party. With his demagogic style and strident rhetoric, Hitler discovered that he possessed hidden talents for haranguing political meetings. Adolf Hitler was thirty years old, and his political career had just begun. He wrote in *Mein Kampf:* "Generally speaking, a man should not take part in politics before he has reached the age of thirty."

In February 1920, the German Workers' Party changed its name to the National Socialist German Workers' Party (Nationalsozialistische Deutsche Arbeiterpartei; NSDAP) and set out its twenty-five-point party program. Hitler imposed himself as party chairman with unlimited powers in the summer of 1921, and having given the new party its symbol—the swastika, and its greeting *Heil!*—he managed with the help of his oratorical and organizational skills to increase membership to more than 3,000 by November 1921. Following his takeover of the party leadership, the personality cult around Hitler became more noticeable as his followers began referring to him as Fuehrer. Hitler, in turn, boosted his personal power by organizing strong-arm squads to keep order at his meetings and break up those of his opponents. Out of these squads grew the storm troopers, organized by Captain Ernst Roehm, and Hitler's black-shirted personal bodyguard, the SS, which became the most powerful organization within the Nazi Party and the Nazi state under the leadership of Heinrich Himmler. Hitler focused his propaganda against the humiliation of the Versailles Treaty, the "November criminals," and Judaism and Marxism, which he tended to regard as amounting to much the same thing. Most of Hitler's ideas were not new, but he disseminated them with extraordinary showmanship, passion, and eloquence.

By November 1923, Hitler was convinced that the Weimar Republic was on the verge of collapse; together with disaffected war hero General Ludendorff and local nationalist groups, he led an unsuccessful putsch to overthrow the Bavarian government in Munich. He was arrested and sentenced to five years' imprisonment for high treason in February 1924. Hitler was released after only nine months in Landsberg Prison, during which time he dictated *Mein Kampf* to his loyal followers Rudolf Hess and Emil Maurice (1897–1945). First published in 1925, it became National Socialism's main ideological tract and stands as testimony to Hitler's primitive Social Darwinist ideas and prejudices. These can be summarized as the struggle to destroy the power of international Jewry, the struggle to annihilate Marxism, and the struggle to obtain "living space" (*Lebensraum*) for Germany at the expense of Russia. *Mein Kampf* is a turgid piece of political demagogy in prose, but it eventually became a best-seller. By 1939 it had been translated into eleven languages and sold more than 5 million copies. (The extent to which *Mein Kampf* constituted a blueprint that the Nazis systematically implemented when they came to power in 1933 remains a source of intense historiographical debate.) The Munich Putsch episode and his period of imprisonment elevated Hitler from an obscure provincial right-wing politician into a national figure, a symbol of implacable opposition to the republic. In January 1925 the ban on the Nazi Party was lifted, and Hitler regained permission to speak in public. At the Bamberg meeting (February 1926), Hitler re-established his absolute leadership by outmaneuvering the "socialist" North German wing of the party under Gregor Strasser. The ensuing reforms enabled the party to widen its appeal and exploit more effectively the popular disaffection that sprang up during the Depression.

Support for the Nazis in national elections between May 1928 and September 1930 rose from 810,127 (2.6 percent of the total) to 6,379,672 votes (18.3 percent)—an eightfold increase. With unemployment exceeding 6 million and the Weimar Republic sinking into its death throes, the 1932 elections in July and November were fought in an atmosphere of growing political violence and disorder. In July, the Nazis emerged as the largest party in the Reichstag, with 37.3 percent of the total vote, while in November they suffered a minor setback when their percentage was reduced to 33.1 percent. However, by January 1933, Hitler had obtained the support of the army and sections of industry, and on 30 January he was constitutionally appointed chancellor by President Hindenburg.

Hitler talked of a "German Revolution" and promised that the Third Reich would last for 1,000 years. Once in power, therefore, he had no intention of becoming a prisoner of the governmental system, and he moved swiftly to establish and consolidate an absolute dictatorship. The Reichstag fire of 27 February 1933 provided Hitler with the pretext to begin consolidating the foundations of a totalitarian one-party state, and the "enabling laws" forced through the Reichstag legalized the regime's intimidating tactics and suspended civil rights in Germany. The extraordinary achievement of Hitler and the Nazis, compared with other fascist and authoritarian regimes of the period, was the speed with which they eliminated opposition. Within eighteen months of coming to power, Hitler had erased all forms of political opposition and incarcerated political opponents; within a year the quasi-autonomy of the regions had been crushed, and in June 1934 the potential threat posed by the strength and unreliability of the SA had been brutally eliminated in the "Night of the Long Knives." On 30 June, numerous SA leaders—on the pretext that they were preparing a coup against the government—were arrested by the Gestapo and SS and immediately shot. The Night of the Long Knives claimed, in all, around eighty-five victims, including Ernst Roehm, Gregor Strasser, and former chancellor General von Schleicher. The main beneficiary of the SA's loss of power was the SS, Hitler's praetorian guard, utterly loyal to the Fuehrer. The power shift within the regime had considerably enhanced Hitler's own position. For individuals and groups that remained, a process of *Gleichschaltung*—by which all political, economic, and cultural activities were forcibly assimilated within the state—ensured that a sufficient degree of conformity would sustain the regime in power until 1945. In August 1934, following the death of Hindenburg, Hitler further consolidated his own position by merging the offices of president and chancellor into the new office of Fuehrer. The "Party of the Fuehrer" would now be extended to become the "Fuehrer state."

By the time Hitler was appointed chancellor in 1933, the edifice of his *Weltanschauung* was in place. It had been constructed as a result of a series of formative and overlapping experiences. Hitler had successfully imposed on his party his racist vision and the need to remove Jews from Germany, as well as for territorial expansion in the East for a German *Herrenvolk*. It would be no exaggeration to use the metaphor of feudal anarchy to describe the system of government during the Third Reich. Invoking Hitler's name was like opening a door—a gateway to power. By delegating power downward but in a random fashion based on access to himself, Hitler was able to outflank the traditional bureaucracy of government and civil service. Provided that they did not threaten his own position as Fuehrer, Hitler allowed subordinates like Himmler, Goering, and Goebbels to mark out their own domains of arbitrary power while multiplying and duplicating offices to a chaotic degree. The traditional view of the Nazi regime as being a monolithic power structure has been largely rejected by later historians and replaced by a more critical, polycratic model, based on the shapelessness, lack of clear direction, and improvisation of Nazi rule. Nevertheless, in the years leading up to war, Hitler enjoyed considerable success both domestically and internationally.

A recurring theme in Nazi propaganda before 1939 was that Hitler was a man of peace, but one who was determined to recover German territories "lost" as a result of the Treaty of Versailles. The Nazi slogan *Deutschland Erwache!* was intended to be a rallying cry for a humiliated and weakened nation to rediscover its glorious past. The signing of the Reich Concordat with the Vatican on 20 July 1933 and the nonaggression treaty with Poland (1934) appeared initially to confirm that view. However, in October 1933, Hitler withdrew Germany from the League of Nations and the Geneva Disarmament Conference. Moreover, in the summer of 1934 he attempted to move into Austria but retreated when the Italian dictator Benito Mussolini sent troops to the frontier to safeguard Austria's independence. In March 1935, Hitler announced that Germany would introduce conscription, with the aim of building a peacetime army of thirty-six divisions, in direct violation of the Treaty of Versailles. From 1936, when Hitler ordered German troops to reoccupy the demilitarized Rhineland—in direct breach of the Versailles (1919) and Locarno (1925) treaties—until the Munich Settlement in 1938, which gave the Sudetenland to Germany, Hitler successfully carried out a series of audacious foreign policy coups that won him widespread support and popularity within Germany. When, in July 1936, civil war broke out in Spain, Hitler gave aid to General Franco. He sent his Luftwaffe to Spain to gain experience in what amounted to a dress rehearsal for World War II. In the Rome-Berlin Pact of October 1936, Germany and Italy joined in a common front against Bolshevism and the Western powers. In March 1938, Hitler achieved the *Anschluss* with Austria by engineering a crisis in Austro-German relations and then sending German troops across the frontier into Austria. The German invasion of Austria was Hitler's first move outside German territory in defiance of the Treaty of Versailles. Shortly afterward, a plebiscite was manipulated so effectively in both Germany and Austria that 99 percent of those voting supported Hitler's actions. Austria was relegated to a mere province of the Greater German Reich. "This is the proudest hour of my life," said Hitler. The concentration camps, the loss of trades union rights, the Nuremberg Laws against the Jews, the persecution of the churches and political dissidents were forgotten by many Germans in the euphoria of Hitler's territorial expansion and bloodless victories. Not only was Hitler now Europe's most powerful dictator but, in addition, he was regarded by his people as a consummate statesman, greater even than Otto von Bismarck (1815–1898).

By mid-1938, Hitler had sufficiently weakened potential opposition from conservative elites and could now initiate an expansionist foreign policy in pursuit of German hegemony. Having dismantled the Czechoslovakian state in March 1939, he took Poland as his next designated target. German grievances against Poland stemmed from the 1919 peace settlements and the loss of the Polish corridor, which now separated East Prussia from the rest of Germany; also, the former German port of Danzig had been made an "open city" under the jurisdiction of the League of Nations. Following the invasion of Czechoslovakia, Britain and France, perceiving Hitler as a persistent aggressor, announced that they would guarantee Poland's independence. Seeking to avoid a war on two fronts, Hitler signed a pact of nonaggression with Soviet Russia on 23 August, with secret clauses on the partition of Poland. When Germany invaded Poland on 1 September, the British government issued an ultimatum to Germany that expired on 3 September. First Britain and then France declared war on the same day, and thus World War II began.

Thenceforth, Hitler devoted his energies to a war that he had unleashed in the pursuit of "living space" (*Lebensraum*) for Germany and the domination of Europe. Hitler put on his soldier's tunic and announced that he would not remove it until Germany was triumphant. The astonishing advance by means of Blitzkrieg of German forces through the Low Countries culminated in the fall of France in June 1940. Intoxicated by the dazzling Blitzkrieg victories, Hitler refused to listen to the warnings of his military and economic advisers that in the long run the war could not be won. His next step was to subjugate Britain by means of aerial bombardment, to be followed by invasion in Operation Sea Lion. The anticipated surrender of Britain failed to materialize when the Royal Air Force prevented the Luftwaffe from securing aerial control over the English Channel. On 22 June 1941, having postponed indefinitely the invasion of Britain, Hitler took possibly the biggest gamble of his career and launched Operation Barbarossa, the invasion of the Soviet Union on a front from the Baltic to the Black Sea. Anticipating a similar victory in the East to that achieved in the West, Hitler had underestimated Russia's resources and resolve. The error of judgment was compounded by Germany's declaration of war on the United States after the Japanese attack on Pearl Harbor on 7 December 1941.

The Barbarossa campaign provided Hitler with the context for the "final solution to the Jewish Question," which had been under consideration since 1939. The leap into genocide was taken in the spring of 1941, when the planning of the invasion of Russia began to be worked out in detail. By late summer of 1941, the dynamics of a war of annihilation in the East and the fate of European Jewry became inexorably linked. At first the German armies carried all before them, encircling Leningrad and reaching within striking distance of Moscow, but by the beginning of 1942, Hitler had begun to lose control of the military situation. In October he prematurely proclaimed that the Soviet Union had been smashed and that she would never rise again. Underestimating the determination and resilience of the Russians, Hitler's final desperate assault on the Caucasus was a disastrous failure. The catastrophe before Moscow in December 1941 led him to dismiss his commander-in-chief, Field Marshall Walther von Brauchitsch (1881–1948), and many other commanders and assume personal control of all military operations himself. Convinced that his own general staff were vacillating—even treacherous—Hitler refused to countenance military defeat or strategic withdrawals and increasingly became prone to hysterical outbursts and misanthropic brooding. With the entry of the United States into the war in December 1941, Hitler's huge military gamble was effectively lost. But he was also engaged in another war—the systematic genocide of the Jews. Within a few months of the launch of Operation Barbarossa, what had been thitherto a hesitant and improvised campaign of mass murder was placed even more firmly under the central control of the SS, directed by Himmler and his deputy Reinhard Heydrich. In December 1941 the first killing installations using mobile "gas vans" were operating at Chelmo in the Warthegau (a part of western Poland annexed to the Reich). However, the "final solution" to the "Jewish question" was not implemented until the Wannsee Conference of 20 January 1942. By the end of March 1942 the mass extermination of Poland's Jewish population was under way in camps such as Belzec, Sobibor, and Treblinka. The most notorious extermination camp of all, Auschwitz-Birkenau, began its systematic mass gassing of Jews in June 1942.

As the extermination of Jews intensified, Germany's military fortunes began to plummet. General Erwin Rommel's defeat at El Alamein and subsequent loss of North Africa was overshadowed by defeat at Stalingrad, where General von Paulus's Sixth Army was cut off and surrendered to the Russians in February 1943. This military disaster was a devastating blow to Hitler and to his prestige in the eyes of the German people. Unwilling to concede defeat, he ordered a total mobilization of the German economy under Albert Speer, in a final effort to reverse the tide of war. Allied bombing, however, was having a telling effect on German industrial production and was beginning to undermine morale. A series of defeats after Stalingrad were followed on 6 June 1944 by Operation Overlord, the Allied invasion of France. Soon a million Allied troops were driving German forces back to their own frontier, while in the East, Soviet troops were advancing relentlessly. Convinced that the war was lost, and disillusioned with Hitler's leadership, a number of high military and civilian officials attempted to assassinate him on 20 July 1944. The plot failed, and Hitler took vicious revenge on the conspirators. He now retreated to his bunker under the Reich Chancellery in Berlin and was rarely seen in public again. Although Hitler was only fifty-six, his health had deteriorated for some time under the impact of drugs prescribed by his quack physician, Dr. Morel, but his resolve to fulfill his ideological objectives remained undiminished. The same hatred and fear that had led to mass extermination was now turned on his own people. In the last weeks of the war, Hitler's vindictive and senseless "Nero Order" for a "scorched earth" policy in the face of the advancing Allied armies descending on Berlin was prevented only by Albert Speer's successful sabotage. On 29 April 1945, Hitler married Eva Braun, his mistress for twelve years, and immediately afterward he dictated his last will and political testament, in which he justified his ideas and actions.

The translation into policy of Hitler's grandiose fixation with territorial expansion led to World War II and untold misery for millions. Hitler's all-consuming anti-Semitism resulted in a process of "cumulative radicalization" that started in Germany with intimidation and persecution and culminated in a network of extermination camps (all outside Germany in occupied Poland) and the slaughter of 6 million Jews (and more than a quarter of a million Gypsies). Similarly, his obsessive anti-Bolshevism culminating in his "war of annihilation" led to the deaths of some 3 million Russian POWs—mostly of disease and starvation. Hitler referred to himself as a man called by Providence to restore Germany to greatness, but he chose not to survive the defeat of his people and committed suicide in the bunker of the Reich Chancellery on 30 April 1945. At the end he complained that the German people had let him down, that they were not worthy of their destiny.

David Welch

See Also: INTRODUCTION; *ANSCHLUSS,* THE; "ANTI-" DIMENSION OF FASCISM, THE; ANTI-SEMITISM; ARCHITECTURE; ART; ARYANISM; AUSCHWITZ (-BIRKENAU); AUSTRIA; AUSTRO-HUNGARIAN EMPIRE/HABSBURG EMPIRE, THE; AUTOBAHNS, THE; AXIS, THE; BARBAROSSA, FREDERICK, HOLY ROMAN EMPEROR; BARBAROSSA, OPERATION; BATTLE OF BRITAIN, THE; BAYREUTH; BERLIN OLYMPICS, THE; BLITZKRIEG; BLOOD; BLOOD AND SOIL; BOLSHEVISM; BORMANN, MARTIN; BRÜNING, HEINRICH; CARLYLE, THOMAS; CATHOLIC CHURCH, THE; CHAMBERLAIN, HOUSTON STEWART; CHURCHILL, SIR WINSTON LEONARD SPENCER; COMBAT 18; CONCENTRATION CAMPS; CZECHOSLOVAKIA; *DEUTSCHLAND ERWACHE!* ("GERMANY AWAKE!"); DICTATORSHIP; DOENITZ, ADMIRAL KARL; *DRANG NACH OSTEN* ("DRIVE TO THE EAST"), THE; DREXLER, ANTON; EL ALAMEIN; ENABLING ACT, THE; EUGENICS; EXPANSIONISM; FÖRSTER-NIETZSCHE, ELISABETH; FRANCO Y BAHAMONDE, GENERAL FRANCISCO; FREDERICK II, THE GREAT; FREEDOM; GERMANNESS (*DEUTSCHHEIT*); GERMANY; GESTAPO, THE; *GLEICHSCHALTUNG;* GOEBBELS, (PAUL) JOSEPH; GOERING, HERMANN; HAMSUN, KNUT; HANFSTAENGL, ERNST FRANZ SEDGWICK ("PUTZI"); HAUSHOFER, KARL ERNST; HEALTH; HEARST, WILLIAM RANDOLPH; HEIDEGGER, MARTIN; *HEIL HITLER!;* HERO, THE CULT OF THE; HESS, RUDOLF; HEYDRICH, REINHARD; HIMMLER, HEINRICH; HINDENBURG, PAUL VON BENECKENDORFF UND VON; HITLER-STALIN PACT, THE; HOLOCAUST, THE; HOLY

ROMAN EMPIRE, THE; HUGENBERG, ALFRED VON; INDUS-
TRY; INFLATION; ITALY; JULY PLOT, THE; KREISAU CIRCLE,
THE; LIEBENFELS, JÖRG ADOLF JOSEF LANZ VON; LEADER
CULT, THE; LEAGUE OF NATIONS, THE; LUDENDORFF,
ERICH; LUEGER, KARL; LUFTWAFFE, THE; MARXISM; *MEIN
KAMPF;* MITFORD FAMILY, THE; MODERNITY; MÜLLER,
BISHOP LUDWIG; MUNICH AGREEMENT/PACT, THE; MU-
NICH (BEER-HALL) PUTSCH, THE; MUSSERT, ANTON ADRI-
AAN; MUSSOLINI, BENITO ANDREA; NATIONALISM;
NAZISM; NEO-NAZISM; NIETZSCHE, FRIEDRICH; NIGHT
OF THE LONG KNIVES, THE; NOVEMBER CRIMINALS/
NOVEMBERBRECHER, THE; NUREMBERG; NUREMBERG
LAWS, THE; NUREMBERG RALLIES, THE; PANGERMANISM;
PAPACY, THE; PAPEN, FRANZ VON; PEARL HARBOR; PIUS
XI, POPE; PIUS XII, POPE; POLAND AND NAZI GERMANY;
PROPAGANDA; RACIAL DOCTRINE; RACISM; RAUSCHNING,
HERMANN; REICHSTAG FIRE, THE; RELIGION; REVOLU-
TION; RIBBENTROP, JOACHIM VON; ROMA AND SINTI,
THE; SA, THE; SCHLEICHER, KURT VON; SCHÖNERER,
GEORG RITTER VON; SCIENCE; *SIEG HEIL!;* SLAVS, THE
(AND GERMANY); SOCIAL DARWINISM; SOCIALISM; SO-
VIET UNION, THE; SPANISH CIVIL WAR, THE; SPEER, AL-
BERT; SS, THE; STALIN, IOSIF VISSARIONOVICH; STALIN-
GRAD; STAUFFENBERG, CLAUS SCHENK GRAF VON;
STRASSER BROTHERS, THE; SUDETENLAND, THE;
SWASTIKA, THE; TECHNOLOGY; THIRD REICH, THE; TO-
TALITARIANISM; TRADITION; *UNTERMENSCHEN* ("SUBHU-
MANS"); VERSAILLES, THE TREATY OF; *VOLK, VÖLKISCH;*
WAFFEN-SS, THE; WAGNER, (WILHELM) RICHARD; WAG-
NER, WINIFRED; WALL STREET CRASH, THE; WANNSEE
CONFERENCE, THE; WARRIOR ETHOS, THE; WEHRMACHT,
THE; WEIMAR REPUBLIC, THE; *WELTANSCHAUUNG;*
WORLD WAR I; WORLD WAR II; YOUTH MOVEMENTS

References

Baynes, N. H., ed. 1942. *The Speeches of Adolf Hitler.* 2 vols.
   Oxford: Oxford University Press.
Bullock, A. 1962. *Hitler: A Study in Tyranny.* London: Penguin.
———. 1991. *Hitler and Stalin: Parallel Lives.* London:
   HarperCollins.
Carr, W. 1978. *Hitler: A Study in Personality and Politics.*
   London: Arnold.
Domarus, M., ed. 1990–2004. *Hitler: Speeches and Proclama-
   tions 1932–1945.* 4 vols. Wauconda, IL: Bolchazy-Carducci.
Fest, J. 1974. *Hitler.* London: Penguin.
Haffner, S. 1979. *The Meaning of Hitler.* London: Weidenfeld
   and Nicolson.
Hamann, B. 1999. *Hitler's Vienna: A Dictator's Apprenticeship.*
   Oxford: Oxford University Press.
Hitler, A. 1939. *Mein Kampf.* London: Hurst and Blackett.
Kershaw, I. 1998. *Hitler 1896–1936: Hubris.* London: Penguin.
———. 2000. *Hitler 1936–1945: Nemesis.* London: Penguin.
Rich, N. 1973–1974. *Hitler's War Aims: Ideology, the Nazi State,
   and the Course of Expansion.* New York: W. W. Norton.
Steinert, M. 1997. *Hitler: A Biography.* New York: W. W. Norton.
Trevor-Roper, H. 1947. *The Last Days of Hitler.* London:
   Macmillan.
Welch, D. 2001. *Hitler: Profile of a Dictator.* London: Routledge.
———. 2002. *The Third Reich: Politics and Propaganda.*
   London: Routledge.

HITLER-STALIN PACT, THE

Totally unexpected agreement between the German
Reich and the Soviet Union signed out of the blue on
23 August 1939 as a preliminary to Hitler's planned assault on Poland. Signatories to the pact were Soviet
commissar for foreign affairs Molotov and German foreign minister Joachim von Ribbentrop. According to
the terms of the pact, neither state would support any
third state in the event of its attacking one of them;
they would consult in matters of common interest; and
neither would have anything to do with any alliance of
powers aimed at the other. There was, in addition, a secret protocol that did not come to public notice until
1948: this divided Eastern Europe into German and
Soviet spheres and handed territorial gains to each state
in the areas between the spheres.

The pact was stunning for Germans and Soviets
alike. Hitler and Stalin had been conducting ideological warfare against each other throughout the 1930s.
Even for the most devoted Nazis it was very strange
that suddenly the Bolsheviks, whom they had been
trained to regard as bestial enemies of civilization,
should now be their allies. They had been schooled to
think not merely of the Soviets as political enemies but
also of the Slavs as nothing more than an inferior race
of *Untermenschen.* Of course Hitler never planned for
the pact to be permanent, and it is highly revelatory of
his Machiavellian political strategy. For him it was a
necessary evil, preventing any possible intervention
from the East during his planned military drive, starting
with the assault on Poland just over a week after the pact
was signed. It meant that Germany did not have to fight
on two fronts, as she had had to do in World War I.
Strangely, Stalin seems to have taken it seriously, since it
is well known that he was not merely highly reluctant to
prepare for a German invasion in 1941 but also, in fact,
reluctant to believe the early reports arriving from the
border when Operation Barbarossa was launched.

Cyprian Blamires

See Also: BARBAROSSA, OPERATION; BOLSHEVISM; CIVILIZA-
   TION; *DRANG NACH OSTEN* ("DRIVE TO THE EAST"), THE;
   GERMANY; HITLER, ADOLF; NAZISM; *LEBENSRAUM;*
   MACHIAVELLI, NICCOLÒ; NAZISM; POLAND AND NAZI
   GERMANY; RACIAL DOCTRINE; RIBBENTROP, JOACHIM
   VON; SLAVS, THE (AND GERMANY); SOVIET UNION, THE;
   STALIN, IOSIF VISSARIONOVICH; *UNTERMENSCHEN* ("SUB-
   HUMANS")

References

Read, A. 1998. *The Deadly Embrace: Hitler, Stalin and the Nazi-Soviet Pact, 1939–41.* London: Michael Joseph.

Vizulis, Izidors. 1990. *The Molotov-Ribbentrop Pact of 1939: The Baltic Case.* Westport, CT: Greenwood.

HITLER YOUTH, THE: *See* YOUTH MOVEMENTS: (GERMANY)
HLINKA, MGR. ANDREJ: *See* SLOVAKIA
HOLLAND: *See* NETHERLANDS, THE

HOLOCAUST (*"SHOAH"*), THE

Roughly translates as "burnt offering" from Hebrew via Greek and Latin to English; usually indicating the mass murder by the Nazis of 6 million Jews between 1941 and 1945. Additional terms to describe the murder of some 10 million "undesirables" under Nazi domination include the "final solution" (of the Jewish Question), genocide, extermination, and the *Shoah*. The murder of other "undesirable" groups, such as Jehovah's Witnesses or Roma and Sinti travelers, anti-Semitic pogroms undertaken by Nazi allies or collaborators, and the development of the "euthanasia" program in Germany and Poland between 1939 and 1941 have also all been historically understood as parts of the "Holocaust." From the Jewish perspective the genocidal attack on them by Hitler and his allies constituted a unique event because of its relation to the millennia-old history of Israel and her struggles with her enemies, and because of the biblical accounts of Israel's role in world history. The term *Holocaust* has a particular resonance for readers of the First (Old) Testament, from which it is derived. For Jews there can be only one "Holocaust."

Already in *Mein Kampf,* Hitler had given voice to his hatred for Jews, declaring: "If at the beginning of the [First] War and during the War twelve or fifteen thousand of these Hebrew corrupters of the people had been held under poison gas, as happened to hundreds of thousands of our very best German workers in the field, the sacrifices of millions at the front would not have been in vain." For some "intentionalists," these and other declarations of vehement anti-Semitism on the part of Nazi functionaries, primarily Hitler, consti-

tutes evidence—and perhaps even prophecy—of a long-term genocidal agenda. Still, the context for such early declarations during the Weimar Republic was political marginality for the Nazis, a fact subject to drastic change only after 1929. Thereafter, much of this racial venom was diluted in a bid for electoral success, and the courting of more mainstream conservative groups in business, the churches, and other political parties ensued. From 1933, however, much of the Nazis' anti-Semitic rhetoric was reflected in actions initiated by the Third Reich: the first anti-Jewish boycotts took place on 1 April 1933; the 1935 Nuremberg Laws defined Jews as "aliens" in Germany; and pogroms on the night of 9–10 November 1938, called *Kristallnacht,* resulted in widespread destruction of property, scores of deaths, and the internment of many thousands of Jews in concentration camps. Given actions like these, some historians understand the Holocaust to have commenced with Hitler's assumption of power on 30 January 1933, reflecting the intent of Nazi elites (and, more contentiously, supported by many "non-Nazi" sectors of the German populace). In contrast, other scholars have emphasized the technological and bureaucratic underpinnings of German society at the time; the intrinsic radicalization and opportunism of the Nazi regime; and the competitive institutional structure of governance (relating to ideas of "social Darwinism" or "working toward the Fuehrer")—suggesting that the internal functioning of the Nazi state was more decisive in the onset of the Holocaust than any underlying Nazi worldview. This perspective, variously called "functionalist" or "structuralist," attributes a central importance to the progressively extreme Nazi policies, expansionism, and fractious organizational features—especially during World War II—rather than the earlier writings and ideological aims of Nazi functionaries. To some degree, the fruitful "intentionalist-functionalist" debate has abated in favor of what has been termed "moderate functionalism"—that is, a recognition that earlier Nazi intentions may have prefigured later actions by perpetrators of the Holocaust, without necessarily meaning that such objectives demonstrate an unalterable program or ideological blueprint.

The installation of the Third Reich in 1933 marked a decisive, arguably revolutionary shift in treatment of those defined as outside the *Volksgemeinschaft.* That is exemplified above all by persecution of Jews as the 1930s progressed: first marginalized and actively humiliated, their initial experience of painful and humiliating harassment then gave way to an active campaign of elimination from German society. Other minority groups to suffer under Nazism—in ways including the imposition of enforced sterilization and internment in the growing networks of concentration camps—were "asocials," Jehovah's Witnesses, Eastern Europeans (especially the Russian "Asiatic horde"), and travelers (or Gypsies). However, the first group to be systematically targeted for destruction were German asylum patients considered "useless eaters" in the increasingly intolerant, pseudo-scientific targeting of the most vulnerable members in German society.

The so-called Euthanasia Campaign, labeled "T-4" for secrecy by participating Nazi doctors and bureaucrats, has sometimes been viewed as the onset of the Holocaust. In early 1939, Philippe Bouhler, the head of the chancellery of the Fuehrer (KdF), devised a scheme whereby institutionalized German children were murdered if judged to be "life unworthy of life" by doctors. By August, this program had been extended to mentally and physically disabled adults, with authorization from Hitler in early October backdated to 1 September 1939. By 1941, at least 70,000 victims had perished in asylums–cum–gas chambers at the institutions of Brandenburg-Gorden Hartheim, Sonnenstein, Bernberg, Hadamar, and Grafeneck. But whereas no directive by Hitler in the wider development of mass murder exists—especially sanctioning genocide against European Jewry undertaken in 1942—a number of precursors found in the Euthanasia Campaign were nevertheless extended to the later industrialized destruction of human beings in extermination centers. For example, shared attributes encompass: attempted secrecy and deception of victims; interagency cooperation and bureaucratic coordination by the Nazis (for identification, transportation, and so on); criteria for selections and mass gassings; collaboration and examination by "ordinary" perpetrators, as well as "unfitness for work" and perpetual humiliation for victims; pillage and disposal of bodies through mass graves or cremation—in short, increasingly effective methods for the assembly-line production of death.

The onslaught against Poland that launched World War II marked an intensification and brutalization of conditions for designated enemies of the Nazi state. From the start, the cultural differences and the sheer number of Jews (some 2 million), as well as progressively unrestrained anti-Semitism, all meant that Nazi policy toward Polish Jewry and other "undesirables" from September 1939 acted as an important catalyst in the development of the Holocaust. The radicalization of population policies geared toward Aryan *Lebensraum* together with the Third Reich's effective colonization of Poland also suggests a policy of "palin-

genetic ultranationalism" in autocratic practice: the identification and the ghettoization of Jews, the transfer of ethnic Germans westward, and, increasingly, the murder of those declared *Untermenschen,* or "subhumans." By the end of 1939, perhaps 50,000 Poles had been murdered, and by the spring of 1940, the Eimann and Lange battalions of Heinrich Himmler's SS had murdered thousands more asylum patients in Poland. Indeed, between the autumn of 1939 and the summer of 1941, Poland became the testing ground for the implementation of industrialized genocide; in the following years roughly 3 million Poles and a further 3 million Polish Jews died under Nazi occupation. As the military conquests of 1940 and 1941 over France and the Low Countries, as well as Norway, Greece, and Yugoslavia, consolidated Nazism's domination over much of Europe, grandiose designs for a murderous millennial "New Order" under German hegemony became steadily clearer, as indicated by an SS handbook of 1941: "The *new ordering of the space of the East* not only affects the *German-Polish problem* and that caused by other ethnic minorities but, because in the East Jewry can be found in its most concentrated form, also raises the *Solution to the Jewish problem*" (Dwork and van Pelt 1996, 22).

Particularly in recent historiography, 1941 is usually recognized as the watershed year in genocidal preparation and initiation of the Holocaust; thereafter, Nazi willingness to murder millions in an ever more comprehensive attempt to "solve" self-imposed problems is unmistakable. With the onset of an ideological war of annihilation against the "Judeo-Bolshevik menace" in the Soviet Union on 22 June 1941, previous "solutions" to socioracial obstacles impeding the construction of a pure "Aryan" community—persecution, ghettoization, enforced emigration, and ultimately, selective killings—were immediately superseded by mass shooting. Four Einsatzgruppen units (special mobile formations whose job it was to implement the liquidation program in occupied territories) operating from the Baltic in the north to the Ukraine in the south, each initially comprising no more than a thousand men, were primarily responsible for the execution of some 1.5 million noncombatants, especially Jews, in a steadily expanding program of murder. In three respects, this was generally in keeping with the Holocaust as a whole. First, the staggering number of victims is indicative of an operation centrally planned from Berlin, substantiated by meticulous Einsatzgruppen reports, as well as vital documents such as the commissar order, essentially sanctioning military warfare on civilian populations in Eastern Europe. Second, the Einsatzgruppen's steadily growing range of targets, initially focused on partisans and Jewish men, but by late summer 1941 extending to, principally, Jewish women and children of all ages. Finally, like the Holocaust as a whole, the attempted secrecy, bureaucratic efficiency, radicalizing techniques and agendas, fragmentation of control and responsibility below Hitler, and, above all, sole consideration for the perpetrators were all evident in Einsatzgruppen killing operations in 1941; they later constituted features replicated on a larger scale in the extermination centers, overwhelmingly located in Poland.

As to the last of these points, the profile of Einsatzgruppen shooters proved notably decisive in the development of the Holocaust. Sensitive to the psychological burdens of shooting innocent people in the nape of the neck day after day, by the autumn of 1941, Nazi planners looked for a better method of systematically exterminating state enemies—again particularly European Jewry (a decision most likely taken in October 1941 and later streamlined at the 20 January 1942 Wannsee Conference, a meeting chaired by Heydrich and organized by his deputy, Eichmann). This was ultimately addressed through the reassignment of more than ninety "T-4" personnel and the widespread adoption of poison gas for killing—first in mobile gas vans designed to murder scores at once with carbon monoxide (used earlier in the "Euthanasia Campaign"), then in extermination camps for hundreds of simultaneous victims through purpose-built carbon monoxide death chambers at the Aktion Reinhard death camps: Belzec, Sobibor, and Treblinka. Finally, the pesticide Zyklon-B was used almost exclusively at Auschwitz. These camps and the facilities accompanying them—death chambers and crematoria, enormous compounds and human vivisections by doctors as well as guards, horrific conditions and nigh-impossible work quotas for those few not "selected" for murder—were collectively responsible for about 2.8 million victims in these four main killing institutions from the spring of 1942 to the winter of 1944. The extermination centers at Chelmo, Majdanek, and elsewhere are frequently viewed as emblematic of the process understood as the Holocaust, yet millions more victims were shot, and many hundreds of thousands of others died through lethal injection, starvation, disease, undocumented killings, and the so-called "death marches" of 1945 toward Germany at the end of World War II. Reflecting this, the postwar Nuremberg Trials adopted legal principles—indeed, the term *genocide* itself—to prosecute a wide range of perpetrators responsible for the planning, management, and operation of the Holocaust.

Energetic discussion continues between scholars over the progression and direction of the Holocaust, especially regarding the intent, evolution, implementation, and bureaucratic depth of population policies undertaken by the Third Reich. Such discussion is part of a wider debate among historians about how to conceptualize events in Europe before and during World War II. While the historical evidence remains indisputable, contentious historiographical issues include the precise dating of the moment when the decision was formally taken by the Nazi leadership to proceed with the "final solution"; the dating of the onset of the Holocaust more generally (the start of the Third Reich in 1933? the invasion of Poland in 1939? the 1941 invasion of the USSR?); the depth and ideological commitment of "ordinary" perpetrators; the extent of European collaboration and resistance, both inside and outside the camps; and the classification of genocide (for example, should non-Jews—such as the disabled, homosexuals, Roma and Sinti travelers, Eastern Europeans, and political opponents—be included together or separately among victims of the Holocaust?). Yet, as a group, none of these historians dispute the essence of the Holocaust: Nazi "racial imperialism" (Browning 2004) directly culminated in violent death for millions of targeted religious, ethnic, and sociopolitical groups, the majority of those European Jews. Disputing this actuality is left to advocates of so-called Holocaust revisionism—frequently a fig leaf for anti-Semitism—fascist ideologues, a particular racist philosophy, or those indifferent to historical evidence.

Insofar as it was planned solely by the German Nazis and implemented by themselves and their allies, the Holocaust cannot be considered a defining feature of generic fascism. Anti-Semitic measures were implemented in Italy only toward the end of the 1930s, after Mussolini had been in power for more than fifteen years, and they did not form a part of the political platform on which he originally campaigned, nor of his program when he came to power. It appears that his acceptance of anti-Semitic ideology was a by-product of Mussolini's later desire to cooperate with the increasingly powerful Nazi state, whose expansionism he had earlier managed to block. It was only under the Salò Republic that Italian participation in the Holocaust developed, and by that point Mussolini had become little more than a puppet of the Germans. The Holocaust was an outcome of the racial doctrine that was one of the distinguishing marks that set German Nazism apart from Italian Fascism, rather than a manifestation of generic fascism.

Matt Feldman

References

Arad, Yitzhak, Israel Gutman, and Abraham Margaliot, eds. 1999. *Documents on the Holocaust.* London: University of Nebraska Press.

Bartov, Omer, ed. 2000. *The Holocaust: Origins, Implementation, Aftermath.* Routledge: London.

Browning, Christopher. 2004. *The Origins of the Final Solution.* London: William Heinemann.

Dwork, Deborah, and Robert Jan van Pelt. 1996. *Auschwitz: 1270 to the Present.* New York: W. W. Norton.

Gilbert, Martin, ed. 2002. *The Routledge Atlas of the Holocaust.* London: Routledge.

Lacqueur, Walter, ed. 2001. *The Holocaust Encyclopedia.* London: Yale University Press.

Lanzmann, Claude. 2003. *Shoah.* (DVD box set of four discs, directed by Claude Lanzmann, unrated; region 1 only.)

Lewy, Guenter. 2001. *Nazi Persecution of the Gypsies.* Oxford: Oxford University Press.

Longerich, Peter. 2003. *The Unwritten Order: Hitler's Role in the Final Solution.* Stroud: Tempus.

Tec, Nechama. 1986. *When the Light Pierced the Darkness: Christian Rescue of Jews in Nazi-occupied Poland.* New York: OUP.

HOLOCAUST DENIAL

Holocaust denial is the most radical aspect of historical revisionism, which tries to rewrite the history of National Socialism in order to shed positive light on that regime in Germany. The denial of the National-Socialist mass murder of Jews is inseparably linked with neo-Nazism, but it has developed strong connections to the Islamist movement as well. The political aim of internationally active Holocaust denial is defamation of the Jews and the subversion of the state of Israel. In the late 1940s the first so-called revisionist books were published in France by Maurice Bardèche and Paul Rassinier, the latter becoming the ideological ancestor of the later generations of "revisionists" who first tried to minimize the extent of National Socialist crimes by doubting the number of victims of the Holocaust. In the late 1970s, alongside growing scientific and public interest in the history of Nazism, "revisionists" began to propagate the denial of the Holocaust as a whole. They produced a great number of publications, most of them camouflaged as the products of a "scientific" concern for historical truth. All of this is based on a rabid anti-Semitism and belief in a worldwide Jewish conspiracy, for it is supposed that documents, witness statements, and concentration camp sites have been tampered with and falsified in order to blackmail the German people into paying enormous sums of indemnification to Israel and the Jews, to force the world to accept the state of Israel, and to defame National Socialism.

Although the first publications on Holocaust denial appeared in Europe, later on the most important centers developed in the United States and Canada, and only recently again in Great Britain, because of the legal situation in those states which does not ban Holocaust denial by law, as do other European countries. Holocaust denial also has a following in Eastern Europe and in the Arab world, where it is explicitly used to question Israel's right of existence.

"Revisionism" and Holocaust denial have developed their own way of arguing. The deniers pick up single details in historical records that are either disputed or actually wrong, and on the basis of such matters of detail they declare the whole of the history of the Holocaust to be a fake. While the first "revisionists" simply invented their own history, the representatives of Holocaust denial often use actual historical documents and scientific literature that they quote either incorrectly or out of context—as the British writer David Irving does. Since the late 1980s, a new kind of pseudoscientific argumentation has been trying to make use of popular belief in the precision of the natural sciences. Typically, it is claimed that it was technically impossible for the Nazis to have murdered people in the gas chambers in the manner stated by official accounts, or that chemical tests have proven that no poisonous gas was used in the relevant buildings in the former extermination camps.

Brigitte Bailer-Galanda

See Also: ANTI-SEMITISM; BARDECHE, MAURICE; CANADA; CONSPIRACY THEORIES; FREY, DR. GERHARD; *HISTORIK-ERSTREIT*, THE; HOLOCAUST, THE; INSTITUTE FOR HISTORICAL REVIEW, THE; IRVING, DAVID JOHN CAWDELL; KÜHNEN, MICHAEL; MIDDLE EAST, THE; NAZISM; NEO-NAZISM; PALESTINE; POSTWAR FASCISM; *PROTOCOLS OF THE ELDERS OF ZION, THE;* REMER, OTTO-ERNST; SCHÖN-HUBER, FRANZ; UNITED STATES, THE (POSTWAR)

References
Lipstadt, Deborah E. 1993. *Denying the Holocaust: The Growing Assault on Truth and Memory.* New York: Free Press.
Vidal-Naquet, Pierre. 1992. *Assassins of Memory: Essays on the Denial of the Holocaust.* New York: Columbia University Press.

HOLY ROMAN EMPIRE, THE

From the eleventh century onward, the official title of the German kingdom or empire that existed from 911 to 1806 and that saw itself as the lawful successor to the Roman Empire; its earlier period was much venerated by certain Nazi ideologues. Alfred Rosenberg recalled that Emperor Otto I (936–973) had been the founder of a "Germanic national church" and had brought the papacy into subjection to himself: "The German Emperor dragged the Papacy out of the mire, raised the Church to honour and ennobled her servants." Rosenberg saw in the Saxon lords the forerunners of the Germanic colonization of territories to the east, which was subsequently driven forward by the German Knightly Orders. A new "German Order" must arise to create a "Holy Germanic Reich of the German nation through absolute obedience to a Germanic leader" and "must define the type of the German of the future." The most bizarre cult of the Saxon lords as colonizers of the East was fostered by Heinrich Himmler, who developed an effusive reverence for King Henry I (919–936) as "the Civilizer of the barbarian Slav peoples." In July 1937 he had the bones of Henry I in Quedlinburg exhumed and solemnly reburied, proposing that he himself be eventually buried next to the honored ruler. Under the influence of astrologers and *völkisch* fantasists close to the SS, whose advice he increasingly sought, Himmler eventually saw himself as the "reincarnation" of Henry I, who was to complete his work of the subjection of the East. In a pretentious celebration of the 1,000th anniversary of Henry's death on 2 May 1936 in Quedlinburg, Himmler celebrated him as forerunner of German expansion to the East and representative of a powerful rule that did not tolerate the Church getting involved in political events. Henry I as founder of an empire had never forgotten "that the strength of the German people lies in purity of blood."

In a speech of 13 September 1937, Hitler stated that in 1933 "the Germanic Reich of the German nation" had been established, and said that his intention was to unite all countries of Germanic race, even Scandinavia and The Netherlands, under one leadership. While admiring the achievement of the great Frankish emperor Charlemagne, his "cultural creativity," his powers of organization, and his renunciation of the freedom of the individual, Hitler reproached the Medieval Holy Roman emperors in general for having been oriented exclusively toward the south and for failing to pursue an *Ostpolitik* comparable to his own.

Markus Hattstein
(translated by Cyprian Blamires)

See Also: BLOOD; COLONIALISM; *DRANG NACH OSTEN* ("DRIVE TO THE EAST"), THE; EXPANSIONISM; GERMANIC RELIGION; GERMANNESS (*DEUTSCHHEIT*); HIMMLER, HEINRICH; HITLER, ADOLF; IMPERIALISM; *MEIN KAMPF;* MOELLER VAN DEN BRUCK, ARTHUR; NORDIC SOUL, THE; RACIAL DOCTRINE; ROME; ROSENBERG, ALFRED; SLAVS, THE (AND GERMANY); SS, THE; THIRD REICH, THE; TRADITION; WARRIOR ETHOS, THE

References
Hahn, H. J. 1995. *German Thought and Culture: From the Holy Roman Empire to the Present Day.* Manchester: Manchester University Press.
Heer, F. 1995. *The Holy Roman Empire.* London: Phoenix Giants.

HOLY SEE, THE: *See* PAPACY, THE

HOMOSEXUALITY

The attitude of fascist movements and regimes was extremely hostile toward (male) homosexuality, and in the 1930s both Italian Fascism and German National Socialism carried out persecutions of homosexuals that, in the latter case, resulted in the murder of tens of thousands. Fascist attitudes toward homosexuality must be seen in the context of a climate of generally fierce social disapproval and the existence of legislation criminalizing homosexual acts in most European and North American states. Thus the German Nazis were able to use Article 175 of the existing criminal code as an adequate tool with which to persecute homosexuals. It should also be said that both major fascist regimes ignored lesbianism: presumably, like Queen Victoria, they thought that it did not exist. The Nazis publicly condemned homosexuality even before the "Roehm Putsch" of July 1934: indeed, as early as May 1933, National Socialist students ransacked Magnus Hirschfeld's Institute for Sexual Research, and it was closed down. But the fact that SS death squads sent to murder SA leaders for allegedly threatening rebellion against Hitler found Roehm and some of his lieutenants in bed with other men undoubtedly intensified Nazi resolve to eliminate the "abominable vice." The roots of Nazi hostility lay in racial ideology, in the belief that homosexuals were a threat to the health and strength of the race because of their failure to carry out their reproductive duties and the danger that their behavior would spread and subvert the racial virility of other men. They were thus counted among other racial and social "undesirables," like Jews, Gypsies, inveterate criminals, and political opponents of Nazism.

The legal basis of the Nazi persecution of homosexuals was Article 175 of the criminal code criminalizing homosexual behavior, which was eventually reinforced by additions to bring any behavior that could be remotely described as "criminal indecency" within its remit. Repeated raids on public places and private homes led to the roundup of many homosexuals in successive waves after 1933. The intensity of Nazi antihomosexual activity may be deduced from the statistics: whereas between 1931 and 1933 only 2,319 convictions had been obtained in the courts under the terms of Article 175, between 1937 and 1939 there were ten times as many (Heger 1986, 7–9). In 1936, Himmler set up a Reich Central Office for Combating Homosexuality and Abortion. Men who were identified as homosexuals, even if not convicted in the courts, were sent to concentration camps. Homosexuals were forced to wear a pink triangle badge and suffered forced labor, inadequate dietary and sanitary conditions, beatings, and death. In 1936, Himmler made a speech pledging to "eliminate" homosexuality from Germany altogether, and in 1942 the death penalty was introduced for homosexual acts.

Fascist Italy had no law criminalizing homosexuality, and an attempt to introduce sanctions against it in the Rocco Code of Criminal Law in 1932 foundered on the argument that such a provision would only "publicize" homosexuality. There was a belief common in Fascist circles that Italians were naturally "manly" and that, consequently, homosexuality hardly existed. Nevertheless, Fascist officials saw the homosexual "threat" in very similar terms to their Nazi counterparts: long before the introduction of the Racial Laws in 1938, homosexuality was classed alongside abortion and birth control as a serious threat to the health of the Italian people. The result was that the persecution of homosexuals was fairly constant from the mid-1930s onward and generally intensified at the beginning of the war (though its level varied from province to province, some prefects—that is, provincial governors—and police chiefs being more zealous than others). Sent into "internal exile," some homosexuals died of poor diet and health conditions on the Tremiti islands. There is clear evidence that Mussolini, as minister of the interior, knew of the police campaign against homosexuals and approved of it.

Modern far-right movements have sometimes echoed the hostility of interwar fascists to homosexuality, and that attitude can be found in virulent form in the lyrics of neo-Nazi rock bands. However, they have also been liable to divide over the issue, which has been known to cause splintering of far-right factions, as in the case of neo-Nazi Michael Kühnen, whose overtures toward homosexuals led to his marginalization within his own movement.

John Pollard

See Also: ASOCIALS; CONCENTRATION CAMPS; FAMILY, THE; FORCED LABOR; GERMANY; HEALTH; HIMMLER, HEINRICH; HOLOCAUST, THE; ITALY; KÜHNEN, MICHAEL; LAW; MUSSOLINI, BENITO ANDREA; NIGHT OF THE LONG KNIVES, THE; POSTWAR FASCISM; RACIAL DOCTRINE; ROCCO, ALFREDO; ROEHM, ERNST; SA, THE; SEXUALITY; SS, THE; WARRIOR ETHOS, THE

References

Ebner, Michael R., 2004. "The Persecution of Homosexual Men under Fascism." In *Gender, Family and Sexuality: The Private Sphere in Italy, 1860–1945*, edited by P. Wilson. Basingstoke: Palgrave-Macmillan.

Heger, H. 1986. *The Men with the Pink Triangle*. London: Gay Men's Press.

Lautman, R. 1998. "The Pink Triangle: Homosexuals as 'Enemies of the State.'" In *The Holocaust and History: The Unknown, the Disputed and the Re-examined*, edited by Michael Berenbaum and Abraham J. Pike. Indianapolis: Indiana University Press.

HONOR: *See EHRE*

HOORNAERT, PAUL (1888–1944)

Leader of Légion Nationale/Nationaal Legioen (LN/NL), a Belgian fascist militia (1923–1941). During World War I, Hoornaert, a lawyer, served as lieutenant in the Belgian army. He opposed the democratization of Belgium, the organized labor movement, and Flemish nationalism. In 1925 he took over the leadership of the LN/NL, which had a few thousand members throughout Belgium. He was hostile to Léon Degrelle and his party Rex, which he condemned as demagogic and lacking in Belgian patriotism. After the German invasion in May 1940, the LN/NL was tolerated initially by the occupation authorities but eventually banned in August 1941. In June 1941, Hoornaert joined the Légion Belge (Belgian Legion), a resistance movement with an extreme-right ideology. In 1942 he was arrested and imprisoned in a German concentration camp, where he suffered great hardship and finally died on 2 August 1944.

Bruno de Wever

See Also: BELGIUM; CONCENTRATION CAMPS; DEGRELLE, LEON; DEMOCRACY; GERMANY; NATIONALISM; REXISM; WORLD WAR I; WORLD WAR II

References
L'Académie Royale des Sciences. 1886–1986. "Hoornaert, Paul." Pp. 423–425 in *Biographie Nationale,* vol. 35. Bruxelles: Académie Royale des Sciences, des Lettres et des Beaux-Arts de Belgique.
Rees, Philip. 1990. *Biographical Dictionary of the Extreme Right since 1890.* Hemel Hempstead: Harvester Wheatsheaf.
Willequet, J. 1986. *La Belgique sous la botte: résistances et collaborations, 1940–1945.* Paris: Editions universitaires.

HORTHY DE NAGYBÁNYA, MIKLÓS (1868–1957)

Right-wing naval officer and governor of Hungary between 1920 and 1944, Horthy came from a well-to-do family from the northeastern part of Hungary. After finishing naval academy he quickly advanced in rank and served in World War I as a captain of various battleships. He was appointed minister of military affairs in the Károlyi government. In 1921 the national assembly elected him to the position of regent with the proviso that the monarchy stayed intact, but Horthy blocked the attempt by Charles V to regain his throne. In 1926 he allowed the formation of a parliament with both upper and lower houses. Not being of royal descent he was not allowed to give noble titles, and for that reason in 1921 he created his own brand of Order of Heroes (*Vitézi Rend*) for those serving in World War I. He extended his power in 1942 when he forced parliament to nominate his own son to the post of deputy governor. From a gentry family himself, he used the upper classes and big business to support his policies. He managed to be on good terms with Italy and Germany, but although he initially entered the war on the side of the Axis, in 1943 he started to take steps to withdraw Hungary from hostilities. At the same time, he was wholly indifferent when the parliament passed anti-Jewish laws leading eventually to mass deportations of Jews in May–June 1944. When the German army occupied Hungary on 19 March 1944, Horthy was pressured to nominate a Nazi-friendly government. After the Arrow Cross takeover, Horthy was forced to resign and was taken to Germany. He was a witness at the Nuremberg Trials but was then allowed to emigrate and lived until his death in Portugal.

László Kurti

See Also: ANTI-SEMITISM; ARROW CROSS, THE; AXIS, THE; GERMANY; HOLOCAUST, THE; HUNGARY; ITALY; MONARCHY; NUREMBERG TRIALS, THE; WORLD WAR I

References
Horthy, Miklós. 1956. *Regent of Hungary.* London: Hutchinson.
Kállay, Miklós. 1954. *Hungarian Premier.* New York: Cambridge University Press.

HUGENBERG, ALFRED (1865–1951)

Industrialist and chairman of the German Nationalist People's Party who helped Hitler to gain power but who very soon became alienated from the Nazi regime. Hugenberg was one of the founders of the Pangerman League and in 1894 was involved in a plan to settle Germans in Poznan, Poland, on land purchased from

Poles. He held the chairmanship of the board of Krupp between 1909 and 1918 and in the 1920s became the leading German media magnate, with a stable of newspapers and publishing companies under his ownership. He opposed parliamentarism and the Weimar Republic constitution and eventually came round to supporting Hitler, who in return made him minister of agriculture in 1933, but he resigned within months.

Cyprian Blamires

See Also: BOURGEOISIE, THE; FINANCE; GERMANY; INDUSTRY; KRUPP VON BOHLEN UND HALBACH, ALFRIED; NATIONALISM; PANGERMANISM; PARLIAMENTARISM; POLAND AND NAZI GERMANY; WEIMAR REPUBLIC, THE

Reference
Leopold, John A. 1977. *Alfred Hugenberg: The Radical Nationalist Campaign against the Weimar Republic.* New Haven: Yale University Press.

HUMAN RIGHTS: *See* **ABSTRACTION**
HUMANITARIANISM: *See* **ABSTRACTION**
HUNGARISM: *See* **ARROW CROSS, THE; HUNGARY; SZÁLASI, FERENC**

Hungarian Ferenc Szálasi formed the Hungarian National Socialist Party in 1937 in conscious imitation of German Nazism. It was one of a number of fascistic movements in interwar Hungary. (Time Life Pictures/Getty Images)

HUNGARY

The roots of Hungarian fascism were firmly anchored to the collapse of the Austro-Hungarian monarchy, with its disillusioned military officer corps, and to the counter-revolution following 1918. This military class—consisting both of career officers and aristocratic families—was entrusted with restoring Hungary's greatness and racial purity. Starting in 1919, they organized several racist and anti-Semitic associations, among which the most important were: MOVE (the Hungarian Association of National Defense), Awakening Hungarians (Ébredo Magyarok), the Irredentist Association, the Association for Territorial Defense, the Hungarian Society for the Defense of Racial Purity (Magyar Tudományos Fajvédo Egyesület), the Etelköz Association (or EX, for short), the Society of the Double-Cross (Kettos-Kereszt Szövetség), and the Christian National Association's secret group "Resurrection" (Feltámadás). The political socialization of Hungarian youth took an extreme form in Levente (Youth Associa-

tion), a paramilitary group able to retain weapons and legalized to train Hungarian youth in military affairs. Both MOVE and Levente were led by the anti-Semitic officer-turned-politician Endre. MOVE was rumored to be planning a coup d'etat in 1937. In 1943 a Race Defenders' College opened under its tutelage, an institute that was connected to the racist National Jewish Research Institute.

The first National Socialist party, Nemzeti Szocialista Párt, was founded by two minor figures—Béla Szász and Miklós Csomós—in 1928. They did not use the swastika but the double-cross and a sword; they did, however, import the green shirt as a party uniform to Hungary. Their slogan was "Courage" (*bátorság*), a play on the greeting of the Social Democrats (*barátság*—friendship). Szász's party was fused with Zoltán Meskó's National Socialist Agrarian and Workers Party in 1933. By the early 1930s there were in fact four fascist parties in Hungary extolling national socialist ideology: the National Socialist Agrarian and Workers Party; the Hungarian National Socialist Workers' Party (1931–1936), led by Zoltán Böszörmény; and the Hungarian National Socialist Party (1933–1938), led by an aristocrat, Count Sándor Festetics. Another aristocrat who was converted to national socialism was Count Fidél Pálffy (1895–1946), who in 1933 founded the Hungarian National Socialist Party, a party that managed to operate under various guises until 1944 but that also utilized the arrow cross as its symbol. This movement was a comprehensive adaptation of the German model, with its own storm troops, SS, and a youth organization. In 1934 the three leaders (Meskó, Pálffy, Festetics) formed a directorium and agreed to adopt the brown shirt and the arrow cross as an accepted symbol.

After meeting Hitler in Germany in 1931, Böszörmény published propaganda extolling the virtues of national socialism. Among his favored ideas were the return of Hungary's borders to their pre-1918 forms, the formation of a "healthy" Hungarian middle class, the limitation of the size of large landholding to 500 hectares, the designation of citizens as "fellow citizen," and the restriction of citizenship to those of Aryan racial stock. In the propaganda of the 1930s, Böszörmény was referred to as "the Hungarian Hitler." The fascist parties' programs closely followed that of Hitler's—racism, anti-Semitism, and militarization—but with an added flavor combining a Hungarian extreme form of nationalism infused with mystic Christian fundamentalism. None of these parties were able to garner enough votes during the 1935 national elections to enter parliament. They were, however, successful in preparing the entrance of Ferenc Szálasi, the only fascist leader with a vision for world domination under the leadership of the Hungarian people. He had already in 1933 published his "Plan for the Construction of the Hungarian State," an ideological program followed two years later by "Goal and Demands." Szálasi planned a complete makeover of the Hungarian state in three years that would be followed by a systematically planned economy. In "Goal and Demands" he proposed the expulsion of all Jews from Hungary and the creation of the Hungarian United Lands, a loose confederation of all pre-1918 territories. In 1935, Szálasi formed his own Party of National Will (Nemzeti Akarat Pártja, NAP), together with Sándor Csia, a fellow fascist. Szálasi launched his Hungarist movement in 1936 based on nationalism, mystic Aryan-Turanian racism combined with anti-Semitism, Christian fundamentalism, and the leadership principle. With all this, it is "perfectly clear that his real preoccupation [was] with the place of Hungary in the world" (Macartney 1957, 161). But that meant not Hungary as she was, but the Great Hungarian dream-state with Magyars as the dominant race leading the others.

Szálasi and Gyula Gömbös (his fellow extreme nationalist, who became prime minister in 1932) were no great friends; the former did not trust Gömbös fully and decided not to run for a seat with his help during the 1935 elections. One year later, at the local elections, Szálasi and other fascist leaders were all defeated at the polls. The government was able to mount a successful, but not very efficient, attack on the extreme right, whose main movements were all disbanded. None of the leaders, however, received jail sentences. But by the fall of 1937 a new and more extreme leadership appeared with such names as László Endre and Kálmán Hubay. With them Szálasi formed another party: the Hungarian National Socialist Party. Their slogan was: God, Homeland, Nation, and "Hungarianness." Endre successfully mounted a political campaign and in 1938 was elected to the post of county deputy governor of Pest county. At this time Hungary's German minorities joined Szálasi's movement: their leader, Ferenc Rothen—a spy for the German Foreign Ministry—became Szálasi's foreign policy advisor. When the Hungarian National Socialist Party was illegalized, new factions formed; by August it reappeared as the Arrow Cross Hungarist Movement, a party supported by the smaller but equally extreme National Front.

Szálasi claimed that his Hungarist idea was not anti-Semitic but "a-Semitic": simply disregarding the Jewish people. He held the view that Hungary and the Hungarians were especially well situated to be a leading race in the world. In order to achieve this, all colonial and imperialistic great powers—the "Judeo-plutocracies" of England, France, the United States, and the Soviet Union—had to be dissolved. Instead, the Latin, German, Slavic, Islamic, and Hungarist political nations should be allowed to form their own *Lebensraum*.

By the late 1930s the extremists were openly organizing rallies and publishing pamphlets and newspapers. In early 1939 they planned a bombing of the Jewish synagogue on Dohány Street in Budapest. Figures like László Baky and Emil Kovarcz, both officers in the gendarmerie, were also involved with the Hungarist Movement. Although the rank-and-file members were workers, lower-middle-class merchants, and public servants, aristocrats such as Lajos Széchenyi and Miklós Serédy also played central roles. Most of Hungary's ethnic Germans, united in the Volksbund and led by Franz Basch (1901–1946), were supporters of the Germanization of Hungary, and soon after Hungary's entrance into the war they began to enlist into the SS.

Secret SS storm troops, the Black Front, and the Order and Defense association were also formed, but they were infiltrated by the police and the leaders arrested. The militarization of Hungary went hand in hand with the anti-Jewish law of 1938. On 2 April the Darányi government announced its Gyor program—a five-year program to rebuild Hungary's military hardware and communications—and the same day the First Jewish Law went into effect. The end of 1938 saw the first open Hungarist rally, with tens of thousands marching on the streets of Budapest. Under this kind of pressure the Teleki government legalized the Arrow Cross Party. During the May 1939 parliamentary elections, the Arrow Cross and other national socialist parties were able to send forty-eight MPs to the parliament. This figure meant that altogether about 900,000 people across the country voted for the fascists. In Budapest and Pest County alone, more than 40 percent of voters opted for Arrow Cross and other fascist candidates. In Budapest the party received 72,383 votes, compared with 95,468 for the government party, and it became the single most important oppositional force to the government.

Because of infighting and personal conflicts, however, many Arrow Cross candidates lost their mandates, and at municipal elections they did not manage to gain enough votes. At the end of 1940 the leaders of various fascist factions agreed to unite and form a single Arrow Cross Party to represent Hungarian national socialism. But the Imrédy government's shift toward Germany created a powerful position against the Arrow Cross by marginalizing its leaders. Many were jailed, while others were forced to immigrate to Germany. By 1942, the National Socialists and the Arrow Cross were also at loggerheads; by 1943 many factions in the countryside were inactive, and the movement—no doubt because of Hungary's tremendous losses on the Eastern Front—counted fewer than 100,000 members nationwide. However, Szálasi and his closest allies did not remain quiet: in 1943 they planned a military coup. By the fall of that year, the German military high command was convinced that the conservative government of Miklós Kállay (installed in power at the behest of Regent Horthy in March 1942 and not sympathetic to Nazism) was incompetent and that a military occupation of the country was inevitable. Before that date, however, military actions were ordered against the Jewish population. During the summer of 1941 almost 16,000 Jews were deported to Galicia and massacred in Kamenec-Podolski. This was the first massacre of the Holocaust to be legitimated by the Hungarian leadership. It was followed by the second massacre, which took place in January 1942 in Délvidék, a region occupied by the Hungarian military and police. They murdered nearly 3,500 people, among them at least 800 Jews.

On 19 March 1944, Hungary was occupied by the Germans. All the national socialist leaders who had immigrated to Germany now returned and actively organized for total war in Hungary, even though the German puppet government of Sztójay did not include any Arrow Cross members. In April, Edmund Veesenmayer, Hungary's Nazi "governor," met Szálasi for the first time. Veesenmayer was able to convince Hungary's ruler, Horthy, to meet Szálasi in May, a meeting that sealed Hungary's fate during the tragic remaining months of the year. All fascist and paramilitary groups were united under MOVE, including the semisecret Association of Fighters of the Eastern Front (KABSZ) and the Turanian Fighters' Association. When, on 15 October 1944, Horthy announced a ceasefire, the Arrow Cross units, armed by the Germans, mounted a successful military coup d'etat. In October 1944, Szálasi issued his Program for National Reconstruction, and he was so taken with Hungary's leading role in the world that he gave a lecture on Japan while the Red Army was approaching Budapest. This was also when his "first book of Hungarism," with the title *The Goal*, was published, in December 1944. He was not, however, directly involved with the mass deportation of Jews in early 1944, and after October, when in office, he did not directly order any executions or deportations. In the spring and early summer, Eichmann and his Sonderkommando deported Hungarian Jews from the provinces to Auschwitz. The deportation of almost a half-million people was actively helped by Hungarian clerks, policemen, and solders. It was Endre who supervised the ghettos and the deportation to the death camps; his colleagues were Zöldi, Baky, and other chief police officers.

After World War II, and with the establishment of state socialism, fascist ideas persisted among Hungarian military and police officers in expatriate communities in North America, Australia, and Western Europe. Many publications and journals were published extolling the virtues of Hungarian racial purity and excusing Hungary's role in the Holocaust. Neo-Nazi and neofascist ideas began to appear in Hungary after the fall of communism in 1989. Skinhead groups and neo-Nazi slogans had in fact already appeared in the small and marginal rock music subculture under the communist regime in the early 1980s, only to be banned. After 1990 new leaders and names appeared, and World War II insignias and songs began to make the rounds. Anti-Semitic and extreme nationalistic rhetoric also reappeared, with swastikas and acts of vandalism in Jewish cemeteries and synagogues across the country. Albert Szabó, Isván Györkös, and György Ekrem Kemál formed the far-right Hungarian Welfare Association, but the party was illegalized, forcing its ideologues to remain silent or to leave Hungary. Characteristic of the 1990s was a demonstration by nationalist skinhead youth in the Castle District of Budapest to commemorate Szálasi's attempt to break out from the Soviet attack on Budapest. The alternative subculture milieu rose again after 2000, with skinhead nationalist groups organizing white power demonstrations and white Christmas concerts. At the beginning of the third millennium a new group surfaced, called Blood and Honor, but its nationalistic and fascist ideology was soon exposed and court action was swift.

László Kürti

See Also: INTRODUCTION; "ANTI-" DIMENSION OF FASCISM, THE; ANTI-SEMITISM; ARROW CROSS, THE; ARYANISM; AUSCHWITZ (-BIRKENAU); AUSTRO-HUNGARIAN EMPIRE/HABSBURG EMPIRE, THE; BLOOD; BÖSZÖRMÉNY, ZOLTÁN; CHRISTIANITY; COMMUNITY; CONCENTRATION CAMPS; EICHMANN, OTTO ADOLF; ENDRE, LÁSZLÓ; EXPANSIONISM; FESTETICS, COUNT SÁNDOR; GERMANY; GHETTOS; GÖMBÖS, GYULA; HITLER, ADOLF; HOLOCAUST, THE; HORTHY DE NAGYBÁNYA, MIKLÓS; IMPERIALISM; LEADER CULT, THE; *LEBENSRAUM;* MESKÓ, ZOLTÁN; MILITARISM; MILITARY DICTATORSHIP; MYSTICISM; NATIONALISM; NAZISM; NEO-NAZISM; PANGERMANISM; PARAMILITARISM; PLUTOCRACY; POSTWAR FASCISM; RACIAL DOCTRINE; REVOLUTION; ROCK MUSIC; SA, THE; SKINHEAD FASCISM; SS, THE; SWASTIKA, THE; SZÁLASI, FERENC; TURANISM; *VOLKSGEMEINSCHAFT,* THE; WHITE SUPREMACISM; WORLD WAR I; WORLD WAR II; YOUTH MOVEMENTS

References
Aczél, Tamás, ed. 1966. *Ten Years After.* London: MacGibbon and Kee.
Dósa, Rudolfné. 1972. *A MOVE. Egy jellegzetes Magyar fasiszta szervezet* [*MOVE: A Special Hungarian Fascist Organization*]. Budapest: Akadémiai.
Jászi, Oszkár. 1921. *Revolution and Counter-revolution in Hungary.* London: P. S. King.
Kürti, László. 2003. "The Uncivility of a Civil Society: Skinhead Youth in Hungary." Pp. 37–54 in *Uncivil Society? Contentious Politics in Post-communist Europe,* edited by Petr Kopecky and Cas Mudde. London: Routledge.
Macartney, C. A. 1937. *Hungary and Her Successors.* London: Royal Institute of International Affairs.
———. 1957. *October Fifteenth: A History of Modern Hungary.* Edinburgh: Edinburgh University Press.
Ormos, Mária. 1990. "The Early Interwar Years, 1921–1938." Pp. 319–338 in *A History of Hungary,* edited by P. Sugar, P. Hanák, and T. Frank. Bloomington: Indiana University Press.
Vago, Bela. 1976. "Fascism in Eastern Europe." In *Fascism: A Reader's Guide,* edited by Walter Laqueur. London: Wildwood House.

HUSSEIN (or HUSAYN), SADDAM (born 1937)

Former president of Iraq and leader of the Iraqi wing of the Ba'th Party; regarded by some as resembling Hitler in his philosophy. Saddam was born in the village of al-Auja, near the town of Tikrit, 175 kilometers north of Baghdad, officially on 28 April 1937. His father disappeared under mysterious circumstances before his birth, and he was brought up by his uncle, an army officer, Khairallah Tulfah. After the July 1958 coup headed by Brigadier Abdel-Karim Qasim, the Ba'th Party faced persecution, and one of those involved in an assassination attempt on Qasim's life, organized by the party in October 1959, was the youthful Saddam Hussein. After the failure of the coup he fled to Syria and then moved to Egypt (both countries were then members of the United Arab Republic). Another attempt to seize power by the Ba'th Party proved successful, enabling it to govern the country by means of ruthless methods from February to November of 1963. During that time Saddam sometimes appeared among the Ba'th hierarchy, although not among the high-ranking leaders. After a period of persecution during which he was jailed and then managed to escape and carry out underground activities, Iraq came under the rule of the Ba'th Party for a second time in July 1968. Saddam Hussein now became formally second-in-command (the so-called strong man), until in July 1979 he assumed unlimited powers (formally as president and head of the Supreme Council of the Revolution).

The Ba'th Party had been established in the 1940s by Syrian, Lebanese, and other Arab nationalists. Its major thinker was Michel 'Aflaq, who attempted to reinterpret Arab history in terms of a new ideological category. "Unity, Freedom and Socialism" were chosen as the main goals of the party. The party was to fight against foreign domination and the Israeli state and to solve class and economic problems in the spirit of the socialist model. All that was to lead to the establishment of the united "Arab Homeland." In 'Aflaq's basic ideological categories we can trace: faith (*iman*) in Arab cultural identity, confrontation with the "imperialist, reactionary and feudal conspiracy," and the downfall of the existing order (*inqilab*).

Saddam Hussein took over 'Aflaq's ideological proposals, adding to them practices and "theories" suited to his own role both as strongman and as president of

Iraq. Arab politics after World War II focused on such leading personalities as Nasser of Egypt, Qasim of Iraq, Boumedienne of Tunisia, and Gaddhafi of Libya. History, ideology, official organizations, and the state apparatus and institutions became instruments of the authoritarian individual. Saddam was an extreme example of this. His cult was crafted with care: newspapers published his image every day on their first pages, and his portraits and statues were in every public place. The cult was so exaggerated that the anniversary of the Ba'th Party foundation in late April was celebrated together with Saddam's alleged birthday. On such occasions newspapers had to hail him as "Saddam the Great," "Hero of the Arab Nation," or "Knight of the Arabs." His vision of Arab history declared that the nation had always had heroes, of whom one was Prophet Muhammad. The implicit idea was that the contemporary hero was Saddam himself. In this intellectual atmosphere, and in the absence of any opposition—even within the Ba'th—objective, rational, and historical arguments were swamped by totalitarian perceptions. History came to be treated in a selective manner, and the science of history was transformed into an instrument serving the political and doctrinal needs of the regime.

The unfavorable result of wars with Israel, and generally speaking of the Palestine question, was at different times interpreted and justified as the effect of the activities of colonialists, imperialists, traitors, feudal landlords, intelligence networks, or the low quality of Soviet armament supplies. The war against Iran (1980–1988) was presented in the news media, official documents, and publications as a series of heroic victories over the "eternal enemy." In March 2003, Iraq was invaded by the forces of a coalition of states headed by the United States, and on 13 December 2003, Saddam was taken into captivity by U.S. forces.

Hassan Jamsheer

See Also: BA'THISM; CONSPIRACY THEORIES; HERO, THE CULT OF THE; HITLER, ADOLF; IRAN; IRAQ; MIDDLE EAST, THE; LEADER CULT, THE; NATIONALISM; NAZISM; PROPAGANDA; QADHAFI (GADDHAFI), MU'AMMAR; PALESTINE; SOCIALISM; TOTALITARIANISM; ZIONISM

References
Farouk-Sluglett, Marion, and Peter Sluglett. 2001. *Iraq since 1958: From Revolution to Dictatorship*. London: I. B. Tauris.
Genocide in Iraq: The Anfal Campaign against the Kurds. 1993. New York: Middle East Watch.
Marr, Phebe. 2004. *The Modern History of Iraq*. 2d ed. Cambridge, MA: Westview.
Makiya, Kanan. 1989. *Republic of Fear: The Inside Story of Saddam's Iraq*. Berkeley: University of California Press.
Tripp, Charles. 2000. *A History of Iraq*. Cambridge: Cambridge University Press.

HYPERNATIONALISM: *See* INTRODUCTION; NATIONALISM

ICELAND

Iceland received its political autonomy from Denmark only in 1918, and cultural nationalism with its romanticization of rural life flourished in Icelandic society during the interwar years. But it did not translate into a far-right political agenda until the early 1930s. An Icelandic Nationalist Movement was created in 1933 by a group of young activists under Nazi influence and by members of the conservative Right on the basis of a common anticommunist agenda. These political forces openly collaborated in the municipal elections in 1934, but the alliance was totally controlled by the conservative Right, or the Independence Party, the largest party in Iceland. It soon became clear that the movement was unable to resolve the tension between a nationalist/conservative agenda and radical/foreign (Nazi) influences. When the Nationalist Party was founded in 1934 many moderate party members returned to the conservative fold.

As a result, the Nationalist Party became radicalized, incorporating corporatist and racist ideas which were imported from Nazi Germany into its program. It not only openly favored the abolition of the parliamentary system and the suppression of the Social Democratic and Communist parties but also harbored some anti-Semitic sentiment. While its social composition is mostly unknown, it pointed in the beginning, at least to a traditional fascist constituency: the lower middle class, including shopkeepers, artisans, and clerks. Its leaders, however, were educated young men who studied in or had some professional dealings with Germany. But as a sign of its marginalization, the party received only 0.7 percent of the vote in the 1934 parliamentary elections, and even less, 0.2 percent, in 1937. By the outbreak of World War II it had ceased to function as a political party. When the British occupied Iceland in 1940, and with the subsequent U.S. military presence during World War II, this minuscule organized form of fascism was totally suppressed. Despite some evidence of cultural and political admiration for Germany, the Icelandic version of fascism never had any impact domestically. Indeed, what has characterized the political system in Iceland since the 1920s is the absence of any far-right party espousing racist or fascist values.

Valur Ingimundarson

See Also: ANTI-SEMITISM; BOLSHEVISM; CONSERVATISM; CORPORATISM; DENMARK; GERMANY; NATIONALISM; NAZISM; PARLIAMENTARISM; RACIAL DOCTRINE; RACISM; RURALISM; SOCIALISM; WORLD WAR II

Reference
Guðmundsson, Ásgeir. 1980. "Iceland." Pp. 743–750 in *Who Were the Fascists: Social Roots of European Fascism,* edited by Stein Ugelvik Larsen, Bernt Hagtvet, and Jan Petter Mykebust. Bergen: Universitetsforlaget.

IG FARBEN

German chemical combine notorious for its association with Zyklon-B, used in the mass gassing of Jews in the Holocaust. In December 1925 seven German enterprises merged into IG Farben to become the biggest chemical company in the world. Some of its top managers had contacts with the NSDAP before 1933, but after the takeover by the Nazis collaboration grew rapidly. IG Farben with its production of synthetic rubber and oil had been the driving force behind the Four-Year Plan by which Germany was to be made ready for war. Close cooperation between the company and the Wehrmacht and the SS was practiced in the exploitation of forced labor. The Degesch subsidiary produced huge amounts of Zyklon-B, the poison used in the gas chambers. Twenty-four managers of the IG Farben combine were tried by the Nuremberg court in 1947–1948. The maximum penalty was eight years, but all had been released by 1951.

Fabian Virchow

See Also: ANTI-SEMITISM; CONCENTRATION CAMPS; FORCED LABOR; HOLOCAUST, THE; INDUSTRY; NAZISM; NUREMBERG TRIALS, THE; SS, THE; WEHRMACHT, THE; ZYKLON-B

References
Borkin, Joseph. 1978. *The Crime and Punishment of IG Farben.* New York: Free Press.
Buscher, Frank M. 1989. *The U.S. War Crimes Trial Program in Germany, 1946–1955.* New York: Greenwood.
Hayes, Peter. 1987. *Industry and Ideology: IG Farben in the Nazi Era.* Cambridge: Cambridge University Press.
Schneckenburger, Artur. 1988. *Die Geschichte des I.G.-Farben-Konzerns.* Cologne: Pahl-Rugenstein.

IMMIGRATION (pre-1945)

Whereas in the postwar era European fascists have exploited the tensions arising from the arrival of many nonwhite immigrants from outside Europe, in the earlier decades of the twentieth century and the last decades of the nineteenth, it was the movement of Jews from Eastern Europe into the countries of Western Europe that provided fuel to fan the flames of fascist agitation, and "immigration" and anti-Semitism amounted to the same issue. The latter part of the nineteenth century saw waves of Jews making the westward trek out of Russia and Eastern Europe, mainly as the result of pogroms, and the dramatic increase in the population of Jews in countries like France and Austria provided a ready opportunity for anti-Semitic agitators to fasten on the Jews as scapegoats for the ills of the day. In the interwar years there was in addition a particular issue with Jewish immigration from Europe into Palestine (*see* MIDDLE EAST, THE). The anxieties this aroused in the indigenous Arab populations were exploited by the Nazis. While expelling their own Jews they did not wish to see the creation of a Jewish homeland (though they had initially favored the idea). The conflict whose flames they helped to fan in Palestine has persisted down to the present.

Cyprian Blamires

See Also: ANTI-SEMITISM; DREYFUS CASE, THE; DRUMONT, EDOUARD ADOLPHE; EXPANSIONISM; IMMIGRATION (POST-1945); LUEGER, KARL; MIDDLE EAST, THE; NATIONALISM; NAZISM; PALESTINE; POSTWAR FASCISM; SCHÖNERER, GEORG RITTER VON

References
Fischer, Klaus P. 1998. *The History of an Obsession: German Judeophobia and the Holocaust.* New York: Continuum.
Malino, Frances, and Bernard Wasserstein. 1985. *The Jews in Modern France.* Hanover, NH: University Press of New England.

IMMIGRATION (post-1945)

Postwar fascists have used the issue of immigration to emphasize the importance of maintaining the cultural integrity of a country, arguing that immigration should be halted, immigrants should be deported, or that benefits such as social security and other political rights should be withheld from foreigners. Nationalists not only want to exclude foreigners; they may also want the actual territory of the nation to be extended to include those who are considered part of the nation, as in Germany, in which the *Republikaner* have called for the return to pre–World War II boundaries. After World War II the economic boom experienced in many European countries led to the importation of labor, originally from other European countries but also eventually from Asia, Africa, the Caribbean, and Turkey. France, the United Kingdom, and The Netherlands encouraged immigration from their former colonies to provide manpower for their industries. In recent decades, immigration has increasingly become a movement of people from the developing to the developed world; it has been driven by the desire to escape from poverty, social instability, and war. A large proportion of these immigrants are arriving from Muslim countries, and several of the host nations in Western Europe have experienced an increased identification with Islam among ethnic minority citizens. Fascists in Europe have seen this more recent immigration as a threat to the cultural homogeneity and national traditions of their countries. They have often exploited increases in the numbers of Muslims to claim that they are defending Christianity against Islam. Opposition to immigration has been one of the common threads within various fascist movements, and it is arguable that it plays the same role for such movements today as anti-Semitism did for interwar Nazism and its imitators.

Family reunification policies and flows of asylum seekers have kept the overall number of immigrants at fairly high levels in Europe, North America, Australia, and other developed countries. Neofascists have responded by calling for the deportation of immigrants, particularly asylum seekers, whom they often claim to be exploiting the system rather than meriting the status of true refugees. Fascists have also opposed changes in citizenship policies that are designed to make it easier for immigrants to naturalize. At the more extreme end of the spectrum, neo-Nazis, particularly skinheads, have been known to target immigrants with violence, and many countries have experienced serious increases in hate crimes toward foreigners and ethnic minority citizens.

Terri Givens

See Also: ANTI-SEMITISM; BLOOD; CONSPIRACY THEORIES; EUROPEANIST FASCISM/RADICAL RIGHT, THE; EXPANSIONISM; FRANCE; GERMANY; GREAT BRITAIN; GREECE; IMMIGRATION (PRE-1945); IMPERIALISM; LE PEN, JEAN-MARIE; MULTICULTURALISM; NATIONAL FRONT (FRANCE); NATIONAL FRONT (UK); NATIONALISM; NEO-NAZISM; POSTWAR FASCISM; RACISM; SKINHEAD FASCISM; XENOPHOBIA

References
Ford, Glyn. 1992. *Fascist Europe.* London: Pluto.
Gellner, Ernest. 1983. *Nations and Nationalism.* Ithaca, NY: Cornell University Press.
Krejcí, Jaroslav. 1995. "Neo-Fascism—West and East." Pp. 1–12 in *The Far Right in Western and Eastern Europe,* edited by Luciano Cheles, Ronnie Ferguson, and Michalina Vaughan. London: Longman.

IMPERIALISM

Territorial expansion became one of the trademark elements of the fascist experience in interwar Europe. Both Mussolini and Hitler sponsored ambitious expansionist ventures, initially in a piecemeal and cautious manner but from the mid-1930s with a dynamic unilateralism that defied embedded standards of international law and order. With the formation of the Axis alliance (1936) the project of fascist expansionism became entangled in the growing opposition of the fascist forces to the Western democracies but also in specific patterns of rivalry between Mussolini and Hitler for the kudos of the most radical regime in Europe. Their efforts and visions—theoretically compatible and complementary, as Hitler had stated in *Mein Kampf,* but often uncoordinated and openly antagonistic—culminated in the territorial reorganization that took place during World War II.

While fascist ideology did not clearly establish imperialism and territorial expansion as primary derivations and priorities of the fascist vision, its radical nationalist core often associated the overriding emphasis on national rebirth with the aggrandizement of the state's territory, in Europe and abroad. The strong belief in the elite qualities of the fascist nations, coupled with historical references to an idealized past, appeared to prescribe expansion through force, thus legitimizing Mussolini's and Hitler's ambitions for political, military, and cultural hegemony over the continent. At the same time, the path to fascist imperialism passed through considerations of increase of national population, economic self-sufficiency, and agricultural productivism—all of which had been adopted by the fascist regimes and pointed to the need for the acquisition of vast space resources. The need for "living space" was articulated in emphatic terms by both Hitler (*Lebensraum*) and Mussolini (*spazio vitale*) throughout the interwar period, providing the legitimacy for territorial claims that went far beyond the narrow scope of anti-Versailles revisionism and of traditional irredentist aspirations.

While on the level of political practice fascist imperialism remained the exclusive preserve of the two established fascist regimes in Italy and Germany, in intellectual terms it also informed the ideological discourses of a plethora of other movements in interwar Europe. In Hungary, the leader of the Arrow Cross, Ferenc Szálasi, articulated a holistic vision of "Hungarism" that predicated the establishment of a

Hungarian political and cultural hegemony over the whole Carpatho-Danubian area. A similar territorial-cultural project was propagated—though with noticeably less vehemence—by the Romanian Iron Guard leaders, contesting the Hungarian claims for their historical predominance in the region. The Belgian radical nationalist movement Verdinaso associated the goal of national rebirth with the territorial reconstitution of the medieval kingdom of Burgundy, thus advocating the need for a wider reorganization of boundaries. For all of these movements imperialism originated from already existing extreme nationalist claims—claims that were subsequently incorporated into the fascist pursuit of national rebirth.

This point may help us to understand why imperialism became an ideological and political priority for some but not for all fascist movements in interwar Europe. Fascist ideology's connection to territorial expansion was conditional and context-specific, not directly causal and deterministic. Only in those cases in which national revival had traditionally been associated with territorial aggrandizement did fascism adopt and subsequently radicalize or extend the claim for territory as an economic, political, or historical resource. By contrast, the ideological discourse of the British Union of Fascists evolved in an intellectual space in which further imperialist pursuits were irrelevant, with the emphasis placed instead on the preservation of Britain's world-hegemonic role rather than on its extension. In a similar vein, the ideology of the Spanish Falange showed little inclination to prescribe territorial expansion, focusing instead on the domestic prerequisites of national regeneration. Even in those cases in which a more-or-less specific territorial vision did exist as a mobilizing myth of indigenous nationalism—such as in Greece and Bulgaria—considerations of feasibility, international balance of power, and political conduct played a crucial role in toning down or even eliminating such expansionist aspirations.

The case of Greece is interesting in that context: while generations of Greek nationalists had consistently advocated a large territorial vision based on the so-called Megali Idea (a partial reconstitution of the Byzantine territorial map at the expense of the Ottoman Empire), the painful defeat of the Greek armies in Anatolia in 1922, coupled with the alignment of interwar Greece with British foreign policy and the lack of military and economic resources for an aggressive pursuit of this agenda, eliminated imperialism from the core of the fascist regeneration discourse of General Ioannis Metaxas's Fourth of August regime (1936–1941).

Therefore, in ideological terms, imperialism remained a by-product of fascist regeneration discourse in those cases in which it dovetailed with autochthonous radical nationalist traditions. On this basis—subsequently strengthened by historical, irredentist, geopolitical, and economic considerations—a number of fascist movements propagated the need for territorial expansion. But only two of them (Fascist Italy and National Socialist Germany) did actively pursue such a vision with all its aggressive and destabilizing implications. By the end of 1941 (the short-lived peak of the fascist "new order"), the territorial map of Europe had been vastly reorganized on the basis of a combination of historical, geopolitical, and racial-anthropological principles. This type of fascist expansionism reflected the dynamism and transient triumph of National Socialist conceptions of space in Europe, only to disintegrate and perish in tandem with the regime's military fortunes in the 1942–1945 period.

In the postwar political environment an overwhelmingly discredited and debilitated (in intellectual terms) fascism sought to realign itself with new visions of regeneration. If territorial expansion as a political claim was bolstered in the interwar period precisely because of the immense territorial changes that followed World War I and the very transient nature of the Versailles settlement, no such opportunities existed after 1945. In fact, not only were there no large-scale territorial redistributions in the aftermath of the Axis defeat but the stability of border arrangements was further fostered by two factors: the forced population transfers with a view to creating more homogeneous nation-states, and the onset of the Cold War. Given that fascism in and of itself did not have an autonomous core of territorial values but acquired them largely by proxy (through indigenous models of nationalism and rebirth), a general postwar consensus on the permanence of the territorial status quo militated against the revival of a new expansionist doctrine among the ranks of the European extreme Right. Postwar fascist ideologies, still in search of a firm intellectual realignment, have pursued very different avenues for conceptualizing their regeneration motto.

Of course, old nationalist utopias die hard. Whimsical irredentist visions (for example, the notion of *Dietschland* in The Netherlands; Vladimir Zhirinovski's vision for a revived Russian empire) continue to underpin a relatively small number of new ideologies of the extreme Right. The gap, however, between utopian visions and political practice or priorities is growing larger, banishing the former to an imaginary sphere that remains divorced from concrete political action. Postwar fascist ideologies appear significantly more intent on exploring possibilities for domestic regeneration (for example, the anti-immigration platform common in many movements and parties) than on engaging with territorial utopias. Some movements have revived territorial debates in order to promote the goal of secession from traditional states and "national" autonomy (for example, Umberto Bossi's notion of "Padania" in northern Italy; the Flemish bloc in Belgium). Overall, however, ethnocentric, or rather ethno-exclusive hypernationalism in the postwar period appears to be seeking a new period of hegemony through more subtle, systemic means, perhaps in anticipation of a more auspicious intellectual and political milieu; in that context, territory matters very little.

Aristotle Kallis

See Also: ARROW CROSS, THE; AXIS, THE; BARBAROSSA, FREDERICK, HOLY ROMAN EMPEROR; BARBAROSSA, OPERATION; BELGIUM; BULGARIA; COLONIALISM; DEMOCRACY; DEMOGRAPHIC POLICY; *DRANG NACH OSTEN* ("DRIVE TO THE EAST"), THE; ELITE THEORY; EXPANSIONISM; FALANGE; GERMANY; GREAT BRITAIN; GREECE; HAUSHOFER, KARL ERNST; HITLER, ADOLF; HOLY ROMAN EMPIRE, THE; HUNGARY; IRREDENTISM; ITALY; LEAGUE OF NATIONS, THE; *LEBENSRAUM;* LEGION OF THE ARCHANGEL MICHAEL, THE; METAXAS, GENERAL IOANNIS; MUSSOLINI, BENITO ANDREA; NATIONALISM; NAZISM; NEW ORDER, THE; PALINGENETIC MYTH; PANGERMANISM; NETHERLANDS, THE; POSTWAR FASCISM; ROMANIA; ROME; RUSSIA; SPAIN; SZÁLASI, FERENC; UTOPIA, UTOPIANISM; VERSAILLES, THE TREATY OF; VLAAMS BLOK; WORLD WAR II

References

Eatwell, R. 2002. "The Rebirth of Right-Wing Charisma? The Cases of Jean-Marie Le Pen and Vladimir Zhirinovsky." *Totalitarian Movements and Political Religions* 3, no. 3: 1–24.
Kallis, A. 2000. *Fascist Ideology: Territory and Expansionism in Italy and Germany, 1919–1945.* London: Routledge.
Knox, M. 2000. *Common Destiny: Dictatorship, Foreign Policy and War in Fascist Italy and Nazi Germany.* Cambridge: Cambridge University Press.
Smith, W. 1986a. *The Ideological Origins of Nazi Imperialism.* Oxford: Oxford University Press.
———. 1986b. *The Ideological Origins of Nazi Imperialism.* New York: Oxford University Press.

INDIA

Fascism with "Sanskrit characters" differs from that associated with Mussolini's Italy or Hitler's Germany. It assumed a "modern" organizational form with the creation of the Rashtriya Swayamsevak Sangh (RSS) in 1925. There is evidence that leaders had contacts with Mussolini and appreciated features of what was occurring in Europe at the time. But the real spur to action was Mohammad Ali Jinnah's advocacy of a two-nation theory and his demand for a separate Muslim state. In response, leaders of the RSS called for the formation of a Hindu nation (Hindu Rashtra) and for a society based exclusively on Hindu culture (Hindutva). Madhv Sadashiv Golwalkar's view that assimilation is virtually impossible has been interpreted widely as advocacy of something approaching an ideology of racial purity. In fact, Golwalkar and other intellectuals in the RSS have contended that India's problems are not due to the forms of worship of Islam or Christianity but to the separate identities that they foster. Golwalkar has written of "the Hindu Race, united together by common traditions, by memories of common glory and disaster, by similar historical, political, social, religious and other experiences." The "fascist" label is applied both because of the goal of racial and cultural purity and because of the means proposed to achieve it.

The assassination of Gandhi in early 1948 by Nathuram Godse, a former RSS member, led to a brief ban on the RSS. Nevertheless, the organization persisted and grew. Today it is the principal proponent of the ideology of *Hindutva.* A variety of associated organizations have been created over the years, collectively known as the Sangh Parivar. In 1951 the Bharatiya Jana Sangh (BJS) was formed as a political party to challenge Congress; in 1966 the Vishva Hindu Parishad (VHP) and its youth wing, the Barjrang Dal, were formed; in 1980, after the demise of the BJS, when it merged into the Janata Party, the Bharatiya Janata Party (BJP) came into being. A wide range of other organizations catering to different sections of the population, but sharing the core views of the RSS, developed over the years. These organizations have been involved in a variety of actions that many have labeled fascist. Two of the most significant were the destruction of the Babri mosque in Ayodhya in late 1992 and the Gujarat riots, sparked by the killing of several *saevaks* (RSS members claiming to be engaged in service to the nation or the people) returning from Ayodhya at Godhra in early 2002. The former was symbolically important because it involved the removal of a mosque built hundreds of years ago supposedly at the site of a temple honoring the place of birth of Ram. The latter was significant because it involved the killing and injury of thousands of Muslims. In both cases, governments did not intervene immediately to stop the destruction, implying complicity. These events symbolized the Sangh Parivar's efforts to purify the country of its "cultural imperfections"—a recurring motif in other fascisms.

This image of "fascism" in India is disputed. Apologists have attributed incidents like the 2002 Gujarat killings to a misunderstanding of the ideals taught by RSS-linked organizations that do not include the elimination of mosques and Muslims. The BJP-dominated government of India from 1999 to 2004 did not engage in behavior characteristic of fascists, though many of its top leaders were members of the RSS. When it was voted out of office in 2004, it abided by the secular constitution and stepped down. Furthermore, a close look at the Sangh Parivar organizations shows considerable pluralism with regard to both means and ends. Those critical of the dominant interpretation of fascism in India contend that fear of a "saffron tide" is politically generated by the secularists to discredit a movement merely seeking to build a nation.

Dean McHenry

See Also: ARYANISM; *BHAGAVADGITA*, THE; FASCIST PARTY, THE; GERMANY; HITLER, ADOLF; ITALY; MUSSOLINI, BENITO ANDREA; NATIONALISM; NAZISM; RACIAL DOCTRINE

References

Bhatt, Chetan. 2001. *Hindu Nationalism: Origins, Ideologies and Modern Myths.* Oxford: Berg.

Chander, Jag Parvesh, ed. 1943. *Gandhi against Fascism.* Lahore: Free India.

Elst, Koenraad. 2001. *The Saffron Swastika: The Notion of Hindu Fascism.* New Delhi: Voice of India.

Golwalkar, M. S. 1945. *We or Our Nationhood Defined.* 3d ed. Nagpur: M. N. Kale.

Hansen, Thomas Blom. 1999. *The Saffron Wave: Democracy and Hindu Nationalism in Modern India.* Princeton: Princeton University Press.

Krishna, Chaitanya, ed. 2003. *Fascism in India: Faces, Fangs and Facts.* New Delhi: Manak.

Zavos, John. 2003. *The Emergence of Hindu Nationalism in India.* Delhi: OUP.

INDIVIDUALISM

Term with very negative connotations in Italian Fascism and National Socialism; it was made responsible for modern "symptoms of decline" associated with ideas such as the "unheroic," "materialism," "egoism," the "subversive," and "rootlessness." National Socialism saw in it an ideology that overvalued the life of the individual, feared any sacrifice for "the whole," and made the individual forget his roots in race, *Volk,* blood, and homeland. Italian fascism understood individualism as an obstacle to the subordination of the individual to the "general will" of the people and the state and to membership of the individual in Fascist organizations. In a speech of 1 December 1921, Mussolini stated that "a centralized, unified state is necessary which subjects the individual to an iron discipline." On the Nazi side, Rosenberg wrote that "race and *Volk* represent not only the very ground of the individual's existence but also the only possible means by which he can be improved." The teaching of "mechanistic individualism," whereby the individual stood by himself and the people were first formed through "coming together," must be overcome through an awareness of rootedness in nation and race (*Volkstum und Stammestum*). But universalism could also be misunderstood in terms of a "supranational construct" or "bloodless combinations of humanity," as taught by the Catholic Church in order to control the peoples from the center through the priests. What was needed was therefore "that the myth of blood and the myth of the soul, race and self, *Volk* and personality, blood and honor, must solely and exclusively permeate, support, and determine the character of the whole of life." True "personality"—understood by the Nazis as the opposite of "rootless individuality"—was possessed only by the person who understood himself as rooted in his race.

In *Mein Kampf,* Adolf Hitler made individualism responsible for "degenerate thinking" and contrasted it with the "readiness to give one's life for the existence of the community." "The state of mind, which subordinates the interest of the ego to the conservation of the community, is really the first premise for every human culture." He called this attitude "true idealism," as a person's readiness to "give his young life for the ideal of his nationality," obeying "the deeper necessity of the preservation of the species, if necessary at the cost of the individual." This quality was marked with the Aryans, while with the Jews individualism was more strongly developed; the Jews were therefore not a "cultured people" but a "parasitic people," because their will and action "did not go beyond the individual's naked instinct of self-preservation" (*Mein Kampf,* ch. 11).

In his later years, Hitler reverted to his attack on an "overvaluation of the individual" again and again: "The life of the individual must not be set at too high a price. If the individual were important in the eyes of nature, nature would take care to preserve him. Amongst the millions of eggs a fly lays, very few are hatched out and yet the race of flies thrives" (*Table Talk,* 1–2.12.41). And he took as his starting point the social chaos to which individualism led: "If men were given complete liberty of action, they would immediately behave like apes. No one of them could bear his neighbour to earn more than he did himself. . . . Slacken the reins of authority, give more liberty to the individual, and you are driving the people along the road to decadence." The limitations of human freedoms "within the framework of an organization which incorporates men of the same race" was by contrast "the real pointer to the degree of civilization attained" (*Table Talk*, 11.4.42).

Markus Hattstein
(translated by Cyprian Blamires)

See Also: INTRODUCTION; ACTUALISM; "ANTI-" DIMENSION OF FASCISM, THE; ARYANISM; BLOOD; CATHOLIC CHURCH, THE; COMMUNITY; CORPORATISM; COSMOPOLITANISM; DECADENCE; DEGENERACY; ENLIGHTENMENT, THE; FASCIST PARTY, THE; GERMANY; HERO, THE CULT OF THE; HITLER, ADOLF; INDUSTRY; INTEGRAL NATIONALISM; ITALY; LEADER CULT, THE; LIBERALISM; MASSES, THE ROLE OF THE; MATERIALISM; MECHANISTIC THINKING; *MEIN KAMPF*; MUSSOLINI, BENITO ANDREA; NATIONALISM; NAZISM; ORGANICISM; PARLIAMENTARISM; RACIAL DOCTRINE; ROOTLESSNESS; ROSENBERG, ALFRED; SOCIAL DARWINISM; STATE, THE; TRADITIONALISM; *VOLK, VÖLKISCH; VOLKSGEMEINSCHAFT,* THE

References

Gentile, E. 1996. *The Sacralization of Politics in Fascist Italy.* London: Harvard University Press.
Griffin, R. 1991. *The Nature of Fascism.* London: Routledge.
———. 1999. "Party Time: Nazism as a Temporal Revolution." *History Today* 49, no. 4: 43–50.
Trevor-Roper, H. R. 2000. *Hitler's Table Talk 1941–1944: His Private Conversations.* Trans. Norman Cameron and R. H. Stevens. New York: Enigma.

INDUSTRY

The role of industry in the advancement of fascist regimes is complex, and has received much scholarly attention in recent years, especially in relation to Nazi Germany. In general, fascists saw the economic structures that had been created by the dominant liberal and laissez-faire ideologies of the industrial era as failing to serve the national interest. In their place they proposed a range of solutions that centered on a binary opposition which argued that a nation's industries must work for what fascists perceived as the national interest, instead of for the private profit of financiers and bankers. The latter were believed by fascists to be corrupting in-

fluences on the national body politic; yet, for the fascist regimes in Italy and Germany at least, they would remain a necessary factor to contend with in order for the state to develop working relationships with capital in the context of the economic realities of managing a nation-state. This was especially important for the two regimes, because they both saw a strong and productive industrial sector as a necessary part of a modern fascist nation-state. Fascists in other countries, who largely failed to move beyond opposition movements, were less constrained in their practices by such concerns. In sum, through a fascist's ideological lens, the ideology sought to create new industrial realities whereby the state, somewhat parasitically, would impose its will on the direction and management of industry, though not via the complete state ownership of the industrial sector; further, the fascist state expected industry's first loyalty to be to the fascist nation and only secondly to private profit.

In Italy, after a period of economic growth in the early to mid-1920s that was favorable to the development of good relations between Fascism and industry, the industrial sector had become weary of the regime by 1925. Around the time of the Matteotti crisis, the poor relationship between industry and the state was indicated not only by the fact that some industrialists were close to defecting from the regime but also by the fact that Fascist unions were becoming increasingly militant toward industry—Fascists even led a strike in Brescia in 1925. Furthermore, industrialists were deeply concerned over the declining lira. As a consequence, Mussolini appointed the industrialist Giuseppe Volpi as finance minister and the banker Giuseppe Belluzzo as the minister for the national economy; in their new roles Volpi and Belluzzo increased foreign (especially U.S.) investment and pursued deflationary and protectionist economic policies. Also, Mussolini struck a new deal between industrialists and the Fascist unions whereby the unions' powers of negotiation were weakened in return for the industrialists' acceptance of exclusive bargaining rights for the Fascist unions.

In the wake of the Wall Street Crash, financial pressures put strains on the liquidity of financial institutions in Italy, and in response to that the Istituto Mobiliare Italiano (IMI) was formed on 4 December 1931. It was not, however, a powerful enough organization to resolve the deepening economic predicament in Italy because, although well funded, it nevertheless lacked sufficient capital to invest in the ailing sectors of Italian industry. Consequently, on 23 January 1933, the regime formed the Istituto per la Ricostruzione Industriale (INI). The establishment of the INI fundamentally altered the relationship between the state and industry. The INI took over the stocks of large corporations as well as companies that were heading toward bankruptcy, leaving only highly profitable sectors outside of effective state control. By the outbreak of the war, state ownership extended to 80 percent of naval construction, 45 percent of steel and 77 percent of pig iron production, 90 percent of shipping, as well as large sectors of telecommunications and electricity (De Grand 2000, 107). The relationship between industrialists and the state was thereby marked by the influence of Fascist ideology's reading of how industry should serve the national ends, and in effect turned the various sectors of industry into national cartels. The relationship was also marked by a growing military influence, and industrialists became increasingly concerned with this development after the invasion of Ethiopia, especially because their interests were tied so closely to the state, which was, in turn, drifting toward Germany's sphere of influence. Further, by 1939 industry was so entwined with the state through the corporate state system that it could not rebel against the Fascist regime.

As in the case of Fascist Italy, in Nazi Germany industry was marked by a mixture of willingness and reluctance with regard to its cooperation with the fascist regime. The rhetoric of the Nazi movement had not opposed capitalism in principle, merely its international and excessive aspects, and Nazism itself operated broadly in the well-established German convention of statist economics that stretched back to the nineteenth century and the development of the nation as a modern economic power. Further, as a Social Darwinist, Hitler was a strong believer in the principle of competition, and felt this to be as applicable to the sphere of industry as any other. Therefore the socialism of the ideology was largely a rhetorical gesture rather than a meaningful description of economic objectives. Despite earlier scholarly assumptions, it is now thought that before the movement came to power Nazism was not heavily supported by industry, at least not until its electoral breakthrough in 1930. Such a conclusion seems legitimate, given that there is a lack of evidence of interest among German industrialists in Nazi overtures before that point. Furthermore, experts in the field, such as Peter Hayes, claim that additional research is needed to develop a more nuanced understanding of this relationship.

Once in power, in order to ensure that its political agenda was served by the private sector, the Nazi regime introduced increased state regulation of industry, but it did not attempt to carry out any sort of economic revolution—though it is likely that business elites, whom Hitler held in low regard, would have been largely eliminated after the war. However, in terms of designs for industry, exactly what Hitler and other Nazis planned after the war is open to much speculation, and evidence in regard to this aspect of the Nazi project is often sketchy and contradictory. From 1936, the armaments industry was augmented by the huge state-owned Herman Göring Reichswerke, a recipient of the massive new investment in armaments under Nazism. Also, private concerns, such as the chemical giant IG Farben and Degussa corporations, found that by cooperating with the state and "working toward the Führer," they could tap into a series of incentives that proved irresistible in the new economic climate in Germany after the Depression and within a dictatorial regime. Through the procurement of government contracts, helping to "Aryanize" business, meeting the requirements for the militarization of the regime, benefiting from forced labor during the Holocaust, and responding to the industrial needs generated by the Holocaust, both firms were typical in being active agents complicit in the regime's atrocities in order to maintain their dominant positions within the economy. The SS also benefited from slave labor. Initially the SS used slave labor merely as a form of punishment, but it later developed the practice more widely at such camps as Auschwitz, Majdanek, and Stutthof, and by the end of the war the SS had become a major supplier of slave labor both to private industry and for the national armaments industry, thereby manifesting a nexus between the needs of private commerce, a racist ideological vision, and the requirements of total warfare. Also, in recent years it has been demonstrated that foreign corporations such as IBM-Germany and Ford-Werke were participants in the atrocities of the regime. The American Military Tribunal at Nuremberg prosecuted representatives of German industries such as Krupp and IG Farben between 1946 and 1949. That was because of their culpability as leading figures who had allowed themselves to be coerced by the regime into helping it to commit war crimes.

Paul Jackson

See Also: ARYANISM; AUSCHWITZ; AUTARKY; AUTOBAHNS; BANKS, THE; CAPITALISM; CORPORATISM; ECONOMICS; EMPLOYMENT; ETHIOPIA; FASCIST PARTY, THE; FINANCE; FORCED LABOR; FORD, HENRY; GOERING, HERMANN; HITLER, ADOLF; HOLOCAUST, THE; HUGENBERG, ALFRED; IG FARBEN; INDIVIDUALISM; INFLATION; ITALY; KRUPP VON BOHLEN UND HALBACH, ALFRIED; LIBERALISM;

MATTEOTTI, GIACOMO; MILITARISM; MODERNITY; MUSSOLINI, BENITO ANDREA; NATIONALISM; NAZISM; NUREMBERG TRIALS, THE; RACISM; SOCIAL DARWINISM; SOCIALISM; SS, THE; STATE, THE; TECHNOLOGY; THYSSEN, FRITZ; TRADES UNIONS; U.S. CORPORATIONS; WALL STREET CRASH, THE

References

Adler, Franklin Hugh. 1995. *Italian Industrialists from Liberalism to Fascism: The Political Development of the Industrial Bourgeoisie, 1906–1934.* Cambridge: Cambridge University Press.

Allen, M. T. 2002. *The Business of Genocide: The SS, Slave Labor, and the Concentration Camps.* Chapel Hill: University of North Carolina Press.

Barkai, Avraham. 1990. *Nazi Economics: Ideology, Theory, and Practice.* Oxford: Berg.

Black, E. 2002. *IBM and the Holocaust: The Strategic Alliance between Nazi Germany and America's Most Powerful Corporation.* London: Time Warner Paperbacks.

De Grand, Alexander. 2000. *Italian Fascism: Its Origins and Development.* London: University of Nebraska Press.

Gregor, N. 1998. *Daimler-Benz in the Third Reich.* New Haven: Yale University Press.

Guérin, D. 1973. *Fascism and Big Business.* New York: Pathfinder.

Nicosia, F. R., and J. Huener, eds. 2004. *Business and Industry in Nazi Germany.* Oxford: Berghahn.

Overy, R. 1994. *War and the Economy in the Third Reich.* Oxford: Oxford University Press.

Payne, Stanley. 1995. *A History of Fascism, 1919–1945.* London: UCL.

Sarti, R. 1971. *Fascism and the Industrial Leadership in Italy: 1919–1940: A Study in The Experience of Private Power under Fascism.* Berkeley: University of California Press.

Turner, H. A. 1987. *German Big Business and the Rise of Hitler.* Oxford: Oxford University Press.

egg cost more than 800 marks, and children played with bundles of banknotes that had become worthless.

In his speeches, Hitler invariably made reference to the economic crisis that helped propel him into power. On 15 February 1933, in Stuttgart, he castigated the "fourteen years" of mediocrity that Germany had been forced to endure since 1919 and, at the same time, he ridiculed the supposed "Christianity" of the country's postwar leaders: "I would ask whether the economic policy of this now superseded system was a Christian policy. Was the inflation an undertaking for which Christians could answer, or has the destruction of German life, of the German peasant as well as of the middle classes, been Christian? . . . When these parties now say: we want to govern for a few more years in order that we can improve the situation, then we say: No! Now it is too late for that! Besides, you had your fourteen years and you have failed." Typically, he blamed inflation on the Jews.

P. J. Davies

See Also: ANTI-SEMITISM; BANKS, THE; CHRISTIANITY; ECONOMICS; GERMANY; HITLER, ADOLF; NAZISM; WALL STREET CRASH, THE; WEIMAR REPUBLIC, THE

References

Barkai, A. 1994. *Nazi Economics: Ideology, Theory and Policy.* Oxford: Berg.

Kitchen, M. 1976. *Fascism.* London: Macmillan.

Sarti, R. 1970. "Mussolini and the Industrial Leadership in the Battle of the Lira (1925–1927)." *Past & Present* (May), pp. 97–112.

Silverman, D. P. 1998. *Hitler's Economy: Nazi Work Creation Programmes 1933–36.* London: Harvard University Press.

Zamagni, G. 1993. *The Economic History of Italy, 1860–1990.* Oxford: Clarendon.

INFLATION

A period of hyperinflation in 1923 caused by financial issues relating to war reparations traumatized the German people and undoubtedly made some of them susceptible to the appeal of Nazism. Many middle-class and lower-middle-class people gravitated toward the Nazis because they had been destroyed economically by the "great inflation" of the post-1918 years. The inflation rate had risen from 1 percent to 32 percent, and in 1918 the German mark had lost 75 percent of its pre-1914 value. In the summer of 1923 hyperinflation reached fantastic levels, and at one point the German mark was trading at 622,000 to the pound. A single

INSTITUTE FOR HISTORICAL REVIEW, THE

Pseudo-academic think tank based in California that is one of the main channels for the distribution of English-language literature questioning the assumption that the mass murder of Jews in World War II was part of a deliberate attempt by the Nazi regime to destroy the Jews of Europe: it calls this "historical revisionism." It also publishes the *Journal for Historical Review* (established in 1980).

Cyprian Blamires

See Also: ANTI-SEMITISM; HOLOCAUST, THE; HOLOCAUST DENIAL; IRVING, DAVID JOHN CAWDELL; NEO-NAZISM; POSTWAR FASCISM; WORLD WAR II

Reference
Shermer, Michael, and Alex Grobman. 2000. *Denying History: Who Says the Holocaust Never Happened and Why Do They Say It?* Berkeley: University of California Press.

INTEGRAL NATIONALISM

The term *integral nationalism* is most closely associated with the protofascist French monarchist Charles Maurras. It represents a form of nationalism that was both "capable of being fully expressed only within the framework of the traditional institutions whose revival he advocated," and that admitted of no higher claims than the nation, seen as a "prior condition of every social and individual good" (Pierce 1966, 12–13). The nation, argued Maurras, "occupies the summit of the hierarchy of political ideas. . . . Subsuming all other large common interests, and making them dependent upon it, it is perfectly clear that all, *in case of conflict,* all interests must yield to it" (Maurras, *Revue d'Action française,* 1901, cited Girardet 1983, 198). The survival of the nation is best assured, argued Maurras, by a traditional hereditary monarchy: "Intelligent nationalists will not hesitate to see it. Hereditary monarchy is the natural, rational constitution in France, the only possible constitution of the central power. Without a king, everything which the royalists wish to conserve will first weaken, then subsequently will necessarily perish" (Maurras, *Le Soleil,* 2 March 1902, cited in ibid., 202).

Integral nationalism was therefore hostile to democracy, the maintenance of which was claimed to lead "inevitably to the dismembering of the nation" (Maurras, cited in ibid., 203): "The Polish Republic and the Athenian Republic, our experience of 1871 and our experience of 1895 are eternal witnesses of it: there is no good democratic republic" (Maurras, *Kiel et Tanger,* cited in ibid., 204). Attacking the French Revolutionary slogan *Liberté, Egalité, Fraternité,* Maurras argued that revolution and romanticism had brought about a cult of the self that marked a break with an eternal order expressed in the idea of the true France, the *pays réel* ("real country") as against the artificial France produced by liberal democracy and universal suffrage, the *pays légal* ("legal country"), which was subject to subversion by Jews, Freemasons, Protestants, and foreigners: "From

above, from below, the Frenchman is blocked. He no longer loses much time complaining because, no matter how high his complaint might go, he sees that it is submitted, before being heard, to some delegates of the four confederal Estates—Jew, Protestant, Mason, foreigner—with which real power is necessarily identified" (Maurras, 6 July 1912, cited in ibid., 210).

A further feature of integral nationalism was support for the decentralization of power to the provinces, to natural communities, and to professional organizations—"The military excepted, all degrees of all orders of the political, administrative, juridical and civil hierarchy must be decentralized" (Maurras, cited ibid., 212)—this latter aspect forming part of a proclaimed synthesis of nationalism with syndicalism that would integrate workers into the national community through the formation of a corporate system breaking with economic liberalism.

Steve Bastow

See Also: ABSTRACTION; ACTION FRANÇAISE; ANTI-SEMITISM; CATHOLIC CHURCH, THE; COMMUNITY; CONSPIRACY THEORIES; CORPORATISM; COUNTER-REVOLUTION; DEMOCRACY; EGALITARIANISM; FRANCE; FREEMASONRY/FREEMASONS, THE; INDIVIDUALISM; LIBERALISM; MAURRAS, CHARLES; MONARCHISM; NATIONALISM; PROTOFASCISM; STATE, THE; SYNDICALISM; TRADITIONALISM; *VOLKSGEMEINSCHAFT,* THE

References
Davies, Peter. 2002. *The Extreme Right in France, 1789 to the Present.* London: Routledge.
Girardet, R. 1983. *Le nationalisme français. Anthologie, 1871–1914.* Paris: Editions du Seuil.
Nolte, E. 1969. *Three Faces of Fascism: Action Française, Italian Fascism, National Socialism.* New York: Signet.
Pierce, R. 1966. *Contemporary French Political Thought.* Oxford: Oxford University Press.
Weber, E. 1962. *Action Française: Royalism and Reaction in Twentieth Century France.* Palo Alto: Stanford University Press.

INTERNATIONAL BRIGADES, THE

Composed of volunteers (intellectuals, workers, journalists, writers, and so forth) of different nationalities who flocked to Spain after the outbreak of the Spanish Civil War to fight against the Nationalist forces of General Franco, which they equated with fascism. The origins of the Brigades lie in the Comintern meeting in Prague of 26 July, when it was agreed to recruit European communist militants. That initiative bore fruit on 22 September, on the occasion of a journey to Moscow by the leader of the French Communist Party, Maurice Thorez. The first *Brigadistas* traveled to Albacete, where the headquarters was established. There are said to have been 60,000 *Brigadistas* from different countries who came to Spain united under the cry "Spain will be the graveyard of fascism." From the start they were integrated into the republican army, but their organizational structure was autonomous under the leadership of their own officers. There was a subdivision into battalions that brought together all those of one nationality, but with the passing of time many *Brigadistas* were integrated into Spanish battalions, remaining there even after the Brigades officially withdrew at the end of 1938. From the summer of 1936 all those left-wing writers, artists, and intellectuals who wanted to make a political commitment in the war joined the Alliance of Anti-fascist Intellectuals led by José Bergamin; that became a public manifestation of the political and ethical commitment of many foreign intellectuals. Celebrated writers of the time such as Dos Passos, Malraux, Hemingway, Stephen Spender, Tristan Tzara, George Orwell, and others actively sought to reinforce international opinion in favor of the republican cause.

Marta Ruiz Jiménez

See Also: ANTIFASCISM; BOLSHEVISM; COMINTERN, THE; FRANCO Y BAHAMONDE, GENERAL FRANCISCO; INTERNATIONAL FASCISM; ORWELL, GEORGE; SPAIN; SPANISH CIVIL WAR, THE

References
Brome, Vincent. 1965. *The International Brigades: Spain 1936–1939.* London: Heinemann.
Jackson, Michael. 1994. *Fallen Sparrows: The International Brigades in the Spanish Civil War.* Copenhagen: SOS Free Stock.
Johnston, Verle Bryant. 1967. *Legions of Babel: The International Brigades in the Spanish Civil War.* Philadelphia: Pennsylvania State University Press.
Stradling, Robert. 2002. *History and Legend: Writing the International Brigades.* Cardiff: University of Wales Press.

INTERNATIONAL FASCISM

It took some time for fascism to be seen, except by the extreme Left, as anything other than an Italian phenomenon. By the early 1930s, however, a consensus started to appear among the Right also, that fascism had an international dimension—and even movements that we would now see as not intrinsically fascist became convinced of their role in this new internationalism. In the 1920s there was little sense of an international movement being formed on the Italian base, and Mussolini does not at this stage seem to have seen Italian Fascism as exportable. The only body devoted to "international fascism," the CINEF (Centre International des Études Fascistes) based in Lausanne under the British enthusiast James Strachey Barnes, consisted mainly of academics; though its name suggests that it was devoted to the wider study of fascism, it served mainly as an apologist for the Italian regime. The only people who seem to have perceived fascism as an international phenomenon (and a dangerous one) were the far Left, with their concept of democratic politicians being "social fascists" who served to pave the way for a fascist takeover.

By the early 1930s, however, all had changed. The rise of antidemocratic forces throughout Europe led to a conviction that they all stemmed from the same source, and enthusiasts began to portray a "new Renaissance" in which "fascist man" would play his part. Even if foreign supporters of Italian Fascism drew serious distinctions between that movement and what they saw as the dangers of "pagan" Nazism, many shared the views of such people as Robert Brasillach in France and Oswald Mosley in Britain, that what had appeared was what the British fascist Sir Oswald Mosley called "the majestic edifice of a new world idea." Mussolini himself, in articles published in the early 1930s, was clearly won over to this new internationalism, while stressing that every country, because of differing circumstances, created a different form of fascism. This was later echoed by Spain's Franco, who—though in reality he was simply an old-style military reactionary—saw himself as "Fascist . . . since that is the word that is used" (Massis 1939, 150). The result was a polarization of Left and Right in Europe, each side seeing the other as a coherent bloc. The Spanish Civil War is a good example of this. Into an essentially Spanish conflict the international Left sent many volunteers to the Republican side, while from as far as Romania came volunteers for the cause of "international fascism," and Italy and Germany gave significant aid. The extent of this polarization, in the eyes of the public, meant that it became more and more difficult for the democratic regimes to maintain friendly diplomatic relations with Italy, which willy-nilly gravitated toward alliance with Germany.

Richard Griffiths

See Also: INTRODUCTION; "ANTI-" DIMENSION OF FASCISM, THE; AXIS, THE; BOLSHEVISM; BRASILLACH, ROBERT; DEMOCRACY; EUROFASCISM; EUROPE; EUROPEANIST FASCISM/RADICAL RIGHT, THE; FASCIST PARTY, THE; FRANCO Y BAHAMONDE, GENERAL FRANCISCO; GERMANY; INTERNATIONAL BRIGADES, THE; INTERNATIONAL FASCIST CONGRESSES, THE; ITALY; MARXIST THEORIES OF FASCISM; MOSLEY, SIR OSWALD; MUSSOLINI, BENITO ANDREA; NATIONALISM; NAZISM; ROMANIA; SPAIN; SPANISH CIVIL WAR, THE

References
Barnes, J. S. 1931. *Fascism.* London: Thornton Butterworth.
Eatwell, Roger. 1996. *Fascism: A History.* London, Vintage.
Griffin, Roger. 1995. *Fascism.* Oxford: Oxford University Press.
Griffiths, Richard. 2000. *An Intelligent Person's Guide to Fascism.* London: Duckworth.
Massis, Henri. 1939. *Chefs.* Paris: Plon.
Mosley, Oswald. 1936. "The World Alternative." *Fascist Quarterly* 2 (July), pp. 377–395.

INTERNATIONAL FASCIST CONGRESSES, THE

By the early 1930s Mussolini's attitude toward fascist internationalism had changed from viewing Italian Fascism in the 1920s as "not merchandise for export" to appreciating the merits of fostering a "Fascist International." To reach that end, Mussolini set up the Circolo Filologico Milanese Centro di Studi Internazionali sul Fascismo in 1932, which propagated a body of literature that detailed Fascism's universal mission for Europe. This sort of discourse was also disseminated in Italian journals such as *Universalità Fascista* and *Anti-Europa.* November 1932 saw the Volta Conference held in Rome on "Europe." Various fascist and other right-wing European ideologues and intellectuals, who were sympathetic both to the Italian regime and the "fascistization" of Europe, attended the conference, including Hermann Goering and Alfred Rosenberg from Germany. Notably, the Nazi delegates disagreed with the Italians over the race issue at Volta, and Nazi representatives took no further part in the attempt to form an Italian-based Fascist International. Following this conference, Mussolini formed the Comitati d'azione per l'Universalità di Roma (CAUR) in 1933 under Euginio Coselschi, in order to organize the strategic developments of the proposed international. The CAUR organized several international conferences, most notably the Fascist International Congress at Montreux

in December 1934. These conferences lacked consensus on the "fascist minimum" needed to decide who should attend, and they were open to all who had "their spirit oriented towards the principles of a political, economic, and social renovation, based on the concepts of the hierarchy of the state and the principles of collaboration between the classes." Representatives included Marcel Bucard, Georges Mercouris, Vidkun Quisling, Ion Moța, and General Eoin O'Duffy.

Despite being organized by the Fascist Party, the Montreux conference had, however, no official representatives from the Italian state. This highlights a key failing of the movement to generate a "Fascist International" from these conferences: the lack of a coherent state-based framework for exporting Italian Fascism. Furthermore, many of the delegates were primarily motivated by the prospect of receiving funding from the Italian regime. What emerged from the conference was a committee for coordinating the development of international fascist projects. This held its first meeting on 30 January 1935 and made its last public announcement on 1 April of that year in Amsterdam. To compound this failure, the formation of the Berlin-Rome Axis in October 1936 thwarted attempts by Italian Fascism to promote its role as the leading nation in the development of continental fascism. In addition, many of the adherents to the international project in Italy were alienated by the imposition of Nazi racial ideals on the dynamic of Italian Fascism, and by 1938 the CAUR had descended in status to a center for the dissemination of anti-Semitic propaganda.

Paul Jackson

See Also: INTRODUCTION; ANTI-SEMITISM; AXIS, THE; BUCARD, MARCEL; GERMANY; INTERNATIONALISM; ITALY; MOȚA, ION; MUSSOLINI, BENITO ANDREA; NATIONALISM; NAZISM; NEW MAN, THE; O'DUFFY, EOIN; QUISLING, VIDKUN; RACIAL DOCTRINE; REVOLUTION; ROSENBERG, ALFRED

References
Ledeen, Michael Arthur. 1972. *Universal Fascism: The Theory and Practice of the Fascist International, 1928–1936.* New York: Howard Fertig.
Payne, Stanley G. 1995. *A History of Fascism, 1914–1945.* London: University College Press.

INTERNATIONALISM: *See*
COSMOPOLITANISM
INTERNET, THE; *See* **CYBERFASCISM**

INTERREGNUM, THE: *See*
NATIONALISM; PALINGENETIC MYTH;
POSTWAR FASCISM; REVOLUTION

INTERVENTIONISM

I. ITALY

Italy and World War I

The key issue that swung Mussolini away from radical socialism and toward a new synthesis of socialism with nationalism was the issue of Italy's response to World War I. Initially opposed to Italian intervention in the war, Mussolini came to regard such an intervention as a means of provoking a situation of revolutionary crisis in his country. His decision to call for intervention both alienated him from classic socialism and his existing socialist allies, and constituted the first stage in his journey toward the creation of the new kind of "national"" socialism or Fascism. Some of his enemies accused him of being in the pay of the Allied powers, but that has never been proved. His change of heart then led him to volunteer himself for the war and to experience for himself the carnage of the trenches and the deficiencies in the national leadership. This strengthened his animosity to the existing establishment in Italy. After the war it gave him sympathy with the feelings of the war veterans and the ability to rally them to his cause. The new Fascist movement was proclaimed to be the vehicle for all who desired to make the terrible suffering of the war worthwhile by restoring Italy's greatness.

Italy and World War II

The issue of Italian intervention in a world war arose a second time in 1939 with the outbreak of hostilities between the Axis and Allied powers. Mindful of his military weakness and seeing Hitler perhaps more as a rival than as an ally, Mussolini kept Italy neutral until 1940. It was only when he saw that the tide of war seemed to be running Germany's way that Mussolini threw in his lot with Hitler, not wanting to lose out on potential advantages from being on the winning side; that decision aroused great hostility in the Fascist Party leadership—most of whom were not particularly sympathetic to German Nazism—and particularly from Galeazzo

Ciano and Dino Grandi. The bitterness it aroused undoubtedly contributed to Mussolini's downfall when the Grand Council of Fascism voted to unseat him in July 1943.

Cyprian Blamires

See Also: INTRODUCTION, *ANSCHLUSS*, THE; AUSTRIA; CIANO, COUNT GALEAZZO; FASCIST PARTY, THE; GRANDI, DINO; ITALY; MUSSOLINI, BENITO ANDREA; NATIONALISM; PACIFISM; SALÒ REPUBLIC, THE; SOCIALISM; WAR VETERANS; WORLD WAR I; WORLD WAR II

References
Bosworth, R. J. B. 2002. *Mussolini.* London: Hodder Arnold.
De Grand, A. 1982. *Italian Fascism: Its Origins and Development.* London: University of Nebraska Press.
Farrell, Nicholas. 2004. *Mussolini.* London: Weidenfeld and Nicholson.

II. UNITED STATES

In the United States at the start of World War II, anti-interventionism was the gospel of far-right sympathizers with Hitler or Mussolini or both. U.S. neutrality was a highly popular stance domestically until the completely unexpected catastrophe of Pearl Harbor, which precipitated U.S. intervention in the war. Anti-interventionism was sometimes also referred to as isolationism.

Cyprian Blamires

See Also: COLLINS, SEWARD; DENNIS, LAWRENCE; GERMAN-AMERICAN BUND, THE; GERMANY; HITLER, ADOLF; ITALY; JAPAN AND WORLD WAR II; LINDBERGH, CHARLES AUGUSTUS; MUSSOLINI, BENITO ANDREA; PEARL HARBOR; PELLEY, WILLIAM DUDLEY; ROOSEVELT, FRANKLIN DELANO; UNITED STATES, THE (PRE-1945); VIERECK, GEORGE SYLVESTER; WINROD, GERALD BURTON; WORLD WAR II

References
Casey, Steven. 2001. *Cautious Crusade: Franklin D Roosevelt, American Public Opinion, and the War against Nazi Germany.* New York: Oxford University Press.
Cole, Wayne S. 1974. *Charles A. Lindbergh and the Battle against Intervention in World War II.* New York: Harcourt Brace.

IRAN

In February 1921, army chief Reza Khan (1878–1944) took power in Persia (as Iran was then known) in a military uprising and in 1925 (as Reza Shah) founded

Reza Shah Pahlavi, interwar ruler of Iran, sometimes referred to as 'the Mussolini of Islam'. He was an admirer of Hitler and an anti-semite who strove to cleanse the language and culture of his 'Aryan' land from anything alien. (Corbis)

the dynasty of the Pahlavi. Soon after Mussolini's March on Rome, the Persian press was calling him the "Mussolini of Islam." Among all the regimes of the Middle East, that of Reza Shah, who welcomed Hitler's rise to power in 1933, bore the strongest outward resemblance to fascism. He undertook a rigid and propagandistically prepared nationalization campaign, made the state and the army swear allegiance to his own person, was a militant anticommunist, and built up a comprehensive secret police apparatus. As a part of his nationalization campaign he officially changed the name of his country from Persia to Iran—or "Land of the Aryans." In 1936 he welcomed the Nuremberg Race Laws; in 1938 there were sporadic pogroms against the Jews in Iran, and the shah sought to cleanse the language and culture of his "pure Aryan land" from everything "alien."

Reza Shah was a huge admirer of Turkey under Mustafa Kemal Atatürk and its orientation to the West. After Turkey concluded an economic treaty with the German Reich in August 1933, relations between Germany and Iran, which had been delicate for a while, improved. The influence of Great Britain—which until

then had been dominant in Iran—was reduced, and Germany sought to acquire a large part of the trade in oil for itself. In November 1936 the Reich finance minister, Hjalmar Schacht, visited Iran, and in December 1937 he was followed by the Reich youth leader, Baldur von Schirach, who arranged an exchange between German and Iranian youth organizations; the shah was increasingly enthusiastic for a national mobilization of the young. Relations between Iran and the USSR and Great Britain quickly deteriorated.

On 8 July 1937, Iran, Turkey, and Afghanistan concluded the "Saadabad" Friendship Pact, which favored the German Reich economically. Germany gained access to Iranian raw materials in return for credit and concessions. In 1938, Germany began to provide Iran with weapons and military aircraft. The Hitler-Stalin Pact of 23 August 1939 was followed on 8 October 1939 by a secret agreement between the German Reich and Iran: Iran provided food and raw materials to Germany, which by now found itself at war; in December 1939, Iran also concluded a Treaty of Friendship with the German ally Japan. However, Iran refused to enter the war on the side of the Axis and officially maintained its policy of neutrality, so that between 1939 and 1941, Germany, Great Britain, and the USSR all wooed the shah to be allowed military bases for a possible extension of the war into the region.

The shah's family were convinced that there would be a military victory for Germany, and there was a great deal of pro-German feeling in Iran. At the same time, Erwin Ettel, since autumn 1939 the German ambassador in Teheran, began to infiltrate German spies into the country. The propaganda of the German regime was supported by radio campaigns from the Deutschen Orientverein. The Orientverein worked on the Shi'ite clergy whom the shah had oppressed; they claimed that Hitler was the twelfth imam of the Shi'ites who had returned, sent by God to the world, in order to destroy Jews and communists. Hitler's struggle was compared with the struggle of the Prophet Mohammed against the Jews. In Teheran, 900 of the 1,200 resident Germans worked actively for National Socialist propaganda, and by May 1940 there were about 4,000 Nazi agents across the country.

The shah welcomed Hitler's invasion of the USSR in June 1941 but experienced difficulties as a result of the alliance of the Soviet Union with Great Britain. Since the British feared German acts of sabotage against the British oil supply and an eventual pro-German putsch, on 14 August 1941 Great Britain and the USSR demanded that the shah expel all Germans, threatening him with military intervention. On 25

August 1941 the British initiated an invasion in the south, while Soviet troops were invading the north of Iran. On 17 September 1941 the shah was forced to abdicate in favor of his son Mohammed Reza Pahlavi and go into exile. In March 1943, German SD agents parachuted into Iran (Operation Franz) and a "Nationalist Organization of Iran" in exile in Germany worked with radio propaganda on behalf of Fascism; however, the new Iranian regime concluded a pact with the Allies on 29 January 1942, and on 9 September 1943 it entered the war against Germany on the side of the Allies.

Markus Hattstein
(translated by Cyprian Blamires)

See Also: INTRODUCTION; ANTI-SEMITISM; ARYANISM; AXIS, THE; BOLSHEVISM; HITLER, ADOLF; HITLER-STALIN PACT, THE; IRAQ; JAPAN AND WORLD WAR II; LEADER CULT, THE; MARCH ON ROME, THE; MIDDLE EAST, THE; MUSSOLINI, BENITO ANDREA; NATIONALIZATION; NAZISM; NUREMBERG LAWS, THE; PALESTINE; PROPAGANDA; RACIAL DOCTRINE; RADIO; SCHIRACH, BALDUR VON; SOVIET UNION, THE; THIRD REICH, THE; TURKEY; WORLD WAR II; YOUTH MOVEMENTS

References

Ghods, M. R. 1989. *Iran in the Twentieth Century: A Political History.* London: Adamantine.

Kamrava, M. 1992. *Political History of Modern Iran.* London: Praeger.

IRAQ

Of the Arab states it was Iraq that was for a short period the closest to the Axis Powers. Germany exploited nationalist feeling there (resentment against the mandate power of Great Britain and Iraqi opposition to a Jewish settlement of Palestine); also, Iraq was the most significant trading partner of the Arabs in Palestine and Jordan. The leading advocate of a rapprochement with fascism was Rashid Ali al-Gailani (1892–1965), who after 1924 was several times justice and interior minister of Iraq and who had emerged as leader of the pan-Arab nationalists in 1930. He was prime minister from 1933 to 1935 and also head of the royal council before again becoming president and interior minister in March 1940. Gailani filled his cabinet with extreme nationalists and sought direct contact with the German regime in August 1940 via the mediation of Italy. Gailani was

fascinated by the nationalistic organization of the masses in Italy and Germany. Between 1933 and 1935 he had done intensive propaganda work among the tribes to get them to forget internecine differences and to sign up to the greater cause of nationalism and pan-Arabism, as well as to stir up dissatisfaction with Great Britain over the Palestine question. In 1940, under the government of Gailani, who was supported by the leader of the Palestinians, the grand mufti of Palestine, Amin Al-Husseini, who had taken refuge in Iraq, there were state-sponsored pogroms against the large Jewish community in Iraq. In response, the British threatened to implement a trade blockade and forced the dismissal of Gailani as prime minister by the regent on 31 January 1941.

On 3 April 1941, Gailani seized power again with the help of the military and imposed a state of emergency, while civil war–type conditions prevailed in the country. The German government now decided in favor of actively providing armaments and military support for Gailani's armed struggle, and on 2 May the British attacked Iraq. On 30 May 1941, Gailani and the grand mufti fled to Teheran and from there in 1942 to Berlin. On 15 February 1942, Gailani had a meeting with Mussolini in Rome to talk about an enlargement of Iraq as the center of Pan-Arabism on the side of the Axis. From Germany, Gailani and the grand mufti called the Arabs to rise up against the Allies on several occasions; in the event of a victory, Germany planned to set up both of them at the head of their countries under a German protectorate. At the end of the war, Gailani fled to Saudi Arabia and returned to Iraq in July 1958 after a putsch as a popular national hero. In the latter decades of the twentieth century, Saddam Hussein headed up a brutal and dictatorial regime in Iraq based on a personality cult and a philosophy that some have compared to Hitler's.

Markus Hattstein
(translated by Cyprian Blamires)

See Also: ANTI-SEMITISM; AXIS, THE; BA'THISM; FASCIST PARTY, THE; GERMANY; HITLER, ADOLF; HUSSEIN, SADDAM; IRAN; ITALY; MASSES, THE ROLE OF THE; MIDDLE EAST, THE; MUSSOLINI, BENITO ANDREA; NATIONALISM; PALESTINE; PROPAGANDA

References

Bengio, O. 1998. *Saddam's Word: Political Discourse in Iraq.* Oxford: Oxford University Press.

Haj, S. 1997. *The Making of Iraq, 1900–1963: Capital, Power and Ideology.* Albany: State University of New York.

Tripp, C. 2000. *A History of Iraq.* Cambridge: Cambridge University Press.

IRELAND

The major Irish flirtation with fascism came in the early to mid-1930s in the form of the Blueshirts. An organization naming itself the Army Comrades Association (ACA) had been formed in January 1932 to serve the needs of army veterans who were alarmed at the threatened loss of their privileges given the successful rise of their former civil war enemies to power. The ACA was moderately successful and attracted many leading politicians from the *Cumann na nGaedheal* Party, which had been voted from power in 1932 and replaced by a *Fianna Fail* government led by Eamon de Valera. The ACA was transformed in July 1933 by the arrival of General Eoin O'Duffy. The former head of the national police force had been sacked by de Valera, as he was seen as favorable to the former government. O'Duffy accepted an invitation to lead the ACA, renamed it the National Guard, and moved its whole ideology toward an open embrace of contemporary European fascist thinking. O'Duffy encouraged leading authoritarian Irish thinkers of the period—namely, Michael Tierney, J. J. Hogan. and Ernest Blythe—to develop policies for the party, and for a brief period he courted the support of W. B. Yeats, who famously penned a series of marching songs for the Blueshirts.

The Blueshirts under O'Duffy successfully combined a series of domestic policies aimed at undermining de Valera and *Fianna Fail* (opposition to the Anglo-Irish economic war, support for farmers, and demands for free speech) with ideologies aimed at transforming and modernizing Irish society. These latter ideas, the work of Tierney, Hogan, and Blythe, were based on an Irish reading of the papal encyclical *Quadragesimo Anno* and the corporatist policies of Mussolini. The central thrust of Blueshirt ideology was that the country had to resist communism vigorously, embrace a new political and social order based around corporatist and vocational structures, and develop an agricultural and industrial base centered on Catholic social action.

In the course of 1933 the movement under O'Duffy grew rapidly and drew the organization into an increasingly violent series of clashes with the agents of *Fianna Fail*. In September 1933, the siege mentality that had built up around the Blueshirts and its ability to mobilize popular support led to a new party being formed. *Fine Gael* was a merger of the Blueshirts, the former party of government, *Cumann na nGaedheal,* and the party of farmers, the National Centre Party. Despite not holding a parliamentary seat, O'Duffy was appointed leader of the party. By mid-1934 the Blueshirts claimed nearly 50,000 members, and it appeared that the new *Fine Gael* party would challenge *Fianna Fail* at the polls. In the event, the Blueshirts suffered a rapid and ignominious collapse. Despite O'Duffy's claims of a new political dawn, the *Fine Gael* candidates did not perform well in the 1934 local government elections, and by August of that year a series of resignations by leading figures had begun. Those who resigned claimed that O'Duffy's leadership was antidemocratic and that there was no support for fascism in the country. O'Duffy was forced to resign at the end of August 1934. The Blueshirts struggled on with ever-diminishing numbers until they were closed down by *Fine Gael* in 1936. In the meantime O'Duffy had gone on to form the National Corporate Party in 1935. This short-lived movement openly embraced fascism but received little popular support; it lasted a matter of only months. The final act in the history of Irish interwar fascism was O'Duffy's excursion, with 700 other supporters, to fight for Franco in Spain.

In Northern Ireland the British Union of Fascists organized in the 1930s but achieved little popular support as a result of the strong particularities of politics there. With the outbreak of the modern troubles in the late 1960s, there were parallels drawn between the workings of Loyalist paramilitary groups and fascism, and there were documented cases of alliances between such groups and British organizations such as Combat 18.

Mike Cronin

See Also: BOLSHEVISM; CATHOLIC CHURCH, THE; COMBAT 18; CORPORATISM; FRANCO Y BAHAMONDE, GENERAL FRANCISCO; GREAT BRITAIN; INTERNATIONAL BRIGADES, THE; MUSSOLINI, BENITO ANDREA; O'DUFFY, EOIN; POLITICAL CATHOLICISM; SPANISH CIVIL WAR, THE; YEATS, WILLIAM BUTLER

References
Broderick, E. 1994. "The Corporate Labour Policy of Fine Gael 1934." *Irish Historical Studies* 29, no. 113: 88–99.
Cronin, M. 1997. *The Blueshirts and Irish Politics.* Dublin: Four Courts.
Loughlin, J. "Northern Ireland and British Fascism in the Inter-War Years." *Irish Historical Studies* 29, no. 116: 537–552.
McGarry, F. 1999. *Irish Politics and the Spanish Civil War.* Cork: Cork University Press.

IRON GUARD, THE: *See* LEGION OF THE ARCHANGEL MICHAEL, THE
IRRATIONALISM: *See* RATIONALISM

IRREDENTISM

A term originating in late-nineteenth-century Italy to describe the program of those Italians who claimed for their newly unified state areas regarded as "Italian" that were still outside the national territory. The term was then applied to any similar claim to "redeem" national territory from foreign rule. Irredentism was the near-inevitable outcome of national-ethnic tensions in Central and Eastern Europe where the post–World War I peace settlement saw the emergence of new or restored states as multinational as the old empires they replaced. It was an integral component of the aims and appeal of interwar nationalist and fascist movements in some Central and Eastern European countries, notably Germany and Hungary.

Philip Morgan

See Also: AUSTRO-HUNGARIAN EMPIRE/HABSBURG EMPIRE, THE; D'ANNUNZIO, GABRIELE; EXPANSIONISM; FIUME; IMPERIALISM; PANGERMANISM; ROME; SLAVS, THE (AND ITALY); WORLD WAR I

Reference
Knox, M. 2000. *Common Destiny: Foreign Policy and War in Fascist Italy and Nazi Germany.* Cambridge: Cambridge University Press.

IRVING, DAVID JOHN CAWDELL (born 1938)

Self-taught historian of World War II who began openly to involve himself with neo-Nazi groups in the mid-1980s. Prior to that he had a long history of association with far-right views. Having established an early reputation for serious scholarship, Irving joined the camp of the Holocaust deniers, to whom this reputation made him something of an icon. He subsequently denied that he held that view and actually sued Holocaust historian Deborah Lipstadt in a London court for attributing the label to him, but he lost the case and has been barred from several countries. In his judgment, British judge Charles Gray described Irving's writing on the Holocaust as "a travesty." In November 2005,

Irving was detained by police in Austria, where a warrant for his arrest had been issued in 1989.

Cyprian Blamires

See Also: HOLOCAUST, THE; HOLOCAUST DENIAL; INSTITUTE FOR HISTORICAL REVIEW, THE; NEO-NAZISM; POSTWAR FASCISM

References
Evans, R. 2001. *Lying about Hitler: History, Holocaust and the David Irving Trial.* New York: Basic.
Lipstadt, D. E. 2005. *History on Trial: My Day in Court with David Irving.* New York: Ecco.

ISLAM, ISLAMIC WORLD, THE: *See* IRAQ; IRAN; MIDDLE EAST, THE; PALESTINE ISOLATIONISM: *See* INTERVENTIONISM ITALIAN SOCIAL REPUBLIC, THE: *See* SALÒ REPUBLIC, THE

ITALY

It was only with the end of World War I that were created the material and objective but also psychological and mental conditions that allowed Fascism to make its appearance on the historical stage in Italy. The war, costing 600,000 dead and massive material damage, had produced traumatic and irreversible changes in the country. It had familiarized an entire generation with blood and violence. It had altered the traditional equilibrium of the social classes. It had determined the appearance on the national political scene of new collective social subjects: young persons, women, former soldiers. It had accentuated the distrust of the popular masses with regard to parliamentarism, traditional political parties, and the liberal ruling class. It had sharpened the ideological conflict between those who had waged the war inspired by patriotic sentiment and those (for example, the socialists and part of the Catholic world) who instead had opposed the intervention of Italy in the conflict. It had ultimately produced a grave economic crisis, from which the only ones to benefit were the speculators and the representatives of the great industrial groups involved in war commissions.

Benito Mussolini had agitated for Italy to enter the war, and indeed for that very reason he had broken his

The Villa Rosa Maltoni in Calambrone, a typical specimen of architecture from the Fascist period in Italy. It was designed by Angiolo Mazzoni as a holiday residence for the children of rail and postal staff. (Alinari Archives/Corbis)

relations with the socialist tradition in which he had been brought up. His political intuition in the midst of the prevalent postwar political and social chaos was to give a voice to all of those who, in the light of the experience of interventionism, the myth of war, and widespread anxieties about a potential Bolshevik-style social revolution, maintained the need for a "national revolution." By this they had in mind a "new state" that would bring to power a new ruling class composed, according to a slogan coined by Mussolini himself for his daily *Il Popolo d'Italia,* of "fighters and producers." Fascism, unthinkable without the social and political chaos of the postwar moment, was thus the politico-ideological movement in which the former soldiers and so-called middle classes (small landowners, professionals, public servants, shopkeepers) eventually joined forces. The war veterans believed themselves legitimated in guiding the country out of consideration for

the sacrifices they had had to make in the course of the war: they considered themselves a social aristocracy born in the trenches. The urban and agrarian petty bourgeoisie, hostile at the same time to socialism and to great capital, looked rather for a party that could embody their own social aspirations and that recognized their dynamic role not just on the economic but also on the political level.

Fascism was born officially in Milan on 23 March 1919, in the course of a public meeting in which participated, under the leadership of Benito Mussolini, a hundred or so individuals, coming mainly from the interventionist Left: republicans, former socialists, former soldiers, Futurists, revolutionary syndicalists, anarchists, and students. The original program of the Fasci still smacked of libertarian, syndicalist, and democratic-radical proposals typical of the politico-intellectual formation of their founder: it declared itself in favor of a work week of eight hours, a minimum wage, the expropriation of uncultivated land, the confiscation of war profits, and the participation of workers in the technical functioning of industry. On this basis the new movement presented as an antiparty and proclaimed itself pragmatic and hostile to ideologies, progressive in inspiration but clearly anti-Bolshevik, patriotic but not nationalist, anticapitalist but advocating industrialism and technical progress. It was a programmatic anticapitalist platform destined very soon to be modified, especially after the noisy failure registered by the Fascists at the elections of 16 November 1919, which had demonstrated the difficulty for the new movement of tuning into the popular masses and the world of labor, which were much more responsive to the revolutionary preaching of the socialist party. The real change in Fascism took place from the middle of 1920, when, having been born with a predominantly urban caste of mind and with a Jacobin-revolutionary core, it began to acquire support from among the small landowners in conflict with the agricultural laborers and with the peasant syndicates; that led it to move toward conservative right-wing positions. In organizational and ideological terms, this qualitative leap was embodied in particular in the birth of *squadrismo:* armed groups, composed mainly of former soldiers and young unemployed, financed and supported by the world of the bosses, which impressed a completely new character on the Italian political struggle through their recourse to violence against their political adversaries, in particular socialists and Catholics. Within a few months, thanks to the power of *squadrismo,* Fascism became a mass political movement, rooted above all in the country areas of the Po Valley and Tuscany, consciously orientated toward the conquest of government on the basis of a political program of nationalist authoritarian stamp, which openly rejected liberal democracy and party-political pluralism.

Notwithstanding the choreography of the March on Rome that led to Mussolini's assumption of power, with thousands of men ready to take power by armed violence, Fascism's appearance in government in October 1922 represented a properly "legal revolution": without violation of the forms of the existing constitution, Mussolini was entrusted by the king with forming a new government only when all other attempts to give life to a politico-parliamentary accord had failed. In reality, this amounted to the mandatory result of a profound politico-institutional crisis that was itself in large part imputable to the climate of "civil war" generated by Fascism. Fascism had managed to impose on the country and on all the institutional actors present on

the scene (from the monarchy to the parties) a political style based not on electoral competition nor on a comparison of rational manifestoes and respect for individual political opinions, but on the systematic use of force, on the cult of the charismatic leader, on the principle of hierarchy, on the exaltation of patriotism, on the ethic of battle, and on contempt for adversaries.

The first Mussolini government was born, formally, as a "coalition government," in which the Fascist ministers were in a definite minority. It included independents, nationalists, liberals, and Catholics from the Popular Party. There were also the two army and navy chiefs: General Armando Diaz and Admiral Paolo Thaon di Revel. This explains the attitude taken at the time by many representatives of liberal, democratic, and socialist antifascism, such as Giovanni Giolitti, Giovanni Amendola, or Filippo Turati, who saw in Mussolini's rise to power not the beginning of a stable political dictatorship but the only solution to save democratic legality and to put an end to violence, taking the country back to normality. It was thought that the Fascist regime would in the worst case be a painful authoritarian parenthesis that would save Italy from chaos and lay the foundations for a return to the democratic dialectic. What most observers failed to grasp was the deeply subversive and revolutionary nature of Fascism, its substantial incompatibility with the rules of liberal democracy and parliamentary politics, and its determination to use the institutions of the liberal state to change the structure of political relationships and give life to a new form of constitutional order. Emblematic from that point of view was the first speech that Mussolini gave to the Chamber of Deputies on 16 November 1922. It was a harsh and threatening speech, in the course of which he reminded the deputies that the real strength of Fascism derived from its autonomous military force: 300,000 "armed youth" ready for anything, even ready to occupy parliament and chase out the enemies of Fascism whether properly elected or no. Mussolini was in effect the head of an "armed party" composed of militiamen accustomed to military conflict and fanatically devoted to their leader, a party whose political objective was not simply the conquest of power but also the destruction of the liberal state, the disbanding of the parties and trades union organizations, and the construction of a "new order" oriented to political values like order, hierarchy, and authority.

But how, and by what stages, did this revolutionary transformation of the Italian political system take place, a transformation that ended in the construction of a totalitarian state whose foundations were the single party, the cult of the leader, the corporatist economic order, and the militarization of the masses? For the purposes of argument, three phases can be distinguished in the twenty years of Fascism. The first ran from 1922 to 1926: from the conquest of power to the definitive dismantling through legal channels of the politico-constitutional structures inherited from the liberal order. It was the *authoritarian* phase of Fascism, in the course of which—thanks to the work of the jurist Alfredo Rocco, the architect of the Fascist state—the parliamentary regime was progressively emptied of powers and competencies in favor of the executive power, wholly concentrated in the hands of Mussolini. In this period a key date is the institution in December 1922 of the Grand Council of Fascism, an essentially consultative political organ destined to play a central role in the "new state" (in December 1928, in fact, the Grand Council became the supreme constitutional organ of the regime, and among its powers there was even that of choosing Mussolini's eventual successor); the constitution in January 1923 of the Milizia Volontaria per la Sicurezza Nazionale, a kind of parallel army of Fascism, within which the paramilitaries and *squadristi* were incorporated; the approval in July 1923 of a majoritarian electoral law (the so-called Acerbo Law), which in the next election, on 6 April 1924, was to enable the Fascist Party and the parties associated with it to obtain a crushing parliamentary majority (374 seats out of 535). At this period, too, the first attempts were made by Fascism to give itself a solid cultural base, so as to legitimate itself on the ideological level. On this terrain the contribution of the philosopher Giovanni Gentile was crucial; in 1925 he organized in Bologna the Fascist Cultural Convention, from which emerged a "manifesto" of support for Mussolini and the new regime signed by numerous men of culture and scholars. Again, it was Gentile—already the author in 1923 (wearing his hat of minister of public instruction in the first Mussolini government) of a fundamental reform of the schools—who, in 1925, produced the definitive plan for the *Enciclopedia italiana,* destined to represent the most ambitious initiative of Fascism in the field of culture. This phase concluded, after the political crisis created by the murder of the socialist deputy Giacomo Matteotti in June 1924, with the publication between January 1925 and November 1926 of a series of repressive measures (the so-called *leggi fascistissime*) that brought about the abolition of freedom of organization, the outlawing of all political parties with the sole exception of the Fascist Party, the introduction of the death penalty for offenses against "the security of the state," and the creation of a special tribunal to judge offenses against Fascism and the state. It was the beginning of the Fascist regime, true and proper.

The second phase, from 1927 to 1936, was the *Caesaristic-dictatorial* one, and it was marked essentially by the progressive fascistization of Italian society, by the affirmation of the cult of Mussolini, by a growing adherence of the masses to the regime, and by its first bellicose undertakings: the conquest of Ethiopia and the proclamation of the empire (1935–1936), and the involvement in the Spanish Civil War on the side of Franco in 1936. A fundamental date in the process of construction and consolidation of the new system of power was in 1929: on 11 February of that year, the Lateran Accords were finally signed, which marked the historic "reconciliation" between the Catholic Church and the Italian state and turned into a great political and propagandistic success, given that the Catholic masses drew definitively close to the regime. On 24 March, in the elections for the renewal of the chamber, the "single" list of 400 deputies set up by the Fascist Grand Council was approved by the Italians by an almost unanimous vote (8.5 million votes in favor, and a mere 100,000 against), which demonstrated how Fascism no longer had any enemies within the country. These two events—the concordat and the "plebiscite"—obviously contributed to build up the charismatic role of Mussolini, who became increasingly the object of a public political cult with mystico-religious echoes. The "Mussolini myth" began to spread among the Italians, and especially among the poor. As for Fascism, it increasingly assumed the form of a real "political religion," based on the mobilization of the masses, on the military education of the young, and on great collective liturgies, and aimed at the construction of a "new Italy," wholly molded to the martial combative spirit of Fascism. It was an objective that obviously called for a state that in its turn was integrally Fascist, from the doctrinaire and organizational point of view. Something that may be considered particularly significant was the approval in April 1927, thanks to the work of Giuseppe Bottai, of the Charter of Labor: this represented the ideological basis of the corporative system that Fascism began to construct in 1930 (with the establishment of the Ministry of Corporations) and that Mussolini considered an original alternative on the level of economic-productive organization both to communist collectivism and liberal/capitalist individualism. It was at this period that power was given to the great mass organizations destined to involve militarily Italians of every class: the Opera nazionale dopolavoro (OND), founded in 1925 and intended to promote initiatives in the areas of welfare, recreation, culture, and sport for the benefit of the workers; and the Opera Nazionale Balilla, which was founded in 1926 and aimed at the welfare and the moral and physical education of young people between the ages of six and eighteen. It was in this period, too, that measures were adopted to fascistize teaching and guarantee for the regime the monopoly of education: in 1928, for example, the decision was taken to introduce the "single state book" for elementary schools; in 1929, it was made obligatory for teachers at every level to swear allegiance to the regime.

The third phase of the Fascist regime, from 1937 to 1945, was the wholly *totalitarian* phase, marked by the politico-military and ideological alliance with Nazi Germany (officially ratified in May 1939) and by the integral fascistization of Italian society at all levels, pursued by Mussolini with the express objective of transforming Italy into an imperial power that could revive on the military level the glories of Ancient Rome. This was a phase destined to culminate in the disastrous involvement in World War II and the "civil war" of 1944–1945, which signaled the traumatic collapse of Fascism and the violent disappearance of the majority of those who had had a role in it. The behavior and the choices that characterized the totalitarian evolution of the regime were varied. Among the most traumatic in terms of its immediate consequences and the wounds it left in the civil fabric and in the public memory of the Italians, was the adoption in November 1938 of the racial anti-Semitic legislation, which had been preceded in July of the same year by the publication of a "manifesto on race" signed by various scientists. With these laws Fascism drew closer to Nazism in discrimination against Jews. Equally eloquent in that same year was the accentuation of a grave diplomatic crisis between the regime and the Holy See, which Fascism intended to block from any activity in the area of education and the formation of the young.

At the moment of the outbreak of World War II (September 1939), Italy opted for neutrality (so-called nonbelligerence): Mussolini did not believe that his country was yet ready to face a war effort that would require, in his judgment, at least two to three more years of preparation. The rapid advance of the Germans on several fronts and a fear of being excluded from peace negotiations induced him to a drastic change of opinion: on 10 June 1940, Italy entered the war, in spite of the opposition of the military chiefs, the hostility of the Church, and the perplexity of many Fascist chiefs—not least Foreign Minister Galeazzo Ciano. Mussolini's

idea, when he attacked France, the English in North Africa, and then Greece, was to wage, as he explicitly stated, a "parallel war" to that of the Third Reich—a war that he hoped would last not more than two years and that, once over, would consecrate Italy as the hegemonic power in the Mediterranean and in the southern Balkans. The military catastrophes of the Axis after the autumn of 1942 produced grave domestic repercussions in Italy: they increased the economic distress of the people and intensified anger with Fascism and its chief. On the night of 25 July 1943 the Grand Council of Fascism voted to restore to King Victor Emmanuel III "the supreme decision-making power," and that in fact marked the collapse of Fascism and its institutions and the political defeat of Mussolini. It was therefore welcomed by the Italians as a liberation, and with the subsequent signing of an armistice (8 September 1943), they thought that they could escape definitively from the conflict. But it was a delusion. Mussolini had been imprisoned but was rescued by the Germans, and he returned to Italy to lead the Salò Republic in the north, the part of the country that had been under military occupation by the Germans; this signaled the beginning of a bloody civil war that for about two years set the "Republican Fascism" of Mussolini and his supporters against the Allies and the fighters of the Italian anti-Fascist resistance. The civil war was ended only in April 1945, with the "liberation" of the main cities from Mussolinian control and the capture and shooting of the leading Fascist chiefs, from Mussolini himself down.

With the end of World War II, Fascism did not disappear from the Italian political scene. In 1947 the veterans of the experience of the Salò Republic established a political party, the Italian Social Movement, that became the politico-electoral rallying point for those who were "nostalgic" for Mussolini. The existence of a neo-Fascist party that was a small but stable presence in the parliamentary-democratic dialectic represented a case unique in Europe for some fifty years. It was an anomaly that eventually finished formally in January 1995 with the dissolution of the Italian Social Movement and the birth of the Alleanza nazionale (An), a political formation led by Gianfranco Fini and programmatically oriented in a national-conservative and post-Fascist direction, now fully integrated, even from the point of view of values, in the democratic life of the country. In the Italy of today the heritage of Fascism is claimed only by small extraparliamentary groups, which have found in Alessandra Mussolini, niece of Il Duce, their point of reference: the ultimate symbol, pathetic and sentimental, of a past that no longer affects political life but that continues nonetheless to weigh on the historical memory of the Italian nation.

Alessandro Campi
(translated by Cyprian Blamires)

See Also: INTRODUCTION; ACERBO LAW, THE; *ANSCHLUSS*, THE; ANTIFASCISM; ANTI-SEMITISM; ARISTOCRACY; AUSTRIA; AVENTINE SECESSION, THE; AXIS, THE; BOLSHEVISM; BOTTAI, GIUSEPPE; CATHOLIC CHURCH, THE; CIANO, COUNT GALEAZZO; CORPORATISM; CROCE, BENEDETTO; CULTURE; D'ANNUNZIO, GABRIELE; ECONOMICS; *ENCICLOPEDIA ITALIANA,* THE; EDUCATION; ETHIOPIA; FARINACCI, ROBERTO; FARMERS; FASCIO, THE; FASCIST PARTY, THE; FEDERZONI, LUIGI; FIUME; FOOTBALL/SOCCER; FRANCO Y BAHAMONDE, GENERAL FRANCISCO; FUTURISM; GENTILE, GIOVANNI; GERMANY; GRAMSCI, ANTONIO; GRAND COUNCIL OF FASCISM, THE; GRANDI, DINO; GUERNICA; HITLER, ADOLF; INTERVENTIONISM; LAW; LEADER CULT, THE; LEISURE; MANIFESTO OF FASCIST INTELLECTUALS, THE; MARCH ON ROME, THE; MARINETTI, FILIPPO TOMMASO; MASSES, THE ROLE OF THE; MATTEOTTI, GIACOMO; MILITARISM; MILIZIA VOLONTARIA PER LA SICUREZZA NAZIONALE (MVSN); MONARCHY; MOVIMENTO SOCIALE ITALIANO, THE; MUSSOLINI, ALESSANDRA; MUSSOLINI, BENITO ANDREA; MYTH; NATIONALISM; NAZISM; NEW ORDER, THE; PAPACY, THE; PARAMILITARISM; PARLIAMENTARISM; PIUS XI, POPE; PIUS XII, POPE; POSITIVISM; POSTWAR FASCISM; PRODUCTIVISM; RACIAL DOCTRINE; RAUTI, GIUSEPPE ("PINO"); RELIGION; REVOLUTION; ROCCO, ALFREDO; ROME; SALÒ REPUBLIC, THE; SARFATTI-GRASSINI, MARGHERITA; SKORZENY, OTTO; SOCIALISM; SPANISH CIVIL WAR, THE; SPORT; *SQUADRISMO;* STRATEGY OF TENSION, THE; THIRD REICH, THE; TOTALITARIANISM; TRADES UNIONS; WAR VETERANS; VICTOR EMMANUEL III/VITTORIO EMANUELE III, KING; WARRIOR ETHOS, THE; WORLD WAR I; WORLD WAR II; YOUTH MOVEMENTS (ITALY)

References

Cannistraro, Philip V., and Brian R. Sullivan. 1993. *Il Duce's Other Woman: The Untold Story of Margherita Sarfatti, Benito Mussolini's Jewish Mistress, and How She Helped Him Come to Power.* New York: William Morrow.

Cassels, A. 1969. *Fascist Italy.* London: Routledge.

De Grand, A. 2000. *Italian Fascism: Its Origins and Development.* London: University of Nebraska Press.

Gentile, E. 1996. *The Sacralization of Politics in Fascist Italy.* London: Harvard University Press.

Griffin, R. 1991. *The Nature of Fascism.* London: Routledge.

Lyttelton, A. 1973. *The Seizure of Power: Fascism in Italy, 1919–1929.* London: Weidenfeld and Nicholson.

Lyttelton, A., ed. 1973. *Italian Fascisms from Pareto to Gentile.* London: Jonathan Cape.

Mack Smith, D. 1968. *The Making of Italy, 1976–1870.* London: Macmillan.

Payne, S. 1995. *A History of Fascism 1914–1945.* London: University College London Press.

Roberts, E. M. 1979. *The Syndicalist Tradition in Italian Fascism.* Manchester: Manchester University Press.

Tannenbaum, E. R. 1972. *The Fascist Experience: Italian Society and Culture 1922–45.* New York: Basic.

JAPAN

Interwar Japan felt the influence of fascism as much as any country outside Western Europe. This influence derived mainly from the emulation of German and Italian models, but the Japanese borrowed from those models selectively, and their knowledge of European fascism was partial. Rather than traveling to Japan as a package, the influence of fascism was uneven. Fascism had its slightest impact on Japan's political movements, a secondary impact on political thought, and its greatest impact on state policy. The Japanese had patterned their country's development after that of the leading Western states since the mid-nineteenth century, and the emulation of German and Italian models in the 1930s continued this practice. In the eyes of some Japanese, Germany and Italy had outdone the liberal democracies in coping with the Great Depression. Moreover, there was a natural confluence of foreign policy interests between Japan, Germany, and Italy. Whereas Japanese imperialism clashed with the imperialism of the Western democracies in interwar Asia, Germany and Italy had no colonies in the region. After Hitler's rise to power in 1933, there was a growing perception in Japan that Nazi Germany represented a new, superior form of society. The Japanese took no interest in fascism anywhere outside Germany and Italy.

Rightist political groups played a big part in Japanese politics in the 1930s, but few adopted the tactics or goals of Europe's fascist movements. Ultranationalist groups dated back to the turn of the century in Japan. They underwent rapid expansion in the early 1930s, when rightists celebrated Japan's military incursion into Manchuria and assassinated several leading politicians. But this expansion occurred before Hitler's rise to power, at a time when European fascism had little visibility in Japan. Most of Japan's right-wingers differed in fundamental ways from the fascist prototype. Most rightist groups in interwar Japan belonged to what Stanley Payne calls the "conservative authoritarian right." Unlike fascists, they eschewed violent tactics and embraced traditional concepts of political legitimacy. Most sought a return to the oligarchical form of constitutional monarchy that had predated Japan's party governments of the 1920s. Some of these groups had respectable and indeed elite support. Fewer in number but no less consequential were adherents of what Payne labels the "radical Right." These were mainly young military officers who conducted a rash of assassinations in the early 1930s. Their final defeat came with the suppression of an attempted coup d'etat in 1936. Although they matched the violence of fascist movements, these radical rightists made no effort to develop a mass base. Moreover, they advocated the return to an obscure, mythical past rather than any new form of authoritarian state. Neither the conservative authoritarian Right nor the radical Right modeled itself on European fascism.

The nearest attempts to build a fascist movement in Japan occurred in the late 1930s. The most successful of them was Seigo Nakano's Eastern Way Society (Tohokai), founded in 1936. Nakano, sometimes called the "Japanese Hitler," traveled to Europe to meet fascist notables, and his followers wore black shirts. However, even this group rejected violent tactics and embraced the traditional doctrine of imperial sovereignty. Although the Eastern Way Society won 2.1 percent of the vote in the 1937 election, that was as close as any right-wing movement came to taking political power in Japan.

Why were rightist movements in general, and fascist movements in particular, not stronger in Japan? Japan had been only a minor participant in World War I, so that the disaffected veterans that provided European fascism with its rank and file were absent. Mass politics was less developed overall than in Western Europe, making it hard to organize a mass movement of any type. Traditional values, based upon loyalty to the emperor, dissuaded most rightists from embracing the secular, voluntaristic norms of fascism or overtly flouting the constitution that the emperor had bestowed upon the nation in 1889. Finally, the police kept extreme rightist elements in check, especially after 1935.

Fascism, however, had a substantial impact on elite political thought in interwar Japan. The main conduits for fascist ideas were bureaucrats, military officers, and intellectuals known as the *kakushin,* or renovationist Right. They included members of the army's Control Faction and officials serving in new interministerial agencies such as the Cabinet Planning Board, which handled planning for total war. Civilian intellectuals of the Showa Research Association, the brain trust of *kakushin* statesman Fumimaro Konoe, also studied fascist thought. *Kakushin* thinkers believed that the world was undergoing a great historical transformation. The era of freedom, which had begun with the French Revolution, had run its course. In its place was emerging a new society that they identified variously as the "national defense state," "totalitarianism," or the "new order." All of these terms originated in contemporary European rightist thought. In the new era, the national community would triumph over individualism, state planning would supersede market competition, and a single political organization of some kind would replace the established political parties. Like the German and Italian fascist thinkers they

studied, *kakushin* elements rejected the institutionalization of conflict characteristic of liberal society. *Kakushin* thinkers ignored fascist movements and focused instead on the economic and military achievements of the German and Italian regimes. They saw the state rather than a movement from below as the main instrument of historical change. Unlike a reticent liberal state or a class-based socialist state, theirs would be an interventionist state standing above classes as the embodiment of the national interest. It would mobilize its subjects for a common purpose, thereby creating a superior new order to replace the wasteful competition of liberal society. *Kakushin* thinkers thought it inevitable that the rising national defense states of Germany, Italy, and Japan would triumph militarily over the declining societies of freedom. When the German army easily swept through Western Europe in the spring of 1940, that world view seemed completely vindicated.

Japan's form of government never came to resemble that of Germany or Italy. No rightist party took power; there was no charismatic leader like Hitler or Mussolini; and the political elite pursued an orderly and at least formally legal transformation from above. It was the military and the bureaucracy that gradually came to dominate Japanese politics in the 1930s, while the influence of political parties waned. But despite the differences in regime structure, the influence of fascist models on Japanese decision-makers soon became evident in every sphere of public policy. Emulating Europe's fascist regimes, the Japanese state pressed social organizations of many types into officially regulated cartels called control associations (*toseikai*). Officials dissolved hundreds of thousands of businesses, including mass media organs, and herded the survivors into these cartels, which were subject to bureaucratic control. The State Total Mobilization Law of 1938, which sanctioned this reorganization, was patterned after a German statute of 1934. To mobilize individuals, the Japanese again mimicked fascist policy. They created a vast complex of monopolistic, state-controlled mass organizations, known collectively as the Imperial Rule Assistance Movement. These organizations targeted people according to their gender, age, occupation, workplace, and place of residence. The state dissolved autonomous trades unions, political parties, youth clubs, and women's interest groups, and forced their members to join the new mass structures. Access to employment, food rations, and other essential goods and services was contingent upon membership. Although there were some modest Japanese precedents for these bodies, German models were paramount. For instance, Japan's Industrial Patriotic Society for industrial workers represented a conscious effort to emulate Hitler's German Labor Front. Whereas party cadres managed these mass organizations in Germany and Italy, military officers and bureaucrats did so in Japan.

The study of fascist models thus led to a statist revolution in wartime Japan. The instigators of change were military-bureaucratic elites rather than cadres of a fascist party. The process of change was an orderly imposition from above rather than a violent uprising from below. And while borrowing much of fascism's condemnation of liberalism, Japan's leaders used traditional, monarchical values to legitimize their new order. Yet the changes they wrought, such as the official cartels and mass organizations, were patterned directly on the policies of the German and Italian fascist regimes. Scholars have used terms such as "military fascism," "Emperor-system fascism," "fascism from above," or simply the term *kakushin* to capture the partial but momentous influence of fascism in Japan.

Gregory Kasza

See Also: INTRODUCTION; AUTARKY; AUTHORITARIANISM; AXIS, THE; CHINA; CLASS; COMMUNITY; CONSERVATISM; CORPORATISM; CULTS OF DEATH; ECONOMICS; FASCIST PARTY, THE; FRENCH REVOLUTION, THE; GERMANY; HIROHITO, EMPEROR; HITLER, ADOLF; INDIVIDUALISM; ITALY; JAPAN AND WORLD WAR II; LABOR FRONT, THE; LEAGUE OF NATIONS, THE; LIBERALISM; MASSES, THE ROLE OF THE; MILITARISM; MISHIMA, YUKIO; MONARCHISM; MUSSOLINI, BENITO ANDREA; NATIONALISM; NAZISM; NEW ORDER, THE; PALINGENETIC MYTH; RADIO; RELIGION; REVOLUTION; STATE, THE; THIRD REICH, THE; TOTALITARIANISM; TRADITION; *VOLKSGEMEINSCHAFT,* THE; VOLUNTARISM; WALL STREET CRASH, THE; WAR VETERANS; WORLD WAR I; WORLD WAR II; YOUTH MOVEMENTS

References

Fletcher, William Miles, III. 1982. *The Search for a New Order: Intellectuals and Fascism in Prewar Japan.* Chapel Hill: University of North Carolina Press.

Kasza, Gregory J. 2001. "Fascism from Above? Japan's *Kakushin* Right in Comparative Perspective." In *Fascism outside Europe: The European Impulse against Domestic Conditions in the Diffusion of Global Fascism,* edited by Stein Ugelvik Larsen. Boulder, CO: Social Science Monographs (distributed by Columbia University Press).

Maruyama, Masao. 1969. *Thought and Behavior in Modern Japanese Politics.* London: Oxford University Press.

Oka, Yoshitake. 1983. *Konoe Fumimaro: A Political Biography.* Tokyo: University of Tokyo Press.

Wilson, George M. 1969. *Radical Nationalist in Japan: Kita Ikki, 1883–1937.* Cambridge: Harvard University Press.

JAPAN AND WORLD WAR II

What gave Japan the image of being a fascist regime in the West was above all her alliance with Germany and Italy in the Axis and her subsequent provocation of war with the United States. This gave rise to the assumption that Japan, too, must be a fascist power. But the origins of Japanese involvement in World War II were not necessarily related to fascism. Historians use the label "the Washington Conference system" to denote the framework of international relations in East Asia in the interwar years. Japan was a signatory to treaties made during the Washington Conference of 1921–1922 that were part of the project to stabilize the world after the conflagration of World War I. Underlying this system was an economic accord that involved the signatories agreeing to accept gold as the medium of international transactions, to link their own currencies to gold, and to uphold currency convertibility. One of the aims of the Washington Conference system was to integrate China into the global economic order, and during the 1920s this process of integration was under way. China's stability was seen as a key to peace in the region, and the signatories to the Washington Conference treaties pledged themselves not to pursue expansionist policies at the expense of China. In the late 1920s foreign capital flowed into China, especially from the United States, to help build the country's infrastructure. Such developments aroused anger among certain elements in Japan, who feared that it was China that was the real beneficiary of the Washington Conference system. They also believed that the system was damaging Japanese interests by binding its national well-being to fluctuations in trade balances and exchange rates.

When Britain and the United States attempted to alter the balance of naval power in the Pacific to Japan's disadvantage in the London Naval Conference of 1930, it caused a domestic political crisis in Japan. Although the minister of the navy supported Japan's ratification of the treaty, the admiralty was strongly opposed. It claimed that the civilian government was violating the navy's constitutional "right of supreme command," and the naval chief of staff reported his objections formally to the emperor. Although Japan finally approved the new treaty, the controversy gave rise to many acts of political terrorism by junior officers in the months that followed. An important shift occurred in the nature of

The USS Arizona *on fire in Pearl Harbor as the Japanese Airforce launches a surprise attack on the unsuspecting American fleet based there. Japan's entry into World War II had much more to do with her imperialistic designs in Asia than with a sympathy for German Nazi or Italian Fascist ideology. (National Archives)*

Japanese imperialism between the London Naval Conference and Japan's military expansion into Manchuria that began in September 1931. Until that time, the Japanese had respected the Western empires in Asia and restricted themselves to seizing territories that the Western powers had neglected to occupy, such as Taiwan and Korea. From that time forward, Japanese policy challenged the Western position in Asia. In domestic politics, the civilian party government's reluctance to push Japan's advantage in Manchuria exacerbated political violence and finally resulted in the assassination of the last party prime minister in 1932. This opened the door to growing military interference in the government. It was these events, which occurred before Hitler's rise to power in Germany and before European fascist models had had much influence in Japan, that put Japan on the road leading to World War II.

The China Incident of 1937 finally involved Japan and China in a total war. Although sparked by a chance encounter between Japanese and Chinese troops, the rapid spread of hostilities was a logical outcome of Japan's Manchurian invasion earlier in the decade, which had led to continual friction with China's Nationalist government. By 1939 the Japanese front in China covered more than 2,000 miles, and the conflict became a huge drain on the Japanese economy. In July 1939 the U.S. government informed Japan that it planned to abrogate the Treaty of Commerce and Navigation, which had been in force since 1911, as of 1940; it was clear that the United States was intending to apply economic sanctions against Japan. The fear of such sanctions was one of the factors that motivated Japan to cast an eye on the abundant natural resources of Southeast Asia. The United States had already looked with anxiety on Japan's decision to send a further three divisions to China in the summer of 1939, and in the early months of 1940 the Japanese decided upon yet another increase in their military presence in China. The spectacular German military successes of that year further emboldened the Japanese, who attributed these victories to

Germany's superior national spirit and to its system of total war mobilization. It was at this point that Japanese statesmen began to pattern many of their mobilization policies after German models, though it was always the military, not any fascist political party, that held the reins of power in Japan.

Japan's acceptance into the Axis alliance with Germany and Italy soon followed. The supporters of this move in Japan argued that it would deter the United States from interfering with Japan's building of a new order in East Asia. Some in Japan saw the country's entry into the Axis as simply a prelude to the expulsion of the European powers from Asia and the seizure of their colonial possessions. While appealing to Japanese nationalists who believed in their country's destiny to be the leading power of the region, entry into the Axis also seemed a solution to the shortage of resources needed to sustain Japan's military operations in China. Foreign Minister Matsuoka Yosuke handled Japan's negotiations with Germany and the Soviet Union. In Moscow he concluded a pact of neutrality with the USSR, mindful of the danger that it might pose to Japanese forces in China. On their side the Soviet leadership were aware that Japan was interested in Southeast Asia and would not wish to provoke conflict with themselves. When Hitler invaded Russia in June 1941 it came as a shock to Matsuoka, in whom Hitler had not confided his intentions. In July the Japanese decided to proceed with their planned move into Indo-China and not to take advantage of the USSR's predicament unless it was clearly defeated.

The reaction to Japan's advance into Indo-China in the West was that the United States and Britain froze Japanese assets. The British and the Dutch agreed that the United States should represent the combined interests of the Western colonial powers in dealing with Japan. But for the United States, any reconciliation with Japan required Japanese withdrawal from China, to which Japan had by now committed around 850,000 troops. At this point it seemed that only a Japanese expansion to the south would make possible Japanese hegemony over the region, making it possible to acquire the requisite natural resources and also cutting off supply routes to the Chinese enemy. The option seemed all the more attractive in the light of the complete cessation of oil shipments from the United States from August of 1941. Many in the Japanese government hoped to achieve economic self-sufficiency in a putative "Greater East Asia Co-Prosperity Sphere." The war in China had stimulated the growth of Japanese heavy industry and her import/export trade within the East Asia region had greatly increased, but this autarki-

cal policy was never very realistic. It was thought that the United States was not prepared for war, and the opinion gained ground in Tokyo that if expansion in the region were contemplated, an early strike against the United States was imperative. A strike in winter was also considered vital, in order to reduce any likelihood of a Soviet move from the other direction. The increasing power of the military in Japanese policy-making meant that the possibility of withdrawing from China to placate the United States was never really an option at all, after so many years of sacrifice. Military planners reported that a strike would have to be made by December 1941 or else postponed to the following spring, by which time the navy's oil stocks would be so depleted as to render it impossible. On 26 November the U.S. government once again notified Japan that an accommodation could not be reached between the two countries unless the Japanese withdrew from China, and that was the last straw for the Japanese military. The decision was taken to launch a pre-emptive strike at U.S. naval power via an attack on its fleet.

After the Pearl Harbor attack of 7 December 1941 on the U.S. fleet, things seemed to be going Japan's way, and the "Greater East Asia Co-Prosperity Sphere" was duly established, with the Japanese soon in control of the European powers' former colonies. However, the United States quickly recovered from the dramatic losses to its navy sustained at Pearl Harbor, and already by the Battle of Midway in mid-1942 the balance of military power had begun to shift in favor of the United States. Meanwhile, Hitler had made the mistake of declaring war on the United States in support of Japan, and that was to prove an expensive error, with huge U.S. resources now committed to the European front as well. Still, a long struggle lay ahead, with the defeat of Japan not being achieved until the dropping of the atomic bombs in August 1945. Japan formally surrendered to the Allied forces on 2 September 1945.

Cyprian Blamires and Gregory Kasza

See Also: AUTARKY; AXIS, THE; CHINA; COLONIALISM; CULTS OF DEATH; GERMANY; GREAT BRITAIN; HIROHITO, EMPEROR; HITLER, ADOLF; IMPERIALISM; ITALY; JAPAN; MILITARISM; MILITARY DICTATORSHIP; PEARL HARBOR; SOVIET UNION, THE; THIRD REICH, THE; UNITED STATES, THE (PRE-1945); VERSAILLES, THE TREATY OF; WORLD WAR I; WORLD WAR II

References
Bergamini, David. 1971. *Japan's Imperial Conspiracy.* New York: William Morrow.
Giffard, Sydney. 1994. *Japan among the Powers.* Newhaven: Yale University Press.

Iriye, Akira. 1987. *The Origins of the Second World War in Asia and the Pacific*. London: Longman.
Williams, David. 2004. *Defending Japan's Pacific War: The Kyoto School Philosophers and Post-White Power*. London: Routledge Curzon.

JEHOVAH'S WITNESSES

The Jehovah's Witness Movement, founded in the United States in the last quarter of the nineteenth century, came into conflict with the Third Reich when Witness beliefs on the nature of the world and its meaning came sharply into conflict with the tenets of National Socialism. Members of the movement believe that the world is in its last days and under the rule of Satan. They are witnesses to their God, Jehovah, on the stage of history while awaiting the end of the current order, and they are dedicated to spreading knowledge of Jehovah and His plans. Members of the organization see their allegiance as being to their God rather than to the political regimes of Satan's world, although they are law abiding and good citizens where their faith allows. They will not swear on oath, vote, bear arms for a civil state, or belong to a political party. In Nazi Germany this stance led members of the group most dramatically to refuse to enlist or to give the *Heil Hitler!* salute. A bitter conflict with the authorities swiftly followed. The Nazis banned Jehovah's Witnesses meetings and missionary work, and some lost their jobs as civil servants; others had their children taken away to be brought up in Nazi homes. Of the 20,000 or so members active in Germany under Hitler's regime, many found themselves or saw their families and cobelievers in prison or concentration camp. Jehovah's Witnesses were among the first Germans to be placed in the camps, where they were often tortured and murdered.

Christine King

See Also: AUSCHWITZ (-BIRKENAU); CONCENTRATION CAMPS; *HEIL HITLER!*; HITLER, ADOLF; HOLOCAUST, THE; NAZISM; RELIGION; THIRD REICH, THE

References

King, Christine E. 2000. "Responses outside the Mainstream Catholic and Protestant Traditions." Pp. 64–67 in *The Holocaust and the Christian World*, edited by Carol Rittner, Stephen D. Smith, and Irena Steinfeldt. London: Kuperard.
Reynaud, Michel, and Sylvie Graffard. 2001. *Jehovah's Witnesses and the Nazis—Persecution, Deportation and Murder 1933–1945*. New York: Cooper Square.

JESUITS, THE

Among Roman Catholic priests, those of the Society of Jesus (the Jesuits) appear to have been the object of particular hostility on the part of members of the Nazi hierarchy. That was not, however, the case in Fascist Italy, where Mussolini actually used a Jesuit, Fr. Pietro Tacchi-Venturi, as a go-between with the Vatican in the early stages of the negotiations for the Lateran Pacts of 1929, and during subsequent crises in church-state relations in 1931 and 1938–1939. Both Himmler and Rosenberg seem to have had a particular aversion to the Jesuits. In the case of the former, a certain element of admiration and envy is also discernible. If Himmler sought role models for the SS in the medieval Teutonic knights, the Society of Jesus, given the caliber of its members and the rigor of their training, its efficient, centralized organization, its information network, and the Jesuits' role as spiritual "shock troops" under the direct allegiance of the pope, might also have seemed an ideal role model. Indeed, Hitler once described Himmler himself as "the Ignatius Loyola" of the SS (St. Ignatius Loyola was the founder of the Jesuits). On the other hand, it was precisely those qualities of the Jesuits that aroused anxiety and hostility in Nazi circles. Additionally, the tightly knit and secretive operations of the Jesuits aroused suspicion: the German Faith Movement, which was allied with the NSDAP, excluded from the ranks of its prospective members Jews, Freemasons, and Jesuits. The presence of a German Jesuit, Fr. Robert Leiber, in the Vatican as a confidential adviser of Pius XII also aroused profound suspicion in Nazi government circles.

During the life of the Nazi dictatorship the Society of Jesus came under growing persecution from the authorities, with a disproportionate number of its priests ending up in concentration camps. In 1937, after the publication of Pius XI's encyclical *Mit Brennender Sorge*, condemning Nazi violations of the *Reichskonkordat*, the Gestapo intensified its campaign against the Roman Catholic Church in general and the Jesuits in particular, calling upon local branch offices to place the Society under special surveillance, while a nationwide card index was compiled to assist in the battle against the Jesuits. After the Austrian *Anschluss* in 1938, the Jesuit-run college in Innsbruck was closed down because it was regarded as a center of resistance to Nazi rule. During the various phases of the campaigns to sequestrate ecclesiastical properties, those of the Jesuits were a particular target. There is even evidence that the Gestapo contemplated a "final solution" for the Jesuits. The Munich Gestapo chief suggested that, "[at] the latest by 1942, the Jesuits will be sent Eastwards to the camps." It is, of course, no accident that this remark should have been made in Catholic Bavaria, where the Jesuits were believed to wield an especially powerful influence.

The role of some Jesuits in opposing National Socialism in Germany also played its part in triggering these persecutions. Although the influential Jesuit journal *Stimmen Der Zeit* followed the usual German Catholic path from opposing National Socialism in early 1933 to acquiescing in the Nazi dictatorship by the year's end, some Jesuits later became prominent in resistance to the regime. Franz Reinisch, a former editor of the journal; Augustinus Roch, father-provincial of the Jesuits in Bavaria; Hermann Wehrle; and Alfred Delp all suffered death for their links with either the Kreisau circle or the instigators of the July Plot. Given the hostility of the Nazi leadership toward the Jesuits, it is entirely appropriate that another Jesuit, the American John Lafarge, was the author of the unpublished encyclical *Humani Generis Unitas* of 1938, which systematically condemned Nazi racial theory.

There was also an ideological reason why the Nazis made the Jesuits a particular target of their venom. The Jesuits represented the most ultramontane, papalist version of Catholicism; they were known for their particular devotion to the papacy; and they therefore supremely embodied the international nature of the Catholic Church, which stood at the opposite pole to fascist hypernationalism. Moreover, they had spearheaded the Counter-Reformation, which had effectively stemmed the flood of escapees from the Catholic Church to the Reformed congregations. Their very existence and ethos represented the most intransigent opposition to the philosophy of Nazism.

John Pollard

See Also: ANTI-SEMITISM; *ANSCHLUSS*, THE; ANTIFASCISM; AUSTRIA; CATHOLIC CHURCH, THE; CHRISTIANITY; CONCENTRATION CAMPS; COSMOPOLITANISM; FASCIST PARTY, THE; FREEMASONRY/FREEMASONS, THE; GERMAN FAITH MOVEMENT, THE; GERMANNESS (*DEUTSCHHEIT*); GERMANY; GESTAPO, THE; HIMMLER, HEINRICH; HITLER, ADOLF; HOLOCAUST, THE; ITALY; JULY PLOT, THE; KREISAU CIRCLE, THE; MUSSOLINI, BENITO ANDREA AMILCARE; NATIONALISM; NAZISM; NORDIC SOUL, THE; PAPACY, THE; PIUS XI, POPE; PIUS XII, POPE; PROTESTANTISM; RACIAL DOCTRINE; ROMAN CATHOLIC CHURCH, THE; ROME; ROSENBERG, ALFRED; SS, THE; THEOLOGY

References
Conway, J. S. 1968. *The Nazi Persecution of the Churches.* London: Weidenfeld and Nicolson.
Lewy, G. 1964. *The Catholic Church and Nazi Germany.* London: Weidenfeld and Nicolson.
Passalecq, G., and B. Suchecky, eds. 1997. *The Hidden Encyclical of Pius XI.* New York: Harcourt Brace.

JEWRY: *See* ANTI-SEMITISM; HOLOCAUST, THE; ZIONISM
JEWS, THE: *See* ANTI-SEMITISM; HOLOCAUST, THE; ZIONISM
JORDAN, COLIN: *See* GREAT BRITAIN: LEESE, ARNOLD SPENCER

JOYCE, WILLIAM (1906–1946)

Director of propaganda for the British Union of Fascists who fled to Germany in 1940, achieving infamy in the United Kingdom thenceforth as the Nazi radio broadcaster "Lord Haw Haw." Despite not officially being a British citizen (he was born in the United States to Irish parents who had taken U.S. citizenship, and he did not come to the United Kingdom until he was in his teens), Joyce was executed for high treason in 1946, the last person to be hanged as a traitor in Britain. His activities continue to arouse interest in more recent times, and recently published biographical works reflect a fascination with his case.

Graham Macklin

See Also: GERMANY; GREAT BRITAIN; MOSLEY, SIR OSWALD; PROPAGANDA; RADIO; WORLD WAR II

References
Kenny, Mary. 2004. *Germany Calling: A Personal Biography.* New York: New Island.
Martland, Peter. 2003. *Lord Haw Haw: The English Voice of Nazi Germany.* London: National Archives.

JUDAISM: *See* ANTI-SEMITISM; HOLOCAUST, THE; ZIONISM

JULY PLOT, THE

Given the cover name *Operation Valkyrie,* the July Plot marks the only significant act of resistance aimed at toppling the Nazi dictatorship (organized by national-conservative forces) during the whole period from 1933 to 1945. On 20 July 1944, Colonel Claus Graf Schenk von Stauffenberg detonated a bomb during a discussion in Hitler's headquarters in East Prussia. This attempted assassination was supposed to signal the beginning of a putsch, but it did not succeed: Hitler was only lightly wounded, the conspirators failed to get control of the radio stations, and the top Wehrmacht generals were indecisive, compared with the reactions of Wehrmacht and Waffen-SS units loyal to Hitler. The July Plot was organized mainly by Wehrmacht officers associated with imperialistic and national racist Nazi policies who had begun to feel moral scruples or who were afraid that in the end Germany would be totally ruined. Their political program comprised an immediate end to the war, a corporate state, and the retention of territories occupied by Nazi Germany. In consequence of the plot, some 600 to 700 people were arrested and more than 180 of them were executed.

Fabian Virchow

See Also: ANTIFASCISM; CANARIS, ADMIRAL WILHELM; CONSERVATISM; CORPORATISM; HITLER, ADOLF; KREISAU CIRCLE, THE; NAZISM; REMER, OTTO-ERNST; STAUFFENBERG, CLAUS SCHENK GRAF VON; TROTT ZU SOLZ, ADAM VON; WAFFEN-SS, THE; WEHRMACHT, THE; WORLD WAR II

References
Dunn, Walter S., Jr. 2003. *Heroes or Traitors: The German Replacement Army, the July Plot, and Adolf Hitler.* Westport, CT: Praeger.
Galante, Pierre. 2002. *Operation Valkyrie: The German Generals' Plot against Hitler.* New York: Cooper Square.
Manvell, Roger. 1964. *The July Plot: The Attempt in 1944 on Hitler's Life and the Men behind It.* London: Bodley Head.

JUNG, CARL GUSTAV (1875–1961)

Celebrated Swiss psychiatrist and founder of analytical psychology, Jung was concerned for the regeneration of the Aryan race and enthusiastic for *völkisch* ideology. In a famous essay of 1936 he argued that Germany was possessed by Wotan, the true God of the German peoples, but that few of them were conscious of the fact. He sometimes expressed himself in ways that suggested he was anti-Semitic, but debate about that aspect of his thinking continues to the present time. He certainly followed Nazi ideologues in regarding Christianity as a "foreign growth" that had been harmfully grafted onto the Germanic stem. His *völkisch* utopianism and Aryanist mysticism reflected the intellectual atmosphere in which he grew up at the end of the nineteenth century. One of his closest disciples (Jolande Jacobi) recorded that he regarded Nazism as "a chaotic precondition for the birth of a new world." It was not to be rejected even if evil, because it was a necessary precondition for the spiritual rebirth of Germany.

Cyprian Blamires

See Also: ANTI-SEMITISM; ARYANISM; FREUD, SIGMUND; GERMANNESS (*DEUTSCHHEIT*); NAZISM; NEW AGE, THE; NORDIC SOUL, THE; PALINGENETIC MYTH; PSYCHOANALYSIS; PSYCHODYNAMICS OF PALINGENETIC MYTH, THE; PSYCHOLOGY; RELIGION; REVOLUTION; UTOPIA, UTOPIANISM; *VOLK, VÖLKISCH*

Reference
Noll, Richard. 1997. *The Aryan Christ: The Secret Life of Carl Jung.* London: Macmillan.

JÜNGER, ERNST (1895–1998)

Prominent German writer whose extreme right-wing nationalistic views brought him close to the Nazis before their advent to power, but whose relationship to them thereafter became more distant. Jünger fought on the Western Front in World War I and was very highly decorated. His postwar writings combined contempt for democracy and for the people with a conviction that through action and heroism (and dictatorship) society could be revolutionized. In 1923 he left the army, becoming editor of the right-wing Stahlhelm newspaper *Die Standarte* and of the journal *Arminius,* through the pages of which he sought to unite all the different nationalist movements. He became sympathetic to the Nazi movement, stressing in articles such as "Nationalismus und Nationalsozialismus" (1927) that while Nazism differed from pure nationalism, the two forces could together create a new Germany. Reluctant to get involved in practical politics, however, he refused a Nazi offer of a seat in the Reichstag in 1927. From 1933 onward, with the Nazis in power, he withdrew into the role of a detached observer, taking little part in politics. It was as though once his ideas were put into action, he found himself out of tune with them. Then, in 1939, he published the novel *Auf den Marmorklippen,* whose ambiguities concealed an allegorical attack on the Nazi regime.

In 1940, mobilized once more, Jünger took part in the invasion of France. From 1941 to 1944 he was at the army headquarters in Paris. Privately, he regretted much of what was going on, including the persecution of the Jews, which he found incompatible with military honor. Nevertheless, he remained a detached observer, temperamentally unable to involve himself. Even at the time of the 1944 generals' plot, when he knew many of the plotters and was aware of their plans, he remained aloof, though sympathetic. Despite his connections,

and his failure to report what was afoot, he was spared by Hitler because of his eminence as a right-wing writer (though removed from active service). In postwar Germany, despite initial problems with the occupying powers, he settled down to his literary career once more, and, as one of Germany's greatest contemporary writers, was showered with honors.

Richard Griffiths

See Also: ANTI-SEMITISM; DEMOCRACY; ELITE THEORY; *EHRE* ("HONOR"); DICTATORSHIP; FRANCE; GERMANY; HITLER, ADOLF; JULY PLOT, THE; MASSES, THE ROLE OF THE; NATIONALISM; NATURE; NAZISM; PALINGENETIC MYTH; REVOLUTION; SOCIALISM; THIRD REICH, THE; WEIMAR REPUBLIC, THE; WORLD WAR I

References
Nevin, Thomas. 1996. *Ernst Jünger and Germany: Into the Abyss, 1914–1945.* Durham: Duke University Press.
Newman, Elliot. 1999. *A Dubious Past: Ernst Jünger and the Politics of Literature after Nazism.* Berkeley: University of California Press.

KALTENBRUNNER, ERNST (1903–1946)

Successor to Heydrich as head of the SD. While studying law, Austrian-born Kaltenbrunner joined a racial nationalist student fraternity. A member of the NS-DAP and the SS from 1932, he played a prominent role in organizing the *Anschluss;* when Austrian chancellor Schuschnigg was forced to retreat in March 1938, Kaltenbrunner was the commander of the SS troops exerting pressure on him. Kaltenbrunner not only became a member of the Reich National Parliament (1938) but, more important, he also became responsible for the police forces in former Austria (renamed the Ostmark) and in late January 1943 successor of Heydrich as the head of the Reich Central Security Office. As he controlled both the police and the large apparatus organizing the mass murder of the European Jews, he was sentenced to death in the Nuremberg Trials and executed on 16 October 1946.

Fabian Virchow

See Also: *ANSCHLUSS*, THE; ANTI-SEMITISM; AUSTRIA; HEYDRICH, REINHARD; HOLOCAUST, THE; NATIONALISM; NAZISM; NUREMBERG TRIALS, THE; SCHUSCHNIGG, KURT VON; SD, THE; SS, THE

References

Black, Peter. 1984. *Ernst Kaltenbrunner, Ideological Soldier of the Third Reich.* Princeton: Princeton University Press.

Matteson, Robert Eliot. 1993. *The Capture and the Last Days of SS General Ernst Kaltenbrunner: Chief of the Nazi Gestapo, Criminal Police, and Intelligence Services.* Saint Paul, MN: R. E. Matteson.

KAMIKAZE: *See* CULTS OF DEATH

KAMPUCHEA

The native name for Cambodia, Kampuchea first gained international prominence when the Communist Party of Kampuchea—better known as the Khmer Rouge (KR)—took power in 1975 and renamed the country Democratic Kampuchea (DK); some have viewed their brand of socialist nationalism as fascistic. Under Pol Pot's leadership, the KR conducted a campaign of mass murder and genocide/democide in which an estimated 2 million people died during its four-year rule from 1975 until 1979. The population of Kampuchea had been 6 to 7 million. When they came to power on 17 April 1975, the KR immediately evacuated more than 2 million people from the Cambodian capital, Phnom Penh,

A child next to the Killing Fields Memorial in Cambodia. The ideology of the Khmer Rouge regime, which unleashed a reign of terror in the country, is sometimes considered to have resemblances to that of interwar fascism. (Corel)

and other cities and relocated them to the countryside. The Constitution of DK was promulgated on 5 January 1976 and declared its foreign policy as one of independence, peace, neutrality, and nonalignment, a position consistent with its intention to support the anti-imperialist struggle of the Third World that had begun with Lenin.

In practice, DK possessed a totalitarian regime in which the Organization or Angkar attempted to control all citizens. On 13 January 1976, Radio Phnom Penh declared: "Against any foe and against every obstacle thou shalt struggle with determination and courage, ready to make every sacrifice, including thy life, for the people, the laborers, and peasants, for the revolution and for Angkar, without hesitation or respite" (Jackson 1989, 66). Private property was abolished, Buddhism was banned, and currency was made illegal. The KR expressed commitment to Angkar through patriotic mottos and slogans. They portrayed Cambodian communism as superior to the

communism of other countries, using the metaphor of engines and horsepower. Pol Pot became prime minister from 1976 to 1979, but he had already become the KR's leader since 1963. DK implemented a radical agricultural revolution based on collectivization, light industry, and cooperative farming. Inspired by Mao's economic program of the five-year plan and the Great Leap Forward, Pol Pot introduced the Four Year Plan on 21 August 1976, emphasizing rapid economic development through agricultural production and light industry. Subsequently his commitment to an accelerated socialist state failed utterly, as a result of his inefficient economic plans, inadequate rationing system, and retrograde developmental polices. The KR's nationalist tendencies have arguably been considered fascist in nature. The KR targeting of the Vietnamese and other ethnic groups such as the Chams (Muslim Cambodians) can be invoked as one example. Under DK, these two groups were perceived as enemies of the communist revolution. During the purges of 1977–1978, the KR targeted and systematically exterminated the Vietnamese resident in Kampuchea because of racial and political animosity between the two countries and the fear that Vietnam would invade and occupy Cambodia. That fear was realized on 7 January 1979.

By 1978, the KR boasted of a kill ratio of one Cambodian to thirty Vietnamese. Extrapolating, 2 million Cambodians could sacrifice themselves in order to exterminate all of Vietnam, which would still leave millions of Cambodians alive. Heder (2004) convincingly demonstrates that the single most important influence on KR doctrine and organizational structure was, in fact, the Vietnamese communists themselves. In the final analysis, several typical features of fascist regimes—such as qualified protection for private property, state toleration of a national religion, and an express rejection of Marxism and Marxism-Leninism in all its variants—were not in evidence during Democratic Kampuchea, and the regime cannot, as such, be considered fascist.

Susan Ear and Sophal Ear

See Also: BUDDHISM; CAPITALISM; DEMOCRACY; ECONOMICS; IMPERIALISM; KHMER ROUGE, THE; MARXISM; MODERNITY; NATIONALISM; POL POT; RACIAL DOCTRINE; RELIGION; REVOLUTION; SOCIALISM; STATE, THE; TECHNOLOGY; TOTALITARIANISM; VIOLENCE; WAR; WARRIOR ETHOS, THE

References
Documentation Center of Cambodia. http://www.dccam.org (accessed 15 June 2004)
Etcheson, Craig. 1984. *The Rise and Demise of Democratic Kampuchea.* Boulder, CO: Westview.
Heder, Steve. 2004. *Cambodian Communism and the Vietnamese Model.* Vol. 1: *Imitation and Independence, 1930–1975.* Bangkok: White Lotus.
Jackson, Karl, ed. 1989. *Cambodia 1975–78: Rendez-vous with Death.* Princeton: Princeton University Press.

KAPP PUTSCH, THE

Attempted antigovernment coup by right-wing conspirators in Germany in March 1920. Wolfgang Kapp (1868–1922) was a journalist who mounted the coup together with General Walther von Lüttwitz (1859–1942). The government fled Berlin but called for a general strike that paralyzed essential services; Kapp soon had to take refuge in Sweden. The putsch had been spearheaded militarily by a naval brigade known as the Ehrhardt Brigade, commanded by Captain Hermann Ehrhardt, a Freikorps leader, and the uniform of its members came with the innovation of the swastika.

Cyprian Blamires

See Also: FREIKORPS, THE; GERMANY; SWASTIKA, THE; WAR VETERANS; WEIMAR REPUBLIC, THE

References
Eley, G. 1980. *Reshaping the German Right.* New Haven: Yale University Press.
Feldman, Gerald D. 1997. *The Great Disorder: Politics, Economics and Society in the German Inflation, 1914–24.* New York: OUP.

KEITEL, WILHELM (1882–1946)

Hitler's most trusted military adviser. Keitel joined the imperial army in 1901 and became head of the Wehrmacht Office in the Reich war department (1935) and then chief of the Wehrmacht headquarters in early 1938. Promoted to Field Marshal in 1940, Keitel was involved in all strategic decisions and spearheaded the penetration of the Wehrmacht with National Socialist ideology. The mass murder of civilians and Soviet POWs and the plundering of the territories occupied by Nazi Germany were carried out on his orders. Keitel was sentenced to death in the Nuremberg Trials and executed.

Fabian Virchow

See Also: BARBAROSSA, OPERATION; GERMANY; HITLER, ADOLF; NAZISM; NUREMBERG TRIALS, THE; SLAVS, THE (AND GERMANY); SOVIET UNION, THE; WEHRMACHT, THE; WORLD WAR II

References
Mueller, Gene. 2003. *Wilhelm Keitel, the Forgotten Field Marshal: With a New Introduction.* New York: Cooper Square.
Schmeller, Helmut J. 1970. *Hitler and Keitel: An Investigation of the Influence of Party Ideology on the High Command of the Armed Forces in Germany between 1938 and 1945.* Hays: Fort Hays Kansas State College.

KELLER, CARLOS (1898–1974)

Chilean of German ancestry who helped to found the Movimiento Nacional Socialista (MNS; National Socialist Party) in 1932. Keller agreed with the anti-Jewish attitudes of the German Nazis, but he criticized their racist beliefs, in part because he rejected such a deterministic outlook and because he supported intermarriage. He wrote two books. The first, *La eternal crisis Chilena,* promoted nationalism and authoritarianism. The second, *La locura de Juan Bernales,* recounted a highly flattering and male view of the history of the MNS. He left the MNS after its failed coup attempt of 1938.

Margaret Power

See Also: ANTI-SEMITISM; CHILE; GERMANY; NATIONALISM; NAZISM; RACIAL DOCTRINE; RACISM; SEXUALITY

KHMER ROUGE, THE

The "Red Khmer" or "Red Cambodians" ruled Democratic Kampuchea as a totalitarian regime from 1975 until 1979. With its origins in the Khmer People's Revolutionary Party (1951), renamed the Khmer Worker's Party (1960) and forerunner to the Communist Party of Kampuchea (1971), the KR had a leadership that was composed of a group of communist guerrillas, a number of whom were French-educated and committed to the nationalist struggle of gaining power in Cambodia by overthrowing Prince Sihanouk's government. They were led by Pol Pot and Nuon Chea, known as Brother Number 1 and Brother Number 2, respectively. On 18 March 1970, Cambodian head of state Prince Norodom Sihanouk was overthrown in a republican coup d'etat and replaced by Lon Nol and Sirik Matak. Sihanouk joined hands with the KR to regain power. Through radio appeals by Sihanouk, the KR gained popularity and momentum from the general population, and it overran the republican government in 1975. On 17 April 1975, the KR evacuated nearly 2 million urban dwellers from Phnom Penh and other cities to the countryside, creating a nationwide agricultural labor camp.

It has been suggested that the KR were not communists but ultranationalists and inherently fascists, but it is clear that while they possessed strong nationalist tendencies, they were fervently committed to Marxist-Leninist ideology, the eradication of class and religion, the elimination of private property, and total political and economic egalitarianism. The end result, however, was mass starvation and executions, disease, and genocide/democide resulting in the deaths of an estimated 2 million out of 6 to 7 million Cambodians. The Vietnamese invasion of 1978–1979 ended the revolution and forced the KR to retreat to the Thai-Cambodian border, where they continued their struggle as part of the Coalition Government of Democratic Kampuchea with royalist and noncommunist allies until the signing of the Paris Peace Accord in 1991. The movement dissolved with the death of Pol Pot in 1998 and the defection of Nuon Chea and other leaders shortly thereafter.

Susan Ear and Sophal Ear

See Also: CAPITALISM; CLASS; DEMOCRACY; DICTATORSHIP; KAMPUCHEA; MARXISM; NATIONALISM; POL POT; RELIGION; REVOLUTION; SOCIALISM; TOTALITARIANISM

References
Chandler, David, and Ben Kiernan, eds. 1983. *Revolution and Its Aftermath in Kampuchea: Eight Essays.* New Haven: Yale University Southeast Asia Studies.
Documentation Center of Cambodia. http://www.dccam.org (accessed 15 June 2004)
Etcheson, Craig. 2005. *After the Killing Fields: Lessons from the Cambodian Genocide.* Westport, CT: Greenwood.
Jackson, Karl, ed. 1989. *Cambodia 1975–78: Rendez-vous with Death.* Princeton: Princeton University Press.

KIRCHENKAMPF, THE: *See* CONFESSING (or CONFESSIONAL) CHURCH, THE; *GLEICHSCHALTUNG*

KOCH, ILSE (1906–1967)

Wife of the SS commandant of the Buchenwald concentration camp, notorious for her sadism toward inmates. The daughter of a laborer, she married Colonel Karl Koch in 1936. She made a hobby out of collecting such items as lampshades and gloves made from the skins of dead camp inmates. In 1951 she was sentenced to life imprisonment but committed suicide in prison in 1967.

Cyprian Blamires

See Also: CONCENTRATION CAMPS; SS, THE

References
Smith, Arthur L. 1995. *Die Hexe von Buchenwald.* Vienna: Böhlau.

KORNEUBURG OATH, THE

The oath was the program of the Austrian Heimwehr, agreed to at a meeting in Korneuburg, Lower Austria, in May 1930. It invoked an Austrian, rather than Pangerman, nationalism, and called for root and branch reform, rejecting Marxist socialism, liberal capitalism, parliamentary democracy, and the party political system alike in favor of a new single-party Heimwehr state and corporate representation. For the Heimwehr's more radical leaders, the oath was meant to unite a regionally based and ideologically undefined anticommunist patriotic movement on a clearly fascist program, distinguishing itself from its conservative political allies in order to contest the forthcoming 1930 elections as an independent political force. Local Heimwehr members, unhappy about adopting the oath, refused to join the abortive 1931 coup of the Styrian movement, led by Walter Pfrimer, who wanted to implement the oath upon seizing power.

Philip Morgan

See Also: "ANTI-" DIMENSION OF FASCISM, THE; AUSTRIA; BOLSHEVISM; CAPITALISM; CORPORATISM; DEMOCRACY; GERMANY; HEIMWEHR, THE; LIBERALISM; MARXISM; NATIONALISM; PANGERMANISM; PARLIAMENTARISM; SOCIALISM; STATE, THE

References
Edmondson, C. Earl. 1982. *Heimwehr and Austrian Politics, 1918–36.* Athens: University of Georgia Press.

KRAFT DURCH FREUDE: *See* LEISURE; LABOR SERVICE, THE

KREISAU CIRCLE, THE

The center of the middle-class civilian resistance to Hitler's dictatorship from 1940. The name referred to the Silesian estate of Count von Moltke, one of the leaders of the resistance to Hitler. The group incorporated some forty people from such different backgrounds as social democrats (Julius Leber), aristocrats (Yorck von Wartenburg), diplomats (Trott zu Solz), and representatives of the Lutheran and Catholic churches. The aim of the group was to prepare the way for a postwar democratic Germany. As Count von Moltke rejected the idea of overthrowing the Nazi dictatorship by violence—he was afraid of a new myth of the stab in the back and had moral scruples about violent rebellion against an established government—this issue played a minor role only at the three big meetings of the Kreisau Circle in 1942 and 1943. The circle produced programmatic papers such as the "Principles of a New Order" or "Punishment of the Disgracers of Law," in which a Christian ethos dominated. This found its expression in a close relationship between church and state, a strong emphasis on the importance of families, and the notion of a democracy of "small communities" in which parishes would play an important role beside neighborhoods, local authority districts, and companies. Basic industries were to be nationalized in a corporative-style mixture of a planned and a market economy. The circle strongly favored reconciliation with European neighbors, the inclusion of Germany in a European context, and the foundation of a European association. The disintegration of the Kreisau Circle was the result of the arrest of Count von Moltke in January 1944. Some of its members took part in the July plot, and many of them were among those convicted and executed in consequence.

Fabian Virchow

See Also: ANTIFASCISM; CATHOLIC CHURCH, THE; CONFESSING (OR CONFESSIONAL) CHURCH, THE; CONSERVATISM; CORPORATISM; ECONOMICS; EUROPE; FAMILY, THE; GERMANY; HITLER, ADOLF; JULY PLOT, THE; LUTHERAN CHURCHES, THE; NAZISM; NOVEMBER CRIMINALS/ *NOVEMBERBRECHER*, THE; STATE, THE; STAUFFENBERG, CLAUS SCHENK GRAF VON; THIRD REICH, THE; TROTT ZU SOLZ, ADAM VON; WEHRMACHT, THE; WORLD WAR II

References
Moltke, Freya von. 2003. *Memories of Kreisau and the German Resistance.* Lincoln: University of Nebraska Press.

Mommsen, Hans. 2003. *Alternatives to Hitler: German Resistance under the Third Reich.* Trans. Angus McKeoch. London: I. B. Tauris.

Roon, Ger van. 1971. *German Resistance to Hitler: Count von Moltke and the Kreisau Circle.* London: Van Nostrand Reinhold.

KRIECK, ERNST (1882–1947)

National Socialist educational theorist. In 1900 he became a schoolmaster in Baden and in 1928 obtained a chair in the Pedagogical Academy at Frankfurt. He was dismissed from this post on account of his agitation on behalf of the National Socialists, but in 1933 he was made professor of pedagogics in Frankfurt and the following year in Heidelberg; he then rose to be rector of the universities of Frankfurt (1933) and Heidelberg (1937–1938). His ambition to become the leading National Socialist pedagogue and philosopher in Germany was blocked by Alfred Rosenberg, and that led to his retirement in 1938. Subsequently, he devoted himself to writing. In numerous publications—among others the polemical tract *Nationalpolitische Erziehung* (*National Political Education,* 1932)—Krieck embodied the National Socialist world view in pedagogy. He advocated the education of youth in National Socialist organizations such as the Hitler Youth, the SA, and the SS and called for the German people to be educated as a "race-conscious nation." He also called for "breeding, selection and culling." In his three-volume *Völkisch-politischen Anthropologie* (1936/1938) he praised the ideal of the "hero ready for sacrifice" and advocated a "specific" German philosophy.

Markus Hattstein
(translated by Cyprian Blamires)

See Also: ARYANISM; BLOOD; EDUCATION; EUGENICS; GERMANNESS (*DEUTSCHHEIT*); GERMANY; HERO, THE CULT OF THE; NAZISM; NORDIC SOUL, THE; RACIAL DOCTRINE; ROSENBERG, ALFRED; SA, THE; SS, THE; UNIVERSITIES (GERMANY); *VOLK, VÖLKISCH;* YOUTH MOVEMENTS

Reference
Blackburn, Gilmer W. 1985. *Education in the Third Reich: A Study of Race and History in Nazi Textbooks.* New York: State University of New York Press.

KRISTALLNACHT (NIGHT OF BROKEN GLASS)

Anti-Jewish night of violence and destruction carried out by the SA during the night from 9 to 10 November 1938. *Kristall* is a reference to the windows of about 7,000 Jewish-owned shops smashed that night. All over Germany and Austria, synagogues were burned to the ground and the homes of Jews were attacked. Joseph Goebbels had instigated the pogroms by a speech calling for retaliation for the murder of German diplomat Ernst von Rath in Paris. The Gestapo and SS arrested approximately 30,000 male Jews and imprisoned them in concentration camps in Buchenwald, Dachau, and Sachsenhausen.

Christophe Müller

See Also: ANTI-SEMITISM; CONCENTRATION CAMPS; GERMANY; GESTAPO, THE; GOEBBELS, (PAUL) JOSEPH; HOLOCAUST, THE; NAZISM; PROPAGANDA; SA, THE; SS, THE

Reference
Read, A. 1989. *Kristallnacht: Unleashing the Holocaust.* London: Michael Joseph.

KRUPP VON BOHLEN UND HALBACH, ALFRIED (1907–1967)

Eldest son of Gustav Krupp (chairman of the board of the Friedrich Krupp company, 1909–1943), became promoting member of the SS in 1931. During the 1930s he was an influential protagonist of heavy industry and received the honorary title of *Wehrwirtschaftsführer* ("work leader in defense products factories"). Later he dealt with the pillage of economic goods in the occupied countries. In 1943, Alfried Krupp became the sole owner of the combine. With this position, he became responsible for the large-scale exploitation of forced labor, and for that he was given a prison sentence of twelve years in the Nuremberg Trials.

Fabian Virchow

See Also: FORCED LABOR; GERMANY; INDUSTRY; NAZISM; NUREMBERG TRIALS, THE; SS, THE; WORLD WAR II

References
Batty, Peter. 2001. *The House of Krupp: The Steel Dynasty that Armed the Nazis.* New York: Cooper Square.
Young, George Gordon. 1960. *The Fall and Rise of Alfried Krupp.* London: Cassell.

KU KLUX KLAN, THE

First emerging in the immediate aftermath of the American Civil War and revived in 1915, the Ku Klux Klan represents the most enduring form of the extreme Right to appear in the United States. It was created by six Confederate veterans in Pulaski, Tennessee, but the exact date of the Klan's inception is disputed. Probably emerging in late 1865, it derived its name partly from the popularity of Greek names for student fraternities (the Greek word for circle is *kuklos*) and partly from the Scottish origin of many white Southerners (hence "clan"). In 1867, the Klan was reorganized under the leadership of former Confederate general Nathan Bedford Forrest. Their identities disguised by white hoods and robes, Klan night-riders whipped, beat, and shot African Americans and white supporters of the federal government. Control of its activities proved difficult, and in 1869, Forrest declared it dissolved. Much of its activity nonetheless continued. Ultimately, federal legislation and mass trials of Klan activists dealt a grievous blow to the organization, which effectively ceased to exist by the early 1870s. The goal of restoring white supremacy in the defeated South, however, was largely achieved.

In 1915, following the enthusiastic reception of *The Birth of a Nation,* D. W. Griffiths's silent movie celebrating the Klan of the 1860s, the organization was relaunched. By the early 1920s it had sunk roots in many states and achieved the largest membership it would ever experience, with estimates ranging from 1 million to more than 6 million. It was influential in election contests in states ranging from Oregon to Texas. It suffered a number of splits, however, and in 1925 was deeply damaged by the publicity surrounding the conviction of its leading Indiana official for the murder of a young woman he had kidnapped and sexually assaulted. By the end of the 1920s, the Klan was a shadow of its former self. In 1944, faced with the government's claim of large amounts in back taxes, it formally declared itself suspended. It continued to exist at state level, and a number of attempts were made to re-

Initiation ceremony for Ku Klux Klan members in Baltimore, 1923. This movement's concerns have traditionally had more to do with the maintenance of racial segregation and white supremacism than with the revolutionary thrust of interwar fascism. (The Illustrated London News Picture Library)

vive it nationally. In 1954, the Supreme Court's Brown ruling against school segregation resulted in an upsurge of activity. Unlike previously, this third period did not involve a single Klan organization. Of the different groups, the most important was the United Klans of America, formed in 1961. United Klans members were heavily involved in a campaign of violence against African Americans and their supporters, but other Klans were also involved, notably the White Knights of the Ku Klux Klan. Black churches were bombed, opponents were beaten, and in the most publicized incident, in 1964, three civil rights activists were murdered in Mississippi. The spread of civil rights activity to the North gave rise to Klan growth outside the South, and in 1960 the different groupings were estimated to total between 35,000 and 50,000. But the passing of civil rights measures and the increase in African American political participation marked the failure of Klan terrorism, and subsequent attempts to revive the organization met with little success.

In the 1970s, two groups attracted media attention. The first, the Knights of the Ku Klux Klan, was led by a history graduate and former Nazi, David Duke. His frequent television appearances and attempt to reinvent the Klan as a movement for white rights proved unsuccessful, and Duke left the Klan, subsequently becoming a Louisiana state legislator. A rival group, the Invisible Empire, Knights of the Ku Klux Klan, offered a more traditional image, only for its leader, Bill Wilkinson, to be revealed as an FBI informant; in 1994 a court case led to the group's dissolution. (Another case, in 1987, ended with a $7 million award against the United Klans.) By the early 1990s, it was estimated that membership in different Klans had fallen to between 5,500 and 6,500. While the Ku Klux Klan has outgrown its Southern origin, and even emerged in other countries—for instance, in Canada and Germany—it has failed to achieve the levels of support of earlier periods.

Martin Durham

See Also: DUKE, DAVID; NAZISM; NEO-NAZISM; RACIAL DOCTRINE; RACISM; UNITED STATES, THE; WHITE SUPREMACISM

References

Dobratz, Betty A., and Stephanie L. Shanks-Meile. 2000. *The White Separatist Movement in the United States: White Power, White Pride.* Baltimore: Johns Hopkins University Press.

Sims, Patsy. 1978. *The Klan.* New York: Stein and Day.

Stanton, Bill. 1992. *Klanwatch: Bringing the Ku Klux Klan to Justice.* Bergenfield, NJ: Mentor.

Wade, Wyn Craig. 1987. *The Fiery Cross: The Ku Klux Klan in America.* New York: Simon and Schuster.

KUHN, FRITZ: *See* GERMAN-AMERICAN BUND, THE

KÜHNEN, MICHAEL (1955–1991)

A relatively influential and high-profile neo-Nazi activist in postwar West Germany, from the mid-1970s until his death in 1991. Unlike a host of other German neofascist, neo-Nazi, national revolutionary, conservative revolutionary, and New Right leaders, several of whom were more sophisticated thinkers, Kühnen was jailed several times and managed to garner a disproportionate amount of media attention because of his penchant for wearing Nazi-style uniforms, using inflammatory Nazi-inspired rhetoric, organizing paramilitary camps, sponsoring acts of terrorism and street violence, and openly celebrating Hitler's birthday.

Kühnen began his political career in the late 1960s in the ranks of the principal West German right-wing electoral party, the Nationaldemokratische Partei Deutschlands (NPD; National Democratic Party of Germany). He was especially active in its Aktion Widerstand (Resistance Action) initiatives opposing the conciliatory policies toward East Germany and the Soviet bloc of the then-chancellor and leader of the *Sozialdemokratische Partei Deutschlands* (SPD; Social Democratic Party of Germany), Willi Brandt. During this period Kühnen made contacts with several leading neo-Nazi activists, including Manfred Roeder of the Deutsche Bürgerinitiative (BBI; German Citizens' Initiative). After the hemorrhaging of the NPD's voter base in the 1972 elections and the subsequent splintering of the entire radical-right milieu, he founded a series of his own neo-Nazi groups. Before doing so, however, he seems to have either temporarily joined or infiltrated the Liga gegen den Imperialismus (League against Imperialism), a Maoist front group established by the recently banned Kommunistische Partei Deutschland/Marxisten-Leninisten (KPD/ML; Communist Party of Germany/Marxist-Leninists), from whom he claims to have learned much about comradeship, propaganda, and organizational techniques.

The most important of these neo-Nazi organizations was the Aktionsfront Nationaler Sozialisten (ANS; National Socialists' Action Front), which he established in November 1977 and hoped eventually to transform into a mass national party. This group was apparently organized, on the Nazi Party model, into a two-tiered structure with both a legal and a clandestine wing. In contrast to certain other extremists, Kühnen also understood the importance of the news media in garnering publicity and new recruits, and thus he regularly granted interviews and assiduously engaged in agitational and propaganda activities. Among his many tactics was the distribution of pamphlets, bulletins (such as *NS Kampfruf*), and leaflets outlining his political agenda, as well as stickers with ANS symbols and catchy, easy-to-remember slogans such as *Wir sind wieder da* ("We're back again!") and *Ausländer raus* ("Foreigners out!"). To help produce these materials he established a close relationship with a German-American Nazi sympathizer based in Nebraska named Gary Rex ("Gerhard") Lauck, self-styled Fuehrer of a tiny organization known as the Nationalsozialistische Deutsche Arbeiterpartei/Aufbau- und Auslandsorganization (NSDAP/AO; National Socialist German Worker's Party/Construction and External Organization), who published large amounts of German-language neo-Nazi material and then shipped it to Germany in violation of that country's laws against the production and dissemination of Nazi propaganda.

As a result of his increasingly public neo-Nazi activities, Kühnen was expelled from the Bundeswehr's cadet college in 1977. From that point on, he devoted most of his efforts to political activism on the fringes of West German society. In 1977 and 1978, ANS members carried out several bank robberies and stole weapons from various military bases, and the following year six of them were arrested, tried, and sentenced to eleven years in prison for those crimes, as well as for hatching bomb plots targeting NATO facilities and a memorial for the victims of the Bergen-Belsen Concentration Camp. Kühnen himself was tried and convicted, but he was sentenced only to four years in prison, for inciting racial hatred and violence. It was during this period of incarceration that, following Hitler's example, he wrote his main ideological treatise, *Die zweite Revolution* (*The Second Revolution,* 1979, an allusion to the aborted 1934 "social revolution" of Ernst Roehm's interwar SA), wherein he sought to update and modify Nazi doctrine, organization, and praxis to make it more relevant in the vastly different context of postwar Europe. This work advocated lifting the ban on the NSDAP, repatriating foreigners, protecting the environment, resisting U.S. "imperialism," and struggling for a neutral and "socialist" Germany. In short, it sought to combine old-style Nazi biological racism and the social revolutionary agenda of the SA with postwar geopolitical "Third Positionism."

In January 1983, following his November 1982 release from prison, Kühnen arranged for a merger between the remnants of the ANS and branches of the Nationale Aktivisten in Fulda, which led to the creation of the Aktionsfront Nationaler Sozialisten/Nationale Aktivisten (ANS/NA; National Socialists' Action Front/National Activists), a new group modeled on the SA. When the German government moved to ban this new organization, which now numbered almost 300 activists in nearly thirty local branches, Kühnen set up a series of cultural circles—the most important of which was the Gesinnungsgemeinschaft der Neuen Front (GdNF; New Front Association of Kin-

dred Spirits)—and successfully infiltrated and took over a small conservative right-wing party, the Freiheitliche Deutsche Arbeiterpartei (FAP; Independent German Worker's Party), in an effort to circumvent the ban. Although he was rearrested and sentenced to three years in prison in 1985, by the time Kühnen was released in March 1988 the FAP had become far larger and more militant under its new neo-Nazi directors. Unfortunately for Kühnen, rival FAP leaders Jürgen Mosler and Volker Heidel had in the meantime carried out a successful internal putsch against him. The rationale for this putsch was that Kühnen, who was homosexual, had openly promoted the recruitment of homosexuals who were unencumbered by traditional families into the neo-Nazi movement in a book entitled *Nazismus und Homosexualität.* (This work was later translated into the French language by gay French neo-Nazi Michel Caignet, a member of Marc Frédériksen's Fédération d'Action Nationaliste et Européenne (FANE; Federation for Nationalist and European Action) and Holocaust denier who was later implicated in various pedophilia scandals in France.) Since the bulk of the FAP adopted the antihomosexual positions of Mosler and Heidel, who were backed by other German neo-Nazi leaders who hoped to weaken Kühnen's influence, the latter was forced to form a new organization with his remaining partisans, the Nationale Sammlung (NS; National Assembly), which he viewed in part as the foundation of a broader electoral party like the Front National in France. When government authorities banned the NS from participating in the March 1989 regional elections in Hesse, Kühnen and his supporters established yet another new organization, the Deutsche Alternative (DA; German Alternative). Soon after he managed to secure the support of a breakaway faction from the FAP, the Nationale Offensive. He then launched *Arbeitsplan Ost,* an ambitious project designed to spread neo-Nazi ideas within the former German Democratic Republic and thereby recruit disgruntled East Germans into a broader countrywide movement. The extent to which his efforts may have fueled the outbreak of neo-Nazi extremism and violence in eastern Germany after the Marxist regime collapsed is unclear, since much of the neo-Nazi resurgence in that region seems to have been a spontaneous reaction in the face of official Stalinist dogma, looming economic uncertainty, the unwelcome presence of foreigners, and psychological alienation and anxiety.

In addition to his propaganda and organizational activities in the East, Kühnen's efforts over the years to transform the parallel apparatus of the GdNF into a broader neo-Nazi umbrella organization were short-circuited by his early HIV-related death in April 1991. Nevertheless, although he attracted much more press attention than was probably warranted, Kühnen was an indefatigable activist who seems to have exerted a disproportionate influence on the fringe neo-Nazi milieu in Cold War Germany.

Jeffrey M. Bale

See Also: AMERICANIZATION; ANTI-SEMITISM; CONCENTRATION CAMPS; CONSERVATISM; ECOLOGY; EUROPEAN NEW RIGHT, THE; GERMANY; HITLER, ADOLF; HOLOCAUST DENIAL; HOMOSEXUALITY; IMMIGRATION; IMPERIALISM; LEADER CULT, THE; MARXISM; NATURE; NAZISM; NEO-NAZISM; PARAMILITARISM; POSTWAR FASCISM; PROPAGANDA; RACIAL DOCTRINE; RACISM; REVOLUTION; ROEHM, ERNST; SA, THE; SOCIALISM; STYLE; TERRORISM; THIRD POSITIONISM; WHITE SUPREMACISM

References

Antifaschistische Autorenkollektiv, ed. 1991. *Drahtzieher im braunen Netz: Die Wiederaufbau der NSDAP.* Berlin: ID-Archiv im ISSG.

Di Lorenzo, Giovanni. 1989. "Wer, bitte, ist Michael Kühnen: Beschreibung eines Phänomens." Pp. 232–247 in *Rechtsextremismus in der Bundesrepublik: Voraussetzungen, Zusammenhänge, Wirkungen,* edited by Wolfgang Benz. Frankfurt: Fischer.

Dudek, Peter, and Hans-Gerd Raschke. 1984. *Entstehung und Entwicklung des Rechtsextremismus in der Bundesrepublik: Zur Tradition einer besonderen politischen Kultur.* 2 vols. Opladen: Westdeutscher.

Kühnen, Michael. 1981. *Homosexualität und Nazismus.*

———. 1987a [1979]. *Die zweite Revolution: Glaube und Kampf.* 2 vols. Lincoln, NE: NSDAP-AO.

———. 1987b. *Politisches Lexikon der Neuen Front.* Butzbach: GdNF.

McGowan, Lee. 2002. *The Radical Right in Germany, 1870 to the Present.* London: Longman.

Mecklenburg, Jens, ed. 1996. *Handbuch deutscher Rechtsextremismus* (esp. pp. 149–150, 269–271, 484–485). Berlin: Elefanten.

Stöss, Richard. 1991. *Politics against Democracy: The Extreme Right in West Germany.* Trans. Lindsay Batson. Oxford: Berg.

Chronology of Fascism

1861   Italy was proclaimed as a Kingdom.

1871   Germany was unified and the Second German Empire was founded under Otto von Bismarck.

In America the Ku Klux Klan was formed, followed by a U.S. congressional inquiry.

1875   In Germany, the Socialist Workers Party was founded.

1879   Austria and Germany signed the 'Dual Alliance'.

1883   Mussolini was born on 29 July.

1886   In France, Boulanger became Minister for War.

Drumont's *La France Juive* was published.

1888   In Germany, Friedrich Wilhelm Viktor Albert von Preußen became Kaiser.

1889   Adolf Hitler was born on 20 April in Braunau am Inn.

1890   Langbehn's *Rembrandt as Teacher* was published.

In Germany, Bismarck was dismissed as Chancellor.

1891   In Germany, the Socialist Party became the Social Democratic Party and adopted a Marxist program.

The Russo-Franco Alliance was signed.

1893   The Pan-German League was founded.

The Gobineau Society was founded.

1895   Le Bon's *Psychology of Crowds* was published.

1898   In France, the term 'socialist nationalism' was first coined by Maurice Barrès.

Germany began a program of naval expansion.

1899   Houston Stewart Chamberlain's *Foundations of the Nineteenth Century* was published.

In France, the *Action Française* was founded by Charles Maurras.

1903   In Italy, Giovanni Giolitti became Prime Minister.

In Germany, The *Wandervögel* movement was founded.

1907   The 'Triple Entente' between Britain, France, and Russia was formed in August.

1908   Sorel's *Reflections on Violence* was published.

Austria annexed Bosnia on 5 October.

In France, the *Action Française* launched their newspaper.

1909   Marinetti's 'Futurist Manifesto' was published.

1910   In Italy, the Italian Nationalist Association was founded by Corradini and Federzoni.

1911–
1912   The *Cercle Proudhon* met.

1911   A German gunboat was sent to Agadir in French-controlled Morocco, creating an international crisis.

1912   In Germany, the SDP became the largest party in the Reichstag.

        In Italy, Mussolini became editor of *Avanti*.

1914   In Bosnia, Archduke Franz Ferdinand was assassinated by Gavrilo Princip of the Young Bosnia movement in Sarajevo on 28 June.

        Austro-Hungary declared war on Serbia on 28 July.

        Germany declared war on Russia on 1 August.

        Germany declared war on France on 3 August.

        Britain declared war on Germany on 4 August.

        The German Army was defeated at the Battle of the Marne on 10 September, marking the failure of the Schlieffen Plan that was designed to secure a quick German victory.

        The Italian Socialist Party ousted Mussolini from the editorship of *Avanti* and from the party after he began to campaign for the entry of Italy into World War I.

        In Italy, the *Fasci di Azione Rivoluzionaria* was founded in October.

1915   Italy entered the war on the side of the Allies in May.

        In the United States, the Ku Klux Klan was reconstituted.

1916   In Germany, Field Marshall Paul von Hindenburg became the Commander-in-Chief of the German Forces in August, and General Erich Ludendorff became his Chief of Staff.

1917   In Russia, Czar Nicholas II abdicated on 16 March after a period of revolutionary fervor.

        The United States declared war on Germany on 6 April.

        In Germany, the Fatherland Party was founded in September.

        Italians suffered hugely traumatic but galvanizing defeat at the Battle of Caporetto between October and November.

        In Russia, the Bolsheviks took power on 7 November.

        The 'Peace Decree' was issued by Lenin on 8 November.

        Russia and Germany agreed an armistice on 16 December.

1918   President Wilson announced his 'Fourteen Points' in January.

        In Argentina, the University Reform movement emerged.

        In South Africa, the *Broederbond* movement was founded.

        The peace treaty of 'Brest-Litovsk' was signed by the USSR and Germany on 14 March.

        In the USSR, civil war broke out in May and the Allied forces sided with the counterrevolutionaries.

        Germany began to negotiate peace with the Allies in October.

        In Germany, sailors based in Kiel revolted.

        In Bavaria, a Republic was declared on 7 November after the Bavarian monarchy was overthrown.

In Germany, Kaiser Wilhelm's abdication was announced on 9 November and the German Republic was proclaimed.

The German government signed an armistice at Compiègne on 11 November, ending World War I.

In Germany, the German Communist Party was founded in December.

1919   The Paris Peace Conference began in January.

In Germany, the 'Spartacist' rising of communists was suppressed by *Freikorps* in January.

In Germany, the National Constitutional Assembly convened in Weimar in February, and Friedrich Ebert became President.

The Comintern was founded in March.

In Hungary, a Soviet Republic was formed in March.

In Italy, Mussolini formed the *Fasci di Combattimento* on 23 March.

In Germany, a Bavarian Soviet regime was proclaimed in April.

The Soviet regime in Bavaria was suppressed in May by both the army and *Freikorps.*

The Treaty of Versailles was signed on the 28 June.

In Germany, the Weimar Constitution was adopted on 31 July.

In Hungary, the Hungarian Soviet Republic was defeated in August by Yugoslav, Romanian, and Czech forces alongside nationalist counterrevolutionaries.

Gabriele D'Annunzio began his occupation of Fiume in September.

In Germany, Hitler joined the German Workers' Party based in Munich on 12 September.

In Italy, Mussolini was defeated in national elections in November.

1920   The Covenant of the League of Nations was agreed in February.

In Germany, the German Workers' Party was renamed the National Socialist German Workers' Party in February, and the '25 Point Program' was adopted by the party on 24 February.

In Germany, the Kapp Putsch attempt occurred in Berlin in March.

In Italy, the 'Red Two Years' reached its pinnacle, and was marked by worker occupation of factories in the summer.

In Italy, Fascism spread into the countryside in the autumn, and *Squadristi* violence escalated.

In the USSR, the civil war ended after an armistice with Poland was signed on 6 October.

In Hungary, Admiral Horthy was elected head of state in December.

D'Annunzio's occupation of Fiume was ended in December.

1921   In Italy, the Italian Communist Party was formed in January.

In Italy, after national elections in May, Mussolini, alongside thirty-five other fascists, was elected to the Italian parliament.

In Italy, the *Arditi del Popolo* was formed in the spring.

The 'Little Entente' between Czechoslovakia, Romania, and Yugoslavia was completed in June.

In Germany, the National Socialist German Workers' Party (NSDAP) or Nazi Party appointed Hitler as party chairman on 29 July.

In Italy, the Italian Fascist Party was formed in November.

1922   In Finland, the Academic Karelia Society was founded.

In the United States, Texas returned a Ku Klux Klan representative to the U.S. Senate.

In Italy, Mussolini was made Prime Minister of Italy on 30 October after the 'March on Rome'.

1923   The French and Belgian armies began their occupation of the industrialized Ruhr region of Germany on 11 January.

In Italy, the Italian Grand Council was created in January.

In Romania, the National Christian Defense League was founded.

In Germany, the Nazi Party held its first Congress in Munich on 27 January.

In Italy, the Italian Nationalists merged with the Fascist Party in March.

Germany experienced a period of hyper-inflation from June, and Gustav Stresemann became Chancellor on 12 August and ended the policy of passive resistance to France.

In Hungary, Gömbös alongside others formed the Party of Racial Defense in August.

The Greek island of Corfu was occupied briefly by the Italian regime in August.

In Spain, Miguel Primo de Rivera successfully mounted a military coup in September.

In Germany, Bavaria broke off diplomatic relations with the central German government in Berlin on 20 October.

In Germany, Hitler led the Nazi Party's failed 'Beer-Hall Putsch' in Munich on 9 November.

In Germany, the inflationary crisis was ended after the introduction of a new currency on 15 November.

In Italy, the Fascist government, Italian industrialists, and Fascist syndicates established the 'Palazzo Chigi' agreement in December.

1924   Fiume was annexed by Italy on 16 March.

Hitler was convicted of high treason on 1 April and sentenced to five years' imprisonment, eligible for parole after six months.

Italian Fascists gained 374 seats, an overwhelming majority in the Italian parliament, in April as a result of the Acerbo electoral law.

The Dawes Plan to revise German reparations was agreed.

In Italy, the Socialist deputy Matteotti was abducted and murdered by Italian Fascists because of his critique of Fascist violence during the April elections.

In Italy, the Aventine Secession began.

In Sweden, the National Socialist League of Freedom and the National Unity Movement were formed.

In Germany, Hitler was released from prison on 20 December.

1925   In Italy, Mussolini resolved the Matteotti crisis by announcing the beginning of the Fascist dictatorship in January.

In France, George Valois founded *Le Faisceau*.

In Germany, the Nazi Party was re-established in February.

In Germany, Hindenburg was elected president on 25 April.

The first volume of Hitler's *Mein Kampf* was published in July.

In Italy, the 'Battle for Grain' was launched in October.

In Germany, the SS protection squad was formed on 9 November.

In Italy, Mussolini gained total executive powers in December.

1926   In Austria, the Nationalist Socialist German Workers' Party formed in April.

In Italy, Syndical Laws were approved by the Fascist regime in April.

In Poland, Josef Pilsudsky staged a military coup in May.

In Portugal, General Gomes de Costa staged a military coup in May.

In Romania, the National Christian Defense League gained six parliamentary seats.

In Italy, the Ministry of Corporations was formed in June.

Germany entered the League of Nations in September.

1927   In France, an Anti-Fascist congress was held in Paris in April.

In Romania, Codreanu formed the Legion of the Archangel Michael in June.

1928   In France, Valois ended *Le Faisceau* in April.

In Germany, the Nazi party polled 2.6 percent of the national vote in May, gaining only 12 seats in the Reichstag.

In France, the *Croix de Feu* (CF) was founded.

In Britain, the Imperial Fascist League was established.

In Italy, the Fascist Grand Council was made into a constitutional organ in December.

1929   In Yugoslavia, King Alexander staged a royal coup in January.

In Estonia, the Vaps movement was formed.

In Sweden, the National Rural Association was formed.

The Italian Fascist Regime and the Vatican signed the Lateran Agreements in February.

The Young Plan was issued in June.

The Wall Street Crash inflicted a worldwide economic downturn from October.

In Finland, the Lapua movement was founded in November.

1930   In Germany, Chancellor Heinrich Brüning (who took office in March) began governing by decree under article 48 of the Weimar Constitution on 16 July.

In Denmark, the Danish National Socialist Workers Party was founded.

In Britain, Oswald Mosley founded his 'New Party'.

In Romania, the Iron Guard was founded by Codreanu to work alongside the Legion of the Archangel Michael.

In Sweden, the Swedish Religious People's Party was established.

In Spain, the *Partido Nacionalista Español* was founded.

In Portugal, the *União Nacional* was established.

In Romania, King Carol returned from exile in June.

In Germany, the Nazis experienced an electoral breakthrough and won over 18 percent of the national vote in the parliamentary elections in September.

1931   In Spain, the monarchy was replaced by a parliamentary republic in January.

In the Netherlands, the Dutch National Socialist Movement was founded.

In Norway, Quisling established the Nordic Folk Awakening movement.

In Spain, the Redondo-Ramos JONS and *La Conquista del Estado* movements were founded.

In Britain, Mosley published his *A National Policy* in March.

In Britain, the 'National Government' was formed in August and the Gold Standard was abandoned in September.

Japan invaded Manchuria in September.

In Britain, Mosley's New Party failed to win a seat in the British General Election.

In Hungary, the Scythe cross movement was formed in December.

In the Netherlands, the Dutch National Socialist Party was formed in December.

In Germany, unemployment rose to 5.6 million.

1932   In Finland, after an attempted Lapua coup in February, the movement was banned and it evolved into the People's Patriotic Movement (IKL).

In Germany, Hitler was defeated by Hindenburg in German presidential elections in March and April.

In Germany, the SA and the SS were prohibited by Brüning in April.

In Germany, von Papen became Chancellor of Germany, replacing Brüning, in May.

In Germany, the ban on the SA and SS was lifted by von Papen.

In Chile, the *Movimiento Nacional Socialista de Chile* (MNS) was founded.

In the Netherlands, the General Dutch Fascist Union was founded.

In France, the *Cartel des Gauches* won the national elections in May.

In Finland, the People's Patriotic Movement was formed in June.

In Yugoslavia, the Ustasha movement was founded.

In Germany, the Nazis won over 37 percent of the national vote in parliamentary elections.

In Portugal, the National Syndicalist movement was founded by Rolão Preto in September.

In Hungary, Horthy appointed Gömbös as Prime Minister in October.

In Britain, after dissolving his New Party in April, Mosley established the British Union of Fascists (BUF) in October.

In Italy, Fascists celebrated the ten year anniversary of the 'March on Rome', which included the famous exhibition of the Fascist Revolution.

In Germany, the Nazis won 33 percent of the national vote in parliamentary elections in November and Communists increased their share of the vote, after which von Papen resigned as Chancellor.

In Germany, von Schleicher became chancellor in December.

1933   In Germany, Hitler was appointed Chancellor on 30 January, von Papen was made his vice-chancellor.

In Germany, the Reichstag was destroyed by fire on 27 February, and, blaming the Communists, Hitler suspended many basic civil liberties the following day.

In Austria, Dollfuss suspended the parliament in March in order to rule by decree.

In Germany, Goebbels launched his Ministry of Popular Enlightenment and Propaganda in March.

In Germany, the first Nazi concentration camp was opened on 20 March in Dachau.

In Germany, Hitler was given full dictatorial powers on 23 March after the Reichstag passed the Enabling Act.

In Finland, *Lapua* gained fourteen seats in the general election.

In France, the *Franciste* movement was formed.

In Germany, *Gleichschaltung* began on 31 March.

In Portugal, Salasar's 'New State' constitution came into effect in April.

In Germany, Nazis organized for Jewish businesses to be boycotted on 1 April.

In Germany, Jews, communists, social democrats, and miscellaneous other political opponents were expelled from the civil service by the Nazis on 7 April.

In Norway, Vidkun Quisling's National Union movement was formed.

In Mexico, the Mexican Revolutionary Action movement was founded.

In Germany, the German Labour Front was established on 2 May.

In Germany, 'un-German' books were burned on 10 May.

In Germany, Nazis became the only legal party on 14 July.

Germany signed a concordat with the Vatican on 20 July.

Germany left the League of Nations and disarmament conference on 14 October.

In Belgium, the Flemish National Front was formed in October.

In Estonia, the Estonian War of Independence Veterans' League received 73 percent of the national vote in a referendum.

In Spain, the *Falange* was formed in October by José Antonio Primo de Rivera.

In the United States, Pelley's Silver Shirts movement was formed.

1934   Germany signed a non-aggression pact with Poland in January.

Mussolini and Hitler met in Venice in June.

In Germany, a purge directed at Ernst Roehm and the SA left over 120 dead on 30 June.

In Britain, the BUF held its Olympia Rally.

In Austria, Dollfuss was murdered by the Austrian Nazis in a failed coup in July.

In Germany, Hitler became *Führer* after the death of Hindenburg in August gave him the opportunity to consolidate the role of President and Chancellor.

The USSR joined the League of Nations in September.

In Switzerland, the Montreux meeting of international fascist movements was held in December.

In Latvia, the Fascist Peasants Union gained power.

1935   In Hungary, Szálasi formed the Party of National Will in January.

In Bolivia, the *Falange Socialista Boliviana* was founded.

In Germany, universal military training was introduced by Hitler on 1 March, in defiance of the Treaty of Versailles.

In Serbia, the *Zbor* movement was founded.

The Franco-Soviet treaty was signed in May.

In Ireland, the National Corporate Party was founded by Eoin O'Duffy in June.

The 'Popular Front' strategy was agreed upon by the USSR at a meeting of the Comintern in August.

In Germany, the Nuremberg Racial Laws that denied Jews political rights were announced in September.

Italy invaded Ethiopia in October, causing the League of Nations to impose sanctions.

In Belgium, the Rex movement was formed.

1936   In Spain, a 'Popular Front' government was formed in February.

The Nazis entered and remilitarized the Rhineland in March.

In France, a 'Popular Front' government was formed in May.

In Italy, Mussolini proclaimed the birth of the Italian Empire after victory in Ethiopia in May.

In Spain, civil war broke out on 31 July after a right wing rising against the Spanish Republic led by Francisco Franco. Later, both Hitler and Mussolini intervened on the side of Franco.

In Germany, the Berlin Olympics began on 1 August.

In Germany in September, Hitler announced the 'Four Year Plan' to prepare Germany's armed forces and economy for war.

The 'Axis' Italo-German treaty was created in October.

The German-Japanese Anti-Comintern Pact was created in November.

In Germany, the Hitler Youth program was made mandatory from December.

1937   The Papal encyclical on 'The Church in Germany' was issued on 14 March.

Hitler and Mussolini met in Vienna.

In Romania, the Legion of the Archangel Michael gained 16 percent of the vote and Antonescu was appointed Chief of General Staff.

Italy joined Germany and Japan in the Anti-Comintern Pact in November.

Under the policy of appeasement, Lord Halifax went to Germany in November seeking a British-German agreement.

1938   In Romania, King Carol abolished the country's parliamentary system in February.

In Argentina, the Argentinian Fascist Party was founded.

Germany annexed Austria in March, Mussolini supported the action.

In Germany and Austria, a plebiscite in April gave over 99 percent approval to the Austrian *Anschluss*.

In Italy, anti-Semitic legislation was introduced in July.

The Sudetenland was transferred from Czechoslovakia to Germany after the Munich Agreement on 29 September.

In Germany, the Nazi *Kristallnacht* pogrom terrorized Jewish communities on 9 November, leaving 267 synagogues and 815 Jewish shops destroyed.

1939   The new Franco regime was officially recognized by Britain on 27 February.

In Romania, Codreanu was killed in a purge of the Legion of the Archangel Michael.

German forces occupied Prague and the whole of Czechoslovakia in March, violating the Munich Agreement.

Albania was occupied by Italy in April.

In response to unauthorized German aggrandisement, the British Prime Minister Neville Chamberlain pledged military support for Poland.

The Anglo-German Naval Treaty and the Non-Aggression Treaty with Poland were both renounced by Germany in May.

In Hungary, the Arrow Cross gained 25 percent of the national vote in elections in May.

The 'Pact of Steel' between Italy and Germany was signed on 22 May.

Danzig (Gdansk) was demanded by the Germans from Poland on 16 August.

The Nazi-Soviet Non-Aggression Pact was agreed on 23 August.

Germany invaded Poland on 1 September, beginning World War II.

Britain declared war on Germany on 3 September.

Warsaw surrendered to Germany on 27 September.

The Nazi euthanasia program was authorised by Hitler in October.

France and Britain declined Hitler's peace offer of accepting the legitimacy of Germany's conquest of Poland on 6 October, and continued the war against Nazi expansionism.

1940   Construction began on the Auschwitz concentration camp in February.

Germany occupied Norway and invaded Denmark in April.

Germany attacked Holland, Belgium, Luxembourg, and France in May.

Italy entered the war on the side of Germany on 10 June.

The French signed an armistice with Germany at Compiègne on 22 June, following which the Vichy regime was established and Pétain became head of state.

Hungary reclaimed Transylvania from Romania in August.

Germany began the 'Battle of Britain' on 13 August.

In Romania, King Carol abdicated and the Iron Guard jointly took power to form the 'National Legionary State' in September.

The Tripartite Pact was signed by Italy, Germany, and Japan in September.

Italy invaded Greece in October.

Soviet Foreign Minister Molotov visited Berlin and met with Hitler in November.

1941   In Romania, Antonescu dissolved the Iron Guard in January after their attempted coup. German forces invaded Greece and Yugoslavia in April.

Rudolf Hess flew to Scotland in May, ostensibly in a bid to bring about peace between Britain and Germany. Replacing him with Bormann, Hitler declared Hess 'mad.'

Hitler issued the 'Commissar Order' on 6 June that called for the liquidation of all Communists in the forthcoming Operation Barbarossa.

Operation Barbarossa commenced and German forces began the invasion of the USSR on 22 June.

In Germany, the Ministry for the Occupied Eastern Territories was created under the leadership of Alfred Rosenberg in July.

In Croatia, the Ustasha came to power.

In Occupied France, foreign Jews began to be rounded up.

The Atlantic Charter was signed by Churchill and Roosevelt in August.

At Auschwitz, the Nazis began experiments with Zyklon-B from September.

In the USSR, Leningrad was surrounded on 4 September.

In Germany, from 19 September Jews were forced to wear a yellow Star of David.

At Chlemno, Nazis began to gas Jews in December.

The Japanese bombed Pearl Harbor on 7 December.

War on the United States was declared by Italy and Germany on 11 December.

In Germany, after the dismissal of Field Marshal Walther von Brauchitsch, Hitler assumed operational command of the German armed forces on 19 December.

1942   The Wannsee Conference was held with the aim of coordinating the genocide programs of the Holocaust on 20 January.

In Norway, Quisling became prime minister in February.

In Czechoslovakia, Heydrich was assassinated on May 27 in Prague.

In Poland, Jews began to be deported from the Warsaw Ghetto to Treblinka from June.

At Auschwitz, mass gassing of Jews began in June.

In the USSR, German forces reached Stalingrad in September.

At El Alamein in Egypt, Rommel's Afrika Korps were forced into retreat in October.

British and American troops landed in North Africa in November.

In Vichy France, German forces occupied the country on 11 November.

In the USSR, the German Sixth Army was encircled at Stalingrad on 23 November.

1943   In the USSR, the German Sixth Army surrendered at Stalingrad on 31 January.

In Poland, the Warsaw Ghetto uprising began in April.

In North Africa, the Afrika Korps surrendered on 12 May.

In Poland, the Warsaw Ghetto uprising was crushed by 16 May and the ghetto was destroyed.

Allied forces landed in Sicily on July 10, leading to Mussolini's removal as head of state and later arrest on 25 July.

Allied forced landed on the Italian mainland on 3 September.

An armistice with Allied forces was announced by the new Italian regime on 8 September.

Mussolini was rescued on 12–13 September by German forces from Gran Sasso, following which the birth of the Italian Social Republic was announced by Mussolini at Salò.

Italy declared war on Germany on 13 October.

1944   In Hungary, German forces occupied the country and Eichmann began a roundup of Hungarian Jews.

Rome was liberated by Allied forces on 4 June.

The D-Day landings began on 6 June.

Colonel Stauffenberg attempted to assassinate Hitler on 20 July.

In Romania, Antonescu's pro-German government fell in August.

The Red Army reached the German borders in East Prussia on 18 August.

Paris was liberated by the Allies on 25 August.

The Anglo-American forces reached Germany's western borders by 15 September.

The German counteroffensive, the Battle of the Bulge, began on 16 December in the Ardennes.

1945   Auschwitz was liberated by the Red Army in January.

In Germany, Hitler made his last broadcast to the German people on 30 January.

At Yalta in the Crimea, Churchill, Roosevelt, and Stalin met on 11 February and decided on the temporary post-war arrangements for Germany.

In Germany, Hitler issued his 'Nero Command' or scorched earth policy on March 19.

In Italy, after the liberation of northern Italy in April, Mussolini was captured by partisans on 26 April and executed on 28 April in Milan.

Hitler committed suicide on 30 April.

Germany unconditionally surrendered on 8 May.

Japan unconditionally surrendered on 2 September after atomic bombs were dropped on Hiroshima and Nagasaki.

In Germany, the Nuremberg War Crimes trials began on 20 November.

1946   In Argentina, Juan Perón was elected President.

In Germany, Nazi war criminals were executed at Nuremberg in October.

In Italy, the *Movimento Sociale Italiano* (MSI) was founded in December.

1947   George Marshall announced the European Recovery Program in June.

1948   In Italy, the Italian Republic was officially proclaimed on 1 January, and its constitution outlawed a return of the Fascist Party.

The USSR blocked land access to Berlin in June in protest at the creation of the separate West German state.

In Ecuador, the *Alianza Revolucionaria Nacionalista Ecuatoriana* (ARNE) was founded.

In South Africa, apartheid was established.

1949   The Soviet blockade of Berlin ended in May.

The Federal Republic of Germany (FRG) was established on 23 May, and Konrad Adenauer became Chancellor on 15 September.

The German Democratic Republic (GDR) was established on 12 October, led by Walter Ulbricht.

Salazar's Portugal entered NATO.

In South Africa, the National Party was created.

1950   In Belgium, the *Mouvement Social Belge* was founded.

Nation Europa was founded.

In West Germany, the far-right *Sozialistiche Reichspartei* was founded.

1951   The European Social Movement was formed at Malmö.

1952   Eva Perón died.

The Federal Republic of Germany (FRG–West Germany) agreed to restitution payments with Israel to the Jewish people.

1953   In the Netherlands, the Dutch National European Socialist Movement was founded.

Evola's *Men Standing among the Ruins* was published.

1954   In France, the *Parti Patriotique Révolutionnaire* was created.

In Britain, the League of Empire Loyalists was founded by A. K. Chesterton.

1955   The Paris Agreements allowed FRG to rearm, though without developing weapons of mass destruction, and also gave full sovereignty to the new state.

The USSR formed the Warsaw Pact in response to FRG rearmament and the rise of NATO.

1956   In Austria, the Freedom Party of Austria (FPÖ) was formed.

1960   In Britain, the British National Party (BNP) was founded.

1961   In Israel, Eichmann was tried and convicted.

The German Democractic Republic (GDR–East Germany) began building the Berlin Wall.

Evola's *To Ride the Tiger* was published.

1962   The World Union of National Socialists was formed.

In Britain, the National Socialist Movement was founded.

1964   In France, *Occident* was founded.

In Germany, the National Democratic Party of Germany was founded.

1966   In Portugal, the Portuguese National Revolutionary Front was formed.

1967   In Britain, the British National Front was established.

In the United States, the leading Nazi sympathizer George Lincoln Rockwell was assassinated; the U.S. government published a report investigating contemporary activities of the Ku Klux Klan.

1968   In France, *Occident* was banned.

In Portugal, Salazar left office.

The Group for Research and Studies on European Civilization (GRECE) was founded.

1969   In France, the *Ordre Nouveau* was born.

In Italy, Almirante became leader of the MSI.

In the United States, the Posse Comitatus movement was founded.

In West Germany, the National Democratic Party gained 4 percent of the vote.

1970   In the United States, Christian Identity ideologue Wesley Smith died.

1971   In the FRG, the *Deutsche Volks Union* was founded.

In the GDR, Walter Ulbricht was replaced by Erich Honecker as head of state.

1972   In Italy, the MSI gained 8.7 percent of the vote in national elections.

In France, Le Pen's *Front National* was founded.

1973   In Belgium, the Flemish *Vlaams-Nationale Raad* was founded.

In Argentina, Perón returned to the position of President.

In Germany, *Wehrsportgruppe Hoffmann* was created.

In South Africa, the African Resistance Movement was formed.

Thies Christopherson's *The Auschwitz Lie* was published.

1974   In Portugal, the dictatorship collapsed.

In France, the *Parti des Forces Nouvelles* (PNF) was formed.

1975   In Spain, the death of Franco ended his dictatorship.

In Cambodia, the Khmer Rouge came to power.

1976   In Belgium, the Belgian Nationalist Student Confederation was created.

1977   In the United States, the Christian Patriot's Defense League was founded.

In Greece, the National Alignment (EP) movement was founded.

In Belgium, the Flemish *Vlaams-Nationale Partij* (VNP) and the *Vlaamse Volkspartij* (VVP) were formed.

In Portugal, the *Movimento Independente para a Reconstrucão Nacional* (MIRN) was founded.

In Germany, the neo-Nazi movement *Aktionsfront Nationaler Sozialisten* (ANS) was formed.

1978 William Pierce's *The Turner Diaries* was published.

Arthur Butz's *The Hoax of the Twentieth Century* was published.

In France, the *Légitime Défence* was created.

In Belgium, the *Vlaams Blok* (VB) and the *Union Démocratique pour le Respect du Travail* (UDRT) were formed.

1979 In Cambodia, after a sustained program of genocide the Khmer Rouge fell from power.

In France, *Sécurité et Liberté* was formed.

In Greece, the United Nationalist Movement was founded.

1980 In Germany, the Thule Seminar was founded.

In Austria, Norbert Burger of the National Democratic Party gained 3.2 percent of the presidential vote.

In the United States, National Socialist sympathizer Harold Covington won 43 percent of the vote in North Carolina.

1982 In Belgium, the Belgian Nationalist Young Students Association was created.

In Britain, the BNP was re-constituted.

1983 In FRG, the *Republikaner* party was founded.

In France, Le Pen's National Front made an electoral breakthrough.

In the United States, the Order movement was founded.

1984 In France, Le Pen's National Front gained over 10 percent in European elections.

1985 In Spain, the *Junta Coordinatora de Fuerzas Nacionales* was created.

In Belgium, the *Front National-Nationaal Front* was formed.

1986 In France, the National Front won thirty-five seats in parliamentary elections.

In Yugoslavia, Milošević issued the SANU Memorandum.

In Austria, Kurt Waldheim ran a controversial election campaign, while Haider took over leadership of the FPÖ.

1987 Klaus Barbie was tried for war crimes.

In Austria, far-right ideologues held 'summit talks' with Haider.

1988 In France, Le Pen received 14.6 percent of the vote in the presidential election.

Fred Leuchter published *The Leuchter Report,* a revisionist history of the Nazi gas chambers.

1989 In Belgium, the Agir movement was founded.

In France, the National Front won a seat in the Dreux parliamentary by election.

In Germany, the Berlin Wall fell, providing a symbolic historical reference point marking the end of the Cold War.

In FRG, the *Republikaner* party won eleven seats in West Berlin in national elections, and six seats in European elections. Also the *Deutsche Alternative, Freundeskreis Freiheit für Deutschland,* and *Nationale List* movements were created.

In Greece, the Nationalist Youth Front was founded.

In Portugal, the *Força National-Nova Monarquia* was formed.

1990 GDR and FRG were united under the West German constitution.

In Denmark, the Party of Well-Being was founded.

In the United States, white supremacist candidate David Duke won 44 percent in a Louisiana election.

In Romania, the Romanian Cradle movement was formed.

In Austria, the FPÖ received over 15 percent in elections.

In Germany, the *Republikaner* party lost its eleven seats in Berlin, and Schönhuber resigned the leadership in May, and was re-elected leader in June.

In Italy, Rauti replaced Fini as leader of the MSI after the party gained a mere 4 percent in local elections.

1991   In Austria, in Vienna local elections the FPÖ won 23 percent of the vote.

In Germany, the *Deutscher Kameradschaftsbund, Nationaler Bloc,* and *Deutsche Liga für Volk und Heimat* were founded.

In South Africa, Apartheid ended.

In the United States, David Duke won 39 percent of the vote in Louisiana governor elections.

In Italy, Fini was re-instated as leader of MSI.

In Romania, the Movement for Romania was formed.

1992   In Croatia, the Croatian Party of Pure Rights and the Croatian Party of Rights Youth Group were founded.

In Romania, the Romanian Party of the National Right was formed.

In Baden–Württemberg in Germany, the *Republikaner* party received 11 percent of the vote.

1993   In Britain, the BNP gained its first councillor in the Isle of Dogs after winning 34 percent of the vote in local elections.

In Italy, the MSI's Fini stood for Mayor of Rome and Alessandra Mussolini stood for the Mayor of Naples.

In Austria, dissenters left the FPÖ, while Haider published *Freiheitlichen Thesen.*

1994   In Austria, the FPÖ polled 22 percent in parliamentary elections.

In Italy, Fini launched Alleanza Nazionale (AN) in January, and in May the AN won 13.5 percent in Italian elections gaining five seats in Berlusconi's cabinet.

In European elections, the French National Front and the German Republikaner party won 10.5 percent and 3.9 percent of the vote respectively.

1995   In Denmark, the Danish People's Party was founded.

In Russia, the *Derzhava* movement was formed.

In the United States, Timothy McVeigh exploded a massive bomb in government offices in Oklahoma.

In France, Le Pen won fifteen percent of the vote in French presidential elections.

1996   In Austria, the FPÖ polled 28 percent in European elections.

In Italy, the AN won 15.7 percent in Italian parliamentary elections and 150,000 attended an AN rally in September in Milan.

1998   In India, Bharatiya Janata made an electoral breakthrough.

1999   In France, friends of Bruno Mégret formed the *Mouvement National Républicain* after splitting with Le Pen's National Front.

In Britain, David Copeland exploded a series of nail bombs in London.

In European elections, the FPÖ in Austria won five seats in the European parliament; elsewhere the *Republikaner* party in Germany polled 1.7 percent, and in France the National front gained 5.7 percent of the vote.

2000   In Italy, Fini became Berlusconi's Deputy Prime Minister.

2001   In Britain, the BNP exploited race riots in Oldham, Burnley, and Bradford.

In Denmark, the Danish People's Party won 22 parliamentary seats.

2002   In France, Le Pen gained 17 percent in the first round of the presidential elections and went through to the second round.

In Britain, the BNP won three council seats in Burnley.

In the Netherlands, the far-right leader Pim Fortuyn was assassinated.

2003   In Italy, Alessandra Mussolini left AN after disagreeing with Fini over his denunciation of fascism.

2004   In Italy, Alessandra Mussolini was elected to the European parliament.

Bibliography

KEY SECONDARY SOURCES ON GENERIC FASCISM

Allardice, G. ed. 1971. *The Place of Fascism in European History.* Englewood Cliffs, NJ: Prentice-Hall.

Almog, S. 1990. *Nationalism and Anti-Semitism in Europe.* Oxford: Pergamon Press.

Bessel, R. 1996. *Fascist Italy and Nazi Germany: Comparison and Contrasts.* Cambridge: Cambridge University Press.

Billig, M. 1978. *Fascists: A Social-psychological View of the National Front.* London: Academic Press in co-operation with European Association of Experimental Social Psychology.

Billig, M. 1979. *Psychology, Racism and Fascism.* Birmingham: A. F. & R. Publications.

Blinkhorn, M. ed. 1990. *Fascists and Conservatives.* London: Unwin Hyman.

Blinkhorn, Martin. 2001. *Fascism and the Right in Europe; 1919–1945.* Harlow: Longman.

Blum, G. 1998. *The Rise of Fascism in Europe.* London: Greenwood Press.

Brooker, P. 1991. *The Faces of Fraternalism: Nazi Germany, Fascist Italy, Imperial Japan.* Oxford: Clarendon Press.

Carsten, F. L. 1971. *The Rise of Fascism.* Berkeley, CA: University of California Press.

Cassels, A. 1975. *Fascism.* Arlington Heights, IL: Harlan Davidson.

Chakotin, S. 1934. *The Rape of the Masses: The Psychology of Totalitarian Propaganda.* London: Routledge.

Cheles, L., Ferguson, R., Vaughan, M. eds. 1991. *Neo-Fascism in Europe.* London: Longman.

Clark, T. 1997. *Art and Propaganda in the Twentieth Century: The Political Image in the Age of Mass Culture.* New York, NY: Harry N. Abrams.

Cohen, Carl. 1972. *Communism, Fascism, Democracy: The Theoretical Foundations.* New York, NY: Random House.

Cullen, S. M. 1986. 'Leaders and Martyrs: Codreanu, Mosley and José Antonio', in *History,* vol. 71.

Davies, P., Lynch, D. 2002. *Routledge Companion to Fascism and the Far Right.* London: Routledge.

De Felice, R. 1977 *Interpretations of Fascism.* London: Harvard University Press.

De Felice, R., Ledeen, M. 1976. *Fascism: An Informal Introduction to its Theory and Practice.* New Brunswick, NJ: Transaction Books.

Deakin, F. W. 1962. *The Brutal Friendship: Mussolini, Hitler and the Fall of Italian Fascism.* London: Weidenfeld and Nicolson.

Delzell, C. F. 1970. *Mediterranean Fascism, 1919–1945.* London: Macmillan.

Durham, M. 1998. *Women and Fascism.* London: Routledge.

Eagleton, T. 1991. *Ideology: An introduction.* London: Verso.

Eatwell, Roger. 2003. *Fascism: A History.* London: Pimlico.

Eatwell, R., Write, A. eds. 1993. *Contemporary Political Ideologies.* London: Pinter.

Eksteins, M. 1989. *Rites of Spring: The Great War and the Birth of the Modern Age.* London: Bantam.

Elliott, W. Y. 1968. *The Pragmatic Revolt in Politics: Syndicalism, Fascism, and the Constitutional State.* New York, NY: Howard Fertig.

Farquharson, J. E. 1976. *The Plough and the Swastika: the NSDAP and Agriculture in Germany, 1928–45.* London: Sage.

Feuer, L. S. 1975. *Ideology and the Ideologists.* Oxford: Blackwell.

Foreman, J. D. 1974. *Fascism: The Meaning and Experience of Reactionary Revolution.* New York, NY: F. Watts.

Fraser, L. 1957. *Propaganda.* London: Oxford University Press.

Gentile, E. 2000. 'The Sacralization of Politics: Definitions, Interpretations and Reflections on the Question of Secular Religion and Totalitarianism,' *Totalitarian Movements and Political Religions* vol. 1, no. 1.

Germani, G. 1978. *Authoritarianism, Fascism and National Populism.* New Brunswick, NJ: Transaction Books.

Golsan, R. ed. 1992. *Fascism, Aesthetics and Culture.* London: University Press of New England.

Greene, N. ed. 1968 *Fascism: An Anthology.* Arlington Heights, IL: Harlan Davidson.

Gregor, A. J. 1969. *The Ideology of Fascism: The Rationale of Totalitarianism.* New York, NY: Free Press.

Gregor, A. J. 1979. *Italian Fascism and Developmental Dictatorship.* Princeton, NJ: Princeton University Press.

Gregor, A. J. 1999. *Phoenix: Fascism in Our Time.* London: Transaction Publishers.

Griffin, R. D. 1991. *The Nature of Fascism.* London: Routledge.

Griffin, R. D. ed. 1995. *Fascism.* Oxford: Oxford University Press.

Griffin, R. D. ed. 1998. *International Fascism: Theories, Causes and the New Consensus.* London: Arnold.

Griffin, R. D., Feldman, M. eds. 2004. *Fascism: Critical Concepts in Social Science* (5 volumes) London: Routledge.

Griffiths, R. 2005. *Fascism.* London: Continuum.

Hainsworth, P. 1992. *The Extreme Right in Europe and the USA.* London: Pinter.

Hamilton, A. 1971. *The Appeal of Fascism. A Study of Intellectuals and Fascism, 1919–1945.* New York, NY: Macmillan.

Hamilton, B. 1987. 'The Elements of the Concept of Ideology,' in *Political Studies,* vol. 35.

Hayes, P. 1973. *Fascism.* London: Allen & Unwin.

Hoffmann, H. 1996. *The Triumph of Propaganda: Film and National Socialism, 1933–1945.* Oxford: Berghahn Books.

Kallis, A. A. 2000. *Fascist Ideology: Territory and Expansionism in Italy and Germany, 1922–1945.* London: Routledge.

Kallis, A. A. ed. 2003. *The Fascism Reader.* London: Routledge.

Kedward, H. R. 1971. *Fascism in Western Europe.* New York, NY: New York University Press.

Kitchen, M. 1976. *Fascism.* London: Macmillan.

Laclau, E. 1977. *Politics and Ideology in Marxist Theory: Capitalism, Fascism, Populism.* London: NLB.

Laqueur, W. ed. 1976. *Fascism: A Reader's Guide: Analyses, Interpretations, Bibliography.* Harmondsworth: Penguin Books.

Larsen, S. U, Hagtvet, B., Myklebust, J. P. eds. 1980. *Who Were the Fascists? Social Roots of European Fascism.* Bergen: Universitetsforlaget.

Lubas, H. ed. 1973. *Fascism: Three Major Regimes.* New York, NY: J. Wiley.

Mangan, J. A. ed. 2000. *Superman Supreme: Fascist Body as Political Icon—Global Fascism.* London: Frank Cass.

Michaelis, M. 1989. 'Fascism, Totalitarianism and the Holocaust. Reflections on Current Interpretations of National Socialist Anti-Semitism,' in *European History Quarterly,* vol. 19.

Milfull, J. ed. 1990. *The Attractions of Fascism: Social Psychology and Aesthetics of the 'Triumph of the Right.'* Oxford: Berg.

Miller, E. A. ed. 1989. *The Legacy of Fascism: Lectures Delivered at the University of Glasgow.* Glasgow: University of Glasgow.

Morgan, P. 2003. *Fascism in Europe, 1919–1945.* London: Routledge.

Mosse, G. L. 1966. 'The Genesis of Fascism', in *Journal of Contemporary History,* vol. 1, no. 1.

Mosse, G. L. 1980. *Masses and Man: Nationalist and Fascist Perceptions of Reality.* New York: H. Fertig.

Mosse, G. L. 1990. *Fallen Soldiers. Reshaping the Memory of the World Wars.* Oxford: Oxford University Press.

Mosse, G. L. 1999. *The Fascist Revolution: Towards a General Theory of Fascism.* New York, NY: H. Fertig.

Mosse, G. L., Laqueur, W. eds 1966 *International Fascism 1920–1945.* New York, NY: Harper & Row.

Mühlberger, D. ed. 1987. *The Social Basis of European Fascist Movements,* London: Croom Helm.

Nathan, P. W. 1943. *The Psychology of Fascism.* London: Faber and Faber.

Nolte, E. 1965. *Three Faces of Fascism: Action Française, Italian Fascism, National Socialism.* London: Weidenfeld and Nicolson.

O'Sullivan, N. 1983. *Fascism.* London: J. M. Dent.

Passmore, K. 2002. *Fascism: A Very Short Introduction.* Oxford: Oxford University Press.

Passmore, K. ed. 2003. *Women, Gender and Fascism in Europe, 1919–1945.* Manchester: Manchester University Press.

Paxton, R. O. 2005. *The Anatomy of Fascism.* London: Penguin.

Payne S. G. 1980. *Fascism: Comparison and Definition.* London: University of Wisconsin Press.

Payne, S.G. 1995. *A History of Fascism, 1914–1945.* London: UCL Press.

Pratkin, A., Aronson, E. 2001. *The Age of Propaganda: The Everyday Use and Abuse of Persuasion.* New York, NY: W.H. Freeman.

Pronay, N., Spring, D. eds. 1982. *Propaganda, Politics, and Film.* London: Macmillan.

Pulzer, P. 1964. *The Rise of Political Anti-Semitism in Germany and Austria.* New York, NY: Wiley.

Rees, R. 1985. *Fascism and Pre-fascism in Europe 1890–1945: A Bibliography of the Extreme Right.* (2 vols.) Brighton, Sussex: Harvester Press.

Renton, D.1999. *Fascism: Theory and Practice.* London: Pluto Press.

Ridley, F. A. 1988. *Fascism Down the Ages: From Caesar to Hitler.* London: Romer.

Robinson, R. A. H. 1995. *Fascism: The International Phenomenon.* London: Historical Association.

Rogger, H., Weber, E. eds. 1965. *The European Right: A Historic Profile.* London: Weidenfeld and Nicolson.

Schueddekopf, O.E. 1973. *Revolutions of Our Time: Fascism.* London: Weidenfeld & Nicolson.

Sternhell, Z. 1994. *The Birth of Fascist Ideology: From Cultural Rebellion to Political Revolution.* Princeton, NJ: Princeton University Press.

Turner, H. A. ed. 1975. *Reappraisals of Fascism.* New York, NY: New Viewpoints.

Turner, S. P., Käsler, D. eds. 1992. *Sociology Responds to Fascism.* London: Routledge.

Weber, E. 1964. *Varieties of Fascism: Doctrines of Revolution in the Twentieth Century.* Princeton, NJ: Van Nostrand.

Weber, E. 1982. 'Decadence on Private Income,' in *Journal of Contemporary History,* vol. 17, no. 1.

Wolff, R. J., Hoensch, J. K. 1987. *Catholics, the State, and the European Radical Right, 1919–1945.* Cambridge: Cambridge University Press.

Woolf, S. J. ed. 1981. *Fascism in Europe.* London: Methuen.

KEY SECONDARY WORKS ON THE INTERWAR FASCIST REGIMES

Italy

Absalom, A.N.L. 1969. *Mussolini and the Rise of Italian Fascism.* London: Methuen.

Adamson, W. L. 1992. 'The Language of Opposition in Early 20th Century Italy: Rhetorical Continuities between Pre-war Florentine Avant-gardism and Mussolini's Fascism,' in *Journal of Modern History,* vol. 64, no. 1.

Adamson, W. L. 1993. *Avant-Garde Florence: From Modernism to Fascism.* London: Harvard University Press.

Anderson, W. L. 1989. 'Fascism and Culture: Avant-Gardes and Secular Religion in the Italian Case,' in *Journal of Contemporary History,* vol. 24.

Antliff, M., Affron, M. 1997. *Fascist Visions: Art and Ideology in Italy and France.* Princeton, NJ: Princeton University Press.

Appollionio, V. ed. 1973. *Futurist Manifestos.* New York, NY: Viking Press.

Baer, G. 1967. *The Coming of the Italo-Ethiopian War.* Cambridge, MA: Harvard University Press.

Binchy, D. A. 1941. *Church and State in Fascist Italy.* London: Oxford University Press.

Bosworth, R. 1998. *The Italian Dictatorship. Problems and Perspectives in the Interpretation of Mussolini's Italy.* London: Arnold.

Braun, M. 2000. *Mario Sironi and Italian Modernism: Art and Politics under Fascism.* Cambridge: Cambridge University Press.

Cannistraro, P. V. 1972. 'Mussolini's Cultural Revolution: Fascist or Nationalist,' in *Journal of Contemporary History,* vol. 7.

Cannistraro, P. V. ed. 1982. *A Historical Dictionary of Fascism.* Westport, CN: Greenwood Press.

Cassels, A. 1969. *Fascist Italy.* London: Routledge & Kegan Paul.

Clark, M. 1984. *Modern Italy, 1871–1982.* London: Longman.

De Grand, A. 1972. 'Curzio Malaparte: The Illusion of the Fascist Revolution,' in *Journal of Contemporary History,* vol. 7, nos 1–2.

De Grand, A. 1976. 'Women Under Italian Fascism,' in *The Historical Journal,* vol. 19.

De Grand, A. 1978. *The Italian Nationalist Association and the Rise of Fascism in Italy.* London: University of Nebraska Press.

De Grand, A. 1982. *Italian Fascism: Its Origins and Development.* London: University of Nebraska Press.

De Grand, A. 1991. 'Cracks in the Facade: The Failure of Fascist Totalitarianism in Italy 1935–1939,' in *European History Quarterly,* vol. 21.

De Grazia, V. 1981. *The Culture of Consent: 'Mass Organizations of Leisure in Fascist Italy.'* Cambridge: Cambridge University Press.

De Grazia, V. 1992. *How Fascism Ruled Women: Italy, 1922–1945.* Berkeley, CA: University of California Press.

Deakin, F. W. 1962. *The Brutal Friendship: Mussolini, Hitler and the Fall of Italian Fascism.* London: Weidenfeld and Nicolson.

Di Scala, Spencer M. 2004. *Italy from Revolution to Republic: 1700 to the Present.* Oxford: Westview.

Ebenstein, W. 1939. *Fascist Italy.* Chicago, IL: American Book Company.

Elwin, W. 1934. *Fascism at Work.* London: M. Hopkinson.

Etlin, R. 1991. *Modernism in Italian Architecture, 1890–1940.* London: MIT Press.

Falasca-Zamponi, S. 1997. *Fascist Spectacle: The Aesthetics of Power in Fascist Italy.* London: University of California Press.

Finer, 1964. *Mussolini's Italy.* London: Frank Cass.

Forgacs, D., ed. 1986. *Rethinking Italian Fascism: Capitalism, Populism and Culture.* London: Lawrence and Wishart.

Forgacs, D. 1990. *Italian Culture in the Industrial Era. 1880–1980. Cultural Industries, Politics and the Public.* Manchester: Manchester University Press.

Gallo, M. 1974. *Mussolini's Italy. Twenty Years of the Fascist Era.* London: Abelard-Schuman.

Gentile, E. 1984. 'The Problem of the Party in Italian Fascism,' in *Journal of Contemporary History,* vol. 19, no. 2.

Gentile, E. 1990. 'Fascism as Political Religion,' in *Journal of Contemporary History,* vol. 25.

Gentile, E. 1996. *The Sacralization of Politics in Fascist Italy.* London: Harvard University Press.

Germino, D. L. 1971. *The Italian Fascist Party in Power: A Study in Totalitarian Rule.* Minneapolis, MN: University of Minnesota Press.

Ginsborg, P. 1990. *A History of Contemporary Italy: Society and Politics, 1943–1988.* Harmondsworth: Penguin.

Gregor, A. J. 1979. *The Young Mussolini and the Intellectual Origins of Fascism.* Berkeley, CA: University of California Press.

Gregor, A. J. 1979. *Italian Fascism and Developmental Dictatorship.* Princeton, NJ: Princeton University Press.

Halperin, S. 1971. *The Separation of Church and State in Italian Thought from Cavour to Mussolini.* New York, NY: Octagon Books.

Halperin, W. 1964. *Mussolini and Italian Fascism.* Princeton, NJ: Van Nostrand.

Hay, J. 1987. *Popular Film Culture in Fascist Italy: The Passing of the Rex.* Bloomington, IN: Indiana University Press.

Hite, J., Hinton, C. 1998. *Fascist Italy.* London: John Murray.

Horn, D. G. 1994. *Social Bodies: Science, Reproduction and Italian Modernity.* Princeton, NJ: Princeton University Press.

Ipsen, C. 1996. *Dictating Demography: The Problem of Population in Fascist Italy.* Cambridge: Cambridge University Press.

Jensen, R.1995. 'Futurism and Fascism,' in *History Today,* vol. 45 no. 11.

Joll, J. 1965. *Three Intellectuals in Politics.* New York, NY: Harper & Row.

Kent, P. 1981. *The Pope and the Duce: The International Impact of the Lateran Agreements.* London: Macmillan Press.

Knight, P. 2003. *Mussolini and Fascism.* London: Routledge.

Knox, M. 2000. *Common Destiny. Foreign Policy and War in Fascist Italy and Nazi Germany.* Cambridge: Cambridge University Press.

Koon, T. 1985. *Believe, Obey, Fight. Political Socialization of Youth in Fascist Italy, 1922–43.* London: University of North Carolina Press.

Landy, M. 2000. *Fascist Film.* Cambridge: Cambridge University Press.

Ledeen, M. A. 1969. 'Italian Youth and Fascism,' in *Journal of Contemporary History,* vol. 4.

Ledeen, M. A. 1971. 'Fascism and the Generation Gap,' in *European Studies Review Quarterly,* vol. 1, no. 3.

Ledeen, M. A. 1976. 'Women under Italian Fascism,' in *Historical Journal,* vol. 19.

Ledeen, M. A. 1976. 'Renzo de Felice and the Controversy over Italian Fascism,' in *Journal of Contemporary History,* vol. 11.

Ledeen, M. A. 1977. *The First Duce: D'Annunzio at Fiume.* London: Johns Hopkins University Press.

Liehm, M. 1984. *Passion and Defiance. Film in Italy from 1942 to the Present.* London: University of California Press.

Lyttleton, A. ed. 1973. *Italian Fascisms from Pareto to Gentile.* London: Cape.

Lyttleton, A. 2004. *The Seizure of Power: Fascism in Italy, 1919–1929.* London: Routledge.

Mack Smith, D. 1979. *Mussolini's Roman Empire.* Harmondsworth: Penguin.

Mack Smith, D. 1981. *Mussolini.* London: Weidenfeld and Nicolson.

Mallett, R. 2003. *Mussolini and the Origins of the Second World War, 1933–1940.* Basingstoke: Palgrave Macmillan.

Matteotti, G. 1969. *The Fascisti Exposed: A Year of Fascist Domination.* London: Independent Labour Party Publication Department.

Melograni, P. 1976. 'The Cult of the Duce in Mussolini's Italy,' in *Journal of Contemporary History,* vol. 11, vol. 4.

Michaelis, M.1978. *Mussolini and the Jews: German-Italian Relations and the Jewish Question in Italy, 1922–1945.* New York, NY: Oxford University Press.

Minio-Paluello, L. 1946. *Education in Fascist Italy.* London: Oxford University Press.

Morgan, P. 1995. *Italian Fascism 1919–1945.* Basingstoke: Macmillan.

Mosse, G. L.1990. 'The Political Culture of Italian Futurism: A General Perspective,' in *Journal of Contemporary History,* vol. 25, nos. 2–3.

Pollard, J. F. 1985. *The Vatican and Italian Fascism 1929–1932.* Cambridge: Cambridge University Press.

Pollard, J. F. 1998. *The Fascist Experience in Italy.* London: Routledge.

Quine, M. 1996. *Population Politics in Twentieth Century Europe: Fascist Dictatorships and Liberal Politics.* London: Routledge.

Quine, Maria. 2002. *Italy's Social Revolution: Charity and Welfare from Liberalism to Fascism.* Basingstoke: Palgrave.

Redman, T. 1991. *Ezra Pound and Italian Fascism.* Cambridge: Cambridge University Press.

Reich, J., Garofalo, P. eds. 2002. *Re-viewing Fascism: Italian Cinema, 1922–43.* Bloomington, IN: Indiana University Press.

Rhodes, A. 1973. *The Vatican in the Age of the Dictators, 1922–1945.* London: Hodder and Stoughton.

Rittner, C., Roth, J. eds. 2002. *Pope Pius XII and the Holocaust.* London: Leicester University Press.

Roberts, D. D. 1979. *The Syndicalist Tradition in Italian Fascism.* Manchester: Manchester University Press.

Robertson, E. M. 1977. *Mussolini as Empire Builder. Europe and Africa, 1932–36.* London: Macmillan.

Robertson, E. M. 1988. 'Race as a Factor in Mussolini's Policy in Africa and Europe,' in *Journal of Contemporary History,* vol. 23, no. 3.

Robson, M. 2000. *Italy: Liberalism and Fascism, 1870–1945.* London: Hodder & Stoughton.

Roth, J. J. 1967. 'The Roots of Italian Fascism: Sorel and Sorelismo,' in *Journal of Modern History,* vol. 39, no. 1.

Salomone, W. ed. 1971. *Italy from the Risorgimento to Fascism: An Enquiry into the Origins of the Totalitarian State.* Newton Abbot: David & Charles.

Sarti, R. 1970. 'Fascist Modernisation in Italy: Traditional or Revolutionary?' in *American Historical Review,* vol. 75, no. 4.

Sbacchi, A. 1985. *Ethiopia under Mussolini. Fascism and the Colonial Experience.* London: Zed.

Segre, C. G. 1987. *Italo Balbo: A Fascist Life.* London: University of California Press.

Settembrini, D. 1976. 'Mussolini and the Legacy of Revolutionary Syndicalism,' in *Journal of Contemporary History,* vol. 11.

Snowden, F. 1989. *The Fascist Revolution in Tuscany, 1919–1922.* Cambridge: Cambridge University Press.

Sorlin, P. 1996. *Italian National Cinema 1896–1996.* London: Routledge.

Stone, M. 1998. *The Patron State. Culture and Politics in Fascist Italy.* Princeton, NJ: Princeton University Press.

Tannenbaum, E. R. 1969. 'The Goals of Italian Fascism,' in *The American Historical Review,* vol. 74.

Tannenbaum, E. R. 1972. *Fascism in Italy: Italian Society and Culture 1922–1945.* London: Allen Lane.

Thompson, D. 1991. *State Control in Fascist Italy: Culture and Conformity.* Manchester: Manchester University Press.

Togliatti, P. 1976. *Lectures on Fascism.* London: Lawrence and Wishart.

Turner, H. A. Jnr. ed. 1975. *Reappraisals of Fascism.* New York, NY: New Viewpoints.

Valli, R. S. 2000. 'The Myth of Squadrismo in the Fascist Regime,' in *Journal of Contemporary History,* vol. 35 no. 2.

Villari, L. 1956. *Italian Foreign Policy Under Mussolini.* London: Holborn Pub. Co.

Visser, R. 1992. 'Fascist Doctrine and the Cult of *Romanità,*' in *Journal of Contemporary History,* vol .27, no. 1.

Vivarelli, R. 1991. 'Interpretations of the Origins of Fascism,' in *Journal of Modern History ,* vol. 63, no. 1.

Wanrooij, B. 1987. 'The Rise and Fall of Italian Fascism as Generational Revolt,' in *Journal of Contemporary History,* vol. 22, no. 3.

Webster, R. 1961. *Christian Democracy in Italy, 1860–1960.* London: Hollis & Carter.

Wiskemann, E. 1969. *Fascism in Italy: Its Development and Influence.* London: Macmillan.

Wolff, R, Hoensch, J. 1987. *Catholics, the State and the European Radical Right, 1919–1945.* Boulder, CO: Social Science Monographs.

Germany

Abraham, D. 1981. *The Collapse of the Weimar Republic: Political Economy and Crisis.* Princeton, NJ: Princeton University Press.

Allen, W. S. 1989. *The Nazi Seizure of Power: The Experience of a Single German Town, 1922–1945.* Harmondsworth: Penguin.

Altner, A. 2002. *Berlin Dance of Death.* Staplehurst: Spellmount.

Aschheim, S. E. 1992. *The Nietzsche Legacy in Germany, 1890–1990.* London: University of California Press.

Ashkenasi, A. 1976. *Modern German Nationalism.* London: Wiley.

Aycoberry, P. 1981. *The Nazi Question: An Essay on the Interpretations of National Socialism, 1922–1975.* London: Routledge and Kegan Paul.

Bankier, D. 1992. *The Germans and the Final Solution: Public Opinion under Nazism.* Oxford: Blackwell.

Barkai, A. 1990. *Nazi Economics: ideology, theory, and policy.* Oxford: Berg.

Barnett, V. 1992. *For the Soul of the People: Protestant Protest against Hitler.* Oxford: Oxford University Press.

Barnouw, D. 1988. *Weimar Intellectuals and the Threat of Modernity.* Bloomington, IN: Indiana University Press.

Bartov, O. 1991. *Hitler's Army: Soldiers, Nazis and War in the Third Reich.* Oxford: Oxford University Press.

Bartov, O. 2001. *The Eastern Front: German Troops and the Barbarisation of Warfare.* Basingstoke: Palgrave.

Bartov, O., ed. 2000. *The Holocaust: Origin, Interpretations, Aftermath.* London: Routledge.

Bauer, Y. 1982. *A History of the Holocaust.* New York, NY: F. Watts.

Bauman, Z. 1989. *Modernity and the Holocaust.* Cambridge: Polity Press.

Bendersky, J. 1983. *Carl Schmitt: Theorist for the Reich.* Princeton, NJ: Princeton University Press.

Bessel, R. 1993. *Germany after the First World War.* Oxford: Clarendon Press.

Bethell, N. 1972. *The War Hitler Won: September 1939.* London: Allen Lane.

Beyerchen, A. D. 1977. *Scientists under Hitler: Politics and the Physics Community in the Third Reich.* London: Yale University Press.

Birken, L. 1995. *Hitler as Philosophe: Remnants of the Enlightenment in National Socialism.* London: Praeger.

Black, R. 1975. *Fascism in Germany: How Hitler Destroyed the World's Most Powerful Labour Movement.* London: Steyne Publications.

Blackbourn, D.1984. *The Peculiarities of German History: Bourgeois Society and Politics in Nineteenth Century Germany.* Oxford: Oxford University Press.

Bracher, K. D. 1973. *The German Dictatorship: The Origins, Structure, and Consequences of National Socialism.* Harmondsworth: Penguin University Books.

Bramsted, E. K. 1965. *Goebbels and National Socialist Propaganda, 1925–1945.* London: Cresset Press.

Bramwell, A. 1985. *Blood and Soil: Walther Darré and Hitler's Green Party.* Bourne End: The Kensal Press.

Breitman, R. 2004. *The Architect of Genocide: Himmler and the Final Solution.* London: Pimlico.

Bridenthal, R. 1984. *When Biology became Destiny. Women in Weimar and Nazi Germany.* New York, NY: Monthly Review Press.

Broszat, M., 1966. *German National Socialism, 1919–45.* Santa Barbara, CA: Clio Press.

Broszat, M., 1981. *The Hitler State.* London: Longman.

Browder, G. C. 1990. *Foundations of the Nazi Police State: The Formation of Sipo and SD.* Lexington, KY: University Press of Kentucky.

Brustein, W. 1996. *The Logic of Evil: The Social Origins of the Nazi Party, 1925–1933.* London: Yale University Press.

Bullock, A., 1990 [1952]. *Hitler: A Study in Tyranny.* London: Penguin Books.

Burden, H. 1967. *The Nuremberg Party Rallies, 1923–39.* London: Pall Mall Press.

Burleigh, M. ed. 1996. *Confronting the Nazi Past: New Debates on Modern German History.* London: Collins & Brown.

Burleigh, M. 2000. *The Third Reich: A New History.* London: Macmillan.

Burleigh, M., Wippermann, W. 1991. *The Racial State: Germany, 1933–1945.* Cambridge: Cambridge University Press.

Burrin, P. 1994. *Hitler and the Jews: The Genesis of the Holocaust.* London: Edward Arnold.

Campbell, B. 1998. *The SA Generals and the Rise of Nazism.* Lexington, KY: University Press of Kentucky.

Carsten, F. 1995. *The German Workers and the Nazis.* Aldershot: Scolar.

Chickering, R. 1984. *We Men Who Feel Most German: A Cultural Study of the Pan-German League, 1886–1914.* London: George Allen & Unwin.

Childers, T. ed. 1986. *The Formation of the Nazi Constituency 1919–1933.* London: Croom Helm.

Crew, D. ed. 1994. *Nazism and German Society, 1933–1945.* London: Routledge.

Deakin, F. W. 1962. *The Brutal Friendship: Mussolini, Hitler and the Fall of Italian Fascism.*

Eley, G. 1980. *Reshaping the German Right.* London: Yale University Press.

Eley, G. 1983. 'What Produces Fascism: Pre-industrial Traditions or the Crisis of the Capitalist State,' in *Politics and Society,* vol. 12, no. 1.

Evans, R. 2003. *The Coming of the Third Reich.* London: Allen Lane.

Fest, J. 1987. *Hitler.* London: Weidenfeld and Nicolson.

Fischer, K. P. 1995. *Nazi Germany: A New History.* London: Constable.

Fisher, C. ed. 1996. *The Rise of National Socialism and the Working Classes in Weimar Germany.* Oxford: Berghahn Books.

Fuechtwanger, E. J. 1995. *From Weimar to Hitler, 1918–1933.* Basingstoke: Macmillan.

Fuechtwanger, E. J. ed. 1973. *Upheaval and Continuity: A Century of German History.* London: Wolff.

Gailus, M. 2003. "Overwhelmed by Their Own Fascination with the 'Ideas of 1933': Berlin's Protestant Social Milieu in the Third Reich," in *German Studies Review,* vol. 26, no. 3.

Giles, G.L. 1985. *Students and National Socialism.* Princeton, NJ: Princeton University Press.

Gregor, N. 1998. *Daimler-Benz in the Third Reich.* London: Yale University Press.

Gregor, N. ed. 2000. *Nazism.* Oxford: Oxford University Press.

Grunberger, R. 1971. *A Social History of the Third Reich.* London: Weidenfeld and Nicolson.

Hake, S. 1993. *The Cinema's Third Machine—Writing on Film in Germany, 1907–1933.* London: University of Nebraska Press.

Harvey, E. 1993. *Youth and the Welfare State in Weimar Germany.* Oxford: Clarendon Press.

Hauner, M. 1978. 'Did Hitler Want a World Dominion?' in *Journal of Contemporary History,* vol. 13.

Herf, J. 1984. *Reactionary Modernism: Technology, Culture and Politics in Weimar and the Third Reich.* Cambridge: Cambridge University Press.

Herzstein, R. E. 1982. *When Nazi Dreams Come True: The Third Reich's Internal Struggle over the Future of Europe after a German Victory: A Look at the Nazi Mentality, 1939–45.* London: Abacus.

Hildebrand, K., 1984. *The Third Reich.* London: Allen & Unwin.

Hinz, B. 1979. *Art in the Third Reich.* Oxford: Basil Blackwell.

Hitler, A. 2003. *Mein Kampf.* New York, NY: Fredonia Classics.

Housden, M. 1997. *Resistance and Conformity in the Third Reich.* London: Routledge.

Hughes, M., Mann, C. 2000. *Fighting Techniques of a Panzergrenadier, 1941–1945: Training, Techniques, and Weapons.* London: Cassell.

James-Chakraborty, K. 2000. *German Architecture for a Mass Audience.* London: Routledge.

Jaskot, P. B. 2000. *The Architecture of Oppression: The SS Forced Labour and Nazi Monumental Building Economy.* London: Routledge.

Jones, L. E. 1998. *German Liberalism and the Dissolution of the Weimar Party System, 1918–1933.* London: University of North Carolina Press.

Kershaw, I. 1987. *The Hitler Myth.* Oxford: Oxford University Press.

Kershaw, I. ed. 1990. *Weimar: Why Did German Democracy Fail?* London: Weidenfeld and Nicolson.

Kershaw, I. 1998. *Hitler, 1889–1936: Hubris.* London: Allen Lane.

Kershaw, I. 2000. *Hitler, 1936–1945: Nemesis.* London: Allen Lane.

Koch, H. 1975. *The Hitler Youth—Origins and Development, 1922–45.* London: Macdonald and Jane's.

Koonz, C. 1986. *Mothers in the Fatherland: Women, the Family and Nazi Politics.* London: Jonathan Cape.

Lane, B. M. 1968 *Architecture and Politics in Germany, 1918–1945.* Cambridge, MA: Harvard University Press.

Laqueur, W. 1962. *Young Germany: A History of the German Youth Movement.* London: Routledge and Kegan Paul.

Lauryssens, S. 2002. *The Man Who Invented the Third Reich: The Life and Times of Moeller van den Bruck.* Stroud : Sutton.

Merkl, P. 1980. *The Making of a Stormtrooper.* Princeton, N.J: Princeton University Press.

Milfull, J. ed. 1990. *The Attractions of Fascism: Social Psychology and Aesthetics of the 'Triumph of the Right.'* New York: Berg.

Mommsen, H. 1996. *The Rise and Fall of Weimar Democracy.* London: University of North Carolina Press .

Mosse, G. L. 1966. *The Crisis of German Ideology.* London: Weidenfeld and Nicolson.

Mosse, G. L. 1978. *Nazism: A Historical and Comparative Analysis of National Socialism.* Oxford: Basil Blackwell.

Mühlberger, D., 1987. *The Social Basis of European Fascist Movements.* London: Croom Helm.

Mühlberger, D. 1991. *Hitler's Followers. Studies in the Sociology of the Nazi Movement.* London: Routledge.

Mühlberger, D. 2003. *Hitler's Voice: The Völkischer Beobachter, 1920–1933.* Oxford: Peter Lang.

Noakes, J., Pridham, G. 1998. *Nazism, 1919–1945* (4 volumes) Exeter: University of Exeter Press.

Orlow, D. 1967. 'The Conversion of Myths into Political Power: The Case of the Nazi Party, 1925–26,' in *The American Historical Review,* no. 72.

Peukert, D. J. K. 1987. *Inside Nazi Germany: Conformity, Opposition and Racism in Everyday Life.* Harmondsworth: Penguin.

Poliakov, L. 1974. *The Aryan Myth.* London: Chatto & Windus.

Pulzer, P. 1964. *The Rise of Political Anti-Semitism in Germany and Austria.* New York, NY: Wiley.

Rabinbach, A. 1976. 'The Aesthetics of Production in the Third Reich,' in *Journal of Contemporary History,* vol. 11, no. 4.

Rauschning, H. 1939. *Hitler Speaks: A Series of Political Conversations with Adolph Hitler on His Real Aims.* London: Thornton Butterworth.

Reimer, R. ed. 2000. *Cultural History through a National Socialist Lens: Essays on the Cinema of the Third Reich.* Woodbridge, Suffolk: Camden House.

Rempel, G. 1989. *Hitler's Children—The Hitler Youth and the SS.* London: University of North Carolina Press.

Rittner, C., Roth, J. eds. 2002. *Pope Pius XII and the Holocaust.* London: Leicester University Press.

Roberts, S. 1938. *The House that Hitler Built.* London: Methuen.

Rogger, H., Weber, E. eds. 1966. *The European Right.* Berkeley, CA: University of California Press.

Rosenbaum, R. 1980. *Explaining Hitler: The Search for the Origins of his Evil.* London: Macmillan.

Rozett, R., Spector, S. 1990. *Encyclopedia of the Holocaust.* New York, NY: Macmillan Library Reference USA.

Schulte-Sass, L. 1996. *Entertaining the Third Reich: Illusions of Wholeness in the Nazi Cinema.* London: Duke University Press.

Shand, J. D. 1984. 'The *Reichsautobahn:* Symbol for the New Reich,' in *Journal of Contemporary History,* vol. 19, no. 2.

Shirer, W. L. 1960. *The Rise and Fall of the Third Reich: A History of Nazi Germany.* New York, NY: Simon and Schuster.

Snyder, Louis L. 1976. *Encyclopedia of the Third Reich.* London: Cassell.

Stachura, P. D. 1975. *Nazi Youth in the Weimar Republic.* Oxford: Clio.

Stachura, P. D. 1983. *Gregor Strasser and the Rise of Nazism.* London: Allen & Unwin.

Stachura, P. D. ed. 1983. *The Nazi Machtergreifung.* London: Allen & Unwin.

Stackelberg, R. 1999. *Hitler's Germany: Origins, Legacies, Interpretations.* London: Routledge.

Stephenson, J. 1975. *Women in Nazi Society.* London: Croom Helm.

Stern, F. 1961. *The Politics of Cultural Despair: A Study in the Rise of the Germanic Ideology.* Berkeley, CA: University of California Press.

Struve, W. 1973. *Elites against Democracy: Leadership Ideals in Bourgeois Political Thought in Germany, 1890–1933.* Princeton, NJ: Princeton University Press.

Taylor, J., W. Shaw. 1987. *A Directory of the Third Reich.* London: Grafton.

Taylor, R. 1974. *The Word in Stone: The Role of Architecture in the National Socialist Ideology.* London: University of California Press.

Taylor R. 1998. *Film Propaganda: Soviet Russia and Nazi Germany.* London: I.B. Tauris.

Traverso, E. 2003. *The Origins of Nazi Violence.* London: New Press.

Vondung, K. 1979. 'Spiritual Revolution and Magic: Speculation and Political Action in National Socialism,' in *Modern Age,* vol. 23, part 4.

Waite, R. 1977. *The Psychopathic God: Adolf Hitler.* New York, NY: Basic Books.

Weber, E., 1964. *Varieties of Fascism: Doctrines of Revolution in the Twentieth Century.* Princeton, NJ: Van Nostrand.

Weindling, P. 1989. *Health, Race and German Politics between National Unification and Nazism, 1870–1945.* Cambridge: Cambridge University Press.

Welch, D. 2002. *The Third Reich: Politics and Propaganda.* London: Routledge.

Williamson, D. G. 1982. *The Third Reich.* Harlow: Longman.

Williamson, G. 1998. *The SS. Hitler's Instrument of Terror.* London: Sidgwick & Jackson.

Zeman, Z. 1973. *Nazi Propaganda.* London: Oxford University Press.

KEY SECONDARY WORKS ON EUROPEAN INTERWAR FASCIST MOVEMENTS BY REGION

The Balkans

Banac, Ivo. 1984. *The National Question: Origin, History, Politics.* Cornell, NY: Ithaca.

Dragnich, A. 1974. *Serbia, Nicola Pasic, and Yugoslavia.* New Brunswick, NJ: Rutgers University Press.

Fischer, Berndt J. 1999. *Albania at War, 1941–1945.* London: Hurst and Company.

Higham, R., Veremis, T. eds. 1993. *The Metaxas Dictatorship: Aspects of Greece, 1936–1940.* Athens: Hellenic Foundation for Defense and Foreign Policy and Speros Basil Vryonis Center for the Study of Hellenism.

Hoptner, J. B. 1962. *Yugoslavia in Crisis, 1934–1941.* New York, NY: Columbia University Press.

Irvine, J. A. 1993. *The Croat Question: Partisan Politics in the Formation of the Yugoslav Socialist State.* Oxford: Westview.

Jelinek, Yeshayahu. 1985. 'Nationalities and Minorities in the Independent State of Croatia,' in *Nationalities Papers,* 7: 2.

Kofas, J. 1981. *Authoritarianism in Greece: The Metaxas Regime.* New York, NY: Eastern European Monographs: Columbia University Press.

MacKensie, D. 1989. *Apis: The Congenial Conspirator.* Boulder, CO: East European Monographs.

Malcolm, Noel. 1995. *Kosovo: A Short History.* London: MacMillan.

Martic, Miloš. 1980. 'Dimitrije Ljotić and the Yugoslav National Movement Zbor, 1935–1945,' in *East European Quarterly,* vol. 16, no. 2.

Mavrogordatos, G. 1983. *Stillborn Republic: Social Conditions and Party Strategies in Greece, 1922–1936.* Berkeley, CA: University of California Press.

Milazzo, M. J. 1975. *The Chetnik Movement and the Yugoslav Resistance.* Baltimore, MD: Johns Hopkins University Press.

Paris, Edmond. 1961. *Genocide in Satellite Croatia: A Record of Racial and Religious Persecutions and Massacres.* Chicago, IL: American Institute for Balkan Affairs.

Perry, D. M. 1988. *The Politics of Terror: The Macedonian Revolutionary Movements, 1893–1903.* London: Duke University Press.

Reinhartz, Dennis. 1986. 'Aryanism in the Independent State of Croatia, 1941–1945: The Historical Basis and Cultural Questions,' in *South Slav Journal,* vol. 9, nos. 3–4.

Sadkovich, James J. 1987. *Italian Support for Croatian Separatism, 1927–1937.* New York, NY: Garland Publishing.

Tomasevich, J. 1975. *War and Revolution in Yugoslavia: The Chetniks.* Stanford, CA: Stanford University Press.

Vatikiotis, P. J. 1998. *Popular Autocracy in Greece, 1936–1941: A Political Biography of General Ioannis Metaxas.* London: Frank Cass.

Vickers, Miranda. 1998. *Between Serb and Albanian: A History of Kosovo.* London: Hurst and Company.

Benelux, France, and Switzerland

Baker, D. N. 1976. 'Two Paths to Socialism: Marcel Déat and Marceau Pivert,' in *Journal of Contemporary History*, vol. 11, no. 1.

Conway, M. 1994. *Collaboration in Belgium. Léon Degrelle and the Rexist Movement.* London: Yale University Press.

Curtis, M. 1959. *Three Against the Third Republic.* Princeton, NJ: Princeton University Press.

Douglas, A.1984. 'Violence and Fascism: The Case of the Faisceau,' in *Journal of Contemporary History*, vol. 19, no. 4.

Gentile, P., Hanspeter, K. 1998. 'Contemporary Radical-Right Parties in Switzerland: History of a Divided Family,' in Betz, H. G., Immerfall, S. eds. *The New Politics of the Right.* New York, NY: St. Martin's Press.

Griffiths R. 1978. 'Anticapitalism and the French Extra—Parliamentary Right, 1870–1940,' in *Journal of Contemporary History*, vol. 13, no. 4.

Hansen, E. 1981. 'Depression Decade Crisis: Social Democracy and Planisme in Belgium and the Netherlands, 1929–1939,' in *Journal of Contemporary History*, vol. 16, no. 2.

Hutton, P. H. 1976. 'Popular Boulangism and the Advent of Mass Politics in France, 1886–90,' in *Journal of Contemporary History*, vol. 11, no. 1.

LeBor, Adam. 1997. *Hitler's Secret Bankers: The Myth of Swiss Neutrality During the Holocaust.* Secaucus, NJ: Birch Lane Press.

Mazgaj, P. 1979. *The Action Française and Revolutionary Syndicalism.* Chapel Hill, NC: University of North Carolina Press.

Mazgaj, P. 1982. 'The Young Sorelians and Decadence,' in *Journal of Contemporary History*, vol. 17, no. 1.

Müller, K. J. 1976. 'French Fascism and Modernisation,' in *Journal of Contemporary History*, vol. 11.

Paxton, R. O. 1982. *Vichy France: Old Guard and New Order, 1940–1944.* New York, NY: Columbia University Press.

Pels, D. 1987. 'Hendrik de Man and the Ideology of Planism,' in *International Review of Social History*, vol. 32.

Shorrock, W. I. 1975. 'France and the Rise of Fascism in Italy,' in *Journal of Contemporary History*, vol. 10.

Soucy, R. J. 1966. 'The Nature of Fascism in France,' in *Journal of Contemporary History*, vol. 1, no. 1.

Soucy, R. J. 1972. *Fascism in France: The Case of Maurice Barrès.* Berkeley, CA: University of California Press.

Soucy, R. J. 1974. 'French Fascist Intellectuals in the 1930s: an Old New Left?' in *French Historical Studies*, vol. 8, no. 3.

Soucy, R. J. 1979. *Fascist Intellectual: Drieu la Rochelle.* Berkeley, CA: University of California Press.

Soucy, R. J. 1980. 'Drieu la Rochelle and the Modernist Anti—Modernism in French Fascism,' in *Modern Language Notes*, vol. 95, no. 4.

Soucy, R. J. 1986. *French Fascism: The First Wave, 1924–33.* London: Yale University Press.

Sternhell, Z. 1973. 'National Socialism and Antisemitism: The Case of Maurice Barrès,' in *Journal of Contemporary History*, vol. 8, no. 4.

Sternhell, Z. 1987. "The 'Anti-materialist' Revision of Marxism as an Aspect of the Rise of Fascist Ideology," in *Journal of Contemporary History*, vol. 22, no. 3.

Sternhell, Z. 1995. *Neither Right nor Left: Fascist Ideology in France.* Princeton, NJ: Princeton University Press.

Sutton, M. 1982. *Nationalism, Positivism and Catholicism: The Politics of Charles Maurras and French Catholics, 1890–1914.* Cambridge: Cambridge University Press.

Central and Eastern Europe

Aczél, T. ed. 1966. *Ten Years After.* London: MacGibbon and Kee.

Batkay, W. M. 1982. *Authoritarian Politics in a Transitional State: Istvan Bethlen and the Unified Party in Hungary.* Boulder, CO: East European Monographs.

Bell, J. D. 1977. *Peasants in Power: Alexander Stamboliski and the Bulgarian Agrarian Union, 1899–1923.* Princeton, NJ: Princeton University Press.

Bischof, G., Pelinka, A., Lassner, A. 2003. *The Dollfuss/Schuschnigg Era in Austria: A Reassessment* (Contemporary Austrian Studies). Somerset, NJ: Transaction Publishers.

Bukey, E. B. 1986. *Hitler's Home Town: Linz, Austria, 1908–1945.* Bloomington, IN: Indiana University Press.

Butnaru, I. C. 1992. *The Silent Holocaust: Romania and its Jews.* London: Greenwood.

Carsten, F. L. 1977. *Fascist Movements in Austria from Schönerer to Hitler.* London: Sage.

Fischer-Galati, S. 1970. *Twentieth Century Rumania.* New York, NY: Columbia University Press.

Gross, J. T. 2001. *Neighbors: The Destruction of the Jewish Community in Jedwabne, Poland.* Princeton, NJ: Princeton University Press.

Hitchins, K. 1994. *Rumania, 1866–1947.* Oxford: Clarendon Press.

Hoebelt, L. 2003. *Defiant Populist: Joerg Haider and the Politics of Austria.* West Lafayette, IN: Purdue University Press.

Innes, A. 2001. *Czechoslovakia: The Short Goodbye.* West Lafayette, IN: Purdue University Press.

Ioanid, R. 1990. *The Sword of the Archangel: Fascist Ideology in Romania.* Boulder, CO: East European Monographs.

Jászi, O. 1921. *Revolution and Counter-revolution in Hungary.* London: P. S. King.

Jellinek, Y. 1976. *The Parish Republic: Hlinka's Slovak People's Party.* Boulder, CO: East European Monographs.

Kelly, D. D. 1995. *The Czech Fascist Movement, 1922–1942.* New York, NY: Columbia University Press.

Kirschbaum, S. J. 1983. *Slovak Politics: Essays on Slovak History in Honour of J. Kirschbaum.* Cleveland, OH: Slovak Institute .

Kirschbaum, S. J. ed. 1999. *Historical Dictionary of Slovakia.* London: Scarecrow Press.

Kitchen, M. 1980. *The Coming of Austrian Fascism.* Montreal: McGill Queens University Press.

Kürti, L. 2003. 'The Uncivility of a Civil Society: Skinhead Youth in Hungary,' in Kopecky, P., Mudde, C. eds. *Uncivil Society? Contentious Politics in Post-communist Europe.* London: Routledge.

Maas, W. B. 1972. *Assassination in Vienna.* New York, NY: Charles Scribner's Sons.

Macartney, C. A. 1937. *Hungary and Her Successors.* London: Royal Institute of International Affairs .

Macartney, C. A. 1957. *October Fifteenth: A History of Modern Hungary.* Edinburgh: Edinburgh University Press.

Mann, M. 2004. *Fascists.* Cambridge: Cambridge University Press.

Mastny, V. 1971. *The Czechs under Nazi Rule: The Failure of National Resistance, 1939–1942.* New York, NY: Columbia University Press.

Miller, M. 1975. *Bulgaria During the Second World War.* Stanford, CA: Stanford University Press.

Nagy-Talavera M. 1970. *The Green Shirts and Others: A History of Fascism in Hungary and Rumania.* Stanford, CA: Hoover Institution Press.

Oliver, H. 1998. *We Were Saved: How the Jews in Bulgaria Were Kept from the Death Camps.* Sofia: Sofia Press.

Parkinson, F. ed. 1989. *Conquering the Past: Austrian Nazism Yesterday and Today.* Detroit, MI: Wayne State University Press.

Pauley, B. 1981. *Hitler and the Forgotten Nazis: A History of Austrian National Socialism.* Chapel Hill, NC: University of North Carolina Press.

Sugar, P. 1971. *Native Fascism in the Successor States, 1918–1945.* Santa Barbara CA: ABC-Clio.

Sugar, P. ed. 1990. *A History of Hungary.* London: Tauris.

Volovici, L. 1976. *Nationalist Ideology and Antisemitism: the Case of Romanian Intellectuals in the 1930s.* Oxford: Pergamon Press.

Great Britain and Ireland

Allen, M. 2000. *Hidden Agenda: How the Duke of Windsor Betrayed the Allies.* London: Macmillan.

Baker, D. 1996. *Ideology of Obsession: A. K. Chesterton and British Fascism.* London: I.B. Tauris.

Benewick, R. 1969. *Political Violence and Public Order: A Study of British Fascism.* London: Allen Lane.

Cronin, M. 1997. *The Blueshirts and Irish Politics.* Dublin: Four Courts Press.

Cross, C. 1966. *The Fascists in Britain.* London: Barrie and Rockliff.

Durham, M. 1992. 'Gender and the British Union of Fascists,' in *Journal of Contemporary History,* vol. 27.

Griffiths, R. 1980. *Fellow Travellers of the Right: British Enthusiasts for Nazi Germany, 1933–9.* London: Constable.

Lewis, D. S. 1987. *Illusions of Grandeur: Mosley, Fascism and British Society, 1931–1981.* Manchester: Manchester University Press.

Linehan, T. 1996. *East End for Mosley.* London: Frank Cass.

Linehan, T. 2000. *British Fascism: Parties, Ideology and Culture.* Manchester: Manchester University Press.

Lunn, K., Thurlow, R. 1980. *British Fascism: Essays on the Radical Right in Inter-war Britain.* London: Croom Helm.

McGarry, F. 1999. *Irish Politics and the Spanish Civil War.* Cork: Cork University Press.

Stone, D. 2002. *Breeding Superman: Nietzsche, Race and Eugenics in Edwardian and Interwar Britain.* Liverpool: Liverpool University Press.

Renton, D. 1998. *Fascism and Anti-Fascism in Britain in the 1940s.* London: Macmillan.

Thurlow, R. 1998. *Fascism in Britain: From Mosley's Blackshirts to the National Front.* London: I.B. Tauris.

Thurlow, R. 2001. *Fascism in Modern Britain.* Stroud: Sutton.

Walker, M. 1981. *The National Front.* London: Routledge and Kegan Paul.

The Iberian Peninsula

Ben-Ami, S. 1983. *Fascism from Above: The Dictatorship of Primo de Rivera in Spain, 1923–1930.* Oxford: Clarendon Press.

Brenan, G. 1960. *The Spanish Labyrinth: An Account of the Social and Political Background of the Civil War.* Cambridge: Cambridge University Press.

Carr, R. 1966. *Spain, 1808–1939.* Oxford: Clarendon Press.

Carr, R., Fusi, J. P. 1979. *Spain: Dictatorship to Democracy.* London: Allen & Unwin.

Coverdale, J. 1975. *Italian Intervention in the Spanish Civil War.* Princeton, NJ: Princeton University Press.

De Blaye, E. 1974. *Franco and the Politics of Spain.* Harmondsworth: Penguin.

Delzell, C. F. ed.1970. *Mediterranean Fascism: 1919–1945.* London: Macmillan.

Foard, D. W. 1975. 'The Forgotten Falangist: Ernesto Gimenez Caballero,' in *Journal of Contemporary History,* vol. 10, no. 1.

Gallo, M. 1973. *Spain under Franco.* London: Allen & Unwin.

Payne, S. G. 1961. *Falange: A History of Spanish Fascism.* London: Oxford University Press.

Payne, S. G. 1999. *Fascism in Spain, 1923–1977.* Madison, WI: University of Wisconsin Press.

Pinto, A. C. 2000. *The Blueshirts: Portuguese Fascists and the New State.* Boulder, CO: Social Science Monographs.

Pinto, A. C. ed. 2003. *Contemporary Portugal: Politics, Society and Culture.* Boulder, CO: Social Science Monographs.

Preston, P. 1994. *The Coming of the Spanish Civil War 1931–1939: Reaction and Revolution in the Second Republic.* London: Routledge.

Preston, P. 1995. *The Politics of Revenge: Fascism and the Military in Twentieth-Century Spain.* London: Routledge.

Preston, P. ed. 1976. *Spain in Crisis: The Evolution and Decline of the Franco Regime.* Hassocks: Harvester.

Preston, P. ed. 1984. *Revolution and War in Spain.* London: Methuen.

Robinson, R.A.H. 1970. *The Origins of Franco's Spain: The Right, the Republic and Revolution, 1931–1936.* Newton Abbot: David & Charles.

Thomas, H. S. 1977. *The Spanish Civil War.* Harmondsworth: Penguin.

Russia, the Soviet Union and the Baltic States

Abramovitch, R. 1962. *The Soviet Revolution, 1880–1963.* London: Allen & Unwin.

Agursky, M. 1987. *The Third Rome: National Bolshevism in the USSR.* Boulder, CO: Westview Press.

Brandenberger, D. 2002. *National Bolshevism: Stalinist Mass Culture and the Formation of Modern Russian National Identity, 1931–1956.* Cambridge, MA: Harvard University Press.

Brent, J., Naumov, V. P. 2003. *Stalin's Last Crime: The Plot Against the Jewish Doctors, 1948–1953.* New York, NY: HarperCollins.

Brudny, Y. 1998. *Reinventing Russia: Russian Nationalism and the Soviet State, 1953–1991.* Cambridge, MA: Harvard University Press.

Bullock, A. 1991. *Hitler and Stalin: Parallel Lives.* London: HarperCollins.

Daniels, R. V. ed. 1965. *The Stalin Revolution: foundations of Soviet totalitarianism.* Lexington, MA: Heath.

Dunlop, J. B. 1976. *The New Russian Revolutionaries.* Belmont, MA: Nordland Publishing Company.

Dunlop, J. B. 1984. *The Faces of Contemporary Russian Nationalism.* Princeton, NJ: Princeton University Press.

Eidintas, A., Zalys, V. 1998. *Lithuania in European Politics: The Years of the First Republic, 1918–1940.* New York, NY: St. Martin's.

Ezergailis, A. 1996. *The Holocaust in Latvia: The Missing Center.* Riga: Historical Institute of Latvia.

Haslam, J. 1984. *The Soviet Union and the Struggle for Collective Security in Europe, 1933–1939.* London: Macmillan.

Kasekamp, A. 1999. 'Radical Right-Wing Movements in the North-East Baltic,' in *Journal of Contemporary History,* vol. 34, no. 4.

Kasekamp, A. 2000. *The Radical Right in Interwar Estonia.* Basingstoke: Macmillan.

Kostyrchenko, G. 1995. *Out of the Red Shadows: Antisemitism in Stalin's Russia.* Amherst, NY: Prometheus.

Laqueur, W. 1994. *Black Hundred: The Rise of the Extreme Right in Russia.* New York, NY: HarperPerennial.

Lewin, M., Kershaw, I. eds. 1997. *Stalinism and Nazism: Dictatorships in Comparison.* Cambridge: Cambridge University Press.

Mastny, V. 1979. *Russia's Road to the Cold War: Diplomacy, Warfare, and the Politics of Communism, 1941–1945.* New York, NY: Columbia University Press.

Mehnert, K. 1952. *Stalin versus Marx: The Stalinist Historical Doctrine.* London: George Allen & Unwin.

Parming, T. 1975. *The Collapse of Liberal Democracy and the Rise of Authoritarianism in Estonia.* London: Sage Publications.

Rauch, G. 1995. *The Baltic States: The Years of Independence, 1970–1940.* London: Hurst.

Rossman, V. 2002. *Russian Intellectual Antisemitism in the Post-Communist Era.* Jerusalem: The Vidal Sassoon International Center for the Study of Antisemitism.

Shenfield, S. D. 2001. *Russian Fascism: Traditions, Tendencies, Movements.* Armonk, NY: M.E. Sharpe.

Stephan, J. J. 1978. *The Russian Fascists: Tragedy and Farce in Exile, 1925–1945.* New York, NY: HarperCollins.

Tucker, R. C. 1990. *Stalin in Power: The Revolution from Above, 1928–1941.* New York, NY: Norton.

Van Ree, E. 2002. *The Political Thought of Joseph Stalin: A Study in Twentieth-Century Revolutionary Patriotism.* London: Routledge.

Weitz, E. D. 2002. 'Racial Politics without the Concept of Race: Reevaluating Soviet Ethnic and National Purges,' in *Slavic Review,* no. 61 (1).

Yanov, A. 1987. *The Russian Challenge and the Year 2000.* New York, NY: Basil Blackwell.

Scandinavia

Berggren, L. 2002. 'Swedish Fascism—Why Bother?' in *Journal of Contemporary History*, vol. 37.

Dahl, H. F. 1995. *Quisling. A Study of Treachery.* London: Cambridge University Press.

Hoidal, O. K. 1999. *Quisling: A Study in Treason.* Cambridge: Cambridge University Press.

Karvonen, L. 1988. *From White to Blue and Black: Finnish Fascism in the Interwar Era.* Helsinki: Finnish Society of Sciences and Letters.

Lindström, U. 1985. *Fascism in Scandinavia, 1920–1940.* Stockholm: Almqvist & Wiksell International.

Milward, A. 1972. *The Fascist Economy in Norway.* Oxford: Clarendon Press.

Rintala, M. 1962. *Three Generations: The Extreme Right Wing in Finnish Politics.* Bloomington, IN: Indiana University.

KEY SECONDARY WORKS ON FASCISM OUTSIDE EUROPE BY REGION

Asia

Berger, G. M. 1977. *Parties out of Power in Japan, 1931–1941.* Princeton, NJ: Princeton University Press.

Chander, J. P. ed. 1943. *Gandhi Against Fascism.* Lahore: Free India Publications.

Chang, M. H. 1985. *The Chinese Blue Shirt Society: Fascism and Developmental Nationalism.* Berkeley, CA: University of California, Berkeley, Institute of East Asian Studies.

Chang, M. H. 2001. *Return of the Dragon: China's Wounded Nationalism.* Boulder, CO: Westview Press.

Crowley, J. 1966. *Japan's Quest for Autonomy: Security and Foreign Policy, 1930–1938.* Princeton, NJ: Princeton University Press.

Eastman, L. E. 1974. *The Abortive Revolution: China Under Nationalist Rule, 1927–1937.* Cambridge, MA: Harvard University Press.

Elst, K. 2001. *The Saffron Swastika, The Notion of Hindu 'Fascism.'* New Delhi: Voice of India.

Etcheson, C. In Press. *After the Killing Fields: Lessons from the Cambodian Genocide.* New York, NY: Praeger.

Fletcher, W. M. 1982. *The Search for a New Order: Intellectuals and Fascism in Pre-war Japan.* Chapel Hill, NC: University of North Carolina Press.

Golwalkar, M.S. 1945. *We or Our Nationhood Defined.* 3rd Edition. Nagpur: M. N. Kale.

Gordon, A. 1991. *Labor and Imperial Democracy in Pre-war Japan.* Oxford: University of California Press.

Hauner, M. 1981. *India in Axis Strategy: Germany, Japan, and Indian Nationalists in the Second World War.* Stuttgart: Klett-Cotta.

Havens, T. R. H. 1974. *Farm and Nation in Modern Japan: Agrarian Nationalism, 1870–1940.* Princeton, NJ: Princeton University Press.

Jackson, K. ed. 1989. *Cambodia 1975–78: Rendez-vous with Death.* Princeton, NJ: Princeton University Press.

Krishna, C. ed. 2003. *Fascism in India: Faces, Fangs and Facts.* New Delhi: Manak Publications.

Maruyama, M. 1969. *Thought and Behavior in Modern Japanese Politics.* London: Oxford University Press.

Mitchell, R. H. 1976. *Thought Control in Pre-war Japan.* Ithaca, NY: Cornell University Press.

Morris, I. ed. 1963. *Japan, 1931–1945: Militarism, Fascism, Japanism?* Boston, MA: Heath.

Oka, Y. 1983. *Konoe Fumimaro: A Political Biography.* Tokyo: University of Tokyo Press.

Scalapino, R. A. 1953. *Democracy and the Party Movement in Pre-war Japan: The Failure of the First Attempt.* Berkeley, CA: University of California Press.

Shillony, B. 1973. *Politics and Culture in Wartime Japan.* Oxford: Clarendon Press.

Wilson, G. M. 1969. *Radical Nationalist in Japan: Kita Ikki, 1883–1937.* Cambridge, MA: Harvard University Press.

Africa

2000. *The Middle East and North Africa 2000: A Survey and Reference Book.* London: Europa Publications.

Bloomberg, C. 1989. *The Afrikaner Broederbond.* Bloomington, IN: Indiana University Press.

Bunting, B. 1969. *The Rise of the South African Reich.* Harmondsworth: Penguin.

Davenport, T.R.H. 1966. *The Afrikaner Bond.* Oxford: Oxford University Press.

Furlong, P. J. 1991. *Between Crown and Swastika.* Middletown, CT: Wesleyan University Press.

Godwin, P. 1993. *"Rhodesians Never Die:" The Impact of War and Political Change on White Rhodesia, c. 1970–1980.* Oxford: Oxford University Press.

Hexham, I. 1981. *The Irony of Apartheid.* Toronto: Edwin Mellen.

Liddell Hart, B. H., ed. 1953. *The Rommel Papers.* London: Collins.

Mockley, A. 1984. *Haile Selassie's War: The Italian-Ethiopian Campaign, 1935–1941.* Oxford: Oxford University Press.

Montgomery, V. 1958. *The Memoirs of Field-Marshall the Viscount Montgomery of Alamein, K.G.* London: Collins.

Moodie, D. 1975. *The Rise of Afrikanerdom.* Berkeley, CA: University of California Press.

Simpson, H. 1980. *The Social Origins of Afrikaner Fascism and Its Apartheid Policy.* Stockholm: Almqvist & Wiksell International.

Van Jaaarsveld, F. A. 1961. *The Awakening of Afrikaner Nationalism.* Cape Town: Human & Rousseau.

Vatcher, W. H., Jr. 1965. *White Laager: The Rise of Afrikaner Nationalism.* London: Pall Mall Press.

Australia and New Zealand

Greason, D. 1994. *I Was a Teenage Fascist.* Ringwood, Victoria: McPhee Gribble.

Leach, M., Stokes, G., Ward, I. eds. 2000. *The Rise and Fall of One Nation.* St Lucia, Queensland: University of Queensland Press.

Moore, A. 1989. *The Secret Army and the Premier: Conservative Paramilitary Organisations in New South Wales 1930–32.* Kensington, New South Wales: New South Wales University Press.

Moore, A. 1995. *The Right Road: A History of Right-Wing Politics in Australia.* Oxford: Oxford University Press.

Middle East

2000. *The Middle East and North Africa 2000: A Survey and Reference Book.* London: Europa Publications.

Abu Jaber, K. 1966. *The Arab Ba'th Socialist Party: History, Ideology, and Organization.* Syracuse, NY: Syracuse University.

Adanir, F. 2001. 'Kemalist Authoritarianism and Fascist Trends in Turkey during the Interwar Period,' in Larsen, S. U. ed. *Fascism Outside Europe.* Boulder, CO: Social Science Monographs.

Al-Khalil, S. 2003. *The Monument: Art, Vulgarity and Responsibility in Iraq.* London: I. B. Tauris.

C.A.R.D.R.I. 1989. *Saddam's Iraq: Revolution or Reaction?* London: Zed Books.

Choueiri, Y. M. 2000. *Arab Nationalism: A History.* Oxford: Blackwell.

Cleveland, W. L. 1994. *A History of the Modern Middle East.* Oxford: Westview Press.

Farouk-Sluglett, M., P. Sluglett, 2001. *Iraq since 1958: From Revolution to Dictatorship.* London: I. B. Tauris.

Genocide in Iraq: The Anfal Campaign Against the Kurds. 1993. New York, NY: Middle East Watch.

Hirszowicz, L. 1966. *The Third Reich and the Arab East.* London: Routledge and Kegan Paul.

Hovannisian, R. G. ed. 1987. *The Armenian Genocide in Perspective.* New Brunswick, NY: Transaction Books.

Jankowski, J. P. 1975. *Egypt's Young Rebels: 'Young Egypt,' 1933–1952.* Stanford, CA: Hoover Institution Press.

Kienle, E. 1990. *Ba'th v Ba'th: The Conflict Between Syria and Iraq, 1968–1989.* London: I. B. Tauris.

Makiya, A. 1989. *Republic of Fear: The Inside Story of Saddam's Iraq.* Berkeley, CA: University of California Press.

Mansfield, P. 1992. *A Modern History of the Middle East.* London: Penguin.

Marr, P. 2004. *The Modern History of Iraq.* Cambridge, MA: Westview Press.

Melson, R. 1992. *Revolution and Genocide: On the Origins of the Armenian Genocide and the Holocaust.* London: University of Chicago Press.

Olson, R. 1982. *The Ba'th and Syria, 1947–1982: The Evolution of Ideology, Party and State.* Princeton, NJ: Kingston.

Schultze, R. 2000. *A Modern History of the Muslim World.* London: I. B. Tauris .

Seale, P. 1986. *The Struggle for Syria.* London: Yale University Press.

Tibi, B. 1990. *Arab Nationalism: A Critical Inquiry.* New York: St. Martin's.

Tripp, C. 2000. *A History of Iraq.* Cambridge: Cambridge University Press.

Zürcher, E. J. 1998. *Turkey: A Modern History.* London: I.B. Tauris.

South and Central America

Alexander, R. J. 1951. *The Perón Era.* London: Gollancz.

Alexander, R. J. 1982. *Bolivia: Past, Present, and Future of Its Politics.* New York, NY: Praeger.

Chomsky, N., Herman, E. 1979. *The Washington Connection and Third World Fascism.* Boston, MA: South End Press.

Collier, D. ed. 1979. *The New Authoritarianism in Latin America.* Princeton, NJ: Princeton University Press.

Crassweller, R. D. 1987. *Perón and the Enigmas of Argentina.* New York, NJ: Norton.

Deutsch, S. M. 1999. *Las Derechas. The Extreme Right in Argentina, Brazil, and Chile, 1890–1939.* Stanford, CA: Stanford University Press.

Falcoff, M., Pike, F. 1982. *The Spanish Civil War: American Hemispheric Perspectives.* Lincoln, NE: University of Nebraska Press.

Hilliker, G. 1971. *The Politics of Reform in Peru: The Aprista and Other Mass Parties of Latin America.* Baltimore, MD: Johns Hopkins Press.

James, D. 1988. *Resistance and Integration. Peronism and the Argentine Working Class, 1946–1976.* Cambridge: Cambridge University Press.

Johnson, J. 1958. *Political Change in Latin America. The Emergence of the Middle Sectors.* Stanford, CA: Stanford University Press.

Jordan, D. 1996. *Nationalism in Contemporary Latin America.* New York: New Press.

Klarén, P. F. 2000. *Peru: Society and Nationhood in the Andes.* Oxford: Oxford University Press.

Klein, H. 1969. *Parties and Political Change in Bolivia, 1880–1952.* Cambridge: Cambridge University Press.

Klein, H. 1982. *Bolivia: The Evolution of a Multi-Ethnic Society.* New York, NY: Oxford University Press.

Klein, H. 2003. *A Concise History of Bolivia.* Cambridge: Cambridge University Press.

Lewis, P. H. 1980. *Paraguay under Stroessner.* Chapel Hill, NC: The University of North Carolina Press.

Malloy, J. M. ed. 1977. *Authoritarianism and Corporatism in Latin America.* Pittsburgh, PA: University of Pittsburgh Press.

Marett, S.R. 1969. *Peru.* New York, NY: Praeger Publishers.

Martz, J. D. 1972. *Ecuador: Conflicting Political Culture and the Quest for Progress.* Boston, MA: Allyn and Bacon, Inc.

McGee, D. S. 1986. *Counterrevolution in Argentina: The Argentine Patriotic League.* Lincoln, NE: University of Nebraska Press.

McGee D. S., Dolkart, R. H. eds. 1993. *The Argentine Right. Its History and Intellectual Origins.* Wilmington, DE: S. R. Books.

McKale, D. 1977. *The Swastika Outside Germany.* Kent, OH: The Kent State University Press.

Miranda, C. R. 1990. *The Stroessner Era: Authoritarian Rule in Paraguay.* Boulder, CO: Westview Press.

Payne, L. A. 2000. *Uncivil Movements. The Armed Right Wing and Democracy in Latin America.* London: The Johns Hopkins University Press.

Power, M. 2002. *Right-Wing Women in Chile. Feminine Power and the Struggle Against Allende, 1964–1973.* University Park, PA: Pennsylvania State University Press.

Rock, D. 1992. *Authoritarian Argentina: The Nationalist Movement, Its History and Impact.* Berkeley, CA: University of California Press.

Rouquié, A. 1987. *The Military and the State in Latin America.* Berkeley, CA: University of California Press.

Schuler, F. E. 1998. *Mexico Between Hitler and Roosevelt. Mexican Foreign Politics in the Age of Lázaro Cárdenas, 1934–1940.* Albuquerque: University of New Mexico Press.

Sherman, J. W. 1997. *The Mexican Right.* Westport CT: Praeger.

Silvert, K. 1961. *The Conflict Society: Reaction and Revolution in Latin America.* New Orleans, LA: The Hauser Press.

Skidmore, T. 1967. *Politics in Brazil, 1930–1964. An Experiment in Democracy.* Oxford: Oxford University Press.

Spektorowski, A. S. 2003. *The Origins of Argentina's Revolution of the Right.* Notre Dame, IN: University of Notre Dame Press.

United States

Barkun, M. 1997. *Religion and the Racist Right. The Origins of the Christian Identity Movement.* London: University of North Carolina Press.

Bell, L. V. 1973. *In Hitler's Shadow: The Anatomy of American Fascism.* Port Washington, NY: Kennikat Press.

Bennett, D. H. 1969. *Demagogues in the Depression: American Radicals and the Union Party, 1932–1936.* New Brunswick, NJ: Rutgers University Press.

Blee, K. M. 2002. *Inside Organized Racism. Women in the Hate Movement.* London: University of California Press.

Brinkley, A. 1982. *Voices of Protest: Huey Long, Father Coughlin, and the Great Depression.* New York, NY: Knopf .

Chalmers, D. M. 1965. *Hooded Americanism: The First Century of the Ku Klux Klan, 1865–1965.* Garden City, NY: Doubleday.

Diggins, J. P. 1972. *Mussolini and Fascism: The View from America.* Princeton, NJ: Princeton University Press.

Dobratz, B. A., Shanks-Meile, S. L. 2000. *The White Separatist Movement in the United States. White Power, White Pride.* Baltimore, MD: Johns Hopkins University Press.

Gardell, M. 2003. *Gods of the Blood. The Pagan Revival and White Separatism.* Durham, NC: Duke University Press.

Gossett, T. F. 1997. *Race: The History of an Idea in America.* London: Oxford University Press.

Handlin, O. 1957. *Race and Nationality in American Life.* Boston, MA: Little Brown.

Jackson, K. T. 1967. *The Ku Klux Klan in the City, 1915–1930.* London: Oxford University Press.

Kaplan, J. ed. 2000. *Encyclopedia of White Power. A Sourcebook on the Radical Racist Right.* Walnut Creek, CA: AltaMira Press.

Levitas, D. 2002. *The Terrorist Next Door. The Militia Movement and the Radical Racist Right.* New York, NY: Thomas Dunne Books.

Nasaw, D. 2000. *The Chief: The Life of William Randolph Hearst.* Boston, MA: Houghton, Mifflin.

Offner, A. A. 1969. *American Appeasement: United States Foreign Policy and Germany, 1933–1938.* Cambridge, MA: Harvard University Press.

Randel, W. P. 1965. *The Ku Klux Klan: A Century of Infamy.* London: H. Hamilton.

Ribuffo, L. P. 1983. *The Old Christian Right: The Protestant Far Right from the Great Depression to the Cold War.* Philadelphia: Temple University Press .

Ribuffo, L. P. ed. 1992. *Right Center Left: Essays in American History.* New Brunswick, NJ: Rutgers University Press.

Schonbach, M. 1985. *Native American Fascism during the 1930s and 1940s: A Study of Its Roots, Its Growth and Its Decline.* New York: Garland .

Sims, P. 1978. *The Klan.* New York: Scarbrough Books.

Stanton, B. 1992. *Klanwatch. Bringing the Ku Klux Klan to Justice.* Bergenfield, New Jersey: Mentor.

Wade, W. C. 1987. *The Fiery Cross. The Ku Klux Klan in America.* New York: Simon and Schuster .

KEY SECONDARY WORKS ON POST-WAR FASCISM

Akenson, D. H. 1992. *God's Peoples: Covenant and Land in South Africa, Israel, and Ulster.* Ithaca and London: Cornell University Press.

Barkun, M. 1997. *Religion and the Racist Right: The Origins of Christian Identity Movement.* Chapel Hill and London: The University of North Carolina Press.

Bar-On, T. 2001. 'The Ambiguities of the Nouvelle Droite, 1968–1999', in *The European Legacy* 6 (3).

Berlet, C. et al. *Right-wing Populism in America: Too Close for Comfort.* London: Guilford Press.

Cheles, L., Ferguson, R., Vaughan, M. eds. 1991. *Neo-Fascism in Europe.* London: Longman.

Cheles, L. et al. eds. 1995. *The Far Right in Western and Eastern Europe.* London: Longman.

Coogan, K. 1999. *Dreamer of the Day: Francis Parker Yockey and the Postwar Fascist International.* New York: Autonomedia.

Eatwell, R. 2003. *Fascism: A History.* London: Pimlico.

Ford, G. ed. 1992. *Fascist Europe. The Rise of Racism and Xenophobia.* London: Pluto Press.

Goodrick-Clarke, N. 2002. *Black Sun: Aryan Cults, Esoteric Nazism, and the Politics of Identity.* London: New York University Press.

Griffin, R. 1991. *The Nature of Fascism.* London: Routledge.

Griffin, R. ed. 1995. *Fascism.* Oxford: Oxford University Press.

Griffin, R. 1998. 'Ce n'est pas Le Pen: The MSI/AN's Estrangement from the Front National's Immigration Policy,' in Westin, C. ed. *Racism, Ideology and Political Organization.* London: Routledge.

Griffin, R. 1999. 'GUD Reactions: The Patterns of Prejudice of a Neo-Fascist *Groupuscule,*' in *Patterns of Prejudice,* vol. 33, no. 2.

Griffin, R. 2000. "Interregnum or Endgame? Radical Right Thought in the 'Post-fascist' Era," in *The Journal of Political Ideologies,* vol. 5, no. 2.

Griffin, R. 2000. "Between Metapolitics and *Apoliteía:* The New Right's Strategy for Conserving the Fascist Vision in the 'Interregnum,'" in *Contemporary French Studies* vol. 8 no. 2.

Griffin, R. 2000. 'Plus ça change! The Fascist Pedigree of the Nouvelle Droite,' in Arnold, E. ed. *The Development of the Radical Right in France.* London: Macmillan.

Griffin, R. 2000. "Interregnum or Endgame? The radical Right in the 'post-fascist' Era." Pp. 163–178 in *Journal of Political Ideologies,* vol. 5, no. 2.

Hainsworth, P. ed. 1992. *The Extreme Right in Europe and the USA.* London: Pinter.

Harris, G. 1990. *The Dark Side of Europe. The Extreme Right Today.* Edinburgh: Edinburgh University Press.

Hockenos, P. 1993. *Free to Hate: The Rise of the Right in Post-Communist Eastern Europe.* London: Routledge.

Kaplan, J. ed. 2000. *Encyclopedia of White Power. A Sourcebook on the Radical Racist Right.* Walnut Creek, CA: AltaMira Press.

Kaplan, J., Weinberg, L. 1998. *The Emergence of a Euro-American Radical Right.* New Brunswick, NJ: Rutgers University Press.

Kitschelt, H. 1995. *The Radical Right in Western Europe: A Comparative Analysis.* Ann Arbor: University of Michigan Press.

Landes, R. ed. 2000. *The Encyclopedia of Millennialism and Millennial Movements.* New York: Routledge.

Laqueur, W. 1996. *Fascism. Past, Present, Future.* Oxford: Oxford University Press.

Lee, M. 1997. *The Beast Reawakens.* London: Little, Brown.

Maclean, N. 1994. *Behind the Mask of Chivalry: The Making of the Second Ku Klux Klan.* Oxford: Oxford University Press.

Merkl, P. H., Weinberg, L. 1997. *The Revival of Right-wing Extremism in the Nineties.* London: Frank Cass.

O'Maolain, C. 1987. *The Radical Right: A World Directory.* Harlow: Longman.

Riboffo, L. P. 1983. *The Old Christian Right: The Protestant Far Right from the Great Depression to the Cold War.* Philadelphia, PA: Temple University Press.

Schmidt, M. 1993. *The New Reich: Violent Extremism in Unified Germany and Beyond.* London: Hutchinson.

Shenfield, S. 2001. *Russian Fascism: Tradition, Tendencies, Movements.* London: M. E. Sharpe.

Simmons, H. 1996. *The French National Front: The Extremist Challenge to Democracy.* Boulder, CO: Westview Press.

Skypietz, I. 1994. 'Right Wing Extremism in Germany', in *German Politics,* vol. 3, no. 1.

Sternhell, Z. et. al. 1994. *The Birth of the Fascist Ideology.* Princeton, NJ: Princeton University Press.

Sunic, T. 1990. *Against Democracy and Equality: The European New Right.* New York, NY: Peter Lang.

Thurlow, R. 1998. *Fascism in Britain: From Mosley's Blackshirts to the National Front.* London. I. B. Tauris.

Thurlow, R. 2001. *Fascism in Modern Britain.* Stroud: Sutton.

Special Issue on Right Wing Extremism in Western Europe. 1988. *West European Politics,* vol. 1, no. 2.

OTHER BOOKS RELATED TO THE STUDY OF FASCIST IDEOLOGY

Adamson, W. L. 1980. *Hegemony and Revolution: A Study of Antonio Gramsci's Political and Cultural Theory.* Berkeley, CA: University of California Press.

Adorno, T. et al. 1950. *The Authoritarian Personality.* New York, NY: Harper.

Albin, M. ed. 1980. *New Directions in Psycho-history: The Adelphi Papers in Honor of Erik H. Erikson.* Lexington, MA: Lexington Books.

Alexander, J. ed. 1989. *Durkheimian Sociology: Cultural Studies.* Cambridge: Cambridge University Press.

Apter, D. 1965. *The Politics of Modernisation.* London: University of Chicago Press.

Arendt, H. 1967. *The Origins of Totalitarianism.* London: Allen & Unwin.

Baradt, L. P. 1991. *Political Ideologies: Their Origins and Impact.* London: Prentice-Hall International.

Bauman, Z. 1991. *Modernity and Ambivalence.* Cambridge: Polity.

Billington, J. S. 1980. *Fire in the Minds of Men: Origins of Revolutionary Faith.* London: Temple Smith.

Cohn, N. 1993. *The Pursuit of the Millennium: Revolutionary Millenarians and Mystical Anarchists of the Middle Ages.* London: Pimlico.

Davies, P. D. Lynch. 2002. *The Routledge Companion to Fascism and the Far Right.* London and New York: Routledge.

Eliade, M. 1987. *The Sacred and the Profane: The Nature of Religion.* London: Harcourt Brace.

Hayes, C. J. H. 1960. *Nationalism: A Religion.* New York, NY: Macmillan.

Koestler, A. 1989. *The Ghost in the Machine.* London: Arkana.

Leed, E. J. 1979. *No Man's Land: Combat and Identity in World War I.* Cambridge: Cambridge University Press.

Rees, Philip. 1990. *Biographical Dictionary of the Extreme Right Since 1890.* New York, NY: Simon & Schuster.

Roshwald, A., Stites, R. eds. 2002. *European Culture in the Great War.* Cambridge: Cambridge University Press.

Scruton, R. 1982. *A Dictionary of Political Thought.* London: Macmillan.

Smith, A. 1979. *Nationalism in the Twentieth Century.* New York, NY: New York University Press.

Stromberg, R. 1966. *An Intellectual History of Modern Europe.* New York, NY: Appleton-Century-Crofts.

Stromberg, R. 1982. *Redemption by War: The Intellectuals and 1914.* Lawrence, KS: Regents Press of Kansas.

Theweleit, K. 1987–1989. *Male Fantasies* (2 Vols.) Cambridge: Polity.

Turner, V. 1975. *The Ritual Process: Structure and Antistructure.* Harmondsworth: Penguin.

Index

Page ranges for main entries appear in boldface type.

Du Toit, S. J., 616
Duarte, Eva. *See* Perón, Evita
Dubrovin, Aleksandr, 580
Duca, Ion, 195, 574
Duce, 251
Il Duce. *See* Mussolini, Benito Andrea
    Amilcare
Dudreville, Leonardo, 59
Dugin, Aleksandr Gel'evich, **182**, 580,
    581, 582, 668
Dühring, (Karl) Eugen, **182**, 469
Duke, David, **182**, 368, 685, 686
Dunkirk, **182–183**
Dunlop, John, 620
Duranton-Crabol, Anne-Marie, 280
Durcansky, Ferdinand, 608
Durkheim, Émile, 142, 613
Düsterberg, Theodor, 634
Dutch Anti-Revolutionary Movement,
    616
Dutch Reformed Christianity, 10
Duverger, Maurice, 83
DVU. *See* Deutsche Volksunion Party
The Dynamics of War and Revolution
    (Dennis), 174

E

East Prussia, 314
Eastern Europe, 206, 734
    forced labor and, 241–242
    ghettos in, 278
    immigration and, 330
    Lutheran Churches in, 397
Eastern Europeans, 318
Eastern Karelia, 237
Eastern Way, 22, 352
Easternness, 155
Eatwell, Roger, 425
Ebeling, Heinrich, 186
Ebert, Friedrich, 721
Eckart, Johann Dietrich, **185**, 578,
    666
Eckhart, "Meister" Johann, **185–186**,
    193, 445
ecofascism. *See* ecology
Ecological-Democratic Party, 187
ecology, **186–187**
    left-wing, 186
    right-wing, 186–187
economic isolationism, 672
economic liberalism, 387
economic nationalism, 672
economic protectionism, 672
economics, **187–190**
    antisocialism and, 189
    autarky and, 188
    corporatism and, 188–189

Four Year Plan Office and, 189–190
    globalization and, 188
    nationalism and, 188
    protectionism and, 188
    Third Way and, 188–189
economy, corporatist theory of, 14
ecosystem, 530
Ecuador, **190**
Edelweiss Pirates, **190**, 601
education, **191–192**, 408, 538
    athletic activity and, 191
    goal of, 191
    sports and, 191
    teachers and, 191–192
Edward III. *See* Windsor, Edward
    Duke of
Effinger, Virgil, 682
egalitarianism, **192**, 199, 200, 404
Egidy, Moritz von, 272
Egoldt, Herbert, 604
Egypt, 84, 420, 421, 576
    military dictatorship, 423
Egyptian society, 6
Ehre ("honor"), **192–193**
Ehrhardt, Hermann, 363
Ehrhardt Brigade, 363
EIAR. *See* Ente Italiano Audizione
    Radio
Eichmann, Otto Adolf, 55, 65, 171,
    194, 199, 319, 458, 497, 725
Eigenart ("individuality"), 187
18 BL, 659
*The Eighteenth Brumaire of Louis
    Bonaparte* (Marx), 112
Einaudi, Luigi, 198, 419
Einstein, Albert, 28, 40, 99, 593
Ekström, Martin, 646, 647
El Alamein, **195**, 315
El Fascio, 534
El Mercurio, 512
Elam, Norah, 233
Elders of Zion, 540
Eleftherofrones, 417
Elemente, 665
Elementi di scienza politica (Mosca),
    433
Eléments, 88, 473
Eléments (Heidegger), 304
Elena, Queen, 586
Eliade, Mircea, **195**, 544
Elias, Alois, 162
Elias, Hendrik, 137
Elías Calles, Plutarco, 418
Eliot, T. S., 138, 532
elite theory, **195–196**
elites, sociology and, 613
elitism, 57

Elizabeth of Russia, 254
Ellison, James, 644
Ellwood, Charles, 613
Ellwood, Robert, 425
e-mail technology, cyberfascism and, 161
Emelianov, Valerii, 620
employment, **196–197**
    autobahn construction and, 196
    immigration and, 197
    women and, 196
Emry, Sheldon, 129
Enabling Act, 106, 124, **197**, 458
Enciclopedia Italiana, **197–198**, 257,
    267, 348, 387, 409, 410, 429,
    443, 612, 715
encryption technology, cyberfascism
    and, 161
Encyclopedia Britannica, 197–198
endecja movement, 517
Endecja (National Democracy), 177
Endre, László, **199**, 325
Engdahl, Per, 81, 647
Engdahl movement, 647
Engels, Friedrich, 182, 606, 611,
    634
ENI. *See* Ente Nazionale Idrocarburi
Enlightenment, 44, 46, 82, **199–200**,
    273, 428, 446, 474, 675, 731
    Christianity and, 200
    Jews and, 200
    liberalism and, 199, 200
    materialism and, 200
    Protestantism and, 200
Enquête sur la Monarchie (Maurras),
    411
ENR. *See* European New Right
Ensor, James, 60
Ente Italiano Audizione Radio (EIAR),
    438
Ente Nazionale Idrocarburi (ENI),
    654
environment, 551. *See also* ecology;
    nature
environmental movement, 187
EON. *See* National Youth
    Organization
equality, 610
era of fascism, 8
Erikson, Erik H., 543–544
Eritrea, 202, 203
Escape from Freedom (Fromm),
    261
ESM. *See* European Social Movement
Essai sur l'inégalite des races humaines
    (*Essay on the Inequality of the
    Human Races,* Gobineau), 62
Essén, Rütger, 647

Gasperi, Alcide de, 525
Gaulle, Charles de, 248, 450, 655, 700
Gautama Buddha, 107
Gautama Sidartha, 107
Gavrilo, Patriarch, 492
Gaxotte, Pierre, 29
Gazzetta Ufficiale del Regno d'Italia, 687
GBM. *See* Greater Britain Movement
GdNF. *See* New Front Association of Kindred Spirits
Gebhardt, Karl, 300
Geelkerken, Cornelis van, 462
Der Gegentypus (Jaensch), 545
Gehlen, Reinhard, 485
Geidl. Rudolf. *See* Gajda, Radola
Der Geist der deutschen Kultur (Troeltsch), 159
Geistchristliche Religionsgemeinschaft, 176
Gemeinschaft (community), 142
gemeinschaftsunfähig, 141
gender. *See* feminism; sexuality; women
General Administration for Theatre and Music, 439
General Electric, 713
General Government. *See* Generalgouvernement
General Motors, 690
General Strike of 1936, 497
General Theater Inspectorate, 658
Generalgouvernement (General Government), **266**
Generalplan Ost, 606
generic fascism, 2
Geneva Convention, 242
Geneva Disarmament Conference, 313
genius, cult of the. *See* hero, cult of the
genocide, 206, 458–459, 594. *See also* Holocaust
genocide classification, 319
Gentile, Emilio, 234, 563, 596, 629
Gentile, Giovanni, 30, 156, 157, 160, 191, 197–198, 200, 213, **266–268**, 348, 387, 401, 412, 443, 444, 463–464, 486, 534, 595, 669, 687, 715
Gentleman's Agreement (film), 48
George, David Lloyd, 302
George, King, 417
George, Stefan, **268–269**
George Circle, 268–269
Georgiev, Kimon, 108
Gerarchia (hierarchy), 192, 257, 708, 716
Gerlach, Hellmut von, 495

Gerlier, Cardinal of Lyon, 123
German Alternative (DA), 369
German Ancestral Heritage Society. *See* Ahnenerbe
German Association of German Scholars, 159
German Christians, 145, 146, **269–270**, 373, 395, 436. *See also* Christianity; German Protestantism; Germanic religion; religion
German Citizens' Initiative (BBI), 369
German Conservative Party-German Right Party (DKP-DRP), 275
German Economic Industries, 633
German Faith Front, 661
German Faith Movement, 36, **271**, 299, 388, 661
German Federation for the Protection of the Homeland (DBH), 187
German Football Federation, 239
German Knightly Orders, 321
German Law for the Restoration of the Career Civil Service, 592
German Monist League, 488
German National People's Party, 413
German National Socialist Worker's Party. *See* NSDAP
German Nazis, 2
German Nazism, 1
  Italian Fascism and, 15–20
  See also Nazism
German Order, 666
German Peace Society (DFG), 495
German Protestant Liberalism, 539
German Protestantism, 145, 146, 395, 396, 397, 539. *See also* Confessing Church; Christianity; religion; German Christians; Germanic religion
German Psychiatric Association, 215
German race, 2
German Red Cross, 722
German Reformation, 61, 98
"German Revolution," 313
German Student Association, 98
German Transmitter/Station, 554
German typeface, 60
German Volk Society, 393
German warrior knights myth, 715
German Women's Order (DFO), 590, 727
German Workers' Party (DAP; Deutsche Arbeiterpartei), 12–13, 16, 179, 185, 232, 312, 456, 578, 645

German-American Bund, **270–271**, 682–683
  membership in, 270
German-American Economic Bulletin, 701
German-Austrian Republic, 67
German-Flemish Labor Community. *See* DeVlag
Germania, 258
Germanic national church, 321
Germanic religion, **272**
Germanic superiority, Wagner and, **712**
Germanism, 551
Germanness (Deutschheit), 61, **273**, 500
Germany, 8, 12, 13, 208–210, **273–277**
  German culture and, **159–160**
  health in, **300–301**
  liberalism in, **385–386**
  medicine in, **412–412**
  music in, **437–438**
  ruralism in, **580**
  Slavs in, **605–606**
  universities in, **688–689**
  youth movements in, **742–743**
  See also Hitler, Adolf; Nazi Germany; Nazism
Germany and England (Webster), 719
Germany's New Religion: The German Faith Movement (Wilhelm, Hauer, and Heim), 539
Gesamtkuntswerk, 711
Gesellschaft (association), 142
Gesetz zur Wiederherstellung des Berufsbeamtentums (Laws for the Restoration of the Civil Service), 63
Gestapo, **277–278**, 278, 595, 601, 638
Gewissen, 431
Geyer, Ludwig, 710
ghettos, **278–279**, 318, 720
Gibbon, Edward, 44
Der Giftpilz, 59
Giliomee, Herman, 617
Giménez Caballero, 660
Gini, Corrado, 172, 206, 613
Giodani, Igino, 669
Giolitti, Giovanni, 12, 15, 239, 347, 441
Gioventù Italiana Cattolica, 743
Gioventù Italiana del Littorio, 229, 443, 670–671
Giral, José, 624

masses
  nationalization of, 731
  role of the, **408–409**
Massis, Henri, 121–122
master race, 273
materialism, 130–131, 192–193, 200,
    208, 404, **409–410**, 429, 445,
    452, 531, 611, 664–665
  Jewish/Catholic, anti-Semitism and,
    45
Matteotti, Giacomo, 74, 98, 147, 156,
    228, 335, 348, 387, **410**, 443,
    611
Matteotti Crisis, 701
Maulnier, Thierry, 103
Mauriac, François, 121
Maurice, Emil, 312
Maurras, Charles, 12, 27, 29, 38, 56,
    90, 154, 181, 201, 244–245,
    257, 338, **411**, 504, 525, 625,
    696
Mayan culture, 8
Mazzini, Giuseppe, 463, 507, 596
McClure, S. S., 683
McDonaldization, 32
McDougall, William, 545
McMahon Pledge, 419
McVeigh, Timothy, 24, 142–143, **400**,
    485–486. *See also* Oklahoma
    bombing
McWilliams, Joseph E., 682, 683
mechanical solidarity, 142
mechanistic thinking, 2, **411–412**
media. *See* film; press; radio
medical refugees, 412
medical research, 412–413
medicine
  alternative, 413
  doctors and, 412
  in Germany, **412–412**
  Holocaust and, 412
  in Italy, **413–414**
  Jewish doctors and, 412, 413
  medical refugees and, 412
  medical research and, 412–413
  physicians organizations and, 413
  racism and, 412–413
  university medical faculties and,
    413
  women and, 412
Mediterranean, 735
Megali Idea, 292, 332
Mégret, Bruno, 380, 450
Mein Kampf (Hitler), 18, 52, 63, 71,
    160, 179, 185, 243, 258, 270,
    283, 312, 317, 331, 334, 382,
    414–416, 438, 456, 468, 500,

509, 578, 591, 612, 639, 645,
    654, 682, 684, 732
  Catholic Church and, 415–416
  idea for, 414
  Marxism and, 415
  racial ideology and, 415
  total sales of, 414
  Western-style democracy and, 415
  youth and, 415
Meiners, Christian, 551
Meir, Golda, 521
Die Meistersinger von Nürnberg
    (Wagner), 710, 711, 712
*Mémoires pour servir à l'histoire du
    jacobinisme* (Barruel), 148–149,
    256
men, sexuality and, 599, 600
Men Standing among the Ruins (Evola),
    217
Mengele, Josef, 31, 65, 92, 204, 205,
    206, 207, **416**, 458, 506
Der Mensch und die Technik (Spengler),
    628, 629
mental illness, 203
Menthon, François de, 480
Mercante, Lieutenant-Colonel, 512,
    513
Mercouris, Georges, 340
Merkl, Peter, 692
Meskó, Zoltán, 324, 325, **416–417**
messianism, 636
Metaphysics and History (Baeumler), 78
Metapo, 665
metapoliticization, of fascism, 23
Metaxas, Ioannis, 291–292, 332, **417**,
    424, 504, 642, 735
methodological empathy, 6–7
Metzger, Tom, 685
Mexican Fascist Party, 418
Mexican Social Democratic Party, 418
Mexicanist Revolutionary Action, 418
Mexico, **417–418**
  Spanish Civil War and, 418
Michael, King, 49
Michael, Prince, 736
Michael (Goebbels), 282
Michelet, Jules, 62
Michels, Roberto, 195, 306, 399,
    418–419, 508, 613, 650
Middle Class Confederation, 418
Middle East, **419–422**, 576
  anti-Semitism in, 48
  Great Britain and, 421
  Palestine and, 420, 421–422
  See also Iran; Iraq; Palestine
Midway, Battle of, 355
Mieli, Aldo, 599

Mihaijlovic, Dragoljub, 492
Mihalache, Ion, 574
Mikhalkov, Sergei, 620
Miklas, Wilhelm, 68
Milan, 12
Milan Triennales, 59
Milch, Erhard, 394, 480
Miliband, Ralph, 407
Milice Socialiste Nationale, 106
militarism, **422**
  Social Darwinism and, 422
military
  science and, 594
  See also militarism; military
    dictatorship
military antifascism, 42
military dictatorship, **423–424**
Militiamen, 148, 149
Milizia Volontaria per la Sicurezza
    Nazionale, 348
Mill, John Stuart, 200, 533, 692
Millán Astray, José, 250
millenarianism, **425**
Ministry of Corporations, 151
Ministry of National Education,
    229
Ministry of Popular Culture, 439
Ministry of Public Enlightenment and
    Propaganda, 235
miscegenation, 221
Mishima, Yukio (pseud. for Hiraoka
    Kimitake), **426**
Mit Brennender Sorge (Pius XI), 119,
    356, 502, 519, 560
Mitford, Algernon Bertram (First Lord
    Redesdale), 426
Mitford, Unity, 426, 427
Mitford family, **426–427**
Mitrovica, Rexhep, 31
mixed marriages, 600
MNFFP. *See* Hungarian National
    Independent Race Defenders'
    Party
MNR. *See* Bolivian National
    Revolutionary Party
MNS. *See* National Socialist
    Movement
MNS. *See* National Socialist Party
Mod subculture, 602–603
modernism, **427–428**
  decadence and, 168, 169
  degeneracy and, 169–170
modernity, 11–12, 17, 19–20,
    429–430
  fascism and, relationship between,
    9–10
  technology and, 653

Organization of Former SS Members. *See* ODESSA

Organizzazione nazionale Dopolavoro, 671

Orientamenti, 217

The Origins of Totalitarianism (Arendt), 53

Orjuna, 745

Orphan Ann, 555

Orthodox Church, 10, **489–492**. *See also individual churches*

Ortiz Pereyra, Manuel, 56

Orwell, George, 7, 339, **493**, 741

Osipov, Vladimir, 620

Osnabrück concentration camp, 143

Ossawabrandweg (OB; Ox Wagon Guard), 10, 21, **493**, 616

Osservatore Romano, 533

Ossietzky, Carl von, 42, 298, 496

Ostara, 312, 389, 660

Ostmark, 34

Ostministerium, 205

Ostwald, Wilhelm, 488

the other, 30

Otto I, 321

Our Contemporary, 620

Our Flag Stays Red (Piratin), 407

Our Path, 597

The Outline of Sanity (G. K. Chesterton), 177

Ovazza, Ettore, 47

Overlord, Operation, 315

Owens, Jesse, 89, 631

OWP. *See* Greater Poland Camp

Ox Wagon Guard. *See* Ossawabrandweg

OZN. *See* National Unity Camp

P

Pacelli, Cardinal, 122, 519

pacifism, 404, **495–496**, 687

Pact of Steel, 75, 735

Pagano, Guiseppe, 59

Pahlavi, Mohammed Reza, 343

Pahlavi dynasty, 342

Pais, Sidonio, 527

Palacio, Juan Carulla Ernesto, 56

Palazzo Vidoni Pact, 150, 151

Palestine, 17, 83, 420, 421–422, **496–498**, 748, 749

immigration and, 330

Jewish homeland in, 420, 421–422

Palestinian National Movement, 496

Palestinians, 23

Pálffy, Count Fidél, 325

palingenesis, 3, 12, 37, 498

palingenetic myth, 4, **498–499**

psychodynamics of, **544**

See also rebirth

palingenetic ultra-nationalism, 3, 318

Pan-Arabism, 218, 496, 497

Pan-German League, 16, **500–501**, 704

Pangerman movement, 87

Pangermanism, 55, 67, 218, 273, 383, **499–501**, 552

Pangermans, 67

Pannevis, Arnoldus, 616

Pan-Slavism, 55, 218

Pan-Slavs, 636

Pantaleone, Maffeo, 507

pan-Turkism, 677

Panunzio, Sergio, 401, **501**, 650

papacy, 120, 124, 134, 198, 321, 349, 357, **501–503**, 576. *See also* Catholic Church; political Catholicism; Vatican

Papen, Franz von, 69, 480, **503**, 524, 566, 588

Papini, Giovanni, 152, 168, 466, **504**, 542

Papon, Maurice, 700

Paracelsus, 668

parafascism, **504–505**

Paraga, Dobroslav, 156

Paraguay, 423, 477, **505–506**

paramilitarism, **506–507**

Pareto, Raffaele, 507

Pareto, Vilfredo, 13, 195, 196, 200, 212, 381, 399, 418, **507–508**, 613

Paris Peace Accord, 364

Paris Peace Conference, 238

Paris World's Fair, 52–53

Park Avenue fascism, 138

parliamentarism, 82, 102, 404, **508–509**

Parti Franciste, 106

Parti Ouvrier, 695

Parti Populaire Français (PPF), 178–179, 225, 245, 246, 247, 531

Parti Social Français (PSF), 21, 245, 246, 247, 249

Parti Socialiste de France (PSdF)-Union Jean Jaurès, 167

Parti Unitaire Français d'Action Socialiste et Nationale (PUF), 106

Partito Nazionale Fascista, 716

Partito Popolare Italiano, 137

Party for Socialist Racial Defense, 199

Party of National Unity, 162

Party of National Will (NAP), 199, 325, 651

Paschoud, Mariette, 649

Pašić, Nikola, 640, 745

pass laws, 579

The Passing of the Great Race (Grant), 207

passo romano. See Roman step

Past and Present (Carlyle), 118

Patent Code of 1936, 654

Patriotic Movement Dignity, 598

patriotism, 227

"Patriotism" (Mishima), 426

Päts, Konstantin, 201, 696

Paul, Saint, 45, 47, 193, 272

Paul VI, 521

Paulus, Field Marshal von, 637

Paulus, General von, 315

Pauwels, Louis, 212

Pavelić, Ante, 123, **510**, 691, 692, 736

Pax Britannica, 14

Paxton, Robert, 653

Payne, Stanley, 7, 37, 251, 351, 452, 472, 514, 563, 642

PCF. *See* French Communist Party

"Peace Note" (Benedict XV), 502

Pearl Harbor, 75, 314, 341, 355, **510–511**, 690, 734

Peasants' League, 21, 178

Peel, Earl, 421

Peel Report, 497

Pejani, Bedri, 31

Pelley, William Dudley, **511**, 682, 683

Pelley's Weekly, 511

Pelloutier, Fernand, 650

Pentagon attack, 686

people with mental handicaps, 141

people with physical handicaps, 141

People's Bank, 105

People's Car (the Volkswagen), 9

People's Court. *See* Volksgericht

People's Labor Union, 619

People's Observer (Völkischer Beobachter), 185, 223, 456

Peoples Party (OeVP), 70, 71

People's Patriotic Movement (IKL), 10, 21

People's Republic of China (PRC), 128

People's Welfare Organization, 722, 726

Perón, Evita (Eva Duarte), 511, 513, 514

Perón, Juan Domingo, 56, **511–512**, 514

rise to power of, 512

Peronism, 22, 56, **512–514**

Peronist government, 22

Peronist Party, 514

Persia, 341–342. See also Iran

Belgium during, 86
Bulgaria and, 108–109
Canada during, 114
Catholic Church and, 519, 520–521
corporatism and, 151
D-Day and, 734
El Alamein and, 195
Ethiopia and, 203
Fascist Party and, 230
film and, 235
film versions of, 17
football/soccer and, 240
France and, 246, 247–248
Franco and, 251–252, 733, 736
freemasonry and, 256
Great Britain and, 353, 354, 355
Guernica and, 293, 294
gypsies and, 571–572
health and, 301
Hitler and, 314–315, 732, 733–736
Hungary and, 324
Iceland and, 329
Italy and, 341, 349
Japan and, **353–355**
Libya and, 389
Lithuania and, 391
Mexico and, 417
Mussolini and, 443–444, 735–736
Nazism and, 458–459
the Netherlands and, 463
Norway and, 475–476
origins of, 733
papacy and, 502–503
Paraguay and, 505–506
Pearl Harbor and, 75, 314, 341, 355, **510–511**, 690, 734
Poland and, 522, 523
Portugal and, 528
post-, 23–25
racial doctrine and, 552
Soviet Union and, 355
Stalin and, 733, 734
Turkey and, 679
United States and, 353, 354, 355, 683

World Wide Web
    postwar fascism and, 529
World Zionist Organization, 747–748
world-view, **723**
Worldwide Websites
    community and, 142–143
Wotansvolk, 685
WTO. *See* World Trade Organization
Wulff, Wilhelm, 483
Wüst, Walter, 89
WVHA, 633

X

xenophobia, 24, 25, 117, **739**

Y

Yalta Conference, 172
Yeats, William Butler, 168, 344, 532, **741**
yellow peril, 95
Yemen, 420
Yockey, Francis Parker, **742**
Yocupicio, Román, 418
Yosuke, Matsuoka, 355
Young, Owen D., 562
Young Egypt Society, 420, 421, 422
Young Guard, 620
Young National Front, 724
Young National Front's Rock Against Communism (RAC), 604
Young Plan, 562
Young Yugoslavia, 745
youth, **742**
    Mein Kampf and, 415
Youth Association, 324
Youth Front, 667
youth movements, 175, 373, 538
    for boys, 742–743
    in Germany, **742–743**
    for girls, 743
    in Italy, **743–747**
youth organizations, 385, 535
    totalitarianism and, 670–671
Yrigoyen, Hipolito, 56
Yugoslav Action, 597
Yugoslav Popular Movement Zbor, 597

Yugoslav Progressive Nationalist Youth (JNNO), 745
Yugoslav Radical Union, 640
Yugoslavia, 23, 108, 155, 156, 238, 318, 492, 597, 640, 691, 735, 736, **745**
    Orguna and, 745
Yzerbedevaart, 176

Z

Zagreb, 155
Zagreb University, 155
ZANU, 566
Zbor movement, 391, 597, 745
Die Zeit, 310
Zeitschrift für Rassenphysiologie, 91
Zetkin, Clara, 140
Zharikov, Sergei, 582
Zhirinovskii, Vladimir Vol'fovich, 332, 530, 581, 582, 643, **747**
Zibordi, Giovanni, 136
Ziegler, Hans Severus, 438
Ziegler, Leopold, 159
Zimbabwe. *See* Rhodesia/Zimbabwe
Zinoviev, Grigorii, 635
Zion, 747
Zionism, 17, 43, 180, 619, 620, **747–749**
Zionist movement, 180
Zionist Occupation Government (ZOG), 129, 647, **749**
Zionist Revisionism, 748
Zionology, 620
Ziuganov, Gennadii, 96, 636
Zmigrodski, Michael, 646
ZOG. *See* Zionist Occupation Government
Zola, Emile, 46, 168, 180
Zolli, Israel, 520
Zubatov, Sergei, 580
Zundel, Ernst, 115–116
Zundelsite, 116
Zur Psychologie des Sozialismus (Man), 400–401
Zurlo, Leopoldo, 658
Zyklon-B, 319, **750**

Editor's Biography

CYPRIAN BLAMIRES
MA (Oxon) D Phil

Cyprian Blamires is a freelance scholar, writer, editor, and translator based in the United Kingdom. He completed a doctoral thesis in the History of Ideas at the University of Oxford under the supervision of one of the most celebrated twentieth century intellectuals, the late Sir Isaiah Berlin. It was the research he did for this thesis—focussing on counter-revolutionary and proto-socialist reactions to the French Revolution—which first sparked his long-standing interest in the ideology of fascism. He has Oxford degrees in European Languages and Literature and in Theology, has taught at Oxford, London, and Leicester Universities, and has held research fellowships in London and Geneva. He has written extensively in English and in French on the history of European thought and is co-editor of two modern editions of works by English philosopher Jeremy Bentham. He has a working knowledge of seven languages, has translated books from Italian, German, and French in the fields of economics, and religion, philosophy and has also translated numerous entries written in these languages for this encyclopedia (as well as authoring numerous entries totalling more than 60,000 words). He is married to an ophthalmic surgeon and has one son, who is a lawyer.